Oxford Dictionary of

Political
Quotations

Oxford Dictionary of

Political
Quotations

THIRD EDITION

edited by **Antony Jay**

OXFORD
UNIVERSITY PRESS

OXFORD
UNIVERSITY PRESS

Great Clarendon Street, Oxford OX2 6DP

Oxford University Press is a department of the University of Oxford.
It furthers the University's objective of excellence in research, scholarship,
and education by publishing worldwide in

Oxford New York

Auckland Cape Town Dar es Salaam Hong Kong Karachi
Kuala Lumpur Madrid Melbourne Mexico City Nairobi
New Delhi Shanghai Taipei Toronto

with offices in

Argentina Austria Brazil Chile Czech Republic France Greece
Guatemala Hungary Italy Japan Poland Portugal Singapore
South Korea Switzerland Thailand Turkey Ukraine Vietnam

Oxford is a registered trade mark of Oxford University Press
in the UK and in certain other countries

Published in the United States
by Oxford University Press Inc., New York

First published 1996
Second edition 2001
Third edition 2006

British Library Cataloguing in Publication Data

Data available

Library of Congress Cataloging in Publication Data

Data available

Designed by Jane Stevenson
Typeset in Photina and Argo
by Inter-active Sciences Ltd
Printed in Great Britain
by Clays Ltd, Bungay, Suffolk

ISBN 0-19-280616-5
ISBN 978-0-19-280616-1

I

Contents

Preface

Enoch Powell once said that 'All political lives, unless they are cut off in midstream at a happy juncture, end in failure . . .'

For the past 10 years, there has existed an essential qualification to Enoch's law—'but only if you have *never* been granted an entry in the *Oxford Dictionary of Political Quotations*'.

Questions of immortality are best left to the gods. But, failing them, this dictionary will do very nicely.

PETER HENNESSY

May 2005

Introduction to the Third Edition

When I took on the editorship of the first edition of the *Oxford Dictionary of Political Quotations*, I saw it as a project. Now, ten years and two editions later, I realize it is a process. Obviously, part of this is the addition of new quotations that reflect events, ideas, and arguments from the years since the last edition went to press; these constitute the majority of the more than 400 citations that appear for the first time in this edition. But there is a second part to the process: the tracking down and digging up of quotations from past generations, quotations which illuminate and enrich our current political communication but which did not find their way into previous editions. This means that each new edition is not only more up-to-date than its predecessor, but also a more comprehensive work of reference.

A look at events since the second edition was published in the spring of 2001 confirms the need for a new edition. They include: the terrorist attacks of 9/11 on New York, wars in Iraq and Afghanistan, the heated debate on the legitimacy of the coalition forces in Iraq, and the weapons of mass destruction, to be followed in Britain by the Hutton Enquiry and the Butler report. George W. Bush retained the US presidency for the Republicans and Tony Blair was re-elected to give New Labour an unprecedented third successive term in office. The Conservative Party leader, Iain Duncan-Smith, the self-styled 'quiet man', resigned after only two years, handing over to Michael Howard who himself announced his resignation after losing the general election, paving the way for the party's fifth leader since 1997. Parliament banned fox-hunting after angry and sometimes violent public protests, the proposed UK national identity card started a passionate debate on civil liberties, and the reform of the House of Lords remained unfinished with the rump of 92 hereditary peers under threat of losing their right to vote. The European Union was enlarged, and as we went to press was thrown into turmoil when referendums in France and the Netherlands both resulted in the rejection of the proposed new European constitution (Nicolas Sarkozy: 'It'll be a small no . . . or a big no').

These events and issues have generated their fair share of quotations which have significantly enlarged this third edition. Some have already given phrases to the language: 'shock and awe', 'axis of evil', 'dodgy dossier', and (most notoriously) 'a good day to bury bad news'. New names have been added, from Hans Blix ('We have not found any smoking guns') and Thabo Mbeki to Dick Cheney ('Direct threats require direct action') and Condoleezza Rice.

All the same, I confess that it is the new discovery of old quotations that gives me the greatest pleasure. One of the difficulties for the political observer is sorting out the passing fashions from the eternal truths. Recent years have supplied plenty of evidence for the view that 'Excessive dealings with tyrants are not good for the security of free states', and the fact that the author was Demosthenes (*c*.384–382 BC) shows that it is not a new discovery.

Equally there are many people in public life who would echo Thomas

Jefferson's observation two centuries ago that 'Nothing can now be believed which is seen in a newspaper. Truth itself becomes suspicious by being put into that polluted vehicle', and the seventeenth-century Cardinal de Retz was not speaking just for his own time when he said 'The head of a party may do what he pleases; as long as he maintains the confidence of his friends he can do no wrong.' Other politicians over the centuries have deserved Oswald Mosley's description by his son Nicholas: 'While the right hand dealt with grandiose ideas and glory, the left hand let the rat out of the sewer.' New material of this kind continues to come to light; it is a pity that two conveniently balancing Churchill quotations on the European issue surfaced just a few days late for inclusion: 'Each time we must choose between Europe and the open sea, we shall always choose the open sea' (1944), and 'If Europe united is to be a living force, Britain will have to play her full part as a member of the European family' (1947). Too late for the third edition, but first in the queue for the fourth.

The second edition owed a considerable debt to Norman Gash for providing a string of quotations that gave Robert Peel a representation in keeping with his eminence and eloquence. In this third edition another scholarly white knight has ridden to the rescue of another nineteenth-century prime minister. Andrew Roberts's classic biography of Lord Salisbury has thrown up an even greater number of quotations that remind us not just of his intellectual power and political experience, but also of his mastery of the English language. To read his entry is to enjoy a crash course in political wisdom. Much of it translates instantly into topical relevance, from 'We do not care to scrutinize too closely the moral boundary which separates a reckless hustings pledge from premeditated fraud' to 'Nobody argues now. They give you an opinion neatly expressed in a single sentence, and that does the work of argument.' Salisbury had views on bureaucracy ('Whitehall will create business for itself as surely as a new railway will create traffic'), House of Lords reform ('The perils of change are so great, the promise of the most hopeful theories is so often deceptive, that it is frequently the wiser part to uphold the existing state of things, if it can be done, even though in point of argument it should be utterly indefensible'), and 'fat cats' ('A highly-paid Chairman is a luxury which should be reserved for the return of a good shareholders' dividend').

Observations like these help the reader to separate the transient from the permanent—as critics of the Iraq war were able to draw on John Adams's observation in 1821 that America 'goes not abroad in search of monsters to destroy.' And one aspect of permanence was underlined by Tony Benn's comment on the role of Lord Cranborne in the reform of the House of Lords: 'The Cecils always come out on top.' That is why I have never seen this Dictionary as simply a work of reference; as I said in my Introduction ten years ago, it is written primarily for the hunters, but also aimed to give pleasure to the browsers and grazers.

I must acknowledge the invaluable help of Peter Hennessy, Anthony Howard, and Andrew Roberts in compiling this edition, and the vigour and rigour of the editors and researchers at the Oxford University Press—especially the PublishingManager for Quotations Dictionaries, Elizabeth Knowles, Susan Ratcliffe, Associate Editor, and Ralph Bates.

ANTONY JAY

Somerset, June 2005

Introduction to the First Edition

'The hard pressed writer in turning over these pages may find and note many excellent phrases, whether to give a pleasing touch of erudition or to save the trouble of thinking for himself.' Bernard Darwin's words in his introduction to the first *Oxford Dictionary of Quotations* are as true today as they were fifty-five years ago. But there are more honourable reasons for using quotations, especially in the world of politics. In mobilizing support for a project or a policy it is especially agreeable to be able to call upon the distinguished dead; their distinction adds intellectual weight and moral force to the argument, and their death makes it impossible for them to appear on television later and say that they meant something completely different.

Even more important, perhaps, than the support of the eminent is the wisdom of the ages. New ideas in politics are always suspect, but recourse to quotation can show that your ideas, far from being new and tender shoots, are rooted deep in the history of political society. Those who argue for punishment as deterrent rather than rehabilitation may find themselves out of the fashion, but a quick look at Aeschylus will enable them to demonstrate the two and a half thousand year pedigree of their belief. Those who oppose closer ties with Europe can quote Bagehot, 'Are they [the English people] not above all nations divided from the rest of the world? . . . Are they not out of the current of common European causes and affairs?' from the nineteenth century, and Gibbon, 'The division of Europe into a number of independent states is productive of the most beneficial consequences to the liberty of mankind,' from the eighteenth, to show that there is nothing new in their belief that there is strength and logic in their resistance, while Europhiles can adduce the dictum of the nineteenth-century Prime Minister Lord Salisbury: 'We are part of the community of Europe and we must do our duty as such.' Just occasionally, too, quotations can be used not just for intellectual support, but for dramatic effect, as if they carried some magical power. Two Prime Ministers in living memory have felt the force of it. The first was Chamberlain in 1940, when Leo Amery quoted Cromwell's historic words to the Rump Parliament 'You have sat too long for any good you have been doing. Depart, I say, and let us have done with you. In the name of God, go!' Chamberlain went. The second was Macmillan in 1963, when a fellow Conservative, Nigel Birch, quoted just as lethally from Browning's *The Lost Leader*:

> Life's night begins; let him never come back to us!
> There would be doubt, hesitation and pain,
> Forced praise on our part—the glimmer of twilight,
> Never glad confident morning again!

Perhaps Macmillan was doomed anyway, but Birch's quotation made certain of his fall as surely as Brutus' dagger.

This Dictionary, it is hoped, will be of service to those who want to support their arguments and opinions with evidence of their distinguished pedigree and ancient lineage, as well as those looking for no more than a pleasing touch of erudition or the avoidance of thought. It is not, however, simply an anthology of political wit and wisdom. It is, first, foremost, and above all, a work of reference. The primary qualification for an entry is not its antiquity or its profundity but its familiarity. There is a bank of political quotations which are part of the currency of political speeches and writings throughout the English-speaking world. All of them should be in these pages, and if they are not (and I am sure time and alert readers will expose some glaring omissions) then the editor is to blame.

Beyond the central core of universally recognized political quotations there is a much wider circle of entries which, while they are quoted from time to time, are not immediately recognizable to all of those to whom they are addressed. These are subject to editorial judgement, and here the editor might try to defend an omission rather than apologize for it. But in both cases the key question has been 'Should this be in a work of reference?' The two principal users for whom the book is intended are those who have encountered or partly recall a quotation and want to verify or source it, and those who are looking for a quotation on a particular subject or from a given writer.

Many works of reference, however, have an appeal to browsers and grazers as well as hunters, and a dictionary of political quotations must be very close to the top of the list; it offers the delight of discovery as well as confirmation and verification. While this one is not designed as an anthology, it is bound to give the reader most of the pleasure of an anthology, and so in many cases I have tried to supply more contextual information than might be necessary in a work of pure reference. Some quotations (for instance Wellington's 'If you believe that you'll believe anything') make little sense to any but the expert reader, unless accompanied by some indication of the context. Others, while intelligible (like Margaret Thatcher's 'Now it must be business as usual'), can become much more interesting with some knowledge of the circumstances in which they were uttered. For the same reason the Dictionary is organized not by theme but by the name of the speaker or writer. I have never myself been entirely at ease with thematic organization—I always have a niggling suspicion that any thematic entry could legitimately have been included under a different heading, and often under several—whereas entries grouped under the name of the source cannot suffer under this disability, and arrangement by source is just as helpful as arrangement by theme for reference purposes. In a collection of political quotations, this form is particularly advantageous, especially for the random dipper: reading through the citations from one individual—Lloyd George, de Tocqueville, Halifax—gives a quick but vivid sense not only of what he said but also of his quality and individuality. So although this is indeed a work of reference, it is hoped that many people will also use it as an illuminating, if wildly unsystematic, compendium of opinions, ideas, and personalities that have marked our progress towards the political society we live in today.

So what makes a quotation into a political quotation? Often, of course, the answer is obvious. General truths about politics are immediate candidates: Aeschylus's 'Everyone's quick to blame the alien', Bacon's 'All rising to great place is by a winding stair', and Burke's 'To tax and to please, no more than to love and be wise, is not given to men.' Then there are quotations specific to an event or an individual which have passed into the language: Disraeli's 'I have climbed to the top of the greasy pole' or Mary Tudor's 'When I am dead and opened, you shall find "Calais" lying in my heart', even though it is more often misquoted than quoted. Some quotations would not merit inclusion but for the source; if you or I had said 'No woman in my time will be Prime Minister' we would hardly expect to find ourselves in the Dictionary. The fact that Margaret Thatcher said it makes all the difference.

There is however a disputed territory between what is obviously a political quotation and what is obviously not. There is nothing remotely political about the words 'I can't tell a lie, Pa; you know I can't tell a lie. I did cut it with my hatchet,' but because it illuminates Washington's character, and because its frequent quotation testifies to his reputation, there can be no question of leaving it out. But what about the sayings of great men when they are writing fiction and the words come from the mouths of their characters, as in Macaulay's poems or Disraeli's novels. Surely it can not be cheating to include them if exclusion would mean omitting 'A Jacobite's Epitaph'? And the 'Two nations' speech in *Sybil* is currently at the heart of the Conservative Party's internal strife.

Another obscure territorial boundary is that which divides, or fails to divide, political quotations from those which, while having large areas that overlap politics, might more properly be classified under headings such as law, warfare, royalty, or economics. If these subjects had their own Oxford quotation dictionaries, there might have been some debate about where to place Adam Smith's observation that 'people of the same trade seldom meet together, even for merriment and diversion, but the conversation ends in a conspiracy against the public, or in some contrivance to raise prices.' Since there is however (as yet) no Oxford Dictionary of Economics Quotations, there was no argument. There is however an excellent *Oxford Book of Political Anecdotes* and, while some anecdotes are the source of quotation, anecdotes as such are not included. Obviously there were temptations. After losing office in 1964 Iain Macleod was a conspicuous absentee from the opposition front bench, which Wilson knew was a cause of much critical comment among Conservative back-benchers. One day however he did appear, to put a challenging question to the Prime Minister. Wilson rose, paused, and then said 'Do you come here often?' It produced one of the biggest laughs ever heard from a party against one of its own front-benchers. But somehow 'Do you come here often?' did not sound like a political quotation; it belongs only in that anecdote and had to be excluded.

Of course not all political quotations are either by politicians or about politics. Lewis Carroll was certainly not a politician and *Alice Through the Looking Glass* is equally certainly not a political work, but 'Jam tomorrow' and 'when I use a word it means just what I choose it to mean' are regularly quoted in political debate—as witness the quotation from Tony Benn, 'Some of that jam we thought was for tomorrow we have already eaten.' The Dictionary would be failing its readers if it left them out. Politicians may no longer quote poetry as freely as they used to, but students of the politics of the recent past will find many quotations from and references to poets, and even today them may encounter Kipling's 'Paying the Dane-geld', Chesterton's 'The Secret People', and copious allusions to the Vicar of Bray. And there is of course one poet who stands out above all the others for frequency of quotation: it is not just the power and range of Shakespeare's writing that makes him so quotable in a political context, it is the fact that so many of his plays are so intensely political in their themes, characters, and conflicts. If readers feel that he is over-represented here, I can only say that I have been acutely aware of the apparently excessive space he has been given, and that the original section was considerably longer. Much weeding has been done, and the surviving entries represent the editor's judgement of those that could not be omitted without loss.

Shakespeare is not the only writer (though he is the only poet) to occupy what might seem to be a disproportionate amount of space. Four great national leaders—Churchill, Disraeli, Jefferson, and Lincoln—have been endlessly quoted by their contemporaries and successors. Certainly they had the gift of language, but it also seems as if the fame they achieved during their lifetime may have led to their words being more diligently recorded and more frequently repeated than those of their less famous contemporaries. There are however two people who figure prominently in these pages without having achieved the same world wide fame. Burke, though he was indeed a statesman, was not in their class, and Bagehot was never even a member of parliament. Both, however, consistently found a way of expressing ideas and arguments that everyone could remember and no one could improve on. Some of their ideas were original, but even those that were not have proved to be endlessly quotable. They exemplify Pope's definition:

> True wit is Nature to advantage dressed.
> What oft was thought, but ne'er so well expressed.

The editor feels no need to apologize for the amount of space they command.

There is one particular danger which confronts all quotation dictionaries: the danger of including only those quotations which have already appeared in other dictionaries. It is of course inevitable that many of the quotations will be found in others collections, but it is equally important that lexicographers should not be endlessly recycling the same material. If quotations are to refresh and invigorate political communication, they should be drawn from a living stream and not a stagnant pond. So while the starting point for this Dictionary was the existing corpus of political quotations held on the files of the Oxford University Press, it was only the starting point. The principal means of bringing in new material was a team of researchers who combed the daily papers and the periodicals, and listened to radio and television programmes, to record every significant quotation they came across and submit it for consideration. Another important source has been correspondence. A living dictionary of quotations will necessarily include quotations from the living, and many of them have been kind enough not only to verify and source entries attributed to them, but also to supply other of their writings and sayings that they have found being quoted. The living have also interceded for the dead: for example, the first draft selection, like all the quotation dictionaries I have encountered, was disturbingly short of quotation from one of Britain's most distinguished Prime Ministers, Robert Peel. It was hard to believe that he had left so few quotable remarks behind him, and a letter to the leading authority on Peel, Professor Norman

Gash, produced evidence that it was not Peel but the record that was at fault. Peel's entry is now of a respectable length. Equally, one of the most politically astute civil servants of the nineteenth century would have remained unrepresented if Lord Dacre had not directed me to Henry Taylor's *The Statesman*.

This leads to the final aspect of the question 'What is a political quotation?', namely does it have to have been quoted, or is it sufficient for it to be quotable? Once you accept quotability as the criterion, you are on a slippery slope, at the bottom of which lie the broad acres of anthologies and commonplace books. The compilers of the first edition of the *Oxford Dictionary of Quotations* were in no doubt: 'During the whole work of selection a great effort was made to restrict the entries to actual current quotations and not to include phrases which the various editors or contributors believed to be quotable or wanted to be quoted.' Of course they were right. And yet even they said only that a great effort was made, not that it was successful in every case. I must confess to not having been quite so purist. Certainly this is essentially a dictionary of what has been quoted, but here and there I have taken one or two small steps down the slippery slope and included lines that I believed modern readers would like to quote. After all, how can one know that they have not been quoted somewhere at some time? I took the liberty of including Laertes's advice to Ophelia about marriage to the heir to the throne:

> His greatness weighed, his will is not his own
> For he himself is subject to his birth.
> He may not, as unvalued persons do,
> Carve for himself, for on his choice depends
> The sanity and health of the whole state;
> And therefore must his choice be circumscribed
> Unto the voice and yielding of that body
> Whereof he is the head.

I had no record of its being politically quoted anywhere, but in view of the continuing current debate about the divorce and remarriage of the Prince of Wales it seemed to me that many people might like to be reminded of it. It was only after it had been passed for the press that I discovered that Stanley Baldwin had quoted that same speech in the House of Commons, in relation to the abdication of King Edward VIII. So the reader will find here a small number— and an exceedingly small percentage—of entries that I cannot swear have been previously quoted, though equally I cannot swear that they have not. They are also another way of stopping the pool of political quotation from stagnating. And another aspect of this question is, when does a political quotation stop being a political quotation? It would have been easy to decide that Bismarck's observation that the Balkan conflict was 'not worth the healthy bones of a single Pomeranian grenadier' had passed into history's out-tray; but it surfaced again in 1995 in a House of Commons debate on the role of the UN forces in Bosnia.

If I may have taken slight liberties with the quotable as opposed to the quoted, this has not been the case with verification and sourcing. My colleagues at the Press have been rigorous and scrupulous about the tracing of quotations, and many promising runners fell at this last fence. They include familiar lines like

Pas d'ennemi à gauche and 'Whoever is in office, the Conservatives are always in power', but among the omissions are a few whose absence I particularly regret. I am sure Bacon said 'Councils to which Time hath not been called, Time will not ratify' (and I am absolutely certain I did not make it up), and I am fairly sure he said 'Great events may have small occasions, but seldom small causes', but no amount of research has been able to track either of them down. I also wish we could have found who it was who said of Gladstone that when making a speech he not only followed every bay and headland along the coastline of his argument, but also insisted on tracking every river to its source. And I believe it was the American scholar Donald Schon who said that government bureaux are memorials to dead problems, but alas I cannot prove it. Another source of regret is the quotations that appeared just too late for inclusion, in particular Shimon Peres's observations 'Television has made dictatorship impossible, but democracy unbearable.' But we were not too late for President Izetbegović's words after signing the Dayton Accord: 'And to my people I say, this may not be a just peace, but it is more just than a continuation of war.'

Perhaps the most problematic of all the quotations are the very recent ones. Ultimately, time is the judge of whether an observation can be accepted as a quotation, and whether 'Tough on crime and tough on the causes of crime' is a full member of the club or merely a short-term visitor, only time will tell. On the other hand, to set an arbitrary limit of ten or twenty years from the first citation as a qualifying period would mean excluding many quotations to which readers would want to refer. I suspect that in any future edition it will be the most topical recent entries that are the least likely to survive.

And what about speech-writers? This is surely a recent problem. It may be that politicians in the past had help from time to time, but it is hard to picture Lincoln or Disraeli or Lloyd George or Churchill asking the boys in the back room to come up with some ideas for the next speech. Today a team of speech writers is part of the standard entourage of an international leader, and on occasions we learn, at least informally, that some famous phrase or other was coined by a hand unconnected to the tongue that uttered it. Should we seek out the names of the writers and give them due recognition? It would be an impossible task, and moreover the reader would look for the phrase under the name of the politician who delivered it. This is also true of quotations that were in circulation some time before a politician gave them national or international currency. Where we can trace the original we attribute it, but it has to be accepted that some of the quotations attributed to politicians were probably not their own coinage. Nevertheless they will always be associated with the words, just as Clark Gable, and not Margaret Mitchell or Sidney Howard, will always be associated with the line 'Frankly, my dear, I don't give a damn' (which would probably be the politician's comment on this question).

The other difficulty presented by the most recent quotations is the possibility that in their original form they reached a national or international audience without ever appearing on a printed page. Radio and television archives are not always accessible, and slow to plough through even when you know exactly what you are looking for; but when you have only an imprecise recollection or reference it can be effectively impossible to locate what would be fairly easy to find in a newspaper or press cuttings library. Of course all the memorable quotations eventually find their way into print, but not always in their original form. The chief whip's famous phrase in Michael Dobbs's *House of Cards*, 'You might very well think that. I couldn't possibly comment', is taken from the television script; it does not appear in the book. Equally, transcripts from radio and television can miss important emphases and nuances: when Neil Kinnock spoke to the Labour Party Conference about Liverpool Council, his stress on 'Labour' in the phrase, 'the grotesque chaos of a Labour council—a *Labour* council—hiring taxis to scuttle round the city handing out redundancy notices to its own workers' did not come through in the press reports as it did in the television news bulletins. And the televising of parliamentary debates has exposed the difference between the semi-incoherence of some members' speeches and the comparative lucidity and logic of the phrasing that appears subsequently in the august pages of Hansard.

Finally I must acknowledge with gratitude the large number of people whose help has been invaluable. Christopher Booker, Simon Heffer, Nigel Rees, and Peter Hennessy all read the whole of the first draft and made numerous comments and suggestions of which many were immediately incorporated. All of them are extremely busy professionals and I was astonished as well as delighted at the amount of time and care they were willing to give to the task. Indeed one of the happiest aspects of an unusually happy assignment has been the willingness of almost everyone I contacted to give up time and take trouble to make the Dictionary as full and accurate as possible. Of those who helped out on specific topics or authors I would like to offer especial thanks to the following: Lord Bauer, Tony Benn, John Biffen, John Blundell, Dr Eamonn Butler, the Bishop of Coventry, Lord Dacre, Lord Deedes, Oliver Everett, Milton Friedman, Norman Gash, Martin Gilbert, Henry Hardy, Lord Healey, Sir Bernard Ingham, Simon Jenkins, Bernard Levin, Kenneth Morgan, Nigel Nicolson, Matthew Parris, Enoch Powell, Stanley Wells, and Chris Wrigley. Above all, I want to thank the editorial team of the Quotations Dictionaries department of the Oxford University Press. Not only have they done the bulk of the work; their knowledge, expertise, and scholarly rigour have contributed immeasurably to the quality of the book.

Any credit for the final result must be shared with all of the above; the blame remains exclusively the editor's.

ANTONY JAY

Somerset, January 1996

How to Use the Dictionary

The sequence of entries is by alphabetical order of author, usually by surname but with occasional exceptions such as imperial or royal titles, or authors known by a pseudonym (**'Saki'**), or a nickname (**Caligula**). In general authors' names are given in the form by which they are best known, so that we have **Harold Macmillan** (not Lord Stockton), **Lord Melbourne** (not William Lamb), and **H. G. Wells** (not Herbert George Wells). Collections such as **Anonymous** and the **Bible** are included in the alphabetical sequence.

Author names are followed by dates of birth and death (where known) and brief descriptions. Cross-references are then given to quotations about that author elsewhere in the text (*on Acheson*: see **Pearson** 200:7). Within each author entry, quotations from speeches are given in date order and appear first; quotations from diaries and letters are included in this chronological sequence, as are quotations from secondary sources to which a date in the author's lifetime can be assigned. Literary and published works, which follow, are arranged in alphabetical order of title, 'a' and 'the' being ignored. Quotations from secondary sources to which no specific date can be assigned come at the end of the entry, and are arranged in alphabetical order of the quotation text. Within the alphabetical sequence there are a number of special category entries, including **Last words**, **Misquotations**, and **Newspaper headlines and leaders**. Quotations in these sections are arranged alphabetically.

Contextual information regarded as essential to a full appreciation of the quotation precedes the relevant text in an italicized note; information providing amplification follows. Bibliographical information as to the source from which the quotation is taken appears in a marginal note.

Cross-references are made both to individual quotations (see **Disraeli** 121:1) and to whole entries. References to specific quotations consist of the author's name followed by the page number and the number of the quotation on the page (**Burke** 63:1). Authors who have their own entries are typographically distinguished by the use of bold (epitaph for John **Adams**, son of Joseph **Kennedy**).

The Index

Both the keywords and the entries following each keyword, including those in foreign languages, are in strict alphabetical order. Singular and plural nouns (with their possessive forms) are grouped separately.

The references show the author's name, usually in abbreviated form (SHAK/Shakespeare), followed by the page number and the number of the quotation on that page: 183:8 therefore means quotation 8 on page 183.

Diane Abbott 1953–
British Labour politician

1 Being an MP is the sort of job all working-class parents want for their children—clean, indoors and no heavy lifting.

in Independent 18 January 1994

Tony Abbott 1966–
Canadian Conservative politician

2 What it is to me is a little rich girl who is basically whoring herself out to the Liberals.
   of Belinda Stronach's crossing the floor to join the Liberal Party

in GlobeandMail.com 18 May 2005 (online edition)

3 There's a right way to say things and there's a wrong way to say things, and I chose the wrong way.
   apologizing for his choice of language in criticizing Belinda Stronach

in CBC Calgary 19 May 2005 (online edition)

Bella Abzug 1920–98
American politician

4 Richard Nixon impeached himself. He gave us Gerald Ford as his revenge.

in Rolling Stone; Linda Botts *Loose Talk* (1980)

Accius 170–c.86 BC
Roman poet and dramatist

5 Let them hate, so long as they fear.

Atreus

Dean Acheson 1893–1971
American politician
on Acheson: see **Pearson** 307:2

6 I will undoubtedly have to seek what is happily known as gainful employment, which I am glad to say does not describe holding public office.

in Time 22 December 1952

7 Great Britain has lost an empire and has not yet found a role.

speech at the Military Academy, West Point, 5 December 1962

8 The first requirement of a statesman is that he be dull.

in Observer 21 June 1970

9 A memorandum is written not to inform the reader but to protect the writer.

in Wall Street Journal 8 September 1977

10 *of President Eisenhower:*
   I doubt very much if a man whose main literary interests were in works by Mr Zane Grey, admirable as they may be, is particularly equipped to be the chief executive of this country, particularly where Indian Affairs are concerned.

attributed

Lord Acton 1834–1902
British historian

11 Power tends to corrupt and absolute power corrupts absolutely.
   often quoted as 'All power corrupts . . . '

letter to Bishop Mandell Creighton, 3 April 1887; see **Pitt** 311:9

12 Great men are almost always bad men, even when they exercise influence and not authority.

letter to Bishop Mandell Creighton, 3 April 1887

Abigail Adams 1744–1818

American letter writer, wife of John **Adams** and mother of John Quincy **Adams**

1 In the new code of laws which I suppose it will be necessary for you to make I desire you would remember the ladies, and be more generous and favourable to them than your ancestors. Do not put such unlimited power into the hands of the husbands. Remember all men would be tyrants if they could.

letter to John Adams, 31 March 1776

2 These are times in which a genius would wish to live. It is not in the still calm of life, or the repose of a pacific station, that great characters are formed . . . Great necessities call out great virtues.

letter to John Quincy Adams, 19 January 1780

3 Patriotism in the female sex is the most disinterested of all virtues. Excluded from honours and from offices, we cannot attach ourselves to the State or Government from having held a place of eminence . . . Yet all history and every age exhibit instances of patriotic virtue in the female sex; which considering our situation equals the most heroic of yours.

letter to John Adams, 17 June 1782

Franklin P. Adams 1881–1960

American journalist and humorist

4 When the political columnists say 'Every thinking man' they mean themselves, and when candidates appeal to 'Every intelligent voter' they mean everybody who is going to vote for them.

Nods and Becks (1944)

5 The trouble with this country is that there are too many politicians who believe, with a conviction based on experience, that you can fool all of the people all of the time.

Nods and Becks (1944)

6 Elections are won by men and women chiefly because most people vote against somebody rather than for somebody.

Nods and Becks (1944)

Gerry Adams 1948–

Northern Irish politician; President of Sinn Féin

7 We want him to be the last British Prime Minister with jurisdiction in Ireland.
    *of Tony **Blair***

in Irish Times 18 October 1997

8 Peace cannot be built on exclusion. That has been the price of the past 30 years.

in Daily Telegraph 11 April 1998

Henry Brooks Adams 1838–1918

American historian

9 Politics, as a practice, whatever its professions, has always been the systematic organization of hatreds.

The Education of Henry Adams (1907)

10 A friend in power is a friend lost.

The Education of Henry Adams (1907)

11 [Charles] Sumner's mind had reached the calm of water which receives and reflects images without absorbing them; it contained nothing but itself.
    *of the American politician and orator Charles **Sumner***

The Education of Henry Adams (1907)

1 The progress of evolution from President Washington to President Grant was alone evidence to upset Darwin.

The Education of Henry Adams (1907)

2 Practical politics consists in ignoring facts.

The Education of Henry Adams (1907)

John Adams 1735–1826

American statesman, 2nd President of the US; husband of Abigail **Adams** and father of John Quincy **Adams**
see also **Last words** 228:6

3 The law, in all vicissitudes of government . . . will preserve a steady undeviating course; it will not bend to the uncertain wishes, imaginations, and wanton tempers of men . . . On the one hand it is inexorable to the cries of the prisoners; on the other it is deaf, deaf as an adder to the clamours of the populace.

argument in defence of the British soldiers in the Boston Massacre Trials, 4 December 1770; see **Sidney** 364:10

4 There is danger from all men. The only maxim of a free government ought to be to trust no man living with power to endanger the public liberty.

Notes for an Oration at Braintree (Spring 1772)

5 *of the Boston Tea Party:*
There is a dignity, a majesty, a sublimity, in this last effort of the patriots that I greatly admire. The people should never rise without doing something to be remembered— something notable and striking.

diary, 17 December 1773

6 A government of laws, and not of men.
later incorporated in the Massachusetts Constitution (1780)

in *Boston Gazette* (1774)

7 I agree with you that in politics the middle way is none at all.

letter to Horatio Gates, 23 March 1776

8 Yesterday, the greatest question was decided which ever was debated in America, and a greater perhaps never was nor will be decided among men. A resolution was passed without one dissenting colony, 'that these United Colonies are, and of right ought to be, free and independent States.'

letter to Abigail Adams, 3 July 1776

9 I must study politics and war that my sons may have liberty to study mathematics and philosophy.

letter to Abigail Adams, 12 May 1780

10 *of the vice-presidency:*
My country has in its wisdom contrived for me the most insignificant office that ever the invention of man contrived or his imagination conceived.

letter to Abigail Adams, 19 December 1793

11 Democracy never lasts long. It soon wastes, exhausts, and murders itself. There never was a democracy that did not commit suicide.

letter to John Taylor, 15 April 1814

12 The fundamental article of my political creed is that despotism, or unlimited sovereignty, or absolute power, is the same in a majority of a popular assembly, an aristocratic council, an oligarchical junto, and a single emperor.

letter to Thomas Jefferson, 13 November 1815

13 The jaws of power are always opened to devour, and her arm is always stretched out, if possible, to destroy the freedom of thinking, speaking, and writing.

A Dissertation on the Canon and the Feudal Law (1765)

1 Liberty cannot be preserved without a general knowledge among the people, who have a right . . . and a desire to know; but besides this, they have a right, an indisputable, unalienable, indefeasible, divine right to that most dreaded and envied kind of knowledge, I mean of the characters and conduct of their rulers.

A Dissertation on the Canon and Feudal Law (1765)

2 The happiness of society is the end of government.

Thoughts on Government (1776)

3 Fear is the foundation of most governments.

Thoughts on Government (1776)

4 The judicial power ought to be distinct from both the legislative and executive, and independent upon both, that so it may be a check upon both, as both should be checks upon that.

Thoughts on Government (1776)

John Quincy Adams 1767–1848
American statesman, 6th President of the US; son of Abigail **Adams** and John **Adams**
see also **Last Words** 228:5

5 Think of your forefathers! Think of your posterity!

Oration at Plymouth 22 December 1802

6 *Fiat justitia, pereat coelum* [Let justice be done, though heaven perish]. My toast would be, may our country be always successful, but whether successful or otherwise, always right.

letter to John Adams, 1 August 1816; see **Decatur** 112:2, **Mansfield** 259:4, **Mottoes** 281:3

7 Wherever the standard of freedom and Independence has been or shall be unfurled, there will her heart, her benedictions and her prayers be. But she [America] goes not abroad in search of monsters to destroy.

speech to House of Representatives, 4 July 1821

8 This house will bear witness to his piety; this town [Braintree, Massachusetts], his birthplace, to his munificence; history to his patriotism; posterity to the depth and compass of his mind.

epitaph for John **Adams**, 1829

Samuel Adams 1722–1803
American revolutionary leader

9 Let us contemplate our forefathers, and posterity, and resolve to maintain the rights bequeathed to us by the former, for the sake of the latter.

speech, 1771

10 What a glorious morning this is.
    on hearing gunfire at Lexington, 19 April 1775

J. K. Hosmer *Samuel Adams* (1886); see **Misquotations** 274:4

11 A nation of shopkeepers are very seldom so disinterested.

Oration in Philadelphia 1 August 1776 (the authenticity of this publication is doubtful); see **Napoleon** 285:1, **Smith** 370:9

12 We cannot make events. Our business is wisely to improve them . . . Mankind are governed more by their feelings than by reason. Events which excite those feelings will produce wonderful effects.

J. N. Rakove *The Beginnings of National Politics* (1979)

Frank Ezra Adcock 1886–1968
British classicist and historian of Greece and Rome

13 Rome under Sulla was like a bus, with half the passengers trying to drive, and the rest trying to collect the fare.

lecture at Cambridge in the 1940s

Joseph Addison 1672–1719

English poet, dramatist, and essayist; co-founder of *The Spectator*

1　　　　What pity is it
That we can die but once to serve our country!

Cato (1713)

2 From hence, let fierce contending nations know
What dire effects from civil discord flow.

Cato (1713)

Konrad Adenauer 1876–1967

German statesman, first Chancellor of the Federal Republic of Germany

3 It was at the Congress of Vienna, when you so foolishly put
Prussia on the Rhine as a safeguard against France and
another Napoleon.
　　identifying England's greatest mistake in its relations with
　　Germany

answering his own question to
Noel Annan in 1945; Noel Annan
*Changing Enemies: the Defeat and
Regeneration of Germany* (1989)

4 A thick skin is a gift from God.

in *New York Times* 30 December
1959

Aeschylus c.525–456 BC

Greek tragedian

5 Do not taint pure laws with mere expediency
Guard well and reverence that form of government
Which will eschew alike licence and slavery.
And from your policy do not wholly banish fear
For what man living, freed from fear, will still be just?

The Eumenides

6 Let war stay abroad; it makes no difficulty in coming, for
the man who will have in him a strong desire for glory. I
disapprove of a bird's battling in its own home.

The Eumenides l. 863

7 Everyone's quick to blame the alien.

The Suppliant Maidens

Herbert Agar 1897–1980

American poet and writer

8 The truth which makes men free is for the most part the
truth which men prefer not to hear.

Time for Greatness (1942)

Spiro T. Agnew 1918–96

American Republican politician

9 I didn't say I wouldn't go into ghetto areas. I've been in
many of them and to some extent I would say this: If you've
seen one city slum you've seen them all.

in *Detroit Free Press* 19 October
1968

10 A spirit of national masochism prevails, encouraged by an
effete corps of impudent snobs who characterize themselves
as intellectuals.

speech in New Orleans, 19
October 1969

11 In the United States today, we have more than our share of
the nattering nabobs of negativism.

speech in San Diego, 11
September 1970

Bertie Ahern 1951–
Irish Fianna Fáil statesman, Taoiseach since 1997

1 It is a day we should treasure. Today is about the promise of a bright future, a day when we hope a line will be drawn under the bloody past.

in Guardian 11 April 1998

Jonathan Aitken 1942–
British Conservative politician

2 If it falls to me to start a fight to cut out the cancer of bent and twisted journalism in our country with the simple sword of truth and the trusty shield of British fair play, so be it.

statement, London, 10 April 1995

3 I realize I am about as welcome in the Tory party as Banquo's ghost.
  on his attempt to become a Tory MP again being stopped by Michael **Howard**

in Sunday Times 15 February 2004

Madeleine Albright 1937–
American diplomat

4 Hallelujah . . . Never again will your fates be tossed around like poker chips on a bargaining table.
  accepting the admission papers for Hungary, Poland, and the Czech Republic to become members of Nato

in Daily Telegraph 13 March 1999

Alcuin c.735–804
English scholar and theologian

5 And those people should not be listened to who keep saying the voice of the people is the voice of God [*Vox populi, vox Dei*], since the riotousness of the crowd is always very close to madness.

letter 164 in Works (1863)

Richard Aldington 1892–1962
English poet, novelist, and biographer

6 Patriotism is a lively sense of collective responsibility. Nationalism is a silly cock crowing on its own dunghill.

The Colonel's Daughter (1931)

Cecil Frances Alexander 1818–95
Irish poet and hymn-writer

7 The rich man in his castle,
The poor man at his gate,
God made them, high or lowly,
And ordered their estate.

'All Things Bright and Beautiful' (1848)

Woody Allen 1935–
American film director, writer, and actor

8 I believe there is something out there watching over us. Unfortunately, it's the government.

Peter McWilliams *Ain't Nobody's Business If You Do* (1993); attributed

Joseph Alsop b. 1910–89
American journalist

1 Gratitude, like love, is never a dependable international emotion.

in *Observer* 30 November 1952

Julian Amery 1919–96
British Conservative politician, son of Leo **Amery**

2 *of a misinterpretation of their role made by some Members of Parliament:*
Representing Parliament in their constituencies rather than their constituents in Parliament.

attributed by Norman Tebbit in 'On the Inner Culture of the Tories'; Subroto Roy and John C. Clarke *Margaret Thatcher's Revolution* (2005)

Leo Amery 1873–1955
British Conservative politician, father of Julian **Amery**

3 *of H. H. **Asquith**:*
For twenty years he has held a season-ticket on the line of least resistance and has gone wherever the train of events has carried him, lucidly justifying his position at whatever point he has happened to find himself.

in *Quarterly Review* July 1914

4 Speak for England.

said to Arthur Greenwood in House of Commons, 2 September 1939; see **Boothby** 51:3

5 I will quote certain other words. I do it with great reluctance, because I am speaking of those who are old friends and colleagues of mine, but they are words which, I think, are applicable to the present situation. This is what Cromwell said to the Long Parliament when he thought it was no longer fit to conduct the affairs of the nation: 'You have sat too long here for any good you have been doing. Depart, I say, and let us have done with you. In the name of God, go.'

in the House of Commons, 7 May 1940; see **Cromwell** 106:1

Fisher Ames 1758–1808
American politician

6 A monarchy is a merchantman which sails well, but will sometimes strike on a rock, and go to the bottom; whilst a republic is a raft which would never sink, but then your feet are always in the water.

attributed to Ames, speaking in the House of Representatives, 1795, but not traced in Ames's speeches

Anacharsis
Scythian prince of the 6th century BC

7 Written laws are like spider's webs; they will catch, it is true, the weak and poor, but would be torn in pieces by the rich and powerful.

Plutarch *Parallel Lives* 'Solon'; see **Shenstone** 362:12, **Swift** 384:5

Count Julius Andrássy 1823–90
Hungarian statesman

8 A fight between a shark and a wolf. They may show any amount of natural animosity but after snapping at each other they could do nothing more than pass on.
on how the Anglo-Russian war would actually be fought

quoted by Lord **Salisbury** in Hatfield Papers; Andrew Roberts *Salisbury: Victorian Titan* (1999)

Kofi Annan 1938–

Ghanaian diplomat, Secretary-General of the United Nation

1 You can do a lot with diplomacy, but of course you can do a lot more with diplomacy backed up by fairness and force.
of the agreement reached with Saddam Hussein over weapons inspections, February 1998

in *Mail on Sunday* 1 March 1998 'Quotes of the Week'

Anonymous

2 All the 'isms are wasms.
said to have been the comment of a Foreign Office spokesman on the signing of the Molotov–Ribbentrop Pact in August 1939

Peter Hennessy *Whitehall* (1990)

3 Beneath that extraordinary exterior there is a little pink, quivering Ted trying to get out.
*comment of a former Cabinet colleague on Edward **Heath***

in 1993; Peter Hennessy *The Prime Minister: the Office and its Holders since 1945* (2000)

4 The best defence against the atom bomb is not to be there when it goes off.

contributor to *British Army Journal*, in *Observer* 20 February 1949

5 But this is terrible—*they*'ve elected a Labour Government, and *the country* will never stand for that!
unidentified lady diner in the Savoy Hotel, 26 July 1945

Michael Sissons and Philip French (eds.) *The Age of Austerity 1945–51* (1964)

6 A community in which power, wealth and opportunity are in the hands of the many not the few, where the rights we enjoy reflect the duties we owe . . . in which the enterprise of the market and the rigour of competition are joined with the forces of partnership and cooperation.

new Clause Four of the Labour Party constitution, passed at a special conference 29 April 1995; see **Anonymous** 12:13

7 A Company for carrying on an undertaking of Great Advantage, but no one to know what it is.

Company Prospectus at the time of the South Sea Bubble (1711)

8 Dalton McGuinty: He's an evil reptilian kitten-eater from another planet.
Canadian Conservative press release attacking the Liberal leader (now premier) during September 2003 Ontario election campaign

in *London Free Press News* 13 September 2003

9 Every country has its own constitution; ours is absolutism moderated by assassination.
of Russia

Ernst Friedrich Herbert, Count Münster, quoting 'an intelligent Russian', in *Political Sketches of the State of Europe, 1814–1867* (1868)

10 Expletive deleted.

Submission of Recorded Presidential Conversations to the Committee on the Judiciary of the House of Representatives by President Richard M. Nixon 30 April 1974

11 Exterminate . . . the treacherous English, walk over General French's contemptible little army.
often attributed to Kaiser Wilhelm II, but most probably fabricated by the British; source of the nickname 'the Old Contemptibles'

Annexe to British Expeditionary Force Routine Orders of 24 September 1914; Arthur Ponsonby *Falsehood in Wartime* (1928)

12 The finest brute votes in Europe.
a 'cynical politician's' view of the parliamentary county members

Walter Bagehot *The English Constitution* (1867) 'The House of Commons'

13 The first and only thing they have to do is to decide how a resigned commission behaves.
unidentified British official in Brussels of the European Commission

in *Daily Telegraph* 18 March 1999

1 For the sake of brevity we have followed the common practice of using the phrase 'Communists' throughout to include Fascists.

Radcliffe Report 'Security Procedures in the Public Service' April 1962

2 Frederick the Great lost the battle of Jena.
*attributing the Prussians' defeat at Jena by **Napoleon** in 1806 to their rigid adherence to the strategy of **Frederick** (who had died in 1786)*

Walter Bagehot *The English Constitution* (1867)

3 Happy is that city which in time of peace thinks of war.
inscription found in the armoury of Venice

Robert Burton *The Anatomy of Melancholy* (1621–51)

4 Hark the herald angels sing
Mrs Simpson's pinched our king.
*contemporary children's rhyme on the abdication of **Edward VIII***

Clement Attlee letter 26 December 1938; Kenneth Harris *Attlee* (1982)

5 Harold wanted to be a combination of the Head of MI5 and News Editor of the *Daily Mirror*.
*Downing Street official shortly after **Wilson**'s resignation*

Peter Hennessy *The Prime Minister: the Office and its Holders since 1945* (2000)

6 Have I said something foolish?

Athenian statesman, on being cheered by the populace

7 Have you heard? The Prime Minister has resigned and Northcliffe has sent for the King.
*a joke (c.1919) suggesting that Lord **Northcliffe**, the press baron and **Lloyd George**'s implacable enemy, would succeed him as Prime Minister*

Hamilton Fyfe *Northcliffe, an Intimate Biography* (1930)

8 Hear ye! Hear ye! All persons are commanded to keep silent, on pain of imprisonment, while the House of Representatives is exhibiting to the Senate of the United States articles of impeachment against William Jefferson Clinton, President of the United States.
formal announcement read by the serjeant-at-arms

in *Guardian* 8 January 1999

9 He may be a minister of the British Government but we are the Walt Disney Corporation and we don't roll over for anyone.
a Disneyland executive commenting on reports that Peter Mandelson might use the theme park's ideas in the Millennium Dome without authorization

in *Sunday Telegraph* 18 January 1998

10 He talked shop like a tenth muse.
*of **Gladstone**'s Budget speech*

G. W. E. Russell *Collections and Recollections* (1898)

11 He who writes the minutes rules the roost.

Civil Service maxim

12 I cannot see the Speaker, Hal, can you?
What! Cannot see the Speaker, I see two!
satirical verse in an opposition newspaper of 1793, referring to the report that William Pitt and Henry Dundas had come into the House of Commons while drunk

William Hague *William Pitt the Younger* (2004) ch. 16

13 The idea that the PM gets integrated advice is nonsense. You could not see a more *unjoined* system. To say they have imported the White House to No. 10—Washington to Downing Street—is absolutely right.
a senior Whitehall figure on the Blair administration, January 2000

Peter Hennessy *The Prime Minister: the Office and its Holders since 1945* (2000)

14 I like Mr Baldwin: he promises nothing and keeps his word.

unattributed

1 I like my Prime Ministers to be a bit inhumane. The PM has insufficient inhumanity . . . He wants to be liked.
*a senior civil servant, shortly after John **Major** had become Prime Minister*

Peter Hennessy *The Prime Minister: the Office and its Holders since 1945* (2000)

2 I never vote. It only encourages them.

elderly American lady quoted by comedian Jack Parr; William Safire *The New Language of Politics* (1968)

3 The iron lady.
*name given to Margaret **Thatcher**, then Leader of the Opposition, by the Soviet Defence Ministry newspaper Red Star, which accused her of trying to revive the cold war*

in *Sunday Times* 25 January 1976

4 It became necessary to destroy the town to save it.
comment by unidentified US Army major on Ben Tre, Vietnam

in Associated Press Report, *New York Times* 8 February 1968

5 It is a pretty pass when the headline in the *Morning Star* reads 'Back the Law Lords.'
to the Lord Chancellor on the Prevention of Terrorism legislation

comment reported by Lord Falconer, speech in House of Lords, 7 March 2005

6 It is becoming difficult to find anyone in the Commission who has even the slightest sense of responsibility.

report on the European Commission; in *Guardian* 17 March 1999

7 *unidentified aide to Gordon Brown commenting on Tony Blair's announcement that if re-elected he would serve a full third term as Prime Minister:*
It's like an African coup. They waited until he [Brown] was out of the country.

in *BBC News* 2 October 2004 (online edition)

8 Just when we thought it was safe to go back in the water, the sharks are circling again.
unidentified British Cabinet Minister on the forthcoming report of the European Convention

in *Daily Telegraph* 11 June 2003 (electronic edition)

9 The King over the Water.
Jacobite toast to the deposed and exiled James II and his heirs

current in the 18th century

10 Liberty is always unfinished business.

title of 36th Annual Report of the American Civil Liberties Union, 1 July 1955–30 June 1956

11 [Like] watching a stream of blood coming from beneath a closed door.
a contemporary expression of the feelings evoked by news of the executions after the Easter Rising

Robert Kee *Ourselves Alone* (1916)

12 Lost is our old simplicity of times,
The world abounds with laws, and teems with crimes.

On the Proceedings Against America (1775)

13 CHILD: Mamma, are Tories born wicked, or do they grow wicked afterwards?
MOTHER: They are born wicked, and grow worse.

G. W. E. Russell *Collections and Recollections* (1898)

14 Men said openly that Christ and His saints slept.
of twelfth-century England during the civil war between Stephen and Matilda

Anglo-Saxon Chronicle for 1137

15 The ministry of all the talents.
name given ironically to William Grenville's coalition of 1806, and also applied to later coalitions

G. W. Cooke *The History of Party* (1837) vol. 3

1 My name is George Nathaniel Curzon,
I am a most superior person.
My face is pink, my hair is sleek,
I dine at Blenheim once a week.
of Lord **Curzon**

The Masque of Balliol (c.1870), in
W. G. Hiscock *The Balliol Rhymes*
(1939, the last two lines are a later
addition); see **Parris** 305:8

2 The nearest thing to death in life
Is David Patrick Maxwell Fyfe,
Though underneath that gloomy shell
He does himself extremely well.
of David Maxwell Fyfe, later Lord **Kilmuir***, and said to have been
current on the Northern circuit in the late 1930s*

E. Grierson *Confessions of a Country
Magistrate* (1972)

3 Never stand when you could sit, and never miss a chance to
relieve yourself.

advice given by a private secretary
or equerry to **George V** or
George VI

4 No man's life, liberty or property are safe while the
legislature is in session.
view of an unidentified New York State Surrogate Court Judge

in 1866; unattributed

5 Now that the Cabinet's gone to its dinner,
The Secretary stays and gets thinner and thinner,
Racking his brains to record and report
What he thinks they think they ought to have thought.

anonymous verse, undated; S. S.
Wilson *The Cabinet Office* (1975)

6 One Cartwright brought a Slave from Russia, and would
scourge him, for which he was questioned: and it was
resolved, That England was too pure an Air for Slaves to
breathe in.

'In the 11th of Elizabeth' (17
November 1568–16 November
1569); John Rushworth *Historical
Collections* (1680–1722)

7 Order reigns in Warsaw.
after the brutal suppression of an uprising

the newspaper *Moniteur* reported,
16 September 1831, 'Order and
calm are completely restored in
the capital'; on the same day
Count Sebastiani, minister of
foreign affairs, declared: 'Peace
reigns in Warsaw'

8 Peace, order, and good government.

British North America Act 1867 sect.
91, introduction

9 A place within the meaning of the Act.

usually taken to be a reference to
the Betting Act 1853, sect. 2,
which banned off-course betting
on horse-races

10 The plan is called 'Shock and Awe', and its goal is 'the
psychological destruction of the enemy's will to fight'.

in *New Yorker* 10 February 2003;
see **Ullman** 403:3

11 Please to remember the Fifth of November,
Gunpowder Treason and Plot.
We know no reason why gunpowder treason
Should ever be forgot.

traditional rhyme on the
Gunpowder Plot (1605)

12 Prudence is the other woman in Gordon's life.
of Gordon **Brown**

unidentified aide, quoted in BBC
News online (Budget Briefing), 20
March 1998

13 Psychological flaws.
on which, according to an unnamed source, Gordon **Brown** *needed
to 'get a grip'*

in *Observer* 18 January 1998;
attributed to Alastair **Campbell** by
Bernard **Ingham** in minutes of the
Parliamentary Select Committee
on Public Administration, 2 June
1998, but denied by Campbell in

1 Reorganizing the Civil Service is like drawing a knife through a bowl of marbles.

evidence to the Committee, 23 June 1998

unattributed comment

2 A revolution which lacks the anchor of ideology or the compass of principle will founder on the rocks of mere personality.
  an unidentified left-winger on the reported feud between New Labour's Gordon Brown and Peter Mandelson

in *The Mail on Sunday* 19 May 1996

3 *Sic transit gloria mundi.*

Thus passes the glory of the world.
  said during the coronation of a new Pope, while flax is burned to represent the transitoriness of earthly glory

used at the coronation of Alexander V in Pisa, 7 July 1409, but earlier in origin

4 The silly, flat, dishwatery utterances of the man who has to be pointed out to intelligent observers as the President of the United States.

review of **Lincoln**'s Gettysburg Address, in *Chicago Times* 20 November 1863; see **Everett** 138:2

5 *Tempora mutantur, et nos mutamur in illis.*

Times change, and we change with them.

William Harrison *Description of Britain* (1577); attributed to the Emperor Lothar I (795–855) in the form '*omnia mutantur, nos et mutamur in illis* [all things change, and we change with them]'

6 There is one thing stronger than all the armies in the world; and that is an idea whose time has come.

in *Nation* 15 April 1943; see **Hugo** 191:2

7 There shall be a Scottish parliament.

first clause of the Scotland Act, 1998; see **Dewar** 116:9

8 *an unnamed Labour MP commenting on the unusually pale eyes of Hugh* **Dalton**:
They have a habit of looking at you intently and conveying unfathomable depths of insincerity.
  sometimes quoted as 'eyes blazing with insincerity'

Patricia Strauss *Bevin and Co. The Leaders of British Labour* (1941)

9 *annotation to a ministerial brief, said to have been read out inadvertently in the House of Lords:*
This is a rotten argument, but it should be good enough for their lordships on a hot summer afternoon.

Lord Home *The Way the Wind Blows* (1976)

10 Those on the opposite side are your opponents; your enemies are on your own side.

traditional advice to a new MP

11 Though I yield to no one in my admiration for Mr Coolidge, I do wish he did not look as if he had been weaned on a pickle.
  of President Calvin **Coolidge**

anonymous remark, in Alice Roosevelt Longworth *Crowded Hours* (1933)

12 'Tis bad enough in man or woman
To steal a goose from off a common;
But surely he's without excuse
Who steals the common from the goose.

'On Inclosures'; in *The Oxford Book of Light Verse* (1938)

13 To secure for the workers by hand or by brain the full fruits of their industry and the most equitable distribution thereof that may be possible upon the basis of the common ownership of the means of production, distribution, and exchange.

Clause Four of the Labour Party's Constitution of 1918 (revised 1929); the commitment to common ownership of services was largely removed in 1995; see **Anonymous** 8:6

1 Under capitalism man exploits man. And under
   Communism it is just the reverse.
   *joke told to J. **Galbraith** at a dinner given for him during his
   lecture tour of Poland by the Polish Economic Society, May 1958*

J. K. Galbraith *A Life in Our Times*
(1981)

2 We hold these truths to be self-evident, that all men are
   created equal, that they are endowed by their Creator with
   certain unalienable rights, that among these are life, liberty
   and the pursuit of happiness.

The American Declaration of
Independence, 4 July 1776

3 We trained hard . . . but it seemed that every time we were
   beginning to form up into teams we would be reorganized. I
   was to learn later in life that we tend to meet any new
   situation by reorganizing; and a wonderful method it can be
   for creating the illusion of progress while producing
   confusion, inefficiency, and demoralization.

modern saying, frequently (and
wrongly) attributed to Petronius
Arbiter

4 We value excellence as well as fairness, independence as
   dearly as mateship.

draft preamble to the Australian
constitution, made public 23
March 1999

5 We wouldn't trust Labour to deliver a pizza—let alone a
   Parliament.
   view of the Scottish Nationalist Party

unattributed; Brian Taylor *The
Scottish Parliament* (1999)

6 What did the President know and when did he know it?

question current at the time of
Watergate, associated particularly
with Howard Baker, Vice-Chairman
of the Senate Watergate
Committee

7 When war enters a country
   It produces lies like sand.

epigraph to Arthur Ponsonby
Falsehood in Wartime (1928)

8 Why is there only one Monopolies Commission?

British graffito; incorporated in the
Official Monster Raving Loony
Party Manifesto, 1987

9 A willing foe and sea room.
   Naval toast in the time of Nelson

W. N. T. Beckett *A Few Naval
Customs, Expressions, Traditions,
and Superstitions* (1931) 'Customs'

10 Winston is back.
   *Board of Admiralty signal to the Fleet on Winston **Churchill**'s
   reappointment as First Sea Lord, 3 September 1939*

Martin Gilbert *Winston S. Churchill*
(1976) vol. 5

11 You may strut, dapper George, but 'twill all be in vain;
   We know 'tis Queen Caroline, not you, that reign.
   *contemporary lampoon on George II and his influential consort
   Caroline of Ansbach*

John, Lord Hervey *Some materials
towards memoirs of the reign of
King George II* (ed. R. Sedgwick,
1931) vol. 1 (see also **Epitaphs**
137:2)

Susan Brownell Anthony 1820–1906

American feminist and political activist

12 The men and women of the North are slaveholders, those of
   the South slaveowners. The guilt rests on the North equally
   with the South.

*Speech on No Union with
Slaveholders* 1857

13 Join the union, girls, and together say *Equal Pay for Equal
   Work*.

in *The Revolution* 8 October 1869

1 Here, in the first paragraph of the Declaration [of Independence], is the assertion of the natural right of all to the ballot; for how can 'the consent of the governed' be given, if the right to vote be denied?
speech in 1873 before her trial for voting

Is It a Crime for a Citizen of the United States to Vote?

Yasser Arafat 1929–2004
Palestinian statesman, President 1996–2004

2 Palestine is the cement that holds the Arab world together, or it is the explosive that blows it apart.

in Time 11 November 1974

John Arbuthnot 1667–1735
Scottish physician and pamphleteer

3 He [the writer] warns the heads of parties against believing their own lies.

The Art of Political Lying (1712)

Hannah Arendt 1906–75
American political philosopher

4 The most radical revolutionary will become a conservative on the day after the revolution.

in New Yorker 12 September 1970

5 Under conditions of tyranny it is far easier to act than to think.

W. H. Auden *A Certain World* (1970)

Marquis d'Argenson 1694–1757
French politician and political essayist

6 *Laisser-faire.*
No interference.
term applied to the doctrine of minimum state intervention in economic affairs

Mémoires et Journal Inédit du Marquis d'Argenson; see **Quesnay** 320:4

Aristophanes c.450–c.385 BC
Greek comic dramatist

7 How about 'Cloudcuckooland'?
naming the capital city of the Birds

The Birds (414 BC) l. 819

8 You have all the characteristics of a popular politician: a horrible voice, bad breeding and a vulgar manner.

The Knights (424 BC) l. 217

9 Under every stone lurks a politician.

Thesmophoriazusae l. 530

Aristotle 384–322 BC
Greek philosopher

10 Therefore, the good of man must be the objective of the science of politics.

Nicomachean Ethics

11 We make war that we may live in peace.

Nicomachean Ethics

12 Politicians also have no leisure, because they are always aiming at something beyond political life itself, power and glory, or happiness.

Nicomachean Ethics

13 Man is by nature a political animal.

Politics

14 He who is unable to live in society, or who has no need because he is sufficient for himself, must be either a beast or a god.

Politics

1 For that some should rule, and others be ruled, is a thing *Politics*
not only necessary but expedient, for from the hour of their
birth some are marked for subjection, others for rule.

2 Poverty is the parent of revolution and crime. *Politics*

3 Where some people are very wealthy and others have *Politics*
nothing, the result will be either extreme democracy or
absolute oligarchy, or despotism will come from either of
those excesses.

4 The most perfect political community is one in which the *Politics*
middle class is in control, and outnumbers both of the other
classes.

5 No tyrant need fear till men begin to feel confident in each *Politics*
other.

Robert Armstrong 1927–
British civil servant; Head of the Civil Service, 1981–7

6 It contains a misleading impression, not a lie. It was being in *Daily Telegraph* 19 November
economical with the truth. 1986; see **Burke** 64:6, **Clark** 94:6
   referring to a letter during the 'Spycatcher' trial, Supreme Court,
   New South Wales, November 1986

William Armstrong 1915–80
British civil servant, Head of the Civil Service 1968–74

7 The business of the Civil Service is the orderly management in 1973: Peter Hennessy *Whitehall*
of decline. (1990)

Matthew Arnold 1822–88
English poet and essayist; son of Thomas **Arnold**

8 Our society distributes itself into Barbarians, Philistines, and *Culture and Anarchy* (1869) preface
Populace; and America is just ourselves, with the
Barbarians quite left out, and the Populace nearly.

9 The men of culture are the true apostles of equality. *Culture and Anarchy* (1869)

10 When I want to distinguish clearly the aristocratic class *Culture and Anarchy* (1869)
from the Philistines proper, or middle class, [I] name the
former, in my own mind *the Barbarians*.

11 That vast portion . . . of the working-class which, raw and *Culture and Anarchy* (1869)
half-developed, has long lain half-hidden amidst its poverty
and squalor, and is now issuing from its hiding-place to
assert an Englishman's heaven-born privilege of doing as he
likes, and is beginning to perplex us by marching where it
likes, meeting where it likes, bawling what it likes, breaking
what it likes—to this vast residuum we may with great
propriety give the name of Populace.

Thomas Arnold 1795–1842
English historian and educator; Headmaster of Rugby School
from 1828; father of Matthew **Arnold**

12 As for rioting, the old Roman way of dealing with that is from an unpublished letter written
always the right one; flog the rank and file, and fling the before 1828
ringleaders from the Tarpeian rock.

Raymond Aron 1905–83
French sociologist and political journalist

1 Political thought, in France, is retrospective or utopian.
L'opium des intellectuels (1955)

John Ashcroft 1942–
American Republican politician, Attorney General of the US 2001–4

2 We may never know why he turned his back on our country and our values, but we cannot ignore that he did. Youth is not absolution for treachery.
on John Walker Lindh, an American who fought for the Taliban
in *Newsweek* 28 January 2002

Paddy Ashdown 1941–
British Liberal Democrat politician

3 There can be no place in a 21st-century parliament for people with 15th-century titles upholding 19th-century prejudices.
in *Independent* 24 November 1998

Herbert Henry Asquith 1852–1928
British Liberal statesman; Prime Minister, 1908–16
on Asquith: see **Churchill** 86:11, **Hennessy** 180:2

4 We had better wait and see.
phrase used repeatedly in speeches in 1910, referring to the rumour that the House of Lords was to be flooded with new Liberal peers to ensure the passage of the Finance Bill
Roy Jenkins *Asquith* (1964)

5 We shall never sheath the sword which we have not lightly drawn until Belgium recovers in full measure all and more than all that she has sacrificed, until France is adequately secured against the menace of aggression, until the rights of the smaller nationalities of Europe are placed upon an unassailable foundation, and until the military domination of Prussia is wholly and finally destroyed.
speech at the Guildhall, London, 9 November 1914

6 There is no more striking illustration of the immobility of British institutions than the House of Commons.
Fifty Years of Parliament (1926) vol. 2

7 The office of the Prime Minister is what its holder chooses and is able to make of it.
Fifty Years of Parliament (1926) vol. 2

8 He is a Chimborazo or Everest among the sandhills of the Baldwin Cabinet.
of Winston **Churchill**
Roy Jenkins *Asquith* (1964)

9 It is fitting that we should have buried the Unknown Prime Minister [Bonar Law] by the side of the Unknown Soldier.
Robert Blake *The Unknown Prime Minister* (1955)

10 [The War Office kept three sets of figures:] one to mislead the public, another to mislead the Cabinet, and the third to mislead itself.
Alistair Horne *Price of Glory* (1962)

Margot Asquith 1864–1945
British political hostess; wife of Herbert **Asquith**

11 Kitchener is a great poster.
More Memories (1933)

12 There is nothing more popular in the House of Commons than to blame yourself. 'I have killed my mother. I will never do it again,' is certain to raise a cheer.
Off the Record (1943)

1 No amount of education will make women first-rate politicians. Can you see a woman becoming a Prime Minister? I cannot imagine a greater calamity for these islands than to be put under the guidance of a woman in 10 Downing Street.

Off the Record (1943)

2 Lord Birkenhead is very clever but sometimes his brains go to his head.

in *Listener* 11 June 1953 'Margot Oxford' by Lady Violet Bonham Carter

3 He can't see a belt without hitting below it.
   *of **Lloyd George***

in *Listener* 11 June 1953 'Margot Oxford' by Lady Violet Bonham Carter

Jacob Astley 1579–1652
English soldier and royalist

4 Gentlemen, ye may now sit and play, for you have done all your work, if you fall not out among yourselves.
   to enemy officers, after being captured at Stow-on-the-Wold, 1646

R. Field *Stow-on-the-Wold, 1646* (1992)

Nancy Astor 1879–1964
American-born British Conservative politician

5 NANCY ASTOR: If I were your wife I would put poison in your coffee.
   WINSTON CHURCHILL: And if I were your husband I would drink it.

Consuelo Vanderbilt *Glitter and Gold* (1952)

Brooks Atkinson 1894–1984
American journalist and critic

6 After each war there is a little less democracy to save.

Once Around the Sun (1951) 7 January

7 In every age 'the good old days' were a myth. No one ever thought they were good at the time. For every age had consisted of crises that seemed intolerable to the people who lived through them.

Once Around the Sun (1951) 8 February

8 There is a good deal of solemn cant about the common interests of capital and labour. As matters stand, their only common interest is that of cutting each other's throat.

Once Around the Sun (1951) 7 September

Clement Attlee 1883–1967
British Labour statesman; Prime Minister, 1945–51
on Attlee: see **Churchill** 92:7, **Churchill** 92:15, **Hennessy** 180:2, **Nicolson** 288:12, **Pimlott** 311:4

9 Why does Mosley always speak to us as though he were a feudal landlord abusing tenants who are in arrears with their rent?
   at a meeting of the Parliamentary Labour Party, 20 November 1930, a few months before Oswald Mosley was expelled from the Party

Hugh Dalton *Political Diary* (1986) 20 November 1930

10 A monologue is not a decision.
   *to Winston **Churchill**, who had complained that a matter had been raised several times in Cabinet*

Francis Williams *A Prime Minister Remembers* (1961)

1 The voice we heard was that of Mr Churchill but the mind was that of Lord Beaverbrook.

speech on radio, 5 June 1945

2 A period of silence on your part would be welcome.
*in reply to a letter from the Chairman of the Labour Party, Harold **Laski**, asking (for the second time and at length) that Attlee should not form a new government until the Parliamentary Labour Party had had the chance to elect a new leader*

letter to Harold Laski, 20 August 1945

3 If the King asks you to form a Government you say 'Yes' or 'No', not 'I'll let you know later!'

Kenneth Harris *Attlee* (1982)

4 *at a Cabinet Meeting, when Aneurin **Bevan** as Minister of Housing complained that he could not get enough people for his building programme:*
BEVAN: Where are all the people I need for my programme?
ATTLEE: Looking for houses, Nye!

Michael Foot *Aneuran Bevan* (1973) vol. 2

5 I should be a sad subject for any publicity expert. I have none of the qualities which create publicity.

Harold Nicolson diary, 14 January 1949

6 *response to a memorandum from the Ministry of Works saying, 'We have read the Cabinet's proposals':*
The Cabinet does not propose, it decides.

Tony Benn diary, 20 May 1974

7 I believe that conscience is a still small voice and not a loudspeaker.

attributed, 1955

8 Few thought he was even a starter
There were many who thought themselves smarter
But he ended PM
CH and OM
An earl and a knight of the garter.
describing himself in a letter to Tom Attlee, 8 April 1956

Kenneth Harris *Attlee* (1982)

9 [Russian Communism is] the illegitimate child of Karl Marx and Catherine the Great.

speech at Aarhus University, 11 April 1956

10 Generally speaking the Press lives on disaster.

attributed, 1956

11 Democracy means government by discussion, but it is only effective if you can stop people talking.

speech at Oxford, 14 June 1957

12 Often the 'experts' make the worst possible Ministers in their own fields. In this country we prefer rule by amateurs.

speech at Oxford, 14 June 1957

13 It's a good maxim that if you have a good dog you don't bark yourself. I had a very good dog in Mr Ernest Bevin.

attributed, 1960

14 *definition of the art of politics:*
Judgement which is needed to make important decisions on imperfect knowledge in a limited time.

attributed

15 A lot of clever people have got everything except judgement.

Francis Williams *A Prime Minister Remembers* (1961)

W. H. Auden 1907–73

English poet

16 To save your world you asked this man to die:
Would this man, could he see you now, ask why?

'Epitaph for the Unknown Soldier' (1955)

17 He knew human folly like the back of his hand,
And was greatly interested in armies and fleets;
When he laughed, respectable senators burst with laughter,
And when he cried the little children died in the streets.

'Epitaph on a Tyrant' (1940); see **Motley** 280:7

1 In the nightmare of the dark
   All the dogs of Europe bark,
   And the living nations wait,
   Each sequestered in its hate.

'In Memory of W. B. Yeats' (1940)

2 Private faces in public places
   Are wiser and nicer
   Than public faces in private places.

Orators (1932) dedication

3 There is no such thing as the State
   And no one exists alone;
   Hunger allows no choice
   To the citizen or the police;
   We must love one another or die.

'September 1, 1939' (1940)

4 Our researchers into Public Opinion are content
   That he held the proper opinions for the time of year;
   When there was peace, he was for peace; when there was
       war, he went.

'The Unknown Citizen' (1940)

5 This marble monument was erected by the state.
   Was he free? Was he happy? The question is absurd:
   Had anything been wrong, we should certainly have heard.

'The Unknown Citizen' (1940)

Augustus 63 BC–AD 14

first Roman emperor
on Augustus: see **Cicero** 93:10

6 Quintilius Varus, give me back my legions.
   *after the annihilation by the German leader Arminius of three
   Roman legions under Quintilius Varus*

Suetonius *Lives of the Caesars*

7 He could boast that he inherited it brick and left it marble.
   of the city of Rome

Suetonius *Lives of the Caesars*

Aung San Suu Kyi 1945–

Burmese political leader

8 It's very different from living in academia in Oxford. We
   called someone vicious in the *Times Literary Supplement*. We
   didn't know what vicious was.
   on returning to Burma (Myanmar)

in *Observer* 25 September 1988
'Sayings of the Week'

9 In societies where men are truly confident of their own
   worth, women are not merely tolerated but valued.

videotape speech at NGO Forum
on Women, China, early
September 1995

Marcus Aurelius AD 121–180

Roman emperor from AD 161

10 Man, you have been a citizen in this world city, what does it
   matter whether for five years or fifty?

Meditations

Jane Austen 1775–1817

English novelist

11 From politics, it was an easy step to silence.

Northanger Abbey (1818)

Ayesha fl. 1492
Moorish princess, mother of the last Sultan of Granada

1 You do well to weep as a woman over what you could not defend as a man.
   reproach to her son Boabdil (Muhammad XI), who had surrendered Granada to Ferdinand and Isabella

traditional attribution; Washington Irving *The Alhambra* (1832; rev. ed. 1851) ch. 18

Isaac Babel 1894–1940
Russian short-story writer

2 Now a man talks frankly only with his wife, at night, with the blanket over his head.

remark *c.*1937; Solomon Volkov *St Petersburg* (1996)

3 They didn't let me finish.

to his wife, on the day of his arrest by the NKVD, 16 May 1939

Francis Bacon 1561–1626
English lawyer, courtier, philosopher, and essayist
see also **Last Words** 226:6

4 To worship the people is to be worshipped.

De Dignitate et Augmentis Scientiarum (1623)

5 He is the fountain of honour.

An Essay of a King (1642); attribution doubtful; see **Bagehot** 22:5

6 In civil business; what first? boldness; what second and third? boldness: and yet boldness is a child of ignorance and baseness.

Essays (1625) 'Of Boldness'

7 There be [some] that can pack the cards and yet cannot play well; so there are some that are good in canvasses and factions, that are otherwise weak men.

Essays (1625) 'Of Cunning'

8 Nothing doth more hurt in a state than that cunning men pass for wise.

Essays (1625) 'Of Cunning'

9 There is surely no greater wisdom than well to time the beginnings and endings of things.

Essays (1625) 'Of Delays'

10 The difficulties in princes' business are many and great, but the greatest difficulty is often in their own mind.

Essays (1625) 'Of Empire'

11 Men in great place are thrice servants: servants of the sovereign or state, servants of fame, and servants of business.

Essays (1625) 'Of Great Place'

12 The rising unto place is laborious, and by pains men come to greater pains; and it is sometimes base, and by indignities men come to dignities. The standing is slippery, and the regress is either a downfall, or at least an eclipse.

Essays (1625) 'Of Great Place'

13 Severity breedeth fear, but roughness breedeth hate. Even reproofs from authority ought to be grave, and not taunting.

Essays (1625) 'Of Great Place'

14 All rising to great place is by a winding stair.

Essays (1625) 'Of Great Place'

15 New nobility is but the act of power, but ancient nobility is the act of time.

Essays (1625) 'Of Nobility'

16 Fame is like a river, that beareth up things light and swollen, and drowns things weighty and solid.

Essays (1625) 'Of Praise'

1 So when any of the four pillars of government are mainly shakened or weakened (which are religion, justice, counsel, and treasure) men had need to pray for fair weather.

Essays (1625) 'Of Seditions and Troubles'

2 The surest way to prevent seditions (if the times do bear it) is to take away the matter of them.

Essays (1625) 'Of Seditions and Troubles'

3 Suspicions amongst thoughts are like bats amongst birds, they ever fly by twilight.

Essays (1625) 'Of Suspicion'

4 Neither is money the sinews of war (as it is trivially said).

Essays (1625) 'Of the True Greatness of Kingdoms'

5 Neither will it be, that a people overlaid with taxes should ever become valiant and martial.

Essays (1625) 'Of the True Greatness of Kingdoms'

6 What is truth? said jesting Pilate; and would not stay for an answer.

Essays (1625) 'Of Truth'

7 All colours will agree in the dark.

Essays (1625) 'Of Unity in Religion'

8 In the youth of a state arms do flourish; in the middle age of a state, learning; and then both of them together for a time; in the declining age of a state, mechanical arts and merchandise.

Essays (1625) 'Of Vicissitude of Things'

9 For also knowledge itself is power.

Meditationes Sacrae 1597) 'Of Heresies'

10 It is well to observe the force and virtue and consequence of discoveries, and these are to be seen nowhere more conspicuously than in those three which were unknown to the ancients, and of which the origins, though recent, are obscure and inglorious; namely, printing, gunpowder, and the magnet [Mariner's Needle]. For these three have changed the whole face and state of things throughout the world.

Novum Organum (1620)

11 There be three things which make a nation great and prosperous: a fertile soil, busy workshops, easy conveyance for men and goods from place to place.

attributed; S. Platt (ed.) *Respectfully Quoted* (1989)

Joan Baez 1941–

American singer and songwriter

12 The only thing that's been a worse flop than the organization of non-violence has been the organization of violence.

Daybreak (1970) 'What Would You Do If?'

Walter Bagehot 1826–77

English economist and essayist

13 In happy states, the Conservative party must rule upon the whole a much longer time than their adversaries. In well-framed politics, innovation—great innovation that is—can only be occasional. If you are always altering your house, it is a sign either that you have a bad house, or that you have an excessively restless disposition—there is something wrong somewhere.

'The Chances for a Long Conservative Régime in England' (1874)

14 Capital must be propelled by self-interest; it cannot be enticed by benevolence.

Economic Studies (1880)

1 The mystic reverence, the religious allegiance, which are essential to a true monarchy, are imaginative sentiments that no legislature can manufacture in any people.

The English Constitution (1867) 'The Cabinet'

2 In such constitutions [as England's] there are two parts . . . first, those which excite and preserve the reverence of the population—the *dignified* parts . . . and next, the *efficient* parts—those by which it, in fact, works and rules.

The English Constitution (1867) 'The Cabinet'

3 No orator ever made an impression by appealing to men as to their plainest physical wants, except when he could allege that those wants were caused by some one's tyranny.

The English Constitution (1867) 'The Cabinet'

4 The Crown is, according to the saying, the 'fountain of honour'; but the Treasury is the spring of business.

The English Constitution (1867) 'The Cabinet'; see **Bacon** 20:5

5 A cabinet is a combining committee—a *hyphen* which joins, a *buckle* which fastens, the legislative part of the state to the executive part of the state.

The English Constitution (1867) 'The Cabinet'

6 It has been said that England invented the phrase, 'Her Majesty's Opposition'; that it was the first government which made a criticism of administration as much a part of the polity as administration itself. This critical opposition is the consequence of cabinet government.

The English Constitution (1867) 'The Cabinet'; see **Hobhouse** 185:13

7 *The Times* has made many ministries.

The English Constitution (1867) 'The Cabinet'

8 The great qualities, the imperious will, the rapid energy, the eager nature fit for a great crisis are not required—are impediments—in common times.

The English Constitution (1867) 'The Cabinet'

9 By the structure of the world we often want, at the sudden occurrence of a grave tempest, to change the helmsman—to replace the pilot of the calm by the pilot of the storm.

The English Constitution (1867) 'The Cabinet'

10 *of Queen* **Victoria** *and the future* **Edward VII**
It is nice to trace how the actions of a retired widow and an unemployed youth become of such importance.

The English Constitution (1867) 'The Monarchy'

11 The best reason why Monarchy is a strong government is, that it is an intelligible government. The mass of mankind understand it, and they hardly anywhere in the world understand any other.

The English Constitution (1867) 'The Monarchy'

12 The characteristic of the English Monarchy is that it retains the feelings by which the heroic kings governed their rude age, and has added the feelings by which the constitutions of later Greece ruled in more refined ages.

The English Constitution (1867) 'The Monarchy'

13 Women—one half the human race at least—care fifty times more for a marriage than a ministry.

The English Constitution (1867) 'The Monarchy'

14 Royalty is a government in which the attention of the nation is concentrated on one person doing interesting actions. A Republic is a government in which that attention is divided between many, who are all doing uninteresting actions. Accordingly, so long as the human heart is strong and the human reason weak, Royalty will be strong because it appeals to diffused feeling, and Republics weak because they appeal to the understanding.

The English Constitution (1867) 'The Monarchy'

15 Throughout the greater part of his life George III was a kind of 'consecrated obstruction'.

The English Constitution (1867) 'The Monarchy'

1 There are arguments for not having a Court, and there are arguments for having a splendid Court; but there are no arguments for having a mean Court.

The English Constitution (1867) 'The Monarchy'

2 The Queen . . . must sign her own death-warrant if the two Houses unanimously send it up to her.

The English Constitution (1867) 'The Monarchy'

3 Above all things our royalty is to be reverenced, and if you begin to poke about it you cannot reverence it . . . Its mystery is its life. We must not let in daylight upon magic.

The English Constitution (1867) 'The Monarchy'

4 The Sovereign has, under a constitutional monarchy such as ours, three rights—the right to be consulted, the right to encourage, the right to warn.

The English Constitution (1867) 'The Monarchy'

5 The only fit material for a constitutional king is a prince who begins early to reign—who in his youth is superior to pleasure—who in his youth is willing to labour—who has by nature a genius for discretion. Such kings are among God's greatest gifts, but they are also among His rarest.

The English Constitution (1867) 'The Monarchy'

6 The order of nobility is of great use, too, not only in what it creates, but in what it prevents. It prevents the rule of wealth—the religion of gold. This is the obvious and natural idol of the Anglo-Saxon.

The English Constitution (1867) 'The House of Lords'

7 A severe though not unfriendly critic of our institutions said that 'the cure for admiring the House of Lords was to go and look at it.'

The English Constitution (1867) 'The House of Lords'

8 If you want to raise a certain cheer in the House of Commons, make a general panegyric on economy; if you want to invite a sure defeat, propose a particular saving.

The English Constitution (1867) 'The House of Lords'

9 Nations touch at their summits.

The English Constitution (1867) 'The House of Lords'

10 The House of Commons lives in a state of perpetual potential choice: at any moment it can choose a ruler and dismiss a ruler. And therefore party is inherent in it, is bone of its bone, and breath of its breath.

The English Constitution (1867) 'The House of Commons'

11 An Opposition, on coming into power, is often like a speculative merchant whose bills become due. Ministers have to make good their promises, and they find a difficulty in so doing.

The English Constitution (1867) 'The House of Commons'

12 It is an inevitable defect, that bureaucrats will care more for routine than for results.

The English Constitution (1867) 'On Changes of Ministry'

13 A bureaucracy is sure to think that its duty is to augment official power, official business, or official members, rather than to leave free the energies of mankind; it overdoes the quantity of government, as well as impairs its quality.

The English Constitution (1867) 'On Changes of Ministry'

14 But would it not have been a miracle if the English people, directing their own policy, and being what they are, had directed a good policy? Are they not above all nations divided from the rest of the world, insular both in situation and in mind, both for good and for evil? Are they not out of the current of common European causes and affairs? Are they not a race contemptuous of others? Are they not a race with no special education or culture as to the modern world, and too often despising such culture? Who could expect such a people to comprehend the new and strange events of foreign places?

The English Constitution (1867) 'On Changes of Ministry'

1 It has been said, not truly, but with a possible approximation to truth, that in 1802 every hereditary monarch was insane.

The English Constitution (1867) 'Its Supposed Checks and Balances'

2 As soon as we see that England is a disguised republic we must see too that the classes for whom the disguise is necessary must be tenderly dealt with.

The English Constitution (1867) 'Its History'

3 The natural impulse of the English people is to resist authority.

The English Constitution (1867) 'Its History'

4 A political country is like an American forest: you only have to cut down the old trees, and immediately new trees come up to replace them; the seeds were waiting in the ground, and they began to grow as soon as the withdrawal of the old ones brought in light and air.

The English Constitution: introduction to the second edition (1872)

5 No real English gentleman, in his secret soul, was ever sorry for the death of a political economist.

Estimates of some Englishmen and Scotchmen (1858)

6 Dullness in matters of government is a good sign, and not a bad one—in particular, dullness in Parliamentary government is a test of its excellence, an indication of its success.

in *Saturday Review* 16 February 1856

7 A constitutional statesman is in general a man of common opinion and uncommon abilities.

in *National Review* July 1856

8 Public opinion is a permeating influence, and it exacts obedience to itself; it requires us to think other men's thoughts, to speak other men's words, to follow other men's habits.

in *National Review* July 1856

9 He believes, with all his heart and soul and strength, that there *is* such a thing as truth; he has the soul of a martyr with the intellect of an advocate.
   of **Gladstone**

in *National Review* July 1860

10 If . . . the country should ever look on the proceedings of Parliament as an intellectual and theatrical exhibition, no merit in our laws, no excellence in our national character, could save our institutions from very serious danger.

in *The Economist* 1861

11 Years of acquiescing in proposals as to which he has not been consulted, of voting for measures which he did not frame, and in the wisdom of which he often did not believe, of arguing for proposals from half of which he dissents— usually de-intellectualize a parliamentary statesman before he comes to half his power.

in *National Review* 1861 'William Pitt'

12 There is no method by which men can be both free and equal.

in *The Economist* 5 September 1863

13 Persecute a sect and it holds together, legalize it and it splits and resplits, till its unity is either null or a non-oppressive bond.

in *The Economist* 27 April 1867

14 The highest and most important capacity in the Leader of the Opposition is to be able on special occasions to resist the mistaken wishes of the party which he leads.

in *The Economist* 1874

15 Policies must 'grow'; they cannot be suddenly made.

in *The Economist* 1874

16 A great Premier must add the vivacity of an idle man to the assiduity of a very laborious one.

in *The Economist* 2 January 1875

1 The being without an opinion is so painful to human nature that most people will leap to a hasty opinion rather than undergo it.

in *The Economist* 4 December 1875

2 In every country the extreme party is most irritated against the party which comes nearest to itself, but does not go so far.

in *The Economist* 22 April 1876

3 Good government depends at least as much on an impartial respect for the rights of all as it does on energy in enforcing respect for the authority which protects those rights.

in *The Economist* 27 May 1876

4 The characteristic danger of great nations, like the Romans or the English, which have a long history of continuous creation, is that they may at last fail from not comprehending the great institutions which they have created.

in *Fortnightly Review* 1 November 1876

5 There never was a worse blunder than the supposition that the more states there are to suffer by a sanguinary quarrel, the sooner will the motives prevail for bringing it to a conclusion.

in *The Economist* 17 March 1877

Ewen Bain 1925-89

Scottish cartoonist

6 No son—they're not the same—devolution takes longer.
   father to his son, who is reading a book on evolution

cartoon caption, in *Scots Independent* January 1978

Jacques Bainville 1879-1936

French historian

7 *of the Treaty of Versailles:*
Written by Bible readers *for* Bible readers.

'Les Consequences Politiques de la Paix' (1920)

Kenneth Baker 1934-

British Conservative politician

8 Why should Scottish and Welsh nationalism be seen as a noble thing, when in England it is seen as something dirty?

in *Sunday Times* 6 January 2000 'Talking Heads'

Michael Bakunin 1814-76

Russian revolutionary and anarchist

9 The urge for destruction is also a creative urge!

in *Jahrbuch für Wissenschaft und Kunst* (1842)

10 We wish, in a word, equality—equality in fact as corollary, or rather, as primordial condition of liberty. From each according to his faculties, to each according to his needs; that is what we wish sincerely and energetically.
   declaration signed by forty-seven anarchists on trial after the failure of their uprising at Lyons in 1870

J. Morrison Davidson *The Old Order and the New* (1890)

James Baldwin 1924-87

American novelist and essayist

11 Freedom is not something that anybody can be given; freedom is something people take and people are as free as they want to be.

Nobody Knows My Name (1961) 'Notes for a Hypothetical Novel'

1 At the root of the American Negro problem is the necessity of the American white man to find a way of living with the Negro in order to be able to live with himself.

in *Harper's Magazine* October 1953 'Stranger in a Village'

2 It comes as a great shock around the age of 5, 6 or 7 to discover that the flag to which you have pledged allegiance, along with everybody else, has not pledged allegiance to you. It comes as a great shock to see Gary Cooper killing off the Indians and, although you are rooting for Gary Cooper, that the Indians are you.

speaking for the proposition that 'The American Dream is at the expense of the American Negro' at the Cambridge Union, England, 17 February 1965

in *New York Times Magazine* 7 March 1965

3 If they take you in the morning, they will be coming for us that night.

in *New York Review of Books* 7 January 1971 'Open Letter to my Sister, Angela Davis'

Stanley Baldwin 1867–1947

British Conservative statesman; Prime Minister, 1923–4, 1924–9, 1935–7
on Baldwin: see **Beaverbrook** 31:9, **Churchill** 90:3, **Churchill** 90:10, **Curzon** 108:2, **Trevelyan** 397:9; *see also* **Kipling** 221:5

4 They [parliament] are a lot of hard-faced men who look as if they had done very well out of the war.

J. M. Keynes *Economic Consequences of the Peace* (1919)

5 A platitude is simply a truth repeated until people get tired of hearing it.

speech in the House of Commons, 29 May 1924

6 There are three classes which need sanctuary more than others—birds, wild flowers, and Prime Ministers.

in *Observer* 24 May 1925

7 'Safety first' does not mean a smug self-satisfaction with everything as it is. It is a warning to all persons who are going to cross a road in dangerous circumstances.

in *The Times* 21 May 1929

8 Had the employers of past generations all of them dealt fairly with their men there would have been no unions.

speech in Birmingham, 14 January 1931

9 I think it is well also for the man in the street to realize that there is no power on earth that can protect him from being bombed. Whatever people may tell him, the bomber will always get through. The only defence is in offence, which means that you have to kill more women and children more quickly than the enemy if you want to save yourselves.

speech in the House of Commons, 10 November 1932

10 Since the day of the air, the old frontiers are gone. When you think of the defence of England you no longer think of the chalk cliffs of Dover; you think of the Rhine. That is where our frontier lies.

speech in the House of Commons, 30 July 1934

11 *of his reasons for excluding* **Churchill** *from the Cabinet:*
If there is going to be a war—and no one can say that there is not—we must keep him fresh to be our war Prime Minister.

letter, 17 November 1935

12 I shall be but a short time tonight. I have seldom spoken with greater regret, for my lips are not yet unsealed. Were these troubles over I would make a case, and I guarantee that not a man would go into the lobby against us.

speech in the House of Commons on the Abyssinian crisis, 10 December 1935; see **Misquotations** 273:7

1 Supposing I had gone to the country and said that Germany was rearming and that we must rearm, does anybody think that this pacific democracy would have rallied to that cry at that moment? I cannot think of anything that would have made the loss of the election from my point of view more certain.

speech in the House of Commons, 12 November 1936

2 *of the advice he had given to* **Edward VIII** *on the possibility of marriage with Mrs Simpson:*
I pointed out to him that the position of the King's wife was different from the position of any other citizen in the country; it was part of the price which the King has to pay. His wife becomes Queen; the Queen becomes Queen of the country; and, therefore, in the choice of a Queen, the voice of the people must be heard.

speech, House of Commons, 10 December 1936 (Abdication Crisis)

3 This House today is a theatre which is being watched by the whole world. Let us conduct ourselves with that dignity which His Majesty is showing in this hour of his trial.

speech, House of Commons, 10 December 1936 (Abdication Crisis)

4 Once I leave, I leave. I am not going to speak to the man on the bridge, and I am not going to spit on the deck.
on resigning

statement to the Cabinet, 28 May 1937

5 You will find in politics that you are much exposed to the attribution of false motive. Never complain and never explain.

Harold Nicolson *Diary* 21 July 1943

6 Do not run up your nose dead against the Pope or the NUM!

Lord Butler *The Art of Memory* (1982); see **Macmillan** 253:11

7 He spent his whole life in plastering together the true and the false and therefrom manufacturing the plausible.
of **Lloyd George**

attributed

Arthur James Balfour 1848–1930

British Conservative statesman; Prime Minister, 1902–5
on Balfour: see **Churchill** 86:11, **Churchill** 91:3, **Lloyd George** 238:6, **Lloyd George** 239:7

8 It is unfortunate, considering that enthusiasm moves the world, that so few enthusiasts can be trusted to speak the truth.

letter to Mrs Drew, 19 May 1891

9 I do not come here to preach any doctrines of passive obedience or non-resistance. You have had to fight for your liberties before. I pray God you may never have to fight for them again. I do not believe that you ever will have to fight for them, but I admit that the tyranny of majorities may be as bad as the tyranny of Kings . . . and I do not think that any rational or sober man will say that what is justifiable against a tyrannical King may not under certain circumstances be justifiable against a tyrannical majority.
watching the Belfast march past of Ulster Loyalists in 1893

in *Times* 5 April 1893

10 When it comes I shall not be sorry. Only let us have separation as well as Home Rule: England cannot afford to go on with the Irishmen in her Parliament.

Wilfrid Scawen Blunt *The Land War in Ireland* (1912)

1 His Majesty's Government view with favour the establishment in Palestine of a national home for the Jewish people, and will use their best endeavours to facilitate the achievement of this object, it being clearly understood that nothing shall be done which may prejudice the civil and religious rights of existing non-Jewish communities in Palestine, or the rights and political status enjoyed by Jews in any other country.

letter to Lord Rothschild, 2 November 1917; see **Weizmann** *414:5*

2 Zionism, be it right or wrong, good or bad, is rooted in age-long traditions, in present need, in future hopes, of far profounder import than the desires and prejudices of the seven hundred thousand Arabs who now inhabit that ancient land.

in August 1919; Max Egremont Balfour (1980)

3 *on being asked what he thought of the behaviour of the German delegation at the signing of the Treaty of Versailles:*
I make it a rule never to stare at people when they are in obvious distress.

Max Egremont Balfour (1980)

4 *replying to Frank Harris, who had claimed that 'all the faults of the age come from Christianity and journalism':*
Christianity, of course . . . but why journalism?

Margot Asquith Autobiography (1920) vol. 1

5 *on the continuing financial dependence of* **Curzon**, *who had failed to become Prime Minister in succession to* **Bonar Law**, *on his second wife Grace Duggan:*
He may have lost the hope of glory, but he still retains the means of Grace.

attributed

6 Biography should be written by an acute enemy.

in Observer 30 January 1927

7 *of an unwelcome supporter:*
He pursues us with malignant fidelity.

Winston Churchill Great Contemporaries (1937)

8 I am more or less happy when being praised, not very uncomfortable when being abused, but I have moments of uneasiness when being explained.

K. Young A. J. Balfour (1963)

9 I never forgive but I always forget.

R. Blake Conservative Party (1970)

10 I thought he was a young man of promise, but it appears he is a young man of promises.
　　describing Churchill

Winston Churchill My Early Life (1930)

E. Digby Baltzell 1915–96

11 There is a crisis in American leadership in the middle of the twentieth century that is partly due, I think, to the declining authority of an establishment which is now based on an increasingly castelike White-Anglo Saxon-Protestant (WASP) upper class.

The Protestant Establishment (1964)

Honoré de Balzac 1799–1850

French novelist

12 Despotism accomplishes great things illegally; liberty doesn't even go to the trouble of accomplishing small things legally.

La Peau de Chagrin (1831)

Lord Bancroft 1922–96
British civil servant; Head of the Civil Service 1978–81

1 Conviction politicians, certainly: conviction civil servants, no.

'Whitehall: Some Personal Reflections', lecture at the London School of Economics 1 December 1983

Joseph Banks 1743–1820
English botanist

2 Who knows but that England may revive in New South Wales when it has sunk in Europe.

letter to Governor Hunter, 30 March 1797

Imamu Amiri Baraka 1934–
American poet and dramatist

3 A man is either free or he is not. There cannot be any apprenticeship for freedom.

in *Kulchur* Spring 1962 'Tokenism'

Ernest Barker 1874–1960
British political scientist

4 Sovereignty is unlimited—unlimited and illimitable.

Principles of Social and Political Theory (1951)

Pat Barker 1943–
English novelist

5 The Somme is like the Holocaust. It revealed things about mankind that we cannot come to terms with and cannot forget. It can never become the past.
   on winning the Booker Prize 1995

in *Athens News* 9 November 1995

Michel Barnier 1951–
French politician

6 Alliance is not allegiance.
   on Europe's relations with America

in *Independent* 29 October 2004

Michael Joseph Barry 1817–89
Irish nationalist writer

7 The wild geese—the wild geese,—'tis long since they flew, O'er the billowy ocean's bright bosom of blue.

in *Spirit of the Nation* (Dublin, 1845)

Bernard Baruch 1870–1965
American financier and presidential adviser

8 Let us not be deceived—we are today in the midst of a cold war.

speech to South Carolina Legislature 16 April 1947; the expression 'cold war' was suggested to him by H. B. Swope, former editor of the *New York World*

9 Vote for the man who promises least; he'll be the least disappointing.

Meyer Berger *New York* (1960)

1 You can talk about capitalism and communism and all that
sort of thing, but the important thing is the struggle
everybody is engaged in to get better living conditions, and
they are not interested too much in government.

in The Times 20 August 1964

2 A political leader must keep looking over his shoulder all the
time to see if the boys are still there. If they aren't still there,
he's no longer a political leader.

in New York Times 21 June 1965

Claude-Frédéric Bastiat 1801–50
French economist

3 All men's impulses, when motivated by legitimate self-
interest, fall into a harmonious social pattern.

Economic Harmonies (1964)

4 Once an abuse exists, everything is arranged on the
assumption that it will last indefinitely; and, as more and
more people come to depend upon it for their livelihood, and
still others depend upon them, a superstructure is erected
that soon comprises a formidable edifice.

in Journal des economistes 1848

Lord Bauer 1915–2002
Hungarian-born British economist

5 Foreign aid is a system of taking money from poor people in
rich countries and giving it to rich people in poor countries.

attributed; not recollected by Lord
Bauer but not repudiated by him.

6 *of foreign aid:*
With every mouth God sends a pair of hands.

saying taken from a Cambridge
Economics Tripos examination
question in the 1930s

Yehuda Bauer 1926–
Czech-born Israeli historian

7 I come from a people who gave the ten commandments to
the world. Time has come to strengthen them by three
additional ones, which we ought to adopt and commit
ourselves to: thou shalt not be a perpetrator; thou shalt not
be a victim; and thou shalt never, but never, be a
bystander.

speech to the German Bundestag,
1998, quoted in his own speech to
the Stockholm International Forum
on the Holocaust, 26 July 2000

Beverley Baxter 1891–1964
British journalist and Conservative politician

8 Beaverbrook is so pleased to be in the Government that he is
like the town tart who has finally married the Mayor!

Henry ('Chips') Channon diary, 12
June 1940

Charles Austin Beard 1874–1948
and **Mary Ritter Beard** 1876–1958

9 At no time, at no place, in solemn convention assembled,
through no chosen agents, had the American people
officially proclaimed the United States to be a democracy . . .
When the Constitution was framed no respectable person
called himself or herself a democrat.

America in Midpassage (1939)

Lord Beaverbrook 1879–1964

Canadian-born British newspaper proprietor and Conservative politician
on Beaverbrook: see **Baxter** 30:8, **Lloyd George** 239:16; *see also* **Kipling** 221:5

1 I hope you will give up the New Party. If you must burn your fingers in public life, go to a bright and big blaze.
to Harold **Nicolson**

letter, 25 June 1931

2 Our cock won't fight.
said to Winston **Churchill**, *of* **Edward VIII**, *during the abdication crisis of 1936*

Frances Donaldson *Edward VIII* (1974)

3 The Daily Express declares that Great Britain will not be involved in a European war this year or next year either.

in *Daily Express* 19 September 1938

4 Now who is responsible for this work of development on which so much depends? To whom must the praise be given? To the boys in the back rooms. They do not sit in the limelight. But they are the men who do the work.

in *Listener* 27 March 1941

5 I ran the paper [the *Daily Express*] purely for propaganda and with no other purpose.
evidence to the Royal Commission on the Press, 18 March 1948

A. J. P. Taylor *Beaverbrook* (1972)

6 [Lloyd George] did not seem to care which way he travelled providing he was in the driver's seat.

The Decline and Fall of Lloyd George (1963)

7 Always threatening resignation, he never signed off.
of Lord Derby

Men and Power (1956)

8 *of Lord* **Curzon**, *who had been created Viceroy of India at the age of thirty-nine:*
For all the rest of his life Curzon was influenced by his sudden journey to heaven at the age of thirty-nine, and then by his return seven years later to earth, for the remainder of his mortal existence.

Men and Power (1956)

9 His conversation turned on the beauty of the mountain rose, and the splendour of hawthorn buds in spring.
of Stanley **Baldwin**

Men and Power (1956)

10 Often undecided whether to desert a sinking ship for one that might not float, he would make up his mind to sit on the wharf for a day.
of Lord **Curzon**

Men and Power (1956)

11 With the publication of his Private Papers in 1952, he [Earl Haig] committed suicide 25 years after his death.
of Earl **Haig**

Men and Power (1956)

12 Churchill on top of the wave has in him the stuff of which tyrants are made.

Politicians and the War (1932)

13 British electors will never vote for a man who doesn't wear a hat.
advice to Tom Driberg

Tom Driberg *Ruling Passions* (1997)

14 *of* **Bonar Law** *and* **Churchill**:
I have had two masters and one of them betrayed me.

A. J. P. Taylor letter, 16 December 1973

Kim Beazley Senior 1917-

Australian Labor politician, father of Kim **Beazley**

1 When I joined the Labor Party it was made up of the cream of the working-class. When I left it was made up of the dregs of the middle-class.

quoted in the Legislative Assembly of New South Wales, 29 April 1992

Kim Beazley 1948-

Australian Labor politician, Party Leader 1995-2001 and since 2005, son of Kim **Beazley** Senior

2 We have never pretended to be a small business party. The Labor Party has never pretended that.

radio interview, 7 July 2000

Margaret Beckett 1943-

British Labour politician

3 Being effective is more important to me than being recognized.

in *Independent on Sunday* 2 January 2000

Henry Becque 1837-99

French dramatist and critic

4 What makes equality such a difficult business is that we only want it with our superiors.

Querelles littéraires (1890)

Brendan Behan 1923-64

Irish dramatist

5 PAT: He was an Anglo-Irishman.
MEG: In the blessed name of God what's that?
PAT: A Protestant with a horse.

The Hostage (1958)

6 When I came back to Dublin, I was courtmartialled in my absence and sentenced to death in my absence, so I said they could shoot me in my absence.

The Hostage (1958)

Lord Belhaven 1656-1708

Scottish politician

7 Good God! What, is this an entire surrender?
   culmination of a speech opposing the Union with England

speech in the Scottish Parliament, 2 November 1706

George Bell 1883-1958

English clergyman, Bishop of Chichester

8 The policy is obliteration, openly acknowledged. This is not a justifiable act of war.
   of the saturation bombing of Berlin

speech, House of Lords, 9 February 1944

Francis Bellamy 1856-1931

American clergyman and editor

9 I pledge allegiance to the flag of the United States of America and to the republic for which it stands, one nation under God, indivisible, with liberty and justice for all.

The Pledge of Allegiance to the Flag (1892)

Hilaire Belloc 1870–1953

British poet, essayist, historian, novelist, and Liberal politician

1 Sir! you have disappointed us!
We had intended you to be
The next Prime Minister but three:
The stocks were sold; the Press was squared;
The Middle Class was quite prepared.
But as it is! . . . My language fails!
Go out and govern New South Wales!

Cautionary Tales (1907) 'Lord Lundy'

2 Here richly, with ridiculous display,
The Politician's corpse was laid away.
While all of his acquaintance sneered and slanged
I wept: for I had longed to see him hanged.

'Epitaph on the Politician Himself' (1923)

3 Whatever happens we have got
The Maxim Gun, and they have not.

The Modern Traveller (1898)

4 The accursed power which stands on Privilege
(And goes with Women, and Champagne, and Bridge)
Broke—and Democracy resumed her reign:
(Which goes with Bridge, and Women and Champagne).

'On a Great Election' (1923)

5 Gentlemen, I am a Catholic . . . If you reject me on account of my religion, I shall thank God that He has spared me the indignity of being your representative.

speech to voters of South Salford, 1906

Saul Bellow 1915–2005

American novelist

6 Sitting tight is power.

The Adventures of Augie March (1953)

Julien Benda 1867–1956

French philosopher and novelist

7 *La trahison des clercs.*
The treachery of the intellectuals.

title of book, 1927

Ruth Fulton Benedict 1887–1948

American anthropologist

8 The tough-minded . . . respect difference. Their goal is a world made safe for differences, where the United States may be American to the hilt without threatening the peace of the world, and France may be France, and Japan may be Japan on the same conditions.

The Chrysanthemum and the Sword (1946)

Peter Benenson 1921–2005

British founder of Amnesty International

9 Better to light a candle than curse the darkness.

at a Human Rights Day ceremony, 10 December 1961 (see also **Stevenson** 380:17)

Ernest Benn 1875–1954

English publisher and economist

1 Politics is the art of looking for trouble, finding it whether it exists or not, diagnosing it incorrectly, and applying the wrong remedy.

attributed

Tony Benn 1925–

British Labour politician
on Benn: see **Levin** 232:7

2 Not a reluctant peer but a persistent commoner.

at a Press Conference, 23 November 1960

3 Some of the jam we thought was for tomorrow, we've already eaten.

attributed, 1969

4 In developing our industrial strategy for the period ahead, we have the benefit of much experience. Almost everything has been tried at least once.

speech in House of Commons, 13 March 1974

5 *on seeing Harold* **Wilson**, *who had resigned as Prime Minister in March, looking 'absolutely shrunk':*
Office is something that builds up a man only if he is somebody in his own right.

diary, 12 April 1976

6 Marxism is now a world faith and must be allowed to enter into a continuous dialogue with other world faiths, including religious faiths.

Karl Marx lecture, 16 March 1982

7 *of the influence of Parliament:*
Through talk, we tamed kings, restrained tyrants, averted revolution.

Anthony Sampson *The Changing Anatomy of Britain* (1982)

8 I did not enter the Labour Party forty-seven years ago to have our manifesto written by Dr Mori, Dr Gallup and Mr Harris.

in *Guardian* 13 June 1988

9 A faith is something you die for; a doctrine is something you kill for: there is all the difference in the world.

in *Observer* 16 April 1989 'Sayings of the Week'

10 *questions habitually asked by Tony Benn on meeting somebody in power:*
What power have you got? Where did you get it from? In whose interests do you exercise it? To whom are you accountable? How do we get rid of you?

'The Independent Mind', lecture at Nottingham, 18 June 1993

11 The Civil Service is a bit like a rusty weathercock. It moves with opinion then it stays where it is until another wind moves it in a different direction.

briefing for 'Cabinet and Premiership' course (Queen Mary and Westfield College), held at the House of Commons 1 March 1995

12 When you get to No. 10, you've climbed there on a little ladder called 'the status quo'. And, when you're there, the status quo looks very good.

at the House of Commons 1 March 1995

13 We should put the spin-doctors in spin clinics, where they can meet other spin patients and be treated by spin consultants. The rest of us can get on with the proper democratic process.

in *Independent* 25 October 1997 'Quote Unquote'

1 The Cecils always end up on top.

of the negotiations between the Labour Party and Lord Cranborne, then Conservative Leader in the Lords, and the agreement that 92 hereditary peers should remain in the reformed house; see also **Cranborne** *104:3*

speech in the House of Commons, 10 November 1999

Alan Bennett 1934-
English dramatist and actor

2 To be Prince of Wales is not a position. It is a predicament.

The Madness of King George (1995 film); in the 1992 play *The Madness of George III* the line was 'To be heir to the throne . . . '

Arnold Bennett 1867-1931
English novelist

3 Seventy minutes had passed before Mr Lloyd George arrived at his proper theme. He spoke for a hundred and seventeen minutes, in which period he was detected only once in the use of an argument.

Things that have Interested Me (1921) 'After the March Offensive'

4 Examine the Honours List and you can instantly tell how the Government feels in its inside. When the Honours List is full of rascals, millionaires, and—er—chumps, you may be quite sure that the Government is dangerously ill.

The Title (1918)

5 Literature's always a good card to play for Honours. It makes people think that Cabinet ministers are educated.

The Title (1918)

A. C. Benson 1862-1925
English writer

6 Land of Hope and Glory, Mother of the Free,
How shall we extol thee who are born of thee?
Wider still and wider shall thy bounds be set;
God who made thee mighty, make thee mightier yet.

'Land of Hope and Glory' written to be sung as the Finale to Elgar's *Coronation Ode* (1902)

Jeremy Bentham 1748-1832
English philosopher

7 Right . . . is the child of law: from real laws come real rights; but from imaginary laws, from laws of nature, fancied and invented by poets, rhetoricians, and dealers in moral and intellectual poisons, come imaginary rights, a bastard brood of monsters.

Anarchical Fallacies (1843)

8 Natural rights is simple nonsense: natural and imprescriptible rights, rhetorical nonsense—nonsense upon stilts.

Anarchical Fallacies (1843)

9 The greatest happiness of the greatest number is the foundation of morals and legislation.

Bentham claims to have acquired the 'sacred truth' either from Joseph Priestley (1733-1804) or Cesare Beccaria (1738-94)

The Commonplace Book (1843)

10 Every law is contrary to liberty.

Principles of the Civil Code (1843)

11 He rather hated the ruling few than loved the suffering many.

of James Mill

H. N. Pym (ed.) *Memories of Old Friends, being Extracts from the Journals and Letters of Caroline Fox* (1882)

Edmund Clerihew Bentley 1875–1956
English writer

1 When their lordships asked Bacon
   How many bribes he had taken
   He had at least the grace
   To get very red in the face.

Baseless Biography (1939) 'Bacon'

2 George the Third
   Ought never to have occurred.
   One can only wonder
   At so grotesque a blunder.

More Biography (1929) 'George the Third'

Lloyd Bentsen 1921–
American Democratic politician

3 *responding to Dan Quayle's claim to have 'as much experience in the Congress as Jack **Kennedy** had when he sought the presidency':*
   Senator, I served with Jack Kennedy. I knew Jack Kennedy. Jack Kennedy was a friend of mine. Senator, you're no Jack Kennedy.

in the vice-presidential debate, 5 October 1988

Peter Berger
American political scientist

4 Capitalism, as an institutional arrangement, has been singularly devoid of plausible myths. By contrast, socialism, its major alternative under modern conditions, has been singularly blessed with myth-generating potency.

in 1986; Anthony Sampson *The Company Man* (1995)

George Berkeley 1685–1753
Irish philosopher and Anglican bishop

5 Westward the course of empire takes its way;
   The first four acts already past,
   A fifth shall close the drama with the day:
   Time's noblest offspring is the last.

'On the Prospect of Planting Arts and Learning in America' (1752); see John Quincy Adams *Oration at Plymouth* (1802): 'Westward the star of empire takes its way'

Irving Berlin 1888–1989
American songwriter

6 God bless America,
   Land that I love,
   Stand beside her and guide her
   Thru the night with a light from above.
   From the mountains to the prairies,
   To the oceans white with foam,
   God bless America,
   My home sweet home.

'God Bless America' (1939)

Isaiah Berlin 1909–97
British philosopher

7 The fundamental sense of freedom is freedom from chains, from imprisonment, from enslavement by others. The rest is extension of this sense, or else metaphor.

Four Essays on Liberty (1969); introduction

1 Injustice, poverty, slavery, ignorance—these may be cured by reform or revolution. But men do not live only by fighting evils. They live by positive goals, individual and collective, a vast variety of them, seldom predictable, at times incompatible.

Four Essays on Liberty (1969)

2 Those who have ever valued liberty for its own sake believed that to be free to choose, and not be chosen for, is an inalienable ingredient in what makes human beings human.

Four Essays on Liberty (1969)

3 Liberty is liberty, not equality or fairness or justice or human happiness or a quiet conscience.

Two Concepts of Liberty (1958)

4 It is this—the 'positive' conception of liberty: not freedom from, but freedom to—which the adherents of the 'negative' notion represent as being, at times, no better than a specious disguise for brutal tyranny.

Two Concepts of Liberty (1958)

5 Few new truths have ever won their way against the resistance of established ideas save by being overstated.

Vico and Herder (1976)

J. D. Bernal 1901–71
Irish-born physicist

6 Men will not be content to manufacture life: they will want to improve on it.

The World, the Flesh and the Devil (1929)

Carl Bernstein 1944–
and Bob Woodward 1943–
American journalists

7 All the President's men.

title of book (1974) on the Watergate scandal

Daniel Berrigan 1921–
American anti-Vietnam War activist

8 This is a war run to show the world, and particularly the Third World, where exactly it stands in relation to our technology.

attributed, 1973

Pierre Berton 1920–2004
Canadian writer

9 The march of social progress is like a long and straggling parade, with the seers and prophets at its head and a smug minority bringing up the rear.

The Smug Minority (1968)

Theobald von Bethmann Hollweg
1856–1921
German statesman, Chancellor 1909–17

10 Just for a word 'neutrality'—a word which in wartime has so often been disregarded—just for a scrap of paper, Great Britain is going to make war on a kindred nation who desires nothing better than to be friends with her.

summary of a report by E. Goschen to Edward Grey in *British Documents on Origins of the War 1898–1914* (1926) vol. 11

Mary McLeod Bethune 1875–1955
American educator

1 If we accept and acquiesce in the face of discrimination, we accept the responsibility ourselves and allow those responsible to salve their conscience by believing that they have our acceptance and concurrence.

Rayford W. Logan (ed.) *What the Negro Wants* (1944) 'Certain Inalienable Rights'

John Betjeman 1906–84
English poet

2 Think of what our Nation stands for,
Books from Boots' and country lanes,
Free speech, free passes, class distinction,
Democracy and proper drains.
Lord, put beneath Thy special care
One-eighty-nine Cadogan Square.

'In Westminster Abbey' (1940)

Aneurin Bevan 1897–1960
British Labour politician

3 This island is made mainly of coal and surrounded by fish. Only an organizing genius could produce a shortage of coal and fish at the same time.

speech at Blackpool 24 May 1945

4 No amount of cajolery, and no attempts at ethical or social seduction, can eradicate from my heart a deep burning hatred for the Tory Party . . . So far as I am concerned they are lower than vermin.

speech at Manchester, 4 July 1948

5 The language of priorities is the religion of Socialism.

speech at Labour Party Conference in Blackpool, 8 June 1949

6 Why read the crystal when he can read the book?
*referring to Robert **Boothby** during a debate on the Sterling Exchange Rate*

in the House of Commons, 29 September 1949

7 [Winston Churchill] does not talk the language of the 20th century but that of the 18th. He is still fighting Blenheim all over again. His only answer to a difficult situation is send a gun-boat.

speech at Labour Party Conference, Scarborough, 2 October 1951

8 The Tories, every election, must have a bogy man. If you haven't got a programme, a bogy man will do. In 1945 it was Harold Laski, in 1951 it is me.

speech in the general election campaign at Stonehouse, Gloucester, 13 October 1951

9 We know what happens to people who stay in the middle of the road. They get run down.

in *Observer* 6 December 1953

10 Damn it all, you can't have the crown of thorns *and* the thirty pieces of silver.
on his position in the Labour Party, c.1956

Michael Foot *Aneurin Bevan* vol. 2 (1973)

11 I am not going to spend any time whatsoever in attacking the Foreign Secretary . . . If we complain about the tune, there is no reason to attack the monkey when the organ grinder is present.
during a debate on the Suez crisis

in the House of Commons, 16 May 1957

12 If you carry this resolution you will send Britain's Foreign Secretary naked into the conference chamber.
speaking against a motion proposing unilateral nuclear disarmament by the United Kingdom

speech at Labour Party Conference in Brighton, 3 October 1957

1 You call that statesmanship? I call it an emotional spasm.
speaking against a motion proposing unilateral nuclear disarmament by the United Kingdom

speech at Labour Party Conference in Brighton, 3 October 1957

2 I know that the right kind of leader for the Labour Party is a desiccated calculating machine who must not in any way permit himself to be swayed by indignation. If he sees suffering, privation or injustice he must not allow it to move him, for that would be evidence of the lack of proper education or of absence of self-control. He must speak in calm and objective accents and talk about a dying child in the same way as he would about the pieces inside an internal combustion engine.
frequently taken as referring to Hugh **Gaitskell**, *although Bevan specifically denied it in an interview with Robin Day on 28 April 1959*

Michael Foot *Aneurin Bevan* vol. 2 (1973)

3 The conquest of the commanding heights of the economy.
recalling his own earlier use of the phrase (possibly originated by Lenin)

at the Labour Party Conference, November 1959

4 The Prime Minister has an absolute genius for putting flamboyant labels on empty luggage.
of Harold **Macmillan**

in the House of Commons, 3 November 1959

5 I read the newspapers avidly. It is my one form of continuous fiction.

in *The Times* 29 March 1960

6 Discontent arises from a knowledge of the possible, as contrasted with the actual.

In Place of Fear (1952)

7 In one sense the Commons is the most unrepresentative of representative assemblies. It is an elaborate conspiracy to prevent the real clash of opinion which exists outside from finding an appropriate echo within its walls. It is a social shock absorber placed between privilege and the pressure of popular discontent.

In Place of Fear (1952)

8 *of his handling of the consultants during the establishment of the National Health Service:*
I stuffed their mouths with gold.

Brian Abel-Smith *The Hospitals 1800–1948* (1964)

9 Listening to a speech by Chamberlain is like paying a visit to Woolworth's: everything in its place and nothing above sixpence.

Michael Foot *Aneurin Bevan* vol. 1 (1962)

10 There are only two ways of getting into the Cabinet. One way is to crawl up the staircase of preferment on your belly; the other way is to kick them in the teeth.

Richard Crossman *Inside View* (1972)

Albert Jeremiah Beveridge 1862–1927

American Republican politician and member of the Senate, who in 1912 chaired the convention that organized the Progressive party and nominated Theodore **Roosevelt** for President

11 This party comes from the grass roots. It has grown from the soil of the people's hard necessities.

address at the Bull Moose Convention in Chicago, 5 August 1912

William Henry Beveridge 1879–1963
British economist

1 Ignorance is an evil weed, which dictators may cultivate among their dupes, but which no democracy can afford among its citizens.

Full Employment in a Free Society (1944)

2 The object of government in peace and in war is not the glory of rulers or of races, but the happiness of the common man.

Social Insurance and Allied Services (1942)

3 Want is one only of five giants on the road of reconstruction . . . the others are Disease, Ignorance, Squalor and Idleness.

Social Insurance and Allied Services (1942)

4 The state is or can be master of money, but in a free society it is master of very little else.

Voluntary Action (1948)

Ernest Bevin 1881–1951
British Labour politician and trade unionist

5 The most conservative man in this world is the British Trade Unionist when you want to change him.

speech, 8 September 1927

6 I hope you will carry no resolution of an emergency character telling a man with a conscience like Lansbury what he ought to do . . . It is placing the Executive in an absolutely wrong position to be taking your conscience round from body to body to be told what you ought to do with it.

in *Labour Party Conference Report* (1935); see **Misquotations** 273:2

7 I am not one of those who decry Eton and Harrow. I was very glad of them in the Battle of Britain.

speech at Blackpool, 1945

8 There never has been a war yet which, if the facts had been put calmly before the ordinary folk, could not have been prevented . . . The common man, I think, is the great protection against war.

in the House of Commons, 23 November 1945

9 *as Minister of Labour to his Civil Servants:*
You've just given me twenty reasons why I can't do this; I'm sure that clever chaps like you can go away and produce twenty good reasons why I can.

oral tradition; Peter Hennessy *Whitehall* (1990)

10 My [foreign] policy is to be able to take a ticket at Victoria Station and go anywhere I damn well please.

in *Spectator* 20 April 1951

11 I didn't ought never to have done it. It was you, Willie, what put me up to it.
to Lord Strang, after officially recognizing Communist China

C. Parrott *Serpent and Nightingale* (1977)

12 If you open that Pandora's Box, you never know what Trojan 'orses will jump out.
on the Council of Europe

Roderick Barclay *Ernest Bevin and the Foreign Office* (1975)

13 *someone had remarked that Aneurin **Bevan** was his own worst enemy:*
Not while I'm alive 'e ain't.
*also attributed to Bevin of Herbert **Morrison***

Roderick Barclay *Ernest Bevin and the Foreign Office* (1975)

Benazir Bhutto 1953–
Pakistani stateswoman; Prime Minister 1988–90 and 1993–96

14 Every dictator uses religion as a prop to keep himself in power.

interview on *60 Minutes*, CBS-TV, 8 August 1986

1 You can't be fuelled by bitterness. It can eat you up, but it cannot drive you.

Daughter of Destiny (1989)

The Bible (Authorized Version)

2 Let my people go.

Exodus

3 Let them live; but let them be hewers of wood and drawers of water unto all the congregation.

Joshua

4 He smote them hip and thigh.

Judges

5 And she named the child I-chabod, saying, The glory is departed from Israel.

I Samuel

6 And Saul said, God hath delivered him into mine hand.

I Samuel

7 He shall know that there is a prophet in Israel.

II Kings

8 Had Zimri peace, who slew his master?

II Kings

9 Thus shall it be done to the man whom the king delighteth to honour.

Esther

10 Great men are not always wise.

Job

11 Where there is no vision, the people perish.

Proverbs

12 The race is not to the swift, nor the battle to the strong.

Ecclesiastes

13 Woe to thee, O land, when thy king is a child.

Ecclesiastes

14 They shall beat their swords into plowshares, and their spears into pruninghooks: nation shall not lift up sword against nation, neither shall they learn war any more.

Isaiah; see **Rendall** 324:6

15 Of the increase of his government and peace there shall be no end.

Isaiah

16 Now, O king, establish the decree, and sign the writing, that it be not changed, according to the law of the Medes and Persians, which altereth not.

Daniel

17 They have sown the wind, and they shall reap the whirlwind.

Hosea

18 Let us now praise famous men, and our fathers that begat us.

Ecclesiasticus

19 Judge not, that ye be not judged.

St Matthew

20 I came not to send peace, but a sword.

St Matthew

21 He that is not with me is against me.

St Matthew; St Luke

22 Render therefore unto Caesar the things which are Caesar's; and unto God the things that are God's.

St Matthew

23 Ye shall hear of wars and rumours of wars: see that ye be not troubled: for all these things must come to pass but the end is not yet.

St Matthew

24 For nation shall rise against nation, and kingdom against kingdom.

St Matthew; St John

25 Those that have turned the world upside down are come hither also.

Acts of the Apostles

26 But Paul said, I am a man which am a Jew of Tarsus, a city in Cilicia, a citizen of no mean city.

Acts of the Apostles

27 Hast thou appealed unto Caesar? unto Caesar shalt thou go.

Acts of the Apostles

1 For where no law is, there is no transgression.   Romans

Georges Bidault 1899–1983
French statesman; Prime Minister, 1946, 1949–50

2 The weak have one weapon: the errors of those who think   in *Observer* 15 July 1962 'Sayings of
they are strong.   the Week'

Ambrose Bierce 1842–c.1914
American writer

3 BATTLE, *n.* A method of untying with the teeth a political   *The Cynic's Word Book* (1906)
knot that would not yield to the tongue.

4 CONSERVATIVE, *n.* A statesman who is enamoured of existing   *The Cynic's Word Book* (1906)
evils, as distinguished from the Liberal, who wishes to
replace them with others.

5 PEACE, *n.* In international affairs, a period of cheating   *The Devil's Dictionary* (1911)
between two periods of fighting.

John Biffen 1930–
British Conservative politician

6 *of Margaret* **Thatcher** *as Prime Minister:*   in *Observer* 9 December 1990
She was a tigress surrounded by hamsters.

7 In politics I think it is wiser to leave five minutes too soon   in *Daily Telegraph* 5 January 1995
than to continue for five years too long.
  resignation letter

John Biggs-Davison 1918–88
British Conservative politician

8 I have never conceived it my duty as a Member of   speech at Chelmsford, 7 November
Parliament to seek to amend the Ten Commandments.   1976

Steve Biko 1946–77
South African anti-apartheid campaigner

9 The most potent weapon in the hands of the oppressor is the   statement as witness, 3 May 1976
mind of the oppressed.

Josh Billings 1818–85
American humorist

10 It is better to know nothing than to know what ain't so.   *Proverb* (1874)

Nigel Birch 1906–81
British Conservative politician

11 *on hearing of the resignation of Hugh* **Dalton**, *Chancellor of the*   Harold Macmillan *Tides of Fortune*
Exchequer in the Labour Government, 13 November 1947:   (1969)
My God! They've shot our fox!

12 For the second time the Prime Minister has got rid of a   letter to *The Times*, 14 July 1962
Chancellor of the Exchequer who tried to get expenditure
under control. Once is more than enough.
  after Harold **Macmillan**'s *dismissal of Selwyn Lloyd in favour of*
  Reginald Maudling

1 On the question of competence and good sense I cannot think that the verdict can be favourable.

*of Harold **Macmillan** and his handling of the Profumo affair; Birch's peroration for this speech was from Browning's 'The Lost Leader': 'Let him never come back to us . . . never glad confident morning again'*

in the House of Commons, 17 June 1963

2 No one could accuse himself of courage more often than the Prime Minister.

*of Harold **Wilson***

in the House of Commons, 2 August 1965

Stanley F. Birch Jr. 1945-

American judge, member of the 11th US Circuit Court of Appeals

3 Despite sincere and altruistic motivation, the legislative and executive branches of our government have acted in a manner demonstrably at odds with our Founding Fathers' blueprint for the governance of a free people—our Constitution.

opinion denying the appeal that the Federal Court reverse the ruling in the Schiavo case, 30 March 2005 (compare **DeLay** 114:1)

Lord Birkenhead see F. E. **Smith**

Otto von Bismarck 1815–98

German statesman
*on Bismarck: see **Taylor** 387:15, **Tenniel** 389:4*

4 If the Princess can leave the Englishwoman at home and become a Prussian, then she may be a blessing to the country.

on the marriage of Victoria, Princess Royal, to Prince Frederick William of Prussia

letter, c.1857

5 The secret of politics? Make a good treaty with Russia.

in 1863, when first in power

A. J. P. Taylor *Bismarck* (1955)

6 Politics is not an exact science.

speech to the Prussian legislature, 18 December 1863

7 Politics is the art of the possible.

in conversation with Meyer von Waldeck, 11 August 1867; see **Galbraith** 150:8

8 Let us . . . put Germany in the saddle! She will know well enough how to ride!

in 1867; Alan Palmer *Bismarck* (1976)

9 The politician has not to revenge what has happened but to ensure that it does not happen again.

c.1871, following public criticism of courtesy shown to the defeated Napoleon III after the battle of Sedan

A. J. P. Taylor *Bismarck* (1955)

10 We will not go to Canossa.

during his quarrel with Pope Pius IX regarding papal authority over German subjects, in allusion to the Emperor Henry IV's submission to Pope Gregory VII at Canossa in Modena in 1077

speech to the Reichstag, 14 May 1872

11 Whoever speaks of Europe is wrong, [it is] a geographical concept.

marginal note on a letter from the Russian Chancellor Gorchakov, November 1876; see **Metternich** 268:3

1 I have always found the word Europe on the lips of those politicians who wanted something from other Powers which they dared not demand in their own names.
  to the Russian Chancellor Gorchakov, who had urged that a rising in Bosnia in 1878 was a European, rather than a German or Russian, question

A. J. P. Taylor *Bismarck* (1955)

2 I do not regard the procuring of peace as a matter in which we should play the role of arbiter between different opinions . . . more that of an honest broker who really wants to press the business forward.
  before the Congress of Berlin

speech to the Reichstag, 19 February 1878

3 A lath of wood painted to look like iron.
  *of Lord **Salisbury** at the Congress of Berlin in 1878*

attributed, but vigorously denied by Sidney Whitman in *Personal Reminiscences of Prince Bismarck* (1902)

4 The old Jew! That is the man.
  *of **Disraeli** at the Congress of Berlin*

attributed

5 Place in the hands of the King of Prussia the strongest possible military power, then he will be able to carry out the policy you wish; this policy cannot succeed through speeches, and shooting-matches, and songs; it can only be carried out through blood and iron.

in the Prussian House of Deputies, 28 January 1886; in a speech on 30 September 1862, Bismarck had used the form 'iron and blood'

6 I am bored; the great things are done. The German *Reich* is made.

A. J. P. Taylor *Bismarck* (1955)

7 Jena came twenty years after the death of Frederick the Great; the crash will come twenty years after my departure if things go on like this.
  *to Kaiser **Wilhelm II** at their last meeting in 1895*

A. J. P. Taylor *Bismarck* (1955)

8 If there is ever another war in Europe, it will come out of some damned silly thing in the Balkans.

reported by the shipping magnate Herr Ballen as being said by Bismarck in his later years; quoted in the House of Commons, 16 August 1945

9 Man cannot create the current of events. He can only float with it and steer.

A. J. P. Taylor *Bismarck* (1955)

10 *of possible German involvement in the Balkans:*
  Not worth the healthy bones of a single Pomeranian grenadier.

George O. Kent *Bismarck and his Times* (1978); see **Harris** 174:2

11 A statesman . . . must wait until he hears the steps of God sounding through events; then leap up and grasp the hem of his garment.

A. J. P. Taylor *Bismarck* (1955)

12 There is a providence that protects idiots, drunkards, children, and the United States of America.

attributed, perhaps apocryphal

13 The tongue in the balance.
  of Germany's position in relation to other European states

A. J. P. Taylor *Bismarck* (1955)

14 When a man says he approves of something in principle, it means he hasn't the slightest intention of putting it into practice.

attributed

Johannes ('Joh') Bjelke-Petersen

1911–2005

New Zealand-born Australian National Party politician, Premier of Queensland, 1968–87

1 Don't you worry about that.   *in Times* 25 April 2005 (obituary)
  habitual response to questions

2 Feeding the chooks.   *in Times* 25 April 2005 (obituary)
  term for a press conference

Hugo La Fayette Black 1886–1971

American judge

3 The First Amendment has erected a wall between church   *in Emerson v. Board of Education*
and state. That wall must be kept high and impregnable. We   1947
could not approve the slightest breach.

4 In revealing the workings of government that led to the   concurring opinion on the
Vietnam War, the newspapers nobly did precisely that   publication of the Pentagon
which the Founders hoped and trusted they would do.   Papers, 1971

William Blackstone 1723–80

English jurist

5 The king never dies.   *Commentaries on the Laws of England* (1765)

6 The royal navy of England hath ever been its greatest   *Commentaries on the Laws of*
defence and ornament; it is its ancient and natural strength;   *England* (1765)
the floating bulwark of the island.

7 That the king can do no wrong, is a necessary and   *Commentaries on the Laws of*
fundamental principle of the English constitution.   *England* (1765)

8 In all tyrannical governments the supreme magistracy, or   *Commentaries on the Laws of*
the right both of making and of enforcing the laws, is vested   *England* (1765)
in one and the same man, or one and the same body of
men; and wherever these two powers are united together,
there can be no public liberty.

9 Herein indeed consists the excellence of the English   *Commentaries on the Laws of*
government, that all parts of it form a mutual check upon   *England* (1765)
each other.

Tony Blair 1953–

British Labour statesman; Prime Minister since 1997
on Blair: see **Mandelson** 134:7, **Newspaper headlines** 287:11,
Thatcher 392:10

10 Labour is the party of law and order in Britain today. Tough   speech at the Labour Party
on crime and tough on the causes of crime.   Conference, 30 September 1993
  as Shadow Home Secretary

11 Those who seriously believe we cannot improve on words   *in Independent* 11 January 1995
written for the world of 1918 when we are now in 1995 are
not learning from our history but living it.
  on the proposed revision of Clause IV

1 Ask me my three main priorities for Government, and I tell you: education, education and education.

speech at the Labour Party Conference, 1 October 1996; see **Michelet** 269:1

2 We are not the masters. The people are the masters. We are the servants of the people . . . What the electorate gives, the electorate can take away.
addressing Labour MPs on the first day of the new Parliament, 7 May 1997

in *Guardian* 8 May 1997; see **Burke** 64:14

3 She was the People's Princess, and that is how she will stay . . . in our hearts and in our memories forever.
*on hearing of the death of **Diana**, Princess of Wales, 31 August 1997*

in *Times* 1 September 1997

4 I am a pretty straight sort of guy.
interviewed on the government's exemption of Formula One racing from the tobacco advertising ban

interviewed on *On the Record* (BBC TV), 17 November 1997

5 I am from the Disraeli school of Prime Ministers in their relations with the Monarch.
*at the Queen's golden wedding celebration, 20 November 1997; see **Elizabeth II** 134:6*

in *Daily Telegraph* 21 November 1997

6 This is not a time for soundbites. We've left them at home. I feel the hand of history upon our shoulders . . . I'm here to try.
arriving in Belfast for the final stage of the Northern Irish negotiations, 8 April 1998

in *Irish Times* 11 April 1998 'This Week They Said'

7 In future, welfare will be a hand-up not a hand-out.

lecture, London, 18 March 1999

8 Arrayed against us: the forces of conservatism, the cynics, the elites, the establishment. On our side, the forces of modernity and justice.

speech to Labour Party Conference, 28 September 1999

9 We need two or three eye-catching initiatives . . . I should be personally associated with as much of this as possible.

leaked memorandum, 29 April 2000; in *Times* 18 July 2000

10 This is not a battle betweeen the United States and terrorism, but between the free and democratic world and terrorism. We therefore here in Britain stand shoulder to shoulder with our American friends in this hour of tragedy and we, like them, will not rest until this evil is driven from our world.

in Downing Street, London, 11 September 2001

11 The state of Africa is a scar on the conscience of the world.

speech to Labour Party Conference, 2 October 2001

12 I believe we're at our best when we are boldest.

speech to the Labour Party Conference, 30 September 2002; see **Brown** 57:8

13 This is not the time to falter.

speech in the House of Commons, 18 March 2003

14 I can only go one way. I've not got a reverse gear.

speech, Labour Party Conference, Bournemouth, 30 September 2003

15 I've listened, and I've learned . . . I, we, the Government are going to focus now relentlessly on the priorities the people have set for us.

speech outside Downing Street, 6 May 2005

William Blake 1757–1827

English poet

1 The strongest poison ever known
Came from Caesar's laurel crown.

'Auguries of Innocence' (c.1803)

2 The whore and gambler by the State
Licensed build that nation's fate
The harlot's cry from street to street
Shall weave old England's winding sheet.

'Auguries of Innocence' (c.1803)

3 He who would do good to another, must do it in minute
particulars
General good is the plea of the scoundrel, hypocrite and
flatterer.

Jerusalem (1815) 'Chapter 3' (plate 55, l. 60)

4 And was Jerusalem builded here
Among these dark Satanic mills?

Milton (1804–10) preface 'And did those feet in ancient time'

5 I will not cease from mental fight,
Nor shall my sword sleep in my hand,
Till we have built Jerusalem,
In England's green and pleasant land.

Milton (1804–10) preface 'And did those feet in ancient time'

Hans Blix 1928–

Swedish diplomat

6 We have not found any smoking guns.
of weapons inspections in Iraq

in *Newsweek* 20 January 2003

7 You can put up a sign on the door, 'beware of the dog',
without having a dog.

in *Guardian* (online edition) 18 September 2003

David Blunkett 1947–

British Labour politician, Minister for Education, 1997–2001;
Home Secretary from 2001

8 Let me say this very slowly indeed. Watch my lips: no
selection by examination or interview under a Labour
government.

in *Daily Telegraph* (electronic edition) 5 October 1995

9 I don't use or recognize the term 'bog standard' but what I
do recognize is the critical importance of honesty about
what some children, in some schools, have had to put up
with over the years.

at Labour spring conference, 17 February 2001; see **Campbell** 72:3

10 We could live in a world which is airy-fairy, libertarian,
where everybody does precisely what they like and we
believe the best of everybody and then they destroy us.

interview on London Weekend Television, 11 November 2001

11 They should go back home and re-create their countries
which we have freed from tyranny, whether it is Kosovo or
now Afghanistan. I have no sympathy whatsoever with
young men in their twenties who do not.
on asylum seekers

in *Observer* 22 September 2002

Alfred Blunt, Bishop of Bradford

1879–1957

English clergyman

1 The benefit of the King's Coronation depends, under God, upon two elements: First on the faith, prayer, and self-dedication of the King himself, and on that it would be improper for me to say anything except to commend him, and ask you to commend him, to God's grace, which he will so abundantly need . . . if he is to do his duty faithfully. We hope that he is aware of his need. Some of us wish that he gave more positive signs of his awareness.
it was this speech that broke the story of **Edward VIII** *and Mrs Simpson which the media had been voluntarily suppressing until then*

speech to Bradford Diocesan Conference, 1 December 1936

David Boaz 1953–

American foundation executive

2 Alcohol didn't cause the high crime rates of the '20s and '30s, Prohibition did. Drugs don't cause today's alarming crime rates, but drug prohibition does.

'The Legalization of Drugs' 27 April 1988

3 Trying to wage war on 23 million Americans who are obviously very committed to certain recreational activities is not going to be any more successful than Prohibition was.

'The Legalization of Drugs' 27 April 1988

Ivan Boesky 1937–

American financier, imprisoned in 1987 for insider dealing

4 Greed is all right . . . Greed is healthy. You can be greedy and still feel good about yourself.

commencement address at the University of California, Berkeley, 18 May 1986; see **Weiser** 414:4

Vernon Bogdanor 1943–

British academic

5 You are giving people a weapon—and if you give a child a weapon you shouldn't be surprised if he shoots you.
on devolution and central government

in *Independent on Sunday* 13 February 2000

Curtis Bok 1897–1962

American federal judge

6 It has been said that a judge is a member of the Bar who once knew a Governor.

The Backbone of the Herring (1941)

Alan Bold 1943–

Scottish poet

7 Scotland, land of the omnipotent No.

'A Memory of Death' (1969)

Henry St John, Lord Bolingbroke
1678–1751
English politician

1 The great mistake is that of looking upon men as virtuous, or thinking that they can be made so by laws.

comment (c.1728) in Joseph Spence Observations, Anecdotes, and Characters (1820)

2 The greatest art of a politician is to render vice serviceable to the cause of virtue.

comment (c.1728) in Joseph Spence Observations, Anecdotes, and Characters (1820)

3 Nations, like men, have their infancy.

On the Study of History letter 5, in Works (1809) vol. 3

Simón Bolívar 1783–1830
Venezuelan patriot and statesman

4 Those who have served the cause of the revolution have ploughed the sea.

attributed

Robert Bolt 1924–95
English dramatist

5 THOMAS MORE: This country's planted thick with laws from coast to coast—Man's laws, not God's—and if you cut them down—and you're just the man to do it—d'you really think you could stand upright in the winds that would blow then?

A Man for All Seasons (1960)

Laetitia Bonaparte 1750–1836
French mother of **Napoleon**

6 *Pourvu que ça dure!*

Let's hope it lasts!
*on her son **Napoleon** becoming Emperor, 1804*

attributed, possibly apocryphal

Andrew Bonar Law 1858–1923
Canadian-born British Conservative statesman, Prime Minister 1922–3
*on Bonar Law: see **Asquith** 16:9, **Beaverbrook** 31:14*

7 If, therefore, war should ever come between these two countries [Great Britain and Germany], which Heaven forbid! it will not, I think, be due to irresistible natural laws, it will be due to want of human wisdom.

in the House of Commons, 27 November 1911

8 There are things stronger than parliamentary majorities. I can imagine no length of resistance to which Ulster will not go, in which I shall not be ready to support them.
at a Unionist meeting at Blenheim in 1912

Robert Blake The Unknown Prime Minister (1955)

9 In war it is necessary not only to be active but to seem active.

*letter to **Asquith**, 1916; Robert Blake The Unknown Prime Minister (1955)*

10 We cannot alone act as the policemen of the world.

letter to Times, 7 October 1922

11 If I am a great man, then all great men are frauds.

Lord Beaverbrook Politicians and the War (1932)

Violet Bonham Carter 1887–1969

British Liberal politician

1 HOW DARE YOU BECOME PRIME MINISTER WHEN I'M AWAY
 GREAT LOVE CONSTANT THOUGHT VIOLET.
   *telegram to her father, H. H. **Asquith**, 7 April 1908*

Mark Bonham Carter and Mark Pottle (eds.) *Lantern Slides* (1996)

Dietrich Bonhoeffer 1906–45

German Lutheran theologian and martyr

2 I have come to the conclusion that I have made a mistake in coming to America. I must live through this difficult period of our national history with the Christian people of Germany. I shall have no right to participate in the reconstruction of Christian life in Germany after the war if I do not share the trials of this time with my people.

letter to Reinhold Niebuhr, July 1939

3 It is the nature, and the advantage, of strong people that they can bring out the crucial questions and form a clear opinion about them. The weak always have to decide between alternatives that are not their own.

Widerstand und Ergebung (1951)

The Book of Common Prayer 1662

4 The Bishop of Rome hath no jurisdiction in this Realm of England.

Articles of Religion (1562) no. 37

Christopher Booker 1937–

English author and journalist

5 In the life of any government, however safe its majority, there comes a moment when the social movements of which it had once been the expression turn inexorably against it . . . After that moment, every mistake it makes becomes magnified; indeed blunders multiply as if feeding on themselves; and both outwardly and inwardly the Government appears to be at the mercy of every wind.

The Neophiliacs (1969)

6 It is a familiar pattern of history that, on the eve of revolutionary crises, the established order veers erratically between liberal concessions and recklessly reactionary steps which seem calculated to cast it in the most unfavourable light and to hasten its own destruction.

The Neophiliacs (1969)

7 Our government has recently unleashed the greatest avalanche of regulations in peacetime history; and wherever we examine their working we see that they are using a sledgehammer to miss a nut.

speech, 1995

Christopher Booker 1937–
and Richard North 1946–

8 Castle of lies: why Britain must get out of Europe.

title of book (1996) on Britain's membership of the European Union

Daniel J. Boorstin 1914–

American writer

1 A pseudo event . . . comes about because someone has
planned, planted, or incited it. Typically, it is not a train
wreck or an earthquake, but an interview.

The Image (1962)

John Wilkes Booth 1838–65

American actor and assassin

2 *Sic semper tyrannis!* The South is avenged.
having shot President **Lincoln**, *14 April 1865*

in *New York Times* 15 April 1865;
the second part of the statement
does not appear in any
contemporary source, and is
possibly apocryphal; see **Mottoes**
281:8

Robert Boothby 1900–86

British Conservative politician

3 *You* speak for Britain!
*to Arthur Greenwood, acting Leader of the Labour Party, after
Neville* **Chamberlain** *had failed to announce an ultimatum to
Germany; perhaps taking up an appeal already voiced by Leo*
Amery

Harold Nicolson diary, 2
September 1939; see **Amery** 7:4

Betty Boothroyd 1929–

British Labour politician; Speaker of the House of Commons
1992–2000

4 My desire to get here [Parliament] was like miners' coal
dust, it was under my fingers and I couldn't scrub it out.

Glenys Kinnock and Fiona Millar
(eds.) *By Faith and Daring* (1993)

5 The level of cynicism about Parliament and the
accompanying alienation of many of the young from the
democratic process is troubling. Let's make a start by
remembering that the function of Parliament is to hold the
executive to account.
in her valedictory statement as Speaker

in the House of Commons, 26 July
2000

James H. Boren 1925–

American bureaucrat

6 Guidelines for bureaucrats: (1) When in charge, ponder. (2)
When in trouble, delegate. (3) When in doubt, mumble.

in *New York Times* 8 November
1970

Jorge Luis Borges 1899–1986

Argentinian writer

7 The Falklands thing was a fight between two bald men over
a comb.

application of a proverbial phrase;
in *Time* 14 February 1983

Cesare Borgia see **Mottoes** 281:1

Robert H. Bork 1927–
American judge and educationalist

1 One of the uses of history is to free us of a falsely imagined   *The Antitrust Paradox* (1978)
past. The less we know of how ideas actually took root and
grew, the more apt we are to accept them unquestioningly,
as inevitable features of the world in which we move.

George Borrow 1803–81
English writer

2 I am invariably of the politics of the people at whose table I   *The Bible in Spain* (1843)
sit, or beneath whose roof I sleep.

James Boswell 1740–95
Scottish lawyer; biographer of Samuel **Johnson**

3 We [Boswell and Johnson] are both *Tories*; both convinced   *Journal of a Tour to the Hebrides* 13
of the utility of monarchical power, and both lovers of that   September 1773
reverence and affection for a sovereign which constitute
loyalty, a principle which I take to be absolutely
extinguished in Britain.

Lucien Bouchard 1938–
Canadian lawyer and politician, Premier of Quebec 1996–2001

4 Canada is divisible because it's not a real country. Canada is   statement at a press conference,
two nations, two peoples, two territories and this one is ours   January 1996
and we're keeping it!
  when asked, after the 1995 Quebec referendum on independence,
  why he felt no guilt about having Quebec separate from the rest of
  Canada

Antoine Boulay de la Meurthe 1761–1840
French statesman

5 *on hearing of the execution of the Duc d'Enghien, 1804:*   C.-A. Sainte-Beuve *Nouveaux Lundis*
It is worse than a crime, it is a blunder.   (1870) vol. 12

Pierre Boulez 1925–
French conductor and composer

6 Revolutions are celebrated when they are no longer   in *Guardian* 13 January 1989
dangerous.

Lord Bowen 1835–94
English judge

7 The man on the Clapham omnibus.   in *Law Reports* (1903); attributed
  the average man

Omar Bradley 1893–1981
American general

8 The way to win an atomic war is to make certain it never   speech to Boston Chamber of
starts.   Commerce, 10 November 1948

1 We have grasped the mystery of the atom and rejected the Sermon on the Mount.

speech on Armistice Day, 1948

2 The world has achieved brilliance without wisdom, power without conscience. Ours is a world of nuclear giants and ethical infants.

speech on Armistice Day, 1948

3 In war there is no second prize for the runner-up.

in *Military Review* February 1950

4 This strategy would involve us in the wrong war, at the wrong place, at the wrong time, and with the wrong enemy.

on General Macarthur's wish to extend the Korean War into China

in *US Congressional Senate Committee on Armed Service* (1951) vol. 2

John Bradshaw 1602–59

English judge at the trial of **Charles I**

5 Rebellion to tyrants is obedience to God.

suppositious epitaph; Henry S. Randall *Life of Thomas Jefferson* (1865) vol. 3; see **Mottoes** 281:6

Edward Stuyvesant Bragg 1827–1912

American politician

6 They love him most for the enemies he has made.

*seconding the presidential nomination of Grover **Cleveland***

speech, 9 July 1884

Louis D. Brandeis 1856–1941

American jurist

7 Fear of serious injury cannot alone justify suppression of free speech and assembly. Men feared witches and burned women. It is the function of speech to free men from the bondage of irrational fears.

in *Whitney v. California* (1927)

8 They [the makers of the Constitution] conferred, as against the Government, the right to be let alone—the most comprehensive of rights and the right most valued by civilized men.

in *Olmstead v. United States* (1928)

9 The greatest dangers to liberty lurk in insidious encroachment by men of zeal, well-meaning but without understanding.

dissenting opinion in *Olmstead v. United States* (1928)

Willy Brandt 1913–92

German statesman, Chancellor of West Germany 1969–74

10 We want to risk more democracy.

speech to parliament after his election as Chancellor, 28 October 1969

11 Where mass hunger reigns, we cannot speak of peace.

World Armament and World Hunger (1986)

William Cowper Brann 1855–98

12 No man can be a patriot on an empty stomach.

The Iconoclast, Old Glory 4 July 1893

Joseph Brant (Thayendanegea) 1742–1807
American-born Canadian Mohawk leader

1 I bow to no man for I am considered a prince among my
own people. But I will gladly shake your hand.
   on being presented to **George III**

attributed

Bertolt Brecht 1898–1956
German dramatist

2 ANDREA: Unhappy the land that has no heroes! . . .
GALILEO: No. Unhappy the land that needs heroes.

Life of Galileo (1939)

3 One observes, they have gone too long without a war here.
Where is morality to come from in such a case, I ask? Peace
is nothing but slovenliness, only war creates order.

Mother Courage (1939)

4 The finest plans are always ruined by the littleness of those
who ought to carry them out, for the Emperors can actually
do nothing.

Mother Courage (1939)

5 War always finds a way.

Mother Courage (1939)

6 Don't tell me peace has broken out, when I've just bought
some new supplies.

Mother Courage (1939)

7 Would it not be easier
In that case for the government
To dissolve the people
And elect another?
   *on the uprising against the Soviet occupying forces in East
Germany in 1953*

'The Solution' (1953)

L. Paul Bremer 1941–
American diplomat, US Administrator for Iraq, 2003–4

8 Ladies and gentlemen, we got him.
   announcing the capture of Saddam **Hussein**, *14 December 2003*

in *Independent* 15 December 2003

William Joseph Brennan Jr. 1906–
American judge

9 Debate on public issues should be uninhibited, robust, and
wide open, and that . . . may well include vehement,
caustic, and sometimes unpleasantly sharp attacks on
government and public officials.

in *New York Times Co. v. Sullivan*
(1964)

Aristide Briand 1862–1932
French statesman

10 The high contracting powers solemnly declare . . . that they
condemn recourse to war and renounce it . . . as an
instrument of their national policy towards each other . . .
The settlement or the solution of all disputes or conflicts of
whatever nature or of whatever origin they may be which
may arise . . . shall never be sought by either side except by
pacific means.

draft, 20 June 1927, later
incorporated into the Kellogg Pact,
1928

Edward Bridges 1892-1969

British civil servant, Cabinet Secretary and Head of the Civil Service

1 I confidently expect that we [civil servants] shall continue to be grouped with mothers-in-law and Wigan Pier as one of the recognized objects of ridicule.

Portrait of a Profession (1950)

John Bright 1811-89

English Liberal politician and reformer

2 The angel of death has been abroad throughout the land; you may almost hear the beating of his wings.
  on the effects of the war in the Crimea

in the House of Commons, 23 February 1855

3 *of British foreign policy:*
A gigantic system of outdoor relief for the aristocracy of Great Britain.

speech at Birmingham, 29 October 1858

4 I am for 'Peace, retrenchment, and reform', the watchword of the great Liberal party 30 years ago.

speech at Birmingham, 28 April 1859; the phrase quoted may be found in Samuel Warren's novel *Ten Thousand a Year* (1841)

5 England is the mother of Parliaments.

speech at Birmingham, 18 January 1865

6 *of Robert Lowe, leader of the dissident Whigs opposed to the Reform Bill of 1866:*
The right hon Gentleman . . . has retired into what may be called his political Cave of Adullam—and he has called about him every one that was in distress and every one that was discontented.

in the House of Commons, 13 March 1866; see I Samuel ch. 22

7 *of Robert Lowe and Edward Horsman:*
This party of two is like the Scotch terrier that was so covered with hair that you could not tell which was the head and which was the tail.

in the House of Commons, 13 March 1866

8 Force is not a remedy.

speech to the Birmingham Junior Liberal Club, 16 November 1880

Vera Brittain 1893-1970

English writer

9 Politics are usually the executive expression of human immaturity.

Rebel Passion (1964)

Russell Brockbank 1913-79

British cartoonist

10 Fog in Channel—Continent isolated.

newspaper placard in cartoon, *Round the Bend with Brockbank* (1948); the phrase 'Continent isolated' was quoted as already current by John Gunther *Inside Europe* (1938)

Fenner Brockway 1888–1988

British Labour politician

1 I have spent three years in prison and three years in Parliament, and I saw character deteriorate more in Parliament than in prison.

Inside the Left (1942)

David Broder 1929–

American columnist

2 Anybody that wants the presidency so much that he'll spend two years organizing and campaigning for it is not to be trusted with the office.

in *Washington Post* 18 July 1973

D. W. Brogan 1900–74

Scottish historian

3 A people that has licked a more formidable enemy than Germany or Japan, primitive North America . . . a country whose national motto has been 'root, hog, or die.'

The American Character (1944)

4 Any well-established village in New England or the northern Middle West could afford a town drunkard, a town atheist, and a few Democrats.

The American Character (1944)

Tom Brokaw 1940–

American journalist

5 We don't just have egg on our face. We have omelette all over our suits.
    *on the networks' premature calls of a win in Florida in the presidential election, first to Al **Gore** and then to George W. **Bush***

in *Atlanta Constitution-Journal* 9 November 2000 (online edition)

Henry Brooke 1703–83

Irish poet and dramatist

6 For righteous monarchs,
Justly to judge, with their own eyes should see;
To rule o'er freemen, should themselves be free.

Earl of Essex (performed 1750, published 1761)

Robert Barnabas Brough 1828–60

English satirical writer

7 My Lord Tomnoddy is thirty-four;
The Earl can last but a few years more.
My Lord in the Peers will take his place:
Her Majesty's councils his words will grace.
Office he'll hold and patronage sway;
Fortunes and lives he will vote away;
And what are his qualifications?—ONE!
He's the Earl of Fitzdotterel's eldest son.

Songs of the Governing Classes (1855) 'My Lord Tomnoddy'

Lord Brougham 1778–1868

Scottish lawyer and politician; Lord Chancellor
on Brougham: see **Melbourne** 266:1, **Melbourne** 266:4

1 In my mind, he was guilty of no error—he was chargeable with no exaggeration—he was betrayed by his fancy into no metaphor, who once said, that all we see about us, King, Lords, and Commons, the whole machinery of the State, all the apparatus of the system, and its varied workings, end in simply bringing twelve good men into a box.

in the House of Commons, 7 February 1828

2 Education makes a people easy to lead, but difficult to drive; easy to govern, but impossible to enslave.

attributed

Heywood Broun 1888–1939

American journalist

3 Just as every conviction begins as a whim so does every emancipator serve his apprenticeship as a crank. A fanatic is a great leader who is just entering the room.

in New York World 6 February 1928

4 Appeasers believe that if you keep on throwing steaks to a tiger, the tiger will turn vegetarian.

attributed

Gordon Brown 1951–

British Labour politician, Chancellor of the Exchequer from 1997
on Brown: see **Anonymous** 11:12, **Anonymous** 11:13

5 Ideas which stress the growing importance of international cooperation and new theories of economic sovereignty across a wide range of areas—macroeconomics, the environment, the growth of post neo-classical endogenous growth theory and the symbiotic relationships between growth and investment in people and infrastructure.

New Labour Economics speech, September 1994, 'winner' of the ironic Plain English No Nonsense Award for 1994

6 It is about time we had an end to the old Britain, where all that matters is the privileges you were born with, rather than the potential you actually have.

speech, 25 May 2000

7 before the Treasury Select Committee, answering the question 'Do you want to be Prime Minister?':
It would be dishonest to say I'd rule out indefinitely the office you refer to.

in Sunday Times 30 July 2000

8 The Labour Party—best when we are boldest, best when we are united, best when we are Labour.

speech to the Labour Party Conference, 29 September 2003; see **Blair** 46:12

9 There is nothing that you could ever say to me now that I could ever believe.
to Tony **Blair**, who in 2004 had allegedly gone back on a promise to resign as Prime Minister.

attributed (although denied in the House of Commons by the Prime Minister); Robert Peston Brown's Britain (2005)

10 There are two kinds of Chancellor. Those who fail and those who get out in time.

habitual saying recalled by Anthony Howard; in Times 8 February 2005

Henry Box Brown b. 1815–

American escaped slave

1 I entered the world a slave—in the midst of a country whose most honoured writings declare that all men have a right to liberty.

Narrative of the Life of Henry Box Brown (1851)

H. Rap Brown 1943–

American Black Power leader

2 I say violence is necessary. It is as American as cherry pie.

speech at Washington, 27 July 1967

John Brown 1800–59

American abolitionist
on Brown: see **Songs** *376:5; see also* **Last words** *228:3*

3 I am yet too young to understand that God is any respecter of persons.
  last speech to the court at his trial

on 2 November 1859

4 If it is deemed necessary that I should forfeit my life for the furtherance of the ends of justice, and mingle my blood further with the blood of my children, and with the blood of millions in this slave country whose rights are disregarded by wicked, cruel, and most unjust enactments, I submit: so let it be done!
  last speech to the court at his trial

on 2 November 1859

Joseph Brown 1821–94

American politician; Confederate Governor of Georgia during the Civil War

5 *refusing to accept the Confederate President Jefferson* **Davis**'s *call for a day of national fasting:*
I entered into this Revolution to contribute my mite to sustain the rights of states and prevent the consolidation of the Government, and I am *still* a rebel . . . no matter who may be in power.

in 1863; Geoffrey C. Ward *The Civil War* (1991)

William Browne 1692–1774

English physician and writer

6 The King to Oxford sent a troop of horse,
For Tories own no argument but force:
With equal skill to Cambridge books he sent,
For Whigs admit no force but argument.

reply to Trapp's epigram, in J. Nichols *Literary Anecdotes* vol. 3; see **Trapp** 397:5

Frederick 'Boy' Browning 1896–1965

British soldier

7 *expressing reservations about the Arnhem 'Market Garden' operation to Field Marshal Montgomery on 10 September 1944:*
I think we might be going a bridge too far.

R. E. Urquhart *Arnhem* (1958)

Robert Browning 1812–89

English poet

1 Just for a handful of silver he left us,
Just for a riband to stick in his coat.
of **Wordsworth**'s *implied abandonment of radical principles by his acceptance of the Laureateship*

'The Lost Leader' (1845)

2 Life's night begins: let him never come back to us!
There would be doubt, hesitation and pain,
Forced praise on our part—the glimmer of twilight,
Never glad confident morning again!

'The Lost Leader' (1845); see **Birch** 43:1

Cathal Brugha 1874–1922

Irish nationalist
on Brugha: see **Collins** 99:8

3 Don't you realize that, if you sign this thing, you will split
Ireland from top to bottom?
to **de Valera**, *December 1921, on the Treaty*

Jim Ring *Erskine Childers* (1996)

Gro Harlem Brundtland 1939–

Norwegian stateswoman; Prime Minister 1981, 1986–89, and 1990–96

4 I do not know of any environmental group in any country
that does not view its government as an adversary.

in *Time* 25 September 1989

John Bruton 1947–

Irish Fine Gael statesman

5 Ministers are behaving like sheep scattered in a fog on a
mountainside.

in 1994, criticizing the Fianna Fáil administration

6 The strategy of the ballot box in one hand and the gun in
the other was . . . originated by the Nazis.

in *Irish Times* 10 October 1996

William Jennings Bryan 1860–1925

American Democratic politician

7 The humblest citizen of all the land, when clad in the
armour of a righteous cause, is stronger than all the hosts of
error.

speech at the Democratic National Convention, Chicago, 1896

8 Destroy our farms and the grass will grow in the streets of
every city in the country.

speech at the Democratic National Convention, Chicago 1896; see **Hoover** 188:5

9 You shall not press down upon the brow of labour this
crown of thorns, you shall not crucify mankind upon a
cross of gold.

speech at the Democratic National Convention, Chicago, 1896; see **Slogans** 368:4

Zbigniew Brzezinski 1928–

American politician

10 Russia can be an empire or a democracy, but it cannot be
both.

in *Foreign Affairs* March/April 1994 'The Premature Partnership'

John Buchan (Lord Tweedsmuir) 1875–1940
Scottish novelist; Governor-General of Canada, 1935–40

1 Have you ever considered what a diabolical weapon that can be—using all the channels of modern publicity to poison and warp men's minds? It is the most dangerous thing on earth . . . Happily, in the long run it defeats itself, but only after it has sown the world with mischief.

The Three Hostages (1924) ch. 4

Frank Buchman 1878–1961
American evangelist; founder of the Moral Re-Armament movement

2 I thank heaven for a man like Adolf Hitler, who built a front line of defence against the anti-Christ of Communism.

in *New York World-Telegram* 26 August 1936

Gerald Bullett 1893–1958
British writer

3 My Lord Archbishop, what a scold you are!
And when your man is down how bold you are!
Of charity how oddly scant you are!
How Lang, O Lord, how full of Cantuar!
 on the role of Cosmo Gordon Lang, Archbishop of Canterbury, in the abdication of Edward VIII

in 1936

Ivor Bulmer-Thomas 1905–93
British Conservative politician

4 *of Harold* **Wilson**:
If he ever went to school without any boots it was because he was too big for them.

speech at the Conservative Party Conference, in *Manchester Guardian* 13 October 1949

Prince Bernhard von Bülow 1849–1929
German statesman, Chancellor of Germany, 1900–9

5 In a word, we desire to throw no one into the shade [in East Asia], but we also demand our own place in the sun.

speech in the Reichstag, 6 December 1897; see **Wilhelm II** 419:9

Edward George Bulwer-Lytton 1803–73
British novelist and politician

6 Here Stanley meets,—how Stanley scorns, the glance!
The brilliant chief, irregularly great,
Frank, haughty, rash,—the Rupert of Debate!
 on Edward Stanley, 14th Earl of **Derby**

The New Timon (1846); see **Disraeli** 119:8

Samuel Dickinson Burchard 1812–91
American Presbyterian minister

7 We are Republicans and don't propose to leave our party and identify ourselves with the party whose antecedents are rum, Romanism, and rebellion.

speech at the Fifth Avenue Hotel, New York, 29 October 1884

Anthony Burgess 1917–93

English novelist and critic

1 The US presidency is a Tudor monarchy plus telephones.

George Plimpton (ed.) *Writers at Work* (4th Series, 1977)

Edmund Burke 1729–97

Irish-born Whig politician and man of letters
on Burke: see **Gibbon** 156:1, **Johnson** 205:5, **O'Brien** 293:2, **Paine** 301:2, **Paine** 301:3; *see also* **Misquotations** 273:5

2 Those who have been once intoxicated with power, and have derived any kind of emolument from it, even though for but one year, can never willingly abandon it.

Letter to a Member of the National Assembly (1791)

3 Tyrants seldom want pretexts.

Letter to a Member of the National Assembly (1791)

4 You can never plan the future by the past.

Letter to a Member of the National Assembly (1791)

5 Men are qualified for civil liberty, in exact proportion to their disposition to put moral chains upon their own appetites.

Letter to a Member of the National Assembly (1791)

6 The king, and his faithful subjects, the lords and commons of this realm,—the triple cord, which no man can break.

A Letter to a Noble Lord (1796)

7 To innovate is not to reform.

A Letter to a Noble Lord (1796)

8 Bodies tied together by so unnatural a bond of union as mutual hatred are only connected to their ruin.

Letter to the Sheriffs of Bristol (1777)

9 I was persuaded that government was a practical thing made for the happiness of mankind, and not to furnish out a spectacle of uniformity to gratify the schemes of visionary politicians.

Letter to the Sheriffs of Bristol (1777)

10 Among a people generally corrupt, liberty cannot long exist.

Letter to the Sheriffs of Bristol (1777)

11 It is a general popular error to imagine the loudest complainers for the public to be the most anxious for its welfare.

Observations on a late Publication on the Present State of the Nation (2nd ed., 1769)

12 There is, however, a limit at which forbearance ceases to be a virtue.

Observations on a late Publication on the Present State of the Nation (2nd ed., 1769)

13 It is the nature of all greatness not to be exact; and great trade will always be attended with considerable abuses.

On American Taxation (1775)

14 To tax and to please, no more than to love and to be wise, is not given to men.

On American Taxation (1775)

15 I have in general no very exalted opinion of the virtue of paper government.

On Conciliation with America (1775)

16 The concessions of the weak are the concessions of fear.

On Conciliation with America (1775)

17 When we speak of the commerce with our colonies, fiction lags after truth; invention is unfruitful, and imagination cold and barren.

On Conciliation with America (1775)

18 The use of force alone is but *temporary*. It may subdue for a moment; but it does not remove the necessity of subduing again; and a nation is not governed, which is perpetually to be conquered.

On Conciliation with America (1775)

1 Nothing less will content me, than *whole America.*

On Conciliation with America (1775)

2 I do not know the method of drawing up an indictment against an whole people.

On Conciliation with America (1775)

3 It is not, what a lawyer tells me I *may* do; but what humanity, reason, and justice, tells me I ought to do.

On Conciliation with America (1775)

4 Freedom and not servitude is the cure of anarchy; as religion, and not atheism, is the true remedy for superstition.

On Conciliation with America (1775)

5 Instead of a standing revenue, you will have therefore a perpetual quarrel.

On Conciliation with America (1775)

6 Parties must ever exist in a free country.

On Conciliation with America (1775)

7 Slavery they can have anywhere. It is a weed that grows in every soil.

On Conciliation with America (1775)

8 Deny them this participation of freedom, and you break that sole bond, which originally made, and must still preserve the unity of the empire.

On Conciliation with America (1775)

9 It is the love of the people; it is their attachment to their government, from the sense of the deep stake they have in such a glorious institution, which gives you your army and your navy, and infuses into both that liberal obedience, without which your army would be a base rabble, and your navy nothing but rotten timber.

On Conciliation with America (1775)

10 Magnanimity in politics is not seldom the truest wisdom; and a great empire and little minds go ill together.

On Conciliation with America (1775)

11 By adverting to the dignity of this high calling, our ancestors have turned a savage wilderness into a glorious empire: and have made the most extensive, and the only honourable conquests; not by destroying, but by promoting the wealth, the number, the happiness of the human race.

On Conciliation with America (1775)

12 I flatter myself that I love a manly, moral, regulated liberty as well as any gentleman.

Reflections on the Revolution in France (1790)

13 Whenever our neighbour's house is on fire, it cannot be amiss for the engines to play a little on our own.

Reflections on the Revolution in France (1790)

14 A state without the means of some change is without the means of its conservation.

Reflections on the Revolution in France (1790)

15 Make the Revolution a parent of settlement, and not a nursery of future revolutions.

Reflections on the Revolution in France (1790)

16 People will not look forward to posterity, who never look backward to their ancestors.

Reflections on the Revolution in France (1790)

17 Those who attempt to level never equalize.

Reflections on the Revolution in France (1790)

18 Government is a contrivance of human wisdom to provide for human *wants*. Men have a right that these wants should be provided for by this wisdom.

Reflections on the Revolution in France (1790)

19 Flattery corrupts both the receiver and the giver.

Reflections on the Revolution in France (1790)

20 *of **Marie-Antoinette**:*
I thought ten thousand swords must have leapt from their scabbards to avenge even a look that threatened her with insult.

Reflections on the Revolution in France (1790)

1 The age of chivalry is gone.—That of sophisters, economists, and calculators, has succeeded; and the glory of Europe is extinguished for ever.

Reflections on the Revolution in France (1790)

2 This barbarous philosophy, which is the offspring of cold hearts and muddy understandings.

Reflections on the Revolution in France (1790)

3 In the groves of *their* academy, at the end of every vista, you see nothing but the gallows.

Reflections on the Revolution in France (1790)

4 Kings will be tyrants from policy when subjects are rebels from principle.

Reflections on the Revolution in France (1790)

5 Because half a dozen grasshoppers under a fern make the field ring with their importunate chink, whilst thousands of great cattle, reposed beneath the shadow of the British oak, chew the cud and are silent, pray do not imagine that those who make the noise are the only inhabitants of the field.

Reflections on the Revolution in France (1790)

6 Society is indeed a contract . . . it becomes a partnership not only between those who are living, but between those who are living, those who are dead, and those who are to be born.

Reflections on the Revolution in France (1790)

7 Nobility is a graceful ornament to the civil order. It is the Corinthian capital of polished society.

Reflections on the Revolution in France (1790)

8 By hating vices too much, they come to love men too little.

Reflections on the Revolution in France (1790)

9 We begin our public affections in our families. No cold relation is a zealous citizen.

Reflections on the Revolution in France (1790)

10 Good order is the foundation of all good things.

Reflections on the Revolution in France (1790)

11 Nothing turns out to be so oppressive and unjust as a feeble government.

Reflections on the Revolution in France (1790)

12 Ambition can creep as well as soar.

Third Letter . . . on the Proposals for Peace with the Regicide Directory (1797)

13 And having looked to government for bread, on the very first scarcity they will turn and bite the hand that fed them.

Thoughts and Details on Scarcity (1800)

14 To complain of the age we live in, to murmur at the present possessors of power, to lament the past, to conceive extravagant hopes of the future, are the common dispositions of the greatest part of mankind.

Thoughts on the Cause of the Present Discontents (1770)

15 I am not one of those who think that the people are never in the wrong. They have been so, frequently and outrageously, both in other countries and in this. But I do say, that in all disputes between them and their rulers, the presumption is at least upon a par in favour of the people.

Thoughts on the Cause of the Present Discontents (1770)

16 The power of the crown, almost dead and rotten as Prerogative, has grown up anew, with much more strength, and far less odium, under the name of Influence.

Thoughts on the Cause of the Present Discontents (1770)

17 We must soften into a credulity below the milkiness of infancy to think all men virtuous. We must be tainted with a malignity truly diabolical, to believe all the world to be equally wicked and corrupt.

Thoughts on the Cause of the Present Discontents (1770)

1 When . . . [people] imagine that their food is only a cover for poison, and when they neither love nor trust the hand that serves it, it is not the name of the roast beef of old England that will persuade them to sit down to the table that is spread for them.

Thoughts on the Cause of the Present Discontents (1770)

2 When bad men combine, the good must associate; else they will fall, one by one, an unpitied sacrifice in a contemptible struggle.

Thoughts on the Cause of the Present Discontents (1770); see **Misquotations** 273:5

3 Of this stamp is the cant of *Not men, but measures*; a sort of charm by which many people get loose from every honourable engagement.

Thoughts on the Cause of the Present Discontents (1770); see **Canning** 73:10

4 Laws, like houses, lean on one another.

A Tract on the Popery Laws (planned c.1765)

5 In all forms of Government the people is the true legislator.

A Tract on the Popery Laws (planned c.1765)

6 Falsehood and delusion are allowed in no case whatsoever: But, as in the exercise of all the virtues, there is an economy of truth.

Two Letters on the Proposals for Peace with the Regicide Directory (9th ed., 1796); see **Armstrong** 15:6

7 All men that are ruined are ruined on the side of their natural propensities.

Two Letters on the Proposals for Peace with the Regicide Directory (9th ed., 1796)

8 If ever there was in all the proceedings of government a rule that is fundamental, universal, invariable it is this: that you ought never to attempt a measure of authority you are not morally sure you can go through with.

in the House of Commons, 9 May 1770

9 The greater the power, the more dangerous the abuse.

speech on the Middlesex Election, 7 February 1771

10 Your representative owes you, not his industry only, but his judgement; and he betrays, instead of serving you, if he sacrifices it to your opinion.

speech, 3 November 1774, in *Speeches at his Arrival at Bristol* (1774)

11 People crushed by law have no hopes but from power. If laws are their enemies, they will be enemies to laws; and those, who have much to hope and nothing to lose, will always be dangerous, more or less.

letter to Charles James Fox, 8 October 1777

12 It is the interest of the commercial world that wealth should be found everywhere.

letter to Samuel Span, 23 April 1778

13 Bad laws are the worst sort of tyranny.

Speech at Bristol, previous to the Late Election (1780)

14 The people are the masters.

in the House of Commons, 11 February 1780; see **Blair** 46:2

15 *of the younger **Pitt**'s maiden speech, February 1781:*
Not merely a chip of the old 'block', but the old block itself.

N. W. Wraxall *Historical Memoirs of My Own Time* (1904 ed.)

16 I feel an insuperable reluctance in giving my hand to destroy any established institution of government, upon a theory, however plausible it may be.

in the House of Commons on Fox's East India Bill, 1 December 1783

17 The people never give up their liberties but under some delusion.

speech at County Meeting of Buckinghamshire, 1784, attributed in E. Latham *Famous Sayings* (1904), with 'except' substituted for 'but'

1 You strike at the whole corps, if you strike at the head.

opening speech, impeachment of Warren Hastings, House of Commons 13 February 1788

2 An event has happened, upon which it is difficult to speak, and impossible to be silent.

speech, 5 May 1789; E. A. Bond (ed.) *Speeches . . . in the Trial of Warren Hastings* (1859) vol. 2

3 At last dying in the last dyke of prevarication.

speech, 7 May 1789; E. A. Bond (ed.) *Speeches . . . in the Trial of Warren Hastings* (1859) vol. 2

4 Somebody has said, that a king may make a nobleman but he cannot make a gentleman.

letter to William Smith, 29 January 1795

5 Those who carry on great public schemes must be proof against the most fatiguing delays, the most mortifying disappointments, the most shocking insults, and, worst of all, the presumptuous judgements of the ignorant upon their designs.

attributed; Benjamin Ward Richardson 'A Biographical Dissertation' ch. 4 in Edwin Chadwick *The Health of Nations* (1887)

George Burns 1896–1996
American comedian

6 Too bad all the people who know how to run the country are busy driving taxi cabs and cutting hair.

in *Daily Mail* 30 September 1997

John Burns 1858–1943
British Liberal politician

7 I have seen the Mississippi. That is muddy water. I have seen the St Lawrence. That is crystal water. But the Thames is liquid history.

in *Daily Mail* 25 January 1943

Robert Burns 1759–96
Scottish poet

8 The rank is but the guinea's stamp,
The man's the gowd for a' that!

'For a' that and a' that' (1790)

9 A fig for those by law protected!
LIBERTY's a glorious feast!
Courts for cowards were erected,
Churches built to please the PRIEST.

'The Jolly Beggars' (1799)

10 Liberty's in every blow!
Let us do—or die!!!

'Robert Bruce's March to Bannockburn' (1799)

11 We labour soon, we labour late,
To feed the titled knave, man;
And a' the comfort we're to get,
Is that ayont the grave, man.

'The Tree of Liberty' (1838)

Burnum Burnum 1936–97
Australian political activist

12 We wish no harm to England's native people. We are here to bring you good manners, refinement and an opportunity to make a *Koompartoo*, a fresh start.
  in 1988, the year of Australia's bicentenary, on planting an Aboriginal flag on the white cliffs of Dover and 'claiming' England for the Aboriginal people

on 26 January 1988; in obituary, *Independent* 20 August 1997

Aaron Burr 1756–1836
American politician

1 Law is whatever is boldly asserted and plausibly maintained.

James Parton *The Life and Times of Aaron Burr* (1857); attributed

Barbara Bush 1925–
American wife of George **Bush**; First Lady 1989–93

2 Somewhere out in this audience may even be someone who will one day follow in my footsteps, and preside over the White House as the President's spouse. I wish him well!

at Wellesley College Commencement, 1 June 1990

3 Remember, they only name things after you when you're dead or really old.
at the naming ceremony for the George Bush Centre for Intelligence

at Wellesley College Commencement, 1 June 1990

George Bush 1924–
American Republican statesman; 41st President of the US, 1989–93; father of George W. **Bush**

4 Is that man crazy? He thinks there's a bug behind all the pictures.
*as Director of the CIA, having visited Harold **Wilson** during Wilson's last premiership*

Peter Hennessy *The Prime Minister: the Office and its Holders since 1945* (2000)

5 I'm President of the United States, and I'm not going to eat any more broccoli!

in *New York Times* 23 March 1990

6 Oh, the vision thing.
responding to the suggestion that he turn his attention from short-term campaign objectives and look to the longer term.

in *Time* 26 January 1987

7 What's wrong with being a boring kind of guy?

during the campaign for the Republican nomination; in *Daily Telegraph* 28 April 1988

8 We are a nation of communities, of tens and tens of thousands of ethnic, religious, social, business, labour union, neighbourhood, regional and other organizations, all of them varied, voluntary, and unique . . . a brilliant diversity spread like stars, like a thousand points of light in a broad and peaceful sky.

acceptance speech at the Republican National Convention in New Orleans, 18 August 1988

9 Read my lips: no new taxes.
accepting the Republican nomination

in *New York Times* 19 August 1988; see **Blunkett** 29:2

10 And now, we can see a new world coming into view. A world in which there is the very real prospect of a new world order.

speech, in *New York Times* 7 March 1991

George W. Bush 1946–
American Republican statesman; 43rd President of the US from 2001; son of George **Bush**

11 New Hampshire has long been known as the bump in the road for front runners—and this year is no exception.
after being defeated in the New Hampshire primary

in *Sunday Times* 6 February 2000

1 It is the office of Lincoln's conscience and Teddy Roosevelt's energy and Harry Truman's integrity and Ronald Reagan's optimism.
accepting his party's presidential nomination

in *Seattle Times* 4 August 2000

2 We will make no distinction between terrorists who committed these acts and those who harbour them.
after the terrorist attacks of 11 September

televised address, 12 September 2001

3 Today we feel what Franklin Roosevelt called the warm courage of national unity. This unity against terror is now extending across the world.
address in Washington National Cathedral, 14 September 2001, at the day of mourning for those killed in the terrorist attacks of 11 September

in *Times* 15 September 2001; see **Roosevelt** 330:8

4 This crusade, this war on terrorism is going to take a while.
the President later retracted his use of the word 'crusade'

at a White House press conference, 16 September 2001

5 States like these . . . constitute an axis of evil, arming to threaten the peace of this world.
of Iraq, Iran, and North Korea

State of the Union address, in *Newsweek* 11 February 2002

6 Let freedom reign!
handwritten note as power in Iraq was officially transferred to the Interim Government

in *Daily Telegraph* 29 June 2004; see also **Mandela** 258:5

7 I earned capital in the campaign, political capital, and I intend to spend it.
on his re-election as President

in *New York Times* 5 November (online edition)

Laura Bush 1946–

American wife of George W. **Bush**, First Lady from 2001

8 *of parents and grandparents encountered on the campaign trail:*
They hold out pictures of their children and they say to George, 'I'm counting on you. I want my son or daughter to respect the president of the United States of America.'

speech at the Republican Convention, 1 August 2000

David Butler 1924–

British political scientist

9 Has he got a resignation in him?
*of James **Callaghan**, to Hugh **Dalton***

Hugh Dalton *Political Diary* (1986) 13 July 1960

Lord Butler of Brockwell 1938–

British civil servant; Cabinet Secretary 1988–97

10 We do have a system in which very great power is given to people if they have a large parliamentary majority as well . . . The deal is that you give people very considerable power for five years, then they can be thrown out. And, in the meantime, if things get bad enough there are ways of getting rid of them. That is the deal of our constitution.

in 1998; Peter Hennessy *The Prime Minister: The Office and its Holders since 1945* (2000)

11 More weight was placed on the intelligence than it could bear.

Review of Intelligence on Weapons of Mass Destruction ('Butler Report') 14 July 2004

R. A. ('Rab') Butler 1902–82

British Conservative politician
on Butler: see **Hennessy** 180:4

1 *on hearing of the appointment of Winston* **Churchill** *as Prime Minister in succession to Neville* **Chamberlain***:*
The good clean tradition of English politics, that of Pitt as opposed to Fox, has been sold to the greatest adventurer of modern political history.

John Colville diary, 10 May 1940

2 REPORTER: Mr Butler, would you say that this [Anthony Eden] is the best Prime Minister we have?
R. A. BUTLER: Yes.
interview at London Airport, 8 January 1956

R. A. Butler *The Art of the Possible* (1971)

3 The Civil Service is a bit like a Rolls-Royce—you know it's the best machine in the world, but you're not quite sure what to do with it.

Anthony Sampson *Anatomy of Britain* (1962)

4 I think a Prime Minister has to be a butcher and know the joints. That is perhaps where I have not been quite competent, in knowing all the ways that you can cut up a carcass.

in *Listener* 28 June 1966

5 In politics you must always keep running with the pack. The moment that you falter and they sense that you are injured, the rest will turn on you like wolves.

Dennis Walters *Not Always with the Pack* (1989)

Isaac Butt 1813–79

Irish nationalist politician

6 The people of this country are not idle. Let no man tell me this, when I see a peasant from Connaught going over to reap the harvest in England.

speech in defence of Thomas F. Meagher, 1848

7 I am not responsible for the member for Meath and cannot control him. I have, however, a duty to discharge to the great nation of Ireland and I think I should discharge it best when I say I disapprove entirely of the conduct of the honourable member for Meath.
of the parliamentary delaying tactics instigated by **Parnell**

in the House of Commons, 12 April 1877

John Byrom 1692–1763

English poet

8 God bless the King, I mean the Faith's Defender;
God bless—no harm in blessing—the Pretender;
But who Pretender is, or who is King,
God bless us all—that's quite another thing.

'To an Officer in the Army, Extempore, Intended to allay the Violence of Party-Spirit' (1773)

Lord Byron 1788–1824

English poet

9 For what were all these country patriots born?
To hunt, and vote, and raise the price of corn?

'The Age of Bronze' (1823)

10 Year after year they voted cent per cent
Blood, sweat, and tear-wrung millions—why? for rent!

'The Age of Bronze' (1823)

11 So he has cut his throat at last!—He! Who?
The man who cut his country's long ago.
on Castlereagh's suicide, c.1822

'Epigram on Lord Castlereagh'

1 The Cincinnatus of the West.
  of George **Washington**

'Ode to Napoleon Bonaparte'
(1814)

2 The arbiter of others' fate
A suppliant for his own!

'Ode to Napoleon Bonaparte'
(1814)

3 I have no consistency, except in politics; and *that* probably
arises from my indifference on the subject altogether.

letter, 16 January 1814

Michael Bywater

4 The American dream is that any citizen can rise to the
highest office in the land. The British dream is that the
Queen drops in for tea.

in *Independent* 20 October 1997

Chuck Cadman 1948–

Canadian Independent politician

5 I'm bound as an independent especially to represent the
views of my constituents.
  *on his reason for voting with the Liberal Government in a key
  budget debate*

in *GlobeandMail.com* 20 May 2005
(online edition)

Julius Caesar 100–44 BC

Roman general and statesman

6 *Gallia est omnis divisa in partes tres.*
  Gaul as a whole is divided into three parts.

De Bello Gallico

7 Men are nearly always willing to believe what they wish.

De Bello Gallico

8 Caesar's wife must be above suspicion.

oral tradition, based on Plutarch
Parallel Lives 'Julius Caesar'

9 Caesar had rather be first in a village than second at Rome.

Francis Bacon *The Advancement of
Learning* (based on Plutarch *Parallel
Lives* 'Julius Caesar')

10 *Iacta alea est.*
  The die is cast.
    at the crossing of the Rubicon

Suetonius *Lives of the Caesars*
'Divus Julius' (often quoted in Latin
'Iacta alea est' but originally
spoken in Greek)

11 *Veni, vidi, vici.*
  I came, I saw, I conquered.

inscription displayed in Caesar's
Pontic triumph, according to
Suetonius *Lives of the Caesars*
'Divus Julius'; or, according to
Plutarch *Parallel Lives* 'Julius
Caesar', written in a letter by
Caesar, announcing the victory of
Zela which concluded the Pontic
campaign

12 *Et tu, Brute?*
  You too, Brutus?

traditional rendering of Suetonius
Lives of the Caesars 'Divus Julius':
'Some have written that when
Marcus Brutus rushed at him, he
said in Greek, "You too, my
child?" '

Joseph Cairns 1920–

British industrialist and politician

1 The betrayal of Ulster, the cynical and entirely
undemocratic banishment of its properly elected Parliament
and a relegation to the status of a fuzzy wuzzy colony is, I
hope, a last betrayal contemplated by Downing Street
because it is the last that Ulster will countenance.
speech on retiring as Lord Mayor of Belfast, 31 May 1972

in Daily Telegraph 1 June 1972

John Caldwell Calhoun 1782–1850

American politician
on Calhoun: see **Jackson** 196:7

2 The very essence of a free government consists in
considering offices as public trusts, bestowed for the good of
the country, and not for the benefit of an individual or
party.

speech 13 February 1835

3 The surrender of life is nothing to sinking down into
acknowledgement of inferiority.

speech in the Senate, 19 February
1847

Caligula (Gaius Julius Caesar Germanicus) AD 12–41

Roman emperor from AD 37

4 Would that the Roman people had but one neck!

Suetonius *Lives of the Caesars*
'Gaius Caligula'

James Callaghan 1912–2005

British Labour statesman; Prime Minister 1976–9
on Callaghan: see **Butler** 67:9, **Jenkins** 201:7; see also
Misquotations 272:5

5 Leaking is what you do; briefing is what *I* do.
*when giving evidence to the Franks Committee on Official Secrecy
in 1971*

Franks Report (1972); oral evidence

6 We say that what Britain needs is a new social contract.
That is what this document [*Labour's Programme for Britain*]
is about.

speech at Labour Party Annual
Conference, 2 October 1972

7 You cannot now, if you ever could, spend your way out of a
recession.

speech at Labour Party
Conference, 28 September 1976

8 You never reach the promised land. You can march towards
it.

in a television interview, 20 July
1978

9 I had known it was going to be a 'winter of discontent'.

television interview, 8 February
1979; see **Newspaper headlines**
287:3

10 It's the first time in recorded history that turkeys have been
known to vote for an early Christmas.
*in the debate resulting in the fall of the Labour government, when
the pact between Labour and the Liberals had collapsed, and the
Nationalists also withdrew their support in the wake of the failure
of the devolution bills*

in the House of Commons, 28
March 1979

1 I doubt if you accumulate much intellectual weight whilst you're in the office [of Prime Minister] . . . I think you rather spend your intellectual capital whilst you're in the office so it's important to take some baggage in.
  to his Principal Private Secretary, towards the end of the 'Winter of Discontent', 1979

in conversation with Michael Cockerell, 1996; Peter Hennessy *The Prime Minister: the Office and its Holders* (2000)

2 I let the country down.
  to his Principal Private Secretary, towards the end of the 'Winter of Discontent', 1979

Kenneth O. Morgan *Callaghan, A Life* (1997)

3 There are times, perhaps once every thirty years, when there is a sea-change in politics. It then does not matter what you say or what you do. There is a shift in what the public wants and what it approves of. I suspect there is now such a sea-change—and it is for Mrs Thatcher.
  during the election campaign of 1979

Kenneth O. Morgan *Callaghan* (1997)

4 *of the popularity of Mrs **Thatcher**:*
  The further you got from Britain, the more admired you found she was.

in *Spectator* 1 December 1990

5 It's never a misfortune to become Prime Minister. It's always the greatest thing in your life. It's absolute heaven— I enjoyed every moment of it until those last few months of the 'Winter of Discontent'.

interview on *Analysis*, BBC Radio 4, 20 June 1991

6 Well, it works, doesn't it? So I think that's the answer, even if it is on the back of an envelope and doesn't have a written constitution with every comma and every semi-colon in place. Because sometimes they can make for difficulties that common sense can overcome.

Peter Hennessy and Simon Coates *The Back of the Envelope* (1991)

7 I certainly didn't go down on one knee. I think she said it's about time we got married.
  on his diamond wedding day, remembering his proposal

in *Daily Telegraph* 29 July 1998

Italo Calvino 1923–85
Italian novelist and short-story writer

8 Revolutionaries are more formalistic than conservatives.

Il Barone Rampante (1957)

Helder Camara 1909–99
Brazilian priest

9 When I give food to the poor they call me a saint. When I ask why the poor have no food they call me a communist.

attributed, 1992

Lord Camden 1714–94
British Whig politician; Lord Chancellor, 1766–70

10 Taxation and representation are inseparable . . . whatever is a man's own, is absolutely his own; no man hath a right to take it from him without his consent either expressed by himself or representative; whoever attempts to do it, attempts an injury; whoever does it, commits a robbery; he throws down and destroys the distinction between liberty and slavery.
  on the taxation of Americans by the British parliament

in the House of Lords, 10 February 1766

Simon Cameron 1799–1889

American politician

1 An honest politician is one who when he's bought stays
  bought.

attributed

Alastair Campbell 1957–

British journalist, Press Secretary to the Prime Minister
1997–2003
see also **Anonymous** 11:13

2 Labour spin doctors aren't supposed to like Tory MPs. But
  Alan Clark was an exceptional man.

in *Mirror* 8 September 1999

3 The day of the bog-standard comprehensive is over.

press briefing, 12 February 2001;
see **Blunkett** 47:9

4 I'm sorry, we don't do God.
  when Tony **Blair** *was asked about his Christian faith in an
  interview for* Vanity Fair *magazine*

in *Daily Telegraph* 5 May 2003

5 We can dance on pinheads till the cows come home.
  *on the importance of his suggested changes to the dossier on Iraq's
  weapons of mass destruction*

in *The Times* 10 January 2004

Lord Campbell of Eskan 1912–

British industrialist

6 The only justification of the [House of] Lords is its
  irrationality: once you try to make it rational, you satisfy no
  one.

Anthony Sampson *The Changing
Anatomy of Britain* (1982)

Thomas Campbell 1777–1844

Scottish poet

7 What millions died—that Caesar might be great!

Pleasures of Hope (1799)

Timothy Campbell 1840–1904

American politician

8 What's the Constitution between friends?
  reported response to President **Cleveland**'s *refusing to support a
  bill on the grounds of its being unconstitutional*

attributed, *c.*1885

Henry Campbell-Bannerman 1836–1908

British Liberal statesman, Prime Minister 1905–8
on Campbell-Bannerman: see **Cecil** 78:8

9 There is a phrase which seems in itself somewhat self-
  evident, which is often used to account for a good deal—
  that 'war is war' But when you come to ask about it, then
  you are told that the war now going on is not war.
  [Laughter] When is a war not a war? When it is carried on
  by methods of barbarism in South Africa.

speech to National Reform Union,
14 June 1901

10 Good government could never be a substitute for
  government by the people themselves.

speech at Stirling, 23 November
1905

Albert Camus 1913–60

French novelist, dramatist, and essayist

1 Politics and the fate of mankind are formed by men without ideals and without greatness. Those who have greatness within them do not go in for politics.

Carnets, 1935–42 (1962)

2 What is a rebel? A man who says no.

The Rebel (1951)

3 All modern revolutions have ended in a reinforcement of the State.

The Rebel (1951)

4 Every revolutionary ends as an oppressor or a heretic.

The Rebel (1951)

Dennis Canavan 1942–

Scottish labour politician

5 Members of Parliament are representatives of the people, we are not party puppets sent down to Westminster to vote simply the way the whips instruct us to.
having failed to be selected as an official Labour candidate for the Scottish assembly

in *Scotsman* 12 November 1998

George Canning 1770–1827

British Tory statesman; Prime Minister, 1827

6 A steady patriot of the world alone,
The friend of every country but his own.
on the Jacobin

'New Morality' (1821)

7 And finds, with keen discriminating sight,
Black's not so black;—nor white so very white.

'New Morality' (1821)

8 Give me the avowed, erect and manly foe;
Firm I can meet, perhaps return the blow;
But of all plagues, good Heaven, thy wrath can send,
Save me, oh, save me, from the candid friend.
*the last two lines were quoted by **Peel** to **Disraeli** in the House of Commons; Disraeli's reply rested on the view that Peel had treated Canning shabbily*

'New Morality' (1821)

9 Pitt is to Addington
As London is to Paddington.

'The Oracle' (c.1803)

10 Away with the cant of 'Measures not men'!—the idle supposition that it is the harness and not the horses that draw the chariot along. If the comparison must be made, if the distinction must be taken, men are everything, measures comparatively nothing.
speech on the Army estimates, 8 December 1802

Speeches of . . . Canning (1828) vol. 2; the phrase 'measures not men' may be found as early as 1742 (in a letter from Chesterfield to Dr Chevenix, 6 March); also in Goldsmith *The Good Natured Man* (1768), 'Measures not men, have always been my mark'; see **Burke** 64:3

11 In matters of commerce the fault of the Dutch
Is offering too little and asking too much.
The French are with equal advantage content,
So we clap on Dutch bottoms just twenty per cent.

dispatch, in cipher, to the English ambassador at the Hague, 31 January 1826

12 I called the New World into existence, to redress the balance of the Old.
speech on the affairs of Portugal

in the House of Commons, 12 December 1826

1 [The Whip's duty is] to make a House, and keep a House, and cheer the minister.

J. E. Ritchie *Modern Statesmen* (1861)

Al Capone 1899–1947
Italian-born American gangster, notorious for his domination of organized crime in Chicago in the 1920s

2 Don't you get the idea I'm one of these goddam radicals. Don't get the idea I'm knocking the American system.

interview, c.1929; Claud Cockburn *In Time of Trouble* (1956)

Benjamin Nathan Cardozo 1870–1938
American judge

3 [The Constitution] was framed upon the theory that the peoples of the several states must sink or swim together, and that in the long run prosperity and salvation are in union and not division.

in *Baldwin v. Seelig* (1935)

Richard Carleton 1943–
Australian journalist

4 How does it feel to have blood on your hands?
  *to Bob **Hawke**, new leader of the Australian Labor Party, after the resignation of Bill **Hayden** as Opposition leader (see **Hayden** 176:1)*

television interview, 3 February 1983

Thomas Carlyle 1795–1881
Scottish historian and political philosopher

5 A witty statesman said, you might prove anything by figures.

Chartism (1839)

6 Surely of all 'rights of man', this right of the ignorant man to be guided by the wiser, to be, gently or forcibly, held in the true course by him, is the indisputablest.

Chartism (1839)

7 In epochs when cash payment has become the sole nexus of man to man.

Chartism (1839)

8 To the very last he [Napoleon] had a kind of idea; that, namely, of *La carrière ouverte aux talents*, The tools to him that can handle them.

Critical and Miscellaneous Essays (1838) 'Sir Walter Scott'

9 The three great elements of modern civilization, Gunpowder, Printing, and the Protestant Religion.

Critical and Miscellaneous Essays (1838) 'The State of German Literature'

10 Two centuries; hardly less; before Democracy go through its due, most baleful, stages of *Quackocracy*.

History of the French Revolution (1837) vol. 1

11 The seagreen Incorruptible.
  *describing **Robespierre***

History of the French Revolution (1837) vol. 2

12 France was long a despotism tempered by epigrams.

History of the French Revolution (1837) vol. 3

13 Aristocracy of the Moneybag.

History of the French Revolution (1837) vol. 3

14 A Parliament speaking through reporters to Buncombe and the twenty-seven millions mostly fools.

Latter-Day Pamphlets (1850) 'Parliaments'; see **Walker** 408:2

15 *of political economy:*
  The Dismal Science.

Latter-Day Pamphlets (1850) 'The Present Time'

1 *of himself:*
Little other than a redtape talking-machine, and unhappy
bag of parliamentary eloquence.

Latter-Day Pamphlets (1850) 'The
Present Time'

2 A Hell in England—the Hell of not making money.

Past and Present (1843)

3 Despotism is essential in most enterprises.

Past and Present (1843)

4 Councillors of state sit plotting, and playing their high
chess-game, whereof the pawns are men.

Sartor Resartus (1858)

5 *of Disraeli:*
A superlative Hebrew conjuror.

Shooting Niagara: and After? (1867)

6 Democracy, which means despair of finding any heroes to
govern you.

attributed

7 Vote by ballot is the dyspepsia of the society.

Simon Heffer *Moral Desperado*
(1995)

Stokely Carmichael 1941–98
and Charles Vernon Hamilton 1929–

8 Black power . . . is a call for black people in this country to
unite, to recognize their heritage, to build a sense of
community.

Black Power (1967)

9 Before a group can enter the open society, it must first close
ranks.

Black Power (1967)

Caroline of Ansbach 1683–1737

German-born Queen of Great Britain and Ireland from 1727, wife
of George II
on Caroline: see **Anonymous** 13:11

10 My dear firstborn is the greatest ass, and the greatest liar,
and the greatest *canaille*, and the greatest beast in the whole
world, and I heartily wish he was out of it.
of her eldest son, Frederick, Prince of Wales, father of **George III**
(he died in 1751, before he could succeed to the throne)

in *Dictionary of National Biography*
(1917–)

Lewis Carroll 1832–98

English writer and logician

11 The rule is, jam to-morrow and jam yesterday—but never
jam today.

Through the Looking-Glass (1872)

12 'When *I* use a word,' Humpty Dumpty said in a rather
scornful tone, 'it means just what I choose it to mean—
neither more nor less.'

Through the Looking-Glass (1872);
see **Shawcross** 361:10

Edward Carson 1854–1935

British lawyer and politician

13 I now enter into compact with you, and with the help of
God you and I joined together . . . will yet defeat the most
nefarious conspiracy that has ever been hatched against a
free people . . . We must be prepared . . . the morning Home
Rule passes, ourselves to become responsible for the
government of the Protestant Province of Ulster.

speech at Craigavon, 23
September 1911

14 My one affection left me is my love for Ireland.
after the death of his wife in 1913

Montgomery Hyde *Carson* (1953)

1 We do not want a sentence of death with a stay of execution for six years.
rejecting the suggestion that the Home Rule Bill should allow the temporary exclusion of Ulster for six years

speech, March 1914

2 From the day I first entered parliament up to the present, devotion to the union has been the guiding star of my political life.

in *Dictionary of National Biography* (1917-)

3 My only great qualification for being put at the head of the Navy is that I am very much at sea.

Ian Colvin *Life of Lord Carson* (1936) vol. 3

Jimmy Carter 1924–

American Democratic statesman, 39th President of the US, 1977–81

4 We should live our lives as though Christ were coming this afternoon.
to a Bible class at Plains, Georgia, March 1976

in *Boston Sunday Herald Advertiser* 11 April 1976

5 I've looked on a lot of women with lust. I've committed adultery in my heart many times. This is something that God recognizes I will do—and I have done it—and God forgives me for it.

in *Playboy* November 1976

John Cartwright 1740–1824

English political reformer

6 One man shall have one vote.

The People's Barrier Against Undue Influence (1780) 'Principles, maxims, and primary rules of politics' no. 68

Thomas Nixon Carver 1865–1961

American economist, who had previously given the course in agricultural economics at Harvard taken over by **Galbraith** in 1934

7 The trouble with radicals is that they only read radical literature, and the trouble with conservatives is that they don't read anything.

'Carver's Law'; J. K. Galbraith *A Life in Our Times* (1981)

Roger Casement 1864–1916

Irish nationalist; executed for treason in 1916

8 Self-government is our right, a thing born in us at birth, a thing no more to be doled out to us, or withheld from us, by another people than the right to life itself—than the right to feel the sun, or smell the flowers, or to love our kind.

statement at the conclusion of his trial, the Old Bailey, London, 29 June 1916

9 Where all your rights become only an accumulated wrong; where men must beg with bated breath for leave to subsist in their own land, to think their own thoughts, to sing their own songs, to garner the fruits of their own labours . . . then surely it is a braver, a saner and truer thing, to be a rebel in act and deed against such circumstances as these than tamely to accept it as the natural lot of men.

statement from prison, 29 June 1916

Barbara Castle 1910–2002

British Labour politician

1 She is so clearly the best man among them.

of Margaret **Thatcher**

diary, 11 February 1975

2 I will fight for what I believe in until I drop dead. And that's what keeps you alive.

in *Guardian* 14 January 1998

Ted Castle 1907–79

British journalist

3 In place of strife.

title of Labour Government White Paper, 17 January 1969; suggested by Castle to his wife, Barbara **Castle**, then Secretary of State for Employment

Fidel Castro 1927–

Cuban statesman, Prime Minister 1959–76 and President since 1976
on Castro: see **Ceauşescu** 78:6

4 Capitalism is using its money; we socialists throw it away.

in *Observer* 8 November 1964

Willa Cather 1873–1947

American novelist

5 Oh, the Germans classify, but the French arrange!

Death Comes For the Archbishop (1927))

Catherine the Great 1729–96

Russian monarch, Empress from 1762

6 I shall be an autocrat: that's my trade. And the good Lord will forgive me: that's his.

attributed

Wyn Catlin

7 Diplomacy is saying 'Nice doggie' until you find a rock.

Laurence J. Peter (ed.) *Quotations for our Time* (1977)

Cato the Elder (or 'the Censor') 234–149 BC

Roman statesman, orator, and writer

8 *Delenda est Carthago.*

Carthage must be destroyed.
words concluding every speech Cato made in the Senate

Pliny the Elder *Naturalis Historia*

Carrie Chapman Catt 1859–1947

American feminist

9 When a just cause reaches its flood-tide . . . whatever stands in the way must fall before its overwhelming power.

speech at Stockholm, *Is Woman Suffrage Progressing?* (1911)

Mr Justice Caulfield 1914–

British judge

1 Remember Mary Archer in the witness box. Your vision of her will probably never disappear. Has she elegance? Has she fragrance? Would she have—without the strain of this trial—a radiance?

summing up of court case between Jeffrey Archer and the *Star*, July 1987, in *The Times* 24 July 1987

Constantine Cavafy 1863–1933

Greek poet

2 What are we waiting for, gathered in the market-place? The barbarians are to arrive today.

'Waiting for the Barbarians' (1904)

3 And now, what will become of us without the barbarians? Those people were a kind of solution.

'Waiting for the Barbarians' (1904)

Edith Cavell 1865–1915

English nurse

4 Patriotism is not enough. I must have no hatred or bitterness towards anyone.
on the eve of her execution by the Germans for assisting in the escape of British soldiers from occupied Belgium

in *The Times* 23 October 1915

Count Cavour 1810–61

Italian statesman

5 We are ready to proclaim throughout Italy this great principle: a free church in a free state.

speech, 27 March 1861

Nicolae Ceauşescu 1918–89

Romanian Communist statesman, first President of the Socialist Republic of Romania 1974–89

6 Fidel Castro is right. You do not quieten your enemy by talking with him like a priest, but by burning him.
at a Communist Party meeting 17 December 1989

in *Guardian* 11 January 1990

Lord Edward Cecil 1867–1918

British soldier and civil servant

7 *definition of a compromise:*
An agreement between two men to do what both agree is wrong.

letter 3 September 1911

Lord Hugh Cecil 1869–1956

British Conservative politician and clergyman, Provost of Eton

8 There is no more ungraceful figure than that of a humanitarian with an eye to the main chance.
*dismissal of a manoeuvre by **Campbell-Bannerman***

in *The Times* 24 June 1901

9 The socialist believes that it is better to be rich than poor, the Christian that it is better to be poor than rich.

Conservatism (1912)

Robert Cecil 1563-1612

English courtier and statesman, son of William Cecil, Lord Burghley

1 Rest content, and give heed to one that hath sorrowed in the bright lustre of a court, and gone heavily even on the best-seeming fair ground . . . I know it bringeth little comfort on earth; and he is, I reckon, no wise man that looketh this way to Heaven.

letter to Sir John Harington; Algernon Cecil *A Life of Robert Cecil* (1915)

Robert Arthur James Gascoyne-Cecil see Salisbury (third Marquess)

Robert Arthur Talbot Gascoyne-Cecil see Salisbury (fifth Marquess)

Robert Michael James Gascoyne-Cecil see Lord Cranborne

Paul Celan 1920-70

German poet

2 *Der Tod ist ein Meister aus Deutschland.*
Death is a master from Germany.

'Deathfugue' (written 1944)

3 There's nothing in the world for which a poet will give up writing, not even when he is a Jew and the language of his poems is German.

letter to relatives, 2 August 1948

Joseph Chamberlain 1836-1914

British Liberal politician, father of Neville **Chamberlain**

4 In politics, there is no use looking beyond the next fortnight.

A. J. Balfour letter to Lord Salisbury, 24 March 1886; see **Wilson** 421:9

5 It is not to your interest to arouse the prejudices of the society in which you hope one day again to take your place . . . Therefore my advice is: Be as Radical as you like. Be Home Ruler if you must. But be a little Jingo if you can.
to his friend Charles Dilke, who was hoping to make a political comeback

Roy Jenkins *Sir Charles Dilke* (1958)

6 Provided that the City of London remains, as it is at present, the clearing-house of the world, any other nation may be its workshop.

speech at the Guildhall, 19 January 1904

7 Learn to think Imperially.
*with reference to Alexander **Hamilton**'s advice to the newly independent United States*

speech at the Guildhall, 19 January 1904; see **Hamilton** 172:3

8 The day of small nations has long passed away. The day of Empires has come.

speech at Birmingham, 12 May 1904

9 We are not downhearted. The only trouble is we cannot understand what is happening to our neighbours.
referring to a constituency which had remained unaffected by an electoral landslide

speech at Smethwick, 18 January 1906

Neville Chamberlain 1869-1940

British Conservative statesman; Prime Minister, 1937-40, son of
Joseph **Chamberlain**
on Chamberlain: see **Bevan** 39:9, **Churchill** 87:9, **Lloyd George**
239:10, **Roberts** 327:7

1 How horrible, fantastic, incredible it is that we should be
digging trenches and trying on gas-masks here because of a
quarrel in a far away country between people of whom we
know nothing.
on Germany's annexation of the Sudetenland

radio broadcast, 27 September
1938

2 This morning I had another talk with the German
Chancellor, Herr Hitler, and here is the paper which bears
his name upon it as well as mine . . . 'We regard the
agreement signed last night and the Anglo-German Naval
Agreement, as symbolic of the desire of our two peoples
never to go to war with one another again.'

speech at Heston Airport, 30
September 1938

3 This is the second time in our history that there has come
back from Germany to Downing Street peace with honour. I
believe it is peace for our time.
*speech from the window of 10 Downing Street, 30 September
1938*

in *The Times* 1 October 1938; see
Disraeli 121:15

4 *the British Ambassador in Berlin had handed the German
government a final note stating that unless the British government
had heard by eleven o'clock that Germany was prepared to withdraw
her troops from Poland, a state of war would exist between the two
countries:*
I have to tell you now that no such undertaking has been
received, and that consequently this country is at war with
Germany.

radio broadcast, 3 September
1939

5 Whatever may be the reason—whether it was that Hitler
thought he might get away with what he had got without
fighting for it, or whether it was that after all the
preparations were not sufficiently complete—however, one
thing is certain—he missed the bus.

speech at Central Hall,
Westminster, 4 April 1940

Nicolas-Sébastien Chamfort 1741-94

French writer

6 If you would find to what extent each condition of society
can corrupt a man, examine what he is when he has
undergone that influence for the longest possible time, that
is to say, when he is old. See what an old courtier is like, an
old priest, an old judge, an old solicitor, an old surgeon.

Maximes et Pensées (1796) ch. 2

Henry ('Chips') Channon 1897-1958

American-born British Conservative politician and diarist

7 I personally think . . . that there will be an unheaval, that
the Throne will sway a little, but that it will survive and
that the King will get away with it. We are working up to
something terrific. What is history unfolding?
during the Abdication crisis of 1936

diary, 22 November 1936

8 There is nowhere in the world where sleep is so deep as in
the libraries of the House of Commons.

diary, 17 December 1937

1 I gather it has now been decided not to embrace the Russian bear, but to hold out a hand and accept its paw gingerly. No more. The worst of both worlds.

diary, 16 May 1939

Charles I 1600–49

British monarch, King of England, Scotland, and Ireland from 1625, son of **James I** and father of **Charles II**
on Charles I: see **Marvell** 262:1

2 Never make a defence or apology before you be accused.

letter to Lord Wentworth, 3 September 1636

3 I see all the birds are flown.
after attempting to arrest the Five Members

in the House of Commons, 4 January 1642

4 Sweet-heart, now they will cut off thy father's head. Mark, child, what I say: they will cut off my head, and perhaps make thee a king. But mark what I say: you must not be a king, so long as your brothers Charles and James do live.
said to Prince Henry

in *Reliquiae Sacrae Carolinae* (1650)

5 You manifestly wrong even the poorest ploughman, if you demand not his free consent.
rejecting the jurisdiction of the High Court of Justice, 21 January 1649

S. R. Gardiner *Constitutional Documents of the Puritan Revolution* (1906 ed.)

6 As to the King, the laws of the land will clearly instruct you for that . . . For the people; and truly I desire their liberty and freedom, as much as any body: but I must tell you, that their liberty and freedom consists in having the government of those laws, by which their life and their goods may be most their own; 'tis not for having share in government [sirs] that is nothing pertaining to 'em. A subject and a sovereign are clean different things . . . If I would have given way to an arbitrary way, for to have all laws changed according to the power of the sword, I needed not to have come here; and therefore I tell you (and I pray God it be not laid to your charge) that I am the martyr of the people.
speech on the scaffold, 30 January 1649

J. Rushworth *Historical Collections* vol. 2 (1701)

7 I die a Christian, according to the profession of the Church of England, as I found it left me by my father.

J. Rushworth *Historical Collections* vol. 2 (1701)

Charles II 1630–85

British monarch, King of England, Scotland and Ireland from 1660, son of **Charles I**
on Charles II: see **Rochester** 328:13

8 It is upon the navy under the good Providence of God that the safety, honour, and welfare of this realm do chiefly depend.

'Articles of War' preamble (probably a popular paraphrase); Geoffrey Callender *The Naval Side of British History* (1952)

9 This is very true: for my words are my own, and my actions are my ministers'.
reply to Lord **Rochester**'s *epitaph on him*

in *Thomas Hearne: Remarks and Collections* (1885–1921) 17 November 1706; see **Epitaphs** 136:3

10 Better than a play.
on the debates in the House of Lords on Lord Ross's Divorce Bill

A. Bryant *King Charles II* (1931)

1 I am sure no man in England will take away my life to make you King.
    to his brother James, afterwards James II

William King *Political & Literary Anecdotes* (1818)

2 I am weary of travelling and am resolved to go abroad no more. But when I am dead and gone I know not what my brother will do: I am much afraid that when he comes to wear the crown he will be obliged to travel again.
    on the difference between himself and his brother

attributed

3 I, who will never use arbitrary government myself, am resolved not to suffer it in others.
    to the Whigs

attributed

4 Not a religion for gentlemen.
    of Presbyterianism

Gilbert Burnet *History of My Own Time* (1724) vol. 1

5 He had been, he said, an unconscionable time dying; but he hoped that they would excuse it.

Lord Macaulay *History of England* (1849) vol. 1

Salmon Portland Chase 1808–73
American lawyer and politician

6 The Constitution, in all its provisions, looks to an indestructible Union composed of indestructible States.

decision in Texas v. White, 1868

Dick Cheney 1941–
American Republican politician, Vice-President of the US from 2001

7 Except for the occasional heart attack, I never felt better.

in June 2003; quoted on *BBC News Online* website, 6 October 2004

8 Direct threats require decisive action.

in *Chicago Sun-Times* 25 January 2004

Mary Chesnut 1823–86
American diarist and Confederate supporter

9 The Confederacy has been done to death by politicians.

in 1863; Ken Burns *The Civil War* (documentary, 1989) episode 4

10 Atlanta is gone. That agony is over. There is no hope but we will try to have no fear.
    after the fall of Atlanta to Sherman's army in 1864

Geoffrey C. Ward *The Civil War* (1991)

Lord Chesterfield 1694–1773
English writer and politician
on Chesterfield: see **Johnson** 204:7, **Walpole** 409:2

11 Women, then, are only children of a larger growth: they have an entertaining tattle, and sometimes wit; but for solid, reasoning good sense, I never knew in my life one that had it, or who reasoned or acted consequentially for four and twenty hours together.

letter, 5 September 1748

12 Politicians neither love nor hate. Interest, not sentiment, directs them.

Letters, 1748

1 I . . . could not help reflecting in my way upon the singular ill-luck of this my dear country, which, as long as ever I remember it, and as far back as I have read, has always been governed by the only two or three people, out of two or three millions, totally incapable of governing, and unfit to be trusted.

in *The World* 7 October 1756

G. K. Chesterton 1874–1936

English essayist, novelist, and poet

2 'My country, right or wrong' is a thing no patriot would ever think of saying except in a desperate case. It is like saying, 'My mother, drunk or sober.'

The Defendant (1901)

3 Tradition means giving votes to the most obscure of all classes, our ancestors. It is the democracy of the dead.

Orthodoxy (1908)

4 Democrats object to men being disqualified by the accident of birth; tradition objects to their being disqualified by the accident of death. Tradition refuses to submit to the small and arrogant oligarchy of those who merely happen to be walking around.

Orthodoxy (1908)

5 All conservatism is based upon the idea that if you leave things alone you leave them as they are. But you do not. If you leave a thing alone you leave it to a torrent of change.

Orthodoxy (1908)

6 Talk about the pews and steeples
And the Cash that goes therewith!
But the souls of Christian peoples . . .
Chuck it, Smith!
   satirizing F. E. **Smith***'s response to the Welsh Disestablishment Bill*

'Antichrist' (1912)

7 They died to save their country and they only saved the world.

'English Graves' (1922)

8 Smile at us, pay us, pass us; but do not quite forget.
For we are the people of England, that never have spoken yet.

'The Secret People' (1915)

9 We only know the last sad squires ride slowly towards the sea,
And a new people takes the land: and still it is not we.

'The Secret People' (1915)

10 They have given us into the hand of new unhappy lords,
Lords without anger and honour, who dare not carry their swords.
They fight us by shuffling papers; they have bright dead alien eyes;
And they look at our labour and laughter as a tired man looks at flies.
And the load of their loveless pity is worse than the ancient wrongs,
Their doors are shut in the evening; And they know no songs.

'The Secret People' (1915)

11 Lancashire merchants whenever they like
Can water the beer of a man in Klondike
Or poison the meat of a man in Bombay;
And that is the meaning of Empire Day.

'Songs of Education: II Geography' (1922)

12 Democracy means government by the uneducated, while aristocracy means government by the badly educated.

in *New York Times* 1 February 1931

Joseph Benedict 'Ben' Chifley 1885–1951

Australian Labor statesman; Prime Minister 1945–9

1 We have a great objective—the light on the hill—which we aim to reach by working for the betterment of mankind not only here but anywhere we may give a helping hand.

speech to the Annual Conference of the New South Wales branch of the Australian Labor Party, 12 June 1949

Lydia Maria Child 1802–80

American abolitionist and suffragist

2 We first crush people to the earth, and then claim the right of trampling on them forever, because they are prostrate.

An Appeal on Behalf of That Class of Americans Called Africans (1833)

3 Woman stock is rising in the market. I shall not live to see women vote, but I'll come and rap at the ballot box.

letter to Sarah Shaw, 3 August 1856

Erskine Childers

British writer and Irish nationalist see **Last words** 226:3

Lawton Chiles 1930–98

American politician

4 You are misunderstood, maligned, viewed by the press as a Pulitzer Prize ready to be won.
    on the problems of investigative journalism for politicians

in *St Petersburg (Florida) Times* 6 March 1991

Jacques Chirac 1932–

French statesman, Prime Minister 1974–6 and 1986–8, President since 1995

5 For its part, France wants you to take part in this great undertaking.
    on European Monetary Union

speech to both Houses of Parliament, 15 May 1996

6 You have been very rude, and I have never been spoken to like this before.
    *to Tony **Blair** at the EU enlargement summit in Brussels*

in *Guardian* online 29 October 2002

7 It is not well-brought-up behaviour. They missed a good opportunity to keep quiet.
    criticizing the support from Central and Eastern European states for the Anglo-American stance on Iraq

in *The Times* 19 February 2003

8 I do not understand this fear.
    repeated comment when taking part in a television show intended to persuade young voters to support the 'yes' campaign in France's referendum on the European constitution, 15 April 2005

in *Times* 16 April 2005 (online edition)

Rufus Choate 1799–1859

American lawyer and politician

9 We join ourselves to no party that does not carry the flag and keep step to the music of the Union.

letter to the Whig Convention, Worcester, Massachusetts, 1 October 1855

10 Its constitution the glittering and sounding generalities of natural right which make up the Declaration of Independence.

letter to the Maine Whig State Central Committee, 9 August 1856

Frank Chodorov 1887–1966

American economist and writer

1 [When people] say 'let's do something about it,' they mean 'let's get hold of the political machinery so that we can do something to somebody else.' And that somebody is invariably you.
'Freedom is Better' (1949)

2 The only way to a world society is through free trade.
'One Worldism' (1950)

Duc de Choiseul 1719–85

French politician

3 A minister who moves about in society is in a position to read the signs of the times even in a festive gathering, but one who remains shut up in his office learns nothing.
Jack F. Bernard *Talleyrand* (1973)

Jean Chrétien 1934–

Canadian Liberal statesman; Prime Minister 1993–2003

4 Leadership means making people feel good.
in *Toronto Star* 7 June 1984

5 The art of politics is learning to walk with your back to the wall, your elbows high, and a smile on your face. It's a survival game played under the glare of lights.
Straight from the Heart (1985)

6 *asked about the kind of proof he needed to be convinced that Iraq had weapons of mass destruction:*
What kind of a proof? . . . A proof is a proof. And when you have a good proof, it's because it's proven.
interview on CBC News, 6 September 2002

7 He's not a moron at all, he's a friend.
after reports of an off-the-record comment on George W. **Bush** *by a Canadian political aide, Françoise* **Ducros**
attributed; reported in *CTVnews* (online edition) 21 November 2002

David Christy 1802–c.68

8 Cotton is King; or, the economical relations of slavery.
title of book, 1855

Clementine Churchill 1885–1977

British wife of Winston **Churchill**

9 Winston . . . has the supreme quality which I venture to say very few of your present or future Cabinet possess, the power, the imagination, the deadliness to fight Germany.
letter to **Asquith** *on Winston* **Churchill**'s *dismissal from the Admiralty, May 1915*
Martin Gilbert *In Search of Churchill* (1994)

Lord Randolph Churchill 1849–94

British Conservative politician
on Churchill: see **Gladstone** 159:2

10 To tell the truth I don't know myself what Tory Democracy is. But I believe it is principally opportunism.
having urged Wilfrid Scawen Blunt in 1885 to stand for Parliament as a Tory Democrat
Elizabeth Longford *A Pilgrimage of Passion* (1979)

11 For the purposes of recreation he [Gladstone] has selected the felling of trees, and we may usefully remark that his amusements, like his politics, are essentially destructive . . . The forest laments in order that Mr Gladstone may perspire.
speech on Financial Reform, delivered in Blackpool, 24 January 1884

1 I decided some time ago that if the G.O.M. [Gladstone] went for Home Rule, the Orange card would be the one to play. Please God it may turn out the ace of trumps and not the two.

often quoted as 'Play the Orange card'; see **Shapiro** *359:16*

letter to Lord Justice FitzGibbon, 16 February 1886

2 Ulster will fight; Ulster will be right.

public letter, 7 May 1886

3 An old man in a hurry.
of **Gladstone**

in an address to the electors of South Paddington, 19 June 1886; see also **Salisbury** 340:9

4 All great men make mistakes. Napoleon forgot Blücher, I forgot Goschen.

when Lord Randolph suddenly resigned the position of Chancellor of the Exchequer in 1886, **Goschen** *had been appointed in his place*

in *Leaves from the Notebooks of Lady Dorothy Nevill* (1907)

5 I never could make out what those damned dots meant.
of decimal points

Winston Churchill *Lord Randolph Churchill* (1906) vol. 2

6 I have tried all forms of excitement, from tip-cat to tiger-shooting; all degrees of gambling, from beggar-my-neighbour to Monte Carlo; but have found no gambling like politics, and no excitement like a big division in the House of Commons.

Robert Rhodes James *An Introduction to the House of Commons* (1961)

Winston Churchill 1874–1965

British Conservative statesman; Prime Minister, 1940–5, 1951–5
on Churchill: see **Asquith** 16:8, **Baldwin** 26:11, **Balfour** 28:10, **Bevan** 38:7, **Butler** 68:1, **Laski** 225:8, **Lloyd George** 239:12, **Lloyd George** 240:2, **Nicolson** 288:12, **Webb** 412:6

7 A labour contract into which men enter voluntarily for a limited and for a brief period, under which they are paid wages which they consider adequate . . . may not be a healthy or proper contract, but it cannot in the opinion of His Majesty's Government be classified as slavery in the extreme acceptance of the word without some risk of terminological inexactitude.

in the House of Commons, 22 February 1906

8 He is one of those orators of whom it was well said, 'Before they get up, they do not know what they are going to say; when they are speaking, they do not know what they are saying; and when they have sat down, they do not know what they have said.'
of Lord Charles Beresford

in the House of Commons, 20 December 1912

9 Business carried on as usual during alterations on the map of Europe.
on the self-adopted 'motto' of the British people

speech at Guildhall, 9 November 1914

10 A drizzle of Empires . . . falling through the air.
of the Austro-Hungarian and Ottoman empires in 1918

Martin Gilbert *In Search of Churchill* (1994)

11 *comparing H. H.* **Asquith** *with Arthur* **Balfour***:*
The difference between him and Arthur is that Arthur is wicked and moral, Asquith is good and immoral.

E. T. Raymond *Mr Balfour* (1920)

12 The whole map of Europe has been changed . . . but as the deluge subsides and the waters fall short we see the dreary steeples of Fermanagh and Tyrone emerging once again.

in the House of Commons, 16 February 1922

1 Anyone can rat, but it takes a certain amount of ingenuity to re-rat.

on rejoining the Conservatives twenty years after leaving them for the Liberals, c.1924

Kay Halle *Irrepressible Churchill* (1966)

2 *of a meeting in 1926 with **Lloyd George**, by then out of office:*
Within five minutes the old relationship between us was completely re-established. The relationship between Master and Servant. And I was the Servant.

Lord Boothby *Recollections of a Rebel* (1978)

3 I decline utterly to be impartial as between the fire brigade and the fire.

replying to complaints of his bias in editing the British Gazette *during the General Strike*

in the House of Commons, 7 July 1926

4 Cultured people are merely the glittering scum which floats upon the deep river of production.

on hearing his son Randolph criticize the lack of culture of the Calgary oil magnates, probably c.1929

Martin Gilbert *In Search of Churchill* (1994)

5 I remember, when I was a child, being taken to the celebrated Barnum's circus, which contained an exhibition of freaks and monstrosities, but the exhibit on the programme which I most desired to see was the one described as 'The Boneless Wonder'. My parents judged that that spectacle would be too revolting and demoralizing for my youthful eyes, and I have waited 50 years to see the boneless wonder sitting on the Treasury Bench.

*of Ramsay **MacDonald***

speech in the House of Commons, 28 January 1931

6 There is not much collective security in a flock of sheep on the way to the butcher.

speech at the New Commonwealth Society luncheon, Dorchester Hotel, 25 November 1936

7 [The Government] go on in strange paradox, decided only to be undecided, resolved to be irresolute, adamant for drift, solid for fluidity, all-powerful to be impotent.

in the House of Commons, 12 November 1936

8 Dictators ride to and fro upon tigers which they dare not dismount. And the tigers are getting hungry.

letter, 11 November 1937

9 The utmost he [Neville Chamberlain] has been able to gain for Czechoslovakia and in the matters which were in dispute has been that the German dictator, instead of snatching his victuals from the table, has been content to have them served to him course by course.

in the House of Commons, 5 October 1938

10 I cannot forecast to you the action of Russia. It is a riddle wrapped in a mystery inside an enigma.

radio broadcast, 1 October 1939

11 *on being asked where to set the podium from which Neville **Chamberlain** was to give an address to local Conservatives:*
It doesn't matter where you put it as long as he has the sun in his eyes and the wind in his teeth.

Martin Gilbert *In Search of Churchill* (1994)

12 An appeaser is one who feeds a crocodile hoping it will eat him last.

in the House of Commons, January 1940

13 *as Prime Minister:*
[I was] conscious of a profound source of relief. I felt as if I was walking with destiny, and that all my past life had been but a preparation for this hour and this trial.

on 10 May 1940

14 I have nothing to offer but blood, toil, tears and sweat.

speech in the House of Commons, 13 May 1940

1 What is our policy? . . . to wage war against a monstrous tyranny, never surpassed in the dark, lamentable catalogue of human crime.

speech in the House of Commons, 13 May 1940

2 We shall not flag or fail. We shall go on to the end. We shall fight in France, we shall fight on the seas and oceans, we shall fight with growing confidence and growing strength in the air, we shall defend our island, whatever the cost may be. We shall fight on the beaches, we shall fight on the landing grounds, we shall fight in the fields and in the streets, we shall fight in the hills; we shall never surrender.

speech in the House of Commons, 4 June 1940

3 Let us therefore brace ourselves to our duty, and so bear ourselves that, if the British Empire and its Commonwealth lasts for a thousand years, men will still say, 'This was their finest hour.'

speech in the House of Commons, 18 June 1940

4 Never in the field of human conflict was so much owed by so many to so few.
on the skill and courage of British airmen

speech in the House of Commons, 20 August 1940

5 Death and sorrow will be the companions of our journey; hardship our garment; constancy and valour our only shield. We must be united, we must be undaunted, we must be inflexible.

speech in the House of Commons, 8 October 1940

6 *comment allegedly made on a long-winded report submitted by Anthony **Eden** on his tour of the Near East:*
As far as I can see you have used every cliché except 'God is Love' and 'Please adjust your dress before leaving.'

in *Life* December 1940

7 What I want is for you to keep the flies off the meat. It becomes bad if they are allowed to settle even for a moment. I am the meat and you must show me the warning light when troubles arise in the Parliamentary and political scene.
to his newly appointed Parliamentary Private Secretary, c.1941

Andrew Roberts *Eminent Churchillians* (1994)

8 It becomes still more difficult to reconcile Japanese action with prudence or even with sanity. What kind of a people do they think we are?

speech to US Congress, 26 December 1941

9 The British nation is unique in this respect. They are the only people who like to be told how bad things are, who like to be told the worst.

speech in the House of Commons, 10 June 1941

10 The people of London with one voice would say to Hitler: 'You have committed every crime under the sun . . . We will have no truce or parley with you, or the grisly gang who work your wicked will. You do your worst—and we will do our best.'

speech at County Hall, London, 14 July 1941

11 Here is the answer which I will give to President Roosevelt . . . Give us the tools and we will finish the job.

radio broadcast 9 February 1941

12 When I warned them [the French Government] that Britain would fight on alone whatever they did, their generals told their Prime Minister and his divided Cabinet, 'In three weeks England will have her neck wrung like a chicken.' Some chicken! Some neck!

speech to Canadian Parliament, 30 December 1941

13 A medal glitters, but it also casts a shadow.
a reference to the envy caused by the award of honours

in 1941; Kenneth Rose *King George V* (1983)

14 I have not become the King's First Minister in order to preside over the liquidation of the British Empire.

speech in London, 10 November 1942

1 Now this is not the end. It is not even the beginning of the
end. But it is, perhaps, the end of the beginning.
  on British success in the North African campaign

speech at the Mansion House,
London, 10 November 1942

2 We make this wide encircling movement in the
Mediterranean, having for its primary object the recovery of
the command of that vital sea, but also having for its object
the exposure of the under-belly of the Axis, especially Italy,
to heavy attack.

speech in the House of Commons,
11 November 1942; see
Misquotations 273:9

3 National compulsory insurance for all classes for all
purposes from the cradle to the grave.

radio broadcast 21 March 1943

4 There is no finer investment for any community than
putting milk into babies.

radio broadcast, 21 March 1943

5 The empires of the future are the empires of the mind.

speech at Harvard, 6 September
1943

6 *on rebuilding the Houses of Parliament:*
We shape our dwellings, and afterwards our dwellings
shape us.

speech in the House of Commons,
28 October 1944

7 I do not see any other way of realizing our hopes about
World Organization in five or six days. Even the Almighty
took seven.
  *to Franklin **Roosevelt** on the likely duration of the Yalta
  conference with **Stalin** in 1945*

The Second World War (1954) vol. 6

8 He devised the extraordinary measure of assistance called
Lend-Lease, which will stand forth as the most unselfish and
unsordid financial act of any country in all history.
  *of President **Roosevelt***

speech in the House of Commons,
17 April 1945

9 *after the General Election of 1945:*
Why should I accept the Order of the Garter from His
Majesty when the people have just given me the order of the
boot?

D. Bardens *Churchill in Parliament*
(1967)

10 *of Aneurin **Bevan**:*
Unless the right hon. gentleman changes his policy and
methods and moves without the slightest delay, he will be
as great a curse to this country in time of peace, as he was a
squalid nuisance in time of war.

speech in the House of Commons,
6 December 1945

11 The Prime Minister has nothing to hide from the President
of the United States
  *on stepping from his bath in the presence of a startled President
  Roosevelt*

as recalled by Roosevelt's son in
Churchill (BBC television series
presented by Martin Gilbert, 1992)
pt. 3

12 From Stettin in the Baltic to Trieste in the Adriatic an iron
curtain has descended across the Continent.
  *the expression 'iron curtain' previously had been applied by others
  to the Soviet Union or her sphere of influence, e.g. Ethel Snowden
  Through Bolshevik Russia (1920), Dr Goebbels Das Reich, 25
  February 1945, and by Churchill himself in a cable to President
  Truman, 4 June 1945*

speech at Westminster College,
Fulton, Missouri, 5 March 1946

13 The first step in the re-creation of the European family must
be a partnership between France and Germany. In this way
only can France recover the moral leadership of Europe.
There can be no revival of Europe without a spiritually great
France and a spiritually great Germany.

speech in Zurich, 19 September
1946

1 Time may be short . . . The fighting has stopped; but the dangers have not stopped. If we are to form the United States of Europe or whatever name or form it may take, we must begin now.

speaking of the threat posed by the atom bomb

speech in Zurich, 19 September 1946

2 *after the Nuremberg war trials:*
From now on I shall have to take care not to lose wars.

attributed

3 I wish Stanley Baldwin no ill, but it would have been much better if he had never lived.

*on being asked to send **Baldwin** an 80th birthday tribute*

Martin Gilbert *In Search of Churchill* (1994)

4 It would be a great reform in politics if wisdom could be made to spread as easily and as rapidly as folly.

speech at the Guildhall, London, 10 September 1947

5 Democracy is the worst form of Government except all those other forms that have been tried from time to time.

speech in the House of Commons, 11 November 1947

6 When I am abroad I always make it a rule never to criticize or attack the Government of my country. I make up for lost time when I am at home.

speech in the House of Commons, 18 April 1947

7 This is the sort of English up with which I will not put.

after an official had gone through one of his papers moving prepositions away from the ends of sentences

Ernest Gowers *Plain Words* (1948) 'Troubles with Prepositions'

8 *on why Clement Attlee was unlikely to go to America to deal with the financial crisis:*
When the mouse is away the cats might play.

Cynthia Gladwyn diary, 17 August 1949

9 Naval tradition? Monstrous. Nothing but rum, sodomy, prayers, and the lash.

often quoted as, 'rum, sodomy, and the lash', as in Peter Gretton Former Naval Person *(1968)*

Harold Nicolson diary, 17 August 1950

10 The candle in that great turnip has gone out.

*in reply to the comment 'One never hears of **Baldwin** nowadays—he might as well be dead'*

Harold Nicolson diary, 17 August 1950

11 The object of Parliament is to substitute argument for fisticuffs.

speech in the House of Commons, 6 June 1951

12 When the English history of the first quarter of the twentieth century is written, it will be seen that the greater part of our fortunes in peace and in war were shaped by this one man.

*of **Lloyd George***

in *Evening Standard* 4 October 1951

13 It is an error to believe that the world began when any particular party or statesman got into office. It has all been going on quite a long time.

speech at the Guildhall, London, 9 November 1951

14 A modest man who has much to be modest about.

*of Clement **Attlee***

in *Chicago Sunday Tribune Magazine of Books* 27 June 1954

15 I am prepared to meet my Maker. Whether my Maker is prepared for the great ordeal of meeting me is another matter.

at a news conference in Washington in 1954

16 To jaw-jaw is always better than to war-war.

speech at the White House, 26 June 1954

17 It was the nation and the race dwelling all round the globe that had the lion's heart. I had the luck to be called upon to give the roar.

speech at Westminster Hall, 30 November 1954

1 I still have the ideas, Walter, but I can't find the words to clothe them.

to Walter Monckton

Tony Benn diary, 15 December 1956

2 *of Lord **Montgomery***:
In defeat unbeatable: in victory unbearable.

Edward Marsh *Ambrosia and Small Beer* (1964)

3 *of **Balfour**'s moving from **Asquith**'s Cabinet to that of **Lloyd George***:
Like a powerful graceful cat walking delicately and unsoiled across a rather muddy street.

Great Contemporaries (1937)

4 *of the career of Lord **Curzon***:
The morning had been golden; the noontide was bronze; and the evening lead. But all were solid, and each was polished till it shone after its fashion.

Great Contemporaries (1937)

5 No part of the education of a politician is more indispensable than the fighting of elections.

Great Contemporaries (1937)

6 *when taking the entrance examination for Harrow, Churchill's answer paper consisted of his own name and a bracketed figure 1 for the first question:*
It was from these slender indications of scholarship that Mr Welldon drew the conclusion that I was worthy to pass into Harrow. It is very much to his credit.

My Early Life (1930)

7 Headmasters have powers at their disposal with which Prime Ministers have never yet been invested.

My Early Life (1930)

8 I am biased in favour of boys learning English. I would make them all learn English: and then I would let the clever ones learn Latin as an honour, and Greek as a treat.

My Early Life (1930)

9 Mr Gladstone read Homer for fun, which I thought served him right.

My Early Life (1930)

10 It may be that vengeance is sweet, and that the gods forbade vengeance to men because they reserved for themselves so delicious and intoxicating a drink. But no one should drain the cup to the bottom. The dregs are often filthy-tasting.

The River War (1899)

11 The influence of the religion [Islam] paralyses the social development of those who follow it. No stronger retrograde force exists in the world.

The River War (1899)

12 In war: resolution. In defeat: defiance. In victory: magnanimity. In peace: goodwill.

The Second World War vol. 1 (1948) epigraph, which according to Edward Marsh in *A Number of People* (1939), occurred to Churchill shortly after the conclusion of the First World War

13 The loyalties which centre upon number one are enormous. If he trips he must be sustained. If he makes mistakes they must be covered. If he sleeps he must not be wantonly disturbed. If he is no good he must be pole-axed. But this last extreme process cannot be carried out every day; and certainly not in the days just after he has been chosen.

The Second World War vol. 2 (1949)

14 It may almost be said, 'Before Alamein we never had a victory. After Alamein we never had a defeat.'

The Second World War (1951) vol. 4

15 I did not suffer from any desire to be relieved of my responsibilities. All I wanted was compliance with my wishes after reasonable discussion.

The Second World War (1951) vol. 4

1 I do not like elections, but it is in my many elections that I have learnt to know and honour the people of this island. They are good through and through.

Thoughts and Adventures (1932)

2 *of the General Election of 1922:*
In the twinkling of an eye I found myself without an office, without a seat, without a party, and without an appendix.

Thoughts and Adventures (1932)

3 *of the qualifications desirable in a prospective politician:*
The ability to foretell what is going to happen tomorrow, next week, next month, and next year. And to have the ability afterwards to explain why it didn't happen.

B. Adler *Churchill Wit* (1965)

4 As to freedom of the press, why should any man be allowed to buy a printing press and disseminate pernicious opinions calculated to embarrass the government?

Piers Brendon *Winston Churchill* (1984)

5 *of his recurring depression:*
Black dog is back again.

attributed

6 An empty taxi arrived at 10 Downing Street, and when the door was opened Attlee got out.
   attributed to Churchill, but strongly repudiated by him

Kenneth Harris *Attlee* (1982)

7 Feed a bee on royal jelly, and it becomes a queen.
   on Attlee's showing unexpected authority as Prime Minister

attributed

8 *of Stanley **Baldwin**:*
He occasionally stumbled over the truth, but hastily picked himself up and hurried on as if nothing had happened.

attributed

9 I am fond of pigs. Dogs look up to us. Cats look down on us. Pigs treat us as equals.

Martin Gilbert *Never Despair* (1988); attributed

10 I have taken more out of alcohol than alcohol has taken out of me.

Quentin Reynolds *By Quentin Reynolds* (1964)

11 I know of no case where a man added to his dignity by standing on it.

attributed

12 If you have ten thousand regulations you destroy all respect for the law.

attributed

13 In the course of my life I have often had to eat my words, and I must confess that I have always found it a wholesome diet.

W. Manchester *The Caged Lion* (1988)

14 Most wars in history have been avoided simply by postponing them.

J. K. Galbraith *A Life in Our Times* (1981)

15 A sheep in sheep's clothing.
   *of Clement **Attlee***

Lord Home *The Way the Wind Blows* (1976)

16 Take away that pudding—it has no theme.

Lord Home *The Way the Wind Blows* (1976)

17 There but for the grace of God, goes God.
   of Stafford Cripps

P. Brendon *Churchill* (1984)

18 *of Alfred Bossom:*
Who is this man whose name is neither one thing nor the other?

attributed

Count Galeazzo Ciano 1903–44

Italian fascist politician; son-in-law of **Mussolini**

1 Victory has a hundred fathers, but defeat is an orphan.

diary, 9 September 1942 (literally 'no-one wants to recognise defeat as his own')

Cicero (Marcus Tullius Cicero) 106–43 BC

Roman orator and statesman
on Cicero: see **Plutarch** 313:5, **Stevenson** 380:16

2 For he delivers his opinions as though he were living in Plato's Republic rather than among the dregs of Romulus.
   of M. Porcius Cato, the Younger

Ad Atticum

3 *Salus populi suprema est lex.*
   The good of the people is the chief law.

De Legibus; see **Selden** 349:3

4 Let war yield to peace, laurels to paeans.

De Officiis

5 In men of the highest character and noblest genius there is to be found an insatiable desire for honour, command, power, and glory.

De Officiis

6 The sinews of war, unlimited money.

Fifth Philippic

7 *O tempora, O mores!*
   Oh, the times! Oh, the manners!

In Catilinam

8 *Civis Romanus sum.*
   I am a Roman citizen.

In Verrem

9 Laws are silent in time of war.

Pro Milone

10 The young man should be praised, decorated, and got rid of.
   *of Octavian, the future Emperor **Augustus***

referred to in a letter from Decimus Brutus to Cicero; *Epistulae ad Familiares*

Edward Hyde, Lord Clarendon 1609–74

English statesman and historian

11 Without question, when he first drew the sword, he threw away the scabbard.
   of John Hampden

The History of the Rebellion (1703) vol. 3

12 He had a head to contrive, a tongue to persuade, and a hand to execute any mischief.
   of Hampden

The History of the Rebellion (1703) vol. 3

13 He . . . would, with a shrill and sad accent, ingeminate the word *Peace, Peace.*
   *of **Falkland***

The History of the Rebellion (1703) vol. 3

14 So enamoured on peace that he would have been glad the King should have bought it at any price.
   *of **Falkland***

The History of the Rebellion (1703) vol. 3

15 He will be looked upon by posterity as a brave bad man.
   *of **Cromwell***

The History of the Rebellion (1703) vol. 6

Alan Clark 1928–99
British Conservative politician
on Clark: see **Campbell** 72:2, **Parris** 305:7

1 In the end we are all sacked and it's always awful. It is as inevitable as death following life. If you are elevated there comes a day when you are demoted. Even Prime Ministers.

diary, 21 June 1983

2 Give a civil servant a good case and he'll wreck it with clichés, bad punctuation, double negatives and convoluted apology.

diary, 22 July 1983

3 Like most Chief Whips he knew who the shits were.
of Michael Jopling

diary, 17 June 1987

4 There's nothing so improves the mood of the Party as the imminent execution of a senior colleague.

diary, 13 July 1990

5 There are no true friends in politics. We are all sharks circling, and waiting, for traces of blood to appear in the water.

diary, 30 November 1990

6 Our old friend economical . . . with the *actualité.*
under cross-examination at the Old Bailey during the Matrix Churchill case

in *Independent* 10 November 1992; see **Armstrong** 15:6

7 Safe is spelled D-U-L-L. Politics has got to be a fun activity.
on being selected as parliamentary candidate for Kensington and Chelsea, 24 January 1997

in *Daily Telegraph* 25 January 1997

8 If I can comport myself with the dignity and competence of Ms Mo Mowlam, I shall be very satisfied.
after surgery for a brain tumour

in *Sunday Times* 6 June 1999 'Talking Heads'

9 Alan died suddenly at Saltwood on Sunday 5th September. He said he would like it to be stated that he regarded himself as having gone to join Tom and the other dogs.

announcement in *The Times* 8 September 1999

Kenneth Clarke 1940–
British Conservative politician

10 Tell your kids to get their scooters off my lawn.
allegedly said to the Party Chairman, Brian Mawhinney; see **Wilson** *421:12*

in *Guardian* 7 December 1996

11 The Government doesn't have a hostile attitude to the single currency. It was a slip of the tongue.
in response to a statement by fellow Conservative Malcolm Rifkind, 19 February 1997

in *Guardian* 20 February 1997

12 I do not wear a bleeper. I can't speak in soundbites. I refuse to repeat slogans. . . . I hate focus groups. I absolutely hate image consultants.

in *New Statesman* 12 February 1999

13 Every Labour government in my lifetime has run out of money.

in *Guardian* 25 April 2005

Karl von Clausewitz 1780–1831
Prussian soldier and military theorist

14 The general unreliability of all information presents a special problem in war: all action takes place, so to speak, in a kind of twilight, which, like fog or moonlight, often tends to make things seem grotesque and larger than they really are.
often alluded to by the phrase 'fog of war'

On War (1832–4) bk 2, ch. 2

1 The closer these practical probabilities drive war toward the absolute, the more the belligerent states are involved and drawn into its vortex, the clearer appear the connections between its separate actions, and the more imperative the need not to take the first step without considering the last.

On War (1832–4) bk. 8, ch. 3

2 War is nothing but a continuation of politics with the admixture of other means.
 commonly rendered 'War is the continuation of politics by other means'

On War (1832–4) bk. 8, ch. 6

Henry Clay 1777–1852
American politician
on Clay: see **Glascock** 160:1, **Jackson** 196:7

3 I am for resistance by the *sword*. No man in the nation desires peace more than I. But I prefer the troubled ocean of war . . . to the tranquil, putrescent pool of ignominious peace.

speech in the US Senate on the Macon Bill, 22 February 1810

4 If you wish to avoid foreign collision, you had better abandon the ocean.

in the House of Representatives, 22 January 1812

5 The gentleman [Josiah Quincy] can not have forgotten his own sentiment, uttered even on the floor of this House, 'peaceably if we can, forcibly if we must'.

speech in Congress, 8 January 1813

6 [Andrew Jackson] is ignorant, passionate, hypocritical, corrupt, and easily swayed by the basest men who surround him.

letter to Francis T. Brooke, 2 August 1833

7 The arts of power and its minions are the same in all countries and in all ages. It marks a victim; denounces it; and excites the public odium and the public hatred, to conceal its own abuses and encroachments.

speech in the Senate, 14 March 1834

8 It has been my invariable rule to do all for the Union. If any man wants the key of my heart, let him take the key of the Union, and that is the key to my heart.

speech in Norfolk, 22 April 1844

9 I had rather be right than be President.

to Senator Preston of South Carolina, 1839

10 I have heard something said about allegiance to the South. I know no South, no North, no East, no West, to which I owe any allegiance . . . The Union, sir, is my country.

speech in the US Senate, 1848

Philip 'Tubby' Clayton 1885–1972
Australian-born British clergyman, founder of Toc H

11 CHAIRMAN: What is service?
 CANDIDATE: The rent we pay for our room on earth.
 admission ceremony of Toc H, a society founded after the First World War to provide Christian fellowship and social service

Tresham Lever *Clayton of Toc H* (1971)

Eldridge Cleaver 1935–98
American political activist

12 What we're saying today is that you're either part of the solution or you're part of the problem.

speech in San Francisco, 1968; R. Scheer *Eldridge Cleaver, Post Prison Writings and Speeches* (1969)

John Cleese 1939– and Connie Booth
British comedy writer and actor; British comedy actress

1 They're Germans. Don't mention the war.

Fawlty Towers 'The Germans' (BBC TV programme, 1975)

Sarah Norcliffe Cleghorn 1876–1959

2 The golf-links lie so near the mill
That almost every day
The labouring children can look out
And watch the men at play.

'For Some Must Watch, While—' (1914)

Georges Clemenceau 1841–1929
French statesman; Prime Minister of France, 1906–9, 1917–20
on Clemenceau: see **Keynes** 214:8, **Lloyd George** 239:5

3 My home policy: I wage war; my foreign policy: I wage war. All the time I wage war.

speech to French Chamber of Deputies, 8 March 1918

4 *to André Tardieu, on being asked why he always gave in to Lloyd George at the Paris Peace Conference, 1918*
What do you expect when I'm between two men of whom one [Lloyd George] thinks he is Napoleon and the other [Woodrow Wilson] thinks he is Jesus Christ?

Harold Nicolson letter, 20 May 1919

5 It is easier to make war than to make peace.

speech at Verdun, 20 July 1919

6 War is too serious a matter to entrust to military men.

attributed to Clemenceau, but also to Briand and Talleyrand; see also **de Gaulle** 113:7

7 *on seeing a pretty girl on his eightieth birthday:*
Oh, to be seventy again!

James Agate diary, 19 April 1938; has also been attributed to Oliver Wendell **Holmes** Jr.

Grover Cleveland 1837–1908
American Democratic statesman; 22nd and 24th President of the US 1885–9 and 1893–7
on Cleveland: see **Bragg** 53:6

8 Your every voter, as surely as your chief magistrate, exercises a public trust.
  'public office is a public trust' was used as the motto of the Cleveland administration

inaugural address, 4 March 1885

9 I have considered the pension list of the republic a roll of honour.

veto of Dependent Pension Bill, 5 July 1888

10 The lessons of paternalism ought to be unlearned and the better lesson taught that, while the people should patriotically and cheerfully support their government, its functions do not include the support of the people.

inaugural address, 4 March 1893

Harlan Cleveland 1918–
American government official

11 The revolution of rising expectations.

phrase coined, 1950; see Arthur Schlesinger *A Thousand Days* (1965)

Hillary Rodham Clinton 1947–

American lawyer, wife of Bill **Clinton**, First Lady of the US
1993–2001

1 I am not standing by my man, like Tammy Wynette. I am
sitting here because I love him, I respect him, and I honour
what he's been through and what we've been through
together.

interview on *60 Minutes*, CBS-TV,
27 January 1992

2 I could have stayed home and baked cookies and had teas.
But what I decided was to fulfil my profession, which I
entered before my husband was in public life.

comment on questions raised by
rival Democratic contender
Edmund G. Brown Jr.; in *Albany
Times-Union* 17 March 1992

3 The great story here . . . is this vast right-wing conspiracy
that has been conspiring against my husband since the day
he announced for president.

interview on *Today* (NBC
television), 27 January 1998

4 A hard dog to keep on the porch.
  on her husband

in *Guardian* 2 August 1999

William Jefferson ('Bill') Clinton 1946–

American Democratic statesman; 42nd President of the US
1993–2001; husband of Hillary Rodham **Clinton**
on Clinton: see **Jackson** 196:11

5 I experimented with marijuana a time or two. And I didn't
like it, and I didn't inhale.

in *Washington Post* 30 March 1992

6 The comeback kid!
  *description of himself after coming second in the New Hampshire
  primary in the 1992 presidential election (since 1952, no
  presidential candidate had won the election without first winning
  in New Hampshire)*

Michael Barone and Grant Ujifusa
*The Almanac of American Politics
1994*

7 The urgent question of our time is whether we can make
change our friend and not our enemy.

inaugural address, 1993

8 I did not have sexual relations with that woman.

in a television interview, *Daily
Telegraph* (electronic edition) 27
January 1998

9 I did have a relationship with Ms Lewinsky that was not
appropriate. In fact, it was wrong.
  broadcast to the American people, 18 August 1998

in *Times* 19 August 1998

10 It depends on what the meaning of 'is' is.
  *videotaped evidence to the grand jury; tapes broadcast 21
  September 1998*

in *Guardian* 22 September 1998

11 The American people have spoken—but it's going to take a
little while to determine exactly what they said.
  on the US presidential election

in *Mail on Sunday* 12 November
2000; compare **Salisbury** 340:3

12 I tried to walk a fine line between acting lawfully and
testifying falsely but I now recognize that I did not fully
accomplish that goal.

in *Daily Telegraph* 20 January 2001

1 I think I did something for the worst possible reason—just
because I could.
on his relationship with Monica Lewinsky

in *Sunday Times* 20 June 2004

Lord Clive 1725–74

British general; Governor of Bengal

2 By God, Mr Chairman, at this moment I stand astonished at
my own moderation!
reply during Parliamentary cross-examination, 1773

G. R. Gleig *The Life of Robert, First Lord Clive* (1848)

3 *while attempting to take his own life, his pistol twice failed to fire:*
I feel that I am reserved for some end or other.

G. R. Gleig *The Life of Robert, First Lord Clive* (1848)

Thomas W. Cobb 1784–1830

American politician

4 If you persist, the Union will be dissolved. You have kindled
a fire which all the waters of the ocean cannot put out,
which seas of blood can only extinguish.
*to James Tallmadge, on his amendment to the bill to admit
Missouri to the Union as a slave state in 1820*

Robert V. Remini *Henry Clay* (1991)

William Cobbett 1762–1835

English political reformer and radical journalist

5 Nouns of number, or multitude, such as Mob, Parliament,
Rabble, House of Commons, Regiment, Court of King's
Bench, Den of Thieves, and the like.

English Grammar (1817) letter 17 'Syntax as Relating to Pronouns'

6 From a very early age, I had imbibed the opinion, that it
was every man's duty to do all that lay in his power to leave
his country as good as he had found it.

Political Register 22 December 1832

7 But what is to be the fate of the great wen of all? The
monster, called . . . 'the metropolis of the empire'?
of London

Rural Rides: The Kentish Journal 5 January 1822

Claud Cockburn 1904–81

British writer and journalist

8 I am prepared to believe that a lot of the people I had cast as
principal figures were really mere cat's-paws. But then a
cat's-paw is a cat's-paw and must expect to be treated as
part of the cat.
of his writing about the 'Cliveden Set'

Crossing the Line (1958)

9 Believe nothing until it has been officially denied.
advice frequently given to the young Claud Cockburn

In Time of Trouble (1956)

George M. Cohan 1878–1942

American songwriter, dramatist, and producer

10 Over there, over there,
Send the word, send the word over there
That the Yanks are coming, the Yanks are coming,
The drums rum-tumming everywhere.

So prepare, say a prayer,
Send the word, send the word to beware.
We'll be over, we're coming over
And we won't come back till it's over, over there.

'Over There' (1917 song)

Edward Coke 1552–1634

English jurist

1 Magna Charta is such a fellow, that he will have no
sovereign.
on the Lords' Amendment to the Petition of Right, 17 May 1628

J. Rushworth *Historical Collections* (1659) vol. 1

Richard Law, Lord Coleraine 1901–80

British writer, son of Andrew **Bonar Law**

2 When all is said, the floating vote lives up to its name. It
floats with the tide; and whoever would influence it must
first influence the tide.

For Conservatives Only (1970)

Samuel Taylor Coleridge 1772–1834

English poet, critic, and philosopher

3 State policy, a cyclops with one eye, and that in the back of
the head!

On the Constitution of the Church and State (1839)

4 In politics, what begins in fear usually ends in folly.

Table Talk (1835) 5 October 1830

Michael Collins 1890–1922

Irish revolutionary

5 That volley which we have just heard is the only speech
which it is proper to make over the grave of a dead Fenian.
*at the funeral of Thomas Ashe, who had died in prison while on
hunger strike*

at Glasnevin cemetery, 30th
September 1917

6 Think—what I have got for Ireland? Something which she
has wanted these past seven hundred years. Will anyone be
satisfied at the bargain? Will anyone? I tell you this—early
this morning I signed my death warrant. I thought at the
time how odd, how ridiculous—a bullet may just as well
have done the job five years ago.
*on signing the treaty establishing the Irish Free State; he was
shot from ambush in the following year*

letter, 6 December 1921

7 *on arriving at Dublin Castle for the handover by British forces on 16
January 1922, and being told that he was seven minutes late:*
We've been waiting 700 years, you can have the seven
minutes.

Tim Pat Coogan *Michael Collins*
(1990); attributed

8 Because of his sincerity, I would forgive him anything.
*after the death of Cathal **Brugha**, July 1922*

Robert Kee *Ourselves Alone* (1976)

9 My own fellow-countrymen won't kill me.
*before leaving for Cork where he was ambushed and killed, 20
August 1922*

James Mackay *Michael Collins*
(1996)

John Robert Colombo 1936–

Canadian writer

1 Canada could have enjoyed:
English government,
French culture,
and American know-how.

Instead it ended up with:
English know-how,
French government,
and American culture.

'O Canada' (1965)

Henry Steele Commager 1902–98

American historian

2 It was observed half a century ago that what is a stone wall
to a layman, to a corporate lawyer is a triumphant arch.
Much the same might be said of civil rights and freedoms.
To the layman the Bill of Rights seems to be a stone wall
against the misuse of power. But in the hands of a
congressional committee, or often enough of a judge, it
turns out to be so full of exceptions and qualifications that it
might be a whole series of arches.

'The Right to Dissent' in *Current History* October 1955; see below

A law, Hinnissey, that might look like a wall to you or me
wud look like a triumphal arch to th'expeeryenced eye iv
a lawyer.

Peter Finley Dunne (1867–1936) 'Mr Dooley on the Power of the Press' in *American Magazine* 1906

Barber B. Conable Jr. 1922–

American Republican politician and banker

3 I guess we have found the smoking pistol, haven't we?
*on hearing a tape of President **Nixon**'s discussion with H. R.*
***Haldeman**, on 23 June 1972, as to how the FBI's investigation*
of the Watergate burglary could be limited

Nigel Rees *Brewer's Quotations* (1994)

Gerry Conlon 1954–

Northern Irish member of the Guildford Four, the first to be released from prison

4 The life sentence goes on. It's like a runaway train that you
can't just get off.
of life after his conviction was quashed by the Court of Appeal

in *Irish Post* 13 September 1997

James M. Connell

Irish socialist songwriter see **Songs** 377:1

Sean Connery 1930–

Scottish actor

5 It is Scotland's rightful heritage that its people should create
a modern Parliament . . . This entire issue is above and
beyond any political party.
of Scottish devolution, in the Referendum campaign

speech in Edinburgh, 7 September 1997; in *Scottish Daily Record* 8 September 1997

1 We have waited nearly 300 years. My hope is that it will evolve with dignity and integrity and it will truly reflect the new voice of Scotland. My position on Scotland has never changed in 30-odd years. Scotland should be nothing less than an equal of other nations of the world.

in Daily Telegraph 27 April 1999

Billy Connolly 1942–

Scottish comedian

2 I don't want a Stormont. I don't want a wee pretendy government in Edinburgh.
   on the prospective Scottish Parliament; often quoted as 'a wee pretendy Parliament'

interview on *Breakfast with Frost* (BBC TV), 9 February 1997

Cyril Connolly 1903–74

English writer

3 M is for Marx
   And Movement of Masses
   And Massing of Arses.
   And Clashing of Classes.

'Where Engels Fears to Tread'

James Connolly 1868–1916

Irish labour leader and nationalist; executed after the Easter Rising, 1916

4 Apostles of freedom are ever idolised when dead, but crucified when alive.

in Workers' Republic August 1898

5 The worker is the slave of capitalist society, the female worker is the slave of that slave.

The Re-conquest of Ireland (1915)

6 The time for Ireland's battle is NOW, the place for Ireland's battle is HERE.

in The Workers' Republic 22 January 1916

7 I can always guarantee that the Irish Citizen Army will fight, but I cannot guarantee that it will be on time.

Diana Norman *Terrible Beauty* (1987)

8 The man who is bubbling over with love and affection for 'Ireland' and can pass unmoved through our streets and witness all the sorrow and suffering . . . without burning to end it, is a fraud and a liar in his heart, no matter how much he loves that combination of chemical elements he is pleased to call 'Ireland'.

Desmond Ryan *James Connolly* (1924)

Joseph Conrad 1857–1924

Polish-born English novelist

9 The terrorist and the policeman both come from the same basket.

The Secret Agent (1907)

10 The scrupulous and the just, the noble, humane, and devoted natures; the unselfish and the intelligent may begin a movement—but it passes away from them. They are not the leaders of a revolution. They are its victims.

Under Western Eyes (1911)

Constitution of the United States 1787

the first ten amendments are known as the Bill of Rights

1 We the people of the United States, in order to form a more perfect Union, establish justice, insure domestic tranquillity, provide for the common defense, promote the general welfare, and secure the blessings of liberty to ourselves and our posterity do ordain and establish this Constitution for the United States of America.

*preamble (see also **Rice** 326:1)*

2 Representatives and direct taxes shall be apportioned among the several States which may be included within this Union, according to their respective numbers, which shall be determined by adding to the whole number of free persons, including those bound to service for a term of years, and excluding Indians not taxed, three fifths of all other persons.

*article 1, sect. 2 (see also **Rice** 326:1)*

3 He shall from time to time give to the Congress information of the state of the Union, and recommend to their consideration such measures as he shall judge necessary and expedient.
   origin of the 'State of the Union' address

article 2, sect. 3 'President shall communicate to Congress'

4 Congress shall make no law respecting an establishment of religion, or prohibiting the free exercise thereof; or abridging the freedom of speech, or of the press; or the right of the people peaceably to assemble, and to petition the government for a redress of grievances.

First Amendment (1791)

5 A well-regulated militia, being necessary to the security of a free State, the right of the people to keep and bear arms, shall not be infringed.

Second Amendment (1791)

6 Nor shall any person subject for the same offense to be twice put in jeopardy of life or limb; nor shall be compelled in any criminal case to be a witness against himself, nor be deprived of life, liberty, or property, without due process of law.

Fifth Amendment (1791)

7 Excessive bail shall not be required, nor excessive fines imposed, nor cruel and unusual punishment inflicted.

Eighth Amendment (1791)

A. J. Cook 1885-1931

English labour leader; Secretary of the Miners' Federation of Great Britain, 1924-31

8 Not a penny off the pay, not a second on the day.
   often quoted with 'minute' substituted for 'second'

speech at York, 3 April 1926

Peter Cook 1937-95

British satirist and performer

9 *sketch satirizing the Prime Minister, Harold **Macmillan**:*
I have recently been travelling round the world—on your behalf, and at your expense—visiting some of the chaps with whom I hope to be shaping your future. I went first to Germany, and there I spoke with the German Foreign Minister, Herr . . . Herr and there, and we exchanged many frank words in our respective languages.

Beyond the Fringe (1961)

Robin Cook 1946–2005
British Labour politician

1 Our foreign policy must have an ethical dimension and must support the demands of other people for the democratic rights on which we insist for ourselves.
mission statement by the new Foreign Secretary, 12 May 1997

in *Times* 13 May 1997

2 Why is it now so urgent that we should take military action to disarm a military capacity that has been there for 20 years, and which we helped to create?
resigning from the government over Iraq

speech in the House of Commons, 17 March 2003

3 They found more dangerous chemicals in Coca-Cola's Dasani mineral water than they did in the whole of Iraq.

speaking at the Edinburgh Book Festival, in *Observer* 29 August 2004

4 New Labour is so programmed to appeal to floating voters that it has forgotten the language with which to appeal to its core voters.

in *Guardian* 8 April 2005

Calvin Coolidge 1872–1933
American Republican statesman; 30th President of the US 1923–9
on Coolidge: see **Anonymous** 12:11, **Mencken** 267:12, **Parker** 304:1

5 There is no right to strike against the public safety by anybody, anywhere, any time.

telegram to Samuel Gompers, 14 September 1919

6 Civilization and profits go hand in hand.

speech in New York, 27 November 1920

7 The chief business of the American people is business.

speech in Washington, 17 January 1925

8 That man has offered me unsolicited advice for six years, all of it bad.
*in 1928, when asked to support the Presidential nomination of his eventual successor Herbert **Hoover***

Donald R. McCoy *Calvin Coolidge: the Quiet President* (1967)

9 They hired the money, didn't they?
on the subject of war debts incurred by England and others

John H. McKee *Coolidge: Wit and Wisdom* (1933)

10 *account (probably apocryphal) supposedly given by Coolidge to his wife of what a preacher had said about sin:*
He was against it.

John H. McKee *Coolidge: Wit and Wisdom* (1933)

11 Nothing is easier than spending the public money. It does not appear to belong to anybody. The temptation is overwhelming to bestow it on somebody.

attributed

Francis M. Cornford 1874–1943
English academic

2 Every public action, which is not customary, either is wrong, or, if it is right, is a dangerous precedent. It follows that nothing should ever be done for the first time.

Microcosmographia Academica (1908)

3 *of propaganda:*
That branch of the art of lying which consists in very nearly deceiving your friends without quite deceiving your enemies.

Microcosmographia Academica (1922 ed.)

Coronation Service

1 We present you with this Book, the most valuable thing that this world affords. Here is wisdom; this is the royal Law; these are the lively Oracles of God.

'The Presenting of the Holy Bible' L. G. Wickham Legge *English Coronation Records* (1901)

Thomas Coventry 1578–1640

English judge

2 The dominion of the sea, as it is an ancient and undoubted right of the crown of England, so it is the best security of the land . . . The wooden walls are the best walls of this kingdom.

speech to the Judges, 17 June 1635

Lord Cranborne (Robert Arthur James Gascoyne-Cecil, Viscount Cranborne) 1946–

British Conservative politician, former Leader in the Lords, son of the 6th Marquess of Salisbury

3 [I was sacked for] running in like an ill-trained spaniel.
of his independent negotiation with the Labour Party on Lords reform, and subsequent dismissal by William **Hague**; *see also* **Benn** 35:1

in *Daily Telegraph* 3 December 1998

4 There was this odd mixture of misery and the limpet—the miserable limpet if you like—which was a great inhibition to his [John Major's] premiership.

on *The Major Years* pt 3, BBC1, 25 October 1999

Crazy Horse (Ta-Sunko-Witko) c.1849–77

American Siouxchief

5 One does not sell the earth upon which the people walk.

Dee Brown *Bury My Heart at Wounded Knee* (1970) ch. 12

Edith Cresson 1934–

French politician and European Commissioner

6 *Je ne regrette rien.*
I have no regrets.
on the inquiry into fraud at the European Commission

in an interview, 16 March 1999; '*Non, je ne regrette rien*' was the title of a song (1960) by Michel Vaucaire, sung by Edith Piaf

7 Perhaps I have been a little careless.
after the appearance of the report into fraud at the European Commission

in an interview, 16 March 1999

Michel Guillaume Jean de Crèvecoeur

1735–1813

French-born immigrant to America

8 What then is the American, this new man? He is either a European, or the descendant of a European, hence that strange mixture of blood, which you will find in no other country . . . Here individuals of all nations are melted into a new race of men, whose labours and posterity will one day cause great changes in the world.

Letters from an American Farmer (1782)

Ivor Crewe 1945–
British political scientist

1 The British public has always displayed a healthy cynicism of MPs. They have taken it for granted that MPs are self-serving impostors and hypocrites who put party before country and self before party.
addressing the Nolan inquiry into standards in public life

in *Guardian* 18 January 1995

George Washington Crile 1864–1943
American surgeon and physiologist

2 France . . . a nation of forty millions with a deep-rooted grievance and an iron curtain at its frontier.

A Mechanistic View of War and Peace (1915)

Julian Critchley 1930–2000
British Conservative politician and journalist

3 He could not see a parapet without ducking beneath it.
*of Michael **Heseltine***

Heseltine (1987)

4 The only safe pleasure for a parliamentarian is a bag of boiled sweets.

in *Listener* 10 June 1982

5 She cannot see an institution without hitting it with her handbag.
*of Margaret **Thatcher***

in *The Times* 21 June 1982

6 Disloyalty is the secret weapon of the Tory Party.

in *Observer* 11 November 1990; see **Kilmuir** 217:2

Oliver Cromwell 1599–1658
English soldier and statesman; Lord Protector from 1653
see also **Last words** 227:7, **Misquotations** 274:1

7 *on being asked by Lord **Falkland** what he would have done if the Grand Remonstrance of 1641 against the King had not passed:*
I would have sold all I had the next morning, and never have seen England more.

Clarendon *History of the Rebellion* (1826)

8 A few honest men are better than numbers.

letter to William Spring, September 1643

9 I would rather have a plain russet-coated captain that knows what he fights for, and loves what he knows, than that which you call 'a gentleman' and is nothing else.

letter to William Spring, September 1643

0 Cruel necessity.
*on the execution of **Charles I***

Joseph Spence *Anecdotes* (1820)

1 For that which you mention concerning liberty of conscience, I meddle not with any man's conscience.
letter to the Governor of Ross in Ireland, 19 October 1649

W. C. Abbott *Writings and Speeches of Oliver Cromwell* (1939) vol. 3

2 I beseech you, in the bowels of Christ, think it possible you may be mistaken.

letter to the General Assembly of the Kirk of Scotland, 3 August 1650

3 The dimensions of this mercy are above my thoughts. It is, for aught I know, a crowning mercy.

letter to William **Lenthall**, Speaker of the Parliament of England, 4 September 1651

1 You have sat too long here for any good you have been doing. Depart, I say, and let us have done with you. In the name of God, go!
    *addressing the Rump Parliament, 20 April 1653 (oral tradition; quoted by Leo **Amery** to Neville **Chamberlain** in the House of Commons, 7 May 1940)*

Bulstrode Whitelock *Memorials of the English Affairs* (1732 ed.)

2 Take away that fool's bauble, the mace.
    at the dismissal of the Rump Parliament, 20 April 1653

Bulstrode Whitelock *Memorials of the English Affairs* (1732 ed.); see **Misquotations** 273:11

3 It's a maxim not to be despised, 'Though peace be made, yet it's interest that keeps peace.'

speech to Parliament, 4 September 1654

4 Necessity hath no law. Feigned necessities, imaginary necessities . . . are the greatest cozenage that men can put upon the Providence of God, and make pretences to break known rules by.

speech to Parliament, 12 September 1654

5 Your poor army, those poor contemptible men, came up hither.

speech to Parliament, 21 April 1657

6 You have accounted yourselves happy on being environed with a great ditch from all the world besides.

speech to Parliament, 25 January 1658

7 Hell or Connaught.
    summary of the choice offered to the Catholic population of Ireland, transported to the western counties to make room for settlers

traditionally attributed

8 None climbs so high as he who knows not whither he is going.

attributed

9 There is no one I am more at a loss how to manage than that Marcus Tullius Cicero, the little man with three names.
    *of Anthony Ashley Cooper, Lord **Shaftesbury***

B. Martyn and Dr Kippis *The Life of the First Earl of Shaftesbury* (1836)

Anthony Crosland 1918–77

British Labour politician

10 Total abstinence and a good filing system are not now the right signposts to the socialist Utopia; or at least, if they are, some of us will fall by the wayside.

The Future of Socialism (1956)

11 Harold knows best. Harold is a bastard, but he is a genius. He's like Odysseus. Odysseus was a bastard, but he managed to steer the ship between Scylla and Charybdis.
    *on Harold **Wilson***

Susan Crosland *Tony Crosland* (1982)

12 If it's the last thing I do, I'm going to destroy every fucking grammar school in England. And Wales, and Northern Ireland.
    c.1965, while Secretary of State for Education and Science.

Susan Crosland *Tony Crosland* (1982)

13 The party's over.
    cutting back central government's support for rates, as Minister of the Environment in the 1970s

Anthony Sampson *The Changing Anatomy of Britain* (1982)

14 In the blood of the socialist there should always run a trace of the anarchist and the libertarian, and not too much of the prig and the prude.

Susan Crosland *Tony Crosland* (1982)

Richard Crossman 1907–74

British Labour politician
on Crossman: see **Dalton** 108:8

1 While there is death there is hope.
on the death of Hugh **Gaitskell** *in 1963*

Tam Dalyell *Dick Crossman* (1989)

2 The Civil Service is profoundly deferential—'Yes, Minister!
No, Minister! If you wish it, Minister!'

Diaries of a Cabinet Minister vol. 1
(1975) 22 October 1964

3 [To strip away] the thick masses of foliage which we call the
myth of democracy.

introduction to *Diaries of a Cabinet
Minister* vol. 1 (1975)

e. e. cummings 1894–1962

American poet

4 a politician is an arse upon
which everyone has sat except a man.

1 x 1 (1944) no. 10

Mario Cuomo 1932–

American Democratic politician

5 You campaign in poetry. You govern in prose.

in *New Republic*, Washington, DC, 8
April 1985

John Philpot Curran 1750–1817

Irish judge

6 The condition upon which God hath given liberty to man is
eternal vigilance; which condition if he break, servitude is at
once the consequence of his crime, and the punishment of
his guilt.

speech on the right of election of
the Lord Mayor of Dublin, 10 July
1790; see **Demosthenes** 114:4

7 *of Robert* **Peel**'s *smile:*
Like the silver plate on a coffin.

quoted by Daniel **O'Connell** in the
House of Commons, 26 February
1835

Edwina Currie 1946–

British Conservative politician

8 I wasn't even in the index.
on the omission of their affair from John **Major**'s *autobiography*

in *The Times* 28 September 2002

John Curtin 1885–1945

Australian Labor statesman; Prime Minister 1941–5

9 Australia looks to America, free of any pangs as to our
traditional links or kinship with the United Kingdom.
*of the threat from Japan, and British reluctance to recall
Australian troops from the Middle East*

in *Herald* (Melbourne) 27
December 1941

Lord Curzon 1859–1925

British Conservative politician; Viceroy of India 1898–1905
on Curzon: **Anonymous** 11:1, **Beaverbrook** 31:8, **Beaverbrook**
31:10; **Churchill** 91:4, **Nehru** 286:1

10 Other countries have but one capital—Paris, Berlin, Madrid.
Great Britain has a series of capitals all over the world, from
Ottawa to Shanghai.

notebook, 1887; Kenneth Rose
Superior Person (1969)

1 When a group of Cabinet Ministers begins to meet separately and to discuss independent action, the death-tick is audible in the rafters.

*in November 1922, shortly before the fall of **Lloyd George**'s Coalition Government*

David Gilmour *Curzon* (1994)

2 Not even a public figure. A man of no experience. And of the utmost insignificance.

*of Stanley **Baldwin**, appointed Prime Minister in 1923 in succession to **Bonar Law***

Harold Nicolson *Curzon: the Last Phase* (1934)

3 Gentlemen do not take soup at luncheon.

E. L. Woodward *Short Journey* (1942)

4 I never knew that the lower classes had such white skins.

supposedly said when watching troops bathing during the First World War

Kenneth Rose *Superior Person* (1969)

Astolphe Louis Léonard, Marquis de Custine 1790–1857

French writer and traveller

5 This empire, vast as it is, is only a prison to which the emperor holds the key.

of Russia

La Russie en 1839; at Peterhof, 23 July 1839

6 Whoever has really seen Russia will find himself content to live anywhere else. It is always good to know that a society exists where no happiness is possible because, by a law of nature, man cannot be happy unless he is free.

La Russie en 1839; at Peterhof, 23 July 1839; conclusion

Richard J. Daley 1902–76

American Democratic politician and Mayor of Chicago

7 The policeman isn't there to create disorder; the policeman is there to preserve disorder.

to the press, on the riots during the Democratic Convention in 1968

Milton N. Rakove *Don't Make No Waves: Don't Back No Losers* (1975)

Hugh Dalton 1887–1962

British Labour politician
*on Dalton: see **Anonymous** 12:8, **Birch** 42:11*

8 I view this able and energetic man with some detachment. He is loyal to his own career but only incidentally to anything or anyone else.

*of Richard **Crossman***

diary, 17 September 1941

Tam Dalyell 1932–

Scottish-born Labour politician

9 Under the new Bill, shall I still be able to vote on many matters in relation to West Bromwich but not West Lothian, as I was under the last Bill, and will my right hon. Friend [James Callaghan, MP for Cardiff] be able to vote on many matters in relation to Carlisle but not Cardiff?

formulation of the 'West Lothian question', identifying the constitutional anomaly that would arise if devolved assemblies were established for Scotland and for Wales but not for England

in the House of Commons, 3 November 1977

1 The West-Lothian-West-Bromwich problem pinpoints a basic design fault in the steering of the devolutionary coach which will cause it to crash into the side of the road.

in the House of Commons, 14 November 1977

2 I make no apology for returning yet again to the subject of the sinking of the *Belgrano*.

on the question of whether the Argentine cruiser Belgrano *had been a legitimate target in the Falklands War*

in the House of Commons, 13 May 1983

George Dangerfield 1904–86
British historian

3 To reform the House of Lords [in 1910] meant to set down in writing a Constitution which for centuries had remained happily unwritten, to conjure a great ghost into the narrow and corruptible flesh of a code.

The Strange Death of Liberal England (1936)

Samuel Daniel 1563–1619
English poet and dramatist

4   Princes in this case
Do hate the traitor, though they love the treason.

The Tragedy of Cleopatra (1594)

Georges Jacques Danton 1759–94
French revolutionary

5 *De l'audace, et encore de l'audace, et toujours de l'audace!*
Boldness, and again boldness, and always boldness!

speech to the Legislative Committee of General Defence, 2 September 1792

6 Thou wilt show my head to the people: it is worth showing.
to his executioner, 5 April 1794

Thomas Carlyle *History of the French Revolution* (1837) vol. 3

Bill Darnell
Canadian environmentalist

7 Make it a *green* peace.
at a meeting of the Don't Make a Wave Committee, which preceded the formation of Greenpeace

in Vancouver, 1970; Robert Hunter *The Greenpeace Chronicle* (1979); see **Hunter** 192:6

Clarence Darrow 1857–1938
American lawyer

8 When I was a boy I was told that anybody could become President. I'm beginning to believe it.

Irving Stone *Clarence Darrow for the Defence* (1941)

Harry Daugherty 1860–1941
American Republican supporter

9 Some twelve or fifteen men, worn out and bleary-eyed for lack of sleep, will sit down about two o'clock in the morning around a table in a smoke-filled room in some hotel and decide the nomination.
the way in which the Republican Party's presidential candidate for the 1920 would be selected if (as in fact happened) no clear nomination emerged from the convention; see **Simpson** *365:4*

attributed (although subsequently denied by Daugherty); William Safire *The New Language of Politics* (1968)

Charles D'Avenant 1656–1714

English dramatist and political economist

1 Custom, that unwritten law,
By which the people keep even kings in awe.

Circe (1677)

Ian Davidson 1950–

Scottish Labour politician

2 Anyone in the Labour Party hierarchy who believes that
new Labour is popular in Scotland should get out more.
after Labour was beaten into third place in the Ayr by-election for
the Scottish Parliament

in *Scotsman* 18 March 2000

Randall Davidson 1848–1930

Scottish-born Anglican clergyman, Archbishop of Canterbury
1903–28

3 There is a good deal more difficulty in dealing with a spoilt
child of sixty or seventy than with a spoilt child of six or
seven.
after having dissuaded Queen Victoria from writing a biography of
her Highland servant John Brown

Andrew Roberts *Salisbury: Victorian*
Titan (1999)

Robertson Davies 1913–95

Canadian novelist

4 I see Canada as a country torn between a very northern,
rather extraordinary, mystical spirit which it fears and its
desire to present itself to the world as a Scotch banker.

The Enthusiasms of Robertson Davies
(1990)

Ron Davies 1946–

British Labour politician

5 It was a moment of madness for which I have subsequently
paid a very, very heavy price.
of the episode on Clapham Common leading to his resignation as
Welsh Secretary

interview with BBC Wales and HTV,
30 October 1998

6 We are what we are. We are all different, the products of
both our genes and our experiences.

personal statement to the House
of Commons, 2 November 1998

Jefferson Davis 1808–89

American statesman; President of the Confederate states 1861–5
on Davis: see **Yancey** 426:3

7 If the Confederacy fails, there should be written on its
tombstone: *Died of a Theory.*

in 1865; Geoffrey C. Ward *The Civil*
War (1991)

Thomas Davis 1814–45

Irish poet and nationalist

8 But the land of their heart's hope they never saw more,
For in far, foreign fields, from Dunkirk to Belgrade
Lie the soldiers and chiefs of the Irish Brigade.

'The Battle-Eve of the Brigade'
(1845)

9 Viva la the New Brigade!
Viva la the Old One, too!
Viva la, the Rose shall fade,
And the shamrock shine for ever new.

'Clare's Dragoons' (1845)

1 And then I prayed I yet might see
Our fetters rent in twain,
And Ireland, long a province, be
A Nation once again.

'A Nation Once Again' (1846)

2 But—hark!—some voice like thunder spake:
The West's awake! the West's awake!

'The West's Asleep' (1845); see **Robinson** 328:10

3 The Wild Geese fly where others walk;
The Wild Geese do what others talk.

'When South Winds Blow' (1845)

4 If we live influenced by wind, and sun, and tree, and not by the passions and deeds of the past, we are a thriftless and hopeless people.

Literary and Historical Essays (1846)

Michael Davitt 1846–1905

Irish nationalist

5 An Englishman of the strongest type moulded for an Irish purpose.
    of Charles Stewart **Parnell**

The Fall of Feudalism in Ireland (1906)

Lord Dawson of Penn 1864–1945

British physician to King **George V**

6 The King's life is moving peacefully towards its close.
    bulletin, drafted on a menu card at Buckingham Palace on the eve of the king's death, 20 January 1936

Kenneth Rose *King George V* (1983)

Stockwell Burt Day 1950–

Canadian Progressive Conservative politician

7 God's law is clear. Standards of education are not set by government, but by God, the Bible, the home and the school.

Alberta Report, 1984

John Dean 1938–

American lawyer and White House counsel during the Watergate affair

8 We have a cancer within, close to the Presidency, that is growing.

from the [Nixon] Presidential Transcripts, 21 March 1973

9 The White House is another world. Expediency is everything.

in *New York Post* 18 June 1973

Régis Debray 1940–

French Marxist theorist

10 International life is right-wing, like nature. The social contract is left-wing, like humanity.

Charles de Gaulle (1994)

Eugene Victor Debs 1855–1926

American socialist

11 When great changes occur in history, when great principles are involved, as a rule the majority are wrong. The minority are right.
    speech at his trial for sedition in Cleveland, Ohio, 11 September 1918

Speeches (1928)

1 While there is a lower class, I am in it; while there is a criminal element, I am of it; while there is a soul in prison, I am not free.
  speech at his trial for sedition in Cleveland, Ohio, 11 September 1918

in Liberator November 1918

Stephen Decatur 1779–1820
American naval officer

2 Our country! In her intercourse with foreign nations, may she always be in the right; but our country, right or wrong.
  Decatur's toast at Norfolk, Virginia, April 1816

A. S. Mackenzie *Life of Stephen Decatur* (1846); see **Adams** 4:6

John de Chastelain 1937–
Canadian soldier and diplomat

3 The pike in the thatch is not quite the same as the surface-to-air missile in the thatch.
  on decommissioning in Northern Ireland

interview in *Daily Telegraph* 11 June 1999

Declaration of Arbroath

4 So long as there shall but one hundred of us remain alive, we will never subject ourselves to the dominion of the English. For it is not glory, it is not riches, neither is it honour, but it is freedom alone that we fight and contend for, which no honest man will lose but with his life.

letter sent by the Scottish Parliament, 6 April 1320, to the pope, asserting the independence of Scotland.

W. F. Deedes 1913–
British Conservative politician and journalist

5 The millennium is going to present us with a very sharp portrait of ourselves: drinking is to continue all night and religious observance, as far as possible, is to be kept at bay.

in *Sunday Times* 15 August 1999

6 One golden rule for people who want to get on in politics is to keep their traps shut in August.

in *Mail on Sunday* 22 August 1999

7 The man who said nobody ever lost money by underrating public taste has been proved wrong.
  on the Millennium Dome

in *Mail on Sunday* 4 June 2000

Daniel Defoe 1660–1731
English novelist and journalist

8 Nature has left this tincture in the blood,
  That all men would be tyrants if they could.

The History of the Kentish Petition (1712–13)

9 Fools out of favour grudge at knaves in place.

The True-Born Englishman (1701) introduction

10 From this amphibious ill-born mob began
  That vain, ill-natured thing, an Englishman.

The True-Born Englishman (1701)

11 Your Roman-Saxon-Danish-Norman English.

The True-Born Englishman (1701)

12 His lazy, long, lascivious reign.
  of **Charles II**

The True-Born Englishman (1701)

13 Great families of yesterday we show,
  And lords whose parents were the Lord knows who.

The True-Born Englishman (1701)

1 And of all plagues with which mankind are curst,
   Ecclesiastic tyranny's the worst.

The True-Born Englishman (1701)

2 When kings the sword of justice first lay down,
   They are no kings, though they possess the crown.
   Titles are shadows, crowns are empty things,
   The good of subjects is the end of kings.

The True-Born Englishman (1701)

Charles de Gaulle 1890–1970

French soldier and statesman; President of France, 1959–69

3 France has lost a battle. But France has not lost the war!

proclamation, 18 June 1940

4 Faced by the bewilderment of my countrymen, by the
   disintegration of a government in thrall to the enemy, by
   the fact that the institutions of my country are incapable, at
   the moment, of functioning, I General de Gaulle, a French
   soldier and military leader, realize that I now speak for
   France.

speech in London, 19 June 1940

5 Since they whose duty it was to wield the sword of France
   have let it fall shattered to the ground, I have taken up the
   broken blade.

speech, 13 July 1940

6 Yes, it is Europe, from the Atlantic to the Urals, it is Europe,
   it is the whole of Europe, that will decide the fate of the
   world.

speech to the people of
Strasbourg, 23 November 1959

7 Politics are too serious a matter to be left to the politicians.
   replying to Clement **Attlee***'s remark that 'De Gaulle is a very
   good soldier and a very bad politician'*

Clement Attlee *A Prime Minister
Remembers* (1961)

8 How can you govern a country which has 246 varieties of
   cheese?

Ernest Mignon *Les Mots du Général*
(1962)

9 Since a politician never believes what he says, he is quite
   surprised to be taken at his word.

Ernest Mignon *Les Mots du Général*
(1962)

10 *Europe des patries.*
    A Europe of nations.

*c.*1962; widely associated with De
Gaulle and taken as encapsulating
his views, although perhaps not
coined by him; J. Lacouture *De
Gaulle: the Ruler* (1991)

11 Treaties, you see, are like girls and roses: they last while
    they last.

speech at Elysée Palace, 2 July
1963

12 *Vive Le Québec Libre.*
    Long Live Free Quebec.
    *quoting the slogan of the separatist movement for an independent
    Quebec*

speech in Montreal, 24 July 1967

13 Authority doesn't work without prestige, or prestige
    without distance.

Le Fil de l'épée (1932) 'Du
caractère'

14 The sword is the axis of the world and its power is absolute.

Vers l'armée de métier (1934)
'Comment?' Commandement 3

15 *on the death of his daughter, who had been born with Down's
    Syndrome:*
    And now she is like everyone else.

in 1948; Jean Lacouture *De Gaulle*
(1965)

16 The EEC is a horse and carriage: Germany is the horse and
    France is the coachman.

attributed; Bernard Connolly *The
Rotten Heart of Europe* (1995)

17 One does not put Voltaire in the Bastille.
    when asked to arrest **Sartre***, in the 1960s*

in *Encounter* June 1975

Tom DeLay 1947–

American Republican politician; Senate Majority Leader since
2002

1 An arrogant, out-of-control, unaccountable judiciary that
thumbed their nose at Congress and the president.
statement issued after the death of the brain-damaged Terri
Schiavo, whose feeding tube was removed by court order; an
extraordinary session of Congress had passed a bill forcing the
Federal Court to review the decision, but appeals for replacement
of the tube were not upheld

in *The Age* (online edition) 2 April
2005

2 I said something in an inartful way, and I shouldn't have
said it that way.
referring to his earlier comments on the judiciary

in *Washington Post* 14 April 2005
(online edition)

Vine Victor Deloria Jr. 1933–

American Standing Rock Sioux

3 This country was a lot better off when the Indians were
running it.

in *New York Times Magazine* 3
March 1970

Demosthenes c.384–c.322 BC

Greek orator and Athenian statesman

4 There is one safeguard known generally to the wise, which
is an advantage and security to all, but especially to
democracies against despots—suspicion.

Philippic; see **Curran** 107:6

5 Excessive dealings with tyrants are not good for the security
of free states.

Second Philippic ch. 21

6 When asked what was first in oratory, [he] replied to his
questioner, 'action,' what second, 'action,' and again third,
'action'.

Cicero *Brutus* ch. 37, sect. 142

Jack Dempsey 1895–1983

American boxer

7 Honey, I just forgot to duck.
to his wife, on losing the World Heavyweight title, 23 September
1926; after a failed attempt on his life in 1981, Ronald **Reagan**
quipped to his wife 'Honey, I forgot to duck'

J. and B. P. Dempsey *Dempsey*
(1977)

Deng Xiaoping 1904–97

Chinese Communist statesman; from 1977 paramount leader of
China

8 The colour of the cat doesn't matter as long as it catches the
mice.

proverbial expression; in *Financial*
Times 18 December 1986

9 I should love to be around in 1997 to see with my own eyes
Hong Kong's return to China.

in 1984; in *Daily Telegraph* 20
February 1997, obituary

Lord Denning 1899–1999

British judge

10 The Treaty [of Rome] is like an incoming tide. It flows into
the estuaries and up the rivers. It cannot be held back.

in 1975; Anthony Sampson *The*
Essential Anatomy of Britain (1992)

1 To every subject of this land, however powerful, I would use Thomas Fuller's words over three hundred years ago, 'Be ye never so high, the law is above you.'

in a High Court ruling against the Attorney-General, January 1977

2 The keystone of the rule of law in England has been the independence of judges. It is the only respect in which we make any real separation of powers.

The Family Story (1981)

3 We shouldn't have all these campaigns to get the Birmingham Six released if they'd been hanged. They'd have been forgotten and the whole community would be satisfied.

in *Spectator* 18 August 1990

4 Properly exercised the new powers of the executive lead to the welfare state; but abused they lead to the totalitarian state.

Anthony Sampson *The Changing Anatomy of Britain* (1982)

Edward Stanley, 14th Earl of Derby
1799–1869
British Conservative statesman; Prime Minister, 1852, 1858–9, 1866–8
on Derby: see **Bulwer-Lytton** 60:6, **Disraeli** 119:8

5 The duty of an Opposition [is] very simple . . . to oppose everything, and propose nothing.

quoting 'Mr Tierney, a great Whig authority', in the House of Commons, 4 June 1841

6 Meddle and muddle.
   summarizing Lord John **Russell***'s foreign policy*

speech on the Address, in the House of Lords 4 February 1864

Proinsias de Rossa
Irish politician

7 If the Three Wise Men arrived here tonight, the likelihood is that they would be deported.
   advocating an amnesty for asylum-seekers

in *Irish Times* 20 December 1997 'This Week They Said'

Camille Desmoulins 1760–94
French revolutionary

8 My age is that of the *bon Sansculotte Jésus*; an age fatal to Revolutionists.
   reply given at his trial

Thomas Carlyle *History of the French Revolution* (1837)

Eamonn de Valera 1882–1975
American-born Irish statesman; Taoiseach 1937–48, 1951–4, and 1957–9, and President of the Republic of Ireland 1959–73
on de Valera: see **Lloyd George** 240:3

9 I am against this Treaty, not because I am a man of war, but because I am a man of peace.

in 1921

10 Whenever I wanted to know what the Irish people wanted, I had only to examine my own heart and it told me straight off what the Irish people wanted.

speech in Dáil Éireann, 6 January 1922

11 Further sacrifice of life would now be in vain . . . Military victory must be allowed to rest for the moment with those who have destroyed the Republic.

message to the Republican armed forces, 24 May 1923

1 I signed it the same way as I signed an autograph for a newspaper.
on taking the oath of allegiance to the King before entering Dáil Éireann

in 1932, attributed

2 If I were told tomorrow, 'You can have a united Ireland if you give up the idea of restoring the national language to be the spoken language of the majority of the people,' I would for myself say no.

speech in the Dáil, 1939

3 That Ireland which we dreamed of would be the home of a people who valued material wealth only as a basis of right living, of a people who were satisfied with frugal comfort and devoted their leisure to the things of the spirit; a land whose countryside would be bright with cosy homesteads, whose fields and villages would be joyous with sounds of industry, the romping of sturdy children, the contests of athletic youths, the laughter of comely maidens; whose firesides would be the forums of the wisdom of serene old age.

St Patrick's Day broadcast, 17 March 1943

4 Mr Churchill is proud of Britain's stand alone, after France had fallen, and before America had entered the war. Could he not find in his heart the generosity to acknowledge that there is a small nation that stood alone, not for one year or two, but for several hundred years, against aggression; that endured spoliation, famines, massacres in endless succession; that was clubbed many times into insensibility but each time, on returning consciousness, took up the fight anew; a small nation that could never be got to accept defeat and has never surrendered her soul?

radio broadcast, 16 May 1945

5 I sometimes admit that when I think of television and radio and their immense power, I feel somewhat afraid.

at the inauguration of Telefís Éireann in 1961

6 Whoever misunderstood Madame, the poor did not.
*of Constance **Markievicz***

Diana Norman *Terrible Beauty* (1987)

7 Women are at once the boldest and most unmanageable revolutionaries.

in conversation, c.1975

Donald Dewar 1937–2000
Scottish Labour politician; First Minister for Scotland from 1999

8 He could start a party in an empty room—and often did—filling it with good cheer, Gaelic songs, and argument.
*of John **Smith***

at John Smith's funeral service, 19 May 1994

9 'There shall be a Scottish parliament.' Through long years, those words were first a hope, then a belief, then a promise. Now they are a reality.
at the official opening of the Scottish Parliament

speech, 1 July 1999; see **Anonymous** 12:7

10 We look forward to the time when this moment will be seen as a turning point: the day when democracy was renewed in Scotland, when we revitalised our place in this our United Kingdom.
at the official opening of the Scottish Parliament

speech, 1 July 1999

11 This is about more than our politics and our laws. This is about who we are, how we carry ourselves.
at the official opening of the Scottish Parliament

speech, 1 July 1999

Thomas E. Dewey 1902-71

American politician and presidential candidate
on Dewey: see **Newspaper headlines** 287:4

1 That's why it's time for a change!
   phrase used extensively in campaigns of 1944, 1948, and 1952

campaign speech in San Francisco,
21 September 1944

Diana, Princess of Wales 1961-97

British princess, former wife of Charles, Prince of Wales

2 I'd like to be a queen in people's hearts but I don't see
   myself being Queen of this country.

interview on *Panorama*, BBC1 TV,
20 November 1995

3 I'm not a political figure . . . I'm a humanitarian figure. I
   always have been and I always will be.
   on taking part in the campaign against landmines

in *Daily Telegraph* 17 January 1997

4 The press is ferocious. It forgives nothing, it only hunts for
   mistakes . . . In my position anyone sane would have left a
   long time ago.
   contrasting British and foreign press

in *Le Monde* 27 August 1997

Porfirio Diaz 1830-1915

Mexican revolutionary and statesman; President of Mexico,
1877-80, 1884-1911

5 Poor Mexico, so far from God and so close to the United
   States.

attributed

A. V. Dicey 1835-1922

British jurist

6 The beneficial effect of state intervention, especially in the
   form of legislation, is direct, immediate, and, so to speak,
   visible, while its evil effects are gradual and indirect, and lie
   out of sight . . . Hence the majority of mankind must almost
   of necessity look with undue favour upon government
   intervention.

*Lectures on the Relation between
Law and Public Opinion* (1914)

Charles Dickens 1812-70

English novelist

7 O let us love our occupations,
   Bless the squire and his relations,
   Live upon our daily rations,
   And always know our proper stations.

The Chimes (1844) 'The Second
Quarter'

8 Annual income twenty pounds, annual expenditure
   nineteen nineteen six, result happiness. Annual income
   twenty pounds, annual expenditure twenty pounds ought
   and six, result misery.

David Copperfield (1850)

9 'It's always best on these occasions to do what the mob do.'
   'But suppose there are two mobs?' suggested Mr Snodgrass.
   'Shout with the largest,' replied Mr Pickwick.

Pickwick Papers (1837)

1 It was the best of times, it was the worst of times, it was the age of wisdom, it was the age of foolishness, it was the epoch of belief, it was the epoch of incredulity, it was the season of Light, it was the season of Darkness, it was the spring of hope, it was the winter of despair, we had everything before us, we had nothing before us, we were all going direct to Heaven, we were all going direct the other way.

A Tale of Two Cities (1859)

of the French Revolution

2 'It is possible—that it may not come, during our lives . . . We shall not see the triumph.' 'We shall have helped it,' returned madame.

A Tale of Two Cities (1859)

3 Detestation of the high is the involuntary homage of the low.

A Tale of Two Cities (1859)

4 My faith in the people governing is, on the whole, infinitesimal; my faith in The People governed is, on the whole, illimitable.

speech at Birmingham and Midland Institute, 27 September 1869

John Dickinson 1732–1808

American politician

5 We have counted the cost of this contest, and find nothing so dreadful as voluntary slavery . . . Our cause is just, our union is perfect.

C. J. Stillé *The Life and Times of John Dickinson* (1891)

declaration of reasons for taking up arms against England, presented to Congress, 8 July 1775

6 Then join hand in hand, brave Americans all,— By uniting we stand, by dividing we fall.

'The Liberty Song' (1768)

Denis Diderot 1713–84

French philosopher and man of letters

7 And [with] the guts of the last priest Let's shake the neck of the last king.

Dithrambe sur fete de rois; see **Meslier** 268:2

Joan Didion 1934–

American writer

8 When we start deceiving ourselves into thinking not that we want something or need something, not that it is a pragmatic necessity for us to have it, but that it is a *moral imperative* that we have it, then is when we join the fashionable madmen, and then is when the thin whine of hysteria is heard in the land, and then is when we are in bad trouble.

Slouching towards Bethlehem (1968) 'On Morality'

John G. Diefenbaker 1895–1979

Canadian Progressive Conservative statesman; Prime Minister 1957–63

9 There can be no dedication to Canada's future without a knowledge of its past.

in *Toronto Star* 9 October 1964

John Dillon 1851–1927

Irish nationalist politician

1 Women's suffrage will, I believe, be the ruin of our Western civilisation. It will destroy the home, challenging the headship of men laid down by God. It may come in your time—I hope not in mine.
  c.1912, to a deputation led by Hanna Sheehy Skeffington

Diana Norman *Terrible Beauty* (1987)

2 I say I am proud of their courage and if you were not so dense and stupid, as some of you English people are, you could have had these men fighting for you . . . It is not murderers who are being executed; it is insurgents who have fought a clean fight, however misguided, and it would have been a damned good thing for you if your soldiers were able to put up as good a fight as did those men in Dublin.
  of those executed after the Easter Rising

speech in the British House of Commons, 11 May 1916

Benjamin Disraeli 1804–81

British Tory statesman and novelist; Prime Minister, 1868, 1874–80
on Disraeli: see **Bismarck** 44:4, **Carlyle** 75:5, **Foot** 142:6, **Palmerston** 303:2; *see also* **Last words** 227:8

3 Between ourselves I could floor them all. This *entre nous*. I was never more confident of anything than that I could carry everything before me in that House. The time will come.
  four years before he entered Parliament

letter, 7 February 1833

4 In the 'Town' yesterday, I am told 'some one asked Disraeli, in offering himself for Marylebone, on what he intended *to stand*. "On my head," was the reply.'

letter, 8 April 1833

5 Though I sit down now, the time will come when you will hear me.
  maiden speech

in the House of Commons, 7 December 1837

6 The Continent will [not] suffer England to be the workshop of the world.

in the House of Commons, 15 March 1838

7 Thus you have a starving population, an absentee aristocracy, and an alien Church, and in addition the weakest executive in the world. That is the Irish Question.

in the House of Commons, 16 February 1844

8 The noble Lord is the Prince Rupert of Parliamentary discussion.
  *of Lord Stanley, later the 14th Earl of **Derby***

in the House of Commons, 24 April 1844; see **Bulwer-Lytton** 60:6

9 The right hon. Gentleman caught the Whigs bathing, and walked away with their clothes.
  *on Robert **Peel**'s abandoning protection in favour of free trade, traditionally the policy of the [Whig] Opposition*

in the House of Commons, 28 February 1845

10 Protection is not a principle, but an expedient.

in the House of Commons, 17 March 1845

1 A Conservative Government is an organized hypocrisy.

in the House of Commons, 17 March 1845; (Bagehot, quoting Disraeli in *The English Constitution* (1867) 'The House of Lords', elaborated on the theme with the words 'so much did the ideas of its "head" differ from the sensations of its "tail" ')

2 He traces the steam-engine always back to the tea-kettle.
  of Robert **Peel**

in the House of Commons, 11 April 1845

3 Justice is truth in action.

in the House of Commons, 11 February 1851

4 I read this morning an awful, though monotonous, manifesto in the great organ of public opinion, which always makes me tremble: Olympian bolts; and yet I could not help fancying amid their rumbling terrors I heard the plaintive treble of the Treasury Bench.

in the House of Commons, 13 February 1851

5 These wretched colonies will all be independent, too, in a few years, and are a millstone round our necks.

letter to Lord Malmesbury, 13 August 1852

6 England does not love coalitions.

in the House of Commons, 16 December 1852

7 Finality is not the language of politics.

in the House of Commons, 28 February 1859

8 It is, I say, in the noble Lord's power to come to some really cordial understanding . . . between this country and France . . . and to put an end to these bloated armaments which only involve states in financial embarrassment.

in the House of Commons, 8 May 1862

9 Colonies do not cease to be colonies because they are independent.

in the House of Commons, 5 February 1863

10 You are not going, I hope, to leave the destinies of the British Empire to prigs and pedants.

in the House of Commons, 5 February 1863

11 Party is organized opinion.

speech at Oxford, 25 November 1864

12 I hold that the characteristic of the present age is craving credulity.

speech at Oxford, 25 November 1864

13 Is man an ape or an angel? Now I am on the side of the angels.

speech at Oxford, 25 November 1864

14 Assassination has never changed the history of the world.

in the House of Commons, 1 May 1865

15 I had to prepare the mind of the country, and . . . to educate our party.

speech at Edinburgh, 29 October 1867

16 Change is inevitable in a progressive country. Change is constant; and the great question is, not whether you still resist change which is inevitable, but whether that change shall be carried out in deference to the manners, the customs, the laws and the traditions of a people, or . . . in deference to abstract principles and arbitrary and general doctrines.

speech at Edinburgh, 29 October 1867

17 There can be no economy where there is no efficiency.

address to his Constituents, 1 October 1868

1 *to Queen Victoria after the publication of* Leaves from the Journal of our Life in the Highlands *in 1868:*
We authors, Ma'am.

Elizabeth Longford *Victoria R.I.* (1964)

2 We have legalized confiscation, consecrated sacrilege, and condoned high treason.
*on **Gladstone**'s Irish policy*

in the House of Commons, 27 February 1871

3 I look upon Parliamentary Government as the noblest government in the world.

speech at Manchester, 3 April 1872

4 I believe that without party Parliamentary government is impossible.

speech at Manchester, 3 April 1872

5 You behold a range of exhausted volcanoes.
of the Liberal Government

speech at Manchester, 3 April 1872

6 Increased means and increased leisure are the two civilizers of man.

speech at Manchester, 3 April 1872

7 The very phrase 'foreign affairs' makes an Englishman convinced that I am about to treat of subjects with which he has no concern.

speech at Manchester, 3 April 1872

8 A University should be a place of light, of liberty, and of learning.

in the House of Commons, 11 March 1873

9 An author who speaks about his own books is almost as bad as a mother who talks about her own children.
at a banquet given in Glasgow on his installation as Lord Rector, 19 November 1873

in *The Times* 20 November 1873

10 Upon the education of the people of this country the fate of this country depends.

in the House of Commons, 15 June 1874

11 He is a great master of gibes and flouts and jeers.
*of Lord **Salisbury***

in the House of Commons, 5 August 1874

12 Mr Gladstone not only appeared but rushed into the debate ... The new Members trembled and fluttered like small birds when a hawk is in the air.

letter to Queen Victoria, March 1875, after an election in which **Gladstone**'s party had lost office;

13 Coffee house babble.
on the Bulgarian Atrocities, 1876

R. W. Seton-Watson *Britain in Europe 1789–1914* (1955)

14 Cosmopolitan critics, men who are the friends of every country save their own.

speech at Guildhall, 9 November 1877

15 Lord Salisbury and myself have brought you back peace— but a peace I hope with honour.
speech on returning from the Congress of Berlin, 16 July 1878

in *The Times* 17 July 1878; see **Chamberlain** 80:3, **Russell** 337:2

16 A series of congratulatory regrets.
of Lord Harrington's Resolution on the Berlin Treaty

at a banquet, Knightsbridge, 27 July 1878

17 A sophistical rhetorician, inebriated with the exuberance of his own verbosity.
*of **Gladstone***

in *The Times* 29 July 1878

18 I admit that there is gossip ... But the government of the world is carried on by sovereigns and statesmen, and not by anonymous paragraph writers ... or by the hare-brained chatter of irresponsible frivolity.

speech at Guildhall, London, 9 November 1878

19 One of the greatest of Romans, when asked what were his politics, replied, *Imperium et Libertas*. That would not make a bad programme for a British Ministry.

speech at Mansion House, London, 10 November 1879

Here the two great interests Imperium & Libertas, res olim insociabiles (saith Tacitus), began to incounter each other.

Winston Churchill (*c.*1620–88) *Divi Britannici* (1675); see **Tacitus** 384:10

1 Take away that emblem of mortality.
on being offered an air cushion to sit on, 1881

Robert Blake *Disraeli* (1966)

2 I will not go down to posterity talking bad grammar.
while correcting proofs of his last Parliamentary speech, 31 March 1881

Robert Blake *Disraeli* (1966)

3 The House of Commons is absolute. It is the State. 'L'État c'est moi.'

Coningsby (1844)

4 What by way of jest they call the Lower House.
of the House of Commons

Coningsby (1844)

5 A government of statesmen or of clerks? Of Humbug or Humdrum?

Coningsby (1844)

6 We owe the English peerage to three sources: the spoliation of the Church; the open and flagrant sale of honours by the elder Stuarts; and the borough-mongering of our own time.

Coningsby (1844)

7 Conservatism discards Prescription, shrinks from Principle, disavows Progress; having rejected all respect for antiquity, it offers no redress for the present, and makes no preparation for the future.

Coningsby (1844)

8 'A sound Conservative government,' said Taper, musingly. 'I understand: 'Tory men and Whig measures.''

Coningsby (1844)

9 Youth is a blunder; Manhood a struggle; Old Age a regret.

Coningsby (1844)

10 It seems to me a barren thing this Conservatism—an unhappy cross-breed, the mule of politics that engenders nothing.

Coningsby (1844); see **Donnelly** 125:5, **Power** 316:6

11 The depositary of power is always unpopular.

Coningsby (1844)

12 Where can we find faith in a nation of sectaries?

Coningsby (1844)

13 No Government can be long secure without a formidable Opposition.

Coningsby (1844)

14 Read no history: nothing but biography, for that is life without theory.

Contarini Fleming (1832)

15 The practice of politics in the East may be defined by one word—dissimulation.

Contarini Fleming (1832)

16 The transient and embarrassed phantom of Lord Goderich.
of Lord Goderich as Prime Minister

Endymion (1880)

17 An insular country, subject to fogs, and with a powerful middle class, requires grave statesmen.

Endymion (1880)

18 As for our majority . . . one is enough.

Endymion (1880)

19 The greatest opportunity that can be offfered to an Englishman—a seat in the House of Commons.

Endymion (1880)

20 The sweet simplicity of the three per cents.

Endymion (1880); see **Stowell** 382:8

21 I believe they went out, like all good things, with the Stuarts.

Endymion (1880)

22 What we anticipate seldom occurs; what we least expected generally happens.

Henrietta Temple (1837)

1 An aristocracy is rather apt to exaggerate the qualities and magnify the importance of a plebeian leader.

Lord George Bentinck (1852)

2 *of Robert **Peel***:
Wanting imagination he lacked prescience . . . His judgement was faultless provided he had not to deal with the future.

Lord George Bentinck (1852)

3 'Two nations; between whom there is no intercourse and no sympathy; who are as ignorant of each other's habits, thoughts, and feelings, as if they were dwellers in different zones, or inhabitants of different planets; who are formed by a different breeding, are fed by a different food, are ordered by different manners, and are not governed by the same laws.' 'You speak of—' said Egremont, hesitatingly, 'THE RICH AND THE POOR.'

Sybil (1845)

4 Pretending that people can be better off than they are is radicalism and nothing else.

Sybil (1845)

5 'Frank and explicit'—that is the right line to take when you wish to conceal your own mind and to confuse the minds of others.

Sybil (1845)

6 The Youth of a Nation are the trustees of Posterity.

Sybil (1845)

7 That fatal drollery called a representative government.

Tancred (1847)

8 A majority is always the best repartee.

Tancred (1847)

9 Progress to what and from where . . . The European talks of progress because by an ingenious application of some scientific acquirements he has established a society which has mistaken comfort for civilization.

Tancred (1847)

10 London is a modern Babylon.

Tancred (1847)

11 We should never lose an occasion. Opportunity is more powerful even than conquerors and prophets.

Tancred (1847)

12 The grovelling tyranny of self-government.

Tancred (1847)

13 There is no act of treachery or meanness of which a political party is not capable; for in politics there is no honour.

Vivian Grey (1826)

14 Experience is the child of thought and thought is the child of action. We cannot learn men from books.

Vivian Grey (1826)

15 I repeat . . . that all power is a trust—that we are accountable for its exercise—that, from the people, and for the people, all springs, and all must exist.

Vivian Grey (1826)

16 Damn your principles! Stick to your party.

attributed to Disraeli and believed to have been said to Edward **Bulwer-Lytton**; E. Latham *Famous Sayings and their Authors* (1904)

17 Everyone likes flattery; and when you come to Royalty you should lay it on with a trowel.

to Matthew **Arnold**, in G. W. E. Russell *Collections and Recollections* (1898) ch. 23

18 I have climbed to the top of the greasy pole.
on becoming Prime Minister

W. Monypenny and G. Buckle *Life of Benjamin Disraeli* vol. 4 (1916)

19 I am dead; dead, but in the Elysian fields.
to a peer, on his elevation to the House of Lords

W. Monypenny and G. Buckle *Life of Benjamin Disraeli* vol. 5 (1920)

20 I never deny; I never contradict; I sometimes forget.
said to Lord Esher of his relations with Queen Victoria

Elizabeth Longford *Victoria R. I* (1964)

1 Never complain and never explain.

J. Morley *Life of William Ewart Gladstone* (1903) vol. 1; see **Fisher** 141:1

2 The palace is not safe when the cottage is not happy.

Robert Blake *Disraeli* (1966)

3 Palmerston is now seventy. If he could prove evidence of his potency in his electoral address he'd sweep the country.
   to the suggestion that capital could be made from one of Palmerston's affairs

Hesketh Pearson *Dizzy* (1951); attributed, probably apocryphal

4 Posterity will do justice to that unprincipled maniac Gladstone—extraordinary mixture of envy, vindictiveness, hypocrisy and superstition; and with one commanding characteristic—whether Prime Minister or Leader of the Opposition, whether preaching, praying, speechifying or scribbling—never a gentleman.

W. Monypenny and G. Buckle *Life of Benjamin Disraeli* vol. 6 (1920)

5 Pray remember, Mr Dean, no dogma, no Dean.

W. Monypenny and G. Buckle *Life of Benjamin Disraeli* vol. 4 (1916)

6 Protection is not only dead, but damned.

W. Monypenny and G. Buckle *Life of Benjamin Disraeli* vol. 3 (1914)

7 The school of Manchester.
   of the free trade politics of Cobden and **Bright**

Robert Blake *Disraeli* (1966)

8 There are three kinds of lies: lies, damned lies and statistics.

attributed to Disraeli in Mark Twain *Autobiography* (1924) vol. 1

9 We came here for fame.
   to John **Bright**, *in the House of Commons*

Robert Blake *Disraeli* (1966)

10 When Gentlemen cease to be returned to Parliament this Empire will perish.

W. Fraser *Disraeli and His Day* (1891)

11 When I want to read a novel, I write one.

W. Monypenny and G. Buckle *Life of Benjamin Disraeli* vol. 6 (1920)

12 You will find as you grow older that courage is the rarest of all qualities to be found in public life.
   to Lady Gwendolen Cecil, telling her that her father Lord **Salisbury** *was the only man of real courage with whom Disraeli had worked*

Lady Gwendolen Cecil *Life of Robert Marquis of Salisbury* (1931)

Milovan Djilas 1911–

Yugoslav political writer and former member of the Yugoslav Communist Party (from which he resigned in April 1954)

13 The Party line is that there is no Party line.
   comment on reforms of the Yugoslavian Communist Party, November 1952

Fitzroy Maclean *Disputed Barricade* (1957)

Michael Dobbs 1948–

British writer

14 You might very well think that. I couldn't possibly comment.
   the Chief Whip's habitual response to questioning

House of Cards (as dramatised for television, 1990)

Frank Dobson 1940–

British Labour politician

15 I trudge the streets rather than trade the soundbite. I . . . would not know a focus group if I met one. I am unspun.

in *Sunday Times* 27 February 2000

1 The ego has landed.
of Ken **Livingstone**'s *independent candidacy for Mayor of London*

in *Times* 7 March 2000

Bubb Dodington 1691–1762
English politician

2 Love thy country, wish it well,
Not with too intense a care,
'Tis enough, that when it fell,
Thou its ruin didst not share.

'Ode' (written 1761) in Joseph
Spence *Anecdotes* (1820)

Elizabeth Dole 1936–
American Republican presidential candidate, wife of Robert
('Bob') **Dole**

3 From what I've seen, the answer is yes.
*on being asked if the country is ready for its first woman
President*

in *Sunday Telegraph* 14 March 1999

Robert Dole 1923–
American Republican politician

4 *announcing his decision to relinquish his Senate seat and step down
as majority leader:*
I will seek the presidency with nothing to fall back on but
the judgement of the people and with nowhere to go but the
White House or home.

on Capitol Hill, 15 May 1996

Ignatius Donnelly 1831–1901
American politician

5 The Democratic Party is like a mule—without pride of
ancestry or hope of posterity.

attributed; see **Disraeli** 122:10,
Power 316:6

John Dos Passos 1896–1970
American novelist

6 America our nation has been beaten by strangers who have
bought the laws and fenced off the meadows and cut down
the woods for pulp and turned our pleasant cities into slums
and sweated the wealth out of our people and when they
want to they hire the executioner to throw the switch.

The Big Money (1936)

William O. Douglas 1898–1980
American judge, Justice of the Supreme Court

7 The Fifth Amendment is an old friend and a good friend. It is
one of the great landmarks in man's struggle to be free of
tyranny, to be decent and civilized.

An Almanac of Liberty (1954)

8 The search . . . for ways and means to make the machine—
and the vast bureaucracy of the corporation state and of
government that runs that machine—the servant of man.
That is the revolution that is coming.

in 1970; Anthony Sampson *The
Company Man* (1995)

Alec Douglas-Home see Home

Frederick Douglass c.1818–95
American former slave and civil rights campaigner

1 Every tone [of the songs of the slaves] was a testimony against slavery, and a prayer to God for deliverance from chains.

Narrative of the Life of Frederick Douglass (1845) ch. 2

2 What, to the American slave, is your Fourth of July? I answer: A day that reveals to him, more than all other days in the year, the gross injustice and cruelty to which he is the constant victim. To him your celebration is a sham.

speech at Rochester, New York, 4 July 1852

3 In all the relations of life and death, we are met by the colour line.

speech at the Convention of Coloured Men, Louisville, Kentucky, 24 September 1883

4 No man can put a chain about the ankle of his fellow man without at last finding the other end fastened about his own neck.

speech at Civil Rights Mass Meeting, Washington, DC, 22 October 1883

Maureen Dowd 1952–
American journalist

5 These are not grounds for impeachment. These are grounds for divorce.
   on the Lewinsky affair.

in *Guardian* 14 September 1998

Margaret Drabble 1939–
English novelist

6 England's not a bad country . . . It's just a mean, cold, ugly, divided, tired, clapped-out, post-imperial, post-industrial slag-heap covered in polystyrene hamburger cartons.

A Natural Curiosity (1989)

Francis Drake c.1540–96
English sailor and explorer

7 The singeing of the King of Spain's Beard.
   on the expedition to Cadiz, 1587

Francis Bacon *Considerations touching a War with Spain* (1629)

8 There is plenty of time to win this game, and to thrash the Spaniards too.

attributed, in *Dictionary of National Biography* (1917–) vol. 5

Joseph Rodman Drake 1795–1820
American poet

9 Forever float that standard sheet!
   Where breathes the foe but falls before us,
   With Freedom's soil beneath our feet,
   And Freedom's banner streaming o'er us?

'The American Flag' in *New York Evening Post*, 29 May 1819 (also attributed to Fitz-Greene Halleck)

William Driver 1803–86

American sailor

1 I name thee Old Glory.

attributed

as the flag was hoisted to the masthead of his ship (Driver was captain of the Charles Doggett, *the ship on which the Bounty mutineers were returned from Tahiti to Pitcairn, and was presented with a large American flag by a band of women in recognition of this)*

John Dryden 1631–1700

English poet, critic, and dramatist

2 Plots, true or false, are necessary things,
To raise up commonwealths and ruin kings.

Absalom and Achitophel (1681)

3 Of these the false Achitophel was first,
A name to all succeeding ages curst.
For close designs and crooked counsels fit,
Sagacious, bold, and turbulent of wit,
Restless, unfixed in principles and place,
In power unpleased, impatient of disgrace.

Absalom and Achitophel (1681)

in Dryden's political satire relating to the Protestant succession 'Achitophel' represented **Shaftesbury**, *and 'Absalom' the Duke of* **Monmouth**

4 A daring pilot in extremity;
Pleased with the danger, when the waves went high
He sought the storms; but for a calm unfit,
Would steer too nigh the sands to boast his wit.

Absalom and Achitophel (1681)

5 In friendship false, implacable in hate:
Resolved to ruin or to rule the state.

Absalom and Achitophel (1681)

6 The people's prayer, the glad diviner's theme,
The young men's vision and the old men's dream!

Absalom and Achitophel (1681)

7 All empire is no more than power in trust.

Absalom and Achitophel (1681)

8 Better one suffer, than a nation grieve.

Absalom and Achitophel (1681)

9 For who can be secure of private right,
If sovereign sway may be dissolved by might?
Nor is the people's judgement always true:
The most may err as grossly as the few.

Absalom and Achitophel (1681)

10 Never was patriot yet, but was a fool.

Absalom and Achitophel (1681)

11 Reason to rule, but mercy to forgive:
The first is law, the last prerogative.

The Hind and the Panther (1687)

12 Either be wholly slaves or wholly free.

The Hind and the Panther (1687)

13 T'abhor the makers, and their laws approve,
Is to hate traitors and the treason love.

The Hind and the Panther (1687)

14 War is the trade of kings.

King Arthur (1691)

15 But treason is not owned when 'tis descried;
Successful crimes alone are justified.

The Medal (1682)

16 But 'tis the talent of our English nation,
Still to be plotting some new reformation.

'The Prologue at Oxford, 1680' (prologue to Nathaniel Lee *Sophonisba*, 2nd ed., 1681)

17 Freedom which in no other land will thrive,
Freedom an English subject's sole prerogative.

Threnodia Augustalis (1685)

1 If by the people you understand the multitude, the *hoi polloi*, 'tis no matter what they think; they are sometimes in the right, sometimes in the wrong: their judgement is a mere lottery.

An Essay of Dramatic Poesy (1668)

Alexander Dubček 1921–92
Czechoslovak statesman; First Secretary of the Czechoslovak Communist Party, 1968–9

2 In the service of the people we followed such a policy that socialism would not lose its human face.

in *Rudé Právo* 19 July 1968

Joachim Du Bellay 1522–60
French poet

3 France, mother of arts, of warfare, and of laws.

Les Regrets (1558) Sonnet no. 9

W. E. B. Du Bois 1868–1963
American social reformer and political activist

4 The cost of liberty is less than the price of repression.

John Brown (1909)

5 The problem of the twentieth century is the problem of the colour line—the relation of the darker to the lighter races of men in Asia and Africa, in America and the islands of the sea.

The Souls of Black Folk (1905)

Françoise Ducros
Canadian political aide

6 What a moron.
off-the-record comment on George W. **Bush***; she subsequently resigned as Jean* **Chrétien***'s director of communications*

attributed; reported in *CTV news* (online edition) 21 November 2002

John Foster Dulles 1888–1959
American international lawyer and politician

7 If . . . the European Defence Community should not become effective; if France and Germany remain apart . . . That would compel an agonizing reappraisal of basic United States policy.

speech to NATO Council in Paris, 14 December 1953

8 The ability to get to the verge without getting into the war is the necessary art. If you cannot master it, you inevitably get into war. If you try to run away from it, if you are scared to go to the brink, you are lost. We've had to look it square in the face—on the question of enlarging the Korean war, on the question of getting into the Indochina war, on the question of Formosa. We walked to the brink and we looked it in the face.
this policy became known as 'brinkmanship'

in *Life* 16 January 1956; see **Stevenson** 380:13

Henry Dundas 1742–1811
Scottish-born politician

9 When it is said that no alternative is left to the New Englanders but to starve or rebel, this is not the fact, for there is another way, to submit.
the word 'starvation' was said to have been coined in relation to this speech, and Dundas became known as 'Starvation Dundas'

in the House of Commons, 1775

John Dunning, Lord Ashburton 1731–83
English lawyer and politician

1 The influence of the Crown has increased, is increasing, and
ought to be diminished.

resolution passed in the House of Commons, 6 April 1780

Ray Durem 1915–63
American poet

2 Some of my best friends are white boys.
when I meet 'em
I treat 'em
just the same as if they was people.

'Broadminded' (written 1951)

John George Lambton, Lord Durham
1792–1840
English Whig politician

3 £40,000 a year a moderate income—such a one as a man
might jog on with.

Thomas Creevey, letter to Elizabeth Ord, 13 September 1821

4 I expected to find a contest between a government and a
people: I found two nations warring in the bosom of a single
state.

Report of the Affairs of British North America (1839)

Esther Dyson
American businesswoman

5 It is cute to have the British pound, it is quaint. But Britain
has more hope if it joins them and fights for what it wants.
on why Britain should join the euro

in Times 6 July 2000

Stephen T. Early 1889–1951

6 Don't Worry Me—I am an 8 Ulcer Man on 4 Ulcer Pay.
card received by Harry Truman

William Hillman Mr President: the First Publication from the Personal Diaries, Private Letters, Papers and Revealing Interviews of Harry S. Truman (1952)

Abba Eban 1915–
Israeli diplomat

7 History teaches us that men and nations behave wisely once
they have exhausted all other alternatives.

speech in London, 16 December 1970

8 *of the British Foreign Office:*
A hotbed of cold feet.

in conversation with Antony Jay

Anthony Eden 1897–1977
British Conservative statesman, Prime Minister 1955–7
on Eden: see **Butler** 68:2, **Muggeridge** 282:7, **Newspaper
headlines** 288:2, **Roberts** 327:6

9 Everyone is always in favour of general economy and
particular expenditure.

in Observer 17 June 1956

10 We are in an armed conflict; that is the phrase I have used.
There has been no declaration of war.
on the Suez crisis

in the House of Commons, 1 November 1956

1 Long experience has taught me that to be criticized is not always to be wrong.
   during the Suez crisis

speech at Lord Mayor's Guildhall banquet; in *Daily Herald* 10 November 1956

Clarissa Eden 1920–

British wife of Anthony **Eden**

2 For the past few weeks I have really felt as if the Suez Canal was flowing through my drawing room.

speech at Gateshead, 20 November 1956

Edward VII 1841–1910

British monarch, King of the United Kingdom from 1901

3 The last King of England.
   introducing his son, the future George V, to Lord Haldane, expressing his pessimism for the survival of the British monarchy

Andrew Roberts *Eminent Churchillians* (1994)

Edward VIII 1894–1972

King of the United Kingdom, 1936; afterwards Duke of Windsor
on Edward VIII: see **George V** 154:3, **Thomas** 393:4

4 These works brought all these people here. Something should be done to get them at work again.
   speaking at the derelict Dowlais Iron and Steel Works, 18 November 1936

in *Western Mail* 19 November 1936; see **Misquotations** 273:10

5 At long last I am able to say a few words of my own . . . you must believe me when I tell you that I have found it impossible to carry the heavy burden of responsibility and to discharge my duties as King as I would wish to do without the help and support of the woman I love.
   radio broadcast following his abdication, 11 December 1936

in *The Times* 12 December 1936

John Edwards 1953–

American Democratic politician, vice-presidential candidate in 2004

6 The president of the United States actually has to be able to walk and chew gum at the same time.

in January 2004; quoted on *BBC News Online* website, 6 October 2004 (see **Johnson** 203:14)

7 We have been 'The Little Engine that Could'. I am proud of what we've done.
   to his supporters, acknowledging defeat in the contest for the Democratic presidential nomination

in *Chicago Tribune* 3 March (online edition)

John Ehrlichman 1925–99

American Presidential assistant to Richard **Nixon**

8 I think we ought to let him hang there. Let him twist slowly, slowly in the wind.
   speaking of Patrick Gray (regarding his nomination as director of the FBI) in a telephone conversation with John Dean

in *Washington Post* 27 July 1973

Albert Einstein 1879–1955

German-born theoretical physicist; originator of the theory of relativity

1 The prestige of government has undoubtedly been lowered considerably by the Prohibition laws. For nothing is more destructive of respect for the government and the law of the land than passing laws which cannot be enforced.

after visiting America in 1921; *The World As I See It* (1935)

2 Nationalism is an infantile sickness. It is the measles of the human race.

Helen Dukas and Banesh Hoffman *Albert Einstein, the Human Side* (1979)

3 One must divide one's time between politics and equations. But our equations are much more important to me.

C. P. Snow 'Einstein' in M. Goldsmith et al. (eds.) *Einstein* (1980)

Dwight D. Eisenhower 1890–1969

American Republican statesman; 34th President of the US
on Eisenhower: see **Acheson** 1:10, **Truman** 401:5

4 People of Western Europe: A landing was made this morning on the coast of France by troops of the Allied Expeditionary Force. This landing is part of the concerted United Nations plan for the liberation of Europe, made in conjunction with our great Russian allies . . . I call upon all who love freedom to stand with us now. Together we shall achieve victory.

broadcast on D-Day, 6 June 1944

5 Every gun that is made, every warship launched, every rocket fired signifies, in the final sense, a theft from those who hunger and are not fed, those who are cold and are not clothed. This world in arms is not spending money alone. It is spending the sweat of its labourers, the genius of its scientists, the hopes of its children.

speech in Washington, 16 April 1953

6 I just will not—I *refuse*—to get into the gutter with that guy.
    explaining why he did not try to restrain Senator **McCarthy**

in 1953; in *American National Biography* (online edition) 'Joseph McCarthy'

7 You have broader considerations that might follow what you might call the 'falling domino' principle. You have a row of dominoes set up. You knock over the first one, and what will happen to the last one is that it will go over very quickly. So you have the beginning of a disintegration that would have the most profound influences.

speech at press conference, 7 April 1954

8 Governments are far more stupid than their people.

attributed, 1958

9 I think that people want peace so much that one of these days governments had better get out of the way and let them have it.

broadcast discussion, 31 August 1959

10 In the councils of government, we must guard against the acquisition of unwarranted influence, whether sought or unsought, by the military-industrial complex. The potential for the disastrous rise of misplaced power exists and will persist.
    farewell broadcast, 17 January 1961

in *New York Times* 18 January 1961

11 No *easy* problems ever come to the president of the United States. If they are easy to solve, someone else has solved them.

quoted by John F. Kennedy, in *Parade* 8 April 1962

George Eliot 1819–80
English novelist

1 An election is coming. Universal peace is declared, and the foxes have a sincere interest in prolonging the lives of the poultry.

Felix Holt (1866)

T. S. Eliot 1888–1965
American-born British poet, critic, and dramatist

2 This is the way the world ends
Not with a bang but a whimper.

'The Hollow Men' (1925)

Queen Elisabeth of Belgium 1876–1965
German-born consort of King Albert of the Belgians

3 Between them [Germany] and me there is now a bloody curtain which has descended forever.
on Germany's invasion of Belgium in 1914

attributed

Elizabeth I 1533–1603
English monarch, Queen of England and Ireland from 1558
see also **Last words** 226:1, **Mottoes** 281:7

4 This judgement I have of you that you will not be corrupted by any manner of gift and that you will be faithful to the state; and that without respect of my private will you will give me that counsel which you think best.
to William Cecil, appointing him her Secretary of State in 1558

Conyers Read *Mr Secretary Cecil and Queen Elizabeth* (1955)

5 The queen of Scots is this day leichter of a fair son, and I am but a barren stock.

to her ladies, June 1566, in Sir James Melville *Memoirs of His Own Life* (1827 ed.)

6 I am your anointed Queen. I will never be by violence constrained to do anything. I thank God that I am endued with such qualities that if I were turned out of the Realm in my petticoat, I were able to live in any place in Christome.

speech to Members of Parliament, 5 November 1566

7 I know what it is to be a subject, what to be a Sovereign, what to have good neighbours, and sometimes meet evil-willers.

speech to a Parliamentary deputation at Richmond, 12 November 1586; J. E. Neale *Elizabeth I and her Parliaments 1584–1601* (1957), from a report 'which the Queen herself heavily amended in her own hand'; see **Misquotations** 273:4

8 I will make you shorter by the head.
*to the leaders of her Council, who were opposing her course towards **Mary** Queen of Scots*

F. Chamberlin *Sayings of Queen Elizabeth* (1923)

9 I know I have the body of a weak and feeble woman, but I have the heart and stomach of a king, and of a king of England too; and think foul scorn that Parma or Spain, or any prince of Europe, should dare to invade the borders of my realm.
speech to the troops at Tilbury on the approach of the Armada, 1588

Lord Somers *A Third Collection of Scarce and Valuable Tracts* (1751)

10 The daughter of debate, that eke discord doth sow.
*on **Mary** Queen of Scots*

George Puttenham (ed.) *The Art of English Poesie* (1589)

1 I will have here but one Mistress, and no Master.
reproving the presumption of the Earl of Leicester

Robert Naunton *Fragmenta Regalia* (1641)

2 My lord, we make use of you, not for your bad legs, but for your good head.
to William Cecil, who suffered from gout

F. Chamberlin *Sayings of Queen Elizabeth* (1923)

3 I do entreat heaven daily for your longer life, else will my people and myself stand in need of cordials too. My comfort hath been in my people's happiness and their happiness in thy discretion.
to William Cecil on his death-bed

F. Chamberlin *Sayings of Queen Elizabeth* (1923)

4 Though God hath raised me high, yet this I count the glory of my crown: that I have reigned with your loves.
the Golden Speech, 1601

in *The Journals of All the Parliaments . . . Collected by Sir Simonds D'Ewes* (1682)

5 God may pardon you, but I never can.
*to the dying Countess of Nottingham, February 1603, for her part in the death of the Earl of **Essex**; the story is almost certainly apocryphal*

David Hume *The History of England under the House of Tudor* (1759) vol. 2

6 Must! Is *must* a word to be addressed to princes? Little man, little man! thy father, if he had been alive, durst not have used that word.
*to Robert **Cecil**, on his saying in her last illness that she must go to bed*

J. R. Green *A Short History of the English People* (1874); Dodd's *Church History of England* vol. 3 (ed. M. A. Tierney, 1840) adds, 'but thou knowest I must die, and that maketh thee so presumptuous'

7 If thy heart fails thee, climb not at all.
*lines after Walter **Ralegh**, written on a window-pane*

Thomas Fuller *Worthies of England* vol. 1; see **Ralegh** 321:5

8 I think that, at the worst, God has not yet ordained that England shall perish.

F. Chamberlin *Sayings of Queen Elizabeth* (1923)

9 I would not open windows into men's souls.

oral tradition, in J. B. Black *Reign of Elizabeth 1558–1603* (1936) (the words very possibly originating in a letter drafted by Bacon)

10 Like strawberry wives, that laid two or three great strawberries at the mouth of their pot, and all the rest were little ones.
describing the tactics of the Commission of Sales, in their dealings with her

Francis Bacon *Apophthegms New and Old* (1625)

11 Madam I may not call you; mistress I am ashamed to call you; and so I know not what to call you; but howsoever, I thank you.
to the wife of the Archbishop of Canterbury, the Queen disapproving of marriage among the clergy

John Harington *A Brief View of the State of the Church of England* (1653)

12 *welcoming Edward de Vere, Earl of Oxford, on his return from seven years self-imposed exile, occasioned by the acute embarrassment to himself of breaking wind in the presence of the Queen:*
My Lord, I had forgot the fart.

John Aubrey *Brief Lives* 'Edward de Vere'

13 *on being asked her opinion of Christ's presence in the Sacrament:*
'Twas God the word that spake it,
He took the bread and brake it;
And what the word did make it;
That I believe, and take it.

S. Clarke *The Marrow of Ecclesiastical History* (1675) 'The Life of Queen Elizabeth'

Elizabeth II 1926–

British monarch, Queen of the United Kingdom from 1952;
daughter of **George VI** and Queen **Elizabeth** the Queen Mother

1 I declare before you all that my whole life, whether it be
long or short, shall be devoted to your service and the
service of our great Imperial family to which we all belong.
*broadcast speech, as Princess Elizabeth, to the Commonwealth
from Cape Town, 21 April 1947*

in *The Times* 22 April 1947

2 *speech at Guildhall, London, on her 25th wedding anniversary:*
I think everybody really will concede that on this, of all
days, I should begin my speech with the words 'My husband
and I'.

in *The Times* 21 November 1972

3 In the words of one of my more sympathetic correspondents,
it has turned out to be an 'annus horribilis'.

speech at Guildhall, London, 24
November 1992

4 The British Constitution has always been puzzling and
always will be.

Peter Hennessy *The Hidden Wiring*
(1995)

5 I for one believe that there are lessons to be drawn from her
life and from the extraordinary and moving reaction to her
death.
*broadcast from Buckingham Palace on the evening before the
funeral of **Diana**, Princess of Wales, 5 September 1997*

in *The Times* 6 September 1997

6 Please don't be too effusive.
*adjuration to the Prime Minister on the speech he was to make to
celebrate her golden wedding, 18 November 1997*

in *Daily Telegraph* 21 November
1997; see **Blair** 46:5

7 *Vive la différence, mais vive l'entente cordiale.*
Long live the difference, but long live the Entente Cordiale.

speech, Paris, 5 April 2004 in *The
Times* 6 April 2004

Queen Elizabeth, the Queen Mother
1900–2002

British Queen Consort of **George VI**, mother of **Elizabeth II**

8 I'm glad we've been bombed. It makes me feel I can look the
East End in the face.
to a London policeman, 13 September 1940

John Wheeler-Bennett *King George
VI* (1958)

9 *on the suggestion that the royal family be evacuated during the
Blitz:*
The Princesses would never leave without me and I couldn't
leave without the King, and the King will never leave.

Penelope Mortimer *Queen Elizabeth*
(1986)

Ebenezer Elliott 1781–1849

English poet known as the 'Corn Law Rhymer'

10 What is a communist? One who hath yearnings
For equal division of unequal earnings.

'Epigram' (1850)

Thomas Edward Ellis 1859–99

British Liberal politician and Welsh nationalist

11 Over and above all, we shall work for a Legislature, elected
by the manhood and womanhood of Wales.

speech at Bala, 1890

Ralph Waldo Emerson 1803–82

American philosopher and poet

1 The two parties which divide the state, the party of Conservatism and that of Innovation, are very old, and have disputed the possession of the world ever since it was made.

'The Conservative' (lecture, 1841)

2 The louder he talked of his honour, the faster we counted our spoons.

The Conduct of Life (1860)
'Worship'

3 When you strike at a king, you must kill him.

attributed to Emerson by Oliver Wendell **Holmes** Jr.; Max Lerner *The Mind and Faith of Justice Holmes* (1943)

Robert Emmet 1778–1803

Irish nationalist

4 Let no man write my epitaph . . . When my country takes her place among the nations of the earth, *then*, and *not till then*, let my epitaph be written.

speech from the dock when condemned to death, 19 September 1803

Friedrich Engels 1820–95

German socialist; founder, with Karl **Marx**, of modern Communism

5 The State is not 'abolished', *it withers away.*

Anti-Dühring (1878)

6 Naturally, the workers are perfectly free; the manufacturer does not force them to take his materials and his cards, but he says to them . . . 'If you don't like to be frizzled in my frying-pan, you can take a walk into the fire'.

The Condition of the Working Class in England in 1844 (1892)

Friedrich Engels

see also **Marx** and **Engels**

Ennius 239–169 BC

Roman writer

7 *Moribus antiquis res stat Romana virisque.*
The Roman state survives by its ancient customs and its manhood.

Annals

8 *Unus homo nobis cunctando restituit rem.*
One man by delaying put the state to rights for us.
referring to the Roman general Fabius Cunctator ('The Delayer')

Annals

▌ Epitaphs *see box overleaf*

Erasmus c.1469–1536

Dutch Christian humanist

9 In the country of the blind the one-eyed man is king.

Adages

Epitaphs

1 Free at last, free at last
Thank God almighty
We are free at last.
*epitaph of Martin Luther **King** (1929–68), Atlanta, Georgia*

anonymous spiritual; see **King** 217:8

2 Go, tell the Spartans, thou who passest by,
That here obedient to their laws we lie.
epitaph for the 300 Spartans killed at Thermopylae, 480 BC

attributed to **Simonides**; Herodotus *Histories* bk. 7, ch. 228

3 Here lies a great and mighty king
Whose promise none relies on;
He never said a foolish thing,
Nor ever did a wise one.
*of **Charles II** (1630–85); an alternative first line reads: 'Here lies our sovereign lord the King'*

John Wilmot, Earl of **Rochester** 'The King's Epitaph'; in C. E. Doble et al. *Thomas Hearne: Remarks and Collections* (1885–1921) 17 November 1706; see **Charles II** 81:9

4 Here lies a valiant warrior
Who never drew a sword;
Here lies a noble courtier
Who never kept his word;
Here lies the Earl of Leicester
Who governed the estates
Whom the earth could never living love,
And the just heaven now hates.
of Robert Dudley, Earl of Leicester (c.1532–88)

attributed to Ben **Jonson** in Silvester Tissington *A Collection of Epitaphs and Monumental Inscriptions* (1857)

5 Here lies Fred,
Who was alive and is dead:
Had it been his father,
I had much rather;
Had it been his brother,
Still better than another;
Had it been his sister,
No one would have missed her;
Had it been the whole generation,
Still better for the nation:
But since 'tis only Fred,
Who was alive and is dead,—
There's no more to be said.
of Frederick Louis, Prince of Wales (1707–1751), son of George II and Caroline of Ansbach

in Horace Walpole *Memoirs of George II* (1847) vol. 1

6 Here lies he who neither feared nor flattered any flesh.
*of John **Knox**, said as he was buried, 26 November 1572*

Earl of Morton (c.1516–81); George R. Preedy *The Life of John Knox* (1940)

7 Here lies wise and valiant dust,
Huddled up, 'twixt fit and just:
Strafford, who was hurried hence
'Twixt treason and convenience.
He spent his time here in a mist,
A Papist, yet a Calvinist . . .
Riddles lie here, or in a word,
Here lies blood; and let it lie
Speechless still, and never cry.

John Cleveland (1613–58) 'Epitaph on the Earl of **Strafford**' (1647)

Epitaphs *continued*

1 I will return. And I will be millions.

inscription on the tomb of Eva **Perón**, Buenos Aires

2 O Death, where is thy sting?
   To take the Queen and leave the King?
   on the death of Caroline of Ansbach, consort of George II, in 1737 (anonymous verse found at the Royal Exchange)

in *Manuscripts of the earl of Egmont: diary of Viscount Percival, afterwards first earl of Egmont* (1920-3) vol. 2 (see also **Anonymous** 13:11)

3 Rest in peace. The mistake shall not be repeated.

inscription on the cenotaph at Hiroshima, Japan

4 A soldier of the Great War known unto God.
   standard epitaph for the unidentified dead of World War One

adopted by the War Graves Commission

5 Their name liveth for evermore.
   *standard inscription on the Stone of Sacrifice in each military cemetery of World War One, proposed by Rudyard **Kipling** as a member of the War Graves Commission*

Charles Carrington *Rudyard Kipling* (rev. ed. 1978)

6 When you go home, tell them of us and say,
   'For your tomorrow we gave our today.'

Kohima memorial to the Burma campaign of the Second World War; in recent years used at Remembrance Day parades in the UK

When you go home, tell them of us and say,
'For your tomorrows these gave their today.'

John Maxwell Edmonds (1875-1958) *Inscriptions Suggested for War Memorials* (1919)

Ludwig Erhard 1897-1977

German statesman, Chancellor of West Germany (1963-6)

7 Without Britain Europe would remain only a torso.

remark on W. German television, 27 May 1962; in *The Times* 28 May 1962

Dudley Erwin 1917-84

Australian politician

8 *claiming that the 'political manoeuvre' which had cost him his job in the reshuffled Government was actually the Prime Minister's secretary:*
It wiggles, it's shapely and its name is Ainsley Gotto.

in *The Times* 14 November 1969

Lord Esher 1913-

English architect and planner

9 When politicians and civil servants hear the word 'culture' they feel for their blue pencils.

speech, House of Lords, 2 March 1960; see **Johst** 205:10

Robert Devereux, Lord Essex 1566-1601

English soldier and courtier, executed for treason

10 Reasons are not like garments, the worse for wearing.

letter to Lord Willoughby, 4 January 1599

William Maxwell Evarts 1818–83
American politician and lawyer

1 The pious ones of Plymouth, who, reaching the Rock, first fell upon their own knees and then upon the aboriginees.

in Louisville Courier-Journal *4* July 1913; a pun which has been variously attributed

Edward Everett 1794–1865
American orator and politician

2 I should be glad if I could flatter myself that I came as near the central idea of the occasion in two hours as you did in two minutes.
   *to Abraham **Lincoln** on the Gettysburg address, which had been publicly criticized while Everett's two hour speech had received adulatory attention in the press*

letter to Lincoln, 20 November 1863; see **Anonymous** 12:4

William Norman Ewer 1885–1976
British writer

3 I gave my life for freedom—This I know:
For those who bade me fight had told me so.

'Five Souls' (1917)

Winifred Ewing 1929–
Scottish Nationalist politician

4 As I took my seat it was said by political pundits that 'a chill ran along the Labour back benches looking for a spine to run up.'
   of her arrival at Westminster after winning the Hamilton by-election in 1967; use of a general political expression

in 1988, attributed; Angela Cran and James Robertson *Dictionary of Scottish Quotations* (1996)

5 The Scottish Parliament which adjourned on 25 March in the year 1707 is hereby reconvened.
   opening speech, as oldest member of the new Parliament

in *Scottish Parliament* 12 May 1999

6 I am an expert in being a minority. I was alone in the House of Commons for three years and alone in the European Parliament for nineteen years, but we are all minorities now.
   opening speech, as oldest member of the new Parliament

in *Scottish Parliament* 12 May 1999

Quintus Fabius Maximus c.275–203 BC
Roman politician and general

7 To be turned from one's course by men's opinions, by blame, and by misrepresentation shows a man unfit to hold an office.

Plutarch *Parallel Lives* 'Fabius Maximus'

Émile Faguet 1847–1916
French writer and critic

8 *commenting on **Rousseau**'s 'Man was born free, and everywhere he is in chains':*
It would be equally correct to say that sheep are born carnivorous, and everywhere they nibble grass.

paraphrasing Joseph de Maistre; *Politiques et Moralistes du Dix-Neuvième Siècle* (1899)

Thomas Fairfax 1621–71
English Parliamentary general

1 Human probabilities are not sufficient grounds to make war upon a neighbour nation.
> *to the proposal in 1650 that the expected attack by the Scots should be anticipated by the invasion of Scotland*

in *Dictionary of National Biography*

Lucius Cary, Lord Falkland 1610–43
English royalist politician

2 When it is not necessary to change, it is necessary not to change.

Discourses of Infallibility (1660) 'A Speech concerning Episcopacy' delivered in 1641

Frantz Fanon 1925–61
French West Indian psychoanalyst and writer

3 The shape of Africa resembles a revolver, and the Congo is the trigger.

attributed

Michael Faraday 1791–1867
English physicist and chemist

4 *to **Gladstone**, when asked about the usefulness of electricity:*
Why sir, there is every possibility that you will soon be able to tax it!

W. E. H. Lecky *Democracy and Liberty* (1899 ed.)

Wallace Fard c.1891–1934
American religious leader, founder of the Nation of Islam

5 The blue-eyed devil white man.

Malcolm X with Alex Haley *The Autobiography of Malcolm X* (1965); see **Malcolm X** 257:1

James A. Farley 1888–1976
American Democratic politician

6 As Maine goes, so goes Vermont.
> *after predicting correctly that Franklin **Roosevelt** would carry all but two states in the election of 1936*

statement to the press, 4 November 1936; see **Proverbs and sayings** 318:3

Farouk 1920–65
Egyptian monarch, King 1936–52

7 The whole world is in revolt. Soon there will be only five Kings left—the King of England, the King of Spades, the King of Clubs, the King of Hearts and the King of Diamonds.

Lord Boyd-Orr *As I Recall* (1966), addressed to the author at a conference in Cairo, 1948

Guy Fawkes 1570–1606
English conspirator in the Gunpowder Plot, 1605

8 A desperate disease requires a dangerous remedy.

on 6 November 1605, in *Dictionary of National Biography* (1917–) vol. 6

Dianne Feinstein 1933–
American Democratic politician

1 Toughness doesn't have to come in a pinstripe suit.

in *Time* 4 June 1984

2 There was a time when you could say the least government was the best—but not in the nation's most populous state.

campaign speech, 15 March 1990

Ferdinand I see **Mottoes** 281:3

Paul Feyerabend 1924–94
Austrian philosopher

3 The time is overdue for adding the separation of state and science to the by now customary separation of state and church. Science is only *one* of the many instruments man has invented to cope with his surroundings. It is not the only one, it is not infallible, and it has become too powerful, too pushy, and too dangerous to be left on its own.

Against Method (1975)

Elizabeth Filkin 1940–
British academic and administrator, Parliamentary Commissioner for Standards, 1999–2001

4 I don't think you can investigate anything too rigorously, because you're not being fair to people unless you do that.

interview, in *Guardian* 16 February 2002

L'Abbé Edgeworth de Firmont 1745–1807
Irish-born priest, confessor to **Louis XVI**

5 Son of Saint Louis, ascend to heaven.
to Louis XVI as he mounted the steps of the guillotine, 1793

attributed

H. A. L. Fisher 1856–1940
English historian

6 Men wiser and more learned than I have discerned in history a plot, a rhythm, a predetermined pattern. These harmonies are concealed from me. I can see only one emergency following upon another as wave follows upon wave, only one great fact with respect to which, since it is unique, there can be no generalizations, only one safe rule for the historian: that he should recognize in the development of human destinies the play of the contingent and the unforeseen.

A History of Europe (1935)

7 Purity of race does not exist. Europe is a continent of energetic mongrels.

A History of Europe (1935)

8 Nothing commends a radical change to an Englishman more than the belief that it is really conservative.

A History of Europe (1935)

John Arbuthnot Fisher 1841–1920
British admiral

9 Sack the lot!
on overmanning and overspending within government departments

letter to *The Times*, 2 September 1919

1 Never contradict
Never explain
Never apologize.

letter to *The Times*, 5 September 1919; see **Disraeli** 124:1

John Fiske 1842–1901

2 The United States—bounded on the north by the Aurora Borealis, on the south by the precession of the equinoxes, on the east by the primeval chaos, and on the west by the Day of Judgement.

Bounding the United States

Gerry Fitt 1926–

Northern Irish politician

3 People [in Northern Ireland] don't march as an alternative to jogging. They do it to assert their supremacy. It is pure tribalism, the cause of troubles all over the world.

in *The Times* 5 August 1994

4 The people have spoken and the politicians have had to listen.
on the outcome of the referendum on the Good Friday agreement

in *Sunday Telegraph* 24 May 1998

F. Scott Fitzgerald 1896–1940

American novelist

5 See that little stream—we could walk to it in two minutes. It took the British a month to walk it—a whole empire walking very slowly, dying in front and pushing forward behind. And another empire walked very slowly backward a few inches a day, leaving the dead like a million bloody rugs.

Tender is the Night (1934)

Ari Fleischer 1960–

American government spokesman, White House Press Secretary 2001–3

6 The problem with guns that are hidden is you can't see their smoke.

on BBC News Online, 10 January 2003; see **Blix** 47:6

Robert, Marquis de Flers 1872–1927 and Arman de Caillavet 1869–1915

French dramatists

7 Democracy is the name we give the people whenever we need them.

L'habit vert, in *La petite illustration série théâtre* 31 May 1913

Andrew Fletcher of Saltoun 1655–1716

Scottish patriot and anti-Unionist
see also **Last words** 227:5

8 I knew a very wise man so much of Sir Chr—'s sentiment, that he believed if a man were permitted to make all the ballads, he need not care who should make the laws of a nation.

'An Account of a Conversation concerning a Right Regulation of Government for the Good of Mankind. In a Letter to the Marquis of Montrose' (1704)

1 The Scots deserve no pity, if they voluntarily surrender their
united and separate interests to the mercy of an united
Parliament, where the English have so vast a majority . . .
their 45 Scots members may dance round to all eternity, in
this trap of their own making.

*State of the Controversy betwixt
United and Separate Parliaments*
(1706)

Dario Fo 1926–
Italian dramatist

2 *Non si paga, non si paga.*
We won't pay, we won't pay.

title of play (1975; translated by
Lino Pertile in 1978 as 'We Can't
Pay? We Won't Pay!' and
performed in London in 1981 as
'*Can't Pay? Won't Pay!*'); see
Slogans 366:12

Ferdinand Foch 1851–1929
French Marshal

3 My centre is giving way, my right is retreating, situation
excellent, I am attacking.
*message sent during the first Battle of the Marne, September
1914*

R. Recouly *Foch* (1919)

4 This is not a peace treaty, it is an armistice for twenty years.
at the signing of the Treaty of Versailles, 1919

Paul Reynaud *Mémoires* (1963)
vol. 2

Michael Foot 1913–
British Labour politician

5 Think of it! A second Chamber selected by the Whips. A
seraglio of eunuchs.

in the House of Commons, 3
February 1969

6 Disraeli was my favourite Tory. He was an adventurer pure
and simple, or impure and complex. I'm glad to say
Gladstone got the better of him.

in *Observer* 16 March 1975 'Sayings
of the Week'

7 It is not necessary that every time he rises he should give his
famous imitation of a semi-house-trained polecat.
of Norman **Tebbit**

in the House of Commons, 2
March 1978

8 *of David* **Steel**, *Leader of the Liberal Party:*
He's passed from rising hope to elder statesman without any
intervening period whatsoever.

in the House of Commons, 28
March 1979

9 A speech from Ernest Bevin on a major occasion had all the
horrific fascination of a public execution. If the mind was
left immune, eyes and ears and emotions were riveted.

Aneurin Bevan (1962) vol. 1

Gerald Ford 1909–
American Republican statesman; 38th President of the US,
1974–7
on Ford: see **Abzug** 1:4, **Johnson** 203:14, **Morton** 280:4

10 If the Government is big enough to give you everything you
want, it is big enough to take away everything you have.

John F. Parker *If Elected* (1960); a
similar remark has been attributed
to Barry **Goldwater**

11 I am a Ford, not a Lincoln.
on taking the vice-presidential oath, 6 December 1973

in *Washington Post* 7 December
1973

1 Our long national nightmare is over. Our Constitution works; our great Republic is a Government of laws and not of men.
on being sworn in as President in succession to Richard **Nixon**

speech on 9 August 1974

2 I believe that truth is the glue that holds Government together, not only our Government, but civilization itself.
on being sworn in as President

speech on 9 August 1974

Howell Forgy 1908–83
American naval chaplain

3 Praise the Lord and pass the ammunition.
at Pearl Harbor, 7 December 1941, as Forgy moved along a line of sailors passing ammunition by hand to the deck (later the title of a song by Frank Loesser, 1942)

in *New York Times* 1 November 1942

E. M. Forster 1879–1970
English novelist

4 If I had to choose between betraying my country and betraying my friend, I hope I should have the guts to betray my country.

Two Cheers for Democracy (1951) 'What I Believe'

5 So Two cheers for Democracy: one because it admits variety and two because it permits criticism. Two cheers are quite enough: there is no occasion to give three. Only Love the Beloved Republic deserves that.

Two Cheers for Democracy (1951) 'What I Believe' ('Love, the beloved republic' borrowed from Swinburne's poem 'Hertha')

Harry Emerson Fosdick 1878–1969
American Baptist minister

6 I renounce war for its consequences, for the lies it lives on and propagates, for the undying hatred it arouses, for the dictatorships it puts in the place of democracy, for the starvation that stalks after it.

Armistice Day Sermon in New York, 1933, in *The Secret of Victorious Living* (1934)

Charles Foster 1828–1904
American politician

7 Isn't this a billion dollar country?
at the 51st Congress, responding to a Democratic gibe about a 'million dollar Congress'

also attributed to Thomas B. Reed, who reported the exchange in *North American Review* March 1892, vol. 154

George Foster 1847–1931
Canadian politician

8 In these somewhat troublesome days when the great Mother Empire stands splendidly isolated in Europe.

in *Official Report of the Debates of the House of Commons of the Dominion of Canada* (1896) vol. 41, for 16 January 1896; on 22 January 1896; see **Newspaper headlines** 288:5

Allan Fotheringham 1932–
Canadian journalist

1 In the Maritimes, politics is a disease, in Quebec a religion, in Ontario a business, on the Prairies a protest and in British Columbia entertainment.

in 1975; *Last Page First* (1999)

2 Canada is ten independent personalities, united only by a common suspicion of Ottawa.

in *Maclean's* 11 February

3 The voters don't know who he is. And . . . neither does he.
predicting electoral defeat for the Canadian Alliance leader, Stockwell **Day**

26 November 2000, prior to the federal election

Charles Fourier 1772–1837
French social theorist

4 The extension of women's rights is the basic principle of all social progress.

Théorie des Quatre Mouvements (1808) vol. 2

Norman Fowler 1938–
British Conservative politician

5 I have a young family and for the next few years I should like to devote more time to them.
often quoted as 'spend more time with my family'

resignation letter to the Prime Minister, in *Guardian* 4 January 1990; see **Thatcher** 392:1

Caroline Fox d. 1774
English wife of Henry Fox, Lord **Holland**, and mother of Charles James **Fox**

6 That little boy will be a thorn in Charles's side as long as he lives.
*seeing in the young William **Pitt** a prospective rival for her son Charles James **Fox***

attributed

Charles James Fox 1749–1806
English Whig politician
on Fox: see **Gibbon** 156:2, **Holland** 186:7, **Johnson** 205:6, **Shaw-Lefevre** 361:12; see also **Last words** 226:9

7 He [Pitt the Younger] was uniformly of an opinion which, though not a popular one, he was ready to aver, that the right of governing was not property but a trust.
*on **Pitt**'s scheme of Parliamentary Reform, 1785*

J. L. Hammond *Charles James Fox* (1903)

8 How much the greatest event it is that ever happened in the world! and how much the best!
on the fall of the Bastille

letter to Richard Fitzpatrick, 30 July 1789

9 Humanity . . . does not consist in a squeamish ear. It belongs to the mind as well as the nerves, and leads a man to take measures for the prevention of cruelty which the hypocritical cant of humanity contents itself in deploring.

speech in a House of Commons debate on the slave trade, 18 April 1791

10 One feels as if there was something missing in the world—a chasm, a blank that cannot be supplied.
on the death of his rival, William Pitt

Lady Bessborough, letter 23 January 1806, in Countess Granville *Lord Granville Leveson Gower: Private Correspondence 1781–1821* (1916) vol. 2

1 *In the last year of his life Fox's friends suggested that he should accept a peerage:*
I will not close my politics in that foolish way.

in *Dictionary of National Biography* (1917–)

Henry Fox see Holland

Anatole France 1844–1924
French novelist and man of letters

2 In every well-governed state, wealth is a sacred thing; in democracies it is the only sacred thing.

L'île des pingouins (1908)

3 They [the poor] have to labour in the face of the majestic equality of the law, which forbids the rich as well as the poor to sleep under bridges, to beg in the streets, and to steal bread.

Le Lys rouge (1894)

Francis I 1494–1547
French monarch, King from 1515

4 Of all I had, only honour and life have been spared.
letter to his mother following his defeat at Pavia, 1525, usually quoted as 'All is lost, save honour'

in *Collection des Documents Inédits sur l'Histoire de France* (1847) vol. 1; see **Misquotations** 272:1

Anne Frank 1929–45
German-born Jewish diarist

5 I want to go on living even after death!

diary, 4 April 1944

Felix Frankfurter 1882–1965
American judge

6 It is a fair summary of history to say that the safeguards of liberty have been forged in controversies involving not very nice people.

dissenting opinion in *United States v. Rabinowitz* (1950)

Benjamin Franklin 1706–90
American politician, inventor, and scientist
on Franklin: see **Turgot** 402:5

7 Idleness and pride tax with a heavier hand than kings and parliaments. If we can get rid of the former, we may easily bear the latter.
on the Stamp Act

letter 11 July 1765

8 We must indeed all hang together, or, most assuredly, we shall all hang separately.
at the signing of the Declaration of Independence, 4 July 1776 (possibly not original)

P. M. Zall *Ben Franklin* (1980)

9 There never was a good war, or a bad peace.

letter to Josiah Quincy, 11 September 1783

10 I wish the bald eagle had not been chosen as the representative of our country; he is a bird of bad moral character . . . like those among men who live by sharping and robbing, he is generally poor, and often very lousy.
The turkey . . . is a much more respectable bird, and withal a true original native of America.

letter to Sarah Bache, 26 January 1784

1 *on being asked, 'have we got a republic or a monarchy?':*
A republic, if you can keep it.

in conversation, 18 September 1787

2 In this world nothing can be said to be certain, except death and taxes.

letter to Jean Baptiste Le Roy, 13 November 1789; see Daniel Defoe *History of the Devil* (1726) 'Things as certain as death and taxes, can be more firmly believed'

3 George Washington, Commander of the American Armies, who, like Joshua of old, commanded the sun and the moon to stand still, and they obeyed him.
toast given at a dinner at Versailles, when the British minister had proposed a toast to **George III**, *likening him to the sun, and the French minister had likened* **Louis XVI** *to the moon*

attributed

4 They that can give up essential liberty to obtain a little temporary safety deserve neither liberty nor safety.

Historical Review of Pennsylvania (1759)

5 No nation was ever ruined by trade.

Thoughts on Commercial Subjects

Lord Franks 1905–92
British philosopher and administrator

6 The Pentagon, that immense monument to modern man's subservience to the desk.

in *Observer* 30 November 1952

7 *on the composition of such bodies as royal commissions and committees of inquiry:*
There is a fashion in these things and when you are in fashion you are asked to do a lot.

in conversation, 24 January 1977; Peter Hennessy *Whitehall* (1990)

8 A secret in the Oxford sense: you may tell it to only one person at a time.

in *Sunday Telegraph* 30 January 1977

Tommy Franks 1945–
American general

9 This will be a campaign unlike any other in history. A campaign characterized by shock, by surprise, by flexibility, by the employment of precise munitions on a scale never before seen, and by the application of overwhelming force.
encapsulated in the phrase 'shock and awe', originally deriving from a Pentagon briefing document by Harlan Ullman and James P. Wade; see **Ullman** *403:3*

briefing in Qatar, 22 March 2003

Malcolm Fraser 1930–
Australian Liberal statesman; Prime Minister 1975–83

10 He [the Prime Minister] has a dangerous reluctance to consult Cabinet, and an obstinate determination to get his own way.
of John Grey Gorton (1911–2002), when resigning from his administration

speech in the Australian Parliament, March 1971

11 Life is not meant to be easy.

5th Alfred Deakin Lecture, 20 July 1971; see **Shaw** 360:3

Michael Frayn 1933–
British writer

1 To be absolutely honest, what I feel really bad about is that I don't feel worse. That's the ineffectual liberal's problem in a nutshell.

in *Observer* 8 August 1965

Frederick the Great 1712–86
Prussian monarch, King from 1740

2 Drive out prejudices through the door, and they will return through the window.

letter to Voltaire, 19 March 1771

3 My people and I have come to an agreement which satisfies us both. They are to say what they please, and I am to do what I please.
his interpretation of benevolent despotism

attributed

4 Rascals, would you live for ever?
to hesitant Guards at Kolin, 18 June 1757

attributed

Cathy Freeman 1973–
Australian athlete

5 I was so angry because they were denying they had done anything wrong, denying that a whole generation was stolen.
of official response to concerns about the 'stolen generation' of Aboriginal children forcibly removed from their families

interview in *Daily Telegraph* 16 July 2000

E. A. Freeman 1823–92
English historian

6 History is past politics, and politics is present history.

Methods of Historical Study (1886)

John Freeth c.1731–1808
English poet

7 The loss of America what can repay?
New colonies seek for at Botany Bay.

'Botany Bay' in *New London Magazine* (1786)

Milton Friedman 1912–
American economist and exponent of monetarism; policy adviser to President **Reagan** 1981–9

8 There is an invisible hand in politics that operates in the opposite direction to the invisible hand in the market. In politics, individuals who seek to promote only the public good are led by an invisible hand to promote special interests that it was no part of their intention to promote.

Bright Promises, Dismal Performance: An Economist's Protest (1983)

9 Few trends could so thoroughly undermine the very foundations of our free society as the acceptance by corporate officials of a social responsibility other than to make as much money for their stockholders as possible.

Capitalism and Freedom (1962)

10 A society that puts equality—in the sense of equality of outcome—ahead of freedom will end up with neither equality nor freedom.

Free to Choose (1980)

1 The high rate of unemployment among teenagers, and especially black teenagers, is both a scandal and a serious source of social unrest. Yet it is largely a result of minimum wage laws . . . We regard the minimum wage law as one of the most, if not the most, antiblack laws on the statute books.

Free to Choose (1980)

2 There's only one place where inflation is made: that's in Washington.

in 1977; attributed

3 Thank heavens we do not get all of the government that we are made to pay for.

attributed; quoted by Lord Harris in the House of Lords, 24 November 1994

Max Frisch 1911–91
Swiss novelist and dramatist

4 *Jeder Bürger ist strafbar, genaugenommen, von einem gewissen Einkommen an.*
Strictly speaking, every citizen above a certain level of income is guilty of some offence.

The Fire Raisers (1953) sc. 3, translated by Michael Bullock

Robert Frost 1874–1963
American poet

5 I never dared be radical when young
For fear it would make me conservative when old.

'Desert Places' (1936)

6 My apple trees will never get across
And eat the cones under his pines, I tell him.
He only says, 'Good fences make good neighbours.'

'Mending Wall' (1914)

Francis Fukuyama 1952–
American historian

7 What we may be witnessing is not just the end of the Cold War but the end of history as such: that is, the end point of man's ideological evolution and the universalism of Western liberal democracy.

in *Independent* 20 September 1989

J. William Fulbright 1905–95
American politician

8 The Soviet Union has indeed been our greatest menace, not so much because of what it has done, but because of the excuses it has provided us for our failures.

in *Observer* 21 December 1958 'Sayings of the Year'

9 A policy that can be accurately, though perhaps not prudently, defined as one of 'peaceful coexistence'.

speech in the US Senate, 27 March 1964

10 We must dare to think 'unthinkable' thoughts. We must learn to explore all the options and possibilities that confront us in a complex and rapidly changing world. We must learn to welcome and not to fear the voices of dissent. We must dare to think about 'unthinkable things' because when things become unthinkable, thinking stops and action becomes mindless.

speech in the US Senate, 27 March 1964

11 The arrogance of power.

title of book, 1966

Alfred Funke 1869–1941
German writer

1 *Gott strafe England!*
God punish England!

Sword and Myrtle (1914)

David Maxwell Fyfe see Kilmuir

Hugh Gaitskell 1906–63
British Labour politician
on Gaitskell: see **Bevan** 39:2, **Crossman** 107:1

2 The subtle terrorism of words.
in a warning given to his Party, c.1957

Harry Hopkins *The New Look* (1963); attributed

3 There are some of us . . . who will fight and fight and fight again to save the Party we love.
opposing the vote in favour of unilateral disarmament

speech at Labour Party Conference, 5 October 1960

4 It means the end of a thousand years of history.
on a European federation

speech at Labour Party Conference, 3 October 1962

John Kenneth Galbraith 1908–
Canadian-born American economist, US Ambassador to India 1961–3

5 The affluent society.

title of book (1958)

6 The conventional wisdom.
ironic term for 'the beliefs that are at any time assiduously, solemnly and mindlessly traded between the conventionally wise'

The Affluent Society (1958)

7 It is a far, far better thing to have a firm anchor in nonsense than to put out on the troubled seas of thought.

The Affluent Society (1958)

8 In a community where public services have failed to keep abreast of private consumption things are very different. Here, in an atmosphere of private opulence and public squalor, the private goods have full sway.

The Affluent Society (1958)

9 The greater the wealth, the thicker will be the dirt.

The Affluent Society (1958)

10 It is not necessary to advertise food to hungry people, fuel to cold people, or houses to the homeless.

American Capitalism (1952)

11 Trickle-down theory—the less than elegant metaphor that if one feeds the horse enough oats, some will pass through to the road for the sparrows.

The Culture of Contentment (1992)

12 You cannot know the intentions of a government that doesn't know them itself.
'Galbraith's First Law of Intelligence', formulated in early 1960s

A Life in Our Times (1981)

13 The reduction of politics to a spectator sport . . . has been one of the more malign accomplishments of television. Television newsmen are breathless on how the game is being played, largely silent on what the game is all about.

A Life in Our Times (1981)

14 The experience of being disastrously wrong is salutary; no economist should be denied it, and not many are.

A Life in Our Times (1981)

15 In public administration good sense would seem to require the public expectation be kept at the lowest possible level in order to minimize eventual disappointment.

A Life in Our Times (1981)

1 After a lifetime in public office, self-censorship becomes not only automatic but a part of one's personality.

A Life in Our Times (1981)

2 Nothing is so firmly established in Puritan and Presbyterian belief as that people cannot be suffering very much if they are out in healthy fresh air—and also safely out of sight.
of the public view of rural as opposed to urban poverty

A Life in Our Times (1981)

3 Of all the races on earth, the Indians have the most nearly inexhaustible appetite for oratory.

A Life in Our Times (1981)

4 One of the recurrent and dangerous influences on our foreign policy—fear of the political consequences of doing the sensible thing, which in many cases is nothing much at all.

A Life in Our Times (1981)

5 One of the little-celebrated powers of Presidents (and other high government officials) is to listen to their critics with just enough sympathy to ensure their silence.

A Life in Our Times (1981)

6 *of the defeat of Germany in World War Two:*
That they were defeated is conclusive testimony to the inherent inefficiencies of dictatorship, the inherent efficiencies of freedom.

in *Fortune* December 1945

7 [Intellectual torpor is] the disease of opposition parties, for initiative and imagination ordinarily lie with responsibility for action.

letter to Adlai Stevenson, September 1953

8 Politics is not the art of the possible. It consists in choosing between the disastrous and the unpalatable.

letter to President **Kennedy**, 2 March 1962; see **Bismarck** 43:7

9 There are times in politics when you must be on the right side and lose.

attributed, 1968

10 Galbraith's law states that anyone who says he won't resign four times, will.

attributed, 1973

George Galloway 1954–
Scottish politician, expelled from the Labour Party in 2003 and now a member of Respect

11 Sir, I salute your courage, your strength, your indefatigability
*to Saddam **Hussein***

in Baghdad, 1994; quoted in *The Scotsman* 20 October 2003 (online edition)

12 Mr Blair, this is for Iraq.
on winning the Bethnal Green and Bow constituency from Labour for the anti-war coalition Respect

victory speech, 6 May 2005

13 I met Saddam Hussein exactly the same number of times as Donald Rumsfeld met him. The difference is that Donald Rumsfeld met him to sell him guns.
appearing before the US Senate Permanent Subcommittee on Investigations, 17 May 2005

in *Times Online* 23 May 2005 (online edition)

Indira Gandhi 1917–84
Indian stateswoman; Prime Minister 1966–77 and 1980–4

14 Politics is the art of acquiring, holding, and wielding power.

attributed, 1975

15 We do not tilt on either side . . . we walk upright.
when asked by a reporter why India 'always tilted towards the Soviet Union'

in Washington, 1982; Inder Malhotra *Indira Gandhi* (1989)

1 I have lived a long life and I am proud that I spent the whole of my life in the service of my people. I am only proud of this and of nothing else. I shall continue to serve until my last breath and when I die, I can say, that every drop of my blood will invigorate India and strengthen it.

speech, Bhubaneshwar, 30 October 1984 (the night before she was assassinated); *Selected Speeches* (1986) vol. 5

Mahatma Gandhi 1869–1948

Indian statesman
on Gandhi: see **Naidu** 283:9, **Nehru** 285:7

2 What difference does it make to the dead, the orphans and the homeless, whether the mad destruction is wrought under the name of totalitarianism or the holy name of liberty or democracy?

Non-Violence in Peace and War (1942) vol. 1

3 The moment the slave resolves that he will no longer be a slave, his fetters fall. He frees himself and shows the way to others. Freedom and slavery are mental states.

Non-Violence in Peace and War (1949) vol. 2

4 Non-violence is the first article of my faith. It is also the last article of my creed.
speech at Shahi Bag, 18 March 1922, on a charge of sedition

in *Young India* 23 March 1922

5 Please go on. It is my day of silence.
note passed to the British Cabinet Mission at a meeting in 1942

Peter Hennessy *Never Again* (1992)

6 *on being asked what he thought of modern civilization:*
That would be a good idea.
while visiting England in 1930

E. F. Schumacher *Good Work* (1979)

Sonia Gandhi 1946–

Italian-born Indian politician

7 There is no question. It is my inner voice, it is my conscience.
on turning down the post of Prime Minister of India

in *Independent* 19 May 2004

James A. Garfield 1831–81

American Republican statesman; 20th President of the US 1881

8 Fellow-citizens: God reigns, and the Government at Washington lives!
speech on the assassination of President **Lincoln**, *1865*

in *Death of President Garfield* (1881)

9 I am not willing that this discussion should close without any mention of the value of a true teacher. Give me a log hut, with only a simple bench, Mark Hopkins [president of Williams College] on one end and I on the other, and you may have all the buildings, apparatus and libraries without him.

address to Williams College Alumni, New York, 28 December 1871

Giuseppe Garibaldi 1807–82

Italian patriot and military leader

10 Men, I'm getting out of Rome. Anyone who wants to carry on the war against the outsiders, come with me. I can offer you neither honours nor wages; I offer you hunger, thirst, forced marches, battles and death. Anyone who loves his country, follow me.

Giuseppe Guerzoni *Garibaldi* (1882) vol. 1 (not a verbatim record)

John Nance Garner 1868–1967
American Democratic politician; vice-president 1933–41

1 The vice-presidency isn't worth a pitcher of warm piss.

O. C. Fisher *Cactus Jack* (1978)

William Lloyd Garrison 1805–79
American anti-slavery campaigner

2 I am in earnest—I will not equivocate—I will not excuse—I will not retreat a single inch—and I will be heard!

in *The Liberator* 1 January 1831 'Salutatory Address'

3 The compact which exists between the North and the South is 'a covenant with death and an agreement with hell'.

resolution adopted by the Massachusetts Anti-Slavery Society, 27 January 1843

James Louis Garvin 1868–1947
British journalist and editor of the *Observer*

4 He spoke for an hour and put the house in his pocket.
*of F. E. **Smith**'s maiden speech in the House of Commons, 12 May 1906*

attributed

Eric Geddes 1875–1937
British politician and administrator

5 The Germans, if this Government is returned, are going to pay every penny; they are going to be squeezed as a lemon is squeezed—until the pips squeak.

speech at Cambridge, 10 December 1918

Martha Gellhorn 1908–98
American journalist

6 *of the defeat of the Spanish Republic:*
I daresay we all became more competent press tourists because of it, since we never again cared so much. You can only love one war; afterward, I suppose, you do your duty.

The Honeyed Peace (1953)

Jean Genet 1910–86
French novelist, poet, and dramatist

7 What we need is hatred. From it our ideas are born.

The Blacks (1959); epigraph

8 Are you there . . . Africa of the millions of royal slaves, deported Africa, drifting continent, are you there? Slowly you vanish, you withdraw into the past, into the tales of castaways, colonial museums, the works of scholars.

The Blacks (1959)

Genghis Khan (Temujin) 1162–1227
Mongol ruler, who took the name Genghis Khan ('ruler of all') in 1206

9 Happiness lies in conquering one's enemies, in driving them in front of oneself, in taking their property, in savouring their despair, in outraging their wives and daughters.

Witold Rodzinski *The Walled Kingdom: A History of China* (1979)

George III 1738–1820

British monarch, King of Great Britain and Ireland from 1760
on George III: see **Walpole** 409:7

1 Born and educated in this country, I glory in the name of Briton.

The King's Speech on Opening the Session 18 November 1760

2 When he has wearied me for two hours he looks at his watch, to see if he may not tire me for an hour more.
of George **Grenville**

in 1765; Horace Walpole *The Reign of George III* (1845)

3 *of America:*
Knavery seems to be so much the striking feature of its inhabitants that it may not in the end be an evil that they become aliens to this kingdom.

draft of letter to Lord Shelburne, 10 November 1782

George IV 1762–1830

British monarch, King of Great Britain and Ireland from 1820

4 PRINCE OF WALES: True blue and Mrs Crewe.
MRS CREWE: Buff and blue and all of you.
toast proposed by George IV when Prince of Wales to Mrs Crewe, in honour of her support for the Whigs and Charles James Fox in the Westminster election of 1784 (buff and blue were the Whig colours)

at a dinner at Carlton House, May 1784; Amanda Foreman *Georgiana Duchess of Devonshire* (1998)

George V 1865–1936

British monarch, King of Great Britain and Ireland from 1910
see also **Last words** 226:8

5 I venture to allude to the impression which seemed generally to prevail among their brethren across the seas, that the Old Country must wake up if she intends to maintain her old position of pre-eminence in her Colonial trade against foreign competitors.

speech at Guildhall, 5 December 1901 (the speech was reprinted in 1911 with the title 'Wake up, England')

6 I pray that my coming to Ireland today may prove to be the first step towards an end of strife among her people, whatever their race or creed. In that hope I appeal to all Irishmen to pause, to stretch out the hand of forbearance and conciliation, to forgive and forget, and to join with me in making for the land they love a new era of peace, contentment and goodwill.

speech to the new Ulster Parliament at Stormont, 22 June 1921; Kenneth Rose *King George V* (1983)

7 I have many times asked myself whether there can be more potent advocates of peace upon earth through the years to come than this massed multitude of silent witnesses to the desolation of war.
message read at Terlincthun Cemetery, Boulogne, 13 May 1922

in *The Times* 15 May 1922

8 You have kept up the dignity of the office without using it to give you dignity.
to the outgoing Prime Minister, Ramsay **MacDonald**

Ramsay MacDonald diary 7 June 1934

9 The complex forms and balanced spirit of our constitution were not the discovery of a single era, still less of a single party or of a single person. They are the slow accretion of centuries, the outcome of patience, tradition and experience.
the words of G. M. Trevelyan in the King's Silver Jubilee address to Parliament, 1935

David Cannadine *G. M. Trevelyan: a Life in History* (1992)

1 I will not have another war. *I will not.* The last one was none of my doing and if there is another one and we are threatened with being brought into it, I will go to Trafalgar Square and wave a red flag myself sooner than allow this country to be brought in.

*c.*1935, in Andrew Roberts *Eminent Churchillians* (1994)

2 *in conversation with Anthony* **Eden**, *23 December 1935, following Samuel Hoare's resignation as Foreign Secretary:*
I said to your predecessor: 'You know what they're all saying, no more coals to Newcastle, no more Hoares to Paris.' The fellow didn't even laugh.

Earl of Avon *Facing the Dictators* (1962)

3 After I am dead, the boy will ruin himself in twelve months.
on his son, the future **Edward VIII**

Keith Middlemas and John Barnes *Baldwin* (1969)

4 *on H. G. Wells's comment on 'an alien and uninspiring court':*
I may be uninspiring, but I'll be damned if I'm an alien!

Sarah Bradford *George VI* (1989); attributed

5 My father was frightened of his mother; I was frightened of my father, and I am damned well going to see to it that my children are frightened of me.

attributed in Randolph S. Churchill *Lord Derby* (1959), but almost certainly apocryphal; see Kenneth Rose *George V* (1983)

George VI 1895–1952

British monarch, King of Great Britain and Northern Ireland from 1936

6 Personally I feel happier now that we have no allies to be polite to and to pamper.
to Queen Mary, 27 June 1940

John Wheeler-Bennett *King George VI* (1958)

7 ATTLEE: I've won the election.
GEORGE VI: I know. I heard it on the Six O'Clock News.
first exchange between the King and his newly elected Labour Prime Minister, 26 July 1945; perhaps apocryphal

Peter Hennessy *Never Again* (1992)

8 Well the Prime Minister has had a very difficult time, I'm sure. What I say is 'Thank God for the Civil Service.'
shortly after Labour's election victory

Hugh Dalton *Political Diary* (1986) 28 July 1945

9 HARRY TRUMAN: You've had a revolution.
GEORGE VI: Oh no! we don't have those here.
during President **Truman**'s *visit to Britain just after Labour's election victory.*

Hugh Dalton *Political Diary* (1986) 28 July 1945

10 Everything is going nowadays. Before long, I shall have to go myself.
on hearing, c.1949, that the Sackville-West family home, Knole Park, was to be sold to the National Trust

Andrew Roberts *Eminent Churchillians* (1994)

Geronimo c.1829–1909

American Apache chief

11 Once I moved about like the wind. Now I surrender to you and that is all.

surrendering to General Crook, 25 March 1886; Dee Brown *Bury My Heart at Wounded Knee* (1970) ch. 17

Edward Gibbon 1737–94

English historian

1 The division of Europe into a number of independent states connected, however, with each other, by the general resemblance of religion, language, and manners, is productive of the most beneficial consequences to the liberty of mankind.

The Decline and Fall of the Roman Empire (1776–88)

2 In elective monarchies, the vacancy of the throne is a moment big with danger and mischief.

The Decline and Fall of the Roman Empire (1776–88)

3 The various modes of worship, which prevailed in the Roman world, were all considered by the people as equally true; by the philosopher, as equally false; and by the magistrate, as equally useful. And thus toleration produced not only mutual indulgence, but even religious concord.

The Decline and Fall of the Roman Empire (1776–88)

4 The principles of a free constitution are irrecoverably lost, when the legislative power is nominated by the executive.

The Decline and Fall of the Roman Empire (1776–88)

5 The ascent to greatness, however steep and dangerous, may entertain an active spirit with the consciousness and exercise of its own powers; but the possession of a throne could never yet afford a lasting satisfaction to an ambitious mind.

The Decline and Fall of the Roman Empire (1776–88)

6 History . . . is, indeed, little more than the register of the crimes, follies, and misfortunes of mankind.

The Decline and Fall of the Roman Empire (1776–88); see **Voltaire** 407:7

7 In every age and country, the wiser, or at least the stronger, of the two sexes, has usurped the powers of the state, and confined the other to the cares and pleasures of domestic life.

The Decline and Fall of the Roman Empire (1776–88)

8 According to the reasoning of tyrants, those who have been esteemed worthy of the throne deserve death, and those who deliberate have already rebelled.

The Decline and Fall of the Roman Empire (1776–88)

9 All taxes must, at last, fall upon agriculture.

quoting Artaxerxes, in *The Decline and Fall of the Roman Empire* (1776–88) ch. 8

10 Whenever the offence inspires less horror than the punishment, the rigour of penal law is obliged to give way to the common feelings of mankind.

The Decline and Fall of the Roman Empire (1776–88) ch. 14

11 Corruption, the most infallible symptom of constitutional liberty.

The Decline and Fall of the Roman Empire (1776–88)

12 In every deed of mischief he had a heart to resolve, a head to contrive, and a hand to execute.
of Comnenus

The Decline and Fall of the Roman Empire (1776–88)

13 Our sympathy is cold to the relation of distant misery.

The Decline and Fall of the Roman Empire (1776–88)

14 Persuasion is the resource of the feeble; and the feeble can seldom persuade.

The Decline and Fall of the Roman Empire (1776–88)

15 All that is human must retrograde if it does not advance.

The Decline and Fall of the Roman Empire (1776–88)

16 The satirist may laugh, the philosopher may preach, but Reason herself will respect the prejudices and habits which have been consecrated by the experience of mankind.

Memoirs of My Life (1796)

1 I admire his eloquence, I approve his politics, I adore his chivalry, and I can even forgive his superstition.
of Edmund **Burke**

letter to Lord Sheffield, 5 February 1791

2 Let him do what he will I must love the dog.
of Charles James **Fox**

letter to Lord Sheffield, 6 January 1793

Kahlil Gibran 1883–1931

Syrian writer and painter

3 Are you a politician who says to himself: 'I will use my country for my own benefit'? . . . Or are you a devoted patriot, who whispers in the ear of his inner self: 'I love to serve my country as a faithful servant.'

The New Frontier (1931); see **Kennedy** 212:8

W. S. Gilbert 1836–1911

English writer of comic and satirical verse

4 All shall equal be.
The Earl, the Marquis, and the Dook,
The Groom, the Butler, and the Cook,
The Aristocrat who banks with Coutts,
The Aristocrat who cleans the boots.

The Gondoliers (1889)

5 When every one is somebodee,
Then no one's anybody.

The Gondoliers (1889) act 2

6 I always voted at my party's call,
And I never thought of thinking for myself at all.

HMS Pinafore (1878)

7 I often think it's comical
How Nature always does contrive
That every boy and every gal,
That's born into the world alive,
Is either a little Liberal,
Or else a little Conservative!

Iolanthe (1882)

8 The House of Peers, throughout the war,
Did nothing in particular,
And did it very well.

Iolanthe (1882)

9 When in that House MPs divide,
If they've a brain and cerebellum too,
They have to leave that brain outside,
And vote just as their leaders tell 'em to.

Iolanthe (1882)

10 The prospect of a lot
Of dull MPs in close proximity,
All thinking for themselves is what
No man can face with equanimity.

Iolanthe (1882)

11 The idiot who praises, with enthusiastic tone,
All centuries but this, and every country but his own.

The Mikado (1885)

12 No Englishman unmoved that statement hears,
Because, with all our faults, we love our House of Peers.

The Pirates of Penzance (1879)

Andrew Gilligan 1968–
British journalist

1 I have spoken to a British official who was involved in the preparation of the dossier, and he told me that until the week before it was published, the draft dossier produced by the intelligence services added little to what was already publicly known. He said: [Voiceover]: 'It was transformed in the week before it was published, to make it sexier'.

BBC Radio 4 Today programme, 29 May 2003; in Guardian 27 June 2003

Ian Gilmour 1926–
British Conservative politician

2 Unfortunately monetarism, like Marxism, suffered the only fate that for a theory is worse than death: it was put into practice.

Dancing with Dogma (1992)

Newton Gingrich 1943–
American Republican politician; Speaker of the House of Representatives from 1995

3 No society can survive, no civilization can survive, with 12-year-olds having babies, with 15-year-olds killing each other, with 17-year-olds dying of Aids, with 18-year-olds getting diplomas they can't read.
  in December 1994, after the Republican electoral victory

in The Times 9 February 1995

4 One of the greatest intellectual failures of the welfare state is the penchant for sacrifice, so long as the only people being asked to sacrifice are working, tax-paying Americans.

in USA Today 16 January 1995

George Gipp 1895–1920
American footballer

5 Win just one for the Gipper.

*catch-phrase later associated with Ronald **Reagan**, who uttered the immortal words in the 1940 film Knute Rockne, All American*

Rudy Giuliani 1944–
American Republican politician, Mayor of New York 1993–2001

6 Freedom is about the willingness of every single human being to cede to lawful authority a great deal of discretion about what you do, and how you do it.

attributed, in Independent 10 July 1999

7 Politics comes at least second, maybe third, maybe fourth, somewhere else. It'll all work itself out some way politically.
  announcing that he and his wife were separating

in Observer 14 May 2000

8 The number of casualties will be more than any of us can bear.
  in the aftermath of the terrorist attacks which destroyed the World Trade Center in New York, and damaged the Pentagon, 11 September 2001

in The Times 12 September 2001

Catherine Gladstone 1812–1900
British wife of William Ewart **Gladstone**

1 *to her husband:*
Oh, William dear, if you weren't such a great man you
would be a terrible bore.

Roy Jenkins *Gladstone* (1995)

William Ewart Gladstone 1809–98
British Liberal statesman; Prime Minister, 1868–74, 1880–5,
1886, 1892–4
on Gladstone: see **Bagehot** 24:9, **Churchill** 85:11, **Churchill** 86:1,
Churchill 91:9, **Disraeli** 121:12, **Disraeli** 121:17, **Foot** 142:6,
Hennessy 180:2, **Labouchere** 223:4, **Macaulay** 246:6,
Salisbury 344:4, **Victoria** 406:4, **Victoria** 406:7

2 Ireland, Ireland! that cloud in the west, that coming storm.

letter to his wife, 12 October 1845

3 This is the negation of God erected into a system of
Government.

*A Letter to the Earl of Aberdeen on
the State Prosecutions of the
Neapolitan Government* (1851)

4 Finance is, as it were, the stomach of the country, from
which all the other organs take their tone.

article on finance, 1858, in H. C. G.
Matthew *Gladstone 1809–1874*
(1986)

5 Your business is not to govern the country but it is, if you
think fit, to call to account those who do govern it.

speech to the House of Commons,
29 January 1869

6 I am come among you 'unmuzzled'.
after his parliamentary defeat at Oxford University

speech in Manchester, 18 July
1865

7 You cannot fight against the future. Time is on our side.
on the Reform Bill

speech, House of Commons, 27
April 1866

8 My mission is to pacify Ireland.
*on receiving the news that he was to form his first cabinet, 1
December 1868*

H. C. G. Matthew *Gladstone
1809–1874* (1986)

9 Swimming for his life, a man does not see much of the
country through which the river winds.

diary, 31 December 1868

10 We have been borne down in a torrent of gin and beer.

letter to his brother, 6 February
1874

11 Human justice is ever lagging after wrong, as the prayers in
Homer came limping after sin.

in *Contemporary Review* December
1876

12 The love of freedom itself is hardly stronger in England than
the love of aristocracy.

in *Nineteenth Century* 1877

13 Let the Turks now carry away their abuses in the only
possible manner, namely by carrying off themselves . . . one
and all, bag and baggage, shall I hope clear out from the
province they have desolated and profaned.

*Bulgarian Horrors and the Question
of the East* (1876)

14 [The British Constitution] presumes more boldly than any
other the good sense and the good faith of those who work
it.

Gleanings of Past Years (1879)
vol. 1

15 [An] Established Clergy will always be a Tory Corps
d'Armée.

letter to Bishop Goodwin, 8
September 1881

1 To the actual, as distinct from the reported, strength of the Empire, India adds nothing. She immensely adds to the responsibility of Government.

H. C. G. Matthew *Gladstone 1875–1898* (1995)

2 There never was a Churchill from John of Marlborough down that had either morals or principles.

in conversation in 1882, recorded by Captain R. V. Briscoe; R. F. Foster *Lord Randolph Churchill* (1981)

3 I would tell them of my own intention to keep my counsel . . . and I will venture to recommend them, as an old Parliamentary hand, to do the same.

in the House of Commons, 21 January 1886

4 This, if I understand it, is one of those golden moments of our history, one of those opportunities which may come and may go, but which rarely returns.
on the Second Reading of the Home Rule Bill

in the House of Commons, 7 June 1886

5 I will venture to say, that upon the one great class of subjects, the largest and the most weighty of them all, where the leading and determining considerations that ought to lead to a conclusion are truth, justice, and humanity—upon these, gentlemen, all the world over, I will back the masses against the classes.

speech in Liverpool, 28 June 1886

6 One prayer absorbs all others: Ireland, Ireland, Ireland.

diary, 10 April 1887

7 Welsh nationality is as great a reality as English nationality.

speech at Swansea, 4 June 1887

8 The blubbering Cabinet.
of the colleagues who wept at his final Cabinet meeting

diary, 1 March 1894; note

9 What that Sicilian mule was to me, I have been to the Queen.
of a mule on which Gladstone rode, which he 'could neither love nor like', although it had rendered him 'much valuable service'

memorandum, 20 March 1894

10 Former Prime Ministers are like great rafts floating untethered in a harbour.

Roy Jenkins *Gladstone* (1995)

11 I absorb the vapour and return it as a flood.
on public speaking

Lord Riddell *Some Things That Matter* (1927 ed.)

12 I am sorry to say that I have a long speech fermenting in me, and I feel as a loaf might in the oven.

Roy Jenkins *Gladstone* (1995)

13 It is not a Life at all. It is a Reticence, in three volumes.
on J. W. Cross's Life of George Eliot

E. F. Benson *As We Were* (1930)

14 [Money should] fructify in the pockets of the people.

H. G. C. Matthew *Gladstone 1809–1874* (1986)

15 There is scarcely a single moral action of a single man of which other men can have such a knowledge, in its ultimate grounds, its surrounding incidents, and the real determining cause of its merits, as to warrant their pronouncing a conclusive judgement upon it.

H. C. G. Matthew *Gladstone 1875–1898* (1995)

16 We are bound to lose Ireland in consequence of years of cruelty, stupidity and misgovernment and I would rather lose her as a friend than as a foe.

Margot Asquith *More Memories* (1933)

Thomas Glascock

American politician

1 *when General Thomas Glascock of Georgia took his seat in the US Senate, a mutual friend expressed the wish to introduce him to Henry **Clay** of Virginia:*
No, sir! I am his adversary, and choose not to subject myself to his fascination.

Robert V. Remini *Henry Clay* (1991)

David Glencross 1936–

British television executive

2 It is unlikely that the government reaches for a revolver when it hears the word culture. The more likely response is to search for a dictionary.

Royal Television Society conference on the future of television, 26–27 November 1988; see **Johst** 205:10

Joseph Goebbels 1897–1945

German Nazi leader

3 We can manage without butter but not, for example, without guns. If we are attacked we can only defend ourselves with guns not with butter.

speech in Berlin, 17 January 1936; see **Goering** 160:5

4 Making noise is an effective means of opposition.

Ernest K. Bramsted *Goebbels and National Socialist Propaganda 1925–45* (1965)

Hermann Goering 1893–1946

German Nazi leader

5 We have no butter . . . but I ask you—would you rather have butter or guns? . . . preparedness makes us powerful. Butter merely makes us fat.

speech at Hamburg, 1936; W. Frischauer *Goering* (1951); see **Goebbels** 160:3

6 I herewith commission you to carry out all preparations with regard to . . . a *total solution* of the Jewish question in those territories of Europe which are under German influence.
instructions to Heydrich, 31 July 1941

W. L. Shirer *The Rise and Fall of the Third Reich* (1962)

Nikolai Gogol 1809–52

Russian writer

7 [Are not] you too, Russia, speeding along like a spirited *troika* that nothing can overtake? . . . Everything on earth is flying past, and looking askance, other nations and states draw aside and make way.

Dead Souls (1842)

Isaac Goldberg 1887–1938

8 Diplomacy is to do and say
The nastiest thing in the nicest way.

The Reflex October 1927

Ludwig Max Goldberger 1848–1913

9 America, the land of unlimited possibilities.

Land of Unlimited Possibilities: Observations on Economic Life in the United States of America (1903)

William Golding 1911–93

English novelist

1 Anyone who moved through those years without understanding that man produces evil as a bee produces honey, must have been blind or wrong in the head.
of the Second World War

The Hot Gates (1965) 'Fable'

Emma Goldman 1869–1940

American anarchist

2 Anarchism, then, really, stands for the liberation of the human mind from the dominion of religion; the liberation of the human body from the dominion of property; liberation from the shackles and restraints of government.

Anarchism and Other Essays (1910)

Oliver Goldsmith 1728–74

Irish writer, poet, and dramatist

3 Ill fares the land, to hast'ning ills a prey,
Where wealth accumulates, and men decay;
Princes and lords may flourish, or may fade;
A breath can make them, as a breath has made;
But a bold peasantry, their country's pride,
When once destroyed, can never be supplied.
A time there was, ere England's griefs began,
When every rood of ground maintained its man;
For him light labour spread her wholesome store,
Just gave what life required, but gave no more;
His best companions, innocence and health;
And his best riches, ignorance of wealth.

The Deserted Village (1770)

4   How wide the limits stand
Between a splendid and a happy land.

The Deserted Village (1770)

5 Such is the patriot's boast, where'er we roam,
His first, best country ever is, at home.

The Traveller (1764)

6 Laws grind the poor, and rich men rule the law.

The Traveller (1764)

7 How small, of all that human hearts endure,
That part which laws or kings can cause or cure!

The Traveller (1764); see **Johnson** 204:5

Barry Goldwater 1909–98

American Republican politician

8 I would remind you that extremism in the defence of liberty is no vice! And let me remind you also that moderation in the pursuit of justice is no virtue!
speech accepting the presidential nomination, 16 July 1964

in *New York Times* 17 July 1964

Maud Gonne 1867–1953

Irish nationalist and actress

9 The Famine Queen.
of Queen Victoria

in *L'Irlande Libre* 1900

Alberto Gonzales 1955–

American lawyer, White House Counsel 2001–5 and US Attorney General since 2005

1 The nature of the new war [against terrorism] places a high premium on other factors, such as the ability to quickly obtain information from captured terrorists and their sponsors in order to avoid further atrocities or war crimes . . . In my judgment, this new paradigm renders obsolete Geneva's strict limitations on questioning of enemy prisoners and renders quaint some of its provisions requiring that captured enemy be afforded such things as commissary privileges, scrip (i.e. advances of monthly pay), athletic uniforms and scientific instruments.

memorandum, 25 January 2002

Amy Goodman 1957–

American journalist

2 Go to where the silence is and say something.
accepting an award from Columbia University for her coverage of the 1991 massacre in East Timor by Indonesian troops

in *Columbia Journalism Review* March/April 1994

Richard Goodwin 1931–

3 People come to Washington believing it's the centre of power. I know I did. It was only much later that I learned that Washington is a steering wheel that's not connected to the engine.

Peter McWilliams *Ain't Nobody's Business If You Do* (1993)

Mikhail Sergeevich Gorbachev 1931–

Soviet statesman; General Secretary of the Communist Party of the USSR 1985–91 and President 1988–91
on Gorbachev: see **Gromyko** 167:6, **Thatcher** 391:7

4 The guilt of Stalin and his immediate entourage before the Party and the people for the mass repressions and lawlessness they committed is enormous and unforgivable.

speech on the seventieth anniversary of the Russian Revolution, 2 November 1987

5 The idea of restructuring [*perestroika*] . . . combines continuity and innovation, the historical experience of Bolshevism and the contemporaneity of socialism.

speech on the seventieth anniversary of the Russian Revolution, 2 November 1987

6 After leaving the Kremlin . . . my conscience was clear. The promise I gave to the people when I started the process of perestroika was kept: I gave them freedom.

Memoirs (1995)

Albert Gore Jnr. 1948–

American Democratic politician, Vice-President 1993–2001; presidential candidate 2000

7 That year, we voted with our hearts to make history by tearing down a mighty wall of division. We made history . . . We will tear down an old wall of division once again.
comparing the Democrats' selection of the Catholic John F. **Kennedy** *in the presidential campaign of 1960 with his own choice of Joseph* **Lieberman**, *an Orthodox Jew, as his running mate*

in *Seattle Times* 9 August 2000

1 I am Al Gore, and I used to be the next president of the United States of America.
addressing Bocconi University in Milan

in *Newsweek* 19 March 2001; see **Carter** 342:6

Maxim Gorky 1868–1936
Russian writer and revolutionary

2 The proletarian state must bring up thousands of excellent 'mechanics of culture', 'engineers of the soul'.

speech at the Writers' Congress 1934; see **Kennedy** 213:7, **Stalin** 378:6

George Joachim, Lord Goschen 1831–1907
British Liberal Unionist politician
on Goschen: see **Churchill** 86:4

3 I have the courage of my opinions, but I have not the temerity to give a political blank cheque to Lord Salisbury.

in the House of Commons, 19 February 1884

Philip Gould 1950–
British Labour Party strategist

4 The New Labour brand has been badly contaminated. It is the object of constant criticism and, even worse, ridicule.

internal memo, May 2000, leaked to the press in July; text printed in *Guardian* 20 July 2000

Ernest Gowers 1880–1966
British public servant

5 It is not easy nowadays to remember anything so contrary to all appearances as that officials are the servants of the public; and the official must try not to foster the illusion that it is the other way round.

Plain Words (1948)

D. M. Graham 1911–99
British broadcaster

6 That this House will in no circumstances fight for its King and Country.
motion for a debate at the Oxford Union, 9 February 1933 (passed by 275 votes to 153)

motion worded by Graham when Librarian of the Oxford Union

James Graham see **Montrose**

Phil Gramm 1942–
American Republican politician

7 Balancing the budget is like going to heaven. Everybody wants to do it, but nobody wants to do what you have to do to get there.

in a television interview, 16 September 1990

8 I did not come to Washington to be loved, and I have not been disappointed.

Michael Barone and Grant Ujifusa *The American Political Almanac* 1994

Bernie Grant 1944–2000
British Labour politician

1 The police were to blame for what happened on Sunday night and what they got was a bloody good hiding.
after the Broadwater Farm riots in which a policeman was killed

as leader of Haringey Council outside Tottenham Town Hall, 8 October 1985

Ulysses S. Grant 1822–85
American Unionist general and statesman; 18th President of the US 1869–77
on Grant: see **Sherman** 363:7

2 I purpose to fight it out on this line, if it takes all summer.
dispatch to Washington, from headquarters in the field, 11 May 1864

P. C. Headley *The Life and Campaigns of General U. S. Grant* (1869)

3 The war is over—the rebels are our countrymen again.
preventing his men from cheering after **Lee**'s *surrender at Appomattox*

on 9 April 1865

4 Let us have peace.
letter to General Joseph R. Hawkey, 29 May 1868, accepting the presidential nomination

P. C. Headley *The Life and Campaigns of General U. S. Grant* (1869)

5 I know no method to secure the repeal of bad or obnoxious laws so effective as their stringent execution.

inaugural address, 4 March 1869

6 Leave the matter of religion to the family altar, the church, and the private school, supported entirely by private contributions. Keep the church and state forever separate.

speech at Des Moines, Iowa, 1875

7 Labour disgraces no man; unfortunately you occasionally find men disgrace labour.

speech at Midland International Arbitration Union, Birmingham, England, 1877

Günter Grass 1927–
German novelist, poet, and dramatist

8 The citizen's first duty is unrest.

The Citizen's First Duty address delivered 1967; in *Speak Out!* (1968)

9 In those days, when every male who could stand half-way erect was being shipped to Verdun to undergo a radical change of posture from the vertical to the eternal horizontal.

The Tin Drum (1959) bk. 1 'Moth and Light Bulb', translated by Ralph Manheim

Henry Grattan 1746–1820
Irish nationalist leader

10 The thing he proposes to buy is what cannot be sold—liberty.
speech in the Irish Parliament against the proposed union, 16 January 1800

in *Dictionary of National Biography*

Frank Graves
Canadian pollster

11 It is like sleeping with an elephant who is an insomniac.
on relations between Canada and the US; see **Trudeau** 400:11

in *Guardian* 1 November 2004

John Chipman Gray 1839–1915

American lawyer

1 Dirt is only matter out of place; and what is a blot on the escutcheon of the Common Law may be a jewel in the crown of the Social Republic.

Restraints on the Alienation of Property (2nd ed., 1895) preface

Muriel Gray 1959–

Scottish writer and broadcaster

2 Of course I want political autonomy but not cultural autonomy. You just have to watch the Scottish Baftas to want to kill yourself.
    explaining her preference for devolution rather than full independence

in *Scotland on Sunday* 14 January 1996

Patrick, Lord Gray d. 1612

3 A dead woman bites not.
    *oral tradition, Gray being said to have pressed hard for the execution of **Mary** Queen of Scots in 1587, with the words 'Mortua non mordet [Being dead, she will bite no more]'*

A. Darcy's 1625 translation of William Camden's *Annals of the Reign of Queen Elizabeth* (1615) vol. 1

Thomas Gray 1716–71

English poet

4 The boast of heraldry, the pomp of pow'r,
    And all that beauty, all that wealth e'er gave,
    Awaits alike th' inevitable hour,
    The paths of glory lead but to the grave.

Elegy Written in a Country Churchyard (1751)

5 Some village-Hampden, that with dauntless breast
    The little tyrant of his fields withstood;
    Some mute inglorious Milton here may rest,
    Some Cromwell guiltless of his country's blood.

Elegy Written in a Country Churchyard (1751)

Th'applause of list'ning senates to command
    The threats of pain and ruin to despise,
    To scatter plenty o'er a smiling land,
    And read their history in a nations eyes,

Their lot forbad: nor circumscribed alone
    Their growing virtues, but their crimes confined;
    Forbad to wade through slaughter to a throne,
    And shut the gates of mercy on mankind.

Horace Greeley 1811–72

American founder and editor of the *New York Tribune*

6 The illusion that times that were are better than those that are, has probably pervaded all ages.

The American Conflict (1864-6)

7 I never said all Democrats were saloon keepers. What I said was that all saloon keepers were Democrats.

attributed

Pauline Green 1948–

British socialist politician, leader of the Socialist Group in the European Parliament

8 The Commission has an established culture that is secretive and authoritarian.

in *Daily Mail* 17 March 1999

Alan Greenspan 1926–

American economist

1 How do we know when irrational exuberance has unduly escalated asset values?

speech in Washington, 5 December 1996

2 An infectious greed seemed to grip much of our business community.
   of the late 1990s

in New York Times 17 July 2002 (online edition)

3 The free lunch has still to be invented.

in Independent 7 May 2004

Pope Gregory VII see Last words 226:12

Dick Gregory 1932–

American comedian

4 You gotta say this for the white race—its self-confidence knows no bounds. Who else could go to a small island in the South Pacific where there's no poverty, no crime, no unemployment, no war and no worry—and call it a 'primitive society'?

From the Back of the Bus (1962)

George Grenville 1712–70

British Whig statesman; Prime Minister 1763–5
on Grenville: see **George III** 153:2, **Walpole** 409:6

5 A wise government knows how to enforce with temper, or to conciliate with dignity.
   speaking against the expulsion of John **Wilkes**

in the House of Commons, 3 February 1769

Lord Grey of Fallodon 1862–1933

British Liberal politician

6 The lamps are going out all over Europe; we shall not see them lit again in our lifetime.
   on the eve of the First World War

25 Years (1925) vol. 2

Arthur Griffith 1871–1922

Irish statesman

7 What I have signed I will stand by, in the belief that the end of the conflict of centuries is at hand.

statement to Dáil Éireann before the debate on the Treaty, December 1921

8 We have brought back the flag; we have brought back the evacuation of Ireland after 700 years by British troops and the formation of an Irish army. We have brought back to Ireland her full rights.

when moving acceptance of the Treaty in the Dáil, December 1921

Roy Griffiths

9 If Florence Nightingale were carrying her lamp through the corridors of the NHS today she would almost certainly be searching for the people in charge.

in Report of the NHS Management Inquiry, DHSS, 1983

John Grigg 1924–2001

British writer and journalist, who as Lord Altrincham disclaimed
his hereditary title in 1963

1 The personality conveyed by the utterances which are put
into her mouth is that of a priggish schoolgirl, captain of the
hockey team, a prefect, and a recent candidate for
confirmation. It is not thus that she will be able to come into
her own as an independent and distinctive character.
  of Queen **Elizabeth II**

in *National and English Review*
August 1958

2 Lloyd George would have a better rating in British
mythology if he had shared the fate of Abraham Lincoln.

attributed, 1963

3 Politicians are exiles from the normal, private world.

attributed, 1964

Joseph ('Jo') Grimond 1913–93

British Liberal politician, Leader of the Liberal Party 1956–67

4 In bygone days, commanders were taught that when in
doubt, they should march their troops towards the sound of
gunfire. I intend to march my troops towards the sound of
gunfire.

speech to the Liberal Party
Assembly, 14 September 1963

5 *on the chance of a pact with the Labour Government:*
Our teeth are in the real meat.

speech to the Liberal Party
Assembly, 1965

Andrei Gromyko 1909–89

Soviet statesman; President of the USSR 1985–8

6 Comrades, this man has a nice smile, but he's got iron teeth.
  of Mikhail **Gorbachev**

speech to Soviet Communist Party
Central Committee, 11 March
1985

Philip Guedalla 1889–1944

British historian and biographer

7 *of the Admiralty committee to examine inventions:*
There they sit, like inverted Micawbers, waiting for
something to turn down.

in a speech at the Oxford Union,
1912; a similar comment has also
been attributed to Winston
Churchill of Treasury staff
(Anthony Sampson *The Anatomy of
Britain Today*)

8 Don't shoot till you see the stripes on their ties.

attributed

Ernesto ('Che') Guevara 1928–67

Argentinian revolutionary and guerrilla leader

9 The Revolution is made by man, but man must forge his
revolutionary spirit from day to day.

Socialism and Man in Cuba (1968)

Nell Gwyn 1650–87

English actress and courtesan

10 Pray, good people, be civil. I am the Protestant whore.
  at Oxford, during the Popish Terror, 1681

B. Bevan *Nell Gwyn* (1969)

William Hague 1961-

British Conservative politician; Leader of the Conservative Party
1997–2001
on Hague: see **Heseltine** 130:7, **Kinnock** 219:2

1 Feather-bedding, pocket-lining, money-grabbing cronies.
   during the debate on lobbyists' influence and 'cronyism'

in the House of Commons, 8 July
1998

2 Let me take you on a journey to a foreign land—to Britain
after a second term of Tony Blair.

speech to Conservative Party
spring conference, Harrogate, 4
March 2001

Earl Haig 1861–1928

British general, Commander in France, 1915–18

3 A very weak-minded fellow I am afraid, and, like the feather
pillow, bears the marks of the last person who has sat on
him!
   *describing the 17th Earl of Derby, in a letter to Lady Haig, 14
January 1918*

R. Blake *Private Papers of Douglas
Haig* (1952)

4 Every position must be held to the last man: there must be
no retirement. With our backs to the wall, and believing in
the justice of our cause, each one of us must fight on to the
end.
   order to British troops, 12 April 1918

A. Duff Cooper *Haig* (1936) vol. 2

Lord Hailsham 1907–2001

British Conservative politician

5 A great party is not to be brought down because of a squalid
affair between a woman of easy virtue and a proved liar.
   on the Profumo affair

in a television interview, 13 June
1963; in *The Times* 14 June 1963

6 I believe there is a golden thread which alone gives meaning
to the political history of the West, from Marathon to
Alamein, from Solon to Winston Churchill and after. This I
chose to call the doctrine of liberty under the law.

in 1975; Anthony Sampson *The
Changing Anatomy of Britain* (1982)

7 The elective dictatorship.
   of the British Constitution

title of the Dimbleby Lecture, 19
October 1976

8 In a confrontation with the politics of power, the soft centre
has always melted away.

in October 1981; Anthony
Sampson *The Changing Anatomy of
Britain* (1982)

9 *of Denis* **Healey**:
A piratical old bruiser with a first-class mind and very bad
manners.

interview in *The Times* 2 June 198

10 The English and, more latterly, the British, have the habit of
acquiring their institutions by chance or inadvertence, and
shedding them in a fit of absent-mindedness.

'The Granada Guildhall Lecture
1987' 10 November 1987; see
Seeley 348:9

11 Conservatives do not believe that the political struggle is the
most important thing in life . . . The simplest of them prefer
fox-hunting—the wisest religion.

The Case for Conservatism (1947)

12 We are a democratically governed republic with a wholly
admirable head of state.

Values: Collapse and Cure (1994)

13 I've known every Prime Minister to a greater or lesser
extent since Balfour, and most of them have died unhappy.

attributed, 1997

Richard Burdon Haldane 1856–1928
British politician, lawyer, and philosopher

1 We have come to the conclusion . . . that in the sphere of civil government the duty of investigation and thought, as preliminary to action, might with great advantage be more definitely added.

Peter Hennessy *Whitehall* (1990)

H. R. Haldeman 1929–93
American Presidential assistant to Richard **Nixon**

2 Once the toothpaste is out of the tube, it is awfully hard to get it back in.
on the Watergate affair, to John Dean, 8 April 1973

in *Hearings Before the Select Committee on Presidential Campaign Activities of US Senate: Watergate and Related Activities* (1973) vol. 4

Edward Everett Hale 1822–1909
American Unitarian clergyman; Senate chaplain for 1903

3 'Do you pray for the senators, Dr Hale?' 'No, I look at the senators and I pray for the country.'

Van Wyck Brooks *New England Indian Summer* (1940)

Matthew Hale 1609–76
English judge

4 Christianity is part of the laws of England.

William Blackstone's summary of Hale's words (Taylor's case, 1676) in *Commentaries* (1769) vol. 4; the origin of the expression has been traced to Sir John Prisot (d. 1460)

Nathan Hale 1755–76
American revolutionary
see also **Last words** 227:1

5 Every kind of service necessary to the public good becomes honourable by being necessary.
his defence of espionage

letter to William Hull, 10 September 1776

Lord Halifax ('the Trimmer') 1633–95
English politician and essayist

6 This innocent word *Trimmer* signifieth no more than this, that if men are together in a boat, and one part of the company would weigh it down on one side, another would make it lean as much to the contrary.

Character of a Trimmer (1685, printed 1688)

7 Men in business are in as much danger from those that work under them, as from those that work against them.

Political, Moral, and Miscellaneous Thoughts and Reflections (1750) 'Instruments of State Ministers'

8 The best way to suppose what may come, is to remember what is past.

Political, Moral, and Miscellaneous Thoughts and Reflections (1750) 'Miscellaneous: Experience'

9 A known liar should be outlawed in a well-ordered government.

Political, Moral, and Miscellaneous Thoughts and Reflections (1750) 'Miscellaneous: Lying'

1 After a revolution, you see the same men in the drawing-room, and within a week the same flatterers.

Political, Moral, and Miscellaneous Thoughts and Reflections (1750) 'Of Courts'

2 Most men make little other use of their speech than to give evidence against their own understanding.

Political, Moral, and Miscellaneous Thoughts and Reflections (1750) 'Of Folly and Fools'

3 There is . . . no fundamental, but that *every supreme power must be arbitrary*.

Political, Moral, and Miscellaneous Thoughts and Reflections (1750) 'Of Fundamentals'

4 The people are never so perfectly backed, but that they will kick and fling if not stroked at seasonable times.

Political, Moral, and Miscellaneous Thoughts and Reflections (1750) 'Of Fundamentals'

5 In corrupted governments the place is given for the sake of the man; in good ones the man is chosen for the sake of the place.

Political, Moral, and Miscellaneous Thoughts and Reflections (1750) 'Of Fundamentals'

6 It is in a disorderly government as in a river, the lightest things swim at the top.

Political, Moral, and Miscellaneous Thoughts and Reflections (1750) 'Of Government'

7 The best definition of the best government is, that it has no inconveniences but such as are supportable; but inconveniences there must be.

Political, Moral, and Miscellaneous Thoughts and Reflections (1750) 'Of Government'

8 If the laws could speak for themselves, they would complain of the lawyers in the first place.

Political, Moral, and Miscellaneous Thoughts and Reflections (1750) 'Of Laws'

9 Malice is of a low stature, but it hath very long arms.

Political, Moral, and Miscellaneous Thoughts and Reflections (1750) 'Of Malice and Envy'

10 In parliaments, men wrangle in behalf of liberty, that do as little care for it, as they deserve it.

Political, Moral, and Miscellaneous Thoughts and Reflections (1750) 'Of Parliaments'

11 The best party is but a kind of conspiracy against the rest of the nation.

Political, Moral, and Miscellaneous Thoughts and Reflections (1750) 'Of Parties'

12 There are men who shine in a faction, and make a figure by opposition, who would stand in a worse light, if they had the preferments they struggle for.

Political, Moral, and Miscellaneous Thoughts and Reflections (1750) 'Of Parties'

13 Party is little less than an inquisition, where men are under such a discipline in carrying on the common cause, as leaves no liberty of private opinion.

Political, Moral, and Miscellaneous Thoughts and Reflections (1750) 'Of Parties'

14 When the people contend for their liberty, they seldom get anything by their victory but new masters.

Political, Moral, and Miscellaneous Thoughts and Reflections (1750) 'Of Prerogative, Power and Liberty'

15 Power is so apt to be insolent and Liberty to be saucy, that they are very seldom upon good terms.

Political, Moral, and Miscellaneous Thoughts and Reflections (1750) 'Of Prerogative, Power and Liberty'

16 If none were to have liberty but those who understand what it is, there would not be many freed men in the world.

Political, Moral, and Miscellaneous Thoughts and Reflections (1750) 'Of Prerogative, Power and Liberty'

17 Men are not hanged for stealing horses, but that horses may not be stolen.

Political, Moral, and Miscellaneous Thoughts and Reflections (1750) 'Of Punishment'

1 Wherever a knave is not punished, an honest man is laughed at.

Political, Moral, and Miscellaneous Thoughts and Reflections (1750) 'Of Punishment'

2 State business is a cruel trade; good nature is a bungler in it.

Political, Moral, and Miscellaneous Thoughts and Reflections (1750) 'Wicked Ministers'

3 To the question, What shall we do to be saved in this World? there is no other answer but this, Look to your Moat.

A Rough Draft of a New Model at Sea (1694)

4 Lord Rochester was made Lord president: which being a post superior in rank, but much inferior both in advantage and credit to that he held formerly, drew a jest from Lord Halifax . . . he had heard of many kicked down stairs, but never of any that was kicked up stairs before.

Gilbert Burnet *History of My Own Time* (written 1683–6) vol. 1 (1724)

Lord Halifax 1881–1959
British Conservative politician and Foreign Secretary

5 *on being asked immediately after the Munich crisis if he were not worn out by the late nights:*
No, not exactly. But it spoils one's eye for the high birds.

attributed

Margaret Halsey 1910–
American writer

6 The English never smash in a face. They merely refrain from asking it to dinner.

With Malice Toward Some (1938)

W. F. ('Bull') Halsey 1882–1959
American admiral

7 The Third Fleet's sunken and damaged ships have been salvaged and are retiring at high speed toward the enemy.
on hearing claims that the Japanese had virtually annihilated the US fleet

report, 14 October 1944; E. B. Potter *Bull Halsey* (1985)

Alexander Hamilton c.1755–1804
American politician
on Hamilton: see **Webster** 413:9

8 A national debt, if it is not excessive, will be to us a national blessing.

letter to Robert Morris, 30 April 1781

9 I believe the British government forms the best model the world ever produced . . . This government has for its object public strength and individual security.

in *Debates of the Federal Convention* 18 June 1787

10 We are now forming a republican government. Real liberty is neither found in despotism or the extremes of democracy, but in moderate government.

in *Debates of the Federal Convention* 26 June 1787

11 Let Americans disdain to be the instruments of European greatness. Let the thirteen States, bound together in a strict and indissoluble Union, concur in erecting one great American system, superior to the control of all transatlantic force or influence, and able to dictate the terms of the connection between the old and the new world!

in *The Federalist* (1787–8) no. 11

1 Why has government been instituted at all? Because the passions of men will not conform to the dictates of reason and justice, without constraint.

in *The Federalist* (1787–8) no. 15

2 To admit foreigners indiscriminately to the rights of citizens ... would be nothing less than to admit the Grecian horse into the citadel of our liberty and sovereignty.

Works (1886) vol.7

3 Learn to think continentally.
   advice to the newly independent United States

attributed; see **Chamberlain** 79:7

Mark Hanna 1837–1904
American Republican politician and businessman

4 *of Theodore **Roosevelt**'s acceding to the Presidency on the assassination of William McKinley*
Now look, that damned cowboy is President of the United States.

in September 1901

Brian Hanrahan 1949–
British journalist

5 I counted them all out and I counted them all back.
   on the number of British aeroplanes joining the raid on Port Stanley

BBC broadcast report, 1 May 1982

William Harcourt 1827–1904
British Liberal politician

6 We are all socialists now.
   *during the passage of Lord **Goschen**'s 1888 budget, noted for the reduction of the national debt*

G. B. Shaw (ed.) *Fabian Essays in Socialism* (1889)

7 The value of the political heads of departments is to tell the permanent officials what the public will not stand.

A. G. Gardiner *The Life of Sir William Harcourt* (1923) vol. 2

Keir Hardie 1856–1915
Scottish Labour politician

8 From his childhood onward this boy [the future Edward VIII] will be surrounded by sycophants and flatterers by the score—[*Cries of* 'Oh, oh!']—and will be taught to believe himself as of a superior creation. [*Cries of* 'Oh, oh!'] A line will be drawn between him and the people whom he is to be called upon some day to reign over. In due course, following the precedent which has already been set, he will be sent on a tour round the world, and probably rumours of a morganatic alliance will follow—[*Loud cries of* 'Oh, oh!' *and* 'Order!']—and the end of it all will be that the country will be called upon to pay the bill. [*Cries of* Divide!]

in the House of Commons, 28 June 1894

9 Woman, even more than the working class, is the great unknown quantity of the race.

speech at Bradford, 11 April 1914

Warren G. Harding 1865–1923
American Republican statesman; 29th President of the US, 1921–3

10 In the great fulfillment we must have a citizenship less concerned about what the government can do for it and more anxious about what it can do for the nation.

speech at the Republican National Convention, 7 June 1916; see **Kennedy** 212:8

1 America's present need is not heroics, but healing; not nostrums but normalcy; not revolution, but restoration.

speech at Boston, 14 May 1920

Thomas Hardy 1840–1928
English novelist and poet

2 A local thing called Christianity.

The Dynasts (1904) pt. 1, act 1, sc. 6

3 War makes rattling good history; but Peace is poor reading.

The Dynasts (1904) pt. 1, act 2, sc. 5

4 'Peace upon earth!' was said. We sing it,
And pay a million priests to bring it.
After two thousand years of mass
We've got as far as poison-gas.

'Christmas: 1924' (1928)

5 The offhand decision of some commonplace mind high in office at a critical moment influences the course of events for a hundred years.

Florence Hardy *The Early Life of Thomas Hardy 1840–91 (1928)*

John Harington 1561–1612
English writer and courtier

6 Treason doth never prosper, what's the reason?
For if it prosper, none dare call it treason.

Epigrams (1618)

Lord Harlech 1918–85
British diplomat, Ambassador to Washington, 1961–5

7 Britain will be honoured by historians more for the way she disposed of an empire than for the way in which she acquired it.

in *New York Times* 28 October 1962

Mary Harney 1953–
Irish politician

8 If you want to push something in politics, you're accused of being aggressive, and that's not supposed to be a good thing for a woman. If you get upset and show it, you're accused of being emotional.

1990s, attributed

Harold II c.1019–66
English monarch, King 1066

9 He will give him seven feet of English ground, or as much more as he may be taller than other men.
    his offer to Harald Hardrada of Norway, invading England, before the battle of Stamford Bridge

Snorri Sturluson *King Harald's Saga* (*c.*1260)

Stephen Harper 1959–
Canadian Conservative politician, Leader of the Conservative Party of Canada

10 I've never really noticed complexity to be Belinda's strong point.
    *responding to Belinda **Stronach**'s comment that he was not sensitive to the complex nature of Canada*

in *CTV.ca* 18 May 2005 (online)

1 Tonight, the Liberals bought a victory, one that will sow the seeds of its own destruction.
*of the budget vote narrowly won by Paul **Martin**'s administration, 19 May 2005*

in *GlobeandMail.com* 20 May 2005 (online edition)

Arthur Harris 1892–1984
British Air Force Marshal

2 I would not regard the whole of the remaining cities of Germany as worth the bones of one British Grenadier.
supporting the continued strategic bombing of German cities

letter to Norman Bottomley, deputy Chief of Air Staff, 29 March 1945; see **Bismarck** 44:10

Robert Harris 1957–
British political journalist

3 The only leaders Labour loves are dead ones.

in *Sunday Times* 11 August 1996

William Henry Harrison 1773–1841
American Whig statesman and soldier, noted for his victory at the battle of Tippecanoe in 1811, and 9th President of the US, 1841, who died of pneumonia one month after his inauguration
*on Harrison: see **Slogans** 368:14, **Songs** 376:4*

4 We admit of no government by divine right . . . the only legitimate right to govern is an express grant of power from the governed.

inaugural address, 4 March 1841

5 A decent and manly examination of the acts of government should be not only tolerated, but encouraged.

inaugural address, 4 March 1841

Minnie Louise Haskins 1875–1957
English teacher and writer

6 And I said to the man who stood at the gate of the year:
'Give me a light that I may tread safely into the unknown.'
And he replied:
'Go out into the darkness and put your hand into the
Hand of God. That shall be to you better than light and safer than a known way.'
*quoted by King **George VI** in his Christmas broadcast, 25 December 1939*

Desert (1908) 'God Knows'

Roy Hattersley 1932–
British Labour politician

7 Opposition is four or five years' humiliation in which there is no escape from the indignity of no longer controlling events.

in *Independent* 25 March 1995 'Quote Unquote'

8 Politicians are entitled to change their minds. But when they adjust their principles some explanation is necessary.

in *Observer* 21 March 1999

Charles Haughey 1925–
Irish Fianna Fáil statesman; Taoiseach 1979–81, 1982, and 1987–92
*on Haughey: see **O'Brien** 293:3*

9 Every TD, from the youngest or newest in the House, dreams of being Taoiseach.

in *Irish Times* 23 May 1970 'This Week They Said'

1 It was a bizarre happening, an unprecedented situation, a grotesque situation, an almost unbelievable mischance.
on the series of events leading to the resignation of the Attorney General; the acronym GUBU *was subsequently coined by Conor Cruise **O'Brien** to describe Haughey's style of government*

at a press conference in 1982; T. Ryle Dwyer *Charlie: the Political Biography of Charles Haughey* (1987) ch. 12

Václav Havel 1936–

Czech dramatist and statesman; President of Czechoslovakia 1989–92 and of the Czech Republic 1993–2003

2 A spectre is haunting eastern Europe: the spectre of what in the West is called 'dissent'.

The Power of the Powerless (1978)

3 I see a renewed focus of politics on real people as something far more profound than merely returning to the everyday mechanisms of western (or if you like bourgeois) democracy.

Václav Havel et al. *The Power of the Powerless* (1985)

4 To respond to evil by committing another evil does not eliminate evil but allows it to go on forever.

letter 5 November 1989

Bob Hawke 1929–

Australian Labor statesman, Prime Minister 1983–91

5 No longer content to be just the lucky country, Australia must now become the clever country.

speech, c.1990; attributed

R. S. Hawker 1803–75

English clergyman and poet

6 And have they fixed the where and when?
And shall Trelawny die?
Here's twenty thousand Cornish men
Will know the reason why!
the last three lines are taken from a traditional rhyme dating from the imprisonment by James II, in 1688, of the seven Bishops, including Trelawny, Bishop of Bristol

'The Song of the Western Men'

Ian Hay 1876–1952

Scottish novelist and dramatist

7 War is hell, and all that, but it has a good deal to recommend it. It wipes out all the small nuisances of peace-time.

The First Hundred Thousand (1915)

John Milton Hay 1838–1905

American politician

8 It has been a splendid little war, begun with the highest motives, carried on with magnificent intelligence and spirit, favoured by that fortune which loves the brave.
on the Spanish-American War of 1898

letter to Theodore Roosevelt, 27 July 1898

9 The open door.
on the completion of the trade policy he had negotiated with China

letter to the Cabinet, 2 January 1900

Bill Hayden 1933–

Australian Labor politician

1 *Hayden had resigned as Opposition leader in 1983 as Malcolm Fraser was in the process of calling the election, but remained convinced that he would have won:*
I am not convinced the Labor Party could not win under my leadership. I believe a drover's dog could lead the Labor Party to victory the way the country is.

John Stubbs *Hayden* (1989)

Friedrich August von Hayek 1899–1992

Austrian-born economist

2 I am certain that nothing has done so much to destroy the juridical safeguards of individual freedom as the striving after this miracle of social justice.

Economic Freedom and Representative Government (1973)

3 The system of private property is the most important guarantee of freedom, not only for those who own property, but scarcely less for those who do not.

The Road to Serfdom (1944)

4 Probably nothing has done so much harm to the liberal cause as the wooden insistence of some liberals on certain rough rules of thumb, above all the principle of *laissez-faire*.

The Road to Serfdom (1944)

5 We need good principles rather than good people. We need fixed rules, not fixers.

Studies in Philosophy, Politics and Economics (1967)

6 One cannot help a country to maintain its standard of life by assisting people to consume more than they produce.

in *Daily Telegraph* 26 August 1976

Alfred Hayes 1911–85

American songwriter

7 I dreamed I saw Joe Hill last night
Alive as you and me.
Says I, 'But Joe, you're ten years dead.'
'I never died,' says he.

'I Dreamed I Saw Joe Hill Last Night' (1936 song)

William Hazlitt 1778–1830

English essayist

8 Talk of mobs! Is there any body of people that has this character in a more consummate degree than the House of Commons? Is there any set of men that determines more by acclamation, and less by deliberation and individual conviction?

'On the Difference between Writing and Speaking'; in *London Magazine* July 1820

9 The greatest test of courage I can conceive is to speak the truth in the House of Commons.

'On the Difference between Writing and Speaking'; in *London Magazine* July 1820

Cuthbert Morley Headlam 1876–1964

British Conservative politician

10 This Parliament is enough to discourage anyone from entering political life—a vast untutored majority with a helpless minority and an extremely uninteresting Government.

diary 27 March 1933

1 We ought to have made up more to the political leaders and their wives—the latter are an unattractive lot, but their influence is greater than one supposes.

diary 28 July 1933

2 Better to break your party on a matter of principle than to let it fall to pieces because you cannot yourself make up your mind what you want to do.

diary 2 April 1934

Denis Healey 1917–
British Labour politician, husband of Edna **Healey**

3 There are going to be howls of anguish from the 80,000 people who are rich enough to pay over 75% [tax] on the last slice of their income.

speech at the Labour Party Conference, 1 October 1973

4 It's no good ceasing to become the world's policeman in order to become the world's parson instead.

at a meeting of the Cabinet at Chequers, 17 November 1974; Peter Hennessy *Whitehall* (1990)

5 *of being criticized by Geoffrey* **Howe** *in the House of Commons:*
Like being savaged by a dead sheep.

in the House of Commons, 14 June 1978

6 *of Margaret* **Thatcher**:
And who is the Mephistopheles behind this shabby Faust [the Foreign Secretary, Geoffrey Howe]? . . . To quote her own backbenchers, the Great She-elephant, She-Who-Must-Be-Obeyed, the Catherine the Great of Finchley, the Prime Minister herself.

in the House of Commons, 27 February 1984

7 The Fabians . . . found socialism wandering aimlessly in Cloud-cuckoo-land and set it working on the gas and water problems of the nearest town or village.
of the parochialism of the Fabians

New Fabian Essays (1952)

8 La Passionaria of middle-class privilege.
of Margaret **Thatcher**

Kenneth Minogue and Michael Biddiss *Thatcherism* (1987)

9 Healey's first law of politics: when you're in a hole, stop digging.

attributed

Edna Healey 1918–
British writer, wife of Denis **Healey**

10 She has no hinterland; in particular she has no sense of history.
of Margaret **Thatcher**

Denis Healey *The Time of My Life* (1989)

Timothy Michael Healy 1855–1931
Irish nationalist politician

11 REDMOND: Gladstone is now master of the Party!
HEALY: Who is to be mistress of the Party?
at the meeting of the Irish Parliamentary Party on 6 December 1890, when the Party split over **Parnell**'s *involvement in the O'Shea divorce; Healy's reference to Katherine O'Shea was particularly damaging to Parnell*

Robert Kee *The Laurel and the Ivy* (1993)

12 I am for doing business and making peace.

letter to Beaverbrook, 1920; Frank Callanan *T. M. Healy* (1996)

13 The Sinns won in three years what we did not win in forty. You cannot make revolutions with rosewater, or omelettes without breaking eggs.

letter to his brother; Frank Callanan *T. M. Healy* (1996); see **Proverbs** 319:8

1 There is the noble Marquis. Like a pike at the bottom of a pool.

of Lord Hartington, apparently asleep on the Opposition bench

Herbert Gladstone *After Thirty Years* (1928)

Seamus Heaney 1939–
Irish poet

2 Don't be surprised
If I demur, for, be advised
My passport's green.
No glass of ours was ever raised
To toast *The Queen.*

rebuking the editors of The Penguin Book of Contemporary British Poetry *for including him among its authors*

Open Letter (1983)

3 Who would connive
in civilised outrage
yet understand the exact
and tribal, intimate revenge.

'Punishment' (1975)

4 My heart besieged by anger, my mind a gap of danger,
I walked among their old haunts, the home ground where they bled;
And in the dirt lay justice like an acorn in the winter
Till its oak would sprout in Derry where the thirteen men lay dead.

of Bloody Sunday, Londonderry, 30 January 1972

'The Road to Derry'

5   The famous
Northern reticence, the tight gag of place
And times: yes, yes. Of the 'wee six' I sing
Where to be saved you only must save face
And whatever you say, you say nothing.

'Whatever You Say Say Nothing' (1975)

William Randolph Hearst 1863–1951
American newspaper publisher and tycoon

6 You furnish the pictures and I'll furnish the war.

message to the artist Frederic Remington in Havana, Cuba, during the Spanish-American War of 1898

attributed

7 The day when this nation ceases to shape its foreign policy primarily for the safety and welfare of the American people will be the day on which its national doom is sealed—and its international doom too.

in *San Francisco Examiner* 7 May 1924

Edward Heath 1916–2005
British Conservative statesman; Prime Minister, 1970–4
on Heath: see **Anonymous** 8:3, **Hennessy** 180:2, **Jenkins** 201:5, **Margach** 260:2, **Thatcher** 390:5

8 Music means everything to me when I'm here alone. And it's the best way of getting that bloody man Wilson out of my hair.

after playing Chopin and Liszt for a visiting journalist, late 1960s

James Margach *The Abuse of Power* (1978)

9 This would, at a stroke, reduce the rise in prices, increase productivity and reduce unemployment.

press release, never actually spoken by Heath, on proposed tax cuts and a freeze on prices in nationalized industries

from Conservative Central Office, 16 June 1970

1 The unpleasant and unacceptable face of capitalism.
on the Lonrho affair

in the House of Commons, 15 May 1973

2 If politicians lived on praise and thanks they'd be forced into some other line of business.

attributed, 1973

3 Rejoice, rejoice, rejoice.
*telephone call to his office on hearing of Margaret **Thatcher**'s fall from power in 1990*

attributed; in *Daily Telegraph* 24 September 1998 (online edition)

4 It was not totally inconceivable that she could have joined me as my wife at No. 10.
of the starlet Jayne Mansfield

in *Sunday Times* 6 February 2000 'Talking Heads'

G. W. F. Hegel 1770-1831
German idealist philosopher

5 Gangrenous limbs cannot be cured with lavender water.

The German Constitution (1798-1802) pt. 9 'The growth of states in the rest of Europe', translated by M. Knox

6 What experience and history teach is this—that nations and governments have never learned anything from history, or acted upon any lessons they might have drawn from it.

Lectures on the Philosophy of World History: Introduction (1830); see **Marx** 262:7

Heinrich Heine 1797-1856
German poet

7 Wherever books will be burned, men also, in the end, are burned.

Almansor (1823)

Joseph Heller 1923-99
American novelist

8 If I'm going to be trivial, inconsequential, and deceitful . . . then I might as well be in government.

Closing Time (1994)

Lillian Hellman 1905-84
American dramatist

9 I cannot and will not cut my conscience to fit this year's fashions.

letter to John S. Wood, 19 May 1952

Leona Helmsley c.1920-
American hotelier

10 Only the little people pay taxes.
reported at her trial for tax evasion

to her housekeeper; in *New York Times* 12 July 1983

Arthur Henderson 1863-1935
British Labour politician

11 *to critics in his own party, when as adviser on labour matters he was made minister without portfolio in **Lloyd George**'s War Cabinet (December 1916):*
I am not here either to please myself or you; I am here to see the war through.

in *Dictionary of National Biography* (1917-)

12 The first forty-eight hours decide whether a Minister is going to run his office or whether his office is going to run him.

Susan Crosland *Tony Crosland* (1982)

Leon Henderson 1895–1956
American economist; appointed by Franklin **Roosevelt** to the
National Defense Advisory Commission in 1940

1 Having a little inflation is like being a little pregnant.

J. K. Galbraith *A Life in Our Times* (1981)

Peter Hennessy 1947–
English historian

2 The model of a modern Prime Minister would be a kind of grotesque composite freak—someone with the dedication to duty of a Peel, the physical energy of a Gladstone, the detachment of a Salisbury, the brains of an Asquith, the balls of a Lloyd George, the word-power of a Churchill, the administrative gifts of an Attlee, the style of a Macmillan, the managerialism of a Heath, and the sleep requirements of a Thatcher. Human beings do not come like that.

The Hidden Wiring (1995)

3 MI5 is a job creation scheme for muscular underachievers from the ancient universities.

in *The Times* 1981, profile of Roger Hollis

4 *of Rab **Butler** in his last years:*
He seemed like a benign and decent beached whale washed up on the harder shores of modern Conservatism.

in *Independent* 8 May 1987

Henri IV (of Navarre) 1553–1610
French monarch, King from 1589

5 I want there to be no peasant in my kingdom so poor that he is unable to have a chicken in his pot every Sunday.

In Hardouin de Péréfixe *Histoire de Henry le Grand* (1681); see **Hoover** 188:4

6 Hang yourself, brave Crillon; we fought at Arques and you were not there.

traditional form given by Voltaire to a letter from Henri to Crillon, 20 September 1597; Henri's actual words were: 'My good man, Crillon, hang yourself for not having been at my side last Monday at the greatest event that's ever been seen and perhaps ever will be seen'

7 Paris is well worth a mass.
when told that, though a Protestant, he must hear mass at Notre-Dame Cathedral to be consecrated king

attributed to Henri IV; alternatively to his minister Sully, in conversation with Henri

8 The wisest fool in Christendom.
*of **James I** of England*

attributed both to Henri IV and **Sully**

Henry II 1133–89
English monarch, King from 1154

9 Will no one rid me of this turbulent priest?
of Thomas Becket, Archbishop of Canterbury, murdered in Canterbury Cathedral, December 1170

oral tradition, conflating a number of variant forms, including G. Lyttelton *History of the Life of King Henry the Second* (1769): 'so many cowardly and ungrateful men in his court, none of whom would revenge him of the injuries he

sustained from one turbulent
priest'

Henry VIII 1491–1547

English monarch, King from 1509

1 This man hath the right sow by the ear.
of Thomas Cranmer, June 1529

in *Acts and Monuments of John Foxe*
['Foxe's Book of Martyrs'] (1570)

2 The King found her [Anne of Cleves] so different from her
picture . . . that . . . he swore they had brought him a
Flanders mare.

Tobias Smollett *A Complete History
of England* (3rd ed., 1759)

Patrick Henry 1736–99

American statesman

3 Caesar had his Brutus—Charles the First, his Cromwell—
and George the Third—('Treason,' cried the Speaker) . . .
may profit by their example. If *this* be treason, make the most
of it.

speech in the Virginia assembly,
May 1765

4 I am not a Virginian, but an American.

in [John Adams's] Notes of
Debates in the Continental
Congress, Philadelphia, 6
September 1774

5 I know not what course others may take; but as for me, give
me liberty, or give me death!

speech in Virginia Convention, 23
March 1775

6 We are not weak if we make a proper use of those means
which the God of Nature has placed in our power . . . The
battle, sir, is not to the strong alone; it is to the vigilant, the
active, the brave.

speech in Virginia Convention,
Richmond, 23 March 1775

7 Guard with jealous attention the public liberty. Suspect
everyone who approaches that jewel. Unfortunately,
nothing will preserve it but downright force. Whenever you
give up that force, you are inevitably ruined.

attributed

A. P. Herbert 1890–1971

English writer and humorist

8 This high official, all allow,
Is grossly overpaid;
There wasn't any Board, and now
There isn't any Trade.

'The President of the Board of
Trade' (1922)

9 Testators would do well to provide some indication of the
particular Liberal Party which they have in mind, such as a
telephone number or a Christian name.

Misleading Cases (1935)

10 People must not do things for fun. We are not here for fun.
There is no reference to fun in any Act of Parliament.

Uncommon Law (1935) 'Is it a Free
Country?'

11 The Common Law of England has been laboriously built
about a mythical figure—the figure of 'The Reasonable
Man'.

Uncommon Law (1935) 'The
Reasonable Man'

Frank Herbert 1920–86
American writer of science fiction

1 If you think of yourselves as helpless and ineffectual, it is certain that you will create a despotic government to be your master. The wise despot, therefore, maintains among his subjects a popular sense that they are helpless and ineffectual.

The Dosadi Experiment (1978)

Herodotus c.485–c.425 BC
Greek historian

2 In peace, children bury their parents; war violates the order of nature and causes parents to bury their children.

Histories

3 The most hateful torment for men is to have knowledge of everything but power over nothing.

Histories

Lord Hervey 1696–1743
English politician and writer

4 Whoever would lie usefully should lie seldom.

Memoirs of the Reign of George II (ed. J. W. Croker, 1848) vol. 1

5 I am fit for nothing but to carry candles and set chairs all my life.

letter to Sir Robert Walpole, 1737

Alexander Ivanovich Herzen 1812–70
Russian writer and revolutionary

6 Communism is a Russian autocracy turned upside down.

The Development of Revolutionary Ideas in Russia (1851)

7 Russia's future will be a great danger for Europe and a great misfortune for Russia if there is no emancipation of the individual. One more century of present despotism will destroy all the good qualities of the Russian people.

The Development of Revolutionary Ideas in Russia (1851)

Michael Heseltine 1933–
British Conservative politician
on Heseltine: see **Critchley** 105:3

8 I knew that, 'He who wields the knife never wears the crown.'

in *New Society* 14 February 1986

9 The market has no morality.

on *Panorama* BBC1 27 June 1988

10 Polluted rivers, filthy streets, bodies bedded down in doorways are no advertisement for a prosperous or caring society.

speech at Conservative Party Conference 10 October 1989

11 The Tory recognizes the contrast between laissez-faire and noblesse oblige.

in *Observer* 18 March 1990 'Sayings of the Week'

12 The fundamental question is is the Conservative Party leadable?
in the aftermath of disastrous electoral defeat

in *Daily Telegraph* 9 June 2001 (electronic edition)

Gordon Hewart 1870–1943

British lawyer and politician

1 A long line of cases shows that it is not merely of some importance, but is of fundamental importance that justice should not only be done, but should manifestly and undoubtedly be seen to be done.

in *Rex v Sussex Justices* 9 November 1923

John Hewitt 1907–87

Northern Irish poet

2 I fear their creed as we have always feared The lifted hand between the mind and truth.

'The Glens' (1948)

3 Kelt, Briton, Roman, Saxon, Dane, and Scot, time and this island tied a crazy knot.

'Ulsterman' (*Collected Poems*, 1991)

4 I'm an Ulsterman, of planter stock. I was born in the island of Ireland, so secondarily I'm an Irishman. I was born in the British archipelago and English is my native tongue, so I am British. The British archipelago consists of offshore islands to the continent of Europe, so I'm European. This is my hierarchy of values.

in *The Irish Times* 4 July 1974

Reinhard Heydrich 1904–42

German Nazi leader

5 Now the rough work has been done we begin the period of finer work. We need to work in harmony with the civil administration. We count on you gentlemen as far as the final solution is concerned.
  on the planned mass murder of eleven million European Jews

speech in Wannsee, 20 January 1942; see **Goering** 160:6

J. R. Hicks 1904–89

British economist

6 The best of all monopoly profits is a quiet life.

Econometrica (1935) 'The Theory of Monopoly'

Jim Hightower 1943–

American politician

7 There's nothing in the middle of the road but yellow stripes and dead armadillos.

attributed, 1984

Charles Hill 1904–89

British Conservative politician, doctor, and broadcaster

8 It does not do to appear clever. Advancement in this man's party is due entirely to alcoholic stupidity.
  advice given in 1959 to the newly elected MP, Julian **Critchley***, whom he had seen reading in the Smoking Room of the House of Commons*

Julian Critchley *A Bag of Boiled Sweets* (1994)

Joe Hill 1879–1915

Swedish-born American labour leader and songwriter
see also **Last words** 227:4

1 You will eat, bye and bye,
  In that glorious land above the sky;
  Work and pray, live on hay,
  You'll get pie in the sky when you die.

'Preacher and the Slave' in *Songs of
the Workers* (Industrial Workers of
the World, 1911)

Paul von Hindenburg 1847–1934

German Field Marshal and statesman, President of the Weimar
Republic 1925–34

2 That man for a Chancellor? I'll make him a postmaster and
  he can lick the stamps with my head on them.
  of **Hitler**

to Meissner, 13 August 1932; J. W.
Wheeler-Bennett *Hindenburg: the
Wooden Titan* (1936)

Emperor Hirohito 1901–89

Japanese monarch, Emperor from 1926

3 The war situation has developed not necessarily to Japan's
  advantage.
  *announcing Japan's surrender, in a broadcast to his people after
  atom bombs had destroyed Hiroshima and Nagasaki*

on 15 August 1945

4 Certainly things happened during the Second World War for
  which I feel personally sorry.

attributed, 1971

Adolf Hitler 1889–1945

German dictator

5 The broad mass of a nation . . . will more easily fall victim to
  a big lie than to a small one.

Mein Kampf (1925) vol. 1

6 The night of the long knives.
  *applied to the massacre of Ernst Roehm and his associates by
  Hitler on 29–30 June 1934, though taken from an early Nazi
  marching song; the phrase was subsequently associated with
  Harold* **Macmillan***'s Cabinet dismissals of 13 July 1962*

speech in the Reichstag, 13 July
1934

7 I go the way that Providence dictates with the assurance of
  a sleepwalker.

speech in Munich, 15 March 1936

8 It is the last territorial claim which I have to make in
  Europe, but it is the claim from which I will not recede and
  which, God-willing, I will make good.
  on the Sudetenland

speech at Berlin Sportpalast, 26
September 1938

9 With regard to the problem of the Sudeten Germans, my
  patience is now at an end!

speech at Berlin Sportpalast, 26
September 1938

10 *to Mussolini, having spent nine hours intermittently in Franco's
  company:*
  Rather than go through that again, I would prefer to have
  three or four teeth taken out.

Paul Preston *Franco* (1993)

Thomas Hobbes 1588-1679

English philosopher

1 By art is created that great Leviathan, called a commonwealth or state, (in Latin *civitas*) which is but an artificial man . . . and in which, the sovereignty is an artificial soul.

Leviathan (1651); introduction

2 I put for a general inclination of all mankind, a perpetual and restless desire of power after power, that ceaseth only in death.

Leviathan (1651)

3 They that approve a private opinion, call it opinion; but they that mislike it, heresy: and yet heresy signifies no more than private opinion.

Leviathan (1651)

4 During the time men live without a common power to keep them all in awe, they are in that condition which is called war; and such a war as is of every man against every man.

Leviathan (1651)

5 For as the nature of foul weather, lieth not in a shower or two of rain; but in an inclination thereto of many days together: so the nature of war consisteth not in actual fighting, but in the known disposition thereto during all the time there is no assurance to the contrary.

Leviathan (1651)

6 No arts; no letters; no society; and which is worst of all, continual fear and danger of violent death; and the life of man, solitary, poor, nasty, brutish, and short.

Leviathan (1651)

7 Force, and fraud, are in war the two cardinal virtues.

Leviathan (1651)

8 Liberties . . . depend on the silence of the law.

Leviathan (1651)

9 The obligation of subjects to the sovereign, is understood to last as long, and no longer, than the power lasteth, by which he is able to protect them.

Leviathan (1651)

10 I put down for one of the most effectual seeds of the death of any state, that the conquerors require not only a submission of men's actions to them for the future, but also an approbation of all their actions past.

Leviathan (1651)

11 They that are discontented under *monarchy*, call it *tyranny*; and they that are displeased with *aristocracy*, call it *oligarchy*: so also, they which find themselves grieved under a *democracy*, call it *anarchy*, which signifies the want of government; and yet I think no man believes, that want of government, is any new kind of government.

Leviathan (1651)

12 The papacy is not other than the ghost of the deceased Roman Empire, sitting crowned upon the grave thereof.

Leviathan (1651)

John Cam Hobhouse 1786-1869

English politician

13 When I invented the phrase 'His Majesty's Opposition' [Canning] paid me a compliment on the fortunate hit.

Recollections of a Long Life (1865) vol. 2, ch. 12; see below; see **Bagehot** 22:6

It is said to be very hard on his majesty's ministers to raise objections to this proposition. For my own part, I think it is more hard on his majesty's opposition (a laugh) to compel them to take this course.

speech, House of Commons, 10 April 1826

Eric Hobsbawm 1917–

British historian

1 This was the kind of war which existed in order to produce
victory parades.
   of the Falklands War

in *Marxism Today* January 1983

August Heinrich Hoffman 1798–1874

German poet

2 *Deutschland über alles.*
Germany above all.

Title of poem (1841)

Lancelot Hogben 1895–1975

English scientist

3 This is not the age of pamphleteers. It is the age of the
engineers. The spark-gap is mightier than the pen.
Democracy will not be salvaged by men who talk fluently,
debate forcefully and quote aptly.

Science for the Citizen (1938)
epilogue

Sarah Hogg 1946–

British political advisor, former head of John Major's policy unit

4 Ministers say one of two things in Cabinet. Some say, 'Look,
Daddy, no hands.' Others say, 'Look, Daddy, me too.'
   unidentified senior official to Sarah Hogg on her arrival to take
   over the Prime Minister's policy unit

in *Sunday Times* 9 April 1995

Simon Hoggart 1946–

British journalist

5 Peter Mandelson is someone who can skulk in broad
daylight.

in *Guardian* 10 July 1998

Patrick Holden 1937–

British businessman: director of the Soil Association

6 Tony Blair and his ministers are operating on a 'pollute
now, pay later' policy. Farm-scale trial plots are rather like
letting a rat with bubonic plague out into the environment
and then seeing what happens.
   on GM foods

in *Independent* 18 June 1999

Henry Fox, Lord Holland 1705–74

English Whig politician
on Holland: see **Walpole** 410:7

7 Let nothing be done to break his spirit. The world will do
that business fast enough.
   of his son Charles James **Fox** *as a child*

attributed

8 If Mr Selwyn calls again, shew him up: if I am alive I shall
be delighted to see him; and if I am dead he would like to
see me.
   during his last illness

J. H. Jesse *George Selwyn and his*
Contemporaries (1844) vol. 3

Oliver Wendell Holmes Jr. 1841–1935
American lawyer

1 The most stringent protection of free speech would not protect a man falsely shouting fire in a theatre and causing a panic.

> *sometimes quoted as, 'shouting fire in a crowded theatre'*

in *Schenck v. United States* (1919)

2 Men must turn square corners when they deal with the Government.

in *Rock Island, Arkansas & Louisiana Ry. v. United States* (1920)

3 I pay my tax bills more readily than any others—for whether the money is well or ill spent I get civilized society for it.

letter to Harold Laski, 12 May 1930

4 A second-class intellect. But a first-class temperament!

> *of Franklin* **Roosevelt**

on 8 March 1933

5 The mind of a bigot is like the pupil of the eye; the more light you pour upon it, the more it will contract.

attributed

Alec Douglas-Home, Lord Home 1903–95
British Conservative statesman; Prime Minister, 1963–4
on Home: see **Peyton** 310:1

6 Oh, they must find someone else, once they get away from this Blackpool hot-house. Even if they can't agree on Rab or Quintin there must be someone else. But please, please, not me!

> *to James Margach during the Conservative Party Conference, October 1963*

James Margach *The Abuse of Power* (1978)

7 When I have to read economic documents I have to have a box of matches and start moving them into position to simplify and illustrate the points to myself.

in *Observer* 16 September 1962

8 As far as the fourteenth earl is concerned, I suppose Mr Wilson, when you come to think of it, is the fourteenth Mr Wilson.

> *replying to Harold* **Wilson**'s *remark (on Home's becoming leader of the Conservative party) that 'the whole [democratic] process has ground to a halt with a fourteenth Earl'*

in *Daily Telegraph* 22 October 1963

9 There are two problems in my life. The political ones are insoluble and the economic ones are incomprehensible.

attributed, 1964

10 Had a letter from your father [Sir Roy Harrod, the economist] today about inflation . . . or deflation—or something.

> *to Dominic Harrod at a Downing Street party*

Peter Hennessy *The Prime Minister: the Office and its Holders since 1945* (2000)

Richard Hooker c.1554–1600
English theologian

11 He that goeth about to persuade a multitude, that they are not so well governed as they ought to be, shall never want attentive and favourable hearers.

Of the Laws of Ecclesiastical Polity (1593)

12 Alteration though it be from worse to better hath in it inconveniences, and those weighty.

Of the Laws of Ecclesiastical Polity (1593)

Geoffrey Hoon 1953–

British Labour politician, Secretary of State for Defence
1999–2005

1 I accept responsibility for everything that goes on in the MoD. But that does not mean I'm to blame for everything.

in Sunday Times 15 February 2004

Herbert Hoover 1874–1964

American Republican statesman, 31st President of the US,
1929–33

2 Our country has deliberately undertaken a great social and economic experiment, noble in motive and far-reaching in purpose.
    on the Eighteenth Amendment enacting Prohibition, often referred to as 'the noble experiment'

letter to Senator W. H. Borah, 23 February 1928

3 The American system of rugged individualism.

speech in New York City, 22 October 1928

4 The slogan of progress is changing from the full dinner pail to the full garage.
    sometimes paraphrased as, 'a car in every garage and a chicken in every pot'

*speech in New York, 22 October 1928; see **Henri IV** 180:5*

5 The grass will grow in the streets of a hundred cities, a thousand towns.
    on proposals 'to reduce the protective tariff to a competitive tariff for revenue'

*speech, 31 October 1932; see **Bryan** 59:8*

6 Older men declare war. But it is youth who must fight and die.

speech at the Republican National Convention, Chicago, 27 June 1944

Bob Hope 1903–2003

American comedian

7 I must say the Senator's victory in Wisconsin was a triumph for democracy. It proves that a millionaire has just as good a chance as anybody else.
    *of John F. **Kennedy**'s electoral victory*

in 1960; William Robert Faith Bob Hope (1983)

Horace 65–8 BC

Roman poet

8 O cives, cives, quarenda pecunia primum est;
Virtus post nummos.
O citizens, first acquire wealth; you can practise virtue afterwards.

*Epistles; see **Pope** 314:6*

Samuel Horsley 1733–1806

English bishop

9 In this country . . . the individual subject . . . 'has nothing to do with the laws but to obey them.'
    defending a maxim he had used earlier in committee

in the House of Lords, 13 November 1795

John Hoskyns 1927–

British businessman; head of the Prime Minister's Policy Unit 1979–82

1 The House of Commons is the greatest closed shop of all . . . For the purposes of government, a country of 55 million people is forced to depend on a talent pool which could not sustain a single multinational company.

'Conservatism is Not Enough' (Institute of Directors Annual Lecture) 25 September 1983

2 The Tory party never panics, except in a crisis.

in *Sunday Times* 19 February 1989

A. E. Housman 1859–1936

English poet

3 These, in the day when heaven was falling,
The hour when earth's foundations fled,
Followed their mercenary calling
And took their wages and are dead.

Their shoulders held the sky suspended;
They stood, and earth's foundations stay;
What God abandoned, these defended,
And saved the sum of things for pay.

Last Poems (1922) no. 37 'Epitaph on an Army of Mercenaries'

Samuel Houston 1793–1863

American politician and military leader

4 The North is determined to preserve this Union. They are not a fiery, impulsive people as you are, for they live in colder climates. But when they begin to move in a given direction . . . they move with the steady momentum and perseverance of a mighty avalanche.
in 1861, warning the people of Texas against secession

Geoffrey C. Ward *The Civil War* (1991)

John Howard 1939–

Australian Liberal statesman; Prime Minister since 1996

5 That's Lazarus with a triple bypass.
asked if he thought he could regain leadership of his party

at a press conference, 9 May 1989; David Barnett *John Howard: Prime Minister* (1997)

6 I want people to reflect on the loss of life. I want them to reflect on what it means in terms of the loss of innocence . . . in relation to this country's dealings with different parts of the world.
on the Bali bombing, 12 October 2002

interview on Australian television (Channel Ten News), 14 October 2002

7 I have said since September 11 last year that you can't rule out the possibility of a terror attack of this sort in Australia. Because of the nature of our society, I believe it is less likely than in many other parts of the world. But I cannot guarantee that it won't happen. I can't.

in *The Age* (electronic edition) 19 October 2002

Michael Howard 1941–

British Conservative politician, Party Leader from 2003

8 I am happy to debate the past with the Prime Minister any day he likes. I have a big dossier on his past, and I did not even have to sex it up.

at Prime Minister's Questions in the House of Commons, 12 November 2003

1 I have said that if people don't deliver they go, and for me
delivering meant winning the election. I didn't do that.
  announcing his intention to resign as Conservative Party Leader

speech at Putney, 6 May 2005

Geoffrey Howe 1926–

British Conservative politician
on Howe: see **Healey** 177:5

2 It is rather like sending your opening batsmen to the crease
only for them to find, the moment the first balls are bowled,
that their bats have been broken before the game by the
team captain.
  resignation speech which precipitated the fall of Margaret   .
  Thatcher

*in the House of Commons, 13
November 1990*

3 The time has come for others to consider their own response
to the tragic conflict of loyalties with which I have myself
wrestled for perhaps too long.
  resignation speech

*in the House of Commons, 13
November 1990*

Julia Ward Howe 1819–1910

American Unitarian lay preacher

4 Mine eyes have seen the glory of the coming of the Lord:
He is trampling out the vintage where the grapes of wrath
  are stored;
He hath loosed the fateful lightning of his terrible swift
  sword:
His truth is marching on.

*'Battle Hymn of the Republic'
(1862)*

5 As He died to make men holy, let us die to make men free.

*'Battle Hymn of the Republic'
(1862)*

Louis McHenry Howe 1871–1936

American Democratic politician

6 You can't adopt politics as a profession, and remain honest.

speech, 17 January 1933

Langston Hughes 1902–67

American writer and poet

7 I, too, sing America.

I am the darker brother.
They send me to eat in the kitchen
When company comes.

'I, Too' (1925)

8 'It's powerful,' he said.
'What?'
'That one drop of Negro blood—because just *one* drop of
  black blood makes a man coloured. *One* drop—you are a
  Negro!'

Simple Takes a Wife (1953)

Robert Hughes 1938–
Australian writer

1 What the convict system bequeathed to later Australian generations was not the sturdy, skeptical independence . . . but an intense concern with social and political respectability. The idea of the 'convict stain', a moral blot soaked into our fabric, dominated all argument about Australian selfhood by the 1840s.

The Fatal Shore (1987) introduction

Victor Hugo 1802–85
French poet, novelist, and dramatist

2 A stand can be made against invasion by an army; no stand can be made against invasion by an idea.

Histoire d'un Crime (written 1851–2, published 1877); see **Anonymous** 12:6

3 Take away *time is money*, and what is left of England? take away *cotton is king*, and what is left of America?

Les Misérables (1862)

David Hume 1711–76
Scottish philosopher

4 Money . . . is none of the wheels of trade: it is the oil which renders the motion of the wheels more smooth and easy.

Essays: Moral and Political (1741–2) 'Of Money'

5 That policy is violent, which aggrandizes the public by the poverty of individuals.

Essays: Moral and Political (1741–2) 'Of Money'

6 Should it be said, that, by living under the dominion of a prince, which one might leave, every individual has given a tacit assent to his authority . . . We may as well assert, that a man by remaining in a vessel, freely consents to the dominion of the master; though he was carried on board while asleep, and must leap into the ocean, and perish, the moment he leaves her.

'Of the Original Contract' (1748)

7 In all ages of the world, priests have been enemies of liberty.

'Of the Parties of Great Britain' (1741–2)

8 It is a just political maxim, that every man must be supposed a knave.

Political Discourses (1751)

John Hume 1937–
Northern Irish politician

9 There's a very thin line between dying for Ireland and killing for Ireland.

in 1994, attributed

Mick Hume
British journalist

10 It is a fitting national symbol, a wonderful structure that stands for nothing, a stunning shell with a hole where its heart should be.
   the editor of Living Marxism *on the Millennium Dome*

in *Independent on Sunday* 9 January 2000

Hubert Humphrey 1911–78
American Democratic politician

11 There are not enough jails, not enough policemen, not enough courts to enforce a law not supported by the people.

speech at Williamsburg, 1 May 1965

1 The right to be heard does not automatically include the right to be taken seriously.

speech to National Student Association at Madison, 23 August 1965

2 Here we are the way politics ought to be in America, the politics of happiness, the politics of purpose and the politics of joy.

speech in Washington, 27 April 1968

3 Compassion is not weakness, and concern for the unfortunate is not socialism.

attributed

Barry Humphries 1934–

Australian entertainer and writer

4 The prigs who attack Jeffrey Archer should bear in mind that we all, to some extent, reinvent ourselves. Jeffrey has just gone to a bit more trouble.

in *Observer* on 19 December 1999 'They said what . . . ?'

G. W. Hunt

English composer of music-hall songs see **Songs** 377:3

Lord Hunt of Tanworth 1919–

British civil servant; Secretary of the Cabinet 1973–9

5 *of British Cabinet government, described as 'a shambles':*
It has got to be, so far as possible, a democratic and accountable shambles.

at a seminar at the Institute of Historical Research, 20 October 1993

Robert Hunter 1941–2005

Canadian writer

6 The word *Greenpeace* had a ring to it—it conjured images of Eden; it said ecology and antiwar in two syllables; it fit easily into even a one-column headline.

Warriors of the Rainbow (1979); see **Darnell** 109:7

Douglas Hurd 1930–

British Conservative politician; Foreign Secretary 1989–95

7 Lord Rothschild roamed like a condottiere through Whitehall, laying an ambush here, there breaching some crumbling fortress which had outlived its usefulness . . . He respected persons occasionally but rarely policies.
    of Lord **Rothschild** *as first Director of the Central Policy Review Staff*

An End to Promises (1979)

8 If President Clinton decides to accelerate the run-down in US forces in Europe—and by implication the priority Washington attaches to Nato—that wedge will be removed. With it will go one of the principal props which have allowed Britain to punch above its weight in the world.

speech at Chatham House; in *Financial Times* 4 February 1993

9 People in the forefront of environmental causes are destroying experimental crops. That's not logical. That's Luddite.

in *Sunday Times* 19 September 1999

Saddam Hussein 1937–

Iraqi statesman; President 1979–2003

1 The mother of battles.
popular interpretation of his description of the approaching Gulf War, given in a speech in Baghdad, 6 January 1991

in *The Times* 7 January 1991 it was reported that Saddam had no intention of relinquishing Kuwait and was ready for the 'mother of all wars'

2 Baghdad is determined to force the Mongols of our age to commit suicide at its gates.

in *Independent* 18 January 2003

3 I am Saddam Hussein, the president of Iraq.
response when asked who he was at the beginning of his trial; the judge ordered the clerk to 'put down "former" in brackets'

in *Guardian* 2 July 2004

Lord Hutton 1931–

British judge, Lord Chief Justice for Northern Ireland

4 I make it clear that it will be for me to decide as I think right within my terms of reference the matters which will be the subject of my investigation.

statement on the terms of the inquiry into the death of Dr David Kelly, 21 July 2003

5 The term 'sexed-up' is a slang expression, the meaning of which lacks clarity in the context of the discussion of the dossier.

statement, 28 January 2004

Aldous Huxley 1894–1963

English novelist

6 So long as men worship the Caesars and Napoleons, Caesars and Napoleons will duly arise and make them miserable.

Ends and Means (1937)

7 Idealism is the noble toga that political gentlemen drape over their will to power.

in *New York Herald Tribune* 25 November 1963

8 The propagandist's purpose is to make one set of people forget that certain other sets of people are human.

attributed

T. H. Huxley 1825–95

English biologist

9 Why, put him in the middle of a moor, with nothing in the world but his shirt, and you could not prevent him being anything he liked.
*of **Gladstone***

Roy Jenkins *Gladstone* (1995)

Douglas Hyde 1860–1949

Irish nationalist

10 The devouring demon of Anglicization in Ireland . . . with its foul jaws has devoured, one after another, everything that was hereditary, national, instructive, ancient, intellectual and noble in our race, our language, our music, our songs, our industries, our dances, and our pastimes—I know, I say, that you will plant your feet firmly, and say with us, 'Back, Demon, back!'

speaking on behalf of the Gaelic League in America, 1904

Henry Hyde 1924–
American Republican politician, leader of the prosecution for the
impeachment of President **Clinton**

1 We hoped that the public would move from its total
indifference to concern. That hope was unrequited.

in *Times* 13 February 1999

Dolores Ibarruri ('La Pasionaria') 1895–1989
Spanish Communist leader

2 *No pasarán.*
They shall not pass.

radio broadcast, Madrid, 19 July
1936; see **Proverbs and saying**
318:15

3 It is better to die on your feet than to live on your knees.

speech in Paris, 3 September 19
also attributed to Emiliano Zapa
see **Roosevelt** 331:3

Henrik Ibsen 1828–1906
Norwegian dramatist

4 The majority never has right on its side. Never I say! That is
one of the social lies that a free, thinking man is bound to
rebel against. Who makes up the majority in any given
country? Is it the wise men or the fools? I think we must
agree that the fools are in a terrible overwhelming majority,
all the wide world over. But, damn it, it can surely never be
right that the stupid should rule over the clever!

An Enemy of the People (1882)

5 You should never have your best trousers on when you go
out to fight for freedom and truth.

An Enemy of the People (1882)

Harold L. Ickes 1874–1952
American lawyer and administrator

6 The trouble with Senator Long . . . is that he's suffering
from halitosis of the intellect. That's presuming Emperor
Long has an intellect.
of Huey **Long**

speech, 1935; G. Wolfskill and J.
Hudson *All But the People: Frankl*
D. Roosevelt and his Critics, 1933–
(1969)

7 Dewey threw his diaper into the ring.
on the Republican candidate for the presidency

in *New York Times* 12 December
1939

8 I am against government by crony.
on resigning as secretary of the interior

in February 1946

Ivan Illich 1926–
American sociologist

9 In a consumer society there are inevitably two kinds of
slaves: the prisoners of addiction and the prisoners of envy.

Tools for Conviviality (1973)

William Ralph Inge 1860–1954
English writer; Dean of St. Paul's, 1911–34

10 The enemies of Freedom do not argue; they shout and they
shoot.

End of an Age (1948)

11 The effect of boredom on a large scale in history is
underestimated. It is a main cause of revolutions, and would
soon bring to an end all the static Utopias and the farmyard
civilization of the Fabians.

End of an Age (1948)

1 It takes in reality only one to make a quarrel. It is useless for the sheep to pass resolutions in favour of vegetarianism, while the wolf remains of a different opinion.

Outspoken Essays: First Series (1919)

2 The nations which have put mankind and posterity most in their debt have been small states—Israel, Athens, Florence, Elizabethan England.

Outspoken Essays: Second Series (1922) 'State, visible and invisible'

3 A man may build himself a throne of bayonets, but he cannot sit on it.
  a similar image was used by Boris **Yeltsin** *at the time of the failed military coup in Russia, August 1991*

Philosophy of Plotinus (1923) vol. 2

Bernard Ingham 1932–
British journalist and public relations specialist; press secretary to Margaret **Thatcher** 1979–90
on Ingham: see **Morgan** 278:10

4 Blood sport is brought to its ultimate refinement in the gossip columns.

speech, 5 February 1986

5 The media . . . is like an oil painting. Close up, it looks like nothing on earth. Stand back and you get the drift.

speech to the Parliamentary Press Gallery, February 1990

6 *at a meeting of the Parliamentary Lobby, noticing that he had a spot of blood on his shirt:*
  My God, I've been stabbed in the front.

recalled in a letter to Antony Jay, January 1995

Eugène Ionesco 1912–94
French dramatist

7 A civil servant doesn't make jokes.

The Killer (1958)

Hastings Lionel ('Pug') Ismay 1887–1965
British general and Secretary to the Committee of Imperial Defence; first Secretary-General of NATO

8 NATO exists for three reasons—to keep the Russians out, the Americans in and the Germans down.
  to a group of British Conservative backbenchers in 1949

Peter Hennessy *Never Again* (1992); oral tradition

Molly Ivins 1944– and Lou Dubose
American journalists

9 Young political reporters are always told there are three ways to judge a politician. The first is to look at the record. The second is to look at the record. And third, look at the record.

Molly Ivins and Lou Dubose *Shrub* (2000)

10 If you think his daddy had trouble with 'the vision thing', wait till you meet this one.
  of presidential candidate George W. **Bush**

Molly Ivins and Lou Dubose *Shrub* (2000)

Alija Izetbegović 1925–2003
Bosnian statesman; President of Bosnia and Herzegovina 1990–2003

11 And to my people I say, this may not be a just peace, but it is more just than a continuation of war.
  after signing the Dayton accord with representatives of Serbia and Croatia

in Dayton, Ohio, 21 November 1995

Andrew Jackson 1767–1845

American Democratic statesman; 7th President of the US, 1829–37
on Jackson: see **Clay** 95:6

1 The individual who refuses to defend his rights when called by his Government, deserves to be a slave, and must be punished as an enemy of his country and friend to her foe.

proclamation to the people of Louisiana from Mobile, 21 September 1814

2 The brave man inattentive to his duty, is worth little more to his country, than the coward who deserts her in the hour of danger.
   to troops who had abandoned their lines during the battle of New Orleans, 8 January 1815

attributed

3 Our Federal Union: it must be preserved.
   toast given on the Jefferson Birthday Celebration, 13 April 1830

Thomas Hart Benton *Thirty Years View* (1856) vol. 1

4 There are no necessary evils in government. Its evils exist only in its abuses.

veto of the Bank Bill, 10 July 183.

5 You are uneasy; you never sailed with *me* before, I see.

James Parton *Life of Jackson* (186 vol. 3

6 One man with courage makes a majority.

attributed

7 *shortly before his death, Jackson was asked if he had left anything undone:*
   I didn't shoot Henry Clay, and I didn't hang John C. Calhoun.

Robert V. Remini *Henry Clay* (1991); attributed

Glenda Jackson 1936–

British Labour politician and actress

8 If I am one of Blair's babes, well I've been called a damn sight worse.

in *Independent on Sunday* 8 Augu 1999

Jesse Jackson 1941–

American Democratic politician and clergyman

9 My right and my privilege to stand here before you has been won—won in my lifetime—by the blood and the sweat of the innocent.

speech at Democratic National Convention, Atlanta, 19 July 198

10 When I look out at this convention, I see the face of America, red, yellow, brown, black, and white. We are all precious in God's sight—the real rainbow coalition.

speech at Democratic National Convention, Atlanta, 19 July 198

11 You can't keep on running from labour, running from blacks, running from cities and expect to inspire them to vote.
   on President **Clinton**, *after the results of the 1994 election*

in *Guardian* 28 November 1994

Robert H. Jackson 1892–1954

American lawyer and judge

12 That four great nations, flushed with victory and stung with injury, stay the hands of vengeance and voluntarily submit their captive enemies to the judgement of the law, is one of the most significant tributes that Power has ever paid to Reason.
   opening statement for the prosecution at Nuremberg

before the International Military Tribunal in Nuremberg, 21 November 1945

James I (James VI of Scotland) 1566–1625

British monarch, King of Scotland from 1567 and of England from 1603

1 No bishop, no King.
to a deputation of Presbyterians from the Church of Scotland, seeking religious tolerance in England

W. Barlow *Sum and Substance of the Conference* (1604)

2 The state of monarchy is the supremest thing upon earth; for kings are not only God's lieutenants upon earth, and sit upon God's throne, but even by God himself they are called gods.

speech to Parliament, 21 March 1610

3 The king is truly *parens patriae*, the polite father of his people.

speech to Parliament, 21 March 1610

4 That which concerns the mystery of the king's power is not lawful to be disputed; for that is to wade into the weakness of Princes and to take away the mystical reverence, that belongs unto them that sit in the throne of God.

'A Speech in the Star Chamber' [speech to the judges] 20 June 1616

5 I will govern according to the common weal, but not according to the common will.

in December, 1621; J. R. Green *History of the English People* vol. 3 (1879)

James V 1512–42

Scottish monarch, King from 1513

6 *of the crown of Scotland (which had come to the Stuarts through the female line), on learning of the birth of his daughter* **Mary** *Queen of Scots, December 1542:*
It came with a lass, and it will pass with a lass.

Robert Lindsay of Pitscottie (*c.*1500–65) *History of Scotland* (1728)

Antony Jay see Lynn and Jay

Douglas Jay 1907–96

British Labour politician
see also **Slogans** 366:15

7 In the case of nutrition and health, just as in the case of education, the gentleman in Whitehall really does know better what is good for people than the people know themselves.

The Socialist Case (1939)

8 He never used one syllable where none would do.
of **Attlee**

Peter Hennessy *Muddling Through* (1996)

Margaret Jay 1939–

British Labour politician, daughter of James **Callaghan**

9 We're simply saying that what may have been right 800 or even 200 years ago is not right now.
on the abolition of the hereditary right to sit in the House of Lords

in *Guardian* 12 November 1999

10 I never aim to be unpredictable.

in *Observer* 20 February 2000 'They Said What . . . ?'

11 Any proposal totally to elect the second chamber under the mistaken view that it would increase the democratic base of parliament would in fact undermine democracy.

in the House of Lords, 7 March 2000

Thomas Jefferson 1743–1826

American Democratic Republican statesman; 3rd President of the US, 1801–9

on Jefferson: see **Kennedy** 213:2, **Last words** 228:6; *see also* **Last words** 228:4, **Mottoes** 281:6

1 We hold these truths to be sacred and undeniable; that all men are created equal and independent, that from that equal creation they derive rights inherent and inalienable, among which are the preservation of life, and liberty, and the pursuit of happiness.

'Rough Draft' of the American Declaration of Independence; J. P. Boyd et al. *Papers of Thomas Jefferson* vol. 1 (1950)

2 Our liberty depends on freedom of the press, and that cannot be limited without being lost.

letter to James Currie, 28 January 1786, in *Papers of Thomas Jefferson* (1954) vol. 9

3 Were it left to me to decide whether we should have a government without newspapers or newspapers without a government, I should not hesitate for a moment to prefer the latter.

letter to Colonel Edward Carrington, 16 January 1787

4 Experience declares that man is the only animal which devours its own kind, for I can apply no milder term to the governments of Europe, and to the general prey of the rich on the poor.

letter to Colonel Edward Carrington, 16 January 1787

5 A little rebellion now and then is a good thing.

letter to James Madison, 30 January 1787

6 The tree of liberty must be refreshed from time to time with the blood of patriots and tyrants. It is its natural manure.

letter to W. S. Smith, 13 November 1787

7 The natural progress of things is for liberty to yield and governments to gain ground.

letter to Colonel Edward Carrington, 27 May 1788

8 If I could not go to Heaven but with a party, I would not go there at all.

letter to Francis Hopkinson, 13 March 1789

9 The republican is the only form of government which is not eternally at open or secret war with the rights of mankind.

letter to William Hunter, 11 March 1790

10 No government ought to be without censors: and where the press is free, no one ever will.

letter to George Washington, 9 September 1792

11 The second office of government is honourable and easy, the first is but a splendid misery.

letter to Elbridge Gerry, 13 May 1797

12 Offices are acceptable here as elsewhere, and whenever a man has cast a longing eye on them [official positions], a rottenness begins in his conduct.

letter to Tench Coxe, 21 May 1799

13 What an augmentation of the field for jobbing, speculating, plundering, office-building and office-hunting would be produced by an assumption of all the state powers into the hands of the general government.

letter, 13 August 1800

14 If the principle were to prevail, of a common law [i.e. a single government] being in force in the U.S. . . . it would become the most corrupt government on the earth.

letter to Gideon Granger, 13 August 1800

1 A wise and frugal government, which shall restrain men from injuring one another, which shall leave them otherwise free to regulate their own pursuits of industry and improvement, and shall not take from the mouth of labour the bread it has earned. This is the sum of good government, and this is necessary to close the circle of our felicities.

first inaugural address, 4 March 1801

2 All, too, will bear in mind this sacred principle, that though the will of the majority is in all cases to prevail, that will to be rightful must be reasonable; that the minority possess their equal rights, which equal law must protect, and to violate would be oppression.

first inaugural address, 4 March 1801

3 Would the honest patriot, in the full tide of successful experiment, abandon a government which has so far kept us free and firm?

first inaugural address, 4 March 1801

4 Peace, commerce, and honest friendship with all nations— entangling alliances with none.

first inaugural address, 4 March 1801

5 Freedom of religion; freedom of the press, and freedom of person under the protection of *habeas corpus*, and trial by juries impartially selected. These principles form the bright constellation which has gone before us, and guided our steps through an age of revolution and reformation.

first inaugural address, 4 March 1801

6 I have learned to expect that it will rarely fall to the lot of imperfect man to retire from this station with the reputation and the favour which bring him into it.

first inaugural address, March 1801

7 If a due participation of office is a matter of right, how are vacancies to be obtained? Those by death are few; by resignation none.

letter to E. Shipman and others, 12 July 1801; see **Misquotations** 272:8

8 If we can prevent the government from wasting the labours of the people, under the pretence of taking care of them, they must become happy.

letter to Thomas Cooper, 29 November 1802

9 Nothing can now be believed which is seen in a newspaper. Truth itself becomes suspicious by being put into that polluted vehicle.

letter to John Norvell, 14 June 1807, in *The Portable Thomas Jefferson* (1977)

10 When a man assumes a public trust, he should consider himself as public property.
    to Baron von Humboldt, 1807

B. L. Rayner *Life of Jefferson* (1834)

11 The care of human life and happiness, and not their destruction, is the first and only legitimate object of good government.

to the Republican Citizens of Washington County, Maryland, 31 March 1809

12 Politics, like religion, hold up the torches of martyrdom to the reformers of error.

letter to James Ogilvie, 4 August 1811

13 I agree with you that there is a natural aristocracy among men. The grounds of this are virtue and talents.

letter to John Adams, 28 October 1813

14 Merchants have no country. The mere spot they stand on does not constitute so strong an attachment as that from which they draw their gains.

letter to Horatio G. Spafford, 17 March 1814

15 If a nation expects to be ignorant and free, in a state of civilization, it expects what never was and never will be.

letter to Colonel Charles Yancey, 6 January 1816

1 If it is believed that these elementary schools will be better managed by the Governor and Council, the commissioners of the literary fund, or any other general authority of the government, than by the parents in each ward, it is a belief against all experience . . . What has destroyed liberty and the rights of man in every government which has ever existed under the sun? The generalizing and concentrating all cares and powers into one body.

letter to Joseph C. Cabell, 2 February 1816

2 But this momentous question [the Missouri Compromise], like a firebell in the night awakened and filled me with terror. I considered it the knell of the Union.

letter to John Holmes, 22 April 1820

3 We have the wolf by the ears; and we can neither hold him, nor safely let him go. Justice is in one scale, and self-preservation in the other.
   on slavery

letter to John Holmes, 22 April 1820

4 I know no safe depository of the ultimate powers of the society but the people themselves; and if we think them not enlightened enough to exercise their control with a wholesome discretion, the remedy is not to take it from them, but to inform their discretion by education.

letter to William Charles Jarvis, 28 September 1820

5 That one hundred and fifty lawyers should do business together ought not to be expected.
   on the United States Congress

Autobiography 6 January 1821

6 To attain all this [universal republicanism], however, rivers of blood must yet flow, and years of desolation pass over; yet the object is worth rivers of blood, and years of desolation.

letter to John Adams, 4 September 1823

7 The generation which commences a revolution can rarely complete it.

letter to John Adams, 4 September 1823, in P. L. Ford *Writings of Thomas Jefferson* (1899) vol. 10

8 Were we directed from Washington when to sow, and when to reap, we should soon want bread.

Autobiography

9 Millions of innocent men, women, and children, since the introduction of Christianity, have been burnt, tortured, fined, imprisoned; yet we have not advanced one inch towards uniformity [of opinion]. What has been the effect of coercion? To make one half the world fools, and the other half hypocrites.

Notes on the State of Virginia (1781–5)

10 Indeed I tremble for my country when I reflect that God is just.

Notes on the State of Virginia (1781–5)

11 To the press alone, chequered as it is with abuses, the world is indebted for all the triumphs which have been gained by reason and humanity over error and oppression.

Virginia and Kentucky Resolutions (1799)

12 No duty the Executive had to perform was so trying as to put the right man in the right place.

J. B. MacMaster *History of the People of the United States* (1883–1913) vol. 2

13 The legitimate powers of government extend to such acts only as are injurious to others. But it does me no injury for my neighbour to say there are twenty gods, or no God. It neither picks my pocket nor breaks my leg.

attributed

14 The policy of the American government is to leave their citizens free, neither restraining nor aiding them in their pursuits.

attributed

Patrick Jenkin 1926–

British Conservative politician

1 People can clean their teeth in the dark, use the top of the stove instead of the oven, all sorts of savings, but they must use less electricity.
  as Minister for Energy, asking the public to save electricity as a miners' strike reduced supplies; often summarized as, 'clean your teeth in the dark'

radio broadcast, 15 January 1974

Roy Jenkins 1920–2003

British politician; co-founder of the Social Democratic Party, 1981

2 The politics of the left and centre of this country are frozen in an out-of-date mould which is bad for the political and economic health of Britain and increasingly inhibiting for those who live within the mould. Can it be broken?

speech to Parliamentary Press Gallery, 9 June 1980

3 *of Margaret **Thatcher**:*
  A First Minister whose self-righteous stubbornness has not been equalled, save briefly by Neville Chamberlain, since Lord North.

in *Observer* 11 March 1990

4 The record does not provide much sustenance for the view that limpet-like Prime Ministers can be easily disposed of by their parties.

in *Guardian* 14 April 1990

5 *of Edward **Heath**:*
  A great lighthouse which stands there, flashing out beams of light, indifferent to the waves which beat against him.

in *Independent* 22 September 1990

6 Nearly all Prime Ministers are dissatisfied with their successors, perhaps even more so if they come from their own party.

Gladstone (1995)

7 There is nobody in politics I can remember and no case I can think of in history where a man combined such a powerful political personality with so little intelligence.
  *of James **Callaghan***

Richard Crossman diary, 5 September 1969

W. Stanley Jevons 1835–82

English economist

8 All classes of society are trades unionists at heart, and differ chiefly in the boldness, ability, and secrecy with which they pursue their respective interests.

The State in Relation to Labour (1882)

John XXIII 1881–1963

Italian cleric, Pope from 1958

9 If civil authorities legislate for or allow anything that is contrary to that order and therefore contrary to the will of God, neither the laws made or the authorizations granted can be binding on the consciences of the citizens, since God has more right to be obeyed than man.

Pacem in Terris (1963)

10 The social progress, order, security and peace of each country are necessarily connected with the social progress, order, security and peace of all other countries.

Pacem in Terris (1963)

1   [In the universal *Declaration of Human Rights* (December, 1948)] in most solemn form, the dignity of a person is acknowledged to all human beings; and as a consequence there is proclaimed, as a fundamental right, the right of free movement in search for truth and in the attainment of moral good and of justice, and also the right to a dignified life.

Pacem in Terris (1963)

Elton John 1947– and Bernie Taupin 1950–

English pop singer and songwriter; songwriter

2   Goodbye England's rose;
May you ever grow in our hearts.
   *rewritten for and sung at the funeral of **Diana**, Princess of Wales, 7 September 1997*

'Candle in the Wind' (song, revised version, 1997)

3   And it seems to me you lived your life
Like a candle in the wind:
Never fading with the sunset
When the rain set in.
And your footsteps will always fall here
On England's greenest hills;
Your candle's burned out long before
Your legend ever will.

'Candle in the Wind' (song, revised version, 1997)

John Paul II 1920–2005

Polish cleric, Pope 1978–2005

4   It would be simplistic to say that Divine Providence caused the fall of communism. It fell by itself as a consequence of its own mistakes and abuses. It fell by itself because of its own inherent weaknesses.
   when asked by the Italian writer Vittorio Missori if the fall of the USSR could be ascribed to God

Carl Bernstein and Marco Politi *His Holiness: John Paul II and the Hidden History of our Time* (1996)

Lyndon Baines Johnson 1908–73

American Democratic statesman; 36th President of the US 1963–9
on Johnson: see **White** 417:6

5   *to a reporter who had queried his embracing Richard **Nixon** on the vice-president's return from a controversial tour of South America in 1958:*
Son, in politics you've got to learn that overnight chicken shit can turn to chicken salad.

Fawn Brodie *Richard Nixon* (1983)

6   I am a free man, an American, a United States Senator, and a Democrat, in that order.

in *Texas Quarterly* Winter 1958

7   I'll tell you what's at the bottom of it. If you can convince the lowest white man that he's better than the best coloured man, he won't notice you're picking his pocket. Hell, give him someone to look down on and he'll empty his pockets for you.
   during the 1960 Presidential campaign, to Bill Moyers

Robert Dallek *Lone Star Rising* (1991)

8   All I have I would have given gladly not to be standing here today.
   *following the assassination of John F. **Kennedy***

first speech to Congress as President, 27 November 1963

1 We have talked long enough in this country about equal rights. We have talked for a hundred years or more. It is time now to write the next chapter, and to write it in the books of law.

speech to Congress, 27 November 1963

2 This administration, here and now declares unconditional war on poverty in America.

State of the Union address to Congress, 8 January 1964

3 For the first time in our history, it is possible to conquer poverty.

speech to Congress, 16 March 1964

4 In your time we have the opportunity to move not only toward the rich society and the powerful society, but upward to the Great Society.

speech at University of Michigan, 22 May 1964

5 We Americans know, although others appear to forget, the risks of spreading conflict. We still seek no wider war.

speech on radio and television, 4 August 1964

6 We are not about to send American boys 9 or 10,000 miles away from home to do what Asian boys ought to be doing for themselves.

speech at Akron University, 21 October 1964

7 Extremism in the pursuit of the Presidency is an unpardonable vice. Moderation in the affairs of the nation is the highest virtue.

speech in New York, 31 October 1964

8 A President's hardest task is not to *do* what is right, but to *know* what is right.

State of the Union address to Congress, 4 January 1965

9 It is not enough to open the gates of opportunity. All of our citizens must have the ability to walk through those gates.
speech at Harvard in 1965

Paul L. Fisher and Ralph L. Lavenstein (eds.) *Race and the News Media* (1967)

10 Better to have him inside the tent pissing out, than outside pissing in.
of J. Edgar Hoover

David Halberstam *The Best and the Brightest* (1972)

11 Come now, let us reason together.

habitual saying

12 Did you ever think that making a speech on economics is a lot like pissing down your leg? It seems hot to you, but it never does to anyone else.
*to J. K. **Galbraith***

J. K. Galbraith *A Life in Our Times* (1981)

13 I don't want loyalty. I want *loyalty*. I want him to kiss my ass in Macy's window at high noon and tell me it smells like roses. I want his pecker in my pocket.
discussing a prospective assistant

David Halberstam *The Best and the Brightest* (1972)

14 So dumb he can't fart and chew gum at the same time.
*of Gerald **Ford***

Richard Reeves *A Ford, not a Lincoln* (1975)

Philander Chase Johnson 1866–1939
American journalist

15 Politics is the art of turning influence into affluence.

Senator Sorghum's Primer of Politics (1906)

Samuel Johnson 1709–84
English poet, critic, and lexicographer

16 Liberty is, to the lowest rank of every nation, little more than the choice of working or starving.

'The Bravery of the English Common Soldier' in *The British Magazine* January 1760

1 If the changes we fear be thus irresistible, what remains but to acquiesce with silence, as in the other insurmountable distresses of humanity? It remains that we retard what we cannot repel, that we palliate what we cannot cure.

A Dictionary of the English Language (1755) preface

2 *Pension.* Pay given to a state hireling for treason to his country.

A Dictionary of the English Language (1755)

3 Among the calamities of war may be jointly numbered the diminution of the love of truth, by the falsehoods which interest dictates and credulity encourages.

The Idler 11 November 1758; see **Proverbs** 320:1

4 How is it that we hear the loudest yelps for liberty among the drivers of negroes?

Taxation No Tyranny (1775)

5 How small of all that human hearts endure,
That part which laws or kings can cause or cure.

lines added to Oliver Goldsmith's *The Traveller* (1764); see **Goldsmith** 161:7

6 I do not much like to see a Whig in any dress; but I hate to see a Whig in a parson's gown.

James Boswell *Journal of a Tour to the Hebrides* (1785) 24 September 1773

7 This man [Lord Chesterfield] I thought had been a Lord among wits; but, I find, he is only a wit among Lords.

James Boswell *Life of Samuel Johnson* (1791) 1754

8 Your levellers wish to level *down* as far as themselves; but they cannot bear levelling *up* to themselves.

James Boswell *Life of Samuel Johnson* (1791) 21 July 1763

9 A woman's preaching is like a dog's walking on his hinder legs. It is not done well; but you are surprised to find it done at all.

James Boswell *Life of Samuel Johnson* (1791) 31 July 1763

10 BOSWELL: So, Sir, you laugh at schemes of political improvement.
JOHNSON: Why, Sir, most schemes of political improvement are very laughable things.

James Boswell *Life of Samuel Johnson* (1791) 26 October 1769

11 So many objections may be made to everything, that nothing can overcome them but the necessity of doing something.

James Boswell *Life of Samuel Johnson* (1791) 1770

12 A decent provision for the poor, is the true test of civilization.

James Boswell *Life of Samuel Johnson* (1791) 1770

13 I would not give half a guinea to live under one form of government rather than another. It is of no moment to the happiness of an individual.

James Boswell *Life of Samuel Johnson* (1791) 31 March 1772

14 Sir, I perceive you are a vile Whig.
    to Sir Adam Fergusson

James Boswell *Life of Samuel Johnson* (1791) 31 March 1772

15 There are few ways in which a man can be more innocently employed than in getting money.

James Boswell *Life of Samuel Johnson* (1791) 27 March 1775

16 George the First knew nothing, and desired to know nothing; did nothing, and desired to do nothing; and the only good thing that is told of him is, that he wished to restore the crown to its hereditary successor.

James Boswell *Life of Samuel Johnson* (1791) 6 April 1775

17 Patriotism is the last refuge of a scoundrel.

James Boswell *Life of Samuel Johnson* (1791) 7 April 1775

18 Politics are now nothing more than means of rising in the world.

James Boswell *Life of Samuel Johnson* (1791) 18 April 1775

19 Every man who attacks my belief, diminishes in some degree my confidence in it, and therefore makes me uneasy; and I am angry with him who makes me uneasy.

James Boswell *Life of Samuel Johnson* (1791) 3 April 1776

1 It is better that some should be unhappy than that none should be happy, which would be the case in a general state of equality.

James Boswell *Life of Samuel Johnson* (1791) 7 April 1776

2 Though we cannot out-vote them we will out-argue them.

James Boswell *Life of Samuel Johnson* (1791) 3 April 1778

3 I have always said, the first Whig was the Devil.

James Boswell *Life of Samuel Johnson* (1791) 28 April 1778

4 A wise Tory and a wise Whig, I believe, will agree. Their principles are the same, though their modes of thinking are different.

James Boswell *Life of Samuel Johnson* (1791) May 1781; written statement given to Boswell

5 If a man were to go by chance at the same time with Burke under a shed, to shun a shower, he would say—'this is an extraordinary man.'
    on Edmund **Burke**

James Boswell *Life of Samuel Johnson* (1791) 15 May 1784

6 Fox divided the kingdom with Caesar; so that it was a doubt whether the nation should be ruled by the sceptre of George III or the tongue of Fox.
    on the Parliamentary defeat of Charles James **Fox**, *and the subsequent dissolution, in 1784*

in *Dictionary of National Biography* (1917-)

7 Mankind are happier in a state of inequality and subordination. Were they to be in this pretty state of equality, they would soon degenerate into brutes.

attributed

Tom Johnston 1881–1965
Scottish Labour politician

8 I have become . . . uneasy lest we should get political power without our first having, or at least simultaneously having, an adequate economy to administer. What purport would there be in our getting a Scots parliament in Edinburgh if it has to administer an emigration system, a glorified Poor Law, and a graveyard!

Memories (1952)

9 They have barred us by barbed wire fences from the bens and glens: the peasant has been ruthlessly swept aside to make room for the pheasant, and the mountain hare now brings forth her young on the hearthstone of the Gael!

Our Scots Noble Families (1909)

Hanns Johst 1890–1978
German dramatist

10 Whenever I hear the word culture . . . I release the safety-catch of my Browning!
    often quoted as: 'Whenever I hear the word culture, I reach for my pistol!', and attributed to Hermann **Goering**

Schlageter (1933); see **Glencross** 160:2

Ieuan Wyn Jones 1949–
Welsh nationalist politician, president of Plaid Cymru

11 The priority for us now is for Wales to gain the same powers as Scotland.
    speech to the Plaid Cymru Party Conference

in *Guardian* 23 September 2000

John Paul Jones 1747–92

American admiral

1 I have not yet begun to fight.
as his ship was sinking, 23 September 1779, having been asked
whether he had lowered his flag

Mrs Reginald De Koven *Life and*
Letters of John Paul Jones (1914)
vol. 1

Mary Harris 'Mother' Jones c.1837–1930

Irish-born American labour activist

2 Pray for the dead and fight like hell for the living!

The Autobiography of Mother Jones
(1925)

Steve Jones 1944–

English geneticist

3 The greenest political party there has ever been was the
Nazi party. The Nazis were great believers in purity, that
nature should not be interfered with.

in *Times Higher Education*
Supplement 27 August 1999

4 Students accept astonishing things happening in human
genetics without turning a hair but worry about GM soya
beans.

in *Times Higher Education*
Supplement 27 August 1999

William Jones 1746–94

English jurist

5 My opinion is, that power should always be distrusted, in
whatever hands it is placed.

letter to Lord Althorpe, 5 October
1782

Ben Jonson c.1573–1637

English dramatist and poet

6 PEOPLE: The Voice of Cato is the voice of Rome.
CATO: The voice of Rome is the consent of heaven!

Catiline his Conspiracy (1611)

Janis Joplin 1943–70

American singer

7 Fourteen heart attacks and he had to die in my week. In MY
week.
*when ex-President **Eisenhower**'s death prevented her photograph*
appearing on the cover of Newsweek

in *New Musical Express* 12 April
1969

Barbara Jordan 1936–96

American Democratic politician

8 The Bill of Rights was not ordained by nature or God. It's
very human, very fragile.

in *New York Times Magazine* 21
October 1990

Thomas Jordan c.1612–85
English poet and dramatist

1 They plucked communion tables down
And broke our painted glasses;
They threw our altars to the ground
And tumbled down the crosses.
They set up Cromwell and his heir—
The Lord and Lady Claypole—
Because they hated Common Prayer,
The organ and the maypole.

'How the War began' (1664)

Chief Joseph (Hinmaton-Yalaktit) c.1840–1904
American Nez Percé chief

2 From where the sun now stands I will fight no more forever.

speech at the end of the Nez Percé war in 1877; Dee Brown *Bury My Heart at Wounded Knee* (1970) ch. 13

3 Good words do not last long unless they amount to something. Words do not pay for my dead people.

on a visit to Washington in 1879; Chester Anders Fee *Chief Joseph* (1936)

Keith Joseph 1918–94
British Conservative politician

4 Problems reproduce themselves from generation to generation . . . I refer to this as a 'cycle of deprivation'.

speech in London to the Pre-School Playgroups Association, 29 June 1972

5 The balance of our population, our human stock, is threatened . . . a high and rising proportion of children are being born to mothers least fitted to bring children into the world and bring them up.

speech in Birmingham, 19 October 1974

6 If we are to be prosperous we need more millionaires and more bankrupts.

maiden speech in the House of Lords, 19 February 1988

7 There are no illegitimate children, only illegitimate parents.
in Kiss Hollywood Good-Bye (1978), Anita Loos attributes an earlier coinage of this statement to the American philanthropist Edna Gladney

speech to National Children's Home, 6 November 1991

Lionel Jospin 1937–
French statesman, Prime Minister of France 1997–2002

8 Yes to the market economy, No to the market society.

in *Independent* 16 September 1998

Joseph Joubert 1754–1824
French essayist and moralist

9 One of the surest ways of killing a tree is to lay bare its roots. It is the same with institutions. We must not be too ready to disinter the origins of those we wish to preserve. All beginnings are small.

Pensées (1842)

10 It's better to debate a question without settling it than to settle a question without debating it.

attributed

Tessa Jowell 1947–
British Labour politician

1 In the last Parliament, the House of Commons had more MPs called John than all the women MPs put together.

in Independent on Sunday 14 March 1999 'Quotes'

James Joyce 1882–1941
Irish novelist

2 Poor Parnell! he cried loudly. My dead king!

A Portrait of the Artist as a Young Man (1916) ch. 1

William Joyce ('Lord Haw-Haw') 1906–46
American-born Fascist supporter and wartime broadcaster from Nazi Germany; executed for treason in 1946

3 Germany calling! Germany calling!
  habitual introduction to propaganda broadcast

broadcasts from Germany to Britain during the Second World War

Juan Carlos I 1938–
Spanish monarch, King from 1975

4 The Crown, the symbol of the permanence and unity of Spain, cannot tolerate any actions by people attempting to disrupt by force the democratic process.
  on the occasion of the attempted coup in 1981

television broadcast at 1.15 a.m., 24 February 1981

5 I will neither abdicate the Crown nor leave Spain. Whoever rebels will provoke a new civil war and will be responsible.
  on the occasion of the attempted coup

television broadcast, 24 February 1981

'Junius'
English 18th-century pseudonymous writer

6 The right of election is the very essence of the constitution.

in Public Advertiser 24 April 1769, letter 11

7 Is this the wisdom of a great minister? or is it the ominous vibration of a pendulum?

in Public Advertiser 30 May 1769, letter 12

8 There is a holy mistaken zeal in politics as well as in religion. By persuading others, we convince ourselves.

in Public Advertiser 19 December 1769, letter 35

9 However distinguished by rank or property, in the rights of freedom we are all equal.

in Public Advertiser 19 March 1770, letter 37

10 The injustice done to an individual is sometimes of service to the public.

in Public Advertiser 14 November 1770, letter 41

11 As for Mr Wedderburne, there is something about him, which even treachery cannot trust.

in Public Advertiser 22 June 1771, letter 49

12 The liberty of the press is the *Palladium* of all the civil, political, and religious rights of an Englishman.

The Letters of Junius (1772 ed.) 'Dedication to the English Nation'

John Junor 1919–97
British journalist

13 Such a graceful exit. And then he had to go and do this on the doorstep.
  *on Harold **Wilson**'s 'Lavender List', the honours list he drew up on resigning the British premiership in 1976*

in Observer 23 January 1990

Juvenal c.AD 60–c.130

Roman satirist

1 *Quis tulerit Gracchos de seditione querentes?*   *Satires*

Who would put up with the Gracchi complaining about
subversion?
> *referring to the Roman tribune Tiberius Sempronius Gracchus
> (163–133 BC) and his brother Gaius Sempronius Gracchus
> (c.153–121 BC), who were responsible for radical social and
> economic legislation, passed against the wishes of the senatorial
> class*

2   *Sed quis custodiet ipsos*   *Satires*
Custodes?

But who is to guard the guards themselves?

3 . . . *Verbosa et grandis epistula venit*   *Satires*
A Capreis.

A huge wordy letter came from Capri.
> *on the Emperor Tiberius's letter to the Senate, which caused the
> downfall of Sejanus in AD 31*

4 . . . *Duas tantum res anxius optat,*   *Satires*
Panem et circenses.

Only two things does he [the modern citizen] anxiously wish
for—bread and circuses.

Franz Kafka 1883–1924

Czech novelist

5 It's often better to be in chains than to be free.   *The Trial* (1925)

Immanuel Kant 1724–1804

German philosopher

6 There is, therefore, only one categorical imperative. It is: *Fundamental Principles of the*
Act only according to that maxim by which you can at the   *Metaphysics of Ethics* (1785)
same time will that it should become a universal law.

7 Out of the crooked timber of humanity no straight thing   *Idee zu einer allgemeinen Geschichte*
was ever made.   *in weltbürgerliche Absicht* (1784)

Gerald Kaufman 1930–

British Labour politician

8 The longest suicide note in history.   Denis Healey *The Time of My Life*
> *on the Labour Party's* New Hope for Britain *(1983)*   (1989)

9 We would prefer to see the House [the Royal Opera House]   report of the Commons' Culture,
run by a philistine with the requisite financial acumen than   Media and Sport Select Committee
by the succession of opera and ballet lovers who have   on Covent Garden, 3 December
brought a great and valuable institution to its knees.   1997

10 Cabinet minutes are studied in Government Departments   *How to be a Minister* (1980)
with the reverence generally reserved for sacred texts, and
can be triumphantly produced conclusively to settle any
arguments.

John Keane 1949–

Australian political scientist

1 Sovereign state power is an indispensable condition of the democratization of civil society . . . a more democratic order cannot be built *through* state power, it cannot be built *without* state power.

Democracy and Civil Society (1988)

Paul Keating 1944–

Australian Labor statesman; Prime Minister 1991–6

2 You look like an Easter Island statue with an arse full of razor blades.
    in the Australian Parliament to the then Prime Minister, Malcolm **Fraser**

Michael Gordon *A Question of Leadership* (1993)

3 This is a recession that Australia had to have.

speaking as Federal Treasurer, 29 November 1990

4 Even as it [Great Britain] walked out on you and joined the Common Market, you were still looking for your MBEs and your knighthoods, and all the rest of the regalia that comes with it. You would take Australia right back down the time tunnel to the cultural cringe where you have always come from.
    addressing Australian Conservative supporters of Great Britain in the Australian Parliament, 27 February 1992

in *House of Representatives Weekly Hansard* [Australia] (1992) no. 1

5 These are the same old fogies who doffed their lids and tugged the forelock to the British establishment.
    of Australian Conservative supporters of Great Britain, 27 February 1992

in *House of Representatives Weekly Hansard* [Australia] (1992) no. 1

6 I'm a bastard. But I'm a bastard who gets the mail through. And they appreciate that.
    in 1994, to a senior colleague

in *Sunday Telegraph* 20 November 1994

7 Leadership is not about being nice. It's about being right and being strong.

in *Time* 9 January 1995

John Keegan 1934–

British military historian

8 It now does look as if air power has prevailed in the Balkans and that the time to redefine how victory in war may be won has come.

in *Daily Telegraph* 4 June 1999

Christine Keeler 1942–

English model and showgirl

9 Being in the public eye, as Monica Lewinsky will be for the rest of her life, is like being the lady with the moustache at the circus. You're a curiosity—and you will never stop being one.

attributed, in *The Times* 13 March 1999

Brian Keenan 1950–

Irish writer and teacher

10 Politics can only be a small part of what we are. It's a *way* of seeing, it's not all-seeing in itself.

An Evil Cradling (1992)

Garrison Keillor 1942–

American humorous writer and broadcaster

1 Ronald Reagan, the President who never told bad news to the American people.

We Are Still Married (1989), introduction

2 My ancestors were Puritans from England. They arrived here in 1648 in the hope of finding greater restrictions than were permissible under English law at that time.

attributed, 1993

Tom Kelly

British government press officer

3 This is now a game of chicken with the Beeb.
on the argument between Downing Street and the BBC about the content of Andrew Gilligan's Today *report; see* **Gilligan** 157:1

email of 10 July 2003; in *Guardian* 19 August 2003 (online edition)

David Kemp 1941–

Australian Liberal politician

4 This is not a bowl of spaghetti and meatballs. This is a diagram that accurately reflects the knots that Australia is going to be tied up in if Kim Beazley ever tries to put into effect this huge grab-bag of promises.
of the diagram accompanying Kim Beazley's unveiling of the Labor Party's 'Knowledge Nation' strategy

on *Lateline* (ABC TV), 2 July 2001

George F. Kennan 1904–2005

American diplomat and historian

5 Government . . . is simply not the channel through which men's noblest impulses are to be realized. Its task, on the contrary, is largely to see to it that the ignoble ones are kept under restraint and not permitted to go too far.

Around the Cragged Hill (1993)

6 A war regarded as inevitable or even probable, and therefore much prepared for, has a very good chance of being eventually fought.

The Cloud of Danger (1977)

Charles Kennedy 1959–

British Liberal Democrat politician, Party Leader from 1999

7 War is not the word; nor is crusade. Resolve is.
of the appropriate response to terrorism; see **Bush** 67:4

speech to the Liberal Democrat Party Conference, 24 December 2001

8 The era of three-party politics right across the UK is now with us.

speech, 6 May 2005

Florynce Kennedy 1916–2000

American lawyer

9 When you want to get to the suites, start in the streets.
her rule for political activism

attributed; in *Los Angeles Times* 28 December 2000 (obituary)

John F. Kennedy 1917–63

American Democratic statesman, 35th President of the US, 1961–3

on Kennedy: see **Bentsen** 36:3, **Hope** 188:7, **Kennedy** 213:12, **Stevenson** 380:16

1 Don't buy a single vote more than necessary. I'll be damned if I'm going to pay for a landslide.
   telegraphed message from his father, read at a Gridiron dinner in Washington, 15 March 1958, and almost certainly JFK's invention

J. F. Cutler *Honey Fitz* (1962)

2 We stand today on the edge of a new frontier . . . But the New Frontier of which I speak is not a set of promises—it is a set of challenges. It sums up not what I intend to offer the American people, but what I intend to ask of them.
   accepting the Democratic nomination

speech in Los Angeles, 15 July 1960; see **Schlossberg** 347:10

3 Let the word go forth from this time and place, to friend and foe alike, that the torch has been passed to a new generation of Americans—born in this century, tempered by war, disciplined by a hard and bitter peace, proud of our ancient heritage—and unwilling to witness or permit the slow undoing of those human rights to which this nation has always been committed, and to which we are committed today at home and around the world.

inaugural address, 20 January 1961

4 Let every nation know, whether it wishes us well or ill, that we shall pay any price, bear any burden, meet any hardship, support any friend, oppose any foe to assure the survival and the success of liberty.

inaugural address, 20 January 1961

5 If a free society cannot help the many who are poor, it cannot save the few who are rich.

inaugural address, 20 January 1961

6 Let us never negotiate out of fear. But let us never fear to negotiate.

inaugural address, 20 January 1961

7 All this will not be finished in the first 100 days. Nor will it be finished in the first 1,000 days, nor in the life of this Administration, nor even perhaps in our lifetime on this planet. But let us begin.

inaugural address, 20 January 1961

8 And so, my fellow Americans: ask not what your country can do for you—ask what you can do for your country. My fellow citizens of the world: ask not what America will do for you, but what together we can do for the freedom of man.

inaugural address, 20 January 1961; Oliver Wendell **Holmes** Jr., speaking at Keene, New Hampshire, 30 May 1884 said: 'We pause to . . . recall what our country has done for each of us and to ask ourselves what we can do for our country in return' (see also **Gibran** 156:3)

9 I believe that this Nation should commit itself to achieving the goal, before this decade is out, of landing a man on the Moon and returning him safely to earth.

supplementary State of the Union message to Congress, 25 May 1961

10 When we got into office, the thing that surprised me most was to find that things were just as bad as we'd been saying they were.

speech at the White House, 27 May 1961

11 Mankind must put an end to war or war will put an end to mankind.

speech to United Nations General Assembly, 25 September 1961

1 Those who make peaceful revolution impossible will make violent revolution inevitable.

speech at the White House, 13 March 1962

2 Probably the greatest concentration of talent and genius in this house except for perhaps those times when Thomas Jefferson ate alone.
of a dinner for the Nobel prizewinners at the White House

in *New York Times* 30 April 1962

3 If we cannot end now our differences, at least we can help make the world safe for diversity.

address at American University, Washington, DC, 10 June 1963

4 No one has been barred on account of his race from fighting or dying for America—there are no 'white' or 'coloured' signs on the foxholes or graveyards of battle.

message to Congress on proposed Civil Rights Bill, 19 June 1963

5 All free men, wherever they may live, are citizens of Berlin, and therefore, as a free man, I take pride in the words *Ich bin ein Berliner* [I am a Berliner].
speaking in the newly divided city of Berlin, and expressing the USA's commitment to the support and defence of West Berlin

speech in West Berlin, 26 June 1963

6 When power leads man toward arrogance, poetry reminds him of his limitations. When power narrows the areas of man's concern, poetry reminds him of the richness and diversity of his existence. When power corrupts, poetry cleanses. For art establishes the basic human truths which must serve as the touchstone of our judgement.

speech at Amherst College, Massachusetts, 26 October 1963

7 In free society art is not a weapon . . . Artists are not engineers of the soul.

speech at Amherst College, Massachusetts, 26 October 1963; see **Gorky** 163:2, **Stalin** 378:6

8 *on being asked how he became a war hero:*
It was involuntary. They sank my boat.

Arthur M. Schlesinger Jr. *A Thousand Days* (1965)

9 Washington is a city of southern efficiency and northern charm.

Arthur M. Schlesinger Jr. *A Thousand Days* (1965)

10 I'm an idealist without illusions.

attributed; see **Macleod** 251:10

Joseph P. Kennedy 1888–1969

American financier and diplomat; father of John F. **Kennedy**
see also **Proverbs** 319:13

11 This is a hell of a long way from East Boston.
to his wife Rose, on a visit to Windsor Castle two weeks after his arrival as Ambassador

in *The Times* 24 January 1995 (obituary of Rose **Kennedy**)

12 We're going to sell Jack like soapflakes.
*when his son John F. **Kennedy** made his bid for the Presidency*

John H. Davis *The Kennedy Clan* (1984)

Robert F. Kennedy 1925–68

American democratic politician; son of Joseph **Kennedy** and brother of John F. **Kennedy**

13 About one-fifth of the people are against everything all the time.

speech at University of Pennsylvania, 6 May 1964

14 What is objectionable, what is dangerous about extremists is not that they are extreme but that they are intolerant.

The Pursuit of Justice (1964)

15 Every society gets the kind of criminal it deserves. What is equally true is that every community gets the kind of law enforcement it insists on.

The Pursuit of Justice (1964)

Rose Kennedy 1890–1995

American wife of Joseph **Kennedy**, mother of John F. **Kennedy** and Robert **Kennedy**

1 It's our money, and we're free to spend it any way we please . . . If you have money you spend it, and win.
*in response to criticism of overlavish funding of her son Robert **Kennedy**'s 1968 presidential campaign*

in *Daily Telegraph* 24 January 1995 (obituary)

2 Now Teddy must run.
*to her daughter, on hearing of the assassination of Robert **Kennedy***

in *The Times* 24 January 1995 (obituary); attributed, perhaps apocryphal

Jomo Kenyatta 1891–1978

Kenyan statesman, Prime Minister of Kenya 1963 and President 1964–78

3 The African is conditioned, by the cultural and social institutions of centuries, to a freedom of which Europe has little conception, and it is not in his nature to accept serfdom forever. He realizes that he must fight unceasingly for his own emancipation; for without this he is doomed to remain the prey of rival imperialisms.

Facing Mount Kenya (1938); conclusion

John Kerry 1943–

American Democratic politician, presidential candidate in 2004

4 It's the wrong war, in the wrong place, at the wrong time.
*of the war in Iraq, echoing the words of Omar **Bradley** on the Korean War in 1951*

campaigning in Canonsburg, Pennsylvania, 6 September 2004; Reuters 6 September 2004 (electronic edition)

5 It's one thing to be certain, but you can be certain and you can be wrong.

televised presidential debate with George W. **Bush**, 30 September 2004; in *New York Times* 1 October 2004 (electronic edition)

Francis Scott Key 1779–1843

American lawyer and verse-writer

6 'Tis the star-spangled banner; O long may it wave O'er the land of the free, and the home of the brave!

'The Star-Spangled Banner' (1814)

John Maynard Keynes 1883–1946

English economist

7 I work for a Government I despise for ends I think criminal.

letter to Duncan Grant, 15 December 1917

8 *of **Clemenceau**:*
He felt about France what Pericles felt of Athens—unique value in her, nothing else mattering; but his theory of politics was Bismarck's. He had one illusion—France; and one disillusion—mankind, including Frenchmen, and his colleagues not least.

The Economic Consequences of the Peace (1919)

9 Like Odysseus, the President looked wiser when he was seated.
*of Woodrow **Wilson***

The Economic Consequences of the Peace (1919)

1 Lenin was right. There is no subtler, no surer means of overturning the existing basis of society than to debauch the currency. The process engages all the hidden forces of economic law on the side of destruction, and does it in a manner which not one man in a million is able to diagnose.

The Economic Consequences of the Peace (1919)

2 Capitalism, wisely managed, can probably be made more efficient for attaining economic ends than any alternative system yet in sight, but . . . in itself it is in many ways extremely objectionable.

The End of Laissez-Faire (1926)

3 Marxian Socialism must always remain a portent to the historians of Opinion—how a doctrine so illogical and so dull can have exercised so powerful and enduring an influence over the minds of men, and, through them, the events of history.

The End of Laissez-Faire (1926)

4 I do not know which makes a man more conservative—to know nothing but the present, or nothing but the past.

The End of Laissez-Faire (1926)

5 The important thing for Government is not to do things which individuals are doing already, and to do them a little better or a little worse; but to do those things which at present are not done at all.

The End of Laissez-Faire (1926)

6 *of* **Lloyd George**:
This extraordinary figure of our time, this syren, this goat-footed bard, this half-human visitor to our age from the hag-ridden magic and enchanted woods of Celtic antiquity.

Essays in Biography (1933) 'Mr Lloyd George'

7 *of* **Lloyd George**:
Who shall paint the chameleon, who can tether a broomstick?

Essays in Biography (1933) 'Mr Lloyd George'

8 It is better that a man should tyrannize over his bank balance than over his fellow-citizens.

General Theory (1936)

9 We take it as a fundamental psychological rule of any modern community that, when its real income is increased, it will not increase its consumption by an equal *absolute* amount.

General Theory (1936)

10 The ideas of economists and political philosophers, both when they are right and when they are wrong, are more powerful than is commonly understood . . . Practical men, who believe themselves to be quite exempt from any intellectual influences, are usually the slaves of some defunct economist. Madmen in authority, who hear voices in the air, are distilling their frenzy from some academic scribbler of a few years back.

General Theory (1947 ed.)

11 But this *long run* is a misleading guide to current affairs. *In the long run* we are all dead.

A Tract on Monetary Reform (1923)

12 I evidently knew more about economics than my examiners.
explaining why he performed badly in the Civil Service examinations

Roy Harrod *Life of John Maynard Keynes* (1951)

13 We threw good housekeeping to the winds. But we saved ourselves and helped save the world.
of Britain in the Second World War

A. J. P. Taylor *English History, 1914–1945* (1965)

14 LADY VIOLET BONHAM CARTER: What do you think happens to Mr Lloyd George when he is alone in the room?
MAYNARD KEYNES: When he is alone in the room there is nobody there.

Lady Violet Bonham Carter *The Impact of Personality in Politics* (Romanes Lecture, 1963)

Reg Keys 1952–

British father of a serviceman killed in Iraq

1 Fighting this campaign has not been an easy task for me but I had to do it for my son . . . I hope . . . the Prime Minister one day will say sorry.

having fought the election in Tony **Blair**'s Sedgefield constituency, 6 May 2005

Ayatollah Ruhollah Khomeini 1900–89

Iranian Shiite Muslim leader, who returned to Iran from exile in 1979 to lead an Islamic revolution which overthrew the Shah

2 If laws are needed, Islam has established them all. There is no need . . . after establishing a government, to sit down and draw up laws.

Islam and Revolution: Writings and Declarations of Imam Khomeini (1981) ' Islamic Government'

Nikita Khrushchev 1894–1971

Soviet statesman; Premier, 1958–64

3 If anyone believes that our smiles involve abandonment of the teaching of Marx, Engels and Lenin he deceives himself. Those who wait for that must wait until a shrimp learns to whistle.

speech in Moscow, 17 September 1955

4 We must abolish the cult of the individual decisively, once and for all.

speech to secret session of the 20th Congress of the Communist Party, 25 February 1956

5 We say this not only for the socialist states, who are more akin to us. We base ourselves on the idea that we must peacefully co-exist. About the capitalist States, it doesn't depend on you whether or not we exist. If you don't like us, don't accept our invitations and don't invite us to come to see you. Whether you like it or not, history is on our side. We will bury you.
speech to Western diplomats at reception in Moscow for Polish leader Mr Gomulka, 18 November 1956; 'We will bury you' in this context means 'we will outlive you'

in *The Times* 19 November 1956

6 If one cannot catch the bird of paradise, better take a wet hen.

in *Time* 6 January 1958

7 Politicians are the same all over. They promise to build a bridge where there is no river.

at a press conference in New York, October 1960

8 We are going to make the imperialists dance like fishes in a saucepan, even without war.

in Vienna, 2 July 1960

9 If you start throwing hedgehogs under me, I shall throw a couple of porcupines under you.

in *New York Times* 7 November 1963

10 Anyone who believes that the worker can be lulled by fine revolutionary phrases is mistaken . . . If no concern is shown for the growth of material and spiritual riches, the people will listen today, they will listen tomorrow, and then they may say: 'Why do you promise us everything for the future? You are talking, so to speak, about life beyond the grave. The priest has already told us about this.'

speech at World Youth Forum, 19 September 1964

David Maxwell Fyfe, Lord Kilmuir 1900–67
British Conservative politician and lawyer
on Kilmuir: see **Anonymous** 11:2

1 Gratitude is not a normal feature of political life.

Political Adventure (1964)

2 Loyalty is the Tory's secret weapon.

Anthony Sampson *Anatomy of Britain* (1962); see **Critchley** 105:6

Anthony King 1934–
British political scientist

3 It is an asteroid hitting the planet and destroying practically all life on earth.
asserting that the word 'landslide' was too weak to describe the scale of Labour's victory

on 'Election Night' (BBC1) 2 May 1997

Martin Luther King 1929–68
American civil rights leader
see also **Epitaphs** 136:1

4 I want to be the white man's brother, not his brother-in-law.

in *New York Journal-American* 10 September 1962

5 Injustice anywhere is a threat to justice everywhere.

letter from Birmingham Jail, Alabama, 16 April 1963

6 I submit to you that if a man hasn't discovered something he will die for, he isn't fit to live.

speech in Detroit, 23 June 1963

7 I have a dream that one day on the red hills of Georgia the sons of former slaves and the sons of former slave owners will be able to sit down together at the table of brotherhood . . .
    I have a dream that my four little children will one day live in a nation where they will not be judged by the colour of their skin but by the content of their character.

speech at Civil Rights March in Washington, 28 August 1963

8 When we let freedom ring, when we let it ring from every village and every hamlet, from every state and every city, we will be able to speed up that day when all of God's children, black men and white men, Jews and Gentiles, Protestants and Catholics, will be able to join hands and sing in the words of the old Negro spiritual, 'Free at last! Free at last! Thank God Almighty, we are free at last!'

speech at Civil Rights March in Washington, 28 August 1963

9 We must learn to live together as brothers or perish together as fools.

speech at St Louis, 22 March 1964

10 I just want to do God's will. And he's allowed me to go up to the mountain. And I've looked over, and I've seen the promised land . . . So I'm happy tonight. I'm not worried about anything. I'm not fearing any man.
speech in Memphis, 3 April 1968, the day before his assassination

in *New York Times* 4 April 1968

11 If we assume that mankind has a right to survive, then we must find an alternative to war and destruction. In our day of space vehicles and guided ballistic missiles, the choice is either nonviolence or nonexistence.

Strength to Love (1963)

12 Nothing in all the world is more dangerous than sincere ignorance and conscientious stupidity.

Strength to Love (1963)

1 The ultimate measure of a man is not where he stands in moments of comfort and convenience, but where he stands at times of challenge and controversy.

Strength to Love (1963)

2 The means by which we live have outdistanced the ends for which we live. Our scientific power has outrun our spiritual power. We have guided missiles and misguided men.

Strength to Love (1963)

3 A riot is at bottom the language of the unheard.

Where Do We Go From Here? (1967)

4 Cowardice asks the question, 'Is it safe?' Expediency asks the question, 'Is it politic?' Vanity asks the question, 'Is it popular?' But Conscience asks the question, 'Is it right?'

*c.*1967; in *Autobiography of Martin Luther King Jr.* (1999)

William Lyon Mackenzie King 1874–1950

Canadian Liberal statesman, Prime Minister 1921–6, 1926–30, and 1935–48

5 If some countries have too much history, we have too much geography.

speech on Canada as an international power, 18 June 1936

6 Not necessarily conscription, but conscription if necessary.

speech, Canadian House of Commons, 7 July 1942

Hugh Kingsmill 1889–1949

English man of letters

7 A nation is only at peace when it's at war.

attributed

Neil Kinnock 1942–

British Labour politician
see also **Newspaper headlines** 287:9

8 Loyalty is a fine quality but in excess it fills political graveyards.
    in June 1976, in opposition to Conference decisions on devolution

G. M. F. Drower *Neil Kinnock* (1984)

9 *of servicemen in the Falklands War, when replying to a heckler who said that Margaret **Thatcher** 'showed guts':*
It's a pity others had to leave theirs on the ground at Goose Green to prove it.

television interview, 6 June 1983

10 If Margaret Thatcher wins on Thursday, I warn you not to be ordinary, I warn you not to be young, I warn you not to fall ill, and I warn you not to grow old.
    on the prospect of a Conservative re-election

speech at Bridgend, 7 June 1983

11 The grotesque chaos of a Labour council hiring taxis to scuttle round the city handing out redundancy notices to its own workers.
    of the actions of the Labour city council in Liverpool

speech at the Labour Party Conference, 1 October 1985

12 I would die for my country but I could never let my country die for me.

speech at Labour Party Conference, 30 September 1986

13 Why am I the first Kinnock in a thousand generations to be able to get to university?
    later plagiarized by the American politician Joe Biden

speech at Llandudno, 15 May 1987

14 There are lots of ways to get socialism, but I think trying to fracture the Labour party by incessant contest cannot be one of them.

in *Guardian* 29 January 1988

1 I don't think anyone could accuse someone who has been leader of the Labour party for more than seven years of being impulsive.

in *Sunday Times* 5 August 1990

2 I have a lot of sympathy with him. I too was once a young, bald Leader of the Opposition.
on William **Hague** *as Tory Leader*

in *Independent* on 3 October 1999

3 Referendums produce results and results have got to be listened to.
on the French rejection of the European Constitution

in *Guardian* 1 June 2005 (online edition)

Rudyard Kipling 1865-1936

English writer and poet

4 Oh, East is East, and West is West, and never the twain shall meet.

'The Ballad of East and West' (1892)

5 All Power, each Tyrant, every Mob
Whose head has grown too large,
Ends by destroying its own job
And works its own discharge.

'The Benefactors' (1919)

6 Winds of the World, give answer! They are whimpering to and fro—
And what should they know of England who only England know?—
The poor little street-bred people that vapour and fume and brag.

'The English Flag' (1892)

7 I could not dig: I dared not rob:
Therefore I lied to please the mob.
Now all my lies are proved untrue
And I must face the men I slew.
What tale shall serve me here among
Mine angry and defrauded young?

'Epitaphs of the War: A Dead Statesman' (1919)

8 As it will be in the future, it was at the birth of Man—
There are only four things certain since Social Progress began:—
That the Dog returns to his Vomit and the Sow returns to her Mire,
And the burnt Fool's bandaged finger goes wabbling back to the Fire.

'The Gods of the Copybook Headings' (1927)

9 And that after this is accomplished, and the brave new world begins
When all men are paid for existing, and no man must pay for his sins,
As surely as Water will wet us, as surely as Fire will burn,
The Gods of the Copybook Headings with terror and slaughter return!

'The Gods of the Copybook Headings' (1927)

10 If you can keep your head when all about you
Are losing theirs and blaming it on you;
If you can trust yourself when all men doubt you,
But make allowance for their doubting too;
If you can wait and not be tired by waiting,
Or being lied about, don't deal in lies,
Or being hated, don't give way to hating,
And yet don't look too good, nor talk too wise;
If you can dream—and not make dreams your master;

'If—' (1910)

If you can think—and not make thoughts your aim,
If you can meet with triumph and disaster
And treat those two impostors just the same . . .

1 If you can talk with crowds and keep your virtue,   'If—' (1910)
  Or walk with Kings—nor lose the common touch.

2 Now this is the Law of the Jungle—as old and as true as the   'The Law of the Jungle' (1895)
    sky;
  And the Wolf that shall keep it may prosper, but the Wolf
    that shall break it must die.

3 Let us admit it fairly, as a business people should,   'The Lesson' (1902)
  We have had no end of a lesson: it will do us no end of
    good.
  of the Boer Wars

4 Ship me somewheres east of Suez, where the best is like the   'Mandalay' (1892)
    worst,
  Where there aren't no Ten Commandments an' a man can
    raise a thirst.

5 A Nation spoke to a Nation,   'Our Lady of the Snows' (1898)
  A Throne sent word to a Throne:
  'Daughter am I in my mother's house,
  But mistress in my own.
  The gates are mine to open,
  As the gates are mine to close,
  And I abide by my Mother's House.'
  Said our Lady of the Snows.

6 God of our fathers, known of old,   'Recessional' (1897)
  Lord of our far-flung battle-line,
  Beneath whose awful Hand we hold
  Dominion over palm and pine—
  Lord God of Hosts, be with us yet,
  Lest we forget—lest we forget!

  The tumult and the shouting dies—
  The captains and the kings depart—
  Still stands Thine ancient Sacrifice,
  An humble and a contrite heart.

7 Far-called our navies melt away—   'Recessional' (1897)
  On dune and headland sinks the fire—
  Lo, all our pomp of yesterday
  Is one with Nineveh, and Tyre!

8 Such boasting as the Gentiles use,   'Recessional' (1897)
  Or lesser breeds without the Law.

9 For frantic boast and foolish word—   'Recessional' (1897)
  Thy mercy on Thy People, Lord.

10 We have fed our sea for a thousand years   'The Song of the Dead' (1896)
   And she calls us, still unfed,
   Though there's never a wave of all her waves
   But marks our English dead:
   We have strawed our best to the weed's unrest
   To the shark and sheering gull.
   If blood be the price of admiralty,
   Lord God, we ha' paid in full!

1 It is always a temptation to a rich and lazy nation,   'What Dane-geld means' (1911)
To puff and look important and to say:-
'Though we know we should defeat you, we have not the
   time to meet you,
We will therefore pay you cash to go away.'

And that is called paying the Dane-geld;
But we've proved it again and again,
That if once you have paid him the Dane-geld
You never get rid of the Dane.

2 Take up the White Man's burden—   'The White Man's Burden' (1899)
Send forth the best ye breed—
Go, bind your sons to exile
To serve your captives' need.

3 Take up the White Man's burden—   'The White Man's Burden' (1899)
And reap his old reward—
The blame of those ye better,
The hate of those ye guard.

4 He was the greatest, as he was the hugest, of the war   *The Light that Failed* (1891) ch. 4
correspondents . . . and he always opened his conversation
with the news that there would be trouble in the Balkans in
the spring.

5 Power without responsibility: the prerogative of the harlot   in *Kipling Journal* December 1971
throughout the ages.
summing up Lord **Beaverbrook**'*s political standpoint* vis-à-vis
the Daily Express, *after he had said to Kipling, 'What I want is*
power. Kiss 'em one day and kick 'em the next'; Stanley **Baldwin**,
Kipling's cousin, subsequently obtained permission to use the
phrase in a speech in London on 18 March 1931

Henry Kissinger 1923–

German-born American politician, US Secretary of State 1973–7

6 There cannot be a crisis next week. My schedule is already   in *New York Times Magazine* 1 June
full.   1969

7 Power is the great aphrodisiac.   in *New York Times* 19 January 1971

8 The illegal we do immediately. The unconstitutional takes a   in *Washington Post* 20 January
little longer.   1977; attributed

9 If I want to talk to Europe who do I call?   attributed saying; quoted by
    Crispin Blunt in *Minutes of the*
    House of Commons Select
    Committee on Defence, 16 February
    2002

10 Ninety percent of the politicians give the other ten percent a   in 1978, attributed
bad name.

11 History has so far shown us only two roads to international   in *The Times* 12 March 1991
stability: domination and equilibrium.

12 The management of a balance of power is a permanent   *White House Years* (1979)
undertaking, not an exertion that has a foreseeable end.

13 We are the President's men and we must behave   M. and B. Kalb *Kissinger* (1974)
accordingly.

14 For other nations, Utopia is a blessed past never to be   attributed
recovered; for Americans it is just beyond the horizon.

1 The main advantage of being famous is that when you bore people at dinner parties they think it is their fault.

James Naughtie in *Spectator* 1 April 1995; attributed

Lord Kitchener 1850–1916

British soldier and statesman
on Kitchener: see **Asquith** 16:11

2 You are ordered abroad as a soldier of the King to help our French comrades against the invasion of a common enemy . . . In this new experience you may find temptations both in wine and women. You must entirely resist both temptations, and, while treating all women with perfect courtesy, you should avoid any intimacy. Do your duty bravely. Fear God. Honour the King.
  message to soldiers of the British Expeditionary Force (1914)

in *The Times* 19 August 1914

3 I don't mind your being killed, but I object to your being taken prisoner.
  *to the Prince of Wales (later **Edward VIII**) on his asking to be allowed to the Front during the First World War*

in *Journals and Letters of Reginald Viscount Esher* vol. 3 (1938) 18 December 1914

John Knox c.1505–72

Scottish Protestant reformer
on Knox: see **Epitaphs** 136:6

4 The first blast of the trumpet against the monstrous regiment of women.
  here, regiment *means 'rule'*

title of pamphlet (1558)

5 *Un homme avec Dieu est toujours dans la majorité.*
  A man with God is always in the majority.

inscription on the Reformation Monument, Geneva; see **Proverbs** 319:6

Philander C. Knox 1853–1921

American lawyer and Republican politician, US Attorney-General 1901–4

6 *Theodore **Roosevelt** had requested a legal justification for his acquisition of the Panama Canal:*
  Oh, Mr. President, do not let so great an achievement suffer from any taint of legality.

Tyler Dennett *John Hay: From Poetry to Politics* (1933)

Helmut Kohl 1930–

German statesman, Chancellor of West Germany (1982–90) and first postwar Chancellor of united Germany (1990–8)

7 I have been underestimated for decades. I have done very well that way.

in *New York Times* 25 January 1987

8 My goal, when the historical hour allows it, is the unity of the nation.
  to crowds in Dresden on the occasion of his first official visit to East Germany, 19 December 1989

in *The Times* 20 December 1989

9 We Germans now have the historic chance to realize the unity of our fatherland.

in *Guardian* 15 February 1990

10 The policy of European integration is in reality a question of war and peace in the 21st century.

speech at Louvain University, 2 February 1996

Karl Kraus 1874–1936

Austrian satirist

1 How is the world ruled and how do wars start? Diplomats tell lies to journalists and then believe what they read.

Aphorisms and More Aphorisms (1909)

Paul Kruger 1825–1904

South African soldier and statesman

2 A bill of indemnity . . . for raid by Dr Jameson and the British South Africa Company's troops. The amount falls under two heads—first, material damage, total of claim, £677,938 3s. 3d.—second, moral or intellectual damage, total of claim, £1,000,000.
    telegram from the South African Republic, communicated to the House of Commons by Joseph **Chamberlain**

in the House of Commons 18 February 1897

Stanley Kubrick 1928–99

American film director

3 The great nations have always acted like gangsters, and the small nations like prostitutes.

in Guardian 5 June 1963

Henry Labouchere 1831–1912

British politician

4 I do not object to the old man always having a card up his sleeve, but I do object to his insinuating that the Almighty has placed it there.
    on **Gladstone**'s 'frequent appeals to a higher power'

Earl Curzon *Modern Parliamentary Eloquence* (1913)

Jean de la Bruyère 1645–96

French satiric moralist

5 When the populace is excited, one cannot conceive how calm can be restored; and when it is peaceful, one cannot see how calm can be disturbed.

Characters (1688) 'Of the Sovereign and the State'

Fiorello La Guardia 1882–1947

American politician, Republican Mayor of New York 1933–45

6 When I make a mistake, it's a beaut!
    on the appointment of Herbert O'Brien as a judge in 1936

William Manners *Patience and Fortitude* (1976)

7 There is no Democratic or Republican way of cleaning the streets.

Charles Garrett *The La Guardia Years, Machine and Reform Politics in New York City* (1961)

John Lahr 1941–

American critic

8 I know in an existential sense that life can change on a dime . . . something has instantly and inexorably changed in American life.
    in the aftermath of the terrorist attacks which destroyed the World Trade Center in New York, and damaged the Pentagon

'Forever Changed', online correspondence with August Wilson in *Slate*, posted 11 September 2001

John Lambert 1619–83

English soldier and Parliamentary supporter

1 The quarrel is now between light and darkness, not who shall rule, but whether we shall live or be preserved or no. Good words will not do with the cavaliers.
speech in the Parliament of 1656 supporting the rule of the major-generals

in *Dictionary of National Biography*

John George Lambton see John George Lambton, Lord Durham

Norman Lamont 1942–

British Conservative politician

2 A price worth paying.
as Chancellor, responding to criticism on the rise in unemployment

in the House of Commons, 16 May 1991

3 The turn of the tide is sometimes difficult to discern. What we are seeing is the return of that vital ingredient— confidence. The green shoots of economic spring are appearing once again.

speech at the Conservative Party Conference, 9 October 1991; see **Misquotations** 273:1

4 My wife said she had never heard me sing in the bath before.
of the aftermath of sterling's exit from the ERM (Exchange Rate Mechanism)

quoted in *Financial Times* 23 September 1992

5 We give the impression of being in office but not in power.
'in office, but not in power' had earlier been used by A. J. P. **Taylor** *of Ramsay* **MacDonald***'s minority government of 1924*

speech in House of Commons, 9 June 1993

Giuseppe di Lampedusa 1896–1957

Italian writer

6 If we want things to stay as they are, things will have to change.

The Leopard (1957)

Bert Lance 1931–

American government official

7 If it ain't broke, don't fix it.

in *Nation's Business* May 1977

Walter Savage Landor 1775–1864

English poet

8 The wise become as the unwise in the enchanted chambers of Power, whose lamps make every face the same colour.

Imaginary Conversations (1824–9)

9 George the First was always reckoned
Vile, but viler George the Second;
And what mortal ever heard
Any good of George the Third?
When from earth the Fourth descended
God be praised the Georges ended!

epigram in *The Atlas*, 28 April 1855

Andrew Lang 1844–1912
Scottish man of letters

1 He uses statistics as a drunken man uses lampposts—for support rather than illumination.

Alan L. Mackay *Harvest of a Quiet Eye* (1977); attributed

William Langland c.1330–c.1400
English poet

2 Brewesters and baksters, bochiers and cokes—
For thise are men on this molde that moost harm wercheth
To the povere peple.
  in an alternative text, 'As bakeres and breweres, bocheres and cokes; / For thyse men don most harm to the mene peple'

The Vision of Piers Plowman

Lao-tzu c.604–c.531 BC
Chinese philosopher; founder of Taoism

3 The best [rulers] are those whose existence is [merely]
  known by the people.
The next best are those who are loved and praised.
The next are those who are feared.
And the next are those who are reviled . . .
[The great rulers] accomplish their task; they complete their
  work.
Nevertheless their people say that they simply follow
  Nature.

Tao-te Ching ch. 17

James Larkin 1867–1947
Irish labour leader

4 Our fathers died that we might be free men. Are we going to allow their sacrifices to be as naught? Or are we going to follow in their footsteps at the Rising of the Moon?

in *Irish Worker* July 1914

5 Hell has no terror for me. I have lived there. Thirty six years of hunger and poverty have been my portion. They cannot terrify me with hell. Better to be in hell with Dante and Davitt than to be in heaven with Carson and Murphy.
  in 1913, during the 'Dublin lockout' labour dispute

Ulick O'Connor *The Troubles* (rev. ed., 1996)

Duc de la Rochefoucauld-Liancourt
1747–1827
French social reformer

6 LOUIS XVI: It is a big revolt.
  LA ROCHEFOUCAULD-LIANCOURT: No, Sire, a big revolution.
    on a report reaching Versailles of the Fall of the Bastille, 1789

F. Dreyfus *La Rochefoucauld-Liancourt* (1903)

Harold Laski 1893–1950
British Labour politician

7 I respect fidelity to colleagues even though they are fit for the hangman.

letter to Oliver Wendell **Holmes** Jr., 4 December 1926

8 He searched always to end a sentence with a climax. He looked for antithesis like a monkey looking for fleas.
  *of Winston **Churchill** at a dinner at the London School of Economics*

letter to Oliver Wendell **Holmes** Jr., 7 May 1927

Last words

1 All my possessions for a moment of time.
Queen **Elizabeth I** (*1533–1603*)

attributed, but almost certainly apocryphal

2 Be of good comfort Master Ridley, and play the man. We shall this day light such a candle by God's grace in England, as (I trust) shall never be put out.
Hugh Latimer (*c.1485–1555*), *prior to being burned for heresy, 16 October 1555*

John Foxe *Actes and Monuments* (1570 ed.)

3 Come closer, boys. It will be easier for you.
Erskine Childers (*1870–1922*), *British writer and Irish nationalist, to the firing squad at his execution*

Burke Wilkinson *The Zeal of the Convert* (1976) ch. 26

4 Die, my dear Doctor, that's the last thing I shall do!
Lord **Palmerston** (*1784–1865*)

E. Latham *Famous Sayings and their Authors* (1904)

5 An emperor ought to die standing.
Vespasian (AD 9–79)

Suetonius *Lives of the Caesars* 'Vespasian'

6 For my name and memory, I leave it to men's charitable speeches, and to foreign nations, and the next ages.
Francis **Bacon** (*1561–1626*)

his last will, 19 December 1625

7 God save Ireland!
called out from the dock by the Manchester Martyrs, William Allen (*d. 1867*), *Michael Larkin* (*d. 1867*), *and William O'Brien* (*d. 1867*)

Robert Kee *The Bold Fenian Men* (1989); see **Sullivan** 383:6

8 How's the Empire?
said by King **George V** (*1865–1936*) *to his private secretary on the morning of his death, probably prompted by an article in* The Times, *which he held open at the imperial and foreign page; Lord Wigram in a memorandum of 20 January 1936 also recorded that the King had said, 'Gentlemen, I am so sorry for keeping you waiting like this. I am unable to concentrate.' The (probably apocryphal) response 'Bugger Bognor' to the suggestion, 'Cheer up, your Majesty, you will soon be at Bognor again', has also been attributed to an earlier illness in 1929*

letter from Lord Wigram, 31 January 1936, in J. E. Wrench *Geoffrey Dawson and Our Times* (1955).

9 I die happy.
Charles James **Fox** (*1749–1806*)

Lord John Russell *Life and Times of C. J. Fox* vol. 3 (1860) ch. 69

10 I find, then, I am but a bad anatomist.
Wolfe Tone (*1763–98*), *who in trying to cut his throat in prison severed his windpipe instead of his jugular, and lingered for several days*

Oliver Knox *Rebels and Informers* (1998)

11 I have a long journey to take, and must bid the company farewell.
Walter **Ralegh** (*c.1552–1618*), *parting words*

E. Thompson *Sir Walter Raleigh* (1935)

12 I have loved justice and hated iniquity: therefore I die in exile.
Pope Gregory VII (*c.1020–85*) *at Salerno, following his conflict with the Emperor Henry IV*

J. W. Bowden *The Life and Pontificate of Gregory VII* (1840) vol. 2

Last words *continued*

1 I only regret that I have but one life to lose for my country.
Nathan Hale (1755–76), prior to his execution by the British for spying, 22 September 1776

Henry Phelps Johnston *Nathan Hale, 1776* (1914)

2 It is a bad cause which cannot bear the words of a dying man.
Sir Henry Vane (1613–62) as drums and trumpets were ordered to sound at his execution to drown anything he might say

Charles Dickens *A Child's History of England* (1853) ch. 35

3 It is well, I die hard, but I am not afraid to go.
*George **Washington** (1732–99)*

on 14 December 1799

4 I will die like a true-blue rebel. Don't waste any time in mourning—organize.
*Joe **Hill** (1879–1915) before his death by firing squad*

farewell telegram to Bill Haywood, 18 November 1915, in *Salt Lake* (Utah) *Tribune* 19 November 1915

5 Lord have mercy on my poor country that is so barbarously oppressed.
*Andrew **Fletcher** of Saltoun, Scottish patriot and anti-Unionist*

September 1716

6 Lord, open the King of England's eyes!
*William **Tyndale** (c.1494–1536), at the stake*

John Foxe *Actes and Monuments* (1570)

7 My design is to make what haste I can to be gone.
*Oliver **Cromwell** (1599–1658)*

John Morley *Oliver Cromwell* (1900)

8 *on his death-bed, declining a proposed visit from Queen Victoria:*
No it is better not. She would only ask me to take a message to Albert.
*Benjamin **Disraeli** (1804–81)*

Robert Blake *Disraeli* (1966)

9 *Ô liberté! Ô liberté! que de crimes on commet en ton nom!*
O liberty! O liberty! what crimes are committed in thy name!
Mme Roland (1754–93), French revolutionary, before being guillotined

A. de Lamartine *Histoire des Girondins* (1847)

10 Oh, my country! how I leave my country!
*William **Pitt** (1759–1806); also variously reported as 'How I love my country'; and 'My country! oh, my country!'*

Earl Stanhope *Life of the Rt. Hon. William Pitt* vol. 3 (1879); Earl Stanhope *Life of the Rt. Hon. William Pitt* (1st ed.), vol. 4 (1862); and G. Rose *Diaries and Correspondence* (1860) 23 January 1806; oral tradition reports:

I think I could eat one of Bellamy's veal pies.

attributed

11 Put out the light.
*Theodore **Roosevelt** (1858–1919)*

on 6 January 1919

12 Remember—.
***Charles I** (1600–49), giving his George (insignia of the Order of the Garter) to Bishop Juxon*

speech on the scaffold, 30 January 1649

13 So little done, so much to do.
*Cecil **Rhodes** (1853–1902), on the day of his death*

Lewis Michell *Life of Rhodes* (1910)

Last words *continued*

1 Strike the tent.
   *Robert E. **Lee** (1807–70), 12 October 1870*

attributed

2 This hath not offended the king.
   *Thomas **More** (1478–1535), lifting his beard aside after laying his head on the block*

Francis Bacon *Apophthegms New and Old* (1625) no. 22

3 This *is* a beautiful country!
   *John **Brown** (1800–59) as he rode to the gallows, seated on his coffin*

at his execution on 2 December 1859

4 This is the Fourth?
   *Thomas **Jefferson** (1743–1826)*

on 4 July 1826

5 This, this is the end of earth. I am content.
   *John Quincy **Adams** (1767–1848) on collapsing in the Senate, 21 February 1848 (he died two days later)*

William H. Seward *Eulogy of John Quincy Adams to Legislature of New York* 1848

6 Thomas—Jefferson—still surv—
   *in fact Thomas **Jefferson** died on the same day*

John **Adams**, 4 July 1826

7 Useless! Useless!
   *John Wilkes **Booth** (1838–65)*

Philip van Doren Stern *The Man Who Killed Lincoln* (1939)

8 Would to God this wound had been for Ireland.
   Patrick Sarsfield (c.1655–93) on being mortally wounded at the battle of Landen, 19 August 1693, while fighting for France

attributed

Hugh Latimer
English Protestant martyr see **Last words** 226:2

William L. Laurence 1888–1977
American journalist

9 At first it was a giant column that soon took the shape of a supramundane mushroom.

on the first atomic explosion in New Mexico, 16 July 1945

Wilfrid Laurier 1841–1919
Canadian Liberal statesman, Prime Minister 1896–1911

10 Had I been born on the banks of the Saskatchewan, I would myself have shouldered a musket to fight against the neglect of governments and the shameless greed of speculators.

addressing meeting in the Champ de Mars, Montreal, 22 November 1885; O.D. Skelton *Life and Letters of Sir Wilfrid Laurier* (1921)

11 The nineteenth century was the century of the United States. I think we can claim that it is Canada that shall fill the twentieth century.

speech in Ottawa, 18 January 1904; see **Trudeau** 400:10

12 Quebec does not have opinions, only sentiments.

Mason Wade *The French Canadians:1760–1967* (1968)

Peter Law 1948–
Welsh-born Labour politician, who campaigned successfully in 2005 as an Independent Labour candidate protesting against the imposition of an all-woman shortlist

13 This is what you get when you don't listen to people.
   having defeated the official Labour candidate for Blaenau Gwent by a substantial majority

speech from the podium, 6 May 2005

T. E. Lawrence 1888–1935

English soldier and writer

1 Poets hope too much, and their politics . . . usually stink after twenty years.

letter to Cecil Day Lewis, November 1934

2 The trouble with Communism is that it accepts too much of today's furniture. I hate furniture.

letter to Cecil Day Lewis, 20 December 1934

Mark Lawson 1962–

British writer and journalist

3 Office tends to confer a dreadful plausibility on even the most negligible of those who hold it.

Joe Queenan *Imperial Caddy* (1992); introduction

Nigel Lawson 1932–

British Conservative politician

4 The Conservative Party has never believed that the business of government is the government of business.

in the House of Commons, 10 November 1981

5 Teenage scribblers.
   of the financial press

in *Financial Times* 28 September 1985

6 It represented the tip of a singularly ill-concealed iceberg, with all the destructive potential that icebergs possess.
   of an article by Alan Walters, the Prime Minister's economic adviser, criticizing the Exchange Rate Mechanism

in the House of Commons following his resignation as Chancellor, 31 October 1989

7 When I was a minister I always looked forward to the Cabinet meeting immensely because it was, apart from the summer holidays, the only period of real rest I got in what was a very heavy job.

'Cabinet Government in the Thatcher Years' (1994)

Kenneth L. Lay 1942–

American businessman, former CEO of Enron

8 I am deeply troubled about asserting these rights, because it may be perceived by some that I have something to hide.
   invoking his Fifth Amendment protection and declining to answer Congress's questions on the Enron collapse

in *Newsweek* 25 February 2002

Emma Lazarus 1849–87

American poet

9 Give me your tired, your poor,
   Your huddled masses yearning to breathe free,
   The wretched refuse of your teeming shore,
   Send these, the homeless, tempest-tossed, to me:
   I lift my lamp beside the golden door.
   inscription on the Statue of Liberty, New York

'The New Colossus' (1883)

Alexandre Auguste Ledru-Rollin 1807–74

French politician

10 Ah well! I am their leader, I really had to follow them!

E. de Mirecourt *Les Contemporains* vol. 14 (1857) 'Ledru-Rollin'

Charles Lee 1731–82
American soldier

1 Beware that your Northern laurels do not change to Southern willows.

to General Horatio Gates after the surrender of Burgoyne at Saratoga

on 17 October 1777

Henry ('Light-Horse Harry') Lee 1756–1818
American soldier and politician

2 A citizen, first in war, first in peace, and first in the hearts of his countrymen.

*of George **Washington***

Funeral Oration on the death of General Washington (1800)

Richard Henry Lee 1732–94
American politician

3 That these united colonies are, and of right ought to be, free and independent states; that they are absolved from all allegiance to the British crown; and that all political connection between them and the State of Great Britain is, and ought to be, totally dissolved.

resolution moved at the Continental Congress on 7 June 1776; adopted 2 July 1776

Robert E. Lee 1807–70
American Confederate general
*see also **Last words** 228:1*

4 It is well that war is so terrible. We should grow too fond of it.

after the battle of Fredericksburg, December 1862

attributed

5 There is nothing left for me to do but to go and see General Grant and I would rather die a thousand deaths.

just before the Confederate surrender at Appomattox in 1865

Geoffrey C. Ward The Civil War (1991)

6 I have fought against the people of the North because I believed they were seeking to wrest from the South its dearest rights. But I have never cherished toward them bitter or vindictive feelings, and I have never seen the day when I did not pray for them.

Geoffrey C. Ward The Civil War (1991)

Curtis E. LeMay 1906–90
American air-force officer

7 They've got to draw in their horns and stop their aggression, or we're going to bomb them back into the Stone Age.

on the North Vietnamese

Mission with LeMay (1965)

Lenin 1870–1924
Russian revolutionary
*see also **Misquotations** 272:4*

8 Imperialism is the monopoly stage of capitalism.

Imperialism as the Last Stage of Capitalism (1916) 'Briefest possible definition of imperialism'

9 One step forward two steps back

title of book 1904

1 No, Democracy is *not* identical with majority rule. Democracy is a *State* which recognizes the subjection of the minority to the majority, that is, an organization for the systematic use of *force* by one class against the other, by one part of the population against another.

State and Revolution (1919)

2 While the State exists, there can be no freedom. When there is freedom there will be no State.

State and Revolution (1919)

3 What is to be done?

title of pamphlet (1902); originally the title of a novel (1863) by N. G. Chernyshevsky

4 We must now set about building a proletarian socialist state in Russia.

speech in Petrograd, 7 November 1917

5 Communism equals Soviet power plus the electrification of the whole country.

report to 8th Congress, 1920

6 Who? Whom?
  definition of political science, meaning 'Who will outstrip whom?'

in *Polnoe Sobranie Sochinenii* (1970) 17 October 1921

7 An end to bossing.

Neil Harding *Lenin's Political Thought* (1981) vol.2

8 A good man fallen among Fabians.
  of George Bernard **Shaw**

Arthur Ransome *Six Weeks in Russia in 1919* (1919) 'Notes of Conversations with Lenin'

9 Liberty is precious—so precious that it must be rationed.

Sidney and Beatrice Webb *Soviet Communism* (1935) vol. 2

William Lenthall 1591–1662
English politician, Speaker of the House of Commons

10 I have neither eye to see, nor tongue to speak here, but as the House is pleased to direct me.
  to **Charles I**, *4 January 1642, on being asked if he had seen any of the five MPs whom the King had ordered to be arrested*

John Rushworth *Historical Collections. The Third Part* vol. 2 (1692)

Alan Jay Lerner 1918–86
American songwriter

11 Don't let it be forgot
That once there was a spot
For one brief shining moment that was known
As Camelot.
  particularly associated with the Kennedy White House

'Camelot' (1960 song); see **Onassis** 294:8

Doris Lessing 1919–
English writer

12 When old settlers say 'One has to understand the country,' what they mean is, 'You have to get used to our ideas about the native.'

The Grass is Singing (1950)

13 When a white man in Africa by accident looks into the eyes of a native and sees the human being (which it is his chief preoccupation to avoid), his sense of guilt, which he denies, fumes up in resentment and he brings down the whip.

The Grass is Singing (1950)

Leslie Lever 1905–77
British Labour politician

1 Generosity is part of my character, and I therefore hasten to assure this Government that I will never make an allegation of dishonesty against it wherever a simple explanation of stupidity will suffice.

Leon Harris *The Fine Art of Political Wit* (1964)

René Lévesque 1922–87
Canadian politician, founder of Parti Québecois

2 Outside Quebec, I don't find two great cultures. I feel like a foreigner. First and foremost, I am a Québecois, and second—with a rather growing sense of doubt—a Canadian.

in *Toronto Star* 1 June 1963

3 A nation is judged by how it treats its minorities.

attributed, 1978; John Robert Colombo *Colombo's New Canadian Quotations* (1987)

Primo Levi 1919–87
Italian novelist and poet

4 Our language lacks words to express this offence, the demolition of a man.
   of a year spent in Auschwitz

If This is a Man (1958)

Bernard Levin 1928–2004
British journalist

5 Since when was fastidiousness a quality useful for political advancement?

If You Want My Opinion (1992)

6 Harold Macmillan, whose elevation was achieved by a brutality, cunning and greed for power normally met only in the conclaves of Mafia *capi*, said, after he had climbed the greasy pole and pushed all his rivals off (*takes out handkerchief containing concealed onion*) that the whole thing was Dead Sea Fruit.

If You Want My Opinion (1992); see **Macmillan** 253:9

7 [Tony] Benn flung himself into the Sixties technology with the enthusiasm (not to say language) of a newly enrolled Boy Scout demonstrating knot-tying to his indulgent parents.

The Pendulum Years (1970)

8 *of Harold **Macmillan** and Harold **Wilson**:*
   Between them, then, Walrus and Carpenter, they divided up the Sixties.

The Pendulum Years (1970)

9 Whom the mad would destroy, they first make gods.
   *of **Mao** Zedong in 1967*

in *The Times* 21 September 1987

10 Once, when a British Minister sneezed, men half a world away would blow their noses. Now when a British Prime Minister sneezes nobody else will even say, 'Bless You.'

in *The Times* 1976

11 What has happened to architecture since the second world war that the only passers-by who can contemplate it without pain are those equipped with a white stick and a dog?

in *The Times* 1983

12 The less the power, the greater the desire to exercise it.

in *The Times* 21 September 1993

1 I have more than once pointed out that no organization with 'Liberation' in its title has ever, or ever will, liberate anyone or anything.

in *The Times* 14 April 1995

Duc de Lévis 1764–1830
French soldier and writer

2 *Gouverner, c'est choisir.*
To govern is to choose.

Maximes et Réflexions (1812 ed.) 'Politique: Maximes de Politique'

David Lewis 1909–81
Canadian politician

3 Louder voices: the corporate welfare bums.

title of book, 1972

4 Welfare is for the needy, not big and wealthy multinational corporations.

Louder Voices: the Corporate Welfare Bums (1972)

Willmott Lewis 1877–1950
British journalist

5 Every government will do as much harm as it can and as much good as it must.
*to Claud **Cockburn***

Claud Cockburn *In Time of Trouble* (1957)

Joseph Lieberman 1942–
American Democratic politician and vice-presidential candidate in 2000

6 His wrongdoing in this sordid saga does not justify making him the first president to be ousted from office in our history.
*voting to acquit President **Clinton***

at the trial for impeachment, 11 February 1999

7 *to the suggestion that he and George W. **Bush** share a stance on issues:*
That's like saying the veterinarian and the taxidermist are in the same business because either way you get your dog back.

speech in Nashville, Tennessee, 8 August 2000

Abbott Joseph Liebling 1904–63

8 Freedom of the press is guaranteed only to those who own one.

in *New Yorker* 14 May 1960

Charles-Joseph, Prince de Ligne 1735–1814
Belgian soldier

9 *Le congrès ne marche pas, il danse.*
The Congress makes no progress; it dances.
of the Congress of Vienna

Auguste de la Garde-Chambonas *Souvenirs du Congrès de Vienne* (1820)

Abraham Lincoln 1809–65
American statesman, 16th President of the US
on Lincoln: see **Stanton** 378:11, **Whitman** 418:3

10 Prohibition . . . goes beyond the bounds of reason in that it attempts to control a man's appetite by legislation, and makes a crime out of things that are not crimes. A Prohibition law strikes a blow at the very principles upon which our government was founded.

speech in the Illinois House of Representatives, 18 December 1840

1 Any people anywhere, being inclined and having the power, have the *right* to rise up, and shake off the existing government, and form a new one that suits them better.

in the House of Representatives, 12 January 1848

2 No man is good enough to govern another man without that other's consent.

speech at Peoria, Illinois, 16 October 1854

3 To give victory to the right, not bloody bullets, but peaceful ballots only, are necessary.

speech, 18 May 1858; see **Misquotations** 272:2

4 'A house divided against itself cannot stand.' I believe this government cannot endure permanently, half slave and half free.

speech, 16 June 1858

5 As I would not be a *slave*, so I would not be a *master*. This expresses my idea of democracy. Whatever differs from this, to the extent of the difference, is no democracy.

fragment, 1 August 1858?

6 I have no purpose to introduce political and social equality between the white and black races. There is a physical difference between the two which, in my judgement, will probably for ever forbid their living together upon the footing of perfect equality; and inasmuch as it becomes a necessity that there must be a difference, I . . . am in favour of the race to which I belong having the superior position.

speech, 21 August 1858

7 When . . . you have succeeded in dehumanizing the Negro, when you have put him down and made it forever impossible for him to be but as the beasts of the field; when you have extinguished his soul and placed him where the ray of hope is blown out in darkness like that which broods over the spirits of the damned, are you quite sure that the demon you have roused will not turn and rend you?

speech at Edwardsville, Illinois, 11 September 1858

8 What is conservatism? Is it not adherence to the old and tried, against the new and untried?

speech, 27 February 1860

9 If we do not make common cause to save the good old ship of the Union on this voyage, nobody will have a chance to pilot her on another voyage.

address at Cleveland, Ohio, 15 February 1861

10 It is safe to assert that no government proper ever had a provision in its organic law for its own termination.

first inaugural address, 4 March 1861

11 I take the official oath to-day with no mental reservations, and with no purpose to construe the Constitution or laws by any hypercritical rules.

first inaugural address, 4 March 1861

12 This country, with its institutions, belongs to the people who inhabit it. Whenever they shall grow weary of the existing government, they can exercise their constitutional right of amending it, or their revolutionary right to dismember or overthrow it.

first inaugural address, 4 March 1861

13 The mystic chords of memory, stretching from every battlefield and patriot grave to every living heart and heartstone all over this broad land, will yet swell the chorus of the Union when again touched, as surely they will be, by the better angels of our nature.

first inaugural address, 4 March 1861

1 I think the necessity of being *ready* increases. Look to it.

the whole of a letter to Governor Andrew Curtin of Pennsylvania, 8 April 1861

2 *on his suspension of habeas corpus:*
The whole of the laws which were required to be faithfully executed, were being resisted, and failing of execution in nearly one-third of the states. Must they be allowed to finally fail of execution, even had it been perfectly clear, that by the means necessary to their execution, some single law, made in such extreme tenderness of the citizen's liberty, that practically, it relieves more of the guilty, than of the innocent, should, to a very limited extent, be violated? To state the question more directly, are all the laws, *but one* [the right to habeas corpus], to go unexecuted and the government itself go to pieces, lest that one be violated?

message to Congress, 4 July 1861

3 My paramount object in this struggle is to save the Union ... If I could save the Union without freeing any slave, I would do it; and if I could save it by freeing all the slaves, I would do it; and if I could save it by freeing some and leaving others alone, I would also do that ... I have here stated my purpose according to my views of official duty and I intend no modification of my oft-expressed personal wish that all men everywhere could be free.

letter to Horace **Greeley**, 22 August 1862

4 On the first day of January in the year of our Lord, one thousand eight hundred and sixty-three, all persons held as slaves within any state, or designated part of a state, the people whereof shall then be in rebellion against the United States shall be then, thenceforward, and forever free.

Preliminary Emancipation Proclamation, 22 September 1862

5 *when asked how he felt about the New York elections:*
Somewhat like the boy in Kentucky who stubbed his toe while running to see his sweetheart. The boy said he was too big to cry, and far too badly hurt to laugh.

in *Frank Leslie's Illustrated Weekly* 22 November 1862

6 Fellow citizens, we cannot escape history ... No personal significance or insignificance can spare one or another of us. The fiery trial through which we pass will light us down in honour or dishonour to the last generation.

annual message to Congress, 1 December 1862

7 In giving freedom to the slave, we assure freedom to the free—honourable alike in what we give and what we preserve. We shall nobly save, or meanly lose, the last, best hope of earth.

annual message to Congress, 1 December 1862

8 Fourscore and seven years ago our fathers brought forth upon this continent a new nation, conceived in liberty, and dedicated to the proposition that all men are created equal ... In a larger sense we cannot dedicate, we cannot consecrate, we cannot hallow this ground. The brave men, living and these dead, who struggled here, have consecrated it far above our power to add or detract. The world will little note, nor long remember, what we say here, but it can never forget what they did here. It is for us, the living, rather to be dedicated here to the unfinished work which they who fought here have thus far so nobly advanced ... we here highly resolve that the dead shall not have died in vain, that this nation, under God, shall have a new birth of freedom; and that government of the people, by the people, and for the people, shall not perish from the earth.

address at the Dedication of the National Cemetery at Gettysburg, 19 November 1863, as reported the following day; the Lincoln Memorial inscription reads 'by the people, for the people'; see **Anonymous** 12:4, **Everett** 138:2, **Webster** 413:5

1 The President tonight has a dream:—He was in a party of plain people, and, as it became known who he was, they began to comment on his appearance. One of them said:— 'He is a very common-looking man.' The President replied:—'The Lord prefers common-looking people. That is the reason he makes so many of them.'

John Hay *Letters of John Hay and Extracts from Diary* (1908) vol 1, 23 December 1863

2 Only those generals who gain success can set up dictators. What I ask of you is military success, and I will risk the dictatorship.
letter appointing Joseph Hooker to command of the Army of the Potomac in 1863

Shelby Foote *The Civil War: Fredericksburg to Meridian* (1991)

3 I claim not to have controlled events, but confess plainly that events have controlled me.

letter to A. G. Hodges, 4 April 1864

4 It is not best to swap horses when crossing streams.

reply to National Union League, 9 June 1864

5 I desire so to conduct the affairs of this administration that if at the end, when I come to lay down the reins of power, I have lost every other friend on earth, I shall at least have one friend left, and that friend shall be down inside me.

reply to the Missouri Committee of Seventy, 1864

6 Fondly do we hope, fervently do we pray, that this mighty scourge of war may speedily pass away. Yet, if God wills that it continue until all the wealth piled by the bond-man's two hundred and fifty years of unrequited toil shall be sunk, and until every drop of blood drawn with the lash shall be paid by another drawn with the sword, as was said three thousand years ago, so still it must be said, 'The judgements of the Lord are true and righteous altogether.'

second inaugural address, 4 March 1865

7 With malice toward none; with charity for all; with firmness in the right, as God gives us to see the right, let us strive on to finish the work we are in: to bind up the nation's wounds; to care for him who shall have borne the battle, and for his widow and his orphan, to do all which may achieve and cherish a just and lasting peace among ourselves, and with all nations.

second inaugural address, 4 March 1865

8 Whenever I hear anyone arguing for slavery, I feel a strong impulse to see it tried on him personally.

address to an Indiana Regiment, 17 March 1865

9 As President, I have no eyes but constitutional eyes; I cannot see you.
reply to the South Carolina Commissioners

attributed

10 People who like this sort of thing will find this the sort of thing they like.
judgement of a book

G. W. E. Russell *Collections and Recollections* (1898)

11 So you're the little woman who wrote the book that made this great war!
on meeting Harriet Beecher Stowe, author of Uncle Tom's Cabin *(1852)*

Carl Sandburg *Abraham Lincoln: The War Years* (1936) vol. 2

12 You cannot help the poor by destroying the rich. You cannot lift the wage earner by pulling down the wage payer.

attributed, but probably apocryphal

13 You may fool all the people some of the time; you can even fool some of the people all the time; but you can't fool all of the people all the time.

Alexander K. McClure *Lincoln's Yarns and Stories* (1904); also attributed to Phineas Barnum; see **Thurber** 394:8

Eric Linklater 1899–1974
Scottish novelist

1 'There won't be any revolution in America,' said Isadore. Nikitin agreed. 'The people are all too clean. They spend all their time changing their shirts and washing themselves. You can't feel fierce and revolutionary in a bathroom.'

Juan in America (1931)

Walter Lippmann 1889–1974
American journalist

2 Private property was the original source of freedom. It still is its main bulwark.

The Good Society (1937)

3 Mr Coolidge's genius for inactivity is developed to a very high point. It is far from being an indolent activity. It is a grim, determined, alert inactivity which keeps Mr Coolidge occupied constantly. Nobody has ever worked harder at inactivity, with such force of character, with such unremitting attention to detail, with such conscientious devotion to the task.

Men of Destiny (1927)

4 The final test of a leader is that he leaves behind him in other men the conviction and the will to carry on.
    Franklin D. Roosevelt died on 12 June 1945

in *New York Herald Tribune* 14 April 1945

5 A free press is not a privilege but an organic necessity in a great society.

address at the International Press Institute Assembly in London, 27 May 1965

6 The will to be free is perpetually renewed in every individual who uses his faculties and affirms his manhood.

Arthur Seldon *The State is Rolling Back* (1994)

Maxim Litvinov 1876–1951
Soviet diplomat

7 Peace is indivisible.
    note to the Allies, 25 February 1920

A. U. Pope *Maxim Litvinoff* (1943)

Ken Livingstone 1945–
British Labour politician

8 If voting changed anything, they'd abolish it.

title of book, 1987; recorded earlier as a saying

9 The problem is that many MPs never see the London that exists beyond the wine bars and brothels of Westminster.

in *The Times* 19 February 1987

10 Politics is a marathon, not a sprint.

in *New Statesman* 10 October 1997

11 I feel like Galileo going before the Inquisition to explain that the sun doesn't revolve around the earth. I hope I have more success.
    at Millbank, prior to appearing before the Labour Party's selection panel for the Mayor of London. He was rejected, but stood as an independent and won

in *Guardian* 17 November 1999

12 I've met serial killers and professional assassins and nobody scared me as much as Mrs T.
    *on Margaret **Thatcher***

in *Observer* 23 January 2000 'They Said What . . . ?'

1 I have been forced to choose between the party I love and have given 31 years of my life to, and upholding the democratic rights of Londoners.
   announcing his independent candidacy for Mayor of London

in *Times* 7 March 2000

2 When Mr Blair invited me down to Chequers two weeks ago to discuss what I would do if I was elected mayor, we had a very pleasant 50 minutes, whilst my nephew and niece wandered around the grounds and did a bit of vandalism.

in *Observer* 12 March 2000 'They Said What . . . ?'

3 Every year the international finance system kills more people than the Second World War. But at least Hitler was mad, you know.

in *Sunday Times* 16 April 2000 'Talking Heads'

Livy 59 BC–AD 17
Roman historian

4 *Vae victis.*

   Down with the defeated!
   cry (already proverbial) of the Gallic King, Brennus, on capturing Rome in 390 BC

Ab Urbe Condita

5 *Pugna magna victi sumus.*

   We have been defeated in a great battle.
   the announcement of disaster for the Romans in Hannibal's ambush at Lake Trasimene in 217 BC

Ab Urbe Condita

David Lloyd George 1863–1945
British Liberal statesman; Prime Minister, 1916–22
on Lloyd George: see **Asquith** 17:3, **Baldwin** 27:7, **Bennett** 35:3, **Churchill** 90:12, **Clemenceau** 96:4, **Grigg** 167:2, **Keynes** 215:6, **Keynes** 215:7, **Taylor** 387:3

6 The leal and trusty mastiff which is to watch over our interests, but which runs away at the first snarl of the trade unions . . . A mastiff? It is the right hon. Gentleman's poodle.
   *on the House of Lords and Arthur **Balfour** respectively*

in the House of Commons, 26 June 1907

7 I have no nest-eggs. I am looking for someone else's hen-roost to rob next year.
   in 1908, as Chancellor

Frank Owen *Tempestuous Journey* (1954)

8 A fully-equipped duke costs as much to keep up as two Dreadnoughts; and dukes are just as great a terror and they last longer.

speech at Newcastle, 9 October 1909

9 The great peaks of honour we had forgotten—Duty, Patriotism, and—clad in glittering white—the great pinnacle of Sacrifice, pointing like a rugged finger to Heaven.

speech at Queen's Hall, London, 19 September 1914

10 *of the House of Lords, c.1911:*
   A body of five hundred men chosen at random from amongst the unemployed.

speech at Newcastle, 9 October 1909

11 I would as soon go for a sunny evening stroll round Walton Heath with a grasshopper, as try to work with Northcliffe.
   *of Lord **Northcliffe**, c.1916*

Frank Owen *Tempestuous Journey* (1954)

1 At eleven o'clock this morning came to an end the cruellest and most terrible war that has ever scourged mankind. I hope we may say that thus, this fateful morning, came to an end all wars.

in the House of Commons, 11 November 1918; see **Wells** 416:4

2 What is our task? To make Britain a fit country for heroes to live in.

speech at Wolverhampton, 23 November 1918

3 Wild men screaming through the keyholes.
of the Versailles Peace Conference

in the House of Commons, 16 April 1919

4 If you want to succeed in politics, you must keep your conscience well under control.

Lord Riddell diary, 23 April 1919

5 M. Clemenceau . . . is one of the greatest living orators, but he knows that the finest eloquence is that which gets things done and the worst is that which delays them.
speech at Paris Peace Conference, 18 January 1919

in *The Times* 20 January 1919

6 Unless I am mistaken, by the steps we have taken [in Ireland] we have murder by the throat.

speech at the Mansion House, 9 November 1920

7 *of Arthur **Balfour**'s impact on history:*
No more than the whiff of scent on a lady's pocket handkerchief.

Thomas Jones, diary, 9 June 1922

8 The world is becoming like a lunatic asylum run by lunatics.

in *Observer* 8 January 1933

9 A politician was a person with whose politics you did not agree. When you did agree, he was a statesman.

speech at Central Hall, Westminster, 2 July 1935

10 Neville has a retail mind in a wholesale business.
*of Neville **Chamberlain***

in 1935; David Dilks *Neville Chamberlain* (1984)

11 *after meeting **Hitler** in 1936:*
Führer is the proper name for him. He is a great and wonderful leader.

Frank Owen *Tempestuous Journey* (1954)

12 Winston would go up to his Creator and say that he would very much like to meet His Son, of Whom he had heard a great deal and, if possible, would like to call on the Holy Ghost. Winston *loves* meeting people.
*of Winston **Churchill***

A. J. Sylvester diary, 2 January 1937

13 The Prime Minister should give an example of sacrifice, because there is nothing which can contribute more to victory than that he should sacrifice the seals of office.
*of Neville **Chamberlain***

in the House of Commons, 7 May 1940

14 Truth against the world.
Welsh proverb; motto taken on becoming Earl Lloyd-George of Dwyfor, January 1945

Donald McCormick *The Mask of Merlin* (1963)

15 Of all the bigotries that savage the human temper there is none so stupid as the anti-Semitic.

Is It Peace? 1923

16 *on being told by Lord **Beaverbrook**'s butler that, 'The Lord is out walking':*
Ah, on the water, I presume.

Lord Cudlipp letter in *Daily Telegraph* 13 September 1993

17 Brilliant—to the top of his boots.
of Earl Haig

attributed

18 Death is the most convenient time to tax rich people.

in *Lord Riddell's Intimate Diary of the Peace Conference and After, 1918–23* (1933)

1 He has sat on the fence so long the iron has entered into his soul.
   of John Simon

attributed

2 He would make a drum out of the skin of his mother in order to sound his own praises.
   of Winston **Churchill**

Peter Rowland *Lloyd George* (1975)

3 Negotiating with de Valera . . . is like trying to pick up mercury with a fork.
   to which **de Valera** *replied, 'Why doesn't he use a spoon?'*

M. J. MacManus *Eamon de Valera* (1944)

4 Sufficient conscience to bother him, but not sufficient to keep him straight.
   of Ramsay **MacDonald**

A. J. Sylvester *Life with Lloyd George* (1975)

5 There is no friendship at the top.

habitual remark, said to be quoting **Gladstone**; A. J. P. Taylor *Lloyd George, Rise and Fall* (1961)

6 *of the 1905 Tory Government:*
   They died with their drawn salaries in their hands.

attributed

John Locke 1632–1704
English philosopher

7 Man . . . hath by nature a power . . . to preserve his property—that is, his life, liberty, and estate—against the injuries and attempts of other men.

Second Treatise of Civil Government (1690)

8 Man being . . . by nature all free, equal, and independent, no one can be put out of this estate, and subjected to the political power of another, without his own consent.

Second Treatise of Civil Government (1690)

9 The great and chief end, therefore, of men's uniting into commonwealths, and putting themselves under government, is the preservation of their property.

Second Treatise of Civil Government (1690)

10 The only way by which any one divests himself of his natural liberty and puts on the bonds of civil society is by agreeing with other men to join and unite into a community.

Second Treatise of Civil Government (1690)

11 This power to act according to discretion for the public good, without the prescription of the law, and sometimes even against it, is that which is called prerogative.

Second Treatise of Civil Government (1690)

Henry Cabot Lodge Jr. 1902–85
American Republican politician

12 It was those damned tea parties that beat me!
   attributing the loss of his 1952 senatorial campaign, against the national Republican trend, to the tea parties given by Rose Kennedy on behalf of her son, the Democratic candidate John F. Kennedy

in obituary of Rose **Kennedy** in *Guardian* 24 January 1995

Huey Long 1893–1935
American Democratic politician

13 For the present you can just call me the Kingfish.

Every Man a King (1933)

14 *answering his opponent's supporters, who said their candidate had gone barefoot as a boy:*
   I can go Mr Wilson one better; I was born barefoot.

T. Harry Williams *Huey Long* (1969)

1 Oh hell, say that I am *sui generis* and let it go at that.
to journalists attempting to analyse his political personality

T. Harry Williams *Huey Long* (1969)

2 The time has come for all good men to rise above principle.

attributed

Lord Longford 1905–2001
British Labour politician and philanthropist

3 You would get second raters, people who could not get into the Commons or the European Parliament or even into the Scottish or Welsh Parliaments. You would get the dregs.
opposing an elected second chamber

in *Observer* 12 March 2000 'They Said What...?'

Alice Roosevelt Longworth 1884–1980
American daughter of Theodore **Roosevelt**

4 Harding was not a bad man. He was just a slob.
*of US President Warren G. **Harding***

Crowded Hours (1933)

Louis XIV (the 'Sun King') 1638–1715
French monarch, King from 1643

5 *L'État c'est moi.*

I am the State.
before the Parlement de Paris, 13 April 1655 (probably apocryphal)

J. A. Dulaure *Histoire de Paris* (1834) vol. 6

6 *Il n'y a plus de Pyrénées.*

The Pyrenees are no more.
on the accession of his grandson to the throne of Spain, 1700

attributed to Louis by Voltaire in *Siècle de Louis XIV* (1753), but to the Spanish Ambassador to France in the *Mercure Galant* (Paris) November 1700

7 I was nearly kept waiting.

attribution queried, among others, by E. Fournier in *L'Esprit dans l'Histoire* (1857)

8 Every time I create an appointment, I create a hundred malcontents and one ingrate.

Voltaire *Siècle de Louis XIV* (1768 ed.) vol. 2

Louis XV 1710–74
French monarch, King from 1715

9 Are the streets being paved with gold over there? I fully expect to awake one morning in Versailles to see the walls of the fortress rising above the horizon.
on the costs of fortifying Louisbourg on Cape Breton Island, Canada, c.1745

attributed

Louis XVI 1754–93
French monarch, King from 1774; deposed in 1789 on the outbreak of the French Revolution and executed in 1793

10 *diary entry for 14 July 1789, the day of the storming of the Bastille:*
Rien.
Nothing.

Simon Schama *Citizens* (1989)

Louis XVIII 1755–1824

French monarch, King from 1814; titular king from 1795

1 Remember that there is not one of you who does not carry in his cartridge-pouch the marshal's baton of the duke of Reggio; it is up to you to bring it forth.
  speech to Saint-Cyr cadets, 9 August 1819

in *Moniteur Universel* 10 August 1819

2 *L'exactitude est la politesse des rois.*
Punctuality is the politeness of kings.

in *Souvenirs de J. Lafitte* (1844), attributed

Louis Philippe 1773–1850

French monarch, King 1830–48

3 Died, has he? Now I wonder what he meant by that?
  *of **Talleyrand***

attributed, perhaps apocryphal

David Low 1891–1963

British political cartoonist

4 I have never met anyone who wasn't against war. Even Hitler and Mussolini were, according to themselves.

in *New York Times Magazine* 10 February 1946

Robert Lowe, Viscount Sherbrooke 1811–92

British Liberal politician

5 I believe it will be absolutely necessary that you should prevail on our future masters to learn their letters.
  on the passing of the 2nd Reform Bill

in the House of Commons, 15 July 1867; see **Misquotations** 274:3

6 The Chancellor of the Exchequer is a man whose duties make him more or less of a taxing machine. He is intrusted with a certain amount of misery which it is his duty to distribute as fairly as he can.

in the House of Commons, 11 April 1870

James Russell Lowell 1819–91

American poet

7 We've a war, an' a debt, an' a flag; an' ef this
Ain't to be inderpendunt, why, wut on airth is?

The Biglow Papers (Second Series, 1867) no. 4 'A Message of Jeff. Davis in Secret Session'

8 Once to every man and nation comes the moment to decide,
In the strife of Truth with Falsehood, for the good or evil side.

'The Present Crisis' (1845)

9 Truth forever on the scaffold, Wrong forever on the throne,—
Yet that scaffold sways the future, and, behind the dim unknown,
Standeth God within the shadow, keeping watch above his own.

'The Present Crisis' (1845)

Lucan AD 39–65

Roman poet

1   *Quis iustius induit arma*   *Pharsalia*
Scire nefas, magno se iudice quisque tuetur:
Victrix causa deis placuit, sed victa Catoni.

It is not granted to know which man took up arms with
more right on his side. Each pleads his cause before a great
judge: the winning cause pleased the gods, but the losing
one pleased Cato.

2 *Stat magni nominis umbra.*   *Pharsalia*

There stands the ghost of a great name.
   of Pompey

3 *Nil actum credens, dum quid superesset agendum.*   *Pharsalia*

Thinking nothing done while anything remained to be done.

Clare Booth Luce 1903–87

American diplomat, politician, and writer

4 But much of what Mr Wallace calls his global thinking is,   maiden speech to the House of
no matter how you slice it, still 'globaloney.' Mr Wallace's   Representatives, 9 February 1943
warp of sense and his woof of nonsense is very tricky cloth
out of which to cut the pattern of a post-war world.
   on Vice-President Henry Wallace's post-war theories

Lucretius (Titus Lucretius Carus) c.94–55 BC

Roman poet

5 *Tantum religio potuit suadere malorum.*   *De Rerum Natura* bk. 1, l. 101

So much wrong could religion induce.

Luiz Inácio Lula da Silva 1945–

Brazilian statesman, President 2003–

6 A war can perhaps be won single-handedly. But peace—   speech, United Nations, 23
lasting peace—cannot be secured without the support of all.   September 2003; in *Guardian*
                                                              (online edition) 24 September
                                                              2003

Martin Luther 1483–1546

German Protestant theologian

7 Here stand I. I can do no other. God help me. Amen.   speech at the Diet of Worms, 18
                                                           April 1521; attributed

8 If I had heard that as many devils would set on me in   to the Princes of Saxony, 21
Worms as there are tiles on the roofs, I should none the less   August 1524
have ridden there.

Rosa Luxemburg 1871–1919

German revolutionary

9 Freedom is always and exclusively freedom for the one who   *Die Russische Revolution* (1918)
thinks differently.

Jack Lynch 1917–
Irish statesman, Taoiseach 1966–73, 1977–9

1 I have never and never will accept the right of a minority who happen to be a majority in a small part of the country to opt out of a nation.

in Irish Times 14 November 1970 'This Week They Said'

Robert Lynd 1879–1949
Anglo-Irish essayist and journalist

2 The belief in the possibility of a short decisive war appears to be one of the most ancient and dangerous of human illusions.

attributed

Jonathan Lynn 1943– and Antony Jay 1930–
English writers

3 'Opposition's about asking awkward questions.' 'Yes . . . and government's about not answering them.'

Yes Minister vol. 1 (1981)

4 The PM—whose motto is . . . 'In Defeat, Malice—in Victory, Revenge!'

Yes Minister vol. 1 (1981)

5 If you wish to describe a proposal in a way that guarantees that a Minister will reject it, describe it as *courageous*.

Yes Minister vol. 1 (1981)

6 The Official Secrets Act is not to protect secrets but to protect officials.

Yes Minister vol. 1 (1981)

7 Diplomacy is about surviving till the next century—politics is about surviving till Friday afternoon.

Yes Prime Minister vol. 1 (1986)

8 *what is known to the Civil Service as the* Politicians' Syllogism:
Step One: We must do something.
Step Two: This is something.
Step Three: Therefore we must do it.

Yes Prime Minister vol. 2 (1987)

Mary McAleese 1951–
Irish stateswoman; President from 1997

9 I sense a mood among the people that they want a president who can speak to them from above politics. It will look at an Ireland where people are not pigeon-holed any more.
after being selected as Fianna Fáil candidate

in Irish Times 20 September 1997

10 Apart from the shamrock, the President should not wear emblems or symbols of any kind.
deciding not to wear a poppy at her inauguration on 11 November 1997

in Guardian 6 November 1997

11 People ask me what does the Celtic Tiger look like; it looks like this place.
visiting Clonaslee in Co. Laois

in Irish Times 13 April 1998

12 The day of the dinosaurs is over. The future belongs to the bridge-builders, not the wreckers.
on the election to the Northern Ireland Assembly

in Irish Times 27 June 1998

13 Those whom we commemorate . . . fell victim to a war against oppression in Europe. Their memory, too, fell victim to a war for independence at home in Ireland . . . Respect for the memory of one set of heroes was often at the expense of respect for the memory of another.
at the Armistice Day commemorations in Belgium

in Irish Times 14 November 1998 'This Week They Said'

Bernadette Devlin McAliskey 1947–

Irish nationalist

1 Expectation of good news from the British government is
never something I have lived with easily. And yet I have it
and I appreciate it. Maybe I should have more faith.
*on the decision by the British Government not to extradite her
daughter, Róisín, to Germany*

in *Irish Times* 14 March 1998 'This
Week They Said'

Dorothy Macardle 1889–1958

Irish nationalist

2 He knew Ireland too little, and the English House of
Commons too well.
of John **Redmond**

Diana Norman *Terrible Beauty*
(1987)

Douglas MacArthur 1880–1964

American general

3 I came through and I shall return.
*on reaching Australia, 20 March 1942, having broken through
Japanese lines en route from Corregidor*

in *New York Times* 21 March 1942

4 In war, indeed, there can be no substitute for victory.

in *Congressional Record* 19 April
1951, vol. 97

5 I still remember the refrain of one of the most popular
barracks ballads of that day, which proclaimed most
proudly that old soldiers never die; they just fade away. I
now close my military career and just fade away.

address to a Joint Meeting of
Congress, 19 April 1951

Lord Macaulay 1800–59

English Whig politician, historian, and poet
on Macaulay: see **Melbourne** 266:7, **Smith** 372:9

6 In order that he might rob a neighbour whom he had
promised to defend, black men fought on the coast of
Coromandel, and red men scalped each other by the Great
Lakes of North America.

Biographical Essays (1857) 'Frederic
the Great'

7 The gallery in which the reporters sit has become a fourth
estate of the realm.

*Essays Contributed to the Edinburgh
Review* (1843) vol. 1 'Hallam'

8 He knew that the essence of war is violence, and that
moderation in war is imbecility.

*Essays Contributed to the Edinburgh
Review* (1843) vol. 1 'John
Hampden'

9 *of Niccolò* **Machiavelli**:
Out of his surname they have coined an epithet for a knave,
and out of his Christian name a synonym for the Devil.

*Essays Contributed to the Edinburgh
Review* (1843) vol. 1 'Machiavelli'

10 Many politicians of our time are in the habit of laying it
down as a self-evident proposition, that no people ought to
be free till they are fit to use their freedom. The maxim is
worthy of the fool in the old story, who resolved not to go
into the water till he had learnt to swim. If men are to wait
for liberty till they become wise and good in slavery, they
may indeed wait for ever.

*Essays Contributed to the Edinburgh
Review* (1843) vol. 1 'Milton'

1 On the rich and the eloquent, on nobles and priests, they [the Puritans] looked down with contempt: for they esteemed themselves rich in a more precious treasure, and eloquent in a more sublime language, nobles by the right of an earlier creation, and priests by the imposition of a mightier hand.

Essays Contributed to the Edinburgh Review (1843) vol. 1 'Milton'

2 We know no spectacle so ridiculous as the British public in one of its periodical fits of morality.

Essays Contributed to the Edinburgh Review (1843) vol. 1 'Moore's *Life of Lord Byron*'

3 We have heard it said that five per cent is the natural interest of money.

Essays Contributed to the Edinburgh Review (1843) vol. 1 'Southey's Colloquies'

4 With the dead there is no rivalry. In the dead there is no change. Plato is never sullen. Cervantes is never petulant. Demosthenes never comes unseasonably. Dante never stays too long. No difference of political opinion can alienate Cicero. No heresy can excite the horror of Bossuet.

Essays Contributed to the Edinburgh Review (1843) vol. 2 'Lord Bacon'

5 An acre in Middlesex is better than a principality in Utopia.

Essays Contributed to the Edinburgh Review (1843) vol. 2 'Lord Bacon'

6 The rising hope of those stern and unbending Tories.
    of **Gladstone**

Essays Contributed to the Edinburgh Review (1843) vol. 2 'Gladstone on Church and State'

7 The history of England is emphatically the history of progress.

Essays Contributed to the Edinburgh Review (1843) vol. 2 'Sir James Mackintosh'

8 On the day of the accession of George the Third, the ascendancy of the Whig party terminated; and on that day the purification of the Whig party began.

Essays Contributed to the Edinburgh Review (1843) vol. 2 'William Pitt, Earl of Chatham'

9 The reluctant obedience of distant provinces generally costs more than it [the territory] is worth.

Essays Contributed to the Edinburgh Review (1843) vol. 2 'The War of Succession in Spain'

10 Every schoolboy knows who imprisoned Montezuma, and who strangled Atahualpa.

Essays Contributed to the Edinburgh Review (1843) vol. 3 'Lord Clive'

11 The Chief Justice was rich, quiet, and infamous.

Essays Contributed to the Edinburgh Review (1843) vol. 3 'Warren Hastings'

12 Thus our democracy was, from an early period, the most aristocratic, and our aristocracy the most democratic in the world.

History of England vol. 1 (1849)

13 Persecution produced its natural effect on them [Puritans and Calvinists]. It found them a sect; it made them a faction.

History of England vol. 1 (1849)

14 [Louis XIV] had shown, in an eminent degree, two talents invaluable to a prince, the talent of choosing his servants well, and the talent of appropriating to himself the chief part of the credit of their acts.

History of England vol. 1 (1849)

15 No man is fit to govern great societies who hesitates about disobliging the few who have access to him for the sake of the many he will never see.

History of England vol. 1 (1849)

16 It was a crime in a child to read by the bedside of a sick parent one of those beautiful collects which had soothed the griefs of forty generations of Christians.

History of England vol. 1 (1849)

1 The Puritan hated bear-baiting, not because it gave pain to the bear, but because it gave pleasure to the spectators.

History of England vol. 1 (1849)

2 It has often been found that profuse expenditure, heavy taxation, absurd commercial restrictions, corrupt tribunals, disastrous wars, seditions, persecutions, conflagrations, inundations, have not been able to destroy capital so fast as the exertions of private citizens have been able to create it.

History of England vol. 1 (1849)

3 Obadiah Bind-their-kings-in-chains-and-their-nobles-with-links-of-iron.

'The Battle of Naseby' (1824)
fictitious author's name

4 Oh, wherefore come ye forth in triumph from the north,
With your hands, and your feet, and your raiment all red?
And wherefore doth your rout send forth a joyous shout?
And whence be the grapes of the wine-press which ye tread?

'The Battle of Naseby' (1824)

5 And the Man of Blood was there, with his long essenced hair,
And Astley, and Sir Marmaduke, and Rupert of the Rhine.

'The Battle of Naseby' (1824)

6 To my true king I offered free from stain
Courage and faith; vain faith, and courage vain.

'A Jacobite's Epitaph' (1845)

7 By those white cliffs I never more must see,
By that dear language which I spake like thee,
Forget all feuds, and shed one English tear
O'er English dust. A broken heart lies here.

'A Jacobite's Epitaph' (1845)

8 Then none was for a party;
Then all were for the state;
Then the great man helped the poor,
And the poor man loved the great:
Then lands were fairly portioned;
Then spoils were fairly sold:
The Romans were like brothers
In the brave days of old.

Lays of Ancient Rome (1842)
'Horatius'

9 Thank you, madam, the agony is abated.
aged four, having had hot coffee spilt over his legs

G. O. Trevelyan *Life and Letters of Lord Macaulay* (1876)

10 The object of oratory alone is not truth, but persuasion.

'Essay on Athenian Orators' in *Knight's Quarterly Magazine* August 1824

11 Nothing is so galling to a people not broken in from the birth as a paternal, or in other words a meddling government, a government which tells them what to read and say and eat and drink and wear.

in *Edinburgh Review* January 1830

12 He has one eminent merit—that of being an enthusiastic admirer of mine—so that I may be the Hero of a novel yet, under the name of Delamere or Mortimer. Only think what an honour.
*of the novelist and politician **Bulwer Lytton***

letter, 5 August 1831

13 I detest him more than cold boiled veal.
of the Tory essayist and politician John Wilson Croker

letter, 5 August 1831

14 We must at present do our best to form a class who may be interpreters between us and the millions whom we govern; a class of persons, Indian in blood and colour, but English in taste, in opinions, in morals, and in intellect.

minute, as Member of Supreme Council of India, 2 February 1835

John McCain 1936–
American Republican politician

1 I will not take the low road to the highest office in the land.
I want the presidency in the best way, not the worst way.
*conceding victory in the South Carolina presidential primary to
George W. **Bush***

in *Guardian* 24 February 2000

Eugene McCarthy 1916–
American Democratic politician

2 Being in politics is like being a football coach. You have to
be smart enough to understand the game, and dumb
enough to think it's important.
while campaigning for the presidency

in an interview, 1968

Joseph McCarthy 1908–57
American politician and anti-Communist agitator

3 I have here in my hand a list of two hundred and five
[people] that were known to the Secretary of State as being
members of the Communist Party and who nevertheless are
still working and shaping the policy of the State
Department.

speech at Wheeling, West Virginia,
9 February 1950

4 McCarthyism is Americanism with its sleeves rolled.

speech in Wisconsin, 1952; Richard
Rovere *Senator Joe McCarthy* (1973)

Mary McCarthy 1912–89
American novelist

5 Bureaucracy, the rule of no one, has become the modern
form of despotism.

in *New Yorker* 18 October 1958

George B. McClellan 1826–85
American soldier and politician

6 All quiet along the Potomac.
said at the time of the American Civil War

attributed

Robert Rutherford ('Colonel')
McCormick 1880–1955
American newspaper editor and publisher

7 The British are no longer important enough for me to
dislike.
*explaining his willingness to give an interview to the British
journalist Woodrow Wyatt*

J. K. Galbraith *A Life in Our Times*
(1981)

John McCrae 1872–1918
Canadian poet and military physician

8 To you from failing hands we throw
The torch; be yours to hold it high.
If ye break faith with us who die
We shall not sleep, though poppies grow
In Flanders Fields.

'In Flanders Fields' (1915)

Hugh MacDiarmid 1892–1978
Scottish poet and nationalist

1 The rose of all the world is not for me.
I want for my part
Only the little white rose of Scotland
That smells sharp and sweet—and breaks the heart.

'The Little White Rose' (1934)

2 Scotland small? Our multiform, our infinite Scotland *small?*
Only as a patch of hillside may be a cliché corner
To a fool who cries 'Nothing but heather!' . . .

Direadh 1 (1974)

Dwight Macdonald 1906–82
American writer and film critic

3 Götterdämmerung without the gods.
of the use of atomic bombs against the Japanese

in *Politics* September 1945 'The Bomb'

John A. Macdonald 1815–91
Scottish-born Canadian Liberal-Conservative statesman, Prime Minister 1867–73 and 1878–91

4 When fortune empties her chamberpot on your head, smile—and say 'we are going to have a summer shower'.

spoken *c.*1875 when Leader of the Opposition

5 A British subject I was born, and a British subject I will die.

speech, 17 February 1891, in Toronto *Empire* 18 February 1891

Ramsay MacDonald 1866–1937
British Labour statesman; Prime Minister, 1924, 1931–5
on MacDonald: see **Churchill** 87:5, **George V** 153:8, **Lloyd George** 240:4, **Nicolson** 286:10; *see also* **Lamont** 224:5

6 Wars are popular. Contractors make profits; the aristocracy glean honour.

in *Labour Leader* 11 March 1915

7 A terror decreed by a Secret Committee is child's play compared with a terror instituted by 'lawful authority'.

in *Socialist Review* January-March 1921

8 We hear war called murder. It is not: it is suicide.

in *Observer* 4 May 1930

9 Tomorrow every Duchess in London will be wanting to kiss me!
after forming the National Government, 25 August 1931

Viscount Snowden *An Autobiography* (1934) vol. 2

10 A body representing the citizenship of the whole nation is charged with so much that it can do nothing swiftly and well.

Carl Cohen *Parliament and Democracy* (1962)

Ian McEwan 1948–
English novelist

11 The committee divided between the theorists, who had done all their thinking long ago, or had had it done for them, and the pragmatists, who hoped to discover what it was they thought in the process of saying it.

The Child in Time (1987)

12 No human society, from the hunter-gatherer to the postindustrial, has come to the attention of anthropologists that did not have its leaders and the led; and no emergency was ever dealt with effectively by democratic process.

Enduring Love (1987)

George McGovern 1922–

American Democratic politician, presidential candidate in 1972

1 Sometimes, when they say you're ahead of your time, it's just a polite way of saying you have a real bad sense of timing.

in *Observer* 18 March 1990 'Sayings of the Week'

Lord McGregor 1921–

British sociologist

2 An odious exhibition of journalists dabbling their fingers in the stuff of other people's souls.
    on press coverage of the marriage of the Prince and Princess of Wales, speaking as Chairman of the Press Complaints Commission

in *The Times* 9 June 1992

Martin McGuinness 1950–

Northern Irish politician

3 My war is over. My job as a political leader is to prevent war.

in *Daily Telegraph* 30 October 2002

Niccolò Machiavelli 1469–1527

Italian political philosopher and Florentine statesman

4 And if, to be sure, sometimes you need to conceal a fact with words, do it in such a way that it does not become known, or, if it does become known, that you have a ready and quick defence.

'Advice to Raffaello Girolami when he went as Ambassador to the Emperor' (October 1522)

5 It is necessary for him who lays out a state and arranges laws for it to presuppose that all men are evil and that they are always going to act according to the wickedness of their spirits whenever they have free scope.

Discourses on the First Ten Books of Livy (1513–17)

6 Success or failure lies in conforming to the times.

Discourses on the First Ten Books of Livy (1513–17)

7 Wars begin when you will, but they do not end when you please.

History of Florence (1521–4)

8 Men should be either treated generously or destroyed, because they take revenge for slight injuries—for heavy ones they cannot.

The Prince (1513)

9 This leads to a debate: is it better to be loved than feared, or the reverse? The answer is that it is desirable to be both, but because it is difficult to join them together, it is much safer for a prince to be feared than loved, if he is to fail in one of the two.

The Prince (1513)

10 Let no one oppose this belief of mine with that well-worn proverb: 'He who builds on the people builds on mud.'

The Prince (1513)

11 Since, then, a prince is necessitated to play the animal well, he chooses among the beasts the fox and the lion, because the lion does not protect himself from traps; the fox does not protect himself from wolves. The prince must be a fox, therefore, to recognize the traps and a lion to frighten the wolves.

The Prince (1513)

12 So long as the great majority of men are not deprived of either property or honour, they are satisfied.

The Prince (1513)

1 There is no other way for securing yourself against flatteries except that men understand that they do not offend you by telling you the truth; but when everybody can tell you the truth, you fail to get respect.

The Prince (1513)

2 In seizing a state, the usurper ought to examine closely into all those injuries which it is necessary for him to inflict, and to do them all at one stroke, so as not to have to repeat them daily; and thus by not unsettling men he will be able to reassure them, and win them to himself by benefits. He who does otherwise, either from timidity or evil advice, is always compelled to keep the knife in his hand.

The Prince (1513)

3 Princes ought to leave affairs of reproach to the management of others, and keep those of grace in their own hands.

The Prince (1513)

Peter MacKay 1965-

Canadian Conservative politician, Deputy Leader of the Conservative Party of Canada

4 My head's clear. My heart's a little banged up, but that will heal

> *after the decision by his former Conservative colleague Belinda* **Stronach***, with whom he had had a romantic relationship, to join the Liberal Party just before a key budget vote*

in an interview with CBC News, 18 May 2005

James Mackintosh 1765-1832

Scottish philosopher and historian

5 Men are never so good or so bad as their opinions.

Dissertation on the Progress of Ethical Philosophy (1830) 'Jeremy Bentham'

6 The Commons, faithful to their system, remained in a wise and masterly inactivity.

> *of the French Commons*

Vindiciae Gallicae (1791)

Iain Macleod 1913-70

British Conservative politician
on Macleod: see **Salisbury** 345:2

7 To have a debate on the National Health Service without the right hon. Gentleman [Aneurin Bevan] would be like putting on Hamlet with no one in the part of the First Gravedigger.

in the House of Commons, 27 March 1952

8 It is some measure of the tightness of the magic circle on this occasion that neither the Chancellor of the Exchequer nor the Leader of the House of Commons had any inkling of what was happening.

> *of the 'evolvement' of Lord* **Home** *as Conservative leader after the resignation of Harold* **Macmillan**

in *The Spectator* 17 January 1964

9 The Conservative Party always in time forgives those who were wrong. Indeed often, in time, they forgive those who were right.

in *The Spectator* 21 February 1964

10 John Fitzgerald Kennedy described himself, in a brilliant phrase, as an idealist without illusions. I would describe the Prime Minister as an illusionist without ideals.

in the House of Commons, 1 March 1966; see **Kennedy** 213:10

1 In Parliament it should not only be the duty but the pleasure of the Opposition to oppose whenever they reasonably can.

in *The Spectator* 26 August 1966

2 I cannot help it if every time the Opposition are asked to name their weapons they pick boomerangs.

in *Dictionary of National Biography* (1917–)

Marshall McLuhan 1911–80
Canadian communications scholar

3 Television brought the brutality of war into the comfort of the living room. Vietnam was lost in the living rooms of America—not the battlefields of Vietnam.

in *Montreal Gazette* 16 May 1975

Comte de Macmahon 1808–93
French military commander and statesman; President of the Third Republic, 1873–9

4 *J'y suis, j'y reste.*
Here I am, and here I stay.
   at the taking of the Malakoff fortress during the Crimean War, 8 September 1855

G. Hanotaux *Histoire de la France Contemporaine* (1903–8) vol. 2

William McMahon 1908–88
Australian statesman, Prime Minister 1971–2

5 Politics is trying to get into office.

L. Oakes and D. Solomon *The Making of an Australian Prime Minister* (1973)

Harold Macmillan 1894–1986
British Conservative statesman; Prime Minister, 1957–63
on Macmillan: see **Bevan** 39:4, **Birch** 42:12, **Birch** 42:12, **Hennessy** 180:2, **Levin** 232:6, **Levin** 232:8, **Macleod** 251:8, **Stockton** 381:11, **Thorpe** 394:6

6 Toryism has always been a form of paternal socialism.
   in 1936

Anthony Sampson *Macmillan* (1967)

7 We . . . are Greeks in this American empire . . . We must run the Allied Forces HQ as the Greeks ran the operations of the Emperor Claudius.
   to Richard **Crossman** *in 1944, after French North Africa had become an American sphere of influence, with* **Eisenhower** *as Supreme Allied Commander*

in *Sunday Telegraph* 9 February 1964

8 The Whips want the safe men . . . I reminded Winston again that it took Hitler to make him PM and me an under-secretary. The Tory Party would do neither.

diary, 13 October 1954

9 There ain't gonna be no war.
   at a London press conference, 24 July 1955, following the Geneva summit

in *News Chronicle* 25 July 1955

10 Forever poised between a cliché and an indiscretion.
   on the life of a Foreign Secretary

in *Newsweek* 30 April 1956

1 Let us be frank about it: most of our people have never had it so good. Go around the country, go to the industrial towns, go to the farms, and you'll see a state of prosperity such as we have never had in my lifetime—nor indeed ever in the history of this country. What is beginning to worry some of us is 'Is it too good to be true?' or perhaps I should say 'Is it too good to last?'

*speech at Bedford, 20 July 1957; see **Slogans** 369:8*

2 I thought the best thing to do was to settle up these little local difficulties, and then turn to the wider vision of the Commonwealth.
   statement at London airport on leaving for a Commonwealth tour, 7 January 1958, following the resignation of the Chancellor of the Exchequer and others

in The Times 8 January 1958

3 The wind of change is blowing through this continent, and, whether we like it or not, this growth of [African] national consciousness is a political fact.

speech at Cape Town, 3 February 1960

4 Can we say that with fifteen representatives, Ambassadors or Ministers, in Nato acting in unanimity, the deterrent would continue to be credible? There might be one finger on the trigger. There would be fifteen fingers on the safety catch.

attributed, 1960

5 As usual the Liberals offer a mixture of sound and original ideas. Unfortunately none of the sound ideas is original and none of the original ideas is sound.

speech to London Conservatives, 7 March 1961

6 He [Aneurin Bevan] enjoys prophesying the imminent fall of the capitalist system and is prepared to play a part, any part, in its burial, except that of mute.

Michael Foot Aneurin Bevan (1962)

7 I was determined that no British government should be brought down by the action of two tarts.
   comment on the Profumo affair, July 1963

Anthony Sampson Macmillan (1967)

8 It is thinking about themselves that is really the curse of the younger generation—they appear to have no other subject which interests them at all.

the 'Tuesday memorandum', a draft of a letter to the Queen, advising on his successor but not sent, 1963; D. R. Thorpe Alec Douglas-Home (1996)

9 Power? It's like a Dead Sea fruit. When you achieve it, there is nothing there.

*Anthony Sampson The New Anatomy of Britain (1971); see **Levin** 232:6*

10 Churchill was fundamentally what the English call unstable—by which they mean anybody who has that touch of genius which is inconvenient in normal times.

attributed, 1975

11 There are three bodies no sensible man directly challenges: the Roman Catholic Church, the Brigade of Guards and the National Union of Mineworkers.

*in Observer 22 February 1981; see **Baldwin** 27:6*

12 First of all the Georgian silver goes, and then all that nice furniture that used to be in the saloon. Then the Canalettos go.
   on privatization

*speech to the Tory Reform Group, 8 November 1985, in The Times 9 November 1985; see **Misquotations** 273:8*

13 It has always seemed to me more artistic, when the curtain falls on the last performance, to accept the inevitable *E finita la commedia.* It is tempting, perhaps, but unrewarding to hang about the greenroom after final retirement from the stage.

At the End of the Day (1973)

1 The opposition of events.
on his biggest problem (see also **Misquotations** *272:7)*

David Dilks *The Office of Prime Minister in Twentieth Century Britain* (1993)

2 *of the office of Prime Minister:*
Sometimes the strain is awful, you have to resort to Jane Austen.

in the Butler Papers; Peter Hennessy *The Hidden Wiring* (1995)

Robert McNamara 1916–

American Democratic politician, Secretary of Defense during the Vietnam War

3 I don't object to it's being called 'McNamara's War' . . . It is a very important war and I am pleased to be identified with it and do whatever I can to win it.

in *New York Times* 25 April 1964

4 We . . . acted according to what we thought were the principles and traditions of this nation. We were wrong. We were terribly wrong.
of the conduct of the Vietnam War by the **Kennedy** *and* **Johnson** *administrations*

speaking in Washington, just before the twentieth anniversary of the American withdrawal from Vietnam; in *Daily Telegraph* (electronic edition) 10 April 1995

Eoin MacNeill 1867–1945

Irish nationalist

5 What we call our country is not a poetical abstraction . . . There is no such person as Caitlin Ni Uallachain or Roisin Dubh or the Sean-bhean Bhocht, who is calling on us to save her.

in February, 1916; Robert Kee *The Bold Fenian Men* (1989)

6 I wish it then to be clearly understood that under present conditions I am definitely opposed to any proposal that may come forward involving insurrection.

memorandum to Irish Volunteers, February 1916

William Macpherson of Cluny 1926–

Scottish lawyer

7 For the purposes of our Inquiry the concept of institutional racism which we apply consists of:
The collective failure of an organisation to provide an appropriate and professional service to people because of their colour, culture, or ethnic origin. It can be seen or detected in processes, attitudes and behaviour which amount to discrimination through unwitting prejudice, ignorance, thoughtlessness and racist stereotyping which disadvantage minority ethnic people.

The Stephen Lawrence Inquiry: Report (February 1999) ch. 6

Salvador de Madariaga 1886–1978

Spanish writer and diplomat

8 Since, in the main, it is not armaments that cause wars but wars (or the fears thereof) that cause armaments, it follows that every nation will at every moment strive to keep its armament in an efficient state as required by its fear, otherwise styled security.

Morning Without Noon (1974) pt. 1, ch. 9

James Madison 1751–1836
American Democratic Republican statesman; 4th President of the US, 1809–17

1 Liberty is to faction what air is to fire, an aliment without which it instantly expires. But it could not be less folly to abolish liberty, which is essential to political life, because it nourishes faction than it would be to wish the annihilation of air, which is essential to animal life, because it imparts to fire its destructive agency.

The Federalist (1787)

2 The diversity in the faculties of men, from which the rights of property originate, is not less an insuperable obstacle to a uniformity of interests. The protection of these faculties is the first object of government. From the protection of different and unequal faculties of acquiring property, the possession of different degrees and kinds of property immediately results.

The Federalist (1787)

3 The accumulation of all powers, legislative, executive, and judiciary, in the same hands, whether of one, a few, or many, and whether hereditary, self-appointed, or elective, may justly be pronounced the very definition of tyranny.

The Federalist (1787)

4 In framing a government, which is to be administered by men over men, the great difficulty lies in this: you must first enable the government to control the governed, and in the next place oblige it to control itself.

attributed

John Maffey 1877–1969
British diplomat

5 *as British Ambassador to Dublin:*
Phrases make history here.

letter, 21 May 1945

Magna Carta
Political charter signed by King John at Runnymede, 1215

6 That the English Church shall be free.

Clause 1

7 No free man shall be taken or imprisoned or dispossessed, or outlawed or exiled, or in any way destroyed, nor will we go upon him, nor will we send against him except by the lawful judgement of his peers or by the law of the land.

Clause 39

8 To no man will we sell, or deny, or delay, right or justice.

Clause 40

Alfred T. Mahan 1840–1914
American naval officer and historian

9 Those far distant, storm-beaten ships, upon which the Grand Army never looked, stood between it and the dominion of the world.

The Influence of Sea Power upon the French Revolution and Empire 1793–1812 (1892) vol. 2

Norman Mailer 1923–
American novelist and essayist

10 The world stood like a playing card on edge . . . One looked at the buildings one passed and wondered if one was to see them again.
looking back at the week of the Cuban Missile Crisis

The Presidential Papers (1964)

1 All the security around the American President is just to make sure the man who shoots him gets caught.

in Sunday Telegraph 4 March 1990

Henry Sumner Maine 1822–88
British jurist

2 War appears to be as old as mankind, but peace is a modern invention.

International Law (Whewell Lectures, 1887)

Joseph de Maistre 1753–1821
French writer and diplomat

3 *Toute nation a le gouvernement qu'elle mérite.*
Every country has the government it deserves.

letter, 15 August 1811

John Major 1943–
British Conservative statesman; Prime Minister, 1990–7
on Major: see **Anonymous** 10:1, **Cranborne** 104:4, **Shephard** 362:13, **Thatcher** 392:6, **Waldegrave** 407:15

4 The first requirement of politics is not intellect or stamina but patience. Politics is a very long-run game and the tortoise will usually beat the hare.

in Daily Express 25 July 1989

5 If the policy isn't hurting, it isn't working.

speech in Northampton, 27 October 1989; see **Slogans** 369:6

6 Society needs to condemn a little more and understand a little less.

interview with *Mail on Sunday* 21 February 1993

7 Fifty years on from now, Britain will still be the country of long shadows on county [cricket] grounds, warm beer, invincible green suburbs, dog lovers, and—as George Orwell said—old maids bicycling to Holy Communion through the morning mist.

speech to the Conservative Group for Europe, 22 April 1993; see **Orwell** 297:1

8 It is time to get back to basics: to self-discipline and respect for the law, to consideration for others, to accepting responsibility for yourself and your family, and not shuffling it off on the state.

speech to the Conservative Party Conference, 8 October 1993

9 So right. OK. We lost.
on election night

in Guardian 3 May 1997

10 When the final curtain comes down, it's time to get off the stage.
outside 10 Downing Street on 2 May, leaving office as Prime Minister and announcing that he would resign as Party Leader

in Guardian 3 May 1997

11 In retrospect, I think her behaviour was intolerable, and I hope none of my successors are treated in that way.
of Margaret **Thatcher**

in Daily Telegraph 11 August 1999

12 Margaret had been at her happiest confronting political dragons: I chose consensus.
contrasting himself with Margaret **Thatcher**

John Major *The Autobiography* (1999)

Bernard Malamud 1914–86
American novelist and short-story writer

13 There's no such thing as an unpolitical man, especially a Jew.

The Fixer (1966)

Malcolm X 1925-65

American civil rights campaigner

1 The white man was *created* a devil, to bring chaos upon this earth.

speech, c.1953; Malcolm X with Alex Haley *The Autobiography of Malcolm X* (1965); see **Fard** 139:5

2 If you're born in America with a black skin, you're born in prison.

in an interview, June 1963

3 We are not fighting for integration, nor are we fighting for separation. We are fighting for recognition as human beings. We are fighting for . . . human rights.

Black Revolution, speech in New York, 1964

4 You can't separate peace from freedom because no one can be at peace unless he has his freedom.

speech in New York, 7 January 1965

5 We are not speaking of any *individual* white man. We are speaking of the *collective* white man's *historical* record.We are speaking of the collective white man's cruelties, and evils, and greeds, that have seen him *act* like a devil toward the non-white man.

Malcolm X with Alex Haley *The Autobiography of Malcolm X* (1965)

Seamus Mallon 1936-

Northern Irish politician

6 A pint of Guinness, or a large whisky, or maybe two.
   when asked how he proposed to celebrate the agreement on Northern Ireland

in *Times* 11 April 1998

7 Sunningdale for slow learners.
   comparing the earlier stages of the Northern Irish talks with the 1973 negotiations towards a power-sharing executive held at Sunningdale College, Berkshire

in *Daily Telegraph* 6 April 1998

Thomas Robert Malthus 1766-1834

English political economist

8 Population, when unchecked, increases in a geometrical ratio. Subsistence only increases in an arithmetical ratio.

Essay on the Principle of Population (1798)

9 The perpetual struggle for room and food.

Essay on the Principle of Population (1798)

10 A man who is born into a world already possessed, if he cannot get subsistence from his parents on whom he has a just demand, and if the society do not want his labour, has no claim of *right* to the smallest portion of food, and, in fact, has no business to be where he is. At Nature's mighty feast there is no vacant cover for him.

Essay on the Principle of Population (1803 ed.)

Earl of Manchester 1602-71

English politician and Parliamentary commander in the Civil War

11 If we beat the King ninety-nine times, yet he is king still and so will his posterity be after him; but if the king beat us once we shall all be hanged, and our posterity made slaves.
   at a Parliamentary Council-of-War, 10 November 1644

in *Calendar of State Papers, Domestic* 1644-5

Lord Mancroft 1914–87
British Conservative politician

1 Cricket—a game which the English, not being a spiritual people, have invented in order to give themselves some conception of eternity.

Bees in Some Bonnets (1979)

Nelson Mandela 1918–
South African statesman, President of South Africa 1994–9

2 I have dedicated my life to this struggle of the African people. I have fought against white domination, and I have fought against black domination. I have cherished the ideal of a democratic and free society in which all persons live together in harmony with equal opportunities. It is an ideal which I hope to live for and to achieve. But if needs be, it is an ideal for which I am prepared to die.

speech at his trial in Pretoria, 20 April 1964

3 I stand here before you not as a prophet but as a humble servant of you, the people. Your tireless and heroic sacrifices have made it possible for me to be here today. I therefore place the remaining years of my life in your hands.

speech in Cape Town, 11 February 1990

4 Through its imperialist system Britain brought about untold suffering of millions of people. And this is an historical fact. To be able to admit this would increase the respect, you know, which we have for British institutions.

in *Guardian* 2 April 1990

5 Let freedom reign. The sun shall never set on so glorious a human achievement.

inaugural address as President of South Africa, 10 May 1994; see also **Bush** 67:6

6 True reconciliation does not consist in merely forgetting the past.
    on healing the bitterness caused by apartheid

speech, 7 January 1996

7 No one is born hating another person because of the colour of his skin, or his background, or his religion. People must learn to hate, and if they can learn to hate, they can be taught to love, for love comes more naturally to the human heart than its opposite.

Long Walk to Freedom (1994)

8 We close the century with most people still languishing in poverty, subjected to hunger, preventable disease, illiteracy and insufficient shelter.
    speaking at a ceremony at his former prison cell on Robben Island

in *Observer* on 2 January 2000

9 One of the things I learnt when I was negotiating was that until I changed myself I could not change others.

in *Sunday Times* 16 April 2000

10 *of Yasser Arafat:*
    He was like a surrealistic painting. He was complex, deep, superficial, rational, irrational, cold, warm.

in *Independent* 14 November 2004

Winnie Madikizela-Mandela 1934–
South African political activist, former wife of Nelson **Mandela**

11 With that stick of matches, with our necklace, we shall liberate this country.
    speech in black townships, 14 April 1986; a 'necklace' was a tyre soaked or filled with petrol, placed around a victim's neck, and set alight

in *Guardian* 15 April 1986

1 Maybe there is no rainbow nation after all because it does not have the colour black.
   at the funeral of a black child reportedly shot dead by a white farmer

in *Irish Times* 25 April 1998 'Quotes of the Week'

Peter Mandelson 1953–

British Labour politician

2 Before this campaign started, it was said that I was facing political oblivion, my career in tatters . . . They underestimated me, because I am a fighter and not a quitter.
   on winning back his Hartlepool seat in the General Election

speech, 8 June 2001

John Manners, Duke of Rutland 1818–1906

English Tory politician and writer

3 Let wealth and commerce, laws and learning die,
   But leave us still our old nobility!

England's Trust (1841)

Lord Mansfield 1705–93

Scottish lawyer and politician

4 The constitution does not allow reasons of state to influence our judgements: God forbid it should! We must not regard political consequences; however formidable soever they might be: if rebellion was the certain consequence, we are bound to say '*fiat justitia, ruat caelum*'.

Rex v. Wilkes, 8 June 1768, in *The English Reports* (1909) vol. 98; see **Adams** 4:6

5 Consider what you think justice requires, and decide accordingly. But never give your reasons; for your judgement will probably be right, but your reasons will certainly be wrong.
   advice to a newly appointed colonial governor ignorant in the law

Lord Campbell *The Lives of the Chief Justices of England* (1849) vol. 2

Mao Zedong 1893–1976

Chinese statesman, chairman of the Communist Party of the Chinese People's Republic 1949–76 and head of state 1949–59

6 Politics is war without bloodshed while war is politics with bloodshed.

lecture, 1938

7 Every Communist must grasp the truth, 'Political power grows out of the barrel of a gun'.

speech, 6 November 1938

8 The atom bomb is a paper tiger which the United States reactionaries use to scare people. It looks terrible, but in fact it isn't . . . All reactionaries are paper tigers.

interview, 1946

9 Letting a hundred flowers blossom and a hundred schools of thought contend is the policy for promoting progress in the arts and the sciences and a flourishing socialist culture in our land.

speech in Peking, 27 February 1957

10 People of the world, unite and defeat the US aggressors and all their running dogs!

'Statement Supporting the People of the Congo against US Aggression' 28 November 1964

John Marchi 1921–

American Republican politician

1 We ought not to permit a cottage industry in the God business.

on hearing that British scientists had successfully cloned a lamb (Dolly)

in *Guardian* 28 February 1997

James Margach d. 1979

British journalist

2 Power, which has the ability to mellow some of those who achieve it . . . in Heath's case changed his personality overnight. When Prime Minister he became authoritarian and intolerant.

The Abuse of Power (1978)

Princess Margaret 1930–2002

British princess, sister of **Elizabeth II**

3 Mindful of the Church's teaching that Christian marriage is indissoluble, and conscious of my duty to the Commonwealth, I have resolved to put these considerations before any others.

announcing her decision not to marry a divorced man, Group Captain Peter Townsend

statement from Clarence House, 31 October 1955; in *The Times* 1 November 1955

Marie-Antoinette 1755–93

French Queen consort of **Louis XVI**

4 *Qu'ils mangent de la brioche.*

Let them eat cake.

on being told that her people had no bread

attributed; in *Confessions* (1740) Rousseau refers to a similar remark being a well-known saying; in *Relation d'un Voyage à Bruxelles et à Coblentz en 1791* (1823), Louis XVIII attributes 'Why don't they eat pastry?' to Marie-Thérèse (1638–83), wife of Louis XIV

Constance Markievicz 1868–1927

Irish nationalist
on Markievicz: see **de Valera** 116:6

5 A good Nationalist should look upon slugs in the garden in much the same way as she looks on the English in Ireland.

in *Bean na hÉireann* November 1908

6 I wish you had the decency to shoot me.

on hearing of the commutation of her death sentence

Diana Norman *Terrible Beauty* (1987)

7 I have seen the stars, and I am not going to follow a flickering will o' the wisp.

rejecting the Treaty in the Dáil debate, 1921

Diana Norman *Terrible Beauty* (1987)

8 How could I ever meet Paddy Pearse or Jim Connolly in the hereafter if I took an oath to a British king?

in 1926, on her refusal to take the oath which would allow her to enter the Dáil

Diana Norman *Terrible Beauty* (1987)

George C. Marshall 1880–1959

American general and statesman, who as US Secretary of State (1947–9) initiated the programme of economic aid to European countries known as the Marshall Plan

1 If man does find the solution for world peace it will be the most revolutionary reversal of his record we have ever known.

biennial report of the Chief of Staff, United States Army, 1 September 1945

2 Our policy is directed not against any country or doctrine but against hunger, poverty, desperation and chaos. Its purpose should be the revival of a working economy in the world so as to permit the emergence of political and social conditions in which free institutions can exist.
   announcing the Marshall Plan

address at Harvard, 5 June 1947

John Marshall 1755–1835

American jurist

3 The power to tax involves the power to destroy.

in *McCulloch v. Maryland* (1819)

4 The people made the Constitution, and the people can unmake it. It is the creature of their own will, and lives only by their will.

in *Cohens v. Virginia* (1821)

Thomas R. Marshall 1854–1925

American politician

5 What this country needs is a really good 5-cent cigar.

in *New York Tribune* 4 January 1920

Thurgood Marshall 1908–93

American Supreme Court judge

6 We must never forget that the only real source of power that we as judges can tap is the respect of the people.

in *Chicago Tribune* 15 August 1981

Paul Martin 1938–

Canadian Liberal statesman, Prime Minister of Canada since 2002

7 The vote could not have been closer. The government has the confidence of the House but I believe it's very important for our part and the opposition that we now make this Parliament work the way that Canadians want it to.
   having won a key budget vote by the narrowest possible margin, 19 May 2005

in *GlobeandMail.com* 20 May 2005 (online edition)

William McChesney Martin Jr. 1906–98

American economist, Chairman of the Federal Reserve, 1951–70

8 The job of the Federal Reserve is to take away the punch bowl just when the party is getting good.

attributed; Paul Volcker interview on PBS, 26 September 2000

Andrew Marvell 1621–78

English poet

9 Choosing each stone, and poising every weight,
Trying the measures of the breadth and height;
Here pulling down, and there erecting new,
Founding a firm state by proportions true.

'The First Anniversary of the Government under His Highness the Lord Protector, 1655'

1 *He* nothing common did or mean
Upon that memorable scene:
But with his keener eye
The axe's edge did try:
Nor called the gods with vulgar spite
To vindicate his helpless right,
But bowed his comely head,
Down as upon a bed.
    on the execution of **Charles I**

'An Horatian Ode upon Cromwell's
Return from Ireland' (written
1650)

2 And now the Irish are ashamed
To see themselves in one year tamed:
So much one man can do,
That does both act and know.

'An Horatian Ode upon Cromwell's
Return from Ireland' (written
1650)

Karl Marx 1818–83

German socialist and political philosopher; co-founder (with
Friedrich **Engels**) of modern Communism

3 Religion . . . is the opium of the people.

*A Contribution to the Critique of
Hegel's Philosophy of Right* (1843–4)
introduction

4 Mankind always sets itself only such problems as it can
solve; since, looking at the matter more closely, it will
always be found that the task itself arises only when the
material conditions for its solution already exist or are at
least in the process of formation.

*A Contribution to the Critique of
Political Economy* (1859) preface

5 It is not the consciousness of men that determines their
being, but, on the contrary, their social being that
determines their consciousness.

*A Contribution to the Critique of
Political Economy* (1859) preface

6 From each according to his abilities, to each according to
his needs.

Critique of the Gotha Programme
(written 1875, but of earlier
origin); see Morelly *Code de la
nature* (1755) , and J. J. L. Blanc
Organisation du travail (1839)
(who, in quoting Saint-Simon,
rejects the notion) for possible
sources

7 Hegel says somewhere that all great events and personalities
in world history reappear in one fashion or another. He
forgot to add: the first time as tragedy, the second as farce.

*The Eighteenth Brumaire of Louis
Bonaparte* (1852); the origin of the
Hegel reference is uncertain, but
see **Hegel** 179:6

8 It is the ultimate aim of this work, to lay bare the economic
law of motion of modern society.

Das Kapital (1st German ed., 1867)
preface (25 July 1865)

9 The philosophers have only interpreted the world in various
ways; the point is to change it.

Theses on Feuerbach (written 1845)

10 What I did that was new was to prove . . . that the class
struggle necessarily leads to the dictatorship of the
proletariat.
    *the phrase 'dictatorship of the proletariat' had been used earlier in
    the Constitution of the World Society of Revolutionary
    Communists (1850), signed by Marx and others*

letter to Georg Weydemeyer 5
March 1852; Marx claimed that
the phrase had been coined by
Auguste Blanqui (1805–81), but it
has not been found in this form in
Blanqui's work

11 All I know is that I am not a Marxist.

attributed in a letter from Friedrich
Engels to Conrad Schmidt, 5
August 1890

Karl Marx 1818–83
and **Friedrich Engels** 1820–95
German socialists, co-founders of modern Communism

1 A spectre is haunting Europe—the spectre of Communism.

The Communist Manifesto (1848)
opening words

2 The history of all hitherto existing society is the history of class struggles.

The Communist Manifesto (1848)

3 In place of the old bourgeois society, with its classes and class antagonists, we shall have an association, in which the free development of each is the free development of all.

The Communist Manifesto (1848)

4 The proletarians have nothing to lose but their chains. They have a world to win. WORKING MEN OF ALL COUNTRIES, UNITE!
   often quoted as 'Workers of the world, unite!'

The Communist Manifesto (1848) *ad fin.*

Mary I (Mary Tudor) 1516–58
Queen of England from 1553

5 When I am dead and opened, you shall find 'Calais' lying in my heart.

in *Holinshed's Chronicles* vol. 4 (1808)

Queen Mary 1867–1953
British princess, Queen Consort of **George V**

6 *This* is a pretty kettle of fish!
   *to the Prime Minister, Stanley **Baldwin**, after **Edward VIII** had told her that he was prepared to give up the throne to marry Mrs Simpson*

James Pope-Hennessy *Life of Queen Mary* (1959)

7 All *this* thrown away for *that.*
   *on returning home to Marlborough House, London after the abdication of her son, King **Edward VIII**, December 1936*

David Duff *George and Elizabeth* (1983)

8 I do not think you have ever realised the shock, which the attitude you took up caused your family and the whole nation. It seemed inconceivable to those who had made such sacrifices during the war that you, as their King, refused a lesser sacrifice.

letter to the Duke of Windsor, the former **Edward VIII**, July 1938

Mary, Queen of Scots 1542–87
Scottish monarch, Queen 1542–67

9 Look to your consciences and remember that the theatre of the world is wider than the realm of England.
   to the commissioners appointed to try her at Fotheringhay, 13 October 1586

Antonia Fraser *Mary Queen of Scots* (1969) ch. 25

10 *En ma fin git mon commencement.*
    In my end is my beginning.
    motto embroidered with an emblem of her mother, Mary of Guise

quoted in a letter from William Drummond of Hawthornden to Ben Jonson in 1619

Philip Massinger 1583–1640
English dramatist

11 Ambition, in a private man a vice,
    Is in a prince the virtue.

The Bashful Lover (licensed 1636, published 1655)

1   Greatness, with private men
Esteemed a blessing, is to me a curse;
And we, whom, for our high births, they conclude
The only freemen, are the only slaves.
Happy the golden mean!

The Great Duke of Florence (licensed 1627, printed 1635)

W. Somerset Maugham 1874–1965

English novelist

2 The geniality of the politician who for years has gone out of his way to be cordial with everyone he meets.

A Writer's Notebook (1949) written in 1938

Richard Mawrey 1942–

British judge

3 *commenting on the government's refusal to revise the rules for postal voting:*
Anyone who has sat through the case I have just tried and listened to evidence of electoral fraud that would disgrace a banana republic would find this statement surprising.

in *Guardian* 4 April 2005

James Maxton 1885–1946

British Labour politician

4 All I say is, if you cannot ride two horses you have no right in the circus.
   opposing disaffiliation of the Scottish Independent Labour Party from the Labour Party, often quoted as 'no right in the bloody circus'

in *Daily Herald* 12 January 1931

Theresa May 1956–

British Conservative politician

5 You know what some people call us: the nasty party.

speech to the Conservative Conference, 7 October 2002

Horace Maybray-King 1901–86

British Labour politician; Speaker of the House of Commons

6 One of the myths of the British Parliament is that there are three parties there. I can assure you from bitter personal experience there are 629.

in *Observer* 9 October 1966 'Sayings of the Week'

Jonathan Mayhew 1720–66

American divine

7 Rulers have no authority from God to do mischief.

A Discourse Concerning Unlimited Submission and Non-Resistance to the Higher Powers (1750)

8 As soon as the prince sets himself up above the law, he loses the king in the tyrant; he does to all intents and purpose unking himself . . . And in such cases, has no more right to be obeyed, than any inferior officer who acts beyond his commission.

A Discourse Concerning Unlimited Submission and Non-Resistance to the Higher Powers (1750)

Giuseppe Mazzini 1805–72
Italian nationalist leader

1 Insurrection—by means of guerrilla bands—is the true
method of warfare for all nations desirous of emancipating
themselves from a foreign yoke.

General Instructions for the Members of Young Italy (1833) sect. 4

2 A nation is the universality of citizens speaking the same
tongue.

in *La Giovine Italia*, 1832

Thabo Mbeki 1942–
South African statesman, President of South Africa since 1999
on Mbeki: see **Sexwale** 350:4

3 I know that none dare challenge me when I say: I am an
African.

statement on behalf of the African
National Congress, 8 May 1996, on
the occasion of the adoption by
the Constitutional Assembly of the
Republic of South Africa
Constitution Bill

Catherine de' Medici 1518–89
Italian-born queen consort of Henri II of France

4 A false report, if believed during three days, may be of great
service to a government.

Isaac D'Israeli *Curiosities of
Literature* 2nd series (1849) vol. 2;
perhaps apocryphal

Robert Megarry 1910–

5 Whereas in England all is permitted that is not expressly
prohibited, it has been said that in Germany all is prohibited
unless expressly permitted and in France all is permitted
that is expressly prohibited. In the European Common
Market (as it then was) no-one knows what is permitted and
it all costs more.

'Law and Lawyers in a Permissive
Society' (5th Riddell Lecture
delivered in Lincoln's Inn Hall 22
March 1972)

Ahmed Meguili
French socialist

6 In 1789 the revolutionaries freed the prisoners and
frightened the king. This is the same thing . . . yet another
divorce between the leaders and the people.
  on the French rejection of the European Constitution

in *The Times* 31 May 2005 'Quotes
of the Day' (online edition)

Golda Meir 1898–1978
Israeli stateswoman, Prime Minister 1969–74

7 Those that perished in Hitler's gas chambers were the last
Jews to die without standing up to defend themselves.

speech to United Jewish Appeal
Rally, New York, 11 June 1967

Lord Melbourne 1779–1848
British Whig statesman; Prime Minister 1834, 1835–41

8 I have always thought complaints of ill-usage contemptible,
whether from a seduced disappointed girl or a turned-out
Prime Minister.
  on being dismissed by William IV

Emily Eden, letter to Mrs Lister, 23
November 1834

1 If left out he would be dangerous, but if taken in, he would be simply destructive.

Lord David Cecil *Lord M* (1954)

*when forming his second administration in 1835, Melbourne omitted the former Lord Chancellor, Lord **Brougham***

2 Universities never reform themselves; everyone knows that.

speech, House of Lords, 11 April 1837

3 What I like about the Order of the Garter is that there is no damned merit about it.

Lord David Cecil *The Young Melbourne* (1939)

4 You domineered too much, you interfered too much with other departments, you encroached upon the provinces of the Prime Minister, you worked, as I believe, with the Press in a manner unbecoming to the dignity of your station.

Lord David Cecil *Lord M* (1954)

*letter to the former Lord Chancellor, Lord **Brougham**, explaining why he had been omitted from Melbourne's second administration*

5 Damn it! Another Bishop dead! I believe they die to vex me.

Lord David Cecil *Lord M* (1954)

6 God help the Minister that meddles with art!

Lord David Cecil *Lord M* (1954)

7 I wish I was as cocksure of anything as Tom Macaulay is of everything.

Earl Cowper *Preface to Lord Melbourne's Papers* (1889)

8 Nobody ever did anything very foolish except from some strong principle.

Lord David Cecil *The Young Melbourne* (1939)

9 Now, is it to lower the price of corn, or isn't it? It is not much matter which we say, but mind, we must all say *the same.*

Walter Bagehot *The English Constitution* (1867)

at the end of a Cabinet meeting to agree a fixed tariff for corn; Melbourne is said to have put his back to the door and opened it only when they agreed

10 Things have come to a pretty pass when religion is allowed to invade the sphere of private life.

G. W. E. Russell *Collections and Recollections* (1898)

on hearing an evangelical sermon

11 This damned morality will undo us all.

Samuel Weintraub *Albert* (1997)

of Prince Albert's wish to establish the Royal Family as a national icon of domestic life

12 What all the wise men promised has not happened, and what all the d—d fools said would happen has come to pass.

H. Dunckley *Lord Melbourne* (1890)

of the Catholic Emancipation Act (1829)

13 What I want is men who will support me when I am in the wrong.

Lord David Cecil *Lord M* (1954)

replying to a politician who said 'I will support you as long as you are in the right'

14 When in doubt what should be done, do nothing.

Lord David Cecil *Lord M* (1954)

15 The whole duty of government is to prevent crime and to preserve contracts.

Lord David Cecil *Lord M* (1954)

Lord Melchett 1948–

British peer, executive director of Greenpeace

16 The menu could not guarantee GM-free food but I ate vegetarian shepherd's pie.

in *Sunday Times* 1 August 1999 'Talking Heads'

on his two days in prison after leading a raid to destroy GM crops

David Mellor 1949–

British Conservative politician and broadcaster

1 I do believe the popular press is drinking in the last chance saloon.

interview on *Hard News* (Channel 4), 21 December 1989

H. L. Mencken 1880–1956

American journalist and literary critic

2 Nothing is so abject and pathetic as a politician who has lost his job, save only a retired stud-horse.

Chrestomathy (1949)

3 Puritanism. The haunting fear that someone, somewhere, may be happy.

Chrestomathy (1949)

4 The whole aim of practical politics is to keep the populace alarmed (and hence clamorous to be led to safety) by menacing it with an endless series of hobgoblins, all of them imaginary.

In Defence of Women (1923)

5 Democracy is the theory that the common people know what they want, and deserve to get it good and hard.

A Little Book in C major (1916)

6 A government can never be the impersonal thing described in text-books. It is simply a group of men like any other. In every 100 of the men composing it there are two who are honest and intelligent, ten obvious scoundrels, and 88 poor fish.

Minority Report (1956)

7 Under democracy one party always devotes its chief energies to trying to prove that the other party is unfit to rule—and both commonly succeed, and are right.

Minority Report (1956)

8 The worst government is often the most moral. One composed of cynics is often very tolerant and humane. But when fanatics are on top there is no limit to oppression.

Minority Report (1956)

9 A good politician is quite as unthinkable as an honest burglar.

Prejudices 4th series (1925)

10 No one in this world, so far as I know—and I have searched the records for years, and employed agents to help me—has ever lost money by underestimating the intelligence of the great masses of the plain people.

in *Chicago Tribune* 19 September 1926

11 The saddest life is that of a political aspirant under democracy. His failure is ignominious and his success is disgraceful.

in *Baltimore Evening Sun* 9 December 1929

12 He [Calvin Coolidge] slept more than any other President, whether by day or by night. Nero fiddled, but Coolidge only snored.

in *American Mercury* April 1933

13 If there had been any formidable body of cannibals in the country he would have promised to provide them with free missionaries fattened at the taxpayer's expense.
   *of Harry **Truman**'s success in the 1948 presidential campaign*

in *Baltimore Sun* 7 November 1948

Robert Gordon Menzies 1894–1978

Australian Liberal statesman, Prime Minister 1939–41 and 1949–66

14 What Great Britain calls the Far East is to us the near north.

in *Sydney Morning Herald* 27 April 1939

Angela Merkel 1954–
German Christian Democrat politician

1 There are 35 years of the GDR [German Democratic
Republic, the former East Germany] in me, and six weeks of
Hamburg. I became a politician when the wall opened.
*of the origins of her political career (she was born in Hamburg,
but her family moved to Brandenburg when she was six weeks
old)*

quoted in *Daily Telegraph* 24 May
2005

Jean Meslier c.1664–1733
French priest

2 I remember, on this matter, the wish made once by an
ignorant, uneducated man . . . He said he wished . . . that
all the great men in the world and all the nobility could be
hanged, and strangled with the guts of priests. For myself
. . . I wish I could have the strength of Hercules to purge the
world of all vice and sin, and to have the pleasure of
destroying all those monsters of error and sin [priests] who
make all the peoples of the world groan so pitiably.
*often quoted as, 'I should like . . . the last king to be strangled
with the guts of the last priest'*

Testament (1864); see **Diderot**
118:7, **Nairn** 283:10

Prince Metternich 1773–1859
Austrian statesman

3 Italy is a geographical expression.
*discussing the Italian question with Lord **Palmerston** in 1847*

*Mémoires, Documents, etc. de
Metternich publiés par son fils*
(1883) vol. 7; see **Bismarck** 43:11

4 *of his own downfall:*
I feel obliged to call to the supporters of the social uprising:
Citizens of a dream-world, nothing is altered. On 14 March
1848, there was merely one man fewer.

*Aus Metternich's Nachgelassenen
Papieren* (ed. A. von Klinkowström
1880) vol. 8

5 Error has never approached my spirit.
addressed to Guizot in 1848

François Pierre G. Guizot *Mémoires*
(1858–67) vol. 4

6 The Emperor is everything, Vienna is nothing.

letter to Count Bombelles, 5 June
1848

7 The greatest gift of any statesman rests not in knowing
what concessions to make, but recognising when to make
them.

Concessionen und Nichtconcessionen
(1852)

8 The word 'freedom' means for me not a point of departure
but a genuine point of arrival. The point of departure is
defined by the word 'order'. Freedom cannot exist without
the concept of order.

Mein Politisches Testament

Anthony Meyer 1920–2004
British Conservative politician

9 I question the right of that great Moloch, national
sovereignty, to burn its children to save its pride.
speaking against the Falklands War, 1982

in *Listener* 27 September 1990

Jules Michelet 1798–1874

French historian

1 What is the first part of politics? Education. The second? Education. And the third? Education.

Le Peuple (1846); see **Blair** 46:1

William Porcher Miles 1822–96

2 'Vote early and vote often,' the advice openly displayed on the election banners in one of our northern cities.

in the House of Representatives, 31 March 1858

John Stuart Mill 1806–73

English philosopher and economist

3 No great improvements in the lot of mankind are possible, until a great change takes place in the fundamental constitution of their modes of thought.

Autobiography (1873)

4 The Conservatives . . . being by the law of their existence the stupidest party.

Considerations on Representative Government (1861)

5 It is but a small portion of the public business of a country which can be well done, or safely attempted, by the central authorities.

Considerations on Representative Government (1861)

6 When society requires to be rebuilt, there is no use in attempting to rebuild it on the old plan.

Dissertations and Discussions vol. 1 (1859) 'Essay on Coleridge'

7 The sole end for which mankind are warranted, individually or collectively, in interfering with the liberty of action of any of their number, is self-protection.

On Liberty (1859)

8 The only freedom worth the name, is that of pursuing our own good in our own way.

On Liberty (1859)

9 The only purpose for which power can be rightfully exercised over any member of a civilized community, against his will, is to prevent harm to others. His own good, either physical or moral, is not a sufficient warrant.

On Liberty (1859)

10 If all mankind minus one were of one opinion, and only one person were of the contrary opinion, mankind would be no more justified in silencing that one person, than he, if he had the power, would be justified in silencing mankind.

On Liberty (1859)

11 A party of order or stability, and a party of progress or reform, are both necessary elements of a healthy state of political life.

On Liberty (1859)

12 The liberty of the individual must be thus far limited; he must not make himself a nuisance to other people.

On Liberty (1859)

13 I am not aware that any community has a right to force another to be civilized.

On Liberty (1859)

14 Liberty consists in doing what one desires.

On Liberty (1859)

15 A State which dwarfs its men, in order that they may be more docile instruments in its hands even for beneficial purposes, will find that with small men no great thing can really be accomplished.

On Liberty (1859)

16 The principle which regulates the existing social relations between the two sexes—the legal subordination of one sex to the other—is wrong in itself, and now one of the chief hindrances to human improvement.

The Subjection of Women (1869)

1 Everyone who desires power, desires it most over those who
are nearest to him, with whom his life is passed, with whom
he has most concerns in common, and in whom any
independence of his authority is oftenest likely to interfere
with his individual preferences.

The Subjection of Women (1869)

Edna St Vincent Millay 1892–1950
American poet

2 Justice denied in Massachusetts.
relating to the trial of Sacco and **Vanzetti** *and their execution on*
22 August 1927

title of poem (1928)

3 The sun that warmed our stooping backs and withered the
weeds uprooted—
We shall not feel it again.
We shall die in darkness, and be buried in the rain.

'Justice Denied in Massachusetts'
(1928)

Alice Duer Miller 1874–1942
American writer

4 I am American bred,
I have seen much to hate here—much to forgive,
But in a world where England is finished and dead,
I do not wish to live.

The White Cliffs (1940)

Arthur Miller 1915–2005
American dramatist

5 The ultimate human mystery may not be anything more
than the claims on us of clan and race, which may yet turn
out to have the power, because they defy the rational mind,
to kill the world.

Timebends (1987)

6 A good newspaper, I suppose, is a nation talking to itself.

in *Observer* 26 November 1961

7 A theatre where no-one is allowed to walk out and everyone
is forced to applause.
describing Eastern Europe

Omnibus (BBC TV) 30 October
1987; in *Independent* 31 October
1987

Charles Wright Mills 1916–62
American sociologist

8 By the power elite, we refer to those political, economic, and
military circles which as an intricate set of overlapping
cliques share decisions having at least national conseqences.
In so far as national events are decided, the power elite are
those who decide them.

The Power Elite (1956)

Lord Milner 1854–1925
British colonial administrator

9 If we believe a thing to be bad, and if we have a right to
prevent it, it is our duty to try to prevent it and to damn the
consequences.

speech in Glasgow, 26 November
1909

John Milton 1608–74
English poet

10 Cromwell, our chief of men.

'To the Lord General Cromwell'
(written 1652)

1 . . . Peace hath her victories
No less renowned than war.

'To the Lord General Cromwell' (written 1652)

2 They also serve who only stand and wait.

'When I consider how my light is spent' (1673)

3 I cannot praise a fugitive and cloistered virtue, unexercised and unbreathed, that never sallies out and sees her adversary, but slinks out of the race, where that immortal garland is to be run for, not without dust and heat.

Areopagitica (1644)

4 Here the great art lies, to discern in what the law is to be to restraint and punishment, and in what things persuasion only is to work.

Areopagitica (1644)

5 Let not England forget her precedence of teaching nations how to live.

The Doctrine and Discipline of Divorce (1643) 'To the Parliament of England'

6 What I have spoken, is the language of that which is not called amiss *The good old Cause*.

The Ready and Easy Way to Establish a Free Commonwealth (2nd ed., 1660)

7 The land had once enfranchised herself from this impertinent yoke of prelaty, under whose inquisitorious and tyrannical duncery no free and splendid wit can flourish.

The Reason of Church Government (1642) bk. 2, introduction

8 None can love freedom heartily, but good men; the rest love not freedom, but licence.

The Tenure of Kings and Magistrates (1649)

9 No man who knows aught, can be so stupid to deny that all men naturally were born free.

The Tenure of Kings and Magistrates (1649)

Comte de Mirabeau 1749–91

French revolutionary

10 War is the national industry of Prussia.

attributed to Mirabeau by Albert Sorel (1842-1906), based on Mirabeau's introduction to *De la monarchie prussienne sous Frédéric le Grand* (1788)

◀ **Misquotations** *see box overleaf*

John Mitchel 1815–75

Irish nationalist

1 Families, when all was eaten and no hope left, took their last look at the sun, built up their cottage doors, that none might see them die nor hear their groans, and were found weeks afterwards, skeletons on their own hearth.
  of the Irish Famine

Jail Journal (1854)

2 I am ready for my fourteen years' ordeal, and for whatsoever the same may bring me—toil, sickness, ignominy, death. Fate, thou art defied.

Jail Journal (1854)

3 Next to the British government, the worst enemy Ireland ever had—or rather the most fatal friend.
  *of Daniel **O'Connell***

The Last Conquest of Ireland (Perhaps) (1861)

Misquotations

1 All is lost save honour.

Of all I had, only honour and life have been spared.

popular summary of the words of **Francis I** of France:

letter to his mother following his defeat at Pavia, 1525; see **Francis I** 145:4

2 The ballot is stronger than the bullet.

popular version of a speech by **Lincoln**, 18 May 1858; see **Lincoln** 234:3

3 The budget should be balanced, the treasury should be refilled, public debt should be reduced, the arrogance of officialdom should be tempered and controlled, assistance to foreign lands should be curtailed lest Rome should become bankrupt, the mobs should be forced to work and not depend on government for subsistence.

attributed to **Cicero** in *Congressional Record* 25 April 1968, but not traced in his works

4 The capitalists will sell us the rope with which to hang them.

They [capitalists] will furnish credits which will serve us for the support of the Communist Party in their countries and, by supplying us materials and technical equipment which we lack, will restore our military industry necessary for our future attacks against our suppliers. To put it in other words, they will work on the preparation of their own suicide.

attributed to **Lenin**, but not found in his published works; I. U. Annenkov, in 'Remembrances of Lenin' includes a manuscript note attributed to Lenin:

in *Novyi Zhurnal/New Review* September 1961

5 Crisis? What Crisis?

I don't think other people in the world would share the view there is mounting chaos.

Sun headline, 11 January 1979, summarizing James **Callaghan**'s remark; see **Newspaper headlines** 287:3

interview at London Airport, 10 January 1979

6 England and America are two countries divided by a common language.

attributed in this and other forms to George Bernard **Shaw**, but not found in Shaw's published writings; see **Wilde** 419:6

7 Events, dear boy. Events.

popular version of Harold Macmillan's summary of a politician's biggest problem (see **Macmillan** 254:1)

8 Few die and none resign.

popular summary of a letter of Thomas **Jefferson**, 1801; see **Jefferson** 199:7

9 A good day to bury bad news.

popular misquotation of Jo **Moore**'s email of 11 September 2001; see **Moore** 278:3

Misquotations *continued*

1 The green shoots of recovery.

popular misquotation of Norman **Lamont**'s upbeat assessment of the economic situation, 9 October 1991; see **Lamont** 224:3

2 Hawking his conscience round the Chancelleries of Europe.

popular version of Ernest **Bevin**'s description of Lansbury, 1935; see **Bevin** 40:6

3 I disapprove of what you say, but I will defend to the death your right to say it.
to the French philosopher Helvétius (1715–71), following the burning of Helvétius's book De l'esprit *in 1759*

attributed to **Voltaire**, but in fact a later summary of his attitude by S. G. Tallentyre in *The Friends of Voltaire* (1907); see **Voltaire** 407:13

4 In trust I have found treason.

traditional concluding words of a speech by **Elizabeth I** to a Parliamentary deputation at Richmond, 12 November 1586; see **Elizabeth I** 132:7

5 It is necessary only for the good man to do nothing for evil to triumph.

attributed (in a number of forms) to **Burke**, but not found in his writings; see **Burke** 64:2

6 Just a heart-beat away from the Presidency of the United States.

popular version of Adlai **Stevenson**'s description of the Vice-Presidency, 23 October 1952; see **Stevenson** 380:11

7 My lips are sealed.

popular version of **Baldwin**'s speech on the Abyssinian crisis, 10 December 1935; see **Baldwin** 26:12

8 Selling off the family silver.

popular summary of Harold **Macmillan**'s attack on privatization, 8 November 1985; see **Macmillan** 253:12

9 The soft underbelly of Europe.

popular version of **Churchill**'s words in the House of Commons, 11 November 1942; see **Churchill** 89:2

10 Something must be done.

popular version of **Edward VIII**'s words at the derelict Dowlais Iron and Steel Works, 18 November 1936; see **Edward VIII** 130:5

11 Take away these baubles.

popular version of **Cromwell**'s words at the dismissal of the Rump Parliament, 20 April 1653; see **Cromwell** 106:2

Misquotations *continued*

1 Warts and all.

popular summary of **Cromwell**'s instructions to the court painter Lely:

Mr Lely, I desire you would use all your skill to paint my picture truly like me, and not flatter me at all; but remark all these roughnesses, pimples, warts, and everything as you see me; otherwise I will never pay a farthing for it.

Horace Walpole *Anecdotes of Painting in England* vol. 3 (1763) ch. 1

2 We are the masters now.

popular misquotation of Hartley **Shawcross**'s speech in the House of Commons, 2 April 1946; see **Shawcross** 361:10

3 We must educate our masters.

popular version of Robert **Lowe**'s comment on the passing of the Reform Bill, 1867; see **Lowe** 242:5

4 What a glorious morning for America.

popular version of the words of **Samuel Adams** on hearing gunfire at Lexington, 19 April 1775; see **Adams** 4:10

5 What are you going to do about it?

supposed reply of 'Boss' **Tweed** to those protesting at the political corruption of New York under the control of the Tweed Ring; see **Nast** 285:5

6 The white heat of technology.

popular version of Harold **Wilson**'s speech at the Labour Party Conference, 1 October 1963; see **Wilson** 421:5

Austin Mitchell 1934–
British Labour politician

7 Welcome to Britain's New Political Order. No passion . . . No Right. No Left. Just multi-hued blancmange.

in *Observer* 11 April 1999 'Sayings of the Week'

George Mitchell 1933–
American politician, chairman of the Northern Ireland peace talks

8 Although he is regularly asked to do so, God does not take sides in American politics.

comment during the hearing of the Senate Select Committee on the Iran-Contra affair, July 1987

9 Nobody ever said it would be easy—and that was an understatement.
on the Northern Ireland peace talks

in *Times* 19 February 1998

10 I am pleased to announce that the two governments and the political parties in Northern Ireland have reached agreement.
announcing the Good Friday agreement

in *Times* 11 April 1998

11 I have that bittersweet feeling that comes in life. I am dying to leave but I hate to go.
after the signing of the Good Friday agreement

in *Times* 11 April 1998

1 Peace, political stability and reconciliation are not too much to ask for. They are the minimum that a decent society provides.

in *Irish Post* 18 April 1998

John Mitchell 1785–1859

English soldier

2 The most important political question on which modern times have to decide is the policy that must now be pursued, in order to maintain the security of Western Europe against the overgrown power of Russia.

Thoughts on Tactics (1838)

John Mitchell 1913–88

lawyer, US Attorney-General to the Nixon administration

3 Katie Graham's gonna get her tit caught in a big fat wringer if that's published.
  on hearing that Katherine Graham's Washington Post *was to reveal the connection between Watergate and the campaign funding for the Committee to Re-Elect the President*

in 1973; Katherine Graham *Personal History* (1997)

Joni Mitchell 1945–

Canadian singer and songwriter

4 Lord, there's danger in this land.
  You get witch-hunts and wars when church and state hold hands.

attributed; Peter McWilliams *Ain't Nobody's Business If You Do* (1993)

François Mitterrand 1916–96

French socialist statesman; President of France 1981–95

5 She has the eyes of Caligula, but the mouth of Marilyn Monroe.
  *of Margaret **Thatcher**, briefing his new European Minister Roland Dumas*

in *Observer* 25 November 1990

George Monbiot 1963–

British environmentalist

6 I saw how hard it is for our own society ever to become wise while old people are ostracized.

No Man's Land (1994)

Walter Mondale 1928–

American Democratic politician

7 When I hear your new ideas I'm reminded of that ad, 'Where's the beef?'
  alluding to an advertising slogan which made an unfavourable comparison between the relative sizes of a small hamburger and a large bun

in a televised debate with Gary Hart, 11 March 1984

8 Political image is like mixing cement. When it's wet, you can move it around and shape it, but at some point it hardens and there's almost nothing you can do to reshape it.

in *Independent on Sunday* 12 May 1991

Duke of Monmouth 1649–85

British peer, illegitimate son of Charles II; focus of the supporters of the Protestant succession in the Exclusion crisis of 1681 (see **Dryden**127:3) and leader of the failed Monmouth rebellion against James II

1 Do not hack me as you did my Lord Russell.
words addressed to his executioner; according to a contemporary account five blows were needed

T. B. Macaulay *History of England* vol. 1 (1849)

Jean Monnet 1888–1979

French economist and diplomat; founder of the European Community

2 Europe has never existed. It is not the addition of national sovereignties in a conclave which creates an entity. One must genuinely *create* Europe.

Anthony Sampson *The New Europeans* (1968)

3 The common market is a process, not a product.

Anthony Sampson *The New Europeans* (1968)

4 I did not understand the politics of Versailles, only the economics.
of the Treaty of Versailles

in an interview in 1971; François Duchêne *Jean Monnet* (1994)

5 A great statesman is one who can work for long-term goals which eventually suit situations as yet unforeseen.

Memoirs (1978)

6 Each man begins the world afresh. Only institutions grow wiser; they store up the collective experience; and, from this experience and wisdom, men subject to the same laws will gradually find, not that their natures change but that their experience does.
a favourite sentiment ascribed by Monnet to the nineteenth-century Genevese diarist Henri Frédéric Amiel

François Duchêne *Jean Monnet* (1994)

7 Institutions govern relationships between people. They are the real pillars of civilization.

François Duchêne *Jean Monnet* (1994)

8 We should not create a nation Europe instead of a nation France.

François Duchêne *Jean Monnet* (1994)

James Monroe 1758–1831

American Democratic Republican statesman, 5th President of the US 1817–25

9 We owe it . . . to the amicable relations existing between the United States and those [European] powers to declare that we should consider any attempt on their part to extend their system to any portion of this hemisphere as dangerous to our peace and safety.
principle that became known as the 'Monroe Doctrine'

annual message to Congress, 2 December 1823

Montaigne 1533–92

French moralist and essayist

10 There is scarcely any less bother in the running of a family than in that of an entire state. And domestic business is no less importunate for being less important.

Essais (1580)

11 Fame and tranquillity can never be bedfellows.

Essais (1580)

1 On the highest throne in the world, we still sit only on our own bottom.

Essais (1580)

Montesquieu 1689–1755
French political philosopher

2 That huge distemper'd body does not support itself by a mild and temperate regimen; but by violent remedies, which are incessantly corroding and exhausting its strength.
   of the Ottoman empire; see **Nicholas I** *286:5*

Lettres Persanes (1721)

3 Thou knowest that ever since the invention of gunpowder . . . I continually tremble lest men should, in the end, uncover some secret which would provide a short way of abolishing mankind, of annihilating peoples and nations in their entirety.

Lettres Persanes (1721)

4 Just as the sea, which seems to want to cover the whole earth, is checked by the grasses and the smallest bits of gravel on the shore, so monarchs, whose power seems boundless, are checked by the slightest obstacles and submit their natural pride to supplication and prayer.

The Spirit of the Laws (1748)

5 Republics end in luxury; monarchies, in poverty.

The Spirit of the Laws (1748)

6 The corruption of each government almost always begins with that of its principles.

The Spirit of the Laws (1748)

7 The principle of democracy is corrupted not only when the spirit of equality is lost but also when the spirit of extreme equality is taken up and each one wants to be the equal of those chosen to command.

The Spirit of the Laws (1748)

8 If a republic is small, it is destroyed by a foreign force; if it is large, it is destroyed by an internal vice.

The Spirit of the Laws (1748)

9 Liberty is the right to do everything the laws permit.

The Spirit of the Laws (1748)

10 It has eternally been observed that any man who has power is led to abuse it.

The Spirit of the Laws (1748)

11 The English have taken their idea of political government from the Germans. This fine system was found in the forests.

The Spirit of the Laws (1748)

12 This state [England] will perish when legislative power is more corrupt than executive power.

The Spirit of the Laws (1748)

13 Royal authority is a great spring that should move easily and noiselessly.

The Spirit of the Laws (1748)

14 In moderate states, there is a compensation for heavy taxes; it is liberty. In despotic states, there is an equivalent for liberty; it is the modest taxes.

The Spirit of the Laws (1748)

15 Lands produce less by reason of their fertility than by reason of the liberty of their inhabitants.

Alexis de Tocqueville *The Ancien Régime* (1856); attributed

Lord Montgomery 1887–1976
British field marshal

16 War is a very rough game, but I think that politics is worse.

attributed, 1956

17 Rule 1, on page 1 of the book of war, is: 'Do not march on Moscow' . . . [Rule 2] is: 'Do not go fighting with your land armies in China.'

in the House of Lords, 30 May 1962

James Graham, Marquess of Montrose

1612–50

Scottish royalist general and poet

1 Great, Good and Just, could I but rate
My grief to thy too rigid fate!

'Epitaph on King Charles I'

2 Let them bestow on every airth a limb;
Then open all my veins, that I may swim
To thee, my Maker! in that crimson lake;
Then place my parboiled head upon a stake—
Scatter my ashes—strew them in the air;—
Lord! since thou know'st where all these atoms are,
I'm hopeful thou'lt recover once my dust,
And confident thou'lt raise me with the just.

'Lines written on the Window of his Jail the Night before his Execution'

Jo Moore

British government adviser

3 It is now a very good day to get out anything we want to
bury.
   email sent in the aftermath of the terrorist action in America, 11 September 2001

in *Daily Telegraph* 10 October ; see also **Misquotations** 272:9

Thomas More 1478–1535

English scholar and saint; Lord Chancellor of England, 1529–32
on More: see **Whittington** 419:1; *see also* **Last words** 228:2

4 Your sheep, that were wont to be so meek and tame, and so
small eaters, now, as I hear say, be become so great
devourers, and so wild, that they eat up and swallow down
the very men themselves.

Utopia (1516); following the marginal précis 'The Disaster Produced by Standing Military Garrisons'

5 Anyone who campaigns for public office becomes
disqualified for holding any office at all.

Utopia (1516)

6 If the parties will at my hands call for justice, then, all were
it my father stood on the one side, and the Devil on the
other, his cause being good, the Devil should have right.

William Roper *Life of Sir Thomas More*

7 'By god's body, master More, *Indignatio principis mors est*
[The anger of the sovereign is death].' 'Is that all, my Lord?'
quoth he [to the Duke of Norfolk]. 'Then in good faith is
there no more difference between your grace and me, but
that I shall die to-day, and you to-morrow.'

William Roper *Life of Sir Thomas More*

8 Is not this house [the Tower of London] as nigh heaven as
my own?

William Roper *Life of Sir Thomas More*

9 I pray you, master Lieutenant, see me safe up, and my
coming down let me shift for my self.
   on mounting the scaffold

William Roper *Life of Sir Thomas More*

Rhodri Morgan 1939–

British Labour politician

10 I thought you were the original professor of rotational
medicine.
   to Bernard **Ingham**, *who was appearing before the Commons public administration select committee*

in *Mail on Sunday* 7 June 1998
'Quotes of the Week'

1 Nice try, but no deal.

    on his party's suggestion that he should stand as deputy to Alun Michael as leader of the new Welsh assembly

    in *Mirror* 6 November 1998

2 We cannot allow the culling of First Secretaries to become Wales's own annual blood sport. My number one target as First Secretary is to survive until the half-term recess at the end of this week.

    on succeeding Alun Michael as First Secretary for Wales

    in *Observer* 20 February 2000 'They Said What . . . ?'

John Morley 1838–1923

British Liberal politician and writer

3 The golden Gospel of Silence is effectively compressed in thirty fine volumes.

    *on **Carlyle**'s History of Frederick the Great (1858–65), Carlyle having written of his subject as 'that strong, silent man'*

    Critical Miscellanies (1886) 'Carlyle'

4 Simplicity of character is no hindrance to subtlety of intellect.

    Life of Gladstone (1903)

5 You have not converted a man, because you have silenced him.

    On Compromise (1874)

6 *of parliamentary life:*
Having the singular peculiarity of being neither business nor rest.

    Recollections (1917) vol. 1

7 The proper memory for a politician is one that knows what to remember and what to forget.

    Recollections (1917)

8 Although in Cabinet all its members stand on an equal footing, speak with equal voices and, on the rare occasions when a division is taken, are counted on the fraternal principle of one man, one vote, yet the head of the Cabinet is *primus inter pares*, and occupies a position which, so long as it lasts, is one of exceptional and peculiar authority.

    Walpole (1889)

Estelle Morris 1952–

British Labour politician

9 I am not good at dealing with the modern media . . . I have not felt I have been as effective as I should be, or as effective as you need me to be.

    resignation letter to Tony Blair, 23 October 2002; in *Guardian* 24 October 2002 (electronic edition)

William Morris 1834–96

English writer, artist, and designer

10 What is this, the sound and rumour? What is this that all
    men hear,
Like the wind in hollow valleys when the storm is drawing
    near,
Like the rolling on of ocean in the eventide of fear?
'Tis the people marching on.

    Chants for Socialists (1885) 'The March of the Workers'

Herbert Morrison 1888–1965

British Labour politician, grandfather of Peter **Mandelson**

11 Work is the call. Work at war speed. Good-night—and go to it.

    broadcast as Minister of Supply, 22 May 1940

12 Socialism is what the Labour Government does.

    attributed

Dwight D. Morrow 1873–1931

American lawyer, banker, and diplomat

1 Any party which takes credit for the rain must not be surprised if its opponents blame it for the drought.

attributed; William Safire *Safire's New Political Dictionary* (1993)

Wayne Lyman Morse 1900–74

American Democratic politician

2 I believe that history will record that we have made a great mistake.
in the Senate debate on the Tonkin Gulf Resolution, which committed the United States to intervention in Vietnam; Morse was the only Senator to vote against the resolution

in *Congressional Record* 6–7 August 1964

Owen Morshead 1893–1977

English librarian

3 The House of Hanover, like ducks, produce bad parents— they trample on their young.
*in conversation with Harold **Nicolson**, biographer of **George V***

Harold Nicolson, letter to Vita Sackville-West, 7 January 1949

Rogers Morton 1914–79

American public relations officer

4 I'm not going to rearrange the furniture on the deck of the Titanic.
*having lost five of the last six primaries as President **Ford**'s campaign manager*

in *Washington Post* 16 May 1976

Nicholas Mosley 1923–

British writer

5 While the right hand dealt with grandiose ideas and glory, the left hand let the rat out of the sewer.
of his father, Oswald Mosley, as leader of the British Union of Fascists

Robert Skidelsky *Oswald Mosley* (1975)

Oswald Mosley 1896–1980

British politician and Fascist leader
*on Mosley: see **Attlee** 17:9*

6 I am not, and never have been, a man of the right. My position was on the left and is now in the centre of politics.

letter to *The Times* 26 April 1968

John Lothrop Motley 1814–77

American historian

7 As long as he lived, he was the guiding-star of a whole brave nation, and when he died the little children cried in the streets.
of William the Silent, Prince of Orange (1533–84)

The Rise of the Dutch Republic (1856); see **Auden** 18:17

Mottoes

1 *Aut Caesar, aut nihil.*
Caesar or nothing.

motto inscribed on the sword of Cesare Borgia (1476–1507)

2 The buck stops here.

motto on the desk of Harry S **Truman**

3 *Fiat justitia et pereat mundus.*
Let justice be done, though the world perish.

motto of Ferdinand I (1503–64), Holy Roman Emperor; Johannes Manlius *Locorum Communium Collectanea* (1563) vol. 2 'De Lege: Octatum Praeceptum'; see **Adams** 4:6, **Watson** 411:9

4 *Honi soit qui mal y pense.*
Evil be to him who evil thinks.

motto of the Order of the Garter, originated by Edward III (1312–77), probably on 23 April of 1348 or 1349

5 *Nemo me impune lacessit.*
No one provokes me with impunity.

motto of the Crown of Scotland and of all Scottish regiments

6 Rebellion to tyrants is obedience to God.

motto of Thomas **Jefferson**, from John **Bradshaw**; see **Bradshaw** 53:5

7 *Semper eadem.*
Ever the same.

motto of **Elizabeth I**

8 *Sic semper tyrannis.*
Thus always to tyrants.

motto of the State of Virginia; see **Booth** 51:2

Lord Mountbatten 1900–79
British sailor, soldier, and statesman

9 Right, now I understand people think you're the Forgotten Army on the Forgotten Front. I've come here to tell you you're quite wrong. You're not the Forgotten Army on the Forgotten Front. No, make no mistake about it. Nobody's ever *heard* of you.
encouragement to troops when taking over as Supreme Allied Commander South-East Asia in late 1943

R. Hough *Mountbatten* (1980)

10 The nuclear arms race has no military purpose. Wars cannot be fought with nuclear weapons. Their existence only adds to our perils.

speech at Strasbourg, 11 May 1979

Marjorie ('Mo') Mowlam 1949–2005
British Labour politician

11 It takes courage to push things forward.
on her decision to visit Loyalist prisoners in The Maze

in *Guardian* 8 January 1998

12 You can't switch on peace like a light.

in *Independent* 6 September 1999

13 Ian Paisley said he pitied my husband having to put up with 'the sinner', which is what he often called me.

in *Sunday Times* 16 April 2000

Daniel P. Moynihan 1927–

American Democratic politician

1 Welfare became a term of opprobrium—a contentious, often vindictive area of political conflict in which liberals and conservatives clashed and children were lost sight of.

in The Washington Post 25 November 1994

Hosni Mubarak 1928–

Egyptian statesman, President since 1981

2 Instead of having one [Osama] bin Laden, we will have 100 bin Ladens.
on the probable result of a western invasion of Iraq

in Newsweek 14 April 2003

Robert Mugabe 1924–

African statesman; Prime Minister of Zimbabwe, 1980–7, President 1987–

3 Cricket civilizes people and creates good gentlemen. I want everyone to play cricket in Zimbabwe; I want ours to be a nation of gentlemen.

in Sunday Times 26 February 1984

4 Our present state of mind is that you are now our enemies.
to white farmers in Zimbabwe

television broadcast, 18 April 2000

5 Blair, keep your England and let me keep my Zimbabwe.

at the Earth Summit in Johannesburg, 2 September 2002

Malcolm Muggeridge 1903–90

British journalist

6 To succeed pre-eminently in English public life it is necessary to conform either to the popular image of a bookie or of a clergyman; Churchill being a perfect example of the former, Halifax of the latter.

The Infernal Grove (1973)

7 He was not only a bore; he bored for England.
*of Anthony **Eden***

Tread Softly (1966)

Robert Muldoon 1921–92

New Zealand statesman, Prime Minister 1975–84

8 When New Zealanders emigrate to Australia, it raises the average IQ of both countries.

attributed

Brian Mulroney 1939–

Canadian Conservative statesman, Prime Minister 1984–93

9 *challenging the Prime Minister, John Turner, for his approval of the patronage appointments made by the retiring Prime Minister, Pierre Trudeau:*
You had an option, sir. You could have said, 'I am not going to do it. This is wrong for Canada. And I am not going to ask Canadians to pay the price.' You had an option, sir, to say no, and you chose to say yes, yes to the old attitudes and the old stories of the Liberal Party.

televised debate between national leaders, 25 July 1984

Rupert Murdoch 1931–

Australian-born American publisher and media entrepreneur

1 I have heard cynics who say he's a very political old monk shuffling around in Gucci shoes.
on the Dalai Lama

in *Daily Telegraph* 7 September 1999

Ed Murrow 1908–65

American broadcaster and journalist

2 I admired your history, doubted your future.
of Britain in the 1930s

radio broadcast; in *Listener* 28 February 1946

3 Future generations who bother to read the official record of proceedings in the House of Commons will discover that British armies retreated from many places, but that there was no retreat from the principles for which your ancestors fought.

radio broadcast; in *Listener* 28 February 1946

4 No one can terrorize a whole nation, unless we are all his accomplices.
*of Joseph **McCarthy***

'See It Now', broadcast, 7 March 1954

5 *of Winston **Churchill**:*
He mobilized the English language and sent it into battle to steady his fellow countrymen and hearten those Europeans upon whom the long dark night of tyranny had descended.

broadcast, 30 November 1954; *In Search of Light* (1967)

6 When the politicians complain that TV turns their proceedings into a circus, it should be made plain that the circus was already there, and that TV has merely demonstrated that not all the performers are well trained.

attributed, 1959

7 Anyone who isn't confused doesn't really understand the situation.
on the Vietnam War

Walter Bryan *The Improbable Irish* (1969)

Benito Mussolini 1883–1945

Italian Fascist dictator

8 We must leave exactly on time . . . From now on everything must function to perfection.
to a stationmaster

Giorgio Pini *Mussolini* (1939) vol. 2

Sarojini Naidu 1879–1949

Indian politician

9 If only Bapu [Gandhi] knew the cost of setting him up in poverty!

A. Campbell-Johnson *Mission with Mountbatten* (1951)

Tom Nairn

Scottish writer

10 As far as I am concerned, Scotland will be reborn when the last minister is strangled with the last copy of the *Sunday Post*.

'The Dreams of Scottish Nationalism'; Karl Miller (ed.) *Memoirs of a Modern Scotland* (1970); see **Meslier** 268:2

Lewis Namier 1888–1960

Polish-born British historian

1 What matters most about political ideas is the underlying emotions, the music, to which ideas are a mere libretto, often of very inferior quality.

Personalities and Powers (1955)

2 No number of atrocities however horrible can deprive a nation of its right to independence, nor justify its being put under the heel of its worst enemies and persecutors.

in 1919; Julia Namier *Lewis Namier* (1971)

Napoleon I 1769–1821

French monarch, Emperor 1804–15

3 What I have done so far is nothing. I am only at the beginning of the career that lies before me.

in May 1796; F. Furcet *The French Revolution 1770–1814* (1996)

4 Think of it, soldiers; from the summit of these pyramids, forty centuries look down upon you.
   speech to the Army of Egypt on 21 July 1798, before the Battle of the Pyramids

Gaspard Gourgaud *Mémoires* (1823) vol. 2 'Égypte—Bataille des Pyramides'

5 It [the Channel] is a mere ditch, and will be crossed as soon as someone has the courage to attempt it.

letter to Consul Cambacérès, 16 November 1803

6 Let us be masters of the Channel for six hours, and we are masters of the world.

c.1803; J. R. Green *History of the English People* (1880) vol. 4, ch. 9

7 A prince who gets a reputation for good nature in the first year of his reign, is laughed at in the second.

letter to the King of Holland, 4 April 1807

8 It is easier to put up with unpleasantness from a man of one's own way of thinking than from one who takes an entirely different point of view.

letter to J. Finckenstein, 14 April 1807

9 I want the whole of Europe to have one currency; it will make trading much easier.

letter to his brother Louis, 6 May 1807

10 It is a matter of great interest what sovereigns are doing; but as to what Grand Duchesses are doing—Who cares?

letter 17 December 1811

11 There is only one step from the sublime to the ridiculous.
   to De Pradt, Polish ambassador, after the retreat from Moscow in 1812

D. G. De Pradt *Histoire de l'Ambassade dans le grand-duché de Varsovie en 1812* (1815)

12 France has more need of me than I have need of France.

speech to the Corps Législatif, Paris, 31 December 1813

13 As to moral courage, I have very rarely met with two o'clock in the morning courage: I mean instantaneous courage.

E. A. de Las Cases *Mémorial de Ste-Hélène* (1823) vol. 1, 4–5 December 1815

14 An army marches on its stomach.

attributed, but probably condensed from a long passage in E. A. de Las Cases *Mémorial de Ste-Hélène* (1823) vol. 4, 14 November 1816; also attributed to **Frederick the Great**

15 *when asked how to deal with the Pope:*
   As though he had 200,000 men.

J. M. Robinson *Cardinal Consalvi* (1987); see **Stalin** 378:7

16 The career open to the talents.

Barry E. O'Meara *Napoleon in Exile* (1822) vol. 1

1 England is a nation of shopkeepers.

Barry E. O'Meara *Napoleon in Exile* (1822) vol. 2; see **Adams** 4:11, **Smith** 370:9

2 Nothing is more contrary to the organization of the mind, of the memory, and of the imagination . . . The new system of weights and measures will be a stumbling block and the source of difficulties for several generations . . . It's just tormenting the people with trivia!!!
 on the introduction of the metric system

Mémoires . . . écrits à Ste-Hélène (1823–5)

3 Not tonight, Josephine.

attributed, but probably apocryphal; R. H. Horne *The History of Napoleon* (1841) vol. 2 describes the circumstances in which the affront may have occurred

4 *of **Talleyrand**:*
A pile of shit in a silk stocking.

attributed

Thomas Nast 1840–1902

German-born American cartoonist, whose work was highly damaging to 'Boss' **Tweed**'s Tammany domination of New York

5 The Boss. 'Well, what are you going to do about it?'
 *caption to a cartoon entitled 'Under the Thumb' showing a giant hand, with **Tweed**'s name on the cufflink, putting its thumb down over Manhattan*

in *Harper's Weekly* 10 June 1871; a later cartoon of 11 November 1871 depicted 'The Tammany Tiger Loose: "What are you going to do about it?"' (see also **Misquotations** 274:5)

Jawaharlal Nehru 1889–1964

Indian statesman

6 At the stroke of the midnight hour, while the world sleeps, India will awake to life and freedom.
 immediately prior to Independence

speech to the Indian Constituent Assembly, 14 August 1947

7 The light has gone out of our lives and there is darkness everywhere.
 *broadcast, 30 January 1948, following **Gandhi**'s assassination*

Richard J. Walsh *Nehru on Gandhi* (1948)

8 I may lose many things including my temper, but I do not lose my nerve.

at a press conference in Delhi, 4 June 1958

9 Democracy and socialism are means to an end, not the end itself.

'Basic Approach'; written for private circulation and reprinted in Vincent Shean *Nehru: the Years of Power* (1960)

10 Normally speaking, it may be said that the forces of a capitalist society, if left unchecked, tend to make the rich richer and the poor poorer and thus increase the gap between them.

'Basic Approach' in Vincent Shean *Nehru . . .* (1960)

11 History is almost always written by the victors and conquerors and gives their viewpoint.

The Discovery of India (1946)

12 There is no easy walk-over to freedom anywhere, and many of us will have to pass through the valley of the shadow again and again before we reach the mountain-tops of our desire.

'From Lucknow to Tripuri' (1939)

1 After every other Viceroy has been forgotten, Curzon will be remembered because he restored all that was beautiful in India.
in conversation with Lord Swinton

Kenneth Rose *Superior Person* (1969)

2 I shall be the last Englishman to rule in India.

J. K. Galbraith *A Life in Our Times* (1981)

Allan Nevins 1890–1971

American historian

3 The former Allies had blundered in the past by offering Germany too little, and offering even that too late, until finally Nazi Germany had become a menace to all mankind.

in *Current History* (New York) May 1935

■ Newspaper headlines and leaders *see box*

opposite

Huey Newton 1942–

American political activist

4 I suggested [in 1966] that we use the panther as our symbol and call our political vehicle the Black Panther Party. The panther is a fierce animal, but he will not attack until he is backed into a corner; then he will strike out.

Revolutionary Suicide (1973)

Nicholas I 1796–1855

Russian monarch, emperor from 1825

5 Turkey is a dying man. We may endeavour to keep him alive, but we shall not succeed. He will, he must die.
origin of the expression 'the sick man of Europe' referring to Ottoman Turkey

F. Max Müller (ed.) *Memoirs of Baron Stockmar* (1873)

6 Russia has two generals in whom she can confide— Generals Janvier [January] and Février [February].

attributed; in *Punch* 10 March 1855

Nicias c.470–413 BC

Greek politician and Athenian general

7 For a city consists in men, and not in walls nor in ships empty of men.
speech to the defeated Athenian army at Syracuse, 413 BC

Thucydides *History of the Peloponnesian Wars*

Harold Nicolson 1886–1968

English diplomat, politician, and writer

8 Ponderous and uncertain is that relation between pressure and resistance which constitutes the balance of power. The arch of peace is morticed by no iron tendons . . . One night a handful of dust will patter from the vaulting: the bats will squeak and wheel in sudden panic: nor can the fragile fingers of man then stay the rush and rumble of destruction.

Public Faces (1932)

9 We shall have to walk and live a Woolworth life hereafter.
anticipating the aftermath of the Second World War

diary, 4 June 1941

10 I am haunted by mental decay such as I saw creeping over Ramsay MacDonald. A gradual dimming of the lights.

diary, 28 April 1947

Newspaper headlines and leaders

1 Bush Wins It.
original headline in the Miami Herald *for 8 November 2000;
changed in final edition to 'It's Not Over Yet'*

in *Daily Telegraph* 9 November 2000

2 *on the suggestion that* **Edward VIII** *could marry Wallis Simpson
without her becoming Queen:*
The constitution is to be amended in order that she [Mrs
Simpson] may carry in solitary prominence the brand of
unfitness for the Queen's Throne.

leader in *The Times* 8 December 1936

3 Crisis? What crisis?
summarizing an interview with James **Callaghan**

headline in *Sun*, 11 January 1979; see **Misquotations** 272:5

4 Dewey defeats Truman.
anticipating the result of the Presidential election, which
Truman *won against expectation*

in *Chicago Tribune* 3 November 1948

5 Downing Street's dodgy dossier of 'intelligence' about Iraq.
*referring to a briefing document on Iraqi weaponry which was
later withdrawn*

leading article, *Observer* 9 February 2003

6 45 Minutes from Attack.

Evening Standard 24 September 2002

7 GOTCHA!
on the sinking of the General Belgrano

headline in *Sun* 4 May 1982

8 Go West, young man, go West!

editorial in *Terre Haute* [Indiana] *Express* (1851), by John L. B. Soule (1815–91)

9 If Kinnock wins today will the last person to leave Britain
please turn out the lights.
on election day, showing Neil Kinnock's head inside a light bulb

headline in *Sun* 9 April 1992

10 In that case, it might be worthwhile for the Czechoslovak
government to consider whether they should exclude
altogether the project, which has found favour in some
quarters, of making Czechoslovakia a more homogeneous
State, by the secession of that fringe of alien populations
who are contiguous to the nation with which they are
united by race.
referring to the Sudeten Germans

leader in *The Times* 7 September 1938

11 Is THIS the most dangerous man in Britain?
headline beside a picture of Tony **Blair**, *attacking his perceived
sympathy for the euro*

in *Sun* 25 June 1998

12 It *is* a moral issue.
leader following the resignation of Profumo

in *The Times* 11 June 1963, written by William Haley (1901–87)

13 It's that man again . . . ! At the head of a cavalcade of
seven black motor cars Hitler swept out of his Berlin
Chancellery last night on a mystery journey.

headline in *Daily Express* 2 May 1939; the acronym ITMA became the title of a BBC radio show, from September 1939

14 It's The Sun wot won it.
following the 1992 general election

headline in *Sun* 11 April 1992

Newspaper headlines and leaders *continued*

1 King's Moll Reno'd in Wolsey's Home Town.
US newspaper headline on the divorce proceedings of Wallis Simpson (later Duchess of Windsor) in Ipswich

Frances Donaldson *Edward VIII* (1974)

2 Most Conservatives, and almost certainly some of the wiser Trade Union leaders, are waiting to feel the *smack of firm government.*
on the government of Anthony Eden

editorial comment in *Sunday Telegraph* 3 January 1956, written by Donald McLachlan

3 Only a sentence, but what a sentence!
on Prince Charles' speech referring to the Falklands

in *La Nación* (Buenos Aires) 11 March 1999

4 Outside the G.O.P.'s big tent, hoping he's let back in.
of the former Republican Robert C. Smith, whose independent campaign for the presidential nomination had failed; G.O.P. = 'Grand Old Party'

headline in *New York Times* 1 November 1999; see **Slogans** 366:9

5 Splendid isolation.

headline in *The Times* 22 January 1896, referring to George **Foster**'s speech in the Canadian House of Commons; see **Foster** 143:8

6 The Sun backs Blair.
the day after the announcement of the general election

headline in *Sun* 18 March 1997

7 Unless the people—the people everywhere—come forward and petition, ay, thunder for reform.
leader on the Reform Bill, possibly written by Edward Sterling (1773–1847), resulting in the nickname 'The Thunderer'

in *The Times* 29 January 1831; the phrase 'we thundered out' had been used earlier, 11 February 1829

8 Wall St. lays an egg.

crash headline, *Variety* 30 October 1929

9 We shall not pretend that there is nothing in his long career which those who respect and admire him would wish otherwise.
on Edward VII's accession to the throne

in *The Times* 23 January 1901, leading article

10 Whose finger do you want on the trigger?
headline alluding to the atom bomb, apropos the failure of both the Labour and Conservative parties to purge their leaders of proven failures

in *Daily Mirror* 21 September 1951

11 Winter of discontent.

headline in *Sun* 30 April 1979; see below; see **Callaghan** 70:9

Now is the winter of our discontent
Made glorious summer by this sun of York.

William Shakespeare (1564–1616) *Richard III* (1591)

Harold Nicolson *continued*

12 *comparing* **Attlee** *as a public speaker with Winston* **Churchill***:*
Like a village fiddler after Paganini.

diary, 10 November 1947

13 I do not think it is quite fair to say that the British businessman has trampled on the faces of the poor. But he has sometimes not been very careful where he put his feet.
replying to a heckler in the North Croydon by-election, 1948

Nigel Nicolson (ed.) *Diaries and Letters of Harold Nicolson 1945–1962* vol. 3 (1968)

14 For seventeen years he did nothing at all but kill animals and stick in stamps.
of **George V** *as a subject for biography*

letter to Vita Sackville-West, 17 August 1949

1 Suez—a smash and grab raid that was all smash and no grab.

in conversation with Antony Jay, November 1956; see also letter to Vita Sackville-West, 8 November 1956, 'Our smash-and-grab raid got stuck at the smash'

Nigel Nicolson 1917-2004

British Conservative politician and writer; son of Harold **Nicolson**

2 There is no place where a man can occupy himself more intensively or usefully, and no place where he can hold down his job by doing so little.
   of the House of Commons

People and Parliament (1958)

3 One final tip to rebels: always have a second profession in reserve.
   reflecting on the vote on the Maastricht Treaty in the House of Commons, in the light of having abstained from voting with the Government on the Suez Crisis in 1956 and subsequently lost his seat

in *The Spectator* 7 November 1992

Reinhold Niebuhr 1892-1971

American theologian

4 Man's capacity for justice makes democracy possible, but man's inclination to injustice makes democracy necessary.

Children of Light and Children of Darkness (1944) foreword

Martin Niemöller 1892-1984

German theologian

5 When Hitler attacked the Jews I was not a Jew, therefore, I was not concerned. And when Hitler attacked the Catholics, I was not a Catholic, and therefore, I was not concerned. And when Hitler attacked the unions and the industrialists, I was not a member of the unions and I was not concerned. Then, Hitler attacked me and the Protestant church—and there was nobody left to be concerned.
   often quoted in the form 'In Germany they came first for the Communists, and I didn't speak up because I wasn't a Communist . . . ' and so on

in *Congressional Record* 14 October 1968

Friedrich Nietzsche 1844-1900

German philosopher and writer

6 I teach you the superman. Man is something to be surpassed.

Also Sprach Zarathustra (1883) prologue

7 Morality is the herd-instinct in the individual.

Die fröhliche Wissenschaft (1882)

8 Master-morality and slave-morality.

Jenseits von Gut und Böse (1886)

9 At the base of all these aristocratic races the predator is not to be mistaken, the splendorous *blond beast*, avidly rampant for plunder and victory.

Zur Genealogie der Moral (1887)

Richard Milhous Nixon 1913–94

American Republican statesman, 37th President of the US
on Nixon: see **Abzug** 1:4, **Anonymous** 8:10, **Conable** 100:3,
Johnson 202:5, **Roosevelt** 330:2, **Stevenson** 381:3, **Ziegler**
428:3

1 She's pink right down to her underwear.
  *in 1950, accusing Helen Gahagan Douglas, his opponent for a
  Senate seat, of Communist sympathies*

Stephen E. Ambrose *Nixon: The
Education of a Politician* (1987); see
Roosevelt 330:2

2 Pat and I have the satisfaction that every dime that we've
got is honestly ours . . . Pat doesn't have a mink coat. But
she does have a respectable Republican cloth coat. And I
always tell her that she'd look good in anything.
  *having been elected as Vice-President in 1952, in response to
  criticisms of his electoral campaign*

speech on television, 23
September 1952

3 *of the post-election gift of a cocker spaniel, named Checkers by his
small daughter:*
One other thing I probably should tell you, because if I don't
they'll probably be saying this about me too, we did get
something—a gift—after the election . . . It was a little
cocker-spaniel dog . . . The kids love that dog and I just
want to say this right now, that regardless of what they say
about it, we're going to keep it.

speech on television, 23
September 1952

4 There is no such thing as a nonpolitical speech by a
politician.

address to Radio-Television
Executives Society, New York City,
14 September 1955

5 You won't have Nixon to kick around any more.
  *at a press conference after losing the election for Governor of
  California, 5 November 1962*

in *New York Times* 8 November
1962

6 There is nothing wrong with this country which a good
election can't fix.
  at a campaign meeting during the Presidential election

in Syracuse, New York, 29 October
1968

7 Let us begin by committing ourselves to the truth, to see it
like it is and tell it like it is, to find the truth, to speak the
truth and to live the truth. That's what we will do.
  nomination acceptance speech in Miami, 1968

in *New York Times* 9 August 1968

8 This is the greatest week in the history of the world since
the Creation.
  welcoming the return of the first men to land on the moon

speech, 24 July 1969

9 The great silent majority.

broadcast, 3 November 1969

10 In our own lives, let each of us ask—not just what
government will do for me, but what can I do for myself?

second inaugural address, 20
January 1973

11 There can be no whitewash at the White House.

television speech on Watergate, 30
April 1973

12 I made my mistakes, but in all my years of public life, I have
never profited, never profited from public service. I've
earned every cent. And in all of my years in public life I
have never obstructed justice . . . I welcome this kind of
examination because people have got to know whether or
not their President is a crook. Well, I'm not a crook.

speech at press conference, 17
November 1973

13 This country needs good farmers, good businessmen, good
plumbers, good carpenters.
  farewell address at White House, 9 August 1974

in *New York Times* 10 August 1974

1 My own view is that taping of conversations for historical purposes was a bad decision.

attributed, 1974

2 I brought myself down. I gave them a sword. And they stuck it in.

television interview, 19 May 1977; David Frost *I Gave Them a Sword* (1978)

3 Foreign aid is the most unpopular damn thing in the world. It is a loser politically.

in *Observer* 21 April 1985 'Sayings of the Week'

4 I played by the rules of politics as I found them. Not taking a higher road than my predecessors and my adversaries was my central mistake.

In the Arena (1990)

5 Defeat doesn't finish a man—quit does. A man is not finished when he's defeated. He's finished when he quits.
  on Edward Kennedy and Chappaquiddick

William Safire *Before the Fall* (1975)

6 When the President does it, that means that it is not illegal.

in conversation; David Frost *I Gave Them a Sword* (1978)

Kwame Nkrumah 1900–72

Ghanaian statesman, Prime Minister 1957–60, President 1960–6

7 Freedom is not something that one people can bestow on another as a gift. They claim it as their own and none can keep it from them.

speech in Accra, 10 July 1953

8 We face neither East nor West: we face forward.

conference speech, Accra, 7 April 1960; *Axioms of Kwame Nkrumah* (1967)

Peggy Noonan 1950–

American writer, speechwriter for Ronald Reagan

9 The battle for the mind of Ronald Reagan was like the trench warfare of World War I. Never have so many fought so hard for such barren terrain.

What I Saw at the Revolution (1990)

Steven Norris 1945–

British Conservative politician

10 You have your own company, your own temperature control, your own music—and don't have to put up with dreadful human beings sitting alongside you.
  on cars compared to public transport

comment to Commons Environment Select Committee, in *Daily Telegraph* 9 February 1995

Christopher North 1785–1854

Scottish literary critic

11 His Majesty's dominions, on which the sun never sets.

in *Blackwood's Magazine* (April 1829) 'Noctes Ambrosianae'

12 Laws were made to be broken.

in *Blackwood's Magazine* (May 1830) 'Noctes Ambrosianae'

13 I cannot sit still, James, and hear you abuse the shopocracy.

in *Blackwood's Magazine* (February 1835) 'Noctes Ambrosianae'

Lord North 1732–92

British statesman, Prime Minister 1770–82

1 His Majesty has thought proper to order a new Commission of the Treasury to be made out, in which I do not see your name.

letter dismissing Charles James **Fox** from office, 1774

2 Oh God! It is all over!
  on receiving the news of Cornwallis's surrender at Yorktown, 19 October 1781

in *Dictionary of National Biography* (1917–)

3 Those persons who have for some time conducted the public affairs are no longer His Majesty's Ministers.
  announcing the fall of his government to the House of Commons

in the House of Commons, 20 March 1782

Lord Northcliffe 1865–1922

British newspaper proprietor

4 The power of the press is very great, but not so great as the power of suppress.
  office message, Daily Mail 1918

Reginald Rose and Geoffrey Harmsworth *Northcliffe* (1959)

5 When I want a peerage, I shall buy it like an honest man.

Tom Driberg *Swaff* (1974)

Sam Nunn 1938–

American Democratic politician

6 Don't ask, don't tell.
  *summary of the **Clinton** administration's compromise policy on homosexuals serving in the armed forces*

in *New York Times* 12 May 1993

Julius Nyerere 1922–99

Tanzanian statesman, President of Tanganyika 1962–4 and of Tanzania 1964–85

7 Should we really let our people starve so we can pay our debts?

in *Guardian* 21 March 1985

8 We are a poor country and we opted for socialist policies, but to build a socialist society you have to have a developed society.

in *Observer* 28 July 1985 'Sayings of the Week'

Michael Oakeshott 1901–91

British academic

9 A plan to resist all planning may be better than its opposite, but it belongs to the same style of politics.
  *of **Hayek**'s The Road to Serfdom*

Rationalism in Politics (1962)

Barack Obama 1959–

American Democratic politician

10 There is not a black America and a white America and Latino American and Asian America; there's the United States of America . . . We worship an awesome God in the blue states, and we don't like federal agents poking round our libraries in the red states.
  on the view of a red and blue America divided by party

in *New York Times* 28 July 2004 (online edition)

Conor Cruise O'Brien 1917–

Irish politician, writer, and journalist

1 The strength of these men was that each of them could look a Pearsean ghost in the eye . . . Each of them, in their youth, had done the thing the ghost asked them to do, in 1916 or 1919–21 or both. That was it; from now on they would do what seemed reasonable to themselves in the interests of the actual people inhabiting the island of Ireland and not of a personified abstraction, or of a disembodied voice, or of a ghost.

of Sean Lemass (1899–1971) and other senior Irish politicians in the 1960s; see **Pearse** *306:8*

Ancestral Voices (1994)

2 The first great act of intellectual resistance to the first great experiment in totalitarian innovation.

of **Burke**'s *writings on the French Revolution*

The Great Melody (1992)

3 If I saw Mr Haughey buried at midnight at a crossroads, with a stake driven through his heart—politically speaking—I should continue to wear a clove of garlic round my neck, just in case.

in *Observer* 10 October 1982

Daniel O'Connell 1775–1847

Irish nationalist leader and social reformer, elected to Parliament in 1828

4 I shall be as brief as I can upon this subject, for it is quite clear, that no man ever yet rose to address a more unwilling audience.

introducing a motion for the Repeal of the Union

speech in the House of Commons, 22 April 1834

5 A NATION is starving.

in 1846; Charles Chevenix Trench *The Great Dan* (1984)

6 He speaks of '98! Their struggle was of blood and defeated in blood. The means they adopted weakened Ireland and enabled England to carry the Union.

in a debate with the Young Irelander, John **Mitchel**, *13 July 1846*

Charles Chevenix Trench *The Great Dan* (1984)

7 I have given my advice to my countrymen, and whenever I feel it necessary I shall continue to do so, careless whether it pleases or displeases this house or any mad person out of it.

in *Dictionary of National Biography* (1917–)

8 There is a moral electricity in the continuous expression of public opinion concentrated on a single point.

R. F. Foster *Modern Ireland* (1988)

Bernard O'Donoghue 1945–

Irish poet and academic

9 We were terribly lucky to catch
The Ceauşescus' execution, being
By sheer chance that Christmas Day
In the only house for twenty miles
With satellite TV. We sat,
Cradling brandies, by the fire
Watching those two small, cranky autocrats
Lying in snow against a blood-spattered wall,
Hardly able to believe our good fortune.

'Carolling' (1995)

1 The reporter told us how
The cross woman's peasant origins
Came out at the last, shouting
At her executioners 'I have been
A mother to you and this is how
You thank me for it.'

'Carolling' (1995)

Jeremiah O'Donovan Rossa 1831–1915
Irish nationalist

2 I don't believe the Saxon will ever relax his grip except by
the persuasion of cold lead and steel.

Robert Kee *The Bold Fenian Men*
(1989)

■ Official advice *see box opposite*

James Ogilvy, Lord Seafield 1664–1730
Scottish lawyer, Lord Chancellor of Scotland

3 Now there's ane end of ane old song.
*as he signed the engrossed exemplification of the Act of Union,
1706*

in *The Lockhart Papers* (1817)

Kevin O'Higgins 1892–1927
Irish nationalist politician

4 We had an opportunity of building up a worthy State that
would attract and, in time, absorb and assimilate the
[Unionist] elements. We preferred to burn our own houses,
blow up our own bridges, rob our own banks . . . Generally
we preferred to practise upon ourselves worse iniquities
than the British had practised on us since Cromwell and
Mountjoy, and now we wonder why the Orangemen are not
hopping like so many fleas across the Border in their anxiety
to come within our fold.

Robert Kee *The Green Flag* (1972)

Abraham Okpik d. 1997
Canadian Inuit spokesman

5 There are very few Eskimos, but millions of Whites, just like
mosquitoes. It is something very special and wonderful to be
an Eskimo—they are like the snow geese. If an Eskimo
forgets his language and Eskimo ways, he will be nothing
but just another mosquito.

attributed, 1966

Tom O'Leary
British archivist, Head of Education at the British National
Archives

6 The Civil Service doesn't do jokes.

in *Times* 1 April 2004

Jacqueline Kennedy Onassis 1929–94
American wife of John F. **Kennedy**, First Lady of the US 1961–3

7 The one thing I do not want to be called is First Lady. It
sounds like a saddle horse.

Peter Colier and David Horowitz
The Kennedys (1984)

8 There'll be great Presidents again—and the Johnsons are
wonderful, they've been wonderful to me—but there'll
never be another Camelot again.

in *Life* 6 December 1963; see
Lerner 231:11

Official advice

1 Careless talk costs lives.

Second World War security poster

2 Dig for Victory.

Second World War slogan; see below:

Let 'Dig for Victory' be the motto of every one with a garden and of every able-bodied man and woman capable of digging an allotment in their spare time.

Reginald Dorman-Smith (1899–1977) radio broadcast, 3 October 1939, in *The Times* 4 October 1939

3 Don't die of ignorance.

Aids publicity campaign, 1987

4 Duck and cover.

US advice in the event of a missile attack, c.1950; associated particularly with children's cartoon character 'Bert the Turtle'

5 Is your journey *really* necessary?

slogan coined to discourage Civil Servants from going home for Christmas, 1939

6 Make do and mend.

wartime slogan, 1940s

7 Smoking can seriously damage your health.
government health warning now required by British law to be printed on cigarette packets

from early 1970s, in form 'Smoking can damage your health'

8 *Taisez-vous! Méfiez-vous! Les oreilles ennemies vous écoutent.*
Keep your mouth shut! Be on your guard! Enemy ears are listening to you.

official notice in France, 1915

Paul O'Neill 1935–

American businessman and Republican politician, US Treasury Secretary 2001–3

9 Like a blind man in a roomful of deaf people.
*of George W. **Bush** in cabinet meetings*

in *Independent* 12 January 2004

Thomas ('Tip') O'Neill 1912–94

American Democratic politician; Speaker of the House of Representatives 1977–87

10 All politics is local.

in *New York Review of Books* 13 March 1989

Lord Onslow 1938–

British peer

11 I will be sad if I either look up or down after my death and don't see my son fast asleep on the same benches on which I have slept.

in *Times* 31 October 1998 'Quotes of the Week'

J. Robert Oppenheimer 1904–67
American physicist

1 I remembered the line from the Hindu scripture, the *Bhagavad Gita* . . . 'I am become death, the destroyer of worlds.'

>   *on the explosion of the first atomic bomb near Alamogordo, New Mexico, 16 July 1945*

Len Giovannitti and Fred Freed *The Decision to Drop the Bomb* (1965)

2 When you see something that is technically sweet, you go ahead and do it and you argue about what to do about it only after you have had your technical success. That is the way it was with the atomic bomb.

in *In the Matter of J. Robert Oppenheimer, USAEC Transcript of Hearing Before Personnel Security Board* (1954)

P. J. O'Rourke 1947–
American humorous writer and journalist

3 Giving money and power to government is like giving whisky and car keys to teenage boys.

Parliament of Whores (1991)

4 Whatever it is that the government does, sensible Americans would prefer that the government does it to somebody else. This is the idea behind foreign policy.

Parliament of Whores (1991)

5 Every government is a parliament of whores. The trouble is, in a democracy the whores are us.

Parliament of Whores (1991)

George Orwell 1903–50
English novelist

6 Man is the only creature that consumes without producing.

Animal Farm (1945)

7 Four legs good, two legs bad.

Animal Farm (1945)

8 All animals are equal but some animals are more equal than others.

Animal Farm (1945)

9 Down here it was still the England I had known in my childhood: the railway cuttings smothered in wild flowers . . . the red buses, the blue policemen—all sleeping the deep, deep sleep of England, from which I sometimes fear that we shall never wake till we are jerked out of it by the roar of bombs.

Homage to Catalonia (1938)

10 Most revolutionaries are potential Tories, because they imagine that everything can be put right by altering the *shape* of society; once that change is effected, as it sometimes is, they see no need for any other.

Inside the Whale (1940) 'Charles Dickens'

11 England . . . resembles a family, a rather stuffy Victorian family, with not many black sheep in it but with all its cupboards bursting with skeletons. It has rich relations who have to be kowtowed to and poor relations who are horribly sat upon, and there is a deep conspiracy of silence about the source of the family income. It is a family in which the young are generally thwarted and most of the power is in the hands of irresponsible uncles and bed-ridden aunts. Still, it is a family. It has its private language and its common memories, and at the approach of an enemy it closes its ranks. A family with the wrong members in control.

The Lion and the Unicorn (1941) pt. 1 'England Your England'

12 Probably the battle of Waterloo *was* won on the playing-fields of Eton, but the opening battles of all subsequent wars have been lost there.

The Lion and the Unicorn (1941) pt. 1 'England Your England'; see **Wellington** 415:11

1 Old maids biking to Holy Communion through the mists of the autumn mornings . . . these are not only fragments, but *characteristic* fragments, of the English scene.

The Lion and the Unicorn (1941) pt. 1 'England Your England'; see **Major** 256:7

2 BIG BROTHER IS WATCHING YOU.

Nineteen Eighty-Four (1949)

3 War is peace. Freedom is slavery. Ignorance is strength.

Nineteen Eighty-Four (1949)

4 Who controls the past controls the future: who controls the present controls the past.

Nineteen Eighty-Four (1949)

5 Don't you see that the whole aim of Newspeak is to narrow the range of thought? In the end we shall make thoughtcrime literally impossible, because there will be no words in which to express it.

Nineteen Eighty-Four (1949)

6 Freedom is the freedom to say that two plus two make four. If that is granted, all else follows.

Nineteen Eighty-Four (1949)

7 Syme was not only dead, he was abolished, an un-person.

Nineteen Eighty-Four (1949)

8 *Doublethink* means the power of holding two contradictory beliefs in one's mind simultaneously, and accepting both of them.

Nineteen Eighty-Four (1949)

9 Power is not a means, it is an end. One does not establish a dictatorship in order to safeguard a revolution; one makes the revolution in order to establish the dictatorship.

Nineteen Eighty-Four (1949)

10 If you want a picture of the future, imagine a boot stamping on a human face—for ever.

Nineteen Eighty-Four (1949)

11 In a Lancashire cotton-town you could probably go for months on end without once hearing an 'educated' accent, whereas there can hardly be a town in the South of England where you could throw a brick without hitting the niece of a bishop.

The Road to Wigan Pier (1937)

12 The typical Socialist is . . . a prim little man with a white-collar job, usually a secret teetotaller and often with vegetarian leanings, with a history of Nonconformity behind him, and, above all, with a social position which he has no intention of forfeiting.

The Road to Wigan Pier (1937)

13 To the ordinary working man, the sort you would meet in any pub on Saturday night, Socialism does not mean much more than better wages and shorter hours and nobody bossing you about.

The Road to Wigan Pier (1937)

14 We of the sinking middle class . . . may sink without further struggles into the working class where we belong, and probably when we get there it will not be so dreadful as we feared, for, after all, we have nothing to lose but our aitches.

The Road to Wigan Pier (1937)

15 The great enemy of clear language is insincerity. When there is a gap between one's real and one's declared aims, one turns as it were instinctively to long words and exhausted idioms, like a cuttlefish squirting out ink.

Shooting an Elephant (1950) 'Politics and the English Language'

16 In our time, political speech and writing are largely the defence of the indefensible.

Shooting an Elephant (1950) 'Politics and the English Language'

17 Political language . . . is designed to make lies sound truthful and murder respectable, and to give an appearance of solidity to pure wind.

Shooting an Elephant (1950) 'Politics and the English Language'

18 The Catholic and the Communist are alike in assuming that an opponent cannot be both honest and intelligent.

in *Polemic* January 1946 'The Prevention of Literature'

1 The quickest way of ending a war is to lose it.

in *Polemic* May 1946 'Second Thoughts on James Burnham'

John Osborne 1929–94
English dramatist

2 There aren't any good, brave causes left. If the big bang does come, and we all get killed off, it won't be in aid of the old-fashioned, grand design. It'll just be for the Brave New-nothing-very-much-thank-you. About as pointless and inglorious as stepping in front of a bus.

Look Back in Anger (1956)

3 Royalty . . . is the gold filling in a mouthful of decay.

'They call it cricket'; T. Maschler (ed.) *Declaration* (1957)

4 This is a letter of hate. It is for you my countrymen, I mean those men of my country who have defiled it. The men with manic fingers leading the sightless, feeble, betrayed body of my country to its death . . . damn you England.

in *Tribune* 18 August 1961

Arthur O'Shaughnessy 1844–81
English poet

5 One man with a dream, at pleasure
Shall go forth and conquer a crown;
And three with a new song's measure
Can trample an empire down.

'Ode' (1874)

6 For each age is a dream that is dying,
Or one that is coming to birth.

'Ode' (1874)

John L. O'Sullivan 1813–95
American journalist and diplomat

7 Understood as a central consolidated power, managing and directing the various general interests of the society, all government is evil, and the parent of evil . . . The best government is that which governs least.

in *United States Magazine and Democratic Review* (1837) introduction; see **Thoreau** 394:1

8 A spirit of hostile interference against us . . . checking the fulfilment of our manifest destiny to overspread the continent allotted by Providence for the free development of our yearly multiplying millions.
on opposition to the annexation of Texas

in *United States Magazine and Democratic Review* (1845) vol. 17

James Otis 1725–83
American politician

9 Taxation without representation is tyranny.
watchword (c.1761) of the American Revolution

in *Dictionary of American Biography*

10 Where liberty is, there is my country.

motto used by James Otis; also attributed to Benjamin **Franklin**; see **Paine** 302:7

Ovid 43–c.17
Roman poet

11 *Video meliora, proboque;*
Deteriora sequor.
I see the better things, and approve; I follow the worse.

Metamorphoses

1 *Teque, rebellatrix, tandem, Germania, magni*
Triste caput pedibus supposuisse ducis!

How you, rebellious Germany, laid your wretched head
beneath the feet of the great general.

Tristia

David Owen 1938-

British Social Democratic politician

2 The price of championing human rights is a little
inconsistency at times.

speech, House of Commons, 30
March 1977

3 We are fed up with fudging and mudging, with mush and
slush. We need courage, conviction, and hard work.

speech to his supporters at Labour
Party Conference in Blackpool, 2
October 1980

Robert Owen 1771-1858

Welsh-born socialist and philanthropist

4 All the world is queer save thee and me, and even thou art a
little queer.
*to his partner W. Allen, on severing business relations at New
Lanark, 1828*

attributed

Count Oxenstierna 1583-1654

Swedish statesman

5 Dost thou not know, my son, with how little wisdom the
world is governed?

letter to his son, 1648; John
Selden, in *Table Talk* (1689) 'Pope',
quotes 'a certain Pope' (possibly
Julius III) saying 'Thou little
thinkest what *a little foolery
governs the whole world!*'

John Page 1743-1808

American politician

6 We know the race is not to the swift nor the battle to the
strong. Do you not think an angel rides in the whirlwind
and directs this storm?
*quoted by George W. **Bush** in his first inaugural address, 20
January 2001*

letter to Thomas Jefferson, 20 July
1776; see also **Bible** 41:12

William Tyler Page 1868-1942

7 I believe in the United States of America as a government of
the people, by the people, for the people, whose just powers
are derived from the consent of the governed; a democracy
in a republic; a sovereign Nation of many sovereign States;
a perfect Union, one and inseparable, established upon those
principles of freedom, equality, justice, and humanity for
which American patriots sacrificed their lives and fortunes. I
therefore believe it is my duty to my country to love it, to
support its Constitution, to obey its laws, to respect its flag,
and to defend it against all enemies.

American's Creed (prize-winning
competition entry, 1918) in
Congressional Record vol. 56

Thomas Paine 1737–1809

English political theorist

1 It is necessary to the happiness of man that he be mentally faithful to himself. Infidelity does not consist in believing, or in disbelieving, it consists in professing to believe what one does not believe.

The Age of Reason pt. 1 (1794)

2 Though we have been wise enough to shut and lock a door against absolute Monarchy, we at the same time have been foolish enough to put the crown in possession of the key.

Common Sense (1776)

3 Government, even in its best state, is but a necessary evil; in its worst state, an intolerable one. Government, like dress, is the badge of lost innocence; the palaces of kings are built upon the ruins of the bowers of paradise.

Common Sense (1776)

4 Monarchy and succession have laid . . . the world in blood and ashes.

Common Sense (1776)

5 Of more worth is one honest man to society, and in the sight of God, than all the crowned ruffians that ever lived.

Common Sense (1776)

6 'Tis not the affair of a city, a county, a province, or a kingdom; but of a continent—of at least one eighth part of the habitable globe. 'Tis not the concern of a day, a year, or an age; posterity are virtually involved in the contest. Now is the seed-time of continental union.

Common Sense (1776)

7 Any submission to, or dependence on, Great Britain, tends directly to involve this continent in European wars and quarrels, and set us at variance with nations who would otherwise seek our friendship, and against whom we have neither anger nor complaint.

Common Sense (1776)

8 *to America:*
Freedom hath been hunted round the globe. Asia and Africa have long expelled her. Europe regards her like a stranger, and England hath given her warning to depart. O! receive the fugitive, and prepare in time an asylum for mankind.

Common Sense (1776)

9 We have it in our power to begin the world over again.

Common Sense (1776)

10 As to religion, I hold it to be the indispensable duty of government to protect all conscientious professors thereof, and I know of no other business which government hath to do therewith.

Common Sense (1776)

11 These are the times that try men's souls. The summer soldier and the sunshine patriot will, in this crisis, shrink from the service of their country; but he that stands it *now*, deserves the love and thanks of men and women.

The Crisis (December 1776) introduction

12 What we obtain too cheap, we esteem too lightly.

The Crisis (December 1776) introduction

13 Wisdom is not the purchase of a day.

The Crisis (December 1776)

14 The religion of humanity.

Letter . . . on the Invasion of England (1804)

1 A total reformation is wanted in England. She wants an expanded mind—a heart which embraces the universe. Instead of shutting herself up in an island, and quarrelling with the world, she would derive more lasting happiness, and acquire more real riches, by generously mixing with it, and bravely saying, I am the enemy of none.

Letter to the Abbé Raynal (1782)

2 As he rose like a rocket, he fell like the stick.
   on Edmund **Burke***'s losing the parliamentary debate on the French Revolution to Charles James* **Fox**

Letter to the Addressers on the late Proclamation (1792)

3 [Edmund Burke] is not affected by the reality of distress touching his heart, but by the showy resemblance of it striking his imagination. He pities the plumage, but forgets the dying bird.
   on **Burke***'s* Reflections on the Revolution in France, *1790*

The Rights of Man (1791)

4 Lay then the axe to the root, and teach governments humanity. It is their sanguinary punishments which corrupt mankind.

The Rights of Man (1791)

5 [In France] all that class of equivocal generation, which in some countries is called *aristocracy*, and in others *nobility*, is done away, and the peer is exalted into MAN.

The Rights of Man (1791)

6 Titles are but nick-names, and every nick-name is a title.

The Rights of Man (1791)

7 The idea of hereditary legislators is as inconsistent as that of hereditary judges, or hereditary juries; and as absurd as an hereditary mathematician, or an hereditary wise man; and as ridiculous as an hereditary poet laureate.

The Rights of Man (1791)

8 Persecution is not an original feature of *any* religion; but it is always the strongly marked feature of all law-religions, or religions established by law.

The Rights of Man (1791)

9 All hereditary government is in its nature tyranny . . . To inherit a government, is to inherit the people, as if they were flocks and herds.

The Rights of Man pt. 2 (1792)

10 With respect to the two Houses, of which the English Parliament is composed, they appear to be effectually influenced into one, and as a legislature, to have no temper of its own. The Minister, whoever he at any time may be, touches it as with an opium wand, and it sleeps obedience.

The Rights of Man pt. 2 (1792)

11 The candidates were not men but principles.

The Rights of Man (1791)

12 What were formerly called revolutions were little more than a change of persons . . . what we now see in the world, from the revolutions of America and France, is a renovation of the natural order of things.

The Rights of Man (1791)

13 The instant formal government is abolished, society begins to act. A general association takes place, and common interest produces common security.

The Rights of Man pt. 2 (1792)

14 *of monarchy:*
   I compare it to something kept behind a curtain, about which there is a great deal of bustle and fuss, and a wonderful air of seeming solemnity; but when, by any accident, the curtain happens to be open, and the company see what it is, they burst into laughter.

The Rights of Man pt. 2 (1792)

1 When, in countries that are called civilized, we see age going to the workhouse and youth to the gallows, something must be wrong in the system of government.

The Rights of Man pt. 2 (1792)

2 My country is the world, and my religion is to do good.

The Rights of Man pt. 2 (1792)

3 I do not believe that any two men, on what are called doctrinal points, think alike who think at all. It is only those who have not thought that appear to agree.

The Rights of Man pt. 2 (1792)

4 To elect, and to reject, is the prerogative of a free people.

in *National Intelligencer* 29 November 1802

5 When moral principles, rather than persons, are candidates for power, to vote is to perform a moral duty, and not to vote is to neglect a duty.

in *Trenton True-American* April 1803

6 A share in two revolutions is living to some purpose.

Eric Foner *Tom Paine and Revolutionary America* (1976)

7 Where Liberty is not, there is my country.

John Keane *Tom Paine* (1995); see **Otis** 298:10

8 When it shall be said in any country in the world, 'My poor are happy; neither ignorance nor distress is to be found among them; my jails are empty of prisoners, my streets of beggars; the aged are not in want, the taxes are not oppressive; the rational world is my friend, because I am the friend of its happiness': when these things can be said, then may that country boast of its constitution and its government.

John Keane *Tom Paine* (1995)

Ian Paisley 1926–

Northern Irish politician and Presbyterian minister

9 Trusting in the God of our fathers and confident that our cause is just, we will never surrender our heritage.

in *Guardian* 21 August 1968

10 I will walk on no grave of Ulster's honoured dead to do a deal with the IRA or the British government.
   speech at the annual conference of the Democratic Unionist Party

in *Irish Times* 6 December 1997 'This Week They Said'

11 The mother of all treachery.
   on the Good Friday agreement

in *Times* 16 April 1998

12 They have graduated from the devil's school. They have destroyed the Act of Union and given the title deeds of Ulster to Dublin on a plate.
   on those Unionists who support the Belfast Agreement

in *Irish Times* 16 May 1998 'This Week They Said'

13 She has become a parrot.
   on the perceived readiness of the Queen to repeat the views of her Prime Minister

in *Daily Telegraph* 27 May 1998

Lord Palmerston 1784–1865

British Whig statesman, Prime Minister 1855–8 and 1859–65
see also **Last words** 226:4

14 We have no eternal allies and we have no perpetual enemies. Our interests are eternal and perpetual, and those interests it is our duty to follow.

in the House of Commons, 1 March 1848

1 I therefore fearlessly challenge the verdict which this House
. . . is to give . . . whether, as the Roman, in days of old, held
himself free from indignity, when he could say *Civis
Romanus sum*; so also a British subject, in whatever land he
may be, shall feel confident that the watchful eye and the
strong arm of England will protect him against injustice and
wrong.

in the House of Commons, 25 June 1850

> *speech in the debate on the protection afforded to the Greek trader
> David Pacifico (1784–1854), who had been born a British
> subject at Gibraltar*

2 You may call it combination, you may call it the accidental
and fortuitous concurrence of atoms.

> *on a projected coalition with* **Disraeli**

in the House of Commons, 5 March 1857

3 The function of a government is to calm, rather than to
excite agitation.

P. Guedalla Gladstone and Palmerston (1928)

4 Lord Palmerston, with characteristic levity had once said
that only three men in Europe had ever understood [the
Schleswig-Holstein question], and of these the Prince
Consort was dead, a Danish statesman (unnamed) was in
an asylum, and he himself had forgotten it.

R. W. Seton-Watson Britain in Europe 1789–1914 (1937)

5 What is merit? The opinion one man entertains of another.

T. Carlyle Shooting Niagara: and After? (1867)

6 *on being told that English has no word equivalent to* sensibilité:
Yes we have. Humbug.

attributed

Christabel Pankhurst 1880–1958

English suffragette; daughter of Emmeline Pankhurst

7 Never lose your temper with the Press or the public is a
major rule of political life.

Unshackled (1959)

8 We are here to claim our right as women, not only to be
free, but to fight for freedom. That it is our right as well as
our duty.

in Votes for Women 31 March 1911

Emmeline Pankhurst 1858–1928

English suffragette leader; founder of the Women's Social and
Political Union, 1903

9 There is something that Governments care far more for than
human life, and that is the security of property, and so it is
through property that we shall strike the enemy . . . I say to
the Government: You have not dared to take the leaders of
Ulster for their incitement to rebellion. Take me if you dare.

speech at Albert Hall, 17 October 1912

10 The argument of the broken window pane is the most
valuable argument in modern politics.

George Dangerfield The Strange Death of Liberal England (1936)

Boris Pankin 1931–

Russian diplomat

11 Recession is when you have to tighten the belt. Depression
is when there is no belt to tighten. We are probably in the
next degree of collapse when there are no trousers as such.

> *of Russia*

in Independent 25 July 1992

Dorothy Parker 1893–1967
American critic and humorist

1 *on being told that Calvin **Coolidge** was dead:*
How do they know?

Malcolm Cowley *Writers at Work* 1st Series (1958)

Martin Parker d. c.1656
English balladmonger

2 But all's to no end, for the times will not mend
Till the King enjoys his own again.

'Upon Defacing of Whitehall' (1671)

Henry Parkes 1815–95
English-born Australian statesman

3 The crimson thread of kinship runs through us all.
  on Australian federation

speech at banquet in Melbourne 6 February 1890; *The Federal Government of Australasia* (1890)

C. Northcote Parkinson 1909–93
English writer

4 Expenditure rises to meet income.

Parkinson's Law (1958)

5 Work expands so as to fill the time available for its completion.

Parkinson's Law (1958)

6 A committee is organic rather than mechanical in its nature: it is not a structure but a plant. It takes root and grows, it flowers, wilts, and dies, scattering the seed from which other committees will bloom in their turn.

Parkinson's Law (1958)

7 Time spent on any item of the agenda will be in inverse proportion to the sum involved.

Parkinson's Law (1958)

8 The man who is denied the opportunity of taking decisions of importance begins to regard as important the decisions he is allowed to take.

Parkinson's Law (1958)

9 Men enter local politics solely as a result of being unhappily married.

Parkinson's Law (1958)

Rosa Parks 1913–
American civil rights activist

10 Our mistreatment was just not right, and I was tired of it.
  of her refusal, in December 1955, to surrender her seat on a segregated bus in Alabama to a white man

Quiet Strength (1994)

Charles Stewart Parnell 1846–91
Irish nationalist leader
*on Parnell: see **Joyce** 208:2, **Yeats** 427:1*

11 Why should Ireland be treated as a geographical fragment of England . . . Ireland is not a geographical fragment, but a nation.

in the House of Commons, 26 April 1875

12 I do not believe, and I never shall believe, that any murder was committed at Manchester.
  objecting to the expression 'the Manchester murders' in alluding to the escape of the Fenians, Kelly and Deasy, in 1867

in the House of Commons, June 1876

1 My policy is not a policy of conciliation, but a policy of retaliation.
in 1877, on his parliamentary tactics in the House of Commons as leader of the Irish party

in *Dictionary of National Biography* (1917-)

2 None of us, whether we are in America or Ireland, or wherever we may be, will be satisfied until we have destroyed the last link which keeps Ireland bound to England.

speech at Cincinnati, 20 February 1880

3 No man has a right to fix the boundary of the march of a nation; no man has a right to say to his country—thus far shalt thou go and no further.

speech at Cork, 21 January 1885

4 Get the advice of everybody whose advice is worth having— they are very few—and then do what you think best yourself.

Conor Cruise O'Brien *Parnell*

Matthew Parris 1949-

British journalist and former politician

5 *of Lady **Thatcher** in the House of Lords:*
A big cat detained briefly in a poodle parlour, sharpening her claws on the velvet.

Look Behind You! (1993)

6 Being an MP feeds your vanity and starves your self-respect.

in *The Times* 9 February 1994

7 Why waste it on some vanilla-flavoured pixie. Bring on the fruitcakes, we want a fruitcake for an unlosable seat. They enliven the Commons.
*the day before the Kensington and Chelsea association chose Alan **Clark** as their parliamentary candidate*

in *Mail on Sunday* 26 January 1997

8 My name is Mandy: Peter B.,
I'm back in charge—don't mess with me.
My cheeks are drawn, my face is bony,
The line I take comes straight from Tony.
on Peter Mandelson's return to government

in *Times* 21 October 1999; see **Anonymous** 11:1

Carolyn Parrish 1946-

Canadian Independent politician

9 Come hell or high water, there's no frigging way I'm going to let one ovary bring the government down.
on her determination to be present for the critical budget vote, despite suffering stomach pains

quoted in *GlobeandMail.com* 20 May 2005 (online edition)

Tony Parsons 1953-

English critic and writer

10 I never saw a beggar yet who would recognise guilt if it bit him on his unwashed ass.

Dispatches from the Front Line of Popular Culture (1994)

Blaise Pascal 1623-62

French mathematician, physicist, and moralist

11 Had Cleopatra's nose been shorter, the whole face of the world would have changed.

Pensées (1909)

Sadashiv Kanoji Patil

Indian politician

1 The Prime Minister is like the great banyan tree. Thousands shelter beneath it, but nothing grows.
*when asked in an interview who would be **Nehru**'s successor*

J. K. Galbraith *A Life in Our Times* (1981)

Chris Patten 1944–

British Conservative politician

2 Attacking the Liberals is a difficult business, involving all the hazards of wrestling with a greased pig at a village fair, and then insulting the vicar.

attributed, 1996

Jeremy Paxman 1950–

British journalist and broadcaster

3 Did you threaten to overrule him?
*question asked 14 times of Michael **Howard**, referring to the sacking of a prison governor by Derek Lewis, Director of the Prison Service*

interview, BBC2 *Newsnight* 13 May 1997

4 No government in history has been as obsessed with public relations as this one . . . Speaking for myself, if there is a message I want to be off it.
after criticism from Alastair Campbell of interviewing tactics in The World at One *and* Newsnight

in *Daily Telegraph* 3 July 1998

5 Labour's attack dog.
*description of the Labour politician John Reid, to which Reid took great exception (see **Reid** 324:5)*

on *Newsnight* programme, 8 March 2005

6 Down here we live under a sort of Scottish Raj . . . I don't see why there is need for them to feel chippy.
on the influence of Scottish MPs at Westminster

in *Scotsman* 14 March 2005

Patrick Pearse 1879–1916

Irish nationalist leader; executed after the Easter Rising
*on Pearse: see **Yeats** 426:5*

7 The fools, the fools, the fools, they have left us our Fenian dead, and while Ireland holds these graves Ireland unfree shall never be at peace.

oration over the grave of the Fenian Jeremiah O'Donovan Rossa, 1 August 1915

8 Here be ghosts that I have raised this Christmastide, ghosts of dead men that have bequeathed a trust to us living men. Ghosts are troublesome things in a house or in a family, as we knew even before Ibsen taught us. There is only one way to appease a ghost. You must do the thing it asks you. The ghosts of a nation sometimes ask very big things and they must be appeased, whatever the cost.

on Christmas Day, 1915; Conor Cruise O'Brien *Ancestral Voices* (1994); see **O'Brien** 293:1

Lester Pearson 1897–1972

Canadian diplomat and Liberal statesman, Prime Minister 1963–8

9 The grim fact is that we prepare for war like precocious giants and for peace like retarded pygmies.

speech in Toronto, 14 March 1955

1 This is the flag of the future, but it does not dishonour the past.
  on Canada obtaining a flag of its own, a project Pearson successfully achieved

speech in the House of Commons, Ottawa, 15 December 1964

2 Not only did he not suffer fools gladly, he did not suffer them at all.
  of Dean **Acheson**

in *Time* 25 October 1971

3 The chief distinction of a diplomat is that he can say no in such a way that it sounds like yes.

Geoffrey Pearson *Seize the Day* (1993)

Robert Peel 1788–1850

British Conservative statesman; Prime Minister, 1834–5, 1841–6
on Peel: see **Curran** 107:7, **Disraeli** 119:9, **Disraeli** 120:2, **Disraeli** 123:2, **Hennessy** 180:2, **Wellington** 415:13

4 What is right must unavoidably be politic.

to Goulburn, 23 September 1822

5 There is no appetite for truth in Ireland.

to Leveson Gower in 1828

6 As minister of the Crown . . . I reserve to myself, distinctly and unequivocally, the right of adapting my conduct to the exigency of the moment, and to the wants of the country.

in the House of Commons, 30 March 1829

7 All my experience in public life is in favour of the employment of what the world would call young men instead of old ones.

to Wellington in 1829

8 The longer I live, the more clearly do I see the folly of yielding a rash and precipitate assent to any political measure.

in the House of Commons, 1830

9 Men, if in office, seemed really to be like the Indians—they inherited all the qualities of those enemies they killed.

in the House of Commons, 1831

10 We are here to consult the interests and not to obey the will of the people, if we honestly believe that that will conflicts with those interests.

in the House of Commons, 1831

11 No man attached to his country could always acquiesce in the opinions of the majority.

in the House of Commons, 1831

12 No government can exist which does not control and restrain the popular sentiments.

in the House of Commons, 1832

13 There will always be found a permanent fund of discontent and dissatisfaction in every country.

in the House of Commons, 1832

14 The hasty inordinate demand for peace might be just as dangerous as the clamour for war.

in the House of Commons, 1832

15 I see no dignity in persevering in error.

in the House of Commons, 1833

16 *of Robert* **Walpole**:
  So far as the great majority of his audience was concerned, he had blocks to cut, and he chose a fitter instrument than a razor to cut them with.

to Mahon in 1833

17 I am not sure that those who clamour most, suffer most.

in the House of Commons, 1834

18 Of all vulgar arts of government, that of solving every difficulty which might arise by thrusting the hand into the public purse is the most delusory and contemptible.

in the House of Commons, 1834

19 The distinction of being without an honour is becoming a rare and valuable one and should not become extinct.

to Graham in 1841

1 A cordial and good understanding between France and England is essential to the peace and welfare of Europe.

in the House of Commons, 1841

2 Speaking with that caution with which I am sometimes taunted but which I find a great convenience.

in the House of Commons, 1842

3 There are those who seem to have nothing else to do but to suggest modes of taxation to men in office.

in the House of Commons, 1842

4 The great art of government is to work by such instruments as the world supplies.

in Cabinet, 1844

5 There are many parties in Ireland who desire to have a grievance and prefer the grievance to the remedy.

to the Queen, 1844

6 Philosophers are very regardless of expense when the public has to bear it.

to Haddington in 1844

7 Priests are not above sublunary considerations. Priests have nephews.

to Graham, 13 August 1845

8 An Irishman has no sense of the ridiculous when office is in question.

to Graham, 28 December 1845

9 There seem to me very few facts, at least ascertainable facts, in politics.

to Lord **Brougham** in 1846

10 Great public measures cannot be carried by the influence of mere reason.

to Lord Radnor in 1846

Charles Péguy 1873–1914
French poet and essayist

11 Tyranny is always better organized than freedom.

Basic Verities (1943) 'War and Peace'

Henry Herbert, Lord Pembroke
c.1534–1601

12 A parliament can do any thing but make a man a woman, and a woman a man.

quoted by his son, the 4th Earl, in a speech on 11 April 1648, proving himself Chancellor of Oxford

William Penn 1644–1718
English Quaker; founder of Pennsylvania

13 It is a reproach to religion and government to suffer so much poverty and excess.

Some Fruits of Solitude (1693)

14 The taking of a bribe or gratuity, should be punished with as severe penalties as the defrauding of the State.

Some Fruits of Solitude (1693)

Samuel Pepys 1633–1703
English diarist

15 I went out to Charing Cross, to see Major-general Harrison hanged, drawn, and quartered; which was done there, he looking as cheerful as any man could do in that condition.

diary, 13 October 1660

16 But methought it lessened my esteem of a king, that he should not be able to command the rain.

diary, 19 July 1662

17 I see it is impossible for the King to have things done as cheap as other men.

diary, 21 July 1662

1 While we were talking came by several poor creatures
  carried by, by constables, for being at a conventicle . . . I
  would to God they would either conform, or be more wise,
  and not be catched!

diary, 7 August 1664

2 Pretty witty Nell.
    of Nell Gwyn

diary, 3 April 1665

Shimon Peres 1923–
Israeli statesman

3 Television has made dictatorship impossible, but democracy
  unbearable.

at a Davos meeting, in *Financial
Times* 31 January 1995

Pericles *c.*495–429 BC
Greek statesman and Athenian general

4 For famous men have the whole earth as their memorial.

Thucydides *History of the
Peloponnesian War*

Eva Perón 1919–52
Argentinian wife of Juan Perón
on Perón: see **Epitaphs** 137:1

5 Keeping books on charity is capitalist nonsense! I just use
  the money for the poor. I can't stop to count it.

Fleur Cowles *Bloody Precedent: the
Peron Story* (1952)

Juan Perón 1895–1974
Argentinian soldier and statesman, President 1946–55 and
1973–4

6 If I had not been born Perón, I would have liked to be
  Perón.

in *Observer* 21 February 1960

Henri Philippe Pétain 1856–1951
French soldier and statesman

7 To write one's memoirs is to speak ill of everybody except
  oneself.

in *Observer* 26 May 1946

Mike Peters
American cartoonist

8 When I go into the voting booth, do I vote for the person
  who is the best President? Or the slime bucket who will
  make my life as a cartoonist wonderful?

in *Wall Street Journal* 20 January
1993

Jamie Petrie and Peter Cunnah
British singers and songwriters

9 Things can only get better.

title of song (1994); see **Slogans**
368:9

Roger Peyrefitte 1907–
French writer

10 The ideal civil servant should always be colourless,
   odourless and tasteless.

Diplomatic Diversions (1953)

Lord Peyton 1919–

British Conservative politician

1 The great thing about Alec Home is that he was not media driven. He would have had some difficulty in spelling the word 'image'.
  *of Lord **Home***

in conversation, 1997; Peter Hennessy *The Prime Minister: the Office and its Holders since 1945* (2000)

Edward John Phelps 1822–1900

American lawyer and diplomat

2 The man who makes no mistakes does not usually make anything.

speech at the Mansion House, London, 24 January 1889

Kim Philby 1912–88

British intelligence officer and Soviet spy

3 To betray, you must first belong.

in *Sunday Times* 17 December 1967

Prince Philip 1921–

British prince, husband of **Elizabeth II**

4 Just at this moment we are suffering a national defeat comparable to any lost military campaign, and what is more it is self-inflicted . . . I think it is about time we pulled our finger out.

speech to businessmen, 17 October 1961

Morgan Phillips 1902–63

British Labour politician

5 The Labour Party owes more to Methodism than to Marxism.

James Callaghan *Time and Chance* (1987)

Wendell Phillips 1811–84

American abolitionist and orator

6 Revolutions are not made; they come. A revolution is as natural a growth as an oak. It comes out of the past. Its foundations are laid far back.

speech, 8 January 1852

7 The best use of laws is to teach men to trample bad laws under their feet.

speech, 12 April 1852

8 One on God's side is a majority.

speech, 1 November 1859

9 Truth is one forever absolute, but opinion is truth filtered through the moods, the blood, the disposition of the spectator.

in *Idols* 4 October 1859

Phocion c.402–317 BC

Athenian soldier

10 DEMOSTHENES: The Athenians will kill thee, Phocion, should they go crazy.
  PHOCION: But they will kill thee, should they come to their senses.

Plutarch *Parallel Lives* 'Phocion'

John Pienaar 1956–
British journalist

1 She is a loose cannon with a sense of direction.
  *of Clare **Short***

in *Observer* 29 February 2004

John Pilger 1939–
Australian journalist

2 It was all too easy for journalists to see Vietnam as a war, rather than a country.

comment, c.1995

Ben Pimlott 1945–2004
English historian and royal biographer

3 If you have a Royal Family you have to make the best of whatever personalities the genetic lottery comes up with.

in *Independent* 13 September 1997 'Quote Unquote'

4 Clement Attlee—top deity in the modern Labour Party's pantheon.

in *Independent on Sunday* 16 March 1997

William Pitt, Earl of Chatham 1708–78
British Whig statesman; Prime Minister, 1766–8
*on Pitt: see **Walpole** 410:1*

5 The atrocious crime of being a young man . . . I shall neither attempt to palliate nor deny.

in the House of Commons, 2 March 1741

6 I must now address a few words to the Solicitor; they shall be few, but they shall be daggers.

to William Murray, the Attorney-General, in the House of Commons, 1755

7 The poorest man may in his cottage bid defiance to all the forces of the Crown. It may be frail—its roof may shake— the wind may blow through it—the storm may enter—the rain may enter—but the King of England cannot enter!

speech, c.March 1763

8 Confidence is a plant of slow growth in an aged bosom: youth is the season of credulity.

in the House of Commons, 14 January 1766

9 Unlimited power is apt to corrupt the minds of those who possess it.

in the House of Lords, 9 January 1770; see **Acton** 1:11

10 There is something behind the throne greater than the King himself.

in the House of Lords, 2 March 1770

11 We have a Calvinistic creed, a Popish liturgy, and an Arminian clergy.

in the House of Lords, 19 May 1772

12 You cannot conquer America.

in the House of Lords, 18 November 1777

13 I invoke the genius of the Constitution!

in the House of Lords, 18 November 1777

14 Shall a people that fifteen years ago was the terror of the world now stoop so low as to tell its ancient inveterate enemy, 'Take all we have, only give us peace?'
  in his last speech in the Lords, shortly before his death, opposing a surrender to the American colonists and their ally France

Basil Williams *William Pitt, Earl of Chatham* (1913)

15 Our watchword is security.

attributed

16 The parks are the lungs of London.

quoted in the House of Commons by William Windham, 30 June 1808

William Pitt 1759–1806

British Tory statesman; Prime Minister, 1783–1801, 1804–6
on Pitt: see **Burke** 64:15, **Fox** 144:6, **Fox** 144:7, **Scott** 348:8; *see also* **Last words** 227:10

1 Lord North will, I hope, in a very little time make room for me in Downing Street, which is the best summer Town House possible.

as newly appointed Chancellor of the Exchequer, 16 July 1782

2 Necessity is the plea for every infringement of human freedom: it is the argument of tyrants; it is the creed of slaves.

in the House of Commons, 18 November 1783

3 We must anew commence the salvation of Europe.

in 1795; in *Dictionary of National Biography* (1917–)

4 We must recollect . . . what it is we have at stake, what it is we have to contend for. It is for our property, it is for our liberty, it is for our independence, nay, for our existence as a nation; it is for our character, it is for our very name as Englishmen, it is for everything dear and valuable to man on this side of the grave.
   on the rupture of the Peace of Amiens and the resumption of war with Napoleon, 22 July 1803

Speeches of the Rt. Hon. William Pitt (1806)

5 England has saved herself by her exertions, and will, as I trust, save Europe by her example.
   replying to a toast in which he had been described as the saviour of his country in the wars with France

R. Coupland *War Speeches of William Pitt* (1915)

6 Roll up that map; it will not be wanted these ten years.
   of a map of Europe, on hearing of **Napoleon**'s *victory at Austerlitz, December 1805*

Earl Stanhope *Life of the Rt. Hon. William Pitt* (1862)

Pius VII 1742–1823

Italian cleric, Pope from 1800

7 We are prepared to go to the gates of Hell—but no further.
   attempting to reach an agreement with **Napoleon**, *c.1800–1*

J. M. Robinson *Cardinal Consalvi* (1987)

Pius XII 1876–1958

Italian cleric; Pope from 1939

8 One Galileo in two thousand years is enough.
   on being asked to proscribe the works of Teilhard de Chardin

attributed; Stafford Beer *Platform for Change* (1975)

Plato 429–347 BC

Greek philosopher

9 What I say is that 'just' or 'right' means nothing but what is in the interest of the stronger party.

spoken by Thrasymachus in *The Republic*

10 One of the penalties for refusing to participate in politics is that you end up being governed by your inferiors.

The Republic

11 When the tyrant has disposed of foreign enemies by conquest or treaty, and there is nothing to fear from them, then he is always stirring up some war or other, in order that the people may require a leader.
   'foreign enemies' here means 'exiled opponents'

The Republic

Pliny the Elder AD 23-79
Roman statesman and scholar

1 *Ex Africa semper aliquid novi.*
Always something new out of Africa.

traditional form of *Semper aliquid novi Africam adferre*; *Historia Naturalis*

George Washington Plunkitt 1842-1924
American Tammany politician

2 There's an honest graft, and I'm an example of how it works. I might sum up the whole thing by sayin': 'I seen my opportunities and I took 'em.'

'Honest Graft and Dishonest Graft' in William L. Riordon *Plunkitt of Tammany Hall* (1905)

3 The politician who steals is worse than a thief. He is a fool. With the grand opportunities all around for a man with a political pull, there's no excuse for stealin' a cent.

'On the Shame of Cities' in William L. Riordon *Plunkitt of Tammany Hall* (1905)

Plutarch c.AD 46-c.120
Greek philosopher and biographer

4 For we are told that when a certain man was accusing both of them to him, he [Caesar] said that he had no fear of those fat and long-haired fellows, but rather of those pale and thin ones.

Parallel Lives 'Anthony'

5 The man who is thought to have been the first to see beneath the surface of Caesar's public policy and to fear it, as one might fear the smiling surface of the sea.
of **Cicero**

Parallel Lives 'Julius Caesar'

Harry Pollitt 1890-1960
British Communist politician

6 *on being asked by Stephen Spender (1909-95) in the 1930s how best a poet could serve the Communist cause:*
Go to Spain and get killed. The movement needs a Byron.

attributed, perhaps apocryphal

Polybius c.200-c.118 BC
Greek historian

7 Those who know how to win are much more numerous than those who know how to make proper use of their victories.

History bk 10

Madame de Pompadour (Antoinette Poisson, Marquise de Pompadour) 1721-64
French favourite of Louis XV of France

8 *Après nous le déluge.*
After us the deluge.

Madame du Hausset *Mémoires* (1824)

Georges Pompidou 1911-74
French statesman; President of France from 1969

9 A statesman is a politician who places himself at the service of the nation. A politician is a statesman who places the nation at his service.

in 1973, attributed

Alexander Pope 1688–1744

English poet

1 Lo! thy dread empire, Chaos! is restored;
   Light dies before thy uncreating word:
   Thy hand, great Anarch! lets the curtain fall;
   And universal darkness buries all.

   The Dunciad (1742)

2 Old politicians chew on wisdom past,
   And totter on in business to the last.

   Epistles to Several Persons 'To Lord Cobham' (1734)

3 Statesman, yet friend to Truth! of soul sincere,
   In action faithful, and in honour clear;
   Who broke no promise, served no private end,
   Who gained no title, and who lost no friend.

   Epistles to Several Persons 'To Mr Addison' (1720)

4 For forms of government let fools contest;
   Whate'er is best administered is best.

   An Essay on Man Epistle 3 (1733)

5 If parts allure thee, think how Bacon shined,
   The wisest, brightest, meanest of mankind:
   Or ravished with the whistling of a name,
   See Cromwell, damned to everlasting fame!

   An Essay on Man Epistle 4 (1734)

6 Get place and wealth, if possible, with grace;
   If not, by any means get wealth and place.

   Imitations of Horace Horace bk. 1, Epistle 1 (1738); see **Horace** 188:8

7 Here thou, great Anna! whom three realms obey,
   Dost sometimes counsel take—and sometimes tea.

   The Rape of the Lock (1714)

Karl Popper 1902–94

Austrian-born philosopher

8 We may become the makers of our fate when we have ceased to pose as its prophets.

   The Open Society and its Enemies (1945) introduction

9 We must plan for freedom, and not only for security, if for no other reason than that only freedom can make security secure.

   The Open Society and its Enemies (1945)

10 There is no history of mankind, there are only many histories of all kinds of aspects of human life. And one of these is the history of political power. This is elevated into the history of the world.

   The Open Society and its Enemies (1945)

11 Marxism is only an episode—one of the many mistakes we have made in the perennial and dangerous struggle for building a better and a freer world.

   The Open Society and its Enemies (rev. ed., 1952)

12 Piecemeal social engineering resembles physical engineering in regarding the *ends* as beyond the province of technology.

   The Poverty of Historicism (1957)

Michael Portillo 1953–

British Conservative politician and broadcaster
on Portillo: see **Heseltine** 130:7

13 A truly terrible night for the Conservatives.
   after losing Enfield South to Labour in the General Election of 1997

   comment, 2 May 1997; Brian Cathcart *Were You Still Up for Portillo?* (1997)

14 You don't look tall if you surround yourself by short grasses.
   *on Iain Duncan **Smith***

   in *Independent* 22 February 2003

Eugène Pottier

French politician see **Songs** 375:5

Colin Powell 1937–

American general and Republican politician, Secretary of State 2001–5

1 Some in our party miss no opportunity to roundly and loudly condemn affirmative action that helped a few thousand black kids get an education, but hardly a whimper is heard from them over affirmative action for lobbyists who load our federal tax codes with preferences for special interest.

speech at the Republican Convention, 31 August 2000

2 Nato is the bedrock of Europe. It is sacrosanct.

in Independent on Sunday 21 January 2001

Enoch Powell 1912–98

British Conservative politician

3 History is littered with the wars which everybody knew would never happen.

speech to the Conservative Party Conference, 19 October 1967

4 Those whom the gods wish to destroy, they first make mad. We must be mad, literally mad, as a nation to be permitting the annual inflow of some 50,000 dependents, who are for the most part the material of the future growth of the immigrant descended population. It is like watching a nation busily engaged in heaping up its own funeral pyre.

speech at Birmingham, 20 April 1968

5 As I look ahead, I am filled with foreboding. Like the Roman, I seem to see 'the River Tiber foaming with much blood'.

*speech at Birmingham, 20 April 1968; see **Virgil** 407:1*

6 No one is forced to be a politician. It can only compare with fox-hunting and writing poetry. These are two things that men do for sheer enjoyment too.

attributed, 1973

7 Judas was paid! I am sacrificing my whole political life.
response to a heckler's call of 'Judas', having advised Conservatives to vote Labour at the coming general election

speech at Bull Ring, Birmingham, 23 February 1974

8 There is a mania in legislation in detecting discrimination. But all life is about discrimination.

attributed, 1975

9 A party . . . is not a faction or club of individuals who associate for mutual assistance in acquiring and retaining office. It is a body of persons who hold, advocate and desire to bring into effect certain political principles and policies.

speech, 30 September 1976

10 Office before honour was the password of Conservative government.
of the 1970–4 Conservative administration

in Spectator 15 October 1977

11 For a politician to complain about the press is like a ship's captain complaining about the sea.

in Guardian 3 December 1984

12 A Tory is someone who thinks institutions are wiser than those who operate them.

in Daily Telegraph 31 March 1986

13 ANNE BROWN: How would you like to be remembered?
ENOCH POWELL: I should like to have been killed in the war.

in a radio interview, 13 April 1986

1 To pretend that you cannot exchange goods and services freely with a Frenchman or an Italian, unless there is an identical standard of bathing beaches or tap water in the different countries is not logic. It is naked aggression.

in Guardian 22 May 1990

2 What is history except a nation's collective memory?

on BBC Radio 4 10 February 1991

3 All political lives, unless they are cut off in midstream at a happy juncture, end in failure, because that is the nature of politics and of human affairs.

Joseph Chamberlain (1977); epilogue

4 To be and to remain a member of the House of Commons was the overriding and undiscussable motivation of my life as a politician.

'Theory and Practice' 1990

5 Lift the curtain and 'the State' reveals itself as a little group of fallible men in Whitehall, making guesses about the future, influenced by political prejudices and partisan prejudices, and working on projections drawn from the past by a staff of economists.

attributed

John O'Connor Power 1848–1919

Irish lawyer and politician

6 *of the Liberal Unionists:*
The mules of politics: without pride of ancestry, or hope of posterity.

H. H. Asquith *Memories and Reflections* (1928); see **Disraeli** 122:10, **Donnelly** 125:5

John Prescott 1938–

British Labour politician
on Prescott: see **Hague** 114:5

7 People like me were branded, pigeon-holed, a ceiling put on our ambitions.
on failing his 11-plus

speech at Ruskin College, Oxford, 13 June 1996; in *Guardian* 14 June 1996

8 We did it! Let's wallow in our victory!
on Tony **Blair***'s warning that the Labour Party should not be triumphalist in victory*

speech to the Labour Party Conference, 29 September 1997

9 The wife does not like her hair blown about.
explaining why he had driven from his hotel to the conference centre at the Labour Party Conference

in *Daily Telegraph* 1 October 1999

10 When plates appear to be moving, everyone positions themselves for it.

in *The Times* 15 May 2004

Richard Price 1723–91

English nonconformist minister

11 Now, methinks, I see the ardour for liberty catching and spreading; a general amendment beginning in human affairs; the dominion of kings changed for the dominion of laws, and the dominion of priests giving way to the dominion of reason and conscience.

A Discourse on the Love of our Country (1790)

Matthew Prior 1664–1721

English poet

12 What is a King?—a man condemned to bear
The public burden of the nation's care.

Solomon (1718)

Romano Prodi 1939–

Italian statesman, President of the European Commission 1999–2004

1 The pillars of the nation state are the sword and the currency, and we changed that. The euro-decision changed the concept of the nation state.

in *Daily Telegraph* 7 April 1999

2 I know very well that the stability pact is stupid, like all decisions that are rigid.
   on the rules underpinning the single currency

interview in *Le Monde* (electronic edition) 17 October 2002

Pierre-Joseph Proudhon 1809–65

French social reformer

3 Property is theft.

Qu'est-ce que la propriété? (1840)

■ Proverbs and sayings *see box overleaf*

Joseph Pulitzer 1847–1911

Hungarian-born American newspaper proprietor and editor

4 Our Republic and its press will rise or fall together.
   referring to the importance of media independence

in *North American Review* May 1904

5 A cynical, mercenary, demagogic, corrupt press will produce in time a people as base as itself.
   inscribed on the gateway to the Columbia School of Journalism in New York

W. J. Granberg *The World of Joseph Pulitzer* (1965)

Vladimir Putin 1952–

Russian statesman, President of the Russian Federation since 2000

6 Please forgive us. We shall win this fight against international terrorism.
   addressing the nation and apologising for failing to save all the hostages in the Moscow theatre siege

in *Sunday Telegraph* 27 October 2002

Pu Yi 1906–67

Chinese monarch, Emperor of China 1908–12; Japan's puppet emperor of Manchuria 1934–45

7 For the past 40 years I had never folded my own quilt, made my own bed, or poured out my own washing. I had never even washed my own feet or tied my shoes.

From Emperor to Citizen (1964)

John Pym 1584–1643

English Parliamentary leader

8 To have granted liberties, and not to have liberties in truth and realities, is but to mock the kingdom.
   *after the battle of Edgehill, in a speech at Guildhall to the citizens of London pointing out the illusory nature of **Charles I**'s promises*

in *Dictionary of National Biography* (1917–)

Proverbs and sayings

1 Action this day.

annotation as used by Winston Churchill at the Admiralty in 1940

2 Are you now, or have you ever been, a member of the Communist Party?

from 1947, the question habitually put by the House Un-American Activities Committee (HUAC) to those appearing before it, now particularly associated with the McCarthy period of the 1950s

3 As Maine goes, so goes the nation.

American political saying, c.1840; see **Farley** 139:6

4 Bad money drives out good.

proverbial expression of a principle attributed to Sir Thomas Gresham (c.1519–79), founder of the Royal Exchange

5 A conservative is a liberal who's been mugged.

American saying, 1980s; see **Wolfe** 424:2

6 Daddy, what did you do in the Great War?

daughter to father in First World War recruiting poster

7 Don't sell America short.

popular version of saying attributed, c.1890s, to John Pierpont Morgan (1837–1913)

8 The enemy of my enemy is my friend.

late 20th century, said to be 'an old Arab proverb'

9 England's difficulty is Ireland's opportunity.

proverbial from mid 19th century

10 An Englishman's home is his castle.

proverbial from late 16th century

11 Every bullet has its billet.

proverbial from late 16th century; attributed to **William III** in John Wesley *Journal* (1827) 6 June 1765

12 The higher the monkey climbs the more he shows his tail.

proverbial from late 14th century

13 If you don't like the heat, get out of the kitchen.
*associated with Harry S **Truman**, but attributed by him to Harry Vaughan, his 'military jester'*

mid 20th century saying; in *Time* 28 April 1952

14 *Il ne faut pas être plus royaliste que le roi.*
You mustn't be more of a royalist than the king.
noted as a current catch-phrase which was not in fact new; 'it was coined under Louis XVI: it chained up the hands of the loyal, leaving free only the arm of the hangman'

François René, Vicomte de Chateaubriand *De la monarchie selon la charte* (1816)

15 *Ils ne passeront pas.*
They shall not pass.
slogan used by French army defence at Verdun in 1916

variously attributed to Marshal Pétain and to General Robert Nivelle; see **Ibarruri** 194:2

16 It'll play in Peoria.
*catchphrase of the **Nixon** administration (early 1970s) meaning 'it will be acceptable to middle America'*

originating in a standard music hall joke of the 1930s

Proverbs and sayings *continued*

1 Justice delayed is justice denied.

late 20th century saying; see **Magna Carta** 255:6

2 Let's run it up the flagpole and see if anyone salutes it.

Reginald Rose *Twelve Angry Men* (1955); recorded as an established advertising expression in the 1960s

3 Lions led by donkeys.
associated with British soldiers during the First World War

attributed to Max Hoffman (1869–1927) in Alan Clark *The Donkeys* (1961); this attribution has not been traced elsewhere, and the phrase is of much earlier origin:

Unceasingly they had drummed into them the utterance of *The Times*: 'You are lions led by packasses.'
of French troops defeated by Prussians

Francisque Sarcey *Paris during the Siege* (1871)

4 Members [of civil service orders] rise from CMG (known sometimes in Whitehall as 'Call Me God') to the KCMG ('Kindly Call Me God') to—for a select few governors and super-ambassadors—the GCMG ('God Calls Me God').

Anthony Sampson *Anatomy of Britain* (1962)

5 Not to be a republican at twenty is proof of want of heart; to be one at thirty is proof of want of head.
often used in the form 'Not to be a socialist . . . '

adopted by **Clemenceau**, and attributed by him to the French historian and politician François Guizot (1787–1874)

6 One man plus the truth makes a majority.

traditional saying; see **Knox** 222:5

7 Politics makes strange bedfellows.

proverbial from mid 19th century

8 Revolutions are not made with rose-water.

proverbial from early 19th century

9 A rising tide lifts all boats.

mid 20th century saying; principally known in the United States and associated with the **Kennedy** family

10 There's no such thing as a free lunch.
*colloquial axiom in US economics from the 1960s, much associated with Milton **Friedman***

first found in printed form in Robert Heinlein *The Moon is a Harsh Mistress* (1966)

11 To succeed in public life you have to be sincere. Once you can fake that, you've got it made.

traditional saying

12 What Manchester says today, the rest of England says tomorrow.

late 19th century saying

13 When the going gets tough, the tough get going.

proverbial from mid 20th century; widely associated with Joseph P. **Kennedy**, J. H. Cutler *Honey Fitz* (1962); also attributed to Knute Rockne

Proverbs and sayings *continued*

1 When war is declared, Truth is the first casualty.

attributed to Hiram Johnson, speaking in the US Senate, 1918, but not recorded in his speech; the first recorded use is as epigraph to Arthur Ponsonby's *Falsehood in Wartime* (1928); see **Johnson** 204:3

2 Your King and Country need you.

recruitment slogan for First World War, coined by Eric Field, July 1914; *Advertising* (1959); see **Songs** 376:8

Pyrrhus 319–272 BC
Greek monarch, King of Epirus from 306 BC

3 One more such victory and we are lost.
on defeating the Romans at Asculum, 279 BC; origin of the phrase 'Pyrrhic victory'

Plutarch *Parallel Lives* 'Pyrrhus'

François Quesnay 1694–1774
French political economist

4 *Vous ne connaissez qu'une seule règle du commerce; c'est (pour me servir de vos propres termes) de laisser passer et de laisser faire tous les acheteurs et tous les vendeurs quelconques.*

You recognize but one rule of commerce; that is (to avail myself of your own terms) to allow free passage and freedom of action to all buyers and sellers whoever they may be.

letter from M. Alpha to de Quesnay, 1767, in L. Salleron *François Quesnay et la Physiocratie* (1958) vol. 2, but not found in de Quesnay's writings; see **Argenson** 14:6

Josiah Quincy 1772–1864
American Federalist politician

5 As it will be the right of all, so it will be the duty of some, definitely to prepare for a separation, amicably if they can, violently if they must.

in *Abridgement of Debates of Congress* 14 January 1811

Yitzhak Rabin 1922–95
Israeli statesman and military leader, Prime Minister 1974–7 and 1992–5

6 We say to you today in a loud and a clear voice: enough of blood and tears. Enough.
to the Palestinians, at the signing of the Israel–Palestine Declaration

in Washington, 13 September, 1993

Lord Radcliffe 1899–1977
British lawyer and public servant

7 Society has become used to the standing armies of power— the permanent Civil Service, the police force, the tax- gatherer—organized on a scale which was unknown to earlier centuries.

Power and the State (BBC Reith Lectures, 1951)

8 Governments always tend to want not really a free press but a managed or well-conducted one.

in 1967; Peter Hennessy *What the Papers Never Said* (1985)

Jean-Pierre Raffarin 1948–

French statesman, Prime Minister 2002–5

1 We have a country which loves ideology, and we need pragmatism.

in *Independent* 11 May 2002

Thomas Rainborowe d. 1648

English soldier and parliamentarian

2 The poorest he that is in England hath a life to live as the greatest he; and therefore truly, Sir, I think it's clear, that every man that is to live under a government ought to first by his own consent to put himself under that government; and I do think that the poorest man in England is not at all bound in a strict sense to that government that he hath not had a voice to put himself under.
during the Army debates at Putney, 29 October 1647

C. H. Firth (ed.) *The Clarke Papers* vol. 1 (1891)

Milton Rakove 1918–83

3 The second law, Rakove's law of principle and politics, states that the citizen is influenced by principle in direct proportion to his distance from the political situation.

in *Virginia Quarterly Review* (1965)

Walter Ralegh c.1552–1618

English explorer and courtier
see also **Last words** 226:11

4 Say to the court, it glows
And shines like rotten wood;
Say to the church, it shows
What's good, and doth no good:
If church and court reply,
Then give them both the lie.

'The Lie' (1608)

5 Fain would I climb, yet fear I to fall.
line written on a window-pane; see **Elizabeth I** *133:7*

Thomas Fuller *History of the Worthies of England* (1662) 'Devonshire'

6 'Tis a sharp remedy, but a sure one for all ills.
on feeling the edge of the axe prior to his execution

D. Hume *History of Great Britain* (1754)

7 So the heart be right, it is no matter which way the head lies.
at his execution, on being asked which way he preferred to lay his head

W. Stebbing *Sir Walter Raleigh* (1891)

John Randolph 1773–1833

American politician

8 God has given us Missouri, and the devil shall not take it from us.
in the debate in the US Senate in 1820 on the admission of Missouri to the Union as a slave state

Robert V. Remini *Henry Clay* (1991)

9 Never were abilities so much below mediocrity so well rewarded; no, not when Caligula's horse was made Consul.
*on John Quincy **Adams**'s appointment of Richard Rush as Secretary of the Treasury*

speech, 1 February 1828

1 He is a man of splendid abilities but utterly corrupt. He shines and stinks like rotten mackerel by moonlight.
of Edward Livingston

W. Cabell Bruce *John Randolph of Roanoke* (1923) vol. 2

2 He rowed to his object with muffled oars.
of Martin Van Buren

W. Cabell Bruce *John Randolph of Roanoke* (1923) vol. 2

3 That most delicious of all privileges—spending other people's money.

William Cabell Bruce *John Randolph of Roanoke* (1923) vol. 2

Ian Rankin 1960–
Scottish novelist

4 We can't really demolish it until they finish building it.
on the Scottish parliament building

in *Independent* 20 July 2002

Dan Rather 1931–
American journalist

5 I worry that patriotism run amok will trample the very values that the country seeks to defend.

in *Independent* 18 May 2002

Irina Ratushinskaya 1954–
Russian poet

6 Russian literature saved my soul. When I was a young girl in school and I asked what is good and what is evil, no one in that corrupt system could show me.

in *Observer* 15 October 1989 'Sayings of the Week'

Sam Rayburn 1882–1961
American politician, Speaker of the US House of Representatives

7 If you want to get along, go along.

Neil MacNeil *Forge of Democracy* (1963)

Nancy Reagan 1923–
American actress and wife of Ronald **Reagan**, First Lady of the US, 1981–9

8 If the President has a bully pulpit, then the First Lady has a white glove pulpit . . . more refined, restricted, ceremonial, but it's a pulpit all the same.

in *New York Times* 10 March 1988; see **Roosevelt** 333:4

Ronald Reagan 1911–2004
American Republican statesman; 40th President of the US, 1981–9
on Reagan: see **Keillor** 211:1, **Noonan** 291:9, **Schroeder** 347:11, **Vidal** 406:9; *see also* **Dempsey** 114:7, **Gipp** 157:5

9 Government is like a big baby—an alimentary canal with a big appetite at one end and no responsibility at the other.
campaigning for the governorship of California, 1965

attributed

10 Politics is just like show business, you have a hell of an opening, coast for a while and then have a hell of a close.

in 1966; Mark Green and Gail MacColl (eds.) *There He Goes Again* (1983)

11 Politics is supposed to be the second oldest profession. I have come to realize that it bears a very close resemblance to the first.

at a conference in Los Angeles, 2 March 1977

1 I've noticed that everybody who is for abortion has already been born.
presidential campaign debate, 21 September 1980

2 I paid for this microphone.
*in 1980, debating for the Republican nomination against George **Bush**; the moderator had ordered Reagan's microphone turned off when he asked for the participation of other candidates, and the refusal to allow this was held to be very damaging to Bush*
Lou Cannon *Ronald Reagan* (1982)

3 *President **Carter** had described a proposal for a national health insurance plan*
JIMMY CARTER: Governor Reagan, again, typically is against such a proposal.
RONALD REAGAN: There you go again!
as Republican challenger debating with President Carter in the 1980 presidential campaign; in *Times* 30 October 1980

4 You can tell a lot about a fellow's character by his way of eating jellybeans.
in *New York Times* 15 January 1981

5 We're the party that wants to see an America in which people can still get rich.
at a Republican congressional dinner, 4 May 1982

6 So in your discussions of the nuclear freeze proposals, I urge you to beware the temptation of pride—the temptation blithely to declare yourselves above it all and label both sides equally at fault, to ignore the facts of history and the aggressive impulses of an evil empire.
speech to the National Association of Evangelicals, 8 March 1983

7 My fellow Americans, I am pleased to tell you I just signed legislation which outlaws Russia forever. The bombing begins in five minutes.
said during radio microphone test, 11 August 1984
in *New York Times* 13 August 1984

8 The taxpayer—that's someone who works for the federal government but doesn't have to take a Civil Service examination.
attributed, 1985

9 We are especially not going to tolerate these attacks from outlaw states run by the strangest collection of misfits, Looney Tunes, and squalid criminals since the advent of the Third Reich.
speech following the hijack of a US plane, 8 July 1985
in *New York Times* 9 July 1985

10 We will never forget them, nor the last time we saw them this morning, as they prepared for the journey and waved goodbye and 'slipped the surly bonds of earth' to 'touch the face of God.'
after the loss of the space shuttle Challenger *with all its crew*
broadcast from the Oval Office, 28 January 1986, quoting from 'High Flight' by the American airman John Gillespie Magee (1922–41)

11 The nine most terrifying words in the English language are, 'I'm from the government and I'm here to help.'
on assistance to farmers
at a press conference in Chicago, 2 August 1986

12 Mr Gorbachev, tear down this wall!
at the Brandenburg Gate in West Berlin, 12 June 1987

13 To grasp and hold a vision, that is the very essence of successful leadership—not only on the movie set where I learned it, but everywhere.
in *The Wilson Quarterly* Winter 1994; attributed

14 I now begin the journey that will lead me into the sunset of my life.
statement to the American people revealing that he had Alzheimer's disease, 1994
in *Daily Telegraph* 5 January 1995

Red Cloud (Mahpiua Luta) 1822–1909
American Sioux chief

1 You have heard the sound of the white soldier's axe upon the Little Piney. His presence here is . . . an insult to the spirits of our ancestors. Are we then to give up their sacred graves to be ploughed for corn? Dakotas, I am for war!

speech at council at Fort Laramie, 1866

John Redmond 1856–1918
Irish politician and nationalist leader

2 *in the Spring of 1914 Redmond was asked by a friend, a priest from Tipperary, if anything could now rob them of Home Rule:*
A European war might do it.

in *Dictionary of National Biography* (1917–)

Joseph Reed 1741–85
American Revolutionary politician

3 I am not worth purchasing, but such as I am, the King of Great Britain is not rich enough to do it.
replying to an offer from Governor George Johnstone of £10,000, and any office in the Colonies in the King's gift, if he were able successfully to promote a Union between the United Kingdom and the American Colonies

W. B. Read *Life and Correspondence of Joseph Reed* (1847)

John Reid 1947–
British Labour politician

4 What enjoyment does a single mother of three living in a council estate get? The only enjoyment sometimes is having a cigarette.

in *Sunday Times* 13 June 2004

5 If you have a PhD and a posh accent from a school like yours, you are regarded as a sophisticate . . . You called me an attack dog because I've got a Glasgow accent.
to Jeremy Paxman (see **Paxman** *306:5)*

on *Newsnight* progamme, 8 March 2005

Montague John Rendall 1862–1950
British member of the first BBC Board of Governors

6 Nation shall speak peace unto nation.

motto of the BBC; see **Bible** 41:14

Jean-François Paul de Gondi, Cardinal de Retz 1613–79
French cardinal

7 There is nothing in the world which does not have its decisive moment, and the masterpiece of good management is to recognize and grasp this moment.

Mémoires (1717) bk. 2

8 There are no small steps in great affairs.

Mémoires (1717) bk. 2

9 Nothing is so uneasy as to be the minister of a prince, of whom one is not the favourite.

Mémoires (1717) bk. 3

10 Fear is, of all passions, that which weakens the judgment most.

Mémoires (1717) bk. 3

11 A man who does not trust himself will never really trust anybody.

Mémoires (1717) bk. 3

1 Every numerous assembly is a mob, influenced by their passions, humours, and affections, which nothing but eloquence ever did or ever can engage.

attributed; Lord Chesterfield *Letters to his Son* 5 December 1749 (1901) vol. 1

2 The head of a party may do what he pleases; as long as he retains the confidence of his own friends, he can never do wrong.

attributed (not found in de Retz's writings); Adam Smith *The Theory of Moral Sentiments* (1759)

Walter Reuther 1907-70

American labour leader

3 If it looks like a duck, walks like a duck and quacks like a duck, then it just may be a duck.
   as a test, during the McCarthy era, of Communist affiliations

attributed

4 Injustice was as common as streetcars. When men walked into their jobs, they left their dignity, their citizenship and their humanity outside.
   on working life in America before the Wagner Act

attributed

Paul Revere 1735-1818

American patriot

5 To the memory of the glorious Ninety-two: members of the Honorable House of Representatives of the Massachusetts Bay who, undaunted by the insolent menaces of villains in power, from a strict regard to conscience and the liberties of their constituents on the 30th June 1768 voted NOT TO RESCIND.
   inscription on Revere's silver 'Liberty' bowl, 1768

attributed

6 [We agreed] that if the British went out by water, we would show two lanterns in the North Church steeple; and if by land, one as a signal; for we were apprehensive it would be difficult to cross the Charles River or get over Boston Neck.
   signals to be used if the British troops moved out of Boston

arrangements agreed with the Charlestown Committee of Safety on 16 April, 1775

Cecil Rhodes 1853-1902

South African statesman
see also **Last words** 227:13

7 Being an Englishman is the greatest prize in the lottery of life.

A. W. Jarvis *Jottings from an Active Life* (1928)

David Ricardo 1772-1823

British economist

8 Rent is that portion of the earth, which is paid to the landlord for the use of the original and indestructible powers of the soil.

On the Principles of Political Economy and Taxation (1817)

Condoleezza Rice 1954-

American Republican politician, National Security Advisor 2001-5, Secretary of State from 2005

9 We don't want the smoking gun to be a mushroom cloud.

interviewed by Wolf Blitzer for CNN, 8 September 2002; quoted on CNN.com 10 January 2003

1 When the Founding Fathers said 'we the people', they did not mean me. My ancestors were three-fifths of a man.

in *Independent* 3 April 2004 (see **Constitution** 102:1, **Constitution** 102:2)

Grantland Rice 1880–1954

American sports writer

2 All wars are planned by old men
In council rooms apart.

'The Two Sides of War' (1955)

Stephen Rice 1637–1715

Irish lawyer

3 I will drive a coach and six horses through the Act of Settlement.

W. King *State of the Protestants of Ireland* (1672)

Tim Rice 1944–

English songwriter

4 Don't cry for me, Argentina.
    from the musical Evita, *based on the life of Eva Perón*

title of song (1976)

Mandy Rice-Davies 1944–

English model and showgirl

5 *at the trial of Stephen Ward, 29 June 1963, on being told that Lord Astor claimed that her allegations, concerning himself and his house parties at Cliveden, were untrue:*
He would, wouldn't he?

in *Guardian* 1 July 1963

Ann Richards 1933–

American Democratic politician

6 That dog won't hunt.
    of Republican policies

keynote speech at the Democratic convention, 1988

7 Poor George, he can't help it—he was born with a silver foot in his mouth.
    of George **Bush**

keynote speech at the Democratic convention, 1988

Johann Paul Friedrich Richter ('Jean Paul') 1763–1825

German novelist

8 Providence has given to the French the empire of the land, to the English that of the sea, and to the Germans that of—the air!

Thomas Carlyle 'Jean Paul Friedrich Richter' in *Edinburgh Review* no. 91 (1827)

Adam Ridley 1942–

British economist, former Director of the Conservative Research Department

9 Parties come to power with silly, inconsistent and impossible policies because they have spent their whole period in opposition forgetting about the real world, destroying the lessons they learnt in government and clambering slowly back on to the ideological plain where they feel happiest.

in *RIPA Report* Winter 1985

Nicholas Ridley 1929–93
British Conservative politician

1 *of the European monetary union:*
This is all a German racket designed to take over the whole of Europe.
> *in an interview with Dominic Lawson, in the aftermath of which Ridley resigned from the Government*

in *Spectator* 14 July 1990

2 Seventeen unelected reject politicians with no accountability to anybody, who are not responsible for raising taxes, just spending money, who are pandered to by a supine parliament which also is not responsible for raising taxes.
> *of the European Commission*

in *Spectator* 14 July 1990

Louis Riel 1844–85
Canadian Métis political leader

3 People say the native stands on the edge of a chasm. It is not he who stands on the edge of a chasm; his claims are not false. They are just . . . Every step the Indian takes is based on a profound step of fairness.

diary, 6 May 1885

4 I have been hunted as an elk for fifteen years.

speaking at the end of his trial, 1 August 1885; *The Queen vs. Louis Riel* (1886)

5 Every day in which I have neglected to prepare myself to die was a day of mental alienation.

interview published in the *Regina Leader* shortly before his execution by hanging on 16 November 1885

Frank Roberts 1907–98
British diplomat

6 Eden . . . was rather like an Arab horse. He used to get terribly het up and excited and he had to be sort of kept down.

in *What Has Become of Us* Wide Vision Productions/Channel 4 television series, 29 March 1994

7 He just didn't understand Hitler or his ruthlessness. We in the Foreign Office kept telling him it was all in *Mein Kampf*, but he wouldn't believe it.
> *on Neville **Chamberlain***

in *Daily Telegraph* 10 January 1998; obituary

George Robertson 1946–
British Labour politician

8 Serbs out, Nato in, refugees back.

summing up the Nato objective in Kosovo, 7 June 1999

Maximilien Robespierre 1758–94
French revolutionary
*on Robespierre: see **Carlyle** 74:11*

9 I am no courtier, nor moderator, nor Tribune, nor defender of the people: I am myself the people.

speech at the Jacobin Club, 27 April 1792

10 *Citoyens, vouliez-vous une revolution sans revolution?*
Citizens, would you want a revolution without revolution?

speech to the Convention, 5 November 1792

11 The general will rules in society as the private will governs each separate individual.

Lettres à ses commettans (2nd series) 5 January 1793

1 Any law which violates the inalienable rights of man is essentially unjust and tyrannical; it is not a law at all.

Déclaration des droits de l'homme 24 April 1793, article 6; this article, in slightly different form, is recorded as having figured in Robespierre's *Projet* of 21 April 1793

2 Any institution which does not suppose the people good, and the magistrate corruptible, is evil.

Déclaration des droits de l'homme 24 April 1793, article 25

3 The revolutionary government is the despotism of liberty against tyranny.

speech, 5 February 1794

4 Wickedness is the root of despotism as virtue is the essence of the Republic.

in the Convention, 7 May 1794

5 One single will is necessary.

private note; S. A. Berville and J. F. Barrière *Papiers inédits trouvés chez Robespierre* vol. 2 (1828)

6 Intimidation without virtue is disastrous; virtue without intimidation is powerless.

J. M. Thompson *The French Revolution*; attributed

Mary Robinson 1944-

Irish Labour stateswoman; President 1990–97

7 Instead of rocking the cradle, they rocked the system.
   in her victory speech, paying tribute to the women of Ireland

in *The Times* 10 November 1990

8 There are 70 million people living on this globe who claim Irish descent. I will be proud to represent them.

inaugural speech as President, 1990

9 May it be a presidency where I the President can sing to you, citizens of Ireland, the joyous refrain of the 14th century Irish poet as recalled by W. B. Yeats: 'I am of Ireland . . . come dance with me in Ireland.'

inaugural speech as President, 1990

10 As a native of Ballina, one of the most western towns in the most western province of the most western nation in Europe, I want to say—'the West's awake.'

inaugural speech as President, 1990; see **Davis** 111:2

11 Now the time has arrived to give thought to the future, to consider how best the Office of President can serve the Irish people as the new millennium approaches.
   announcing that she would not seek a second term of office

in *Irish Times* 13 March 1997

Boyle Roche 1743–1807

Irish politician

12 Mr Speaker, I smell a rat; I see him forming in the air and darkening the sky; but I'll nip him in the bud.

attributed

Lord Rochester 1647–80

English poet
see also **Epitaphs** 136:3

13 A merry monarch, scandalous and poor.

'A Satire on King Charles II' (1697)

Almiro Rodrigues 1932–

Portuguese judge, presiding at the War Crimes Tribunal in The Hague

1 Individually you agreed to evil.

sentencing the Bosnian Serb General Radislav Krstic for his part in the massacre of Bosnian Muslims at Srebenica in July 1995

at The Hague, 2 August 2001

Sue Rodriguez 1951–94

Canadian activist for the legalization of assisted suicide

2 If I cannot give consent to my own death, then whose body is this? Who owns my life?

appealing to a subcommittee of the Canadian Commons, November 1992, as the victim of a terminal illness

in *Globe and Mail* 5 December 1992

Will Rogers 1879–1935

American actor and humorist

3 Politics has got so expensive that it takes a lot of money to even get beat with nowadays.

Daily Telegrams 28 June 1931

4 The more you read and observe about this Politics thing, you got to admit that each party is worse than the other. The one that's out always looks the best.

Illiterate Digest (1924)

5 A conservative is a man who has plenty of money and doesn't see why he shouldn't always have plenty of money . . . A Democrat is a fellow who never had any money but doesn't see why he shouldn't have some money.

Alex Ayres (ed.) *The Wit and Wisdom of Will Rogers* (1993)

6 I am not a member of any organized political party—I am a Democrat.

P. J. O'Brien *Will Rogers* (1935)

7 I don't know jokes—I just watch the government and report the facts.

'A Rogers Thesaurus' in *Saturday Review* 25 August 1962

8 Communism is like prohibition, it's a good idea but it won't work.

in 1927; *Weekly Articles* (1981) vol. 3

Mme Roland 1754–93

French revolutionary see **Last words** 227:9

Oscar Romero 1917–80

Salvadorean Roman Catholic priest, Archbishop of San Salvador

9 When a dictatorship seriously violates human rights and attacks the common good of the nation, when it becomes unbearable and closes all channels of dialogue, of understanding, of rationality, when this happens, the Church speaks of the legitimate right of insurrectional violence.

Alan Riding 'The Cross and the Sword in Latin America' (1981)

Eleanor Roosevelt 1884–1962

American humanitarian and diplomat
on Roosevelt: see **Stevenson** 380:17

10 Is there anything we can do for you? For you are the one in trouble now.

*to Harry **Truman**, who became President on the death of Franklin D. **Roosevelt***

in conversation, 12 April 1945

1 I cannot believe that war is the best solution. No one won the last war, and no one will win the next war.

letter to Harry Truman, 22 March 1948

2 I have always felt that anyone who wanted an election so much that they would use those methods did not have the character that I really admired in public life.
*on the tactics used by Richard **Nixon** in his 1950 Senatorial campaign against the actress and politician Helen Gahagan Douglas*

on 'Meet the Press' (NBC TV), 16 September 1956

3 No one can make you feel inferior without your consent.

in Catholic Digest August 1960

Franklin D. Roosevelt 1882–1945
American Democratic statesman, President of the US 1933–45
on Roosevelt: see **Churchill** 89:8, **Holmes** 187:4, **Truman** 400:12

4 These unhappy times call for the building of plans that . . . build from the bottom up and not from the top down, that put their faith once more in the forgotten man at the bottom of the economic pyramid.

radio address, 7 April 1932

5 I pledge you, I pledge myself, to a new deal for the American people.
accepting the presidential nomination

speech to the Democratic Convention in Chicago, 2 July 1932

6 The only thing we have to fear is fear itself.

inaugural address, 4 March 1933

7 In the field of world policy I would dedicate this Nation to the policy of the good neighbour.

inaugural address, 4 March 1933

8 We face the arduous days that lie before us in the warm courage of national unity.

*inaugural address, 4 March 1933; see **Bush** 67:3*

9 This generation of Americans has a rendezvous with destiny.

speech accepting renomination as President, 27 June 1936

10 I have seen war. I have seen war on land and sea. I have seen blood running from the wounded. I have seen men coughing out their gassed lungs. I have seen the dead in the mud. I have seen cities destroyed. I have seen 200 limping, exhausted men come out of line—the survivors of a regiment of 1,000 that went forward 48 hours before. I have seen children starving. I have seen the agony of mothers and wives. I hate war.

speech at Chautauqua, NY, 14 August 1936

11 I see one-third of a nation ill-housed, ill-clad, ill-nourished.

second inaugural address, 20 January 1937

12 The only sure bulwark of continuing liberty is a government strong enough to protect the interests of the people, and a people strong enough and well enough informed to maintain its sovereign control over its government.

'Fireside Chat' radio broadcast, 14 April 1938

13 When peace has been broken anywhere, the peace of all countries everywhere is in danger.

'Fireside Chat' radio broadcast, 3 September 1939

14 I am reminded of four definitions: A Radical is a man with both feet firmly planted—in the air. A Conservative is a man with two perfectly good legs who, however, has never learned to walk forward. A Reactionary is a somnambulist walking backwards. A Liberal is a man who uses his legs and his hands at the behest—at the command—of his head.

radio address to New York Herald Tribune Forum, 26 October 1939

15 On this tenth day of June 1940 the hand that held the dagger has struck it into the back of its neighbour.
on hearing that Italy had declared war on France

address at the University of Virginia, Charlottesville, 10 June 1940

1 I have said this before, but I shall say it again and again and again: Your boys are not going to be sent into any foreign wars.

speech in Boston, 30 October 1940

2 We have the men—the skill—the wealth—and above all, the will . . . We must be the great arsenal of democracy.

'Fireside Chat' radio broadcast, 29 December 1940

3 We, too, born to freedom, and believing in freedom, are willing to fight to maintain freedom. We, and all others who believe as deeply as we do, would rather die on our feet than live on our knees.
  on receiving the degree of Doctor of Civil Law from Oxford

on 19 June 1941; see **Ibarruri** *194:3*

4 We look forward to a world founded upon four essential human freedoms. The first is freedom of speech and expression—everywhere in the world. The second is freedom of every person to worship God in his own way—everywhere in the world. The third is freedom from want . . . everywhere in the world. The fourth is freedom from fear . . . anywhere in the world.

message to Congress, 6 January 1941

5 Yesterday, December 7, 1941—a date which will live in infamy—the United States of America was suddenly and deliberately attacked by naval and air forces of the Empire of Japan.

address to Congress, 8 December 1941

6 Books can not be killed by fire. People die, but books never die. No man and no force can abolish memory . . . In this war, we know, books are weapons. And it is a part of your dedication always to make them weapons for man's freedom.

'Message to the Booksellers of America' 6 May 1942

7 The American people are quite competent to judge a political party that works both sides of the street.

campaign speech in Boston, 4 November 1944

8 We have learned that we cannot live alone, at peace; that our own well-being is dependent on the well-being of other nations, far away. We have learned that we must live as men, and not as ostriches, nor as dogs in the manger. We have learned to be citizens of the world, members of the human community.

fourth inaugural address, 20 January 1945

9 Oh Lord, give us faith. Give us faith in Thee; faith in our sons; faith in each other; faith in our united crusade.

address to the nation, D-Day, 6 June 1944

10 It is fun to be in the same decade with you.
  cabled reply to Winston Churchill, acknowledging congratulations on his 60th birthday in 1942. Churchill was then 67

W. S. Churchill The Hinge of Fate (1950)

11 You've convinced me. Now go out and put pressure on me.

attributed; Peter Hennessy Whitehall (1990)

12 The work, my friend, is peace. More than an end of this war—an end to the beginnings of all wars.
  undelivered address for Jefferson Day, 13 April 1945, the day after Roosevelt died

Public Papers (1950) vol. 13

13 The only limit to our realization of tomorrow will be our doubts of today. Let us move forward with strong and active faith.
  undelivered address for Jefferson Day, 13 April 1945, final lines

Public Papers (1950) vol. 13

Theodore Roosevelt 1858–1919

American Republican statesman, 26th President of the US 1901–9
on Roosevelt: see **Hanna** 172:4, **Knox** 222:6; *see also* **Last words**
227:11

1 I wish to preach, not the doctrine of ignoble ease, but the
doctrine of the strenuous life.

speech to the Hamilton Club,
Chicago, 10 April 1899

2 I am as strong as a bull moose and you can use me to the
limit.

*'Bull Moose' subsequently became the popular name of the
Progressive Party*

letter to Mark **Hanna**, 27 June
1900

3 McKinley has no more backbone than a chocolate éclair!

*of William McKinley (1843–1901), Republican statesman and
25th President of the US, whose assassination brought about the
accession of Roosevelt*

H. T. Peck *Twenty Years of the
Republic* (1906)

4 The first requisite of a good citizen in this Republic of ours is
that he shall be able and willing to pull his weight.

speech in New York, 11 November
1902

5 There is a homely old adage which runs: 'Speak softly and
carry a big stick; you will go far.' If the American nation
will speak softly, and yet build and keep at a pitch of the
highest training a thoroughly efficient navy, the Monroe
Doctrine will go far.

speech in Chicago, 3 April 1903

6 A man who is good enough to shed his blood for the
country is good enough to be given a square deal
afterwards. More than that no man is entitled to, and less
than that no man shall have.

speech at the Lincoln Monument,
Springfield, Illinois, 4 June 1903;
see **Slogans** 369:3

7 Far and away the best prize that life offers is the chance to
work hard at work worth doing.

address at the State Fair, Syracuse,
New York Labour Day, 7
September 1903

8 You can no more make an agreement with those leaders of
Colombia than you can nail currant jelly to the wall. And
the failure to nail currant jelly to the wall is not due to the
nail. It's due to the currant jelly.

at the time of the Panama revolution, 1903

attributed by Edmund Morris, John
F. Kennedy Presidential Historians
Forum, 5 March 2002

9 The men with the muckrakes are often indispensable to the
well-being of society; but only if they know when to stop
raking the muck.

speech in Washington, 14 April
1906

10 It is not the critic who counts; not the man who points out
how the strong man stumbles, or where the doer of deeds
could have done better. The credit belongs to the man who
is actually in the arena.

'Citizenship in a Republic', speech
at the Sorbonne, Paris, 23 April
1910

11 We stand at Armageddon and we battle for the Lord.

speech at Progressive Party
Convention, Chicago, 17 June 1912

12 There is no room in this country for hyphenated
Americanism . . . The one absolutely certain way of bringing
this nation to ruin, of preventing all possibility of its
continuing to be a nation at all, would be to permit it to
become a tangle of squabbling nationalities.

speech in New York, 12 October
1915

13 One of our defects as a nation is a tendency to use what
have been called 'weasel words'. When a weasel sucks eggs
the meat is sucked out of the egg. If you use a 'weasel word'
after another, there is nothing left of the other.

speech in St Louis, 31 May 1916

1 Foolish fanatics . . . the men who form the lunatic fringe in all reform movements.

Autobiography (1913)

2 To announce that there must be no criticism of the president, or that we are to stand by the president, right or wrong, is not only unpatriotic and servile, but is morally treasonable to the American public.

in *Kansas City Star* 7 May 1918

3 No man is justified in doing evil on the ground of expediency.

Works (1925) vol. 15 'Latitude and Longitude among Reformers'

4 I have got such a bully pulpit!
  his personal view of the presidency

in *Outlook* (New York) 27 February 1909; see **Reagan** 322:8

Lord Rosebery 1847–1929
British Liberal statesman; Prime Minister, 1894–5

5 There is no need for any nation, however great, leaving the Empire, because the Empire is a commonwealth of nations.

speech in Adelaide, Australia, 18 January 1884

6 I have never known the sweets of place with power, but of place without power, of place with the minimum of power—that is a purgatory, and if not a purgatory it is a hell.

in *The Spectator* 6 July 1895

7 Imperialism, sane Imperialism, as distinguished from what I may call wild-cat Imperialism, is nothing but this—a larger patriotism.

speech, City of London Liberal Club, 5 May 1899

8 It is beginning to be hinted that we are a nation of amateurs.

Rectorial address at Glasgow University, 16 November 1900

9 No one outside an asylum wishes to be rid of it.
  of the British Empire

Rectorial address at Glasgow University, 16 November 1900

10 I must plough my furrow alone.
  speech on remaining outside the Liberal Party leadership, 19 July 1901

in *The Times* 20 July 1901

11 There are two supreme pleasures in life. One is ideal, the other real. The ideal is when a man receives the seals of office from his Sovereign. The real pleasure comes when he hands them back.

Sir Robert Peel (1899)

Ethel Rosenberg 1916–53
and Julius Rosenberg 1918–53
American husband and wife; convicted of spying for the Russians

12 We are innocent . . . To forsake this truth is to pay too high a price even for the priceless gift of life.
  petition for executive clemency, filed 9 January 1953

Ethel Rosenberg *Death House Letters* (1953)

13 We are the first victims of American Fascism.
  letter from Julius to Emanuel Bloch before the Rosenbergs' execution, 19 June 1953

Testament of Ethel and Julius Rosenberg (1954)

Dick Ross
British economist, former Deputy Director of the Central Policy Review Staff

14 You must think the unthinkable, but always wear a dark suit when presenting the results.

in the early 1970s; Peter Hennessy *Whitehall* (1990)

Christina Rossetti 1830–94
English poet

1 Our Indian Crown is in great measure the trapping of a splendid misery.
   on the siege of Kandahar

letter to Amelia Heimann, 29 July 1880

Jean Rostand 1894–1977
French biologist

2 Stupidity, outrage, vanity, cruelty, iniquity, bad faith, falsehood—we fail to see the whole array when it is facing in the same direction as we.

Pensées d'un biologiste (1939)

Lord Rothschild 1910–90
British administrator and scientist
on Rothschild: see **Hurd** 192:7

3 Politicians often believe that their world is the real one. Officials sometimes take a different view.
   on resigning as Director of the Central Policy Review Staff

in *The Times* 13 October 1974

4 The promises and panaceas that gleam like false teeth in the party manifestoes.

Meditations of a Broomstick (1977)

Jean-Jacques Rousseau 1712–78
French philosopher and novelist

5 The social contract

title of book, 1762

6 Man was born free, and everywhere he is in chains.

The Social Contract (1762)

7 Slaves become so debased by their chains as to lose even the desire of breaking from them.

The Social Contract (1762)

Maude Royden 1876–1956
English religious writer

8 The Church should go forward along the path of progress and be no longer satisfied only to represent the Conservative Party at prayer.

address at Queen's Hall, London, 16 July 1917

Richard Rumbold c.1622–85
English republican conspirator

9 I never could believe that Providence had sent a few men into the world, ready booted and spurred to ride, and millions ready saddled and bridled to be ridden.
   on the scaffold

T. B. Macaulay *History of England* vol. 1 (1849)

Donald Rumsfeld 1932–
American Republican politician and businessman, Defense Secretary from 2001

10 When they are being moved from place to place, will they be restrained in a way so that they are less likely to be able to kill an American soldier? You bet. Is it inhumane to do that? No. Would it be stupid to do anything else? Yes.
   on al-Qaeda prisoners being held in Cuba

in *The Times* 26 January 2002

1 You're thinking of Europe as Germany and France. I don't. I think that's old Europe. If you look at the entire Nato Europe today, the centre of gravity is shifting to the east.
to journalists who asked him about European hostility to a possible war, 22 January 2003

in *Independent* 21 February 2003

2 Stuff happens.
on looting in Iraq

press conference, 11 April 2003

3 You go to war with the Army you have. They're not the Army you might want or wish to have at a later time.

briefing to troops at a Town Hall Meeting in Kuwait, 8 December 2004

Robert Runcie 1921–2000
English Protestant clergyman; Archbishop of Canterbury

4 People are mourning on both sides of this conflict. In our prayers we shall quite rightly remember those who are bereaved in our own country and the relations of the young Argentinian soldiers who were killed. Common sorrow could do something to reunite those who were engaged in this struggle. A shared anguish can be a bridge of reconciliation. Our neighbours are indeed like us.

service of thanksgiving at the end of the Falklands war, St. Paul's Cathedral, London, 26 July 1982

Dean Rusk 1909–94
American politician; Secretary of State, 1961–9

5 We're eyeball to eyeball, and I think the other fellow just blinked.
on the Cuban missile crisis, 24 October 1962

in *Saturday Evening Post* 8 December 1962

6 Only one-third of human beings are asleep at one time, and the other two-thirds are awake and up to some mischief somewhere.

attributed, 1966

7 Scratch any American and underneath you'll find an isolationist.

to the British Foreign Secretary, George Brown; Tony Benn diary 12 January 1968

8 It has been said that power tends to corrupt, but that loss of power tends to corrupt absolutely.

attributed, 1968; see **Acton** 1:11

John Ruskin 1819–1900
English art and social critic

9 We Communists of the old school think that our property belongs to everybody, and everybody's property to us; so of course I thought the Louvre belonged to me as much as to the Parisians, and expected they would have sent word over to me, being an Art Professor, to ask whether I wanted it burnt down. But no message or intimation to that effect ever reached me.

Fors Clavigera (1871)

10 You have founded an entire Science of Political Economy, on what you have stated to be the constant instinct of man—the desire to defraud his neighbour.

Fors Clavigera (1871)

11 Visible governments are the toys of some nations, the diseases of others, the harness of some, the burdens of more, the necessity of all.

Fors Clavigera (1871)

12 I am, and my father was before me, a violent Tory of the old school; Walter Scott's school, that is to say, and Homer's.

Praeterita (1885)

1 The first duty of a State is to see that every child born therein shall be well housed, clothed, fed and educated, till it attain years of discretion.

Time and Tide (1867)

2 All mastership is not alike in principle; there are just and unjust masterships.

Time and Tide (1867)

3 You want to have voices in Parliament! Your voices are not worth a rat's squeak, either in Parliament or out of it, till you have some ideas to utter with them.

Time and Tide (1867)

4 It ought to be quite as natural and straightforward a matter for a labourer to take his pension from his parish, because he has deserved well of his parish, as for a man in higher rank to take his pension from his country, because he has deserved well of his country.

Unto this Last (1862) preface

5 The force of the guinea you have in your pocket depends wholly on the default of a guinea in your neighbour's pocket. If he did not want it, it would be of no use to you.

Unto this Last (1862)

6 Government and co-operation are in all things the laws of life; anarchy and competition the laws of death.

Unto this Last (1862)

7 Whereas it has long been known and declared that the poor have no right to the property of the rich, I wish it also to be known and declared that the rich have no right to the property of the poor.

Unto this Last (1862)

Bertrand Russell 1872–1970

British philosopher and mathematician

8 Envy is the basis of democracy.

The Conquest of Happiness (1930)

9 One should as a rule respect public opinion in so far as is necessary to avoid starvation and to keep out of prison, but anything that goes beyond this is voluntary submission to an unnecessary tyranny.

The Conquest of Happiness (1930)

10 Next to enjoying ourselves, the next greatest pleasure consists in preventing others from enjoying themselves, or, more generally, in the acquisition of power.

Sceptical Essays (1928)

11 The opinions that are held with passion are always those for which no good ground exists; indeed the passion is the measure of the holder's lack of rational conviction.

Sceptical Essays (1928)

12 If the Communists conquered the world it would be very unpleasant for a while, but not for ever.

attributed, 1958

13 Few people can be happy unless they hate some other person, nation, or creed.

attributed

14 Religion may in most of its forms be defined as the belief that the gods are on the side of the Government.

attributed

15 The trouble with the world is that the stupid are cocksure and the intelligent are full of doubt.

attributed

Lord John Russell 1792–1878

British Whig statesman; Prime Minister 1846–52, 1865–6
on Russell: see **Derby** 115:6, **Smith** 372:7

1 It is impossible that the whisper of a faction should prevail
against the voice of a nation.
    *reply to an Address from a meeting of 150,000 persons at
Birmingham on the defeat of the second Reform Bill, October
1831*

S. Walpole *Life of Lord John Russell*
(1889)

2 If peace cannot be maintained with honour, it is no longer
peace.

speech at Greenock, 19 September
1853; see **Disraeli** 121:15

3 Among the defects of the Bill, which were numerous, one
provision was conspicuous by its presence and another by
its absence.

speech to the electors of the City
of London, April 1859

Anwar al-Sadat 1918–81

Egyptian statesman, President 1970–81

4 Peace is much more precious than a piece of land.

speech in Cairo, 8 March 1978

Mohammed al-Sahhaf

Iraqi politician, Minister of Information in Saddam **Hussein**'s
government, nicknamed 'Comical Ali'

5 Baghdad is safe, protected. There are no American infidels
in Baghdad.
    press briefing during the war in Iraq

in *Sunday Telegraph* 13 April 2003

6 I now inform you that you are too far from reality.
    final briefing to the press in Baghdad

in *Sunday Telegraph* 13 April 2003

Andrei Sakharov 1921–89

Russian nuclear physicist

7 Every day I saw the huge material, intellectual and nervous
resources of thousands of people being poured into the
creation of a means of total destruction, something capable
of annihilating all human civilization. I noticed that the
control levers were in the hands of people who, though
talented in their own ways, were cynical.

Sakharov Speaks (1974)

Saki (Hector Hugh Munro) 1870–1916

Scottish writer

8 We all know that Prime Ministers are wedded to the truth,
but like other married couples they sometimes live apart.

The Unbearable Bassington (1912)

Lord Salisbury (Robert Arthur Talbot Gascoyne-Cecil, third Marquess of Salisbury) 1830–1903

British Conservative statesman; Prime Minister 1855–6, 1886–92,
1895–1902
on Salisbury: see **Bismarck** 44:3, **Disraeli** 121:11, **Goschen** 163:3,
Hennessy 180:2

9 She has given us foreign invasions, domestic rebellions; and
in quieter times the manly sport of landlord shooting.
    on Ireland

in *Saturday Review*, 1857

1 The witness of history is uniform to this, that Nemesis may spare the sagacious criminal, but never fails to overtake the weak, the undecided and the over-charitable fool.

in Saturday Review 10 March 1860

2 They believe intensely in amiable theories, they loved the sympathy and applause of their fellow men, they were kind-hearted, and charitably fancied everybody as well meaning as themselves; and therefore—so far as it can be said of any single man—they were the proximate causes of a civil convulsion which, for the horror of its calamities, stands alone in the history of the world.
of those he regarded as weak-willed liberals

in Saturday Review 10 March 1860

3 Free institutions, carried beyond the point which the culture of the nation justifies, cease to produce freedom. There is the freedom that makes each man free; and there is the freedom, so called, which makes each man the slave of the majority.

in Saturday Review 10 March 1860

4 The distribution of property and the distribution of political power are inseparably connected. If power is not made to go with property, property will, in the long run, infallibly follow power.

in Quarterly Review April 1860

5 We do not care to scrutinise too closely, the moral boundary which separates a reckless hustings pledge from premeditated fraud.

in Saturday Review February 1861

6 The axioms of the last age are the fallacies of the present, the principles which save one generation may be the ruin of the next. There is nothing abiding in political science but the necessity of truth, purity and justice.
*on Salisbury's ultimate political hero, William **Pitt** the Younger*

in Quarterly Review April 1861

7 No man was ever so yielding without ever being weak, or so stern without being obstinate.
*of William **Pitt** the Younger*

in Quarterly Review April 1861

8 There is nothing dramatic in the success of a diplomatist. His victories are made up of a series of microscopic advantages: of a judicious suggestion here, or an opportune civility there: of a wise concession at one moment, and a farsighted persistence at another; of sleepless tact, immovable calmness, and patience that no folly, no provocation, no blunders can shake.
on Lord Castlereagh

in Quarterly Review January 1862

9 *of intervention in the domestic quarrels of other countries:*
There is no practice which the experience of nations more uniformly condemns, and none which governments more consistently pursue.

in Quarterly Review April 1862

10 The common tendency of mankind is not towards union, but secession. The promptings of neighbourly jealousy find a readier ear than the dull suggestions of statesmanlike policy.
on America

in Quarterly Review October 1862

11 No one is fit to be trusted with a secret who is not prepared, if necessary, to tell an untruth to defend it.

in Saturday Review 15 November 1862

12 The just Nemesis which generally decrees that partisans shall be forced to do in office precisely that which they most loudly decried in opposition.

in Quarterly Review January 1862

1 In a carefully balanced structure like the European system of nations, each State has a vested right in the complete and real independence of its neighbour.

in *Quarterly Review* 1862

2 It is the same with all efforts to root up any evil by the expenditure of money. To attach a money value to the existence of an evil, even for the purpose of extirpating it, can have no other end than that of multiplying the evil.

in *Saturday Review* 10 January 1863

3 War, in whatever form it comes, is a horrible and barbarous thing. It must produce slaughter and rapine; it must often reduce the free to dependence, and the prosperous to ruin; it must frequently condemn proud and renowned nationalities to insignificance or to extinction.

in *Quarterly Review* April 1863

4 The politician who 'yields' to public opinion is simply a dishonourable man. No 'voice of the people', however distinct and powerful, can absolve a man from the guilt of professing doctrines in which he does not believe.

in *Saturday Review* 31 October 1863

5 Directly man has satisfied his most elementary material wants, the first aspiration of his amiable heart is for the privilege of being able to look down upon his neighbours.

in *Saturday Review* 1864

6 First rate men will not canvas mobs: and mobs will not elect first rate men.

in 1866; Andrew Roberts *Salisbury: Victorian Titan* (1999)

7 If it had been money instead of political support they had been dealing with there is not a jury in the country that would not have found them guilty of getting it upon false pretences.
of Derby and Disraeli

letter to his brother Lord Eustace Cecil, September 1867

8 To expect political support as a consequence of good Government is an optimist's dream. Good government avoids one of the causes of hate: but it does not inspire love.
of imperial rather than domestic government

in 1867; Andrew Roberts *Salisbury: Victorian Titan* (1999)

9 Too clever by half.
*of **Disraeli**'s amendment on Disestablishment*

speech, House of Commons, 30 March 1868; see **Salisbury** 345:2

10 [The] perils of change are so great, the promise of the most hopeful theories is so often deceptive, that it is frequently the wiser part to uphold the existing state of things, if it can be done, even though in point of argument it should be utterly indefensible.

in *Quarterly Review* October 1871

11 I have a profound distrust of government inspectors, and I am generally disposed to find them wrong.

to the Rev. Nathaniel Woodard, 1871; Andrew Roberts *Salisbury: Victorian Titan* (1999)

12 Horny-handed sons of toil.

in *Quarterly Review* October 1873; later popularized in the US by Denis Kearney (1847–1907)

13 English policy is to float lazily downstream, occasionally putting out a diplomatic boathook to avoid collisions.

letter to Lord Lytton, 9 March 1877

14 The commonest error in politics sticking to the carcasses of dead policies. When a mast falls overboard, you do not try to save a rope here and a spar there, in memory of its former utility; you can cut away the hamper altogether.

letter to Lord Lytton, 23 April 1877

1 These gentlemen of the press much exaggerate their own power . . . they bear much the relation to a man's unpopularity that flies do to a wound. If the wound exits, they can aggravate it and make it malignant, but they do not make the wound.

letter to Lord Lytton, 23 April 1877

2 No lesson seems to be so deeply inculcated by the experience of life as that you never should trust experts. If you believe the doctors, nothing is wholesome: if you believe the theologians, nothing is innocent: if you believe the soldiers, nothing is safe. They all require to have their strong wine diluted by a very large admixture of insipid common sense.

letter to Lord Lytton, 15 June 1877

3 One of the nuisances of the ballot is that when the oracle has spoken you never know what it means.

to G. M. Sandford, October 1877

4 If our ancestors had cared for the rights of other people, the British Empire would not have been made.

in J. Vincent (ed.) *Derby Diaries 1869–1878* (1994) 8 March 1878

5 The agonies of a man who has to finish a difficult negotiation, and at the same time to entertain four royalties at a country house can be better imagined than described.

letter to Lord Lyons, 5 June 1878

6 What with deafness, ignorance of French, and Bismarck's extraordinary mode of speech, Beaconsfield has the dimmest idea of what is going on—understands everything crossways—and imagines a perpetual conspiracy.
   letter to Lady Salisbury from the Congress of Berlin, 23 June 1878

Lady Gwendolen Cecil *Life of Robert, Marquis of Salisbury* (1921–32)

7 Whatever happens will be for the worse, and therefore it is in our interest that as little should happen as possible.

said to Lord Dufferin about events in Persia, December 1879; Andrew Roberts *Salisbury: Victorian Titan* (1999)

8 The Italians have very much the huffiness which you see occasionally in the governess of a family. They are always thinking themselves slighted.

letter to Sir Augustus Paget, 1879; Andrew Roberts *Salisbury: Victorian Titan* (1899)

9 There are marks of hurry which in so old a man are inexplicable. I suppose he still cherishes his belief in an early monastic retreat from this wicked world—and is feverishly anxious to annihilate all his enemies before he takes it.
   on Gladstone

letter to Arthur Balfour, 16 June 1880; compare **Churchill** 86:3

10 The duty was to represent the permanent as opposed to the passing feeling of the English nation.
   on the House of Lords

speech to Hackney Conservative Club, November 1880

11 I wish the English army may be equal to all the work his peace-loving policy has given it.
   *of **Gladstone***

letter to the Rev. Charles Conybeare, February 1881

12 As a rule I observe that the places where we win seats are the places where no Tory Leader has spoken.

letter to Arthur Balfour, 22 September 1881

13 To those who have found breakfast with difficulty and do not know where to find dinner, intricate questions of politics are a matter of comparatively secondary interest.

in 1881; Andrew Roberts *Salisbury: Victorian Titan* (1999)

14 A party whose mission it is to live entirely upon the discovery of grievances are apt to manufacture the element upon which they subsist.

speech at Edinburgh, 24 November 1882

15 Sobriety is a very good thing and philanthropy is a very good thing, but freedom is better than either.

speech at Kingston-upon-Thames, 15 June 1883

1 By a free country, I mean a country where people are allowed, so long as they do not hurt their neighbours, to do as they like. I do not mean a country where six men may make five men do exactly as they like.

speech to the Kingston and District Working Men's Conservative Association, June 1883

2 Possession of Ireland is our peculiar punishment, our unique affliction, among the family of nations. What crime have we committed, with what particular vice is our national character chargeable, that this chastisement should have befallen us?

in *Quarterly Review* October 1883

3 They who have the absolute power of preventing lamentable events, and knowing what is taking place, refuse to exercise that power, are responsible for what happens.

in the House of Lords, 12 February 1884

4 My epitaph must be: 'Died of writing inane letters to empty-headed Conservative Associations'. It is a miserable death to look forward to.

letter to Lady Janetta Manners, 1884 (Belvoir Papers)

5 Treaties do not affect to overrule the general impulses of populations.

speech at Newport, 7 October 1885

6 People imagine that where an evil exists, the Queen, the Lords and the Commons should stop it. I wonder they have not brought in an Act of Parliament to stop unfavourable weather on the occasion of political demonstrations.

speech at Newport, 7 October 1885

7 Nobody argues now. They give you an opinion neatly expressed in a single sentence, and that does the work of argument. My belief is that a fallacy in two lines will carry you further that a mathematical demonstration in two pages.

speech to Conservative Conference, St James's Hall Piccadilly, 15 May 1886

8 We have got back to the dangerous period of the year when Ministers go to baths, and revolutions take place in the Balkan peninsula.

letter to Sir Augustus Paget, July 1887

9 I was delighted to see you had run Wilfrid Blunt in. The great heart of the people always chuckles when a gentleman gets into the clutches of the law.
   *congratulating Arthur **Balfour** (Chief Secretary for Ireland) after the poet and diarist had been arrested for defying the Crimes Act*

letter to Balfour, 26 October 1887

10 Upon those points upon which they are precise they are not agreed, and upon those points upon which they are agreed they are not precise.
   challenging the Fair Traders to produce a detailed programme

speech to the National Unionist and Conservative Constituency Association Conference at Derby, 19 December 1887

11 We are part of the community of Europe and we must do our duty as such.

speech at Caernarvon, 10 April 1888

12 I do believe politicians would be far more ready to resign office if they did not feel that their doing so would give such infinite pleasure to their adversaries.

letter to the Duchess of Rutland, 8 March 1889

13 It may wear the appearance of some religious movement or pretend to the authority of some great moral effect. But underneath that cloak there is concealed that steady enemy of human liberty—the desire of men, whenever they may grasp a bit of power, to force others to conform their ideas to their own.
   warning to the Primrose League about the spirit of tyranny

in May 1889; Andrew Roberts *Salisbury: Victorian Titan* (1999)

1 We have been engaged in drawing lines upon maps where no white man's foot has ever trod. We have been giving away mountains and rivers and lakes to each other, only hindered by the small impediment that we never knew exactly where the mountains and rivers and lakes were.

speech at the Mansion House, August 1890

2 Parliament is a potent engine, and its enactments must always do something, but they very seldom do what the originators of these enactments meant. [Therefore most legislation] will have the effect of surrounding the industry which it touches with precautions and investigations, inspections and regulations, in which it will be slowly enveloped and stifled.

in *Times* March 1891

3 The use of Conservatism was to delay changes 'till they became harmless.

in Lady Rayleigh diary, 5 February 1892; Andrew Roberts *Salisbury: Victorian Titan* (1999)

4 The only true lasting benefit which the statesman can give the poor man is so to shape matters that the greatest possible liberty for the exercise of his own moral and intellectual qualities should be offered to him by law.
  on Joseph **Chamberlain***'s pressure to introduce old age pensions*

speech at Exeter, February 1892

5 The educationist is one of the daughters of the horse leech: and if you let him suck according to his will, he will soon have swallowed the slender increase of sustenance you are not tendering to the Voluntary schools . . . You had much better give no grant at all, and let the money go to build an ironclad.

letter to Arthur Balfour, November 1896

6 There is not such thing as a fixed policy, because policy like all organic entities is always in the making.

in 1896; Andrew Roberts *Salisbury: Victorian Titan* (1999)

7 Where property is in question I am guilty . . . of erecting individual liberty as an idol, and of resenting all attempts to destroy or fetter it; but when you pass from liberty to life, in no well-governed State, in no State governed according to the principles of common humanity, are the claims of mere liberty allowed to endanger the lives of the citizens.

in the House of Lords, 29 July 1897

8 If you consider the position of the Russians ethically, it is as bad as can be. Negotiating with them is like catching soaped eels.

to Joseph Chamberlain, 1899; Andrew Roberts *Salisbury: Victorian Titan* (1999)

9 It interests me that you are struck with the 'damned nigger' element in the British society of Bombay. It is bad enough in official and military circles here. I look upon it as not only offensive and unworthy but as representing what is now, and will be in a highly magnified proportion, a serious political danger. But I preach in the wilderness.
  to his former private secretary, now Governor of Bombay

letter to Lord Northcote, June 1900 Andrew Roberts *Salisbury: Victorian Titan* (1999)

10 I had secretly indulged the hope that we should be beaten in this election. A spell in Opposition is so good for bracing up the Conservative fibre of our party.

letter to Lord Granby, 6 October 1900

11 In making appointments I can count on a Scotchman not falling below a certain level, they may not be very clever, but they are safe not to be stupid. There is a strong resemblance between the Scotch and the Jews. They both begin as fighters, then become very religious and finally are devoted to money-making.

in Lady Rayleigh diary, 1900; Andrew Roberts *Salisbury: Victorian Titan* (1999)

1 England is, I believe, the only country in which, during a great war, eminent men write and speak publicly as if they belonged to the enemy.

speech, November 1901; Andrew Roberts *Salisbury: Victorian Titan* (1999)

2 It is a Party shackled by tradition; all the cautious people, all the timid, all the unimaginative, belong to it. It stumbles slowly and painfully from precedent to precedent with its eyes fixed on the ground.
   of the Conservative Party

letter to Lord Milner, 1901; Milner Papers

3 [The Admiralty would always] follow the progress of science at a respectful distance, always arriving at an appreciation of each successive invention just soon enough to find that it is obsolete, and never yielding their adhesion to anything new until the time has come to defend it against the claims of something newer.

Andrew Roberts *Salisbury: Victorian Titan* (1999)

4 By office boys for office boys.
   of the Daily Mail

H. Hamilton Fyfe *Northcliffe, an Intimate Biography* (1930)

5 Christianity forced its way up from being the religion of slaves and outcastes, to become the religion of the powerful and rich; but somehow it seems to have lost the power of forcing its way down again.

Andrew Roberts *Salisbury: Victorian Titan* (1999)

6 Confidence of success is almost success, and obstacles often fall by themselves before a determination to overcome them.
   moral written in a Hatfield tenant's autograph book

Andrew Roberts *Salisbury: Victorian Titan* (1999)

7 Did you ever hear of a man who having got rid of a boil on the back of his neck ever wants it back again?
   on the possibility of Lord Randolph Churchill's re-employment

Robert Rhodes James *Lord Randolph Churchill* (1959)

8 Dizzy intends to pursue the old game of talking Green in the House and Orange in the Lobby.

Andrew Roberts *Salisbury: Victorian Titan* (1999)

9 'Eat and be eaten' is the great law of political as of animated nature.

Andrew Roberts *Salisbury: Victorian Titan* (1999)

10 An emotion will shoot electrically through a crowd which might have appealed to each man by himself in vain.

Andrew Roberts *Salisbury: Victorian Titan* (1999)

11 The English aristocracy is a wonderful institution, not for its power, which is nothing, nor for its achievements, which are few, but for the gigantic impression it is able to make upon weak minds. Practically, its political power has dwindled to the prerogative of occasionally obstructing a theological measure for a limited period . . . [but it is] one of the stock nightmares of morbid brains. It takes its place with Antichrist and irremissible sin among the dismal spectres that haunt a disturbed imagination.

Andrew Roberts *Salisbury: Victorian Titan* (1999) 493

12 A highly-paid chairman is a luxury which should be reserved for the return of a good shareholders' dividend.

Andrew Roberts *Salisbury: Victorian Titan* (1999)

13 Hostility to Radicalism, incessant, implacable hostility, is the essential definition of Conservatism.

Andrew Roberts *Salisbury: Victorian Titan* (1999)

14 I am an utter unbeliever that anything that is violent will have permanent results.

Andrew Roberts *Salisbury: Victorian Titan* (1999)

1 If these gentlemen had their way, they would soon be asking me to defend the moon against a possible attack from Mars.

of his senior military advisers, and their tendency to see threats which did not exist

Robert Taylor *Lord Salisbury* (1975)

2 An indiscreet admirer is a far more intolerable nuisance than an acrimonious enemy.

Andrew Roberts *Salisbury: Victorian Titan* (1999)

3 In this country we have got to look upon Budget promises as made of the same stuff as lovers' oaths.

Andrew Roberts *Salisbury: Victorian Titan* (1999)

4 I rank myself no higher in the scheme of things than a policeman—whose utility would disappear if there were no criminals.

comparing his role in the Conservative Party with that of **Gladstone**

Lady Gwendolen Cecil *Biographical Studies . . . of Robert, Third Marquess of Salisbury* (1962)

5 It's difficult enough to go around doing what is right without going around trying to do good.

Andrew Roberts *Salisbury: Victorian Titan* (1999)

6 I wish party government was at the bottom of the sea. It is only insincerity codified.

Arthur Hardinge *Life of Henry Herbert, 4th Earl of Carnarvon* (1925) vol. 2

7 One of the difficulties about great thinkers is that they so often think wrong.

Andrew Roberts *Salisbury: Victorian Titan* (1999)

8 A parapet which gives way when you lean upon it is more dangerous than no parapet at all.

on his private uncertainty of the degree to which he could rely on colleagues' support for the Reform Bill

Andrew Roberts *Salisbury: Victorian Titan* (1999)

9 The result of recent experience is that 'if you wish to keep a secret you must say nothing 1. To Cabinet Ministers. 2. To Foreign Diplomats. 3. To the War Office'.

in minutes to Lord Bertie

Andrew Roberts *Salisbury: Victorian Titan* (1999)

10 To defend a bad policy as an 'error of judgement' does not excuse it—the right functioning of a man's judgement is his most fundamental responsibility.

Gwendolen Cecil *Life of Robert, Marquis of Salisbury* (1921–32) vol. 3

11 To loot somebody or something is the common object, under a thick varnish of pious phrases.

rediscovering his fear of socialism

Andrew Roberts *Salisbury: Victorian Titan* (1999)

12 A treaty is in most cases the result of an employment of force openly applied or covertly threatened.

Andrew Roberts *Salisbury: Victorian Titan* (1999)

13 A very useful institution. It fosters a wholesome taste for bright colours, and gives old men who have good legs an excuse for showing them.

of the Order of the Garter, which had been awarded to both his father and grandfather as well as the early Cecils

in Houghton Papers; Andrew Roberts *Salisbury: Victorian Titan* (1999)

14 When a man says that he agrees with me in principle, I am quite certain that he does not agree with me in practice.

Andrew Roberts *Salisbury: Victorian Titan* (1999)

15 When great men get drunk with a theory, it is the little men who have the headache.

on political theorists

Andrew Roberts *Salisbury: Victorian Titan* (1899)

16 [Whitehall] will create business for itself surely as a new railway will create traffic.

Andrew Roberts *Salisbury: Victorian Titan* (1999)

Lord Salisbury (Robert Arthur James Gascoyne-Cecil, fifth Marquess of Salisbury) 1893–1972

British Conservative politician

1 I never shared the optimistic views of some of our friends
that the old gentleman would be willing to retire gracefully
into the background.
of Winston Churchill in 1946

John Ramsden *The Age of Churchill and Eden, 1940–1957* (1995)

2 Too clever by half.
*of Iain **Macleod**, Colonial Secretary, 'in his relationship to the
white communities of Africa'*

in the House of Lords, 7 March 1961; see **Salisbury** 339:9

Sallust 86–35 BC

Roman historian

3 *Alieni appetens, sui profusus.*
Greedy for the property of others, extravagant with his own.

Catiline

4 *Quieta movere magna merces videbatur.*
To stir up undisputed matters seemed a great reward in
itself.

Catiline

5 *Esse quam videri bonus malebat.*
He preferred to be rather than to seem good.
of Cato

Catiline

6 *Urbem venalem et mature perituram, si emptorem invenerit.*
A venal city ripe to perish, if a buyer can be found.
of Rome

Jugurtha

7 *Punica fide.*
With Carthaginian trustworthiness.
meaning treachery

Jugurtha

Alex Salmond 1954–

Scottish Nationalist politician
*on Salmond: see **Steel** 379:3*

8 Nobody ever celebrated Devolution Day.
asserting his belief in full independence

in *Independent* 2 April 1992

9 I do not want to be separate from anything. I want for my
country to be joined in co-operation and mutual respect—
on a footing of equality—with all the nations of Europe.

in *Scotsman* 27 November 1998

10 The Scottish parliament is our passport to independence.
*outgoing speech as party leader to the Scottish Nationalist Party
Conference*

in *Guardian* 23 September 2000

Anthony Sampson 1926–2004

British author and journalist

11 A secret tome of *The Great and the Good* is kept, listing
everyone who has the right, safe qualifications of
worthiness, soundness and discretion; and from this tome
came the stage army of committee people.

Anatomy of Britain Today (1965)

Lord Sandwich 1718–92

British politician and diplomat; First Lord of the Admiralty

1 If any man will draw up his case, and put his name at the foot of the first page, I will give him an immediate reply. Where he compels me to turn over the sheet, he must wait my leisure.
  on appeals made by officers to the Navy Board

N. W. Wraxall *Memoirs* (1884) vol. 1

George Santayana 1863–1952

Spanish-born philosopher and critic

2 Fanaticism consists in redoubling your effort when you have forgotten your aim.

The Life of Reason (1905); introduction

3 Those who cannot remember the past are condemned to repeat it.

The Life of Reason (1905)

Jacques Santer 1937–

Luxembourgeois politician, former head of the European Commission

4 I note with considerable satisfaction that I am whiter than white.
  of the inquiry into fraud at the European Commission

at a news conference, 16 March 1999

Nicolas Sarkozy 1955–

French politician

5 The referendum? It'll be a small no . . . or a big no.

attributed in *Guardian* 27 May 2005 (online edition)

Patrick Sarsfield c.1655–93

Irish Jacobite
see also **Last words** 228:8

6 As low as we now are, change kings with us, and we will fight it over again with you.
  to English officers during negotiations for the Treaty of Limerick, 1690

in *Dictionary of National Biography* (1917–)

Jean-Paul Sartre 1905–80

French philosopher, novelist, dramatist, and critic

7 When the rich wage war it's the poor who die.

Le Diable et le bon Dieu (1951)

Sayings see Proverbs and sayings

Hugh Scanlon 1913–

British trade union leader

8 Of course liberty is not licence. Liberty in my view is conforming to majority opinion.

television interview, 9 August 1977

Arthur Scargill 1938-

British trades-union leader

1 Parliament itself would not exist in its present form had people not defied the law.

evidence to House of Commons Select Committee on Employment, 2 April 1980

2 I wouldn't vote for Ken Livingstone if he were running for mayor of Toytown.

in *Guardian* 3 May 2000

Lord Scarman 1911-2004

British judge

3 The people as a source of sovereign power are in truth only occasional partners in the constitutional minuet danced for most of the time by Parliament and the political party in power.

The Shape of Things to Come (1989)

4 A government above the law is a menace to be defeated.

Why Britain Needs a Written Constitution 1992

5 Men still feel the need to keep the government in order. The feeling is deep, and as old as man.

Why Britain Needs a Written Constitution 1992

6 *on the need for a written constitution:*
No bevy of men, not even parliament, could always be trusted to safeguard human rights.

in conversation, 1982; Anthony Sampson *The Essential Anatomy of Britain* (1992)

7 When times are abnormally alive with fear and prejudice, the common law is at a disadvantage: it cannot resist the will, however frightened and prejudiced it may be, of parliament.
after delivering a lecture advocating the establishment of a Bill of Rights

in conversation, 20 July 1992; Anthony Sampson *The Essential Anatomy of Britain* (1992)

Arthur M. Schlesinger Jr. 1917-

American historian

8 The answer to the runaway Presidency is not the messenger-boy Presidency. The American democracy must discover a middle way between making the President a czar and making him a puppet.

The Imperial Presidency (1973) preface

9 Suppose . . . that Lenin had died of typhus in Siberia in 1895 and Hitler had been killed on the western front in 1916. What would the twentieth century have looked like now?

The Cycles of American History (1986)

Caroline Kennedy Schlossberg 1958-

American writer, daughter of John F. **Kennedy**

10 Now it is our turn to prove that the New Frontier was not a place in time, but a timeless call.

speech at the Democratic Convention, 15 August 2000; see **Kennedy** 212:2

Patricia Schroeder 1940-

American Democratic politician

11 Ronald Reagan . . . is attempting a great breakthrough in political technology—he has been perfecting the Teflon-coated Presidency. He sees to it that nothing sticks to him.

speech in the US House of Representatives, 2 August 1983

E. F. Schumacher 1911–77
German-born economist

1 It was not the power of the Spaniards that destroyed the
Aztec Empire but the disbelief of the Aztecs in themselves.

Roots of Economic Growth (1962)

2 Small is beautiful. A study of economics as if people
mattered.

title of book, 1973

Carl Schurz 1829–1906
American soldier and politician

3 My country, right or wrong; if right, to be kept right; and if
wrong, to be set right!

speech, US Senate, 29 February
1872

Claud Schuster 1869–1956
British civil servant

4 *of the relationship between the Prime Minister and the Cabinet:*
Like the procreation of eels, [it] is slippery and mysterious.

G. H. L. Le May *The Victorian
Constitution* (1979)

H. Norman Schwarzkopf III 1934–
American general, Commander of US forces in the Gulf War

5 Seven months ago I could give a single command and
541,000 people would immediately obey it. Today I can't
get a plumber to come to my house.

in *Newsweek* 11 November 1991;
see **Truman** 401:5

C. P. Scott 1846–1932
British journalist; editor of the *Manchester Guardian*, 1872–1929

6 Comment is free, but facts are sacred.

in *Manchester Guardian* 5 May
1921; see **Stoppard** 382:4

Sir Walter Scott 1771–1832
Scottish novelist and poet

7 Breathes there the man, with soul so dead,
Who never to himself hath said,
This is my own, my native land!
Whose heart hath ne'er within him burned,
As home his footsteps he hath turned
From wandering on a foreign strand!

The Lay of the Last Minstrel (1805)

8 Now is the stately column broke,
The beacon-light is quench'd in smoke,
The trumpet's silver sound is still,
The warder silent on the hill!
  on the death of Pitt

Marmion (1808); introduction to
canto 1

John Seeley 1834–95
English historian

9 We [the English] seem, as it were, to have conquered and
peopled half the world in a fit of absence of mind.

The Expansion of England (1883);
see **Hailsham** 168:10

John Selden 1584–1654

English historian and antiquary

1 Ignorance of the law excuses no man; not that all men know the law, but because 'tis an excuse every man will plead, and no man can tell how to confute him.

Table Talk (1689) 'Law'

2 A king is a thing men have made for their own sakes, for quietness' sake. Just as in a family one man is appointed to buy the meat.

Table Talk (1689) 'Of a King'

3 There is not anything in the world so much abused as this sentence, *Salus populi suprema lex esto*.

Table Talk (1689) 'People'; see **Cicero** 93:3

Arthur Seldon 1916–

British economist

4 Government of the busy by the bossy for the bully.
   subheading on over-government

Capitalism (1990)

W. C. Sellar 1898–1951
and R. J. Yeatman 1898–1968

British writers

5 The Cavaliers (Wrong but Wromantic) and the Roundheads (Right but Repulsive).

1066 and All That (1930)

6 The Rump Parliament—so called because it had been sitting for such a long time.

1066 and All That (1930)

7 Charles II was always very merry and was therefore not so much a king as a Monarch.

1066 and All That (1930)

8 The National Debt is a very Good Thing and it would be dangerous to pay it off, for fear of Political Economy.

1066 and All That (1930)

9 Most memorable . . . was the discovery (made by all the rich men in England at once) that women and children could work twenty-five hours a day in factories without many of them dying or becoming excessively deformed. This was known as the Industrial Revelation.

1066 and All That (1930)

10 Gladstone . . . spent his declining years trying to guess the answer to the Irish Question; unfortunately whenever he was getting warm, the Irish secretly changed the Question.

1066 and All That (1930)

11 AMERICA was thus clearly top nation, and History came to a .

1066 and All That (1930)

Seneca ('the Younger') c.4 BC–AD 65

Roman philosopher and poet

12 *Non habemus illos hostes, sed facimus.*
   They are not enemies when we acquire them; we make them so.
   on slaves

Epistulae Morales no. 47, sect. 5

Gitta Sereny 1923–

Hungarian-born British writer and journalist

1 *to Albert Speer, who having always denied knowledge of the
Holocaust had said that he was at fault in having 'looked away':*
You cannot look away from something you don't know. If
you looked away, then you knew.

recalled on BBC2 *Reputations*, 2
May 1996

William Seward 1801–72

American politician

2 I know, and all the world knows, that revolutions never go
backward.

speech at Rochester, 25 October
1858

Edward Sexby d. 1658

English conspirator

3 Killing no murder briefly discourst in three questions.

title of pamphlet (an apology for
tyrannicide, 1657)

Tokyo Sexwale 1953–

South African politician and businessman

4 The president's shoes are huge and Thabo has tiny feet.
   *of Thabo **Mbeki** as President of South Africa*

quoted on *BBC News Online*
website, 7 August 2001

5 If blacks get hurt, I get hurt. If whites get hurt, that's my
wife, and if you harm coloured people, you're looking for
my children. Your unity embodies who I am.

quoted in *Biographies of Special
South Africans* (website
www.zar.co.za)

Anthony Ashley Cooper, Lord Shaftesbury 1621–83

English peer, in the English Civil War, adherent first of the royalist
and then (from 1644) of the Parliamentary cause; in the reign of
Charles II, supporter of **Monmouth**'s claim to the succession
on Shaftesbury: see **Cromwell** 106:9, **Dryden** 127:3

6 *refusing the claims of Cromwell's House of Lords:*
Admit lords, and you admit all.

in *Dictionary of National Biography*
(1917–)

William Shakespeare 1564–1616

English dramatist

7 What's the matter, you dissentious rogues,
That, rubbing the poor itch of your opinion,
Make yourselves scabs?

Coriolanus (1608)

8   He that depends
Upon your favours swims with fins of lead,
And hews down oaks with rushes.

Coriolanus (1608)

9 Hear you this Triton of the minnows? mark you
His absolute 'shall'?

Coriolanus (1608)

10 What is the city but the people?

Coriolanus (1608)

11 You common cry of curs! whose breath I hate
As reek o' the rotten fens, whose loves I prize
As the dead carcases of unburied men
That do corrupt my air,—I banish you.

Coriolanus (1608)

1   Despising,
For you, the city, thus I turn my back:
There is a world elsewhere.

Coriolanus (1608)

2   The beast
With many heads butts me away.

Coriolanus (1608)

3 Let me have war, say I; it exceeds peace as far as day does
night; it's spritely, waking, audible, and full of vent. Peace is
a very apoplexy, lethargy: mulled, deaf, sleepy, insensible; a
getter of more bastard children than war's a destroyer of
men.

Coriolanus (1608)

4   I think he'll be to Rome
As is the osprey to the fish, who takes it
By sovereignty of nature.

Coriolanus (1608)

5 Why should we pay tribute? If Caesar can hide the sun from
us with a blanket, or put the moon in his pocket, we will
pay him tribute for light; else, sir, no more tribute.

Cymbeline (1609–10)

6   The art o' th' court,
As hard to leave as keep, whose top to climb
Is certain falling, or so slipp'ry that
The fear's as bad as falling.

Cymbeline (1609–10)

7 But in the gross and scope of my opinion,
This bodes some strange eruption to our state.

Hamlet (1601)

8 His greatness weighed, his will is not his own,
For he himself is subject to his birth.
He may not, as unvalued persons do,
Carve for himself, for on his choice depends
The sanity and health of the whole state;
And therefore must his choice be circumscribed
Unto the voice and yielding of that body
Whereof he is the head.

Hamlet (1601)

9 Something is rotten in the state of Denmark.

Hamlet (1601)

10 The time is out of joint; O cursèd spite,
That ever I was born to set it right!

Hamlet (1601)

11 For who would bear the whips and scorns of time,
The oppressor's wrong, the proud man's contumely,
The pangs of disprized love, the law's delay,
The insolence of office, and the spurns
That patient merit of the unworthy takes,
When he himself might his quietus make
With a bare bodkin? . . .
Thus conscience doth make cowards of us all.

Hamlet (1601)

12 Madness in great ones must not unwatched go.

Hamlet (1601)

13   Indeed this counsellor
Is now most still, most secret, and most grave,
Who was in life a foolish prating knave.

Hamlet (1601)

14 And where the offence is let the great axe fall.

Hamlet (1601)

15 The great man down, you mark his favourite flies;
The poor advanced makes friends of enemies.

Hamlet (1601)

16   Diseases desperate grown,
By desperate appliances are relieved,
Or not at all.

Hamlet (1601)

1 We go to gain a little patch of ground,   *Hamlet* (1601)
That hath in it no profit but the name.

2   Rightly to be great   *Hamlet* (1601)
Is not to stir without great argument,
But greatly to find quarrel in a straw
When honour's at the stake.

3 There's such divinity doth hedge a king,   *Hamlet* (1601)
That treason can but peep to what it would.

4 Rebellion lay in his way, and he found it.   *Henry IV, Part 1* (1597)

5 It was always yet the trick of our English nation, if they *Henry IV, Part 2* (1597)
have a good thing, to make it too common.

6 Uneasy lies the head that wears a crown.   *Henry IV, Part 2* (1597)

7 O England! model to thy inward greatness,   *Henry V* (1599)
Like little body with a mighty heart,
What might'st thou do, that honour would thee do,
Were all thy children kind and natural!
But see thy fault!

8 A little touch of Harry in the night.   *Henry V* (1599)

9 Discuss unto me; art thou officer?   *Henry V* (1599)
Or art thou base, common and popular?

10 I think the king is but a man, as I am: the violet smells to *Henry V* (1599)
him as it doth to me.

11 I am afeard there are few die well that die in a battle; for *Henry V* (1599)
how can they charitably dispose of any thing when blood is
their argument?

12 Every subject's duty is the king's; but every subject's soul is *Henry V* (1599)
his own.

13 Upon the king! let us our lives, our souls,   *Henry V* (1599)
Our debts, our careful wives,
Our children, and our sins lay on the king!
We must bear all. O hard condition!

14   What infinite heart's ease   *Henry V* (1599)
Must kings neglect, that private men enjoy!
And what have kings that privates have not too,
Save ceremony, save general ceremony?

15 Put forth thy hand, reach at the glorious gold.   *Henry VI, Part 2* (1592)

16 Is this the fashion of the court of England?   *Henry VI, Part 2* (1592)
Is this the government of Britain's isle,
And this the royalty of Albion's king?

17 I say it was never merry world in England since gentlemen *Henry VI, Part 2* (1592)
came up.

18 The first thing we do, let's kill all the lawyers.   *Henry VI, Part 2* (1592)

19 Is not this a lamentable thing, that of the skin of an   *Henry VI, Part 2* (1592)
innocent lamb should be made parchment? that parchment,
being scribbled o'er, should undo a man?

1 Thou hast most traitorously corrupted the youth of the realm in erecting a grammar school: and whereas, before, our forefathers had no other books but the score and the tally, thou hast caused printing to be used; and, contrary to the king, his crown and dignity, thou hast built a paper-mill.

Henry VI, Part 2 (1592)

2 Peace! impudent and shameless Warwick, peace; Proud setter up and puller down of kings.

Henry VI, Part 3 (1592)

3   You know his nature, That he's revengeful; and I know, his sword Hath a sharp edge; it's long, and 't may be said, It reaches far, and where 'twill not extend, Thither he darts it.
    the Duke of Norfolk of Cardinal Wolsey

Henry VIII (1613)

4 Farewell! a long farewell, to all my greatness!

Henry VIII (1613)

5   I have ventured, Like little wanton boys that swim on bladders, This many summers in a sea of glory, But far beyond my depth . . . Vain pomp and glory of this world, I hate ye: I feel my heart new opened. O how wretched Is that poor man that hangs on princes' favours! There is, betwixt that smile we would aspire to, That sweet aspect of princes, and their ruin, More pangs and fears than wars or women have; And when he falls, he falls like Lucifer, Never to hope again.

Henry VIII (1613)

6 Cromwell, I charge thee, fling away ambition: By that sin fell the angels; how can man then, The image of his Maker, hope to win by't? Love thyself last: cherish those hearts that hate thee; Corruption wins not more than honesty. Still in thy right hand carry gentle peace, To silence envious tongues: be just, and fear not. Let all the ends thou aim'st at be thy country's, Thy God's, and truth's: then if thou fall'st, O Cromwell! Thou fall'st a blessed martyr.

Henry VIII (1613)

7 Had I but served my God with half the zeal I served my king, he would not in mine age Have left me naked to mine enemies.

Henry VIII (1613)

8 In her days every man shall eat in safety Under his own vine what he plants; and sing The merry songs of peace to all his neighbours.

Henry VIII (1613)

9 You blocks, you stones, you worse than senseless things! O you hard hearts, you cruel men of Rome, Knew you not Pompey?

Julius Caesar (1599)

10 CAESAR: Speak; Caesar is turned to hear.
SOOTHSAYER: Beware the ides of March.

Julius Caesar (1599)

11   Ye gods, it doth amaze me, A man of such a feeble temper should So get the start of the majestic world, And bear the palm alone.

Julius Caesar (1599)

1 Why, man, he doth bestride the narrow world
Like a Colossus; and we petty men
Walk under his huge legs, and peep about
To find ourselves dishonourable graves.
Men at some time are masters of their fates:
The fault, dear Brutus, is not in our stars,
But in ourselves, that we are underlings.

Julius Caesar (1599)

2 'Brutus' will start a spirit as soon as 'Caesar'.
Now in the names of all the gods at once,
Upon what meat doth this our Caesar feed,
That he is grown so great?

Julius Caesar (1599)

3 When could they say, till now, that talked of Rome,
That her wide walls encompassed but one man?
Now is it Rome indeed and room enough,
When there is in it but one only man.

Julius Caesar (1599)

4 Let me have men about me that are fat;
Sleek-headed men and such as sleep o' nights;
Yond' Cassius has a lean and hungry look;
He thinks too much: such men are dangerous.

Julius Caesar (1599)

5 Such men as he be never at heart's ease,
Whiles they behold a greater than themselves,
And therefore are they very dangerous.

Julius Caesar (1599)

6 Th' abuse of greatness is, when it disjoins
Remorse from power.

Julius Caesar (1599)

7   'Tis a common proof,
That lowliness is young ambition's ladder,
Whereto the climber-upward turns his face;
But when he once attains the upmost round,
He then unto the ladder turns his back,
Looks in the clouds, scorning the base degrees
By which he did ascend.

Julius Caesar (1599)

8   O conspiracy!
Sham'st thou to show thy dangerous brow by night,
When evils are most free?

Julius Caesar (1599)

9 Let us be sacrificers, but not butchers, Caius.

Julius Caesar (1599)

10 But when I tell him he hates flatterers,
He says he does, being then most flattered.

Julius Caesar (1599)

11 CAESAR: The ides of March are come.
SOOTHSAYER: Ay, Caesar; but not gone.

Julius Caesar (1599)

12 If I could pray to move, prayers would move me;
But I am constant as the northern star,
Of whose true-fixed and resting
There is no fellow in the firmament.
The skies are painted with unnumbered sparks,
They are all fire and every one doth shine,
But there's but one in all doth hold his place:
So, in the world; 'tis furnished well with men,
And men are flesh and blood, and apprehensive;
Yet in the number I do know but one
That unassailable holds on his rank,
Unshaked of motion: and that I am he.

Julius Caesar (1599)

13 *Et tu, Brute?* Then fall, Caesar!

Julius Caesar (1599)

14 Ambition's debt is paid.

Julius Caesar (1599)

1 CASSIUS: How many ages hence   *Julius Caesar* (1599)
   Shall this our lofty scene be acted o'er,
   In states unborn, and accents yet unknown!
   BRUTUS: How many times shall Caesar bleed in sport.

2 Waving our red weapons o'er our heads   *Julius Caesar* (1599)
   Let's all cry 'Peace, freedom, and liberty!'

3 O mighty Caesar! dost thou lie so low?   *Julius Caesar* (1599)
   Are all thy conquests, glories, triumphs, spoils,
   Shrunk to this little measure?

4   Caesar's spirit, ranging for revenge,   *Julius Caesar* (1599)
   With Ate by his side, come hot from hell,
   Shall in these confines, with a monarch's voice
   Cry, 'Havoc!' and let slip the dogs of war;
   That this foul deed shall smell above the earth
   With carrion men, groaning for burial.

5 Not that I loved Caesar less, but that I loved Rome more.   *Julius Caesar* (1599)

6 As he was valiant, I honour him: but, as he was ambitious,   *Julius Caesar* (1599)
   I slew him.

7 Friends, Romans, countrymen, lend me your ears;   *Julius Caesar* (1599)
   I come to bury Caesar, not to praise him.
   The evil that men do lives after them,
   The good is oft interrèd with their bones;
   So let it be with Caesar. The noble Brutus
   Hath told you Caesar was ambitious;
   If it were so, it was a grievous fault;
   And grievously hath Caesar answered it.

8 He was my friend, faithful and just to me: *Julius Caesar* (1599)
   But Brutus says he was ambitious;
   And Brutus is an honourable man.

9 When that the poor have cried, Caesar hath wept;   *Julius Caesar* (1599)
   Ambition should be made of sterner stuff.

10   On the Lupercal   *Julius Caesar* (1599)
   I thrice presented him a kingly crown
   Which he did thrice refuse: was this ambition?

11 You all did love him once, not without cause.   *Julius Caesar* (1599)

12 But yesterday the word of Caesar might   *Julius Caesar* (1599)
   Have stood against the world; now lies he there,
   And none so poor to do him reverence.

13 This was the most unkindest cut of all.   *Julius Caesar* (1599)

14 O! what a fall was there, my countrymen;   *Julius Caesar* (1599)
   Then I, and you, and all of us fell down,
   Whilst bloody treason flourished over us.

15 I come not, friends, to steal away your hearts: *Julius Caesar* (1599)
   I am no orator, as Brutus is;
   But, as you know me all, a plain, blunt man,
   That love my friend.

16 For I have neither wit, nor words, nor worth,   *Julius Caesar* (1599)
   Action, nor utterance, nor power of speech,
   To stir men's blood; I only speak right on;
   I tell you that which you yourselves do know.

1   But were I Brutus,   *Julius Caesar* (1599)
And Brutus Antony, there were an Antony
Would ruffle up your spirits, and put a tongue
In every wound of Caesar, that should move
The stones of Rome to rise and mutiny.

2 Now let it work; mischief, thou art afoot,   *Julius Caesar* (1599)
Take thou what course thou wilt!

3 He shall not live; look, with a spot I damn him.   *Julius Caesar* (1599)

4 This is a slight unmeritable man,   *Julius Caesar* (1599)
Meet to be sent on errands.

5 There is a tide in the affairs of men,   *Julius Caesar* (1599)
Which, taken at the flood, leads on to fortune;
Omitted, all the voyage of their life
Is bound in shallows and in miseries.
On such a full sea are we now afloat,
And we must take the current when it serves,
Or lose our ventures.

6 O Julius Caesar! thou art mighty yet!   *Julius Caesar* (1599)
Thy spirit walks abroad, and turns our swords
In our own proper entrails.

7 This was the noblest Roman of them all;   *Julius Caesar* (1599)
All the conspirators save only he
Did that they did in envy of great Caesar;
He, only, in a general honest thought
And common good to all, made one of them.
His life was gentle, and the elements
So mixed in him that Nature might stand up
And say to all the world, 'This was a man!'

8 This England never did, nor never shall,   *King John* (1591–8)
Lie at the proud foot of a conqueror,
But when it first did help to wound itself.
Now these her princes are come home again,
Come the three corners of the world in arms,
And we shall shock them: nought shall make us rue,
If England to itself do rest but true.

9 Let go thy hold when a great wheel runs down a hill, lest it   *King Lear* (1605–6)
break thy neck with following; but the great one that goes
upward, let him draw thee after.

10 A dog's obeyed in office.   *King Lear* (1605–6)

11   Get thee glass eyes;   *King Lear* (1605–6)
And, like a scurvy politician, seem
To see the things thou dost not.

12 MALCOLM: Nothing in his life   *Macbeth* (1606)
Became him like the leaving it: he died
As one that had been studied in his death
To throw away the dearest thing he owed
As 'twere a careless trifle.
DUNCAN: There's no art
To find the mind's construction in the face;
He was a gentleman on whom I built
An absolute trust.

1 Thou wouldst be great;   *Macbeth* (1606)
Art not without ambition, but without
The illness should attend it. What thou wouldst highly,
That wouldst thou holily; wouldst not play false,
And yet wouldst wrongly win.

2 Besides, this Duncan   *Macbeth* (1606)
Hath borne his faculties so meek, hath been
So clear in his great office, that his virtues
Will plead like angels trumpet-tongued, against
The deep damnation of his taking-off.

3 I have no spur   *Macbeth* (1606)
To prick the sides of my intent, but only
Vaulting ambition, which o'erleaps itself,
And falls on the other.

4 Confusion now hath made his masterpiece! *Macbeth* (1606)

5 Thou hast it now: King, Cawdor, Glamis, all, *Macbeth* (1606)
As the weird women promised; and, I fear,
Thou play'dst most foully for't.

6 LADY MACBETH: Things without all remedy *Macbeth* (1606)
Should be without regard: what's done is done.
MACBETH: We have scotched the snake, not killed it:
She'll close and be herself.

7 Duncan is in his grave;   *Macbeth* (1606)
After life's fitful fever he sleeps well;
Treason has done his worst: nor steel, nor poison,
Malice domestic, foreign levy, nothing,
Can touch him further.

8 Stands Scotland where it did?   *Macbeth* (1606)

9 Liberty plucks justice by the nose; *Measure for Measure* (1604)
The baby beats the nurse, and quite athwart
Goes all decorum.

10 We must not make a scarecrow of the law, *Measure for Measure* (1604)
Setting it up to fear the birds of prey,
And let it keep one shape, till custom make it
Their perch and not their terror.

11 'Tis one thing to be tempted, Escalus, *Measure for Measure* (1604)
Another thing to fall. I not deny,
The jury, passing on the prisoner's life,
May in the sworn twelve have a thief or two
Guiltier than him they try.

12 No ceremony that to great ones 'longs, *Measure for Measure* (1604)
Not the king's crown, nor the deputed sword,
The marshal's truncheon, nor the judge's robe,
Become them with one half so good a grace
As mercy does.

13 O! it is excellent   *Measure for Measure* (1604)
To have a giant's strength, but it is tyrannous
To use it like a giant.

1   Man, proud man,   *Measure for Measure* (1604)
Drest in a little brief authority,
Most ignorant of what he's most assured,
His glassèd essence, like an angry ape,
Plays such fantastic tricks before high heaven,
As make the angels weep.

2 The quality of mercy is not strained,   *The Merchant of Venice* (1596–8)
It droppeth as the gentle rain from heaven
Upon the place beneath.

3 A substitute shines brightly as a king   *The Merchant of Venice* (1596–8)
Until a king be by, and then his state
Empties itself, as doth an inland brook
Into the main of waters.

4 We were not born to sue, but to command.   *Richard II* (1595)

5 How long a time lies in one little word!   *Richard II* (1595)
Four lagging winters and four wanton springs
End in a word; such is the breath of kings.

6 This royal throne of kings, this sceptered isle,   *Richard II* (1595)
This earth of majesty, this seat of Mars,
This other Eden, demi-paradise,
This fortress built by Nature for herself
Against infection and the hand of war,
This happy breed of men, this little world,
This precious stone set in the silver sea,
Which serves it in the office of a wall,
Or as a moat defensive to a house,
Against the envy of less happier lands,
This blessèd plot, this earth, this realm, this England.

7 The caterpillars of the commonwealth.   *Richard II* (1595)

8 Not all the water in the rough rude sea   *Richard II* (1595)
Can wash the balm from an anointed king;
The breath of worldly men cannot depose
The deputy elected by the Lord.

9 Is not the king's name twenty thousand names?   *Richard II* (1595)
Arm, arm, my name! A puny subject strikes
At thy great glory.

10 For God's sake, let us sit upon the ground   *Richard II* (1595)
And tell sad stories of the death of kings.

11   For within the hollow crown   *Richard II* (1595)
That rounds the mortal temples of a king
Keeps Death his court, and there the antick sits,
Scoffing his state and grinning at his pomp.

12 What must the king do now? Must he submit?   *Richard II* (1595)
The king shall do it: must he be deposed?
The king shall be contented: must he lose
The name of king? o' God's name, let it go.

13 You may my glories and my state depose,   *Richard II* (1595)
But not my griefs; still am I king of those.

14 Now mark me how I will undo myself.   *Richard II* (1595)

15 With mine own tears I wash away my balm,   *Richard II* (1595)
With mine own hands I give away my crown.

1 Mine eyes are full of tears, I cannot see: *Richard II* (1595)
   And yet salt water blinds them not so much
   But they can see a sort of traitors here.
   Nay, if I turn my eyes upon myself,
   I find myself a traitor with the rest.

2 Now is the winter of our discontent *Richard III* (1591)
   Made glorious summer by this sun of York.

3 Grim-visaged war hath smoothed his wrinkled front; *Richard III* (1591)
   And now, instead of mounting barbèd steeds,
   To fright the souls of fearful adversaries,—
   He capers nimbly in a lady's chamber
   To the lascivious pleasing of a lute.

4 Since every Jack became a gentleman *Richard III* (1591)
   There's many a gentle person made a Jack.

5 Woe to the land that's governed by a child! *Richard III* (1591)

6 Talk'st thou to me of 'ifs'? Thou art a traitor: *Richard III* (1591)
   Off with his head!

7 I am not in the giving vein to-day. *Richard III* (1591)

8 Men shut their doors against a setting sun. *Timon of Athens* (c.1607)

9 A stone is soft as wax, tribunes more hard than stones. *Titus Andronicus* (1590)
   A stone is silent and offendeth not,
   And tribunes with their tongues doom men to death.

10 Rome is but a wilderness of tigers. *Titus Andronicus* (1590)

11 The heavens themselves, the planets, and this centre *Troilus and Cressida* (1602)
    Observe degree, priority, and place,
    Insisture, course, proportion, season, form,
    Office, and custom, in all line of order.

12   O! when degree is shaked, *Troilus and Cressida* (1602)
    Which is the ladder to all high designs,
    The enterprise is sick.

13 Take but degree away, untune that string, *Troilus and Cressida* (1602)
    And, hark! what discord follows.

14 A plague of opinion! a man may wear it on both sides, like a *Troilus and Cressida* (1602)
    leather jerkin.

15 How my achievements mock me! *Troilus and Cressida* (1602)

Robert Shapiro 1942–

American lawyer

16 *of the change of strategy embraced after Johnnie Cochran took over* in *The Times* 5 October 1995; see
    from him the leadership of the defence team at the trial of O. J. **Churchill** 86:1
    Simpson:
    Not only did we play the race card, we played it from the
    bottom of the deck.
        to which Cochran responded, 'We didn't play the race card, we
        played the credibility card'

Ariel Sharon 1928–

Israeli Likud statesman, Prime Minister from 2001

17 I'm not going to make any compromise whatsoever. in *Sunday Times* 12 August 2001
    on relations with the Palestinians

George Bernard Shaw 1856–1950

Irish dramatist
see also **Misquotations** 272:6

1 All great truths begin as blasphemies. — *Annajanska* (1919)

2 What Englishman will give his mind to politics as long as he can afford to keep a motor car? — *The Apple Cart* (1930)

3 Life is not meant to be easy, my child; but take courage: it can be delightful. — *Back to Methuselah* (rev. ed., 1930); *see also* **Fraser** 146:11

4 He [the Briton] is a barbarian, and thinks that the customs of his tribe and island are the laws of nature. — *Caesar and Cleopatra* (1901)

5 SWINDON: What will history say?
BURGOYNE: History, sir, will tell lies as usual. — *The Devil's Disciple* (1901)

6 Your friend the British soldier can stand up to anything except the British War Office. — *The Devil's Disciple* (1901)

7 A government which robs Peter to pay Paul can always depend on the support of Paul. — *Everybody's Political What's What?* (1944)

8 Go anywhere in England where there are natural, wholesome, contented, and really nice English people; and what do you always find? That the stables are the real centre of the household. — *Heartbreak House* (1919)

9 The captain is in his bunk, drinking bottled ditch-water; and the crew is gambling in the forecastle. She will strike and sink and split. Do you think the laws of God will be suspended in favour of England because you were born in it? — *Heartbreak House* (1919)

10 It is evident that if the incomes of the rich were taken from them and divided among the poor as we stand at present, the poor would be very little less poor; the supply of capital would cease because nobody could afford to save; the country houses would fall into ruins; and learning and science and art and literature and all the rest of what we call culture would perish. — *The Intelligent Woman's Guide to Socialism and Capitalism* (1928)

11 You have to choose (as a voter) between trusting to the natural stability of gold and the natural stability of the honesty and intelligence of the members of the Government. And, with due respect for these gentlemen, I advise you, as long as the Capitalist system lasts, to vote for gold. — *The Intelligent Woman's Guide to Socialism and Capitalism* (1928)

12 Money is indeed the most important thing in the world; and all sound and successful personal and national morality should have this fact for its basis. — *The Irrational Knot* (1905) preface

13 An Irishman's heart is nothing but his imagination. — *John Bull's Other Island* (1907)

14 He knows nothing; and he thinks he knows everything. That points clearly to a political career. — *Major Barbara* (1907)

15 Nothing is ever done in this world until men are prepared to kill one another if it is not done. — *Major Barbara* (1907)

16 Englishmen never will be slaves: they are free to do whatever the Government and public opinion allow them to do. — *Man and Superman* (1903)

17 In the arts of peace Man is a bungler. — *Man and Superman* (1903)

1 Revolutions have never lightened the burden of tyranny: they have only shifted it to another shoulder.

Man and Superman (1903) 'The Revolutionist's Handbook' foreword

2 Democracy substitutes election by the incompetent many for appointment by the corrupt few.

Man and Superman (1903) 'Maxims: Democracy'

3 Liberty means responsibility. That is why most men dread it.

Man and Superman (1903) 'Maxims: Liberty and Equality'

4 The art of government is the organization of idolatry.

Man and Superman (1903) 'Maxims: Idolatry'

5 The reasonable man adapts himself to the world: the unreasonable one persists in trying to adapt the world to himself. Therefore all progress depends on the unreasonable man.

Man and Superman (1903) 'Maxims: Reason'

6 Titles distinguish the mediocre, embarrass the superior, and are disgraced by the inferior.

Man and Superman (1903) 'Maxims for Revolutionists: Titles'

7 Anarchism is a game at which the police can beat you.

Misalliance (1914)

8 You'll never have a quiet world till you knock the patriotism out of the human race.

O'Flaherty V.C. (1919)

9 Assassination is the extreme form of censorship.

The Showing-Up of Blanco Posnet (1911) 'Limits to Toleration'

Hartley Shawcross 1902–2003
British Labour politician

10 'But,' said Alice, 'the question is whether you can make a word mean different things.' 'Not so,' said Humpty-Dumpty, 'the question is which is to be the master. That's all.' We are the masters at the moment, and not only at the moment, but for a very long time to come.

in the House of Commons, 2 April 1946; see **Carroll** 75:12, **Misquotations** 274:2

11 I don't think it was right. It was victors' justice.
  of the Nuremberg Trials

interviewed on his 95th birthday, in *Daily Telegraph* 10 February 1997

Charles Shaw-Lefevre 1794–1888

12 What is that fat gentleman in such a passion about?
  as a child, on hearing Charles James **Fox** *speak in Parliament*

G. W. E. Russell *Collections and Recollections* (1898)

Francis Sheehy-Skeffington 1878–1916
Irish nationalist

13 A crank is a small engine that causes revolutions.
  on being described as a crank

Owen Dudley Edwards and Fergus Pyle *1916: the Easter Rising* (1968)

Lord Shelburne 1737–1805
British Whig politician; Prime Minister

14 The country will neither be united at home nor respected abroad, till the reins of government are lodged with men who have some little pretensions to common sense and common honesty.

in the House of Lords, 22 November 1770

15 *of the defence of the king's speech at the opening of the parliamentary session:*
  Nothing more than a string of sophisms, no less wretched in their texture than insolent in their tenor.

in the House of Lords, 31 October 1776

1 The sun of Great Britain will set whenever she acknowledges the independence of America . . . the independence of America would end in the ruin of England.

in the House of Lords, October 1782

Percy Bysshe Shelley 1792–1822
English poet

2 Let there be light! said Liberty,
And like sunrise from the sea,
Athens arose!

Hellas (1822)

3 I met Murder on the way—
He had a mask like Castlereagh.

'The Mask of Anarchy' (1819)

4 'My name is Ozymandias, king of kings:
Look on my works, ye Mighty, and despair!'

'Ozymandias' (1819)

5 Kingly conclaves stern and cold
Where blood with guilt is bought and sold.

Prometheus Unbound (1820)

6 Men of England, wherefore plough
For the lords who lay ye low?

'Song to the Men of England' (written 1819)

7 The seed ye sow, another reaps;
The wealth ye find, another keeps;
The robes ye weave, another wears;
The arms ye forge, another bears.

'Song to the Men of England' (written 1819)

8 An old, mad, blind, despised, and dying king.

'Sonnet: England in 1819' (written 1819)

9 The accident of her birth neither made her life more virtuous nor her death more worthy of grief.

An Address to the People on the Death of the Princess Charlotte (1817)

10 Tyranny entrenches itself within the existing interests of the most refined citizens of a nation and says 'If you dare trample upon these, be free.'

A Philosophical View of Reform (written 1819–20)

11 Monarchy is only the string that ties the robber's bundle.

A Philosophical View of Reform (written 1819–20)

William Shenstone 1714–63
English poet and essayist

12 Laws are generally found to be nets of such a texture, as the little creep through, the great break through, and the middle-sized are alone entangled in.

Works in Verse and Prose (1764) vol. 2 'On Politics'; see **Anacharsis** 7:7, **Swift** 384:5

Gillian Shephard 1940–
British Conservative politician

13 John Major's self-control in Cabinet was rigid. The most angry thing he would ever do was to throw down his pencil.

in Sunday Times on 21 November 1999 'Talking Heads'

Philip Henry Sheridan 1831–88
American Union cavalry commander in the Civil War

14 The only good Indian is a dead Indian.
at Fort Cobb, January 1869

attributed; perhaps already proverbial

Richard Brinsley Sheridan 1751–1816

Irish dramatist and Whig politician

1 The newspapers! Sir, they are the most villainous—licentious—abominable—infernal—Not that I ever read them—No—I make it a rule never to look into a newspaper.

The Critic (1779)

2 The throne *we* honour is the *people's choice.*

Pizarro (1799)

3 The Right Honourable gentleman is indebted to his memory for his jests, and to his imagination for his facts.
in reply to Mr Dundas

in the House of Commons; T. Moore *Life of Sheridan* (1825) vol. 2

Tommy Sheridan

Scottish Socialist politician

4 I'm not surprised about Donald Dewar and the Labour Party being reluctant to let the photographers stay. The closer you get to Mr Dewar, the more you see what a Tory he is.
on the decision to ban photographers from the debating chamber of the Scottish Parliament

in *Scotsman* 18 March 2000

William Tecumseh Sherman 1820–91

American general; from 1864 chief Union commander in the west in succession to Ulysses S. **Grant**

5 I will never again command an army in America if we must carry along paid spies. I will banish myself to some foreign country first.
a reference to war correspondents

letter to his wife, February 1863

6 War is the remedy our *enemies* have chosen, and I say let us give them all they want.

in 1864; Geoffrey C. Ward *The Civil War* (1991)

7 [Grant] stood by me when I was crazy, and I stood by him when he was drunk; and now we stand by each other always.
*of his relationship with his fellow Union commander, Ulysses S. **Grant***

in 1864; Geoffrey C. Ward *The Civil War* (1991)

8 I will not accept if nominated, and will not serve if elected.
on being urged to stand as Republican candidate in the 1884 presidential election

telegram to General Henderson; *Memoirs* (4th ed., 1891)

9 I think we understand what military fame is. To be killed on the field of battle and have our name spelled wrong in the newspapers.

Ken Burns *The Civil War* (documentary, 1989) episode 9

Emanuel Shinwell 1884–1986

British Labour politician

10 We know that the organised workers of the country are our friends. As for the rest, they don't matter a tinker's cuss.

speech to the Electrical Trades Union conference at Margate, 7 May 1947

Jonathan Shipley 1714–88

English clergyman, Bishop of St Asaph

1 I look upon North America as the only great nursery of freemen left on the face of the earth.

  in 1774, after voting against the alteration of the constitution of Massachusetts, proposed as a punishment for the tea-ship riots at Boston

in *Dictionary of National Biography*

William Shippen 1673–1743

English Jacobite politician

2 Robin and I are two honest men: he is for King George and I for King James, but those men in long cravats [Sandys, Rushout, Pulteney, and their following] only desire places under one or the other.

  view of his relationship with his political opponent Robert **Walpole**

in *Dictionary of National Biography* (1917–)

Clare Short 1946–

British Labour politician

3 *contrasting Tony Blair's political advisers with elected politicians:* I sometimes call them the people who live in the dark. Everything they do is in hiding . . . Everything we do is in the light. They live in the dark.

in *New Statesman* 9 August 1996

4 It will be golden elephants next.

  suggesting that the government of Montserrat was 'talking mad money' in claiming assistance for evacuating the island

in *Observer* 24 August 1997

5 Reckless with our government; reckless with his own future, position and place in history. It's extraordinarily reckless.

  when asked if she thought that Tony **Blair** *was acting recklessly on Iraq*

in an interview on *Westminster Hour* (BBC Radio 4), 9 March 2003

6 I think everyone agrees we would have done better with a different leader.

comment, 6 May 2005, the morning after the British general election

Algernon Sidney 1622–83

English conspirator, executed for his alleged part in the Rye House Plot, 1683

7 Liars ought to have good memories.

Discourses concerning Government (1698)

8 Men lived like fishes; the great ones devoured the small.

Discourses concerning Government (1698)

9 'Tis not necessary to light a candle to the sun.

Discourses concerning Government (1698)

10 The law is established, which no passion can disturb. 'Tis void of desire and fear, lust and anger . . . 'Tis deaf, inexorable, inflexible.

Discourses concerning Government (1698) ch. 3, sect. 15; see **Adams** 3:3

Emmanuel Joseph Sieyès 1748–1836

French abbot and statesman

1 *La mort, sans phrases.*

Death, without rhetoric.
> *on voting in the French Convention for the death of* **Louis XVI**, *16 January 1793*

attributed to Sieyès, but afterwards repudiated by him (*Le Moniteur* 20 January 1793 records his vote as 'La mort')

2 *when asked what he had done during the French Revolution:*
J'ai vécu.

I survived.

F. A. M. Mignet *Notice historique sur la vie et les travaux de M. le Comte de Sieyès* (1836)

Jim Sillars 1937–

Scottish Nationalist politician

3 I think the greatest problem we have is that we will sing Flower of Scotland at Hampden or Murrayfield, and that we have too many 90-minute patriots.

interview on Scottish Television, 23 April 1992

Simonides

Greek poet see **Epitaphs** 136:2

Kirke Simpson

American journalist

4 [Warren] Harding of Ohio was chosen by a group of men in a smoke-filled room early today as Republican candidate for President.

news report, 12 June 1920; see **Daugherty** 365:4

C. H. Sisson 1914–2003

English poet

5 Here lies a civil servant. He was civil
To everyone, and servant to the devil.

The London Zoo (1961)

Sitting Bull (Tatanka Iyotake) c.1831–90

American Sioux chief

6 The Black Hills belong to me. If the whites try to take them, I will fight.

Dee Brown *Bury My Heart at Wounded Knee* (1970) ch. 12

Noel Skelton 1880–1935

British Conservative politician

7 To state as clearly as may be what means lie ready to develop a property-owning democracy, to bring the industrial and economic status of the wage-earner abreast of his political and educational, to make democracy stable and four-square.

in *The Spectator* 19 May 1923

Slogans

1 All power to the Soviets.
    workers in Petrograd, 1917

2 All the way with LBJ.
    US Democratic Party campaign slogan supporting Lyndon
    Baines **Johnson**
    in *Washington Post* 4 June 1960

3 *Arbeit macht frei.*
    Work makes free.
    on the gates of Dachau concentration camp, and subsequently on
    those of Auschwitz
    inscription, 1933

4 Are you thinking what we're thinking?
    Conservative Party, 2005

5 Ban the bomb.
    US anti-nuclear slogan, 1953 onwards
    adopted by the Campaign for Nuclear Disarmament

6 A bayonet is a weapon with a worker at each end.
    British pacifist slogan (1940)

7 Better red than dead.
    slogan of nuclear disarmament campaigners, late 1950s

8 A bigger bang for a buck.
    Charles E. **Wilson**'s defence policy, in *Newsweek* 22 March 1954

9 The big tent.
    slogan used by the Republican Party to denote a policy of
    inclusiveness
    recorded from 1990; see also **Newspaper headlines** 288:4

10 Black is beautiful.
    slogan of American civil rights campaigners, mid-1960s

11 Burn, baby, burn.
    Black extremist slogan in use during the Los Angeles riots, August 1965

12 Can't pay, won't pay.
    anti-Poll Tax slogan, *c.*1990; see **Fo** 142:2

13 *Deutschland hat einen neuen Kanzler.*
    Germany has a new Chancellor.
    added to a poster of Gerhard Schröder in West Berlin, 28
    September 1998
    in *Guardian* 29 September 1998

14 *Ein Reich, ein Volk, ein Führer.*
    One realm, one people, one leader.
    Nazi Party slogan
    early 1930s

15 Fair shares for all, is Labour's call.
    slogan for the North Battersea by-election, 1946, coined by
    Douglas **Jay**
    Douglas Jay *Change and Fortune* (1980)

16 Fifty-four forty, or fight!
    slogan of expansionist Democrats in the presidential campaign of
    1844, in which the Oregon boundary definition was an issue (in
    1846 the new Democratic president, James K. Polk,
    compromised on the 49th parallel with Great Britain)
    William Allen (1803–79), American Democratic politician, speech in the US Senate, 1844

17 Forward not back.
    Labour Party, 2005

18 Free by '93.
    Scottish National Party, general election campaign, 1992

Slogans *continued*

1 Give us back our eleven days.
protesting against the adoption of the Gregorian Calendar in 1752, and in this form associated with Hogarth's cartoon showing a rowdy Oxfordshire election of 1754

David Ewing Duncan *The Calendar* (1998)

2 Hey, hey, LBJ, how many kids have you killed today?
*anti-Vietnam War marching slogan during the presidency of Lyndon **Johnson***

Jacquin Sanders *The Draft and the Vietnam War* (1966)

3 I like Ike.
*used when General **Eisenhower** was first seen as a potential presidential nominee*

US button badge, 1947; coined by Henry D. Spalding (d. 1990)

4 I'm backing Britain.
slogan coined by workers at the Colt factory, Surbiton, Surrey, and subsequently used in a national campaign

in *The Times* 1 January 1968

5 It's morning again in America.

slogan for Ronald **Reagan**'s election campaign, 1984; coined by Hal Riney (1932–); in *Newsweek* 6 August 1984

6 It's Scotland's oil.

Scottish National Party, 1972

7 It's the economy, stupid.

on a sign put up at the 1992 **Clinton** presidential campaign headquarters by campaign manager James Carville

8 Keep the bastards honest.

coined by the Australian politician Don Chipp (1925–), on leaving the Liberal Party to form the Australian Democrats

9 *Kraft durch Freude.*
Strength through joy.

German Labour Front slogan, from 1933; coined by Robert Ley (1890–1945)

10 Labour isn't working.
caption to Conservative Party poster, 1978–9, showing a long queue outside an unemployment office

Philip Kleinman *The Saatchi and Saatchi Story* (1987)

11 Labour's double whammy.

Conservative Party election slogan 1992

12 The land for the people.

Communist slogan, *c.*1917

13 Let Reagan be Reagan.

Republican campaign slogan, 1980s

14 *Liberté! Égalité! Fraternité!*
Freedom! Equality! Brotherhood!
motto of the French Revolution (though of earlier origin)

the Club des Cordeliers passed a motion, 30 June 1793, 'that owners should be urged to paint on the front of their houses, in large letters, the words: Unity, indivisibility of the Republic, Liberty, Equality, Fraternity or death'; in *Journal de Paris* no. 182 (from 1795 the words 'or death' were dropped)

15 Life's better with the Conservatives. Don't let Labour ruin it.

Conservative Party election slogan, 1959

Slogans *continued*

1 Lousy but loyal.

London East End slogan at George V's Jubilee (1935)

2 Make love not war.

student slogan, 1960s

3 New Labour, new danger.

Conservative slogan, 1996

4 No crown of thorns, no cross of gold.

American Democratic party, 1900; see **Bryan** 59:9

5 *the defenders of the besieged city of Derry to the Jacobite army of James II, April 1689:*
No surrender!
   adopted as a slogan of Protestant Ulster

Jonathan Bardon *A History of Ulster* (1992)

6 Not in my name.

protesters against the war in Iraq, 2003

7 The personal is political.

1970s feminist slogan, attributed to Carol Hanisch (1945–)

8 Power to the people.

slogan of the Black Panther movement, from c.1968 onwards

9 Things can only get better.

Labour campaign slogan, 1997; see **Petrie** 309:9

10 Think globally, act locally.

Friends of the Earth slogan, c.1985

11 *in response to a Republican slogan, 'Thinking feller, vote for McKellar':*
Think some more and vote for Gore.

American Democratic slogan in Senate campaign, Tennessee, 1952; coinage is attributed to Pauline LaFon **Gore** on behalf of her husband Albert Gore Sr.

12 Thirteen years of Tory misrule.

unofficial Labour party election slogan, also in the form 'Thirteen wasted years', 1964

13 Three acres and a cow.
   regarded as the requirement for self-sufficiency; associated with the radical politician Jesse Collings (1831–1920) and his land reform campaign begun in 1885

Jesse Collings in the House of Commons, 26 January 1886, although used earlier by Joseph **Chamberlain** in a speech at Evesham (in *The Times* 17 November 1885), by which time it was already proverbial

14 Tippecanoe and Tyler, too.
   *presidential campaign song for William Henry **Harrison**, 1840*

attributed to A. C. Ross (fl. 1840); see **Songs** 376:4

15 Ulster says no.
   slogan coined in response to the Anglo-Irish Agreement of 15 November 1985

in *Irish Times* 25 November 1985

16 Vote Blair, get Brown.

reflecting the rivalry of Tony **Blair** and Gordon **Brown**, and suggested variously as a threat and a promise to floating voters

Slogans *continued*

1 Votes for women.
*adopted when it proved impossible to use a banner with the longer slogan 'Will the Liberal Party Give Votes for Women?' made by Emmeline **Pankhurst** (1858–1928), Christabel **Pankhurst** (1880–1958), and Annie Kenney (1879–1953)*

slogan of the women's suffrage movement, from 13 October 1905; Emmeline Pankhurst *My Own Story* (1914)

2 War will cease when men refuse to fight.
pacifist slogan (often quoted as 'Wars will cease . . . ')

from c.1936

3 We demand that big business give people a square deal.

Theodore Roosevelt, 1901; see **Roosevelt** 332:6

4 We want eight, and we won't wait.
on the construction of Dreadnoughts

quoted in George Wyndham's speech in *The Times* 29 March 1909

5 Would you buy a used car from this man?

campaign slogan directed against Richard **Nixon**, 1968

6 Yes it hurt, yes it worked.

Conservative Party slogan, 1996; see **Major** 256:5

7 Yesterday's men (they failed before!).

Labour Party slogan, referring to the Conservatives, 1970; coined by David Kingsley, Dennis Lyons, and Peter Lovell-Davis

8 You never had it so good.

Democratic Party slogan during the 1952 US election campaign; see **Macmillan** 253:1

Gillian Slovo 1952–

South African writer

9 In most families it is the children who leave home. In mine it was the parents.
of her anti-apartheid activist parents, Joe Slovo and Ruth First

Every Secret Thing (1997)

Joseph Roberts Smallwood 1900–91

Canadian journalist and politician, Premier of Newfoundland 1949–70

10 I am king of my own little island, and that's all I've ever wanted to be.

Richard Gwyn *Smallwood: The Unlikely Revolutionary* (1968)

Adam Smith 1723–90

Scottish philosopher and economist

11 Little else is requisite to carry a state to the highest degree of opulence from the lowest barbarism, but peace, easy taxes, and a tolerable administration of justice; all the rest being brought about by the natural course of things.

in 1755; *Essays on Philosophical Subjects* (1795)

12 And thus, *Place*, that great object which divides the wives of aldermen, is the end of half the labours of human life; and is the cause of all the tumult and bustle, all the rapine and injustice, which avarice and ambition have introduced into this world.

Theory of Moral Sentiments (1759)

1 [The man of system] seems to imagine that he can arrange the different members of a great society with as much ease as the hand arranges the different pieces upon a chessboard; he does not consider that the pieces upon the chessboard have no other principle of motion besides that which the hand impresses upon them; but that, in the great chessboard of human society, every single piece has a principle of motion of its own, altogether different from that which the legislator might choose to impress upon it.

Theory of Moral Sentiments (1759)

2 It is not from the benevolence of the butcher, the brewer, or the baker, that we expect our dinner, but from their regard to their own interest. We address ourselves not to their humanity but their self love, and never talk to them of our necessities but of their advantages.

Wealth of Nations (1776)

3 People of the same trade seldom meet together, even for merriment and diversion, but the conversation ends in a conspiracy against the public, or in some contrivance to raise prices.

Wealth of Nations (1776)

4 Great nations are never impoverished by private, though they sometimes are by public prodigality and misconduct. The whole, or almost the whole public revenue, is in most countries employed in maintaining unproductive hands.

Wealth of Nations (1776)

5 What is prudence in the conduct of every private family, can scarce be folly in that of a great kingdom. If a foreign country can supply us with a commodity cheaper than we ourselves can make it, better buy it of them with some part of the produce of our own industry, employed in a way in which we have some advantage.

Wealth of Nations (1776)

6 Every individual necessarily labours to render the annual revenue of society as great as he can. He generally, indeed, neither intends to promote the public interest, nor knows how much he is promoting it. By preferring the support of domestic to that of foreign industry, he intends only his own security; and by directing that industry in such a manner as its produce may be of the greatest value, and he is in this, as in many other cases, led by an invisible hand to promote an end which was no part of his intention.

Wealth of Nations (1776)

7 That insidious and crafty animal, vulgarly called a statesman or politician, whose councils are directed by the momentary fluctuations of affairs.

Wealth of Nations (1776)

8 The natural effort of every individual to better his own condition . . . is so powerful, that it is alone, and without any assistance, not only capable of carrying on the society to wealth and prosperity, but of surmounting a hundred impertinent obstructions with which the folly of human laws too often encumbers its operations.

Wealth of Nations (1776)

9 To found a great empire for the sole purpose of raising up a people of customers, may at first sight appear a project fit only for a nation of shopkeepers. It is, however, a project altogether unfit for a nation of shopkeepers; but extremely fit for a nation whose government is influenced by shopkeepers.

Wealth of Nations (1776); see **Adams** 4:11, **Napoleon** 285:1

1 Consumption is the sole end and purpose of all production; and the interest of the producer ought to be attended to only so far as it may be necessary for promoting that of the consumer.
Wealth of Nations (1776)

2 Those parts of education, it is to be observed, for the teaching of which there are no public institutions, are generally the best taught.
Wealth of Nations (1776)

3 There is no art which one government sooner learns of another than that of draining money from the pockets of the people.
Wealth of Nations (1776)

Alfred Emanuel Smith 1873–1944
American politician

4 The crowning climax to the whole situation is the undisputed fact that William Randolph Hearst gave him the kiss of death.
*on **Hearst**'s support for Ogden Mills, Smith's unsuccessful opponent for the governorship of New York State*
in *New York Times* 25 October 1926

5 All the ills of democracy can be cured by more democracy.
speech in Albany, 27 June 1933

6 No sane local official who has hung up an empty stocking over the municipal fireplace, is going to shoot Santa Claus just before a hard Christmas.
comment on the New Deal
in *New Outlook* December 1933

F. E. Smith, Lord Birkenhead 1872–1930
British Conservative politician and lawyer
*on Smith: see **Asquith** 17:2*

7 Does anyone suppose that any of us enjoy the prospect of playing a part for which so many of us are not obviously suited? I myself am a middle-aged lawyer, more at home, and I may perhaps add more highly remunerated, in the law courts than I am likely to be on the parade ground.
of his role in the Ulster Volunteer Force
speech to the House of Commons, 1913

8 The world continues to offer glittering prizes to those who have stout hearts and sharp swords.
Rectorial address, Glasgow University, 7 November 1923

9 We have the highest authority for believing that the meek shall inherit the earth; though I have never found any particular corroboration of this aphorism in the records of Somerset House.
Contemporary Personalities (1924) 'Marquess Curzon'

10 Nature has no cure for this sort of madness [Bolshevism], though I have known a legacy from a rich relative work wonders.
Law, Life and Letters (1927)

11 Austen [Chamberlain] always played the game, and he always lost it.
Lord Beaverbrook *Men and Power* (1956)

Iain Duncan Smith 1954–
British Conservative politician, Leader of the Conservative Party 2001–3
*on Smith: see **Portillo** 314:14*

12 Do not underestimate the determination of a quiet man.
speech to the Conservative Party Conference, 10 October 2002

Ian Smith 1919–

Rhodesian statesman; Prime Minister of Rhodesia (now
Zimbabwe), 1964–79

1 I don't believe in black majority rule in Rhodesia—not in a
thousand years.

broadcast speech, 20 March 1976

John Smith 1938–94

Scottish-born Labour politician, Leader of the Labour Party from
1992
on Smith: see **Dewar** 116:8

2 I am a doer and I want to do things, but there exists the
terrible possibility in politics that you might never win.

in You 22 March 1992

3 The settled will of the Scottish people.
of the creation of a Scottish parliament

*speech at the Scottish Labour
Conference, 11 March 1994*

Samuel Francis Smith 1808–95

American poet and divine

4 My country, 'tis of thee,
Sweet land of liberty,
Of thee I sing:
Land where my fathers died,
Land of the pilgrims' pride,
From every mountain-side
Let freedom ring.

'America' (1831)

Sydney Smith 1771–1845

English clergyman and essayist

5 The moment the very name of Ireland is mentioned, the
English seem to bid adieu to common feeling, common
prudence, and common sense, and to act with the barbarity
of tyrants, and the fatuity of idiots.

Letters of Peter Plymley (1807)

6 Tory and Whig in turns shall be my host,
I taste no politics in boiled and roast.

*letter to John Murray, November
1834*

7 Lord John . . . would perform the operation for the stone—
build St Peter's or assume—(with or without ten minutes
notice) the command of the Channel Fleet; and no one
would discover by his manner that the patient had died, the
church tumbled down, and the Channel Fleet been knocked
to atoms.
of Lord John **Russell**

*Letters to Archdeacon Singleton
(1837–40) vol. 2*

8 Daniel Webster struck me much like a steam-engine in
trousers.

Lady Holland Memoir (1855)

9 He [Macaulay] has occasional flashes of silence, that make
his conversation perfectly delightful.

Lady Holland Memoir (1855)

10 Minorities . . . are almost always in the right.

*H. Pearson The Smith of Smiths
(1934)*

Tobias Smollett 1721–71

Scottish novelist

11 I think for my part one half of the nation is mad—and the
other not very sound.

*The Adventures of Sir Launcelot
Greaves (1762)*

1 Mourn, hapless Caledonia, mourn
Thy banished peace, thy laurels torn.

'The Tears of Scotland' (1746)

Jan Christiaan Smuts 1870–1950

South African soldier and statesman, Prime Minister 1919–24 and
1939–48

2 There is no doubt that mankind is once more on the move.
The very foundations have been shaken and loosened, and
things are again fluid. The tents have been struck, and the
great caravan of humanity is once more on the march.
on the League of Nations

W. K. Hancock *Smuts* (1968)

C. P. Snow 1905–80

English novelist and scientist

3 The official world, the corridors of power.

Homecomings (1956)

Philip Snowden 1864–1937

British Labour politician

4 This is not Socialism. It is Bolshevism run mad.
on the Labour Party's 1931 election programme

radio broadcast, 17 October 1931

5 It would be desirable if every Government, when it comes to
power, should have its old speeches burnt.

C. E. Bechofer Roberts ('Ephesian')
Philip Snowden (1929)

Socrates 469–399 BC

Greek philosopher

6 Most excellent man, are you who are a citizen of Athens,
the greatest of cities and the most famous for wisdom and
power, not ashamed to care for the acquisition of wealth
and for reputation and honour, when you neither care nor
take thought for wisdom and truth and the perfection of
your soul?

Plato *Apology*

7 And I tell you that virtue does not come from money, but
from virtue comes money and all other good things to man,
both to the individual and to the state.

Plato *Apology*

8 I am not Athenian or Greek but a citizen of the world.

Plutarch *Moralia* bk. 7 'On Exile'

Alexander Solzhenitsyn 1918–

Russian novelist

9 You only have power over people as long as you don't take
everything away from them. But when you've robbed a man
of *everything* he's no longer in your power—he's free again.

The First Circle (1968)

10 The Gulag Archipelago.
*referring to the political prison camps dotted around the Soviet
Union*

title of book (1973–5)

11 The thoughts of a prisoner—they're not free either. They
keep returning to the same things.

*One Day in the Life of Ivan
Denisovich* (1962)

12 Mankind's salvation lies exclusively in everyone's making
everything his business, in the people of the East being
anything but indifferent to what is thought in the West, and
in the people of the West being anything but indifferent to
what happens in the East.

Nobel Prize Lecture, 1970

1 In our country the lie has become not just a moral category but a pillar of the State.

interview in 1974; in appendix to The Oak and the Calf (1975)

2 Yes, we are still the prisoners of communism, and yet, for us in Russia, Communism is a dead dog, while for many people in the West it is still a living lion.

broadcast on BBC Russian Service, in Listener 15 February 1979

Anastasio Somoza 1925–80
Nicaraguan dictator

3 *replying to an accusation of ballot-rigging:*
You won the elections, but I won the count.

in Guardian 17 June 1977; *see* **Stoppard** 382:2

■ Songs *see box opposite*
see also **Benson** 35:6

Susan Sontag 1933–2004
American writer

4 The white race *is* the cancer of human history, it is the white race, and it alone—its ideologies and inventions—which eradicates autonomous civilizations wherever it spreads, which has upset the ecological balance of the planet, which now threatens the very existence of life itself.

in Partisan Review Winter 1967

Lord Soper 1903–98
British peer and Methodist minister

5 *of the quality of debate in the House of Lords:*
It is, I think, good evidence of life after death.

in Listener 17 August 1978

Robert Southey 1774–1843
English poet and writer

6 Now tell us all about the war,
And what they fought each other for.

'The Battle of Blenheim' (1800)

7 'And everybody praised the Duke,
Who this great fight did win.'
'But what good came of it at last?'
Quoth little Peterkin.
'Why that I cannot tell,' said he,
'But 'twas a famous victory.'

'The Battle of Blenheim' (1800)

8 The death of Nelson was felt in England as something more than a public calamity; men started at the intelligence, and turned pale, as if they had heard of the loss of a dear friend.

The Life of Nelson (1813)

Lord Spencer 1964–
English peer

9 She needed no royal title to continue to generate her particular brand of magic.
tribute at the funeral of his sister, **Diana**, *Princess of Wales, 7 September 1997*

in Guardian 8 September 1997

Songs

1 *Allons, enfants de la patrie,*
Le jour de gloire est arrivé . . .
Aux armes, citoyens!
Formez vos bataillons!

Come, children of our country, the day of glory has arrived
. . . To arms, citizens! Form your battalions!

'La Marseillaise' (25 April 1792),
written by Claude-Joseph Rouget
de Lisle (1760–1836)

2 Among our ancient mountains,
And from our lovely vales,
Oh, let the prayer re-echo:
'God bless the Prince of Wales!'

'God Bless the Prince of Wales'
(1862 song), written by George
Linley (1798–1865)

3 Ara! but why does King James stay behind?
Lilli burlero bullen a la
Ho! by my shoul 'tis a Protestant wind
Lilli burlero bullen a la.
a Williamite song in mockery of Richard Talbot, newly created
Earl of Tyrconnell by the Catholic James II in Dublin in 1688;
the refrain parodies the Irish language

'A New Song' (1687), written by
Thomas, Lord **Wharton**; Thomas
Kinsella *The New Oxford Book of*
Irish Verse (1986); attribution to
Wharton has been disputed

4 Belgium put the kibosh on the Kaiser.

title of song (1914), written by
Alf Ellerton

5 *Debout! les damnés de la terre!*
Debout! les forçats de la faim!
La raison tonne en son cratère,
C'est l'éruption de la fin . . .
Nous ne sommes rien, soyons tout!
C'est la lutte finale
Groupons-nous, et, demain,
L'Internationale
Sera le genre humain.

On your feet, you damned souls of the earth! On your feet,
inmates of hunger's prison! Reason is rumbling in its
crater, and its final eruption is on its way . . . We are
nothing, let us be everything! This is the final conflict: let
us form up and, tomorrow, the International will
encompass the human race.

'L'Internationale' (1871) by the
French politician Eugène Pottier
(1818–87)

6 From the halls of Montezuma,
To the shores of Tripoli,
We fight our country's battles,
On the land as on the sea.

'The Marines' Hymn' (1847)

7 God save our gracious king!
Long live our noble king!
God save the king!
Send him victorious,
Happy, and glorious,
Long to reign over us:
God save the king!

'God save the King', attributed
to various authors of the mid
eighteenth century, including
Henry Carey (*c.*1687–1743);
Jacobite variants, such as James
Hogg 'The King's Anthem' in
Jacobite Relics of Scotland Second
Series (1821) also exist

Songs *continued*

1 Confound their politics,
Frustrate their knavish tricks.

'God save the King', attributed to various authors; see **Songs** 375:7 above

2 I met wid Napper Tandy, and he took me by the hand,
And he said, 'How's poor ould Ireland, and how does she stand?'
She's the most disthressful country that iver yet was seen,
For they're hangin' men an' women for the wearin' o' the Green.

'The Wearin' o' the Green' (*c*.1795 ballad)

3 In good King Charles's golden days,
When loyalty no harm meant;
A furious High-Churchman I was,
And so I gained preferment.
Unto my flock I daily preached,
Kings are by God appointed,
And damned are those who dare resist,
Or touch the Lord's Anointed.
And this is law, I will maintain,
Unto my dying day, Sir,
That whatsoever King shall reign,
I will be the Vicar of Bray, sir!

'The Vicar of Bray' in *British Musical Miscellany* (1734) vol. 1

4 The iron-armed soldier, the true-hearted soldier,
The gallant old soldier of Tippecanoe.
presidential campaign song for William Henry **Harrison**, *1840*

attributed to George Pope Morris (1802–64); see **Slogans** 368:14

5 John Brown's body lies a mould'ring in the grave,
His soul is marching on.
inspired by the execution of the abolitionist John **Brown**, *after the raid on Harper's Ferry, on 2 December 1859*

song (1861), variously attributed to Charles Sprague Hall, Henry Howard Brownell, and Thomas Brigham Bishop

6 Keep the Home-fires burning,
While your hearts are yearning,
Though your lads are far away
They dream of Home.
There's a silver lining
Through the dark cloud shining;
Turn the dark cloud inside out,
Till the boys come Home.

'Till the Boys Come Home!' (1914 song by Lena Guilbert Ford); music by Ivor Novello

7 Lloyd George knew my father,
My father knew Lloyd George.

two-line comic song, sung to the tune of 'Onward, Christian Soldiers' and possibly by Tommy Rhys Roberts (1910–75)

8 Oh! we don't want to lose you but we think you ought to go
For your King and your Country both need you so;
We shall want you and miss you but with all our might and main
We shall cheer you, thank you, kiss you
When you come back again.

'Your King and Country Want You' (1914 song), written by Paul Alfred Rubens (1875–1917)

Songs *continued*

1 The people's flag is deepest red;
It shrouded oft our martyred dead,
And ere their limbs grew stiff and cold,
Their heart's blood dyed its every fold.
Then raise the scarlet standard high!
Within its shade we'll live or die.
Tho' cowards flinch and traitors sneer,
We'll keep the red flag flying here.

'The Red Flag' (1889), written by the Irish socialist songwriter James M. Connell (1852–1929)

2 So on the Twelfth I proudly wear the sash my father wore.

'The Sash My Father Wore', traditional Orange song

3 We don't want to fight, but, by jingo if we do,
We've got the ships, we've got the men, we've got the money too.
We've fought the Bear before, and while Britons shall be true,
The Russians shall not have Constantinople.

We Don't Want to Fight (music hall song by G. W. Hunt, 1878)

4 We're gonna hang out the washing on the Siegfried Line.

title of song (1939) by Jimmy Kennedy and Michael Carr

5 We shall not be moved.

title of labour and civil rights song (1931) adapted from an earlier gospel hymn

6 We shall overcome.
revived in 1946 as a protest song by Black tobacco workers, and in 1963 during the Black Civil Rights Campaign

title of song, originating from before the American Civil War, adapted as a Baptist hymn ('I'll Overcome Some Day', 1901) by C. Albert Tindley

Lord Spencer *continued*

7 We, your blood family, will do all we can to continue the imaginative way in which you were steering these two exceptional young men so that their souls are not simply immersed by duty and tradition but can sing openly as you planned.
referring to his nephews, Prince William and Prince Harry

in *Guardian* 8 September 1997

Oswald Spengler 1880–1936
German historian

8 Socialism is nothing but the capitalism of the working class.

The Hour of Decision (1933)

Edmund Spenser c.1552–99
English poet

9 Ill can he rule the great, that cannot reach the small.

The Faerie Queen (1596)

Steven Spielberg 1947–
American film director and producer

10 I think that today's youth have a tendency to live in the present and work for the future—and to be totally ignorant of the past.

in *Independent on Sunday* 22 August 1999

Benjamin Spock 1903–98
American paediatrician

1 To win in Vietnam, we will have to exterminate a nation.

Dr Spock on Vietnam (1968)

Cecil Spring-Rice 1859–1918
British diplomat; Ambassador to Washington from 1912

2 I vow to thee, my country—all earthly things above—
Entire and whole and perfect, the service of my love,
The love that asks no question: the love that stands the test,
That lays upon the altar the dearest and the best:
The love that never falters, the love that pays the price,
The love that makes undaunted the final sacrifice.

'I Vow to Thee, My Country'
(written on the eve of his
departure from Washington, 12
January 1918)

3 Wilson is the nation's shepherd and McAdoo his crook.
*of President Woodrow **Wilson** and his secretary of the treasury, a
remark considered unfortunate in the light of British attempts to
draw the US into the First World War*

Robert Skidelsky *John Maynard
Keynes* vol. 1 (1983)

Joseph Stalin 1879–1953
Soviet dictator

4 The State is an instrument in the hands of the ruling class,
used to break the resistance of the adversaries of that class.

Foundations of Leninism (1924)

5 There is the question: Can Socialism *possibly* be established
in one country alone by that country's unaided strength?
The question must be answered in the affirmative.

Problems of Leninism (1926)

6 There are various forms of production: artillery,
automobiles, lorries. You also produce 'commodities',
'works', 'products'. Such things are highly necessary.
Engineering things. For people's souls. 'Products' are highly
necessary too. 'Products' are very important for people's
souls. You are engineers of human souls.

speech to writers at **Gorky**'s
house, 26 October 1932; A. Kemp-
Welch *Stalin and the Literary
Intelligentsia, 1928–39* (1991); see
Gorky 163:2, **Kennedy** 213:7

7 The Pope! How many divisions has *he* got?
*on being asked to encourage Catholicism in Russia by way of
conciliating the Pope*

on 13 May 1935; W. S. Churchill
The Gathering Storm (1948); see
Napoleon 284:15

8 There is one eternally true legend—that of Judas.
at the trial of Radek in 1937

Robert Payne *The Rise and Fall of
Stalin* (1966)

9 One death is a tragedy, one million is a statistic.

attributed

Charles E. Stanton 1859–1933
American soldier

10 *Lafayette, nous voilà!*
Lafayette, we are here.
at the tomb of Lafayette in Paris, 4 July 1917

in *New York Tribune* 6 September
1917

Edwin McMasters Stanton 1814–69
American lawyer

11 Now he belongs to the ages.
*of Abraham **Lincoln**, following his assassination, 15 April 1865*

I. M. Tarbell *Life of Abraham Lincoln*
(1900)

David Steel 1938–

British Liberal politician; Leader of the Liberal Party 1976–88
on Steel: see **Foot** 142:8

1 I have the good fortune to be the first Liberal leader for over half a century who is able to say to you at the end of our annual assembly: go back to your constituencies and prepare for government.

speech to the Liberal Party Assembly, 18 September 1981

2 It is the settled will of the majority of people in Scotland that they want not just the symbol, but the substance of the return of democratic control over internal affairs.
   on the announcement that the Stone of Destiny would be returned to Scotland

in *Scotsman* 4 July 1996

3 Mr Salmond is looking increasingly like a maiden in distress waiting to be rescued by James Bond. I do not think it is going to happen.
   referring to Sean Connery's support for the Scottish National Party

in *Daily Telegraph* 27 April 1999

Lincoln Steffens 1866–1936

American journalist

4 I have seen the future; and it works.
   following a visit to the Soviet Union in 1919

Letters (1938) vol. 1; see J. M. Thompson *Russia, Bolshevism and the Versailles Treaty* (1954), where it is recalled that Steffens had composed the expression before he had even arrived in Russia

Gertrude Stein 1874–1946

American writer

5 In the United States there is more space where nobody is than where anybody is. That is what makes America what it is.

The Geographical History of America (1936)

James Fitzjames Stephen 1829–94

English lawyer

6 The way in which the man of genius rules is by persuading an efficient minority to coerce an indifferent and self-indulgent majority.

Liberty, Equality and Fraternity (1873)

James Stephens 1882–1950

Irish poet and nationalist

7 People say: 'Of course, they will be beaten.' The statement is almost a query, and they continue, 'but they are putting up a decent fight.' For being beaten does not matter greatly in Ireland, but not fighting does matter.

The Insurrection in Dublin (1916)

8 In my definition they were good men—men, that is, who willed no evil. No person living is the worse off for having known Thomas MacDonagh.

The Insurrection in Dublin (1916)

Adlai Stevenson 1900–65
American Democratic politician

1 I am not a politician, I am a citizen.
speech during the 1948 election campaign

Bert Cochran *Adlai Stevenson* (1969)

2 We must be patient—making peace is harder than making war.

speech to Chicago Council on Foreign Relations, 21 March 1946

3 I suppose flattery hurts no one, that is, if he doesn't inhale.

television broadcast, 30 March 1952

4 Better we lose the election than mislead the people.
on accepting the Democratic nomination in 1952

Herbert Muller *Adlai Stevenson* (1968)

5 Let's talk sense to the American people. Let's tell them the truth, that there are no gains without pains.
accepting the Democratic nomination

speech at the Democratic National Convention, Chicago, Illinois, 26 July 1952

6 If they [the Republicans] will stop telling lies about the Democrats, we will stop telling the truth about them.

speech during 1952 Presidential campaign; J. B. Martin *Adlai Stevenson and Illinois* (1976)

7 A hungry man is not a free man.

speech at Kasson, Minnesota, 6 September 1952

8 There is no evil in the atom; only in men's souls.

speech at Hartford, Connecticut, 18 September 1952

9 In America any boy may become President and I suppose it's just one of the risks he takes.

speech in Indianapolis, 26 September 1952

10 A free society is a society where it is safe to be unpopular.

speech in Detroit, 7 October 1952

11 The Republican party did not have to . . . encourage the excesses of its Vice-Presidential nominee [Richard Nixon]— the young man who asks you to set him one heart-beat from the Presidency of the United States.

speech at Cleveland, Ohio, 23 October 1952; see **Misquotations** 273:6

12 A funny thing happened to me on the way to the White House.
speech in Washington, 13 December 1952, following his defeat in the Presidential election

Alden Whitman *Portrait: Adlai E. Stevenson* (1965)

13 We hear the Secretary of State [John Foster Dulles] boasting of his brinkmanship—the art of bringing us to the edge of the abyss.

speech in Hartford, Connecticut, 25 February 1956; see **Dulles** 128:8

14 The idea that you can merchandize candidates for high office like breakfast cereal—that you can gather votes like box tops—is, I think, the ultimate indignity to the democratic process.

speech at the Democratic National Convention, 18 August 1956

15 You have taught me a lesson I should have learned long ago—to take counsel always of your courage and never of your fears.
on losing the Presidential nomination in 1960

Herbert J. Muller *Adlai Stevenson* (1968)

16 Do you remember that in classical times when Cicero had finished speaking, the people said, 'How well he spoke', but when Demosthenes had finished speaking, they said, 'Let us march.'
*introducing John F. **Kennedy** in 1960*

Bert Cochran *Adlai Stevenson* (1969)

17 She would rather light a candle than curse the darkness, and her glow has warmed the world.
*on learning of Eleanor **Roosevelt**'s death*

in *New York Times* 8 November 1962

1 Eggheads of the world unite; you have nothing to lose but your yolks.

perhaps a reworking of 'Eggheads of the world, arise—I was even going to add that you have nothing to lose but your yolks', speech at Oakland, 1 February 1956

attributed

2 If I had any epitaph that I would rather have more than another, it would be to say that I had disturbed the sleep of my generation.

epigraph to Jack W. Germand and Jules Witcover *Wake Us When It's Over* (1985)

3 The kind of politician who would cut down a redwood tree, and then mount the stump and make a speech on conservation.

*of Richard **Nixon***

Fawn M. Brodie *Richard Nixon* (1983)

4 A politician is a person who approaches every subject with an open mouth.

attributed

5 The sound of tireless voices is the price we pay for the right to hear the music of our own opinions.

in *The Guide to American Law* (1984)

Robert Louis Stevenson 1850-94
Scottish novelist

6 Politics is perhaps the only profession for which no preparation is thought necessary.

Familiar Studies of Men and Books (1882)

Sting 1951-
English rock singer, songwriter, and actor

7 If I were a Brazilian without land or money or the means to feed my children, I would be burning the rain forest too.

in *International Herald Tribune* 14 April 1989

Caskie Stinnett 1911-
American writer

8 A diplomat . . . is a person who can tell you to go to hell in such a way that you actually look forward to the trip.

Out of the Red (1960)

Lord St John of Fawsley 1929-
British Conservative politician and author

9 The monarchy has become our only truly popular institution at a time when the House of Commons has declined in public esteem and the Lords is a matter of controversy. The monarchy is, in a real sense, underpinning the other two estates of the realm.

in *The Times* 1 February 1982

Baroness Stocks 1891-1975
British educationist

10 The House of Lords is a perfect eventide home.

My Commonplace Book (1970)

Lord Stockton 1943-
British peer, grandson of Harold **Macmillan**

11 As an old man he only had nightmares about two things: the trenches in the Great War and what would have happened if the Cuban Missile Crisis had gone wrong.

*of Harold **Macmillan***

in 1998; Peter Hennessy *The Prime Minister: the Office and its Holders since 1945* (2000)

I. F. Stone 1907-89
American journalist

1 The difference between burlesque and the newspapers is that the former never pretended to be performing a public service by exposure.

I. F. Stone's Weekly 7 September 1952

Tom Stoppard 1937-
British dramatist

2 It's not the voting that's democracy, it's the counting.

Jumpers (1972); see **Somoza** 374:3

3 The House of Lords, an illusion to which I have never been able to subscribe—responsibility without power, the prerogative of the eunuch throughout the ages.

Lord Malquist and Mr Moon (1966); see **Kipling** 221:5

4 Comment is free but facts are on expenses.

Night and Day (1978); see **Scott** 348:6

5 I'm with you on the free press. It's the newspapers I can't stand.

Night and Day (1978)

6 War is capitalism with the gloves off and many who go to war know it but they go to war because they don't want to be a hero.

Travesties (1975)

William Stoughton 1631-1701
American clergyman

7 God hath sifted a nation that he might send choice grain into this wilderness.

election sermon in Boston, 29 April 1669

Lord Stowell 1745-1836
English jurist

8 The elegant simplicity of the three per cents.

Lord Campbell *Lives of the Lord Chancellors* (1857); see **Disraeli** 122:20

9 A precedent embalms a principle.
an opinion, while Advocate-General, 1788

quoted by Disraeli in the House of Commons, 22 February 1848

Thomas Wentworth, Lord Strafford
1593-1641
English statesman

10 The authority of a King is the keystone which closeth up the arch of order and government which, once shaken, all the frame falls together in a confused heap of foundation and battlement.

Hugh Trevor-Roper *Historical Essays* (1952)

John Whitaker ('Jack') Straw 1946-
British Labour politician

11 What you have within the UK is three small nations who've been under the cosh of the English.

in *Sunday Times* 6 January 2000 'Talking Heads'

12 There is no list, and Syria isn't on it.
on the US description of Syria as a rogue state

speech, Qatar; in *Guardian* 15 April 2003 (online edition)

Barbra Streisand 1942-
American singer and actress

1 We elected a President, not a Pope.
   to journalists at the White House, 5 February 1998

reported by James Naughtie, BBC Radio 4, Today programme, 6 February 1998

Belinda Stronach 1966-
Canadian Conservative politician, who in May 2005 crossed the floor to join the Liberals

2 The political crisis affecting Canada is too risky and dangerous for blind partnership.
   of the Conservative Party's decision to align itself with the separatist Bloc Québécois against the Liberal government of Paul **Martin**

at a news conference announcing her defection to the Liberals, 17 May 2005

3 I do not believe that the party leader [Stephen Harper] is truly sensitive to the needs of each part of the country and just how big and complex Canada is.

at a news conference announcing her defection to the Liberals, 17 May 2005 (see **Harper** 173:10)

Simeon Strunsky 1879-1948

4 People who want to understand democracy should spend less time in the library with Aristotle and more time on buses and in the subway.

No Mean City (1944)

Louis Sullivan 1933-
American politician, Secretary of Health and Human Services

5 *on the probable nature of a nationalized health service:*
   What we would have is a combination of the compassion of the Internal Revenue Service and the efficiency of the post office.

in *Newsweek* February 1992

Timothy Daniel Sullivan 1827-1914
Irish writer and politician

6 'God save Ireland!' said the heroes;
   'God save Ireland', say they all:
   Whether on the scaffold high
   Or the battlefield we die,
   Oh, what matter when for Erin dear we fall.

'God Save Ireland' (1867); see **Last words** 226:7

Maximilien de Béthune, Duc de Sully 1559-1641
French statesman

7 Tilling and grazing are the two breasts by which France is fed.

Mémoires (1638)

8 The English take their pleasures sadly after the fashion of their country.

attributed

Arthur Hays Sulzberger 1891-1968
American newspaper proprietor

9 We tell the public which way the cat is jumping. The public will take care of the cat.
   on journalism

in *Time* 8 May 1950

Charles Sumner 1811–74

American politician and orator
on Sumner: see **Adams** 2:11

1 Where Slavery is, there Liberty cannot be; and where Liberty is, there Slavery cannot be.

'Slavery and the Rebellion'; speech at Cooper Institute 5 November 1864

2 There is the National flag. He must be cold, indeed, who can look upon its folds rippling in the breeze without pride of country. If in a foreign land, the flag is companionship, and country itself, with all its endearments.

Are We a Nation? 19 November 1867

Hannen Swaffer 1879–1962

British journalist

3 Freedom of the press in Britain means freedom to print such of the proprietor's prejudices as the advertisers don't object to.

said to Tom Driberg *c.*1928; Tom Driberg *Swaff* (1974)

Jonathan Swift 1667–1745

Irish poet and satirist

4 It is the folly of too many, to mistake the echo of a London coffee-house for the voice of the kingdom.

The Conduct of the Allies (1711)

5 Laws are like cobwebs, which may catch small flies, but let wasps and hornets break through.

A Critical Essay upon the Faculties of the Mind (1709); see **Anacharsis** 7:7, **Shenstone** 362:12

6 I cannot but conclude the bulk of your natives to be the most pernicious race of little odious vermin that nature ever suffered to crawl upon the surface of the earth.

Gulliver's Travels (1726) 'A Voyage to Brobdingnag'

7 And he gave it for his opinion, that whoever could make two ears of corn or two blades of grass to grow upon a spot of ground where only one grew before, would deserve better of mankind, and do more essential service to his country than the whole race of politicians put together.

Gulliver's Travels (1726) 'A Voyage to Brobdingnag'

8 I have been assured by a very knowing American of my acquaintance in London, that a young healthy child well nursed is at a year old a most delicious, nourishing, and wholesome food, whether stewed, roasted, baked, or boiled, and I make no doubt that it will equally serve in a fricassee, or a ragout.

A Modest Proposal for Preventing the Children of Ireland from being a Burden to their Parents or Country (1729)

9 Party is the madness of many for the gain of a few.

Thoughts on Various Subjects (1711)

Tacitus c.AD 56–after 117

Roman senator and historian

10 *Res olim dissociabiles miscuerit, principatum ac libertatem.*

He [Nerva] has united things long incompatible, the principate and liberty.

Agricola; see **Disraeli** 121:19

11 *Nunc terminus Britanniae patet, atque omne ignotum pro magnifico est.*

Now the boundary of Britain is revealed, and everything unknown is held to be glorious.
  reporting the speech of a British leader, Calgacus

Agricola

1 They make a wilderness and call it peace.

Agricola

2 Those whose habit it is to admire what is forbidden ought to know that there can be great men even under bad emperors, and that duty and discretion, if coupled with energy and a career of action, will bring a man to no less glorious summits than are attained by perilous paths and ostentatious deaths that do not benefit the Commonwealth.

Agricola ch. 42 (translated by A. R. Birling)

3 You were indeed fortunate, Agricola, not only in the distinction of your life, but also in the lucky timing of your death.

Agricola

4 *Sine ira et studio.*

With neither anger nor partiality.

Annals

5 The more corrupt the republic, the more numerous the laws.

Annals

6 These times having the rare good fortune that you may think what you like and say what you think.

Histories

7 *Maior privato visus dum privatus fuit, et omnium consensu capax imperii nisi imperasset.*

He seemed much greater than a private citizen while he still was a private citizen, and by everyone's consent capable of reigning if only he had not reigned.
   of the Emperor Galba

Histories

8 The gods are on the side of the stronger.

Histories; see **Voltaire** 407:9

William Howard Taft 1857–1930

American Republican statesman, 27th President of the US, 1909–13

9 Next to the right of liberty, the right of property is the most important individual right guaranteed by the Constitution and the one which, united with that of personal liberty, has contributed more to the growth of civilization than any other institution established by the human race.

Popular Government (1913)

Charles-Maurice de Talleyrand 1754–1838

French statesman
on Talleyrand: see **Louis Philippe** 242:3, **Napoleon** 285:4

10 *of the Bourbons after returning from exile:*
They have learnt nothing, and forgotten nothing.
   a similar comment on the courtiers of **Louis XVIII**, *attributed to the French general Dumouriez, was quoted by* **Napoleon** *in his Declaration to the French on his return from Elba*

oral tradition, attributed to Talleyrand by the Chevalier de Panat, January 1796

11 *on hearing of* **Napoleon**'*s costly victory at Borodino,* 1812:
This is the beginning of the end.

Sainte-Beuve *M. de Talleyrand* (1870); attributed

12 It is not an event, it is an item of news.
   on hearing of the death of **Napoleon** *in* 1821

Philip Henry Stanhope *Notes of Conversations with the Duke of Wellington* (1888) 1 November 1831

13 Above all, gentlemen, not the slightest zeal.

P. Chasles *Voyages d'un critique à travers la vie et les livres* (1868) vol. 2

1 That, Sire, is a question of dates.
often quoted as, 'treason is a matter of dates'; replying to the Tsar's criticism of those who 'betrayed the cause of Europe'

Duff Cooper *Talleyrand* (1932)

2 What a sad old age you are preparing for yourself.
to a young diplomat who boasted of his ignorance of whist

J. Amédée Pichot *Souvenirs Intimes sur M. de Talleyrand* (1870) 'Le Pour et le Contre'

Wilbert Joseph ('Billy') Tauzin 1943–

American Republican politician

3 In many respects, this case appears to be eerily similar to the accounting hocus-pocus that occurred at Enron.
on the WorldCom collapse

in *BBC News* 28 June 2002 (electronic edition)

R. H. Tawney 1880–1962

British economic historian

4 The characteristic virtue of Englishmen is power of sustained practical activity and their characteristic vice a reluctance to test the quality of that activity by reference to principles.

The Acquisitive Society (1921)

5 Militarism . . . is fetish worship. It is the prostration of men's souls and the laceration of their bodies to appease an idol.

The Acquisitive Society (1921)

6 That seductive border region where politics grease the wheels of business and polite society smiles hopefully on both.

Business and Politics under James I (1958)

7 Those who dread a dead-level of income or wealth . . . do not dread, it seems, a dead-level of law and order, and of security for life and property.

Equality (1931)

8 Freedom for the pike is death for the minnows.

Equality (ed. 3 1938)

9 Private property is a necessary institution, at least in a fallen world; men work more and dispute less when goods are private than when they are common. But it is to be tolerated as a concession to human frailty, not applauded as desirable in itself.

Religion and the Rise of Capitalism (1926) ch. 1, sect. 1

10 Both the existing economic order, and too many of the projects advanced for reconstructing it, break down through their neglect of the truism that, since even quite common men have souls, no increase in material wealth will compensate them for arrangements which insult their self-respect and impair their freedom. A reasonable estimate of economic organisation must allow for the fact that, unless industry is to be paralysed by recurrent revolts on the part of outraged human nature, it must satisfy criteria which are not purely economic.

Religion and the Rise of Capitalism (1926) conclusion

11 Democracy a society where ordinary men exercise initiative. Dreadful respect for superiors. Mental enlargement . . . Real foe to be overcome . . . fact that large section of the public *like* plutocratic government, and are easily gullible. How shake them!

unpublished fragment of Chicago lecture (1939), read at Tawney's funeral

12 *declining the offer of a peerage:*
What harm have I ever done to the Labour Party?

in *Evening Standard* 18 January 1962

A. J. P. Taylor 1906-90

British historian

1 History gets thicker as it approaches recent times.
English History 1914–45 (1965) Bibliography

2 In the Second World War the British people came of age. This was a people's war . . . Few now sang *Land of Hope and Glory*. Few even sang *England Arise*. England had risen all the same.
English History, 1914–1945 (1965)

3 He aroused every feeling except trust.
of Lloyd George
English History 1914–1945 (1965)

4 The politician performs upon the stage; the historian looks behind the scenery.
Englishmen and Others (1956)

5 The First World War had begun—imposed on the statesmen of Europe by railway timetables. It was an unexpected climax to the railway age.
The First World War (1963)

6 *of the period after the First World War:*
Civilization was held together by the civilized behaviour of ordinary people . . . In reality the masses were calmer and more sensible than those who ruled over them.
From Sarajevo to Potsdam (1966)

7 A racing tipster who only reached Hitler's level of accuracy would not do well for his clients.
The Origins of the Second World War (1961)

8 Human blunders, however, usually do more to shape history than human wickedness.
The Origins of the Second World War (1961)

9 With Hitler guilty, every other German could claim innocence.
The Origins of the Second World War (1961)

10 If men are to respect each other for what they are, they must cease to respect each other for what they own.
Politicians, Socialism and Historians (1980)

11 Crimea: The War That Would Not Boil.
Rumours of Wars (1952); originally the title of an essay in *History Today* 2 February 1951

12 Conformity may give you a quiet life; it may even bring you a University Chair. But all change in history, all advance, comes from the nonconformist. If there had been no trouble makers, no Dissenters, we should still be living in caves.
The Troublemakers (1957)

13 Without democracy socialism would be worth nothing, but democracy is worth a great deal even when it is not socialist.
in *Manchester Guardian* 7 March 1941

14 The British political system has no room for the rogue elephant.
in *History Today* July 1951 'Lord Palmerston'

15 Bismarck was a political genius of the highest rank, but he lacked one essential quality of the constructive statesman: he had no faith in the future.
in *Encyclopedia Britannica* (1954)

16 Appeasement was a sensible course, even though it was tried with the wrong man; and it remains the noblest word in the diplomatist's vocabulary.
in *Manchester Guardian* 30 September 1958

17 Like Johnson's friend Edwards, I, too have tried to be a Marxist but common sense kept breaking in.
'Accident Prone' in *Journal of Modern History* 1977

Henry Taylor 1800–86

British writer

1 It is of far greater importance to a statesman to make one friend who will hold out with him for twenty years, than to find twenty followers in each year, losing as many.

The Statesman (1836)

2 No statesman, be he as discreet as he may, will escape having ascribed to him, as the result of interviews, promises and understandings which it was not his purpose to convey; and yet in a short time he will be unable to recollect what was said with sufficient distinctness to enable him to give a confident contradiction.

The Statesman (1836)

3 The conscience of a statesman should be rather a strong conscience than a tender conscience.

The Statesman (1836)

4 It is very certain that there may be met with, in public life, a species of conscience which is all bridle and no spurs.

The Statesman (1836)

5 The hand which executes a measure should belong to the head which propounds it.

The Statesman (1836)

6 One who would thrive by seeking favours from the great, should never trouble them for small ones.

The Statesman (1836)

7 [A statesman] should steer by the compass, but he must lie with the wind.

The Statesman (1836)

8 A secret may be sometimes best kept by keeping the secret of its being a secret.

The Statesman (1836)

9 To choose that which will bring him the most credit with the least trouble, has hitherto been the sole care of the statesman in office.

The Statesman (1836)

10 Good nature and kindness towards those with whom they come in personal contact, at the expense of public interests, that is of those whom they never see, is the besetting sin of public men.

The Statesman (1836)

11 He who has once advanced by a stride will not be content to advance afterwards by steps. Public servants, therefore, like racehorses, should be well fed with reward, but not to fatness.

The Statesman (1836)

12 Men in high places, from having less personal interest in the characters of others—being safe from them—are commonly less acute observers, and with their progressive elevation in life become, as more and more indifferent to what other men are, so more and more ignorant of them.

The Statesman (1836)

Norman Tebbit 1931–

British Conservative politician
on Tebbit: see **Foot** 142:7

13 I grew up in the Thirties with our unemployed father. He did not riot, he got on his bike and looked for work.

speech at Conservative Party Conference, 15 October 1981

14 The cricket test—which side do they cheer for? . . . Are you still looking back to where you came from or where you are?
  on the loyalties of Britain's immigrant population

interview in *Los Angeles Times*, reported in *Daily Telegraph* 20 A▮ 1990

Tecumseh 1768–1813
American Shawnee chief

1 Where today are the Pequot? Where are the Narragansett, the Mohican, the Pokanoket, and many other once powerful tribes of our people? They have vanished before the avarice and oppression of the white man, as snow before the summer sun.

Dee Brown *Bury My Heart at Wounded Knee* (1970) ch. 1

Richard Grenville, 2nd Earl Temple
1711–79
English aristocrat and politician

2 A dead minister, the most respectable that ever existed, weighs very light in the scale against any living one.
   *to his nephew, William **Pitt** the Younger*

letter, 18 July 1779

William Temple 1881–1944
English theologian; Archbishop of Canterbury from 1942

3 In place of the conception of the power-state we are led to that of the welfare-state.

Citizen and Churchman (1941)

John Tenniel 1820–1914
English draughtsman

4 Dropping the pilot.
   *cartoon caption, and title of poem, on **Bismarck**'s dismissal from office by Kaiser **Wilhelm II***

in *Punch* 29 March 1890

Lord Tennyson 1809–92
English poet

5 Kind hearts are more than coronets,
  And simple faith than Norman blood.

'Lady Clara Vere de Vere' (1842) st. 7

6 　　　　Forward, forward let us range,
  Let the great world spin for ever down the ringing grooves
     of change.

'Locksley Hall' (1842)

7 The last great Englishman is low.

'Ode on the Death of the Duke of Wellington' (1852)

8 O good grey head which all men knew!

'Ode on the Death of the Duke of Wellington' (1852)

9 O fall'n at length that tower of strength
  Which stood four-square to all the winds that blew!

'Ode on the Death of the Duke of Wellington' (1852)

10 That world-earthquake, Waterloo!

'Ode on the Death of the Duke of Wellington' (1852)

11 Who never sold the truth to serve the hour,
   Nor paltered with Eternal God for power.

'Ode on the Death of the Duke of Wellington' (1852)

12 Not once or twice in our rough island-story,
   The path of duty was the way to glory.

'Ode on the Death of the Duke of Wellington' (1852)

13 Authority forgets a dying king.

'The Passing of Arthur' (1869)

14 The old order changeth, yielding place to new,
   And God fulfils himself in many ways,
   Lest one good custom should corrupt the world.

'The Passing of Arthur' 1869

1 A land of settled government,
A land of just and old renown,
Where Freedom slowly broadens down
From precedent to precedent.

'You ask me, why, though ill at ease' (1842)

Terence c.190–159 BC

Roman comic dramatist

2 *Quot homines tot sententiae: suus cuique mos.*

There are as many opinions as there are people: each has his own correct way.

Phormio

Margaret Thatcher 1925–

British Conservative stateswoman; Prime Minister, 1979–90
on Thatcher: see **Anonymous** 10:3, **Biffen** 42:7, **Callaghan** 71:3, **Critchley** 105:5, **Healey** 177:6, **Healey** 177:8, **Healey** 177:10, **Hennessy** 180:2, **Kinnock** 218:10, **Major** 256:11, **Mitterrand** 275:5, **Parris** 305:5, **West** 416:10

3 No woman in my time will be Prime Minister or Chancellor or Foreign Secretary—not the top jobs. Anyway I wouldn't want to be Prime Minister. You have to give yourself 100%.
on her appointment as Shadow Education Spokesman

in *Sunday Telegraph* 26 October 1969

4 In politics if you want anything said, ask a man. If you want anything done, ask a woman.

in *People* (New York) 15 September 1975

5 I'll always be fond of dear Ted, but there's no sympathy in politics.
of her predecessor, Edward **Heath**

attributed, 1975

6 I stand before you tonight in my red chiffon evening gown, my face softly made up, my fair hair gently waved . . . the Iron Lady of the Western World! Me? A cold war warrior? Well, yes—if that is how they wish to interpret my defence of values and freedoms fundamental to our way of life.
referring to 'the iron lady' as the name given to her by the Soviet defence ministry newspaper Red Star, *which accused her of trying to revive the cold war*

speech at Finchley, 31 January 1976

7 Pennies don't fall from heaven. They have to be earned on earth.

in *Observer* 18 November 1979 'Sayings of the Week'

8 I don't mind how much my Ministers talk, as long as they do what I say.

in *Observer* 27 January 1980

9 We have to get our production and our earnings in balance. There's no easy popularity in what we are proposing, but it is fundamentally sound. Yet I believe people accept there is no real alternative.
popularly encapsulated in the acronym TINA

speech at Conservative Women's Conference, 21 May 1980

10 To those waiting with bated breath for that favourite media catch-phrase, the U-turn, I have only this to say. 'You turn if you want; the lady's not for turning.'

speech at Conservative Party Conference in Brighton, 10 October 1980

11 Economics are the method; the object is to change the soul.

in *Sunday Times* 3 May 1981

12 We have to see that the spirit of the South Atlantic—the real spirit of Britain—is kindled not only by war but can now be fired by peace. We have the first prerequisite. We know that we can do it—we haven't lost the ability. That is the Falklands Factor.

speech in Cheltenham, 3 July 1982

1 Let me make one thing absolutely clear. The National Health Service is safe with us.

speech at Conservative Party Conference, 8 October 1982

2 Just rejoice at that news and congratulate our armed forces and the Marines. Rejoice!
on the recapture of South Georgia, usually quoted as, 'Rejoice, rejoice!'

to newsmen outside 10 Downing Street, 25 April 1982

3 It is exciting to have a real crisis on your hands, when you have spent half your political life dealing with humdrum issues like the environment.
on the Falklands campaign, 1982

speech to Scottish Conservative Party conference, 14 May 1982

4 I was asked whether I was trying to restore Victorian values. I said straight out I was. And I am.

speech to the British Jewish Community, 21 July 1983, referring to an interview with Brian Walden on 17 January 1983

5 Now it must be business as usual.
on the steps of Brighton police station a few hours after the bombing of the Grand Hotel, Brighton; often quoted as 'We shall carry on as usual'

in *The Times* 13 October 1984

6 In church on Sunday morning—it was a lovely morning and we haven't had many lovely days—the sun was coming through a stained glass window and falling on some flowers, falling right across the church. It just occurred to me that this was the day I was meant not to see. Then all of a sudden I thought, 'there are some of my dearest friends who are not seeing this day.'
after the Brighton bombing

television interview, 15 October 1984

7 *of Mikhail **Gorbachev**:*
We can do business together.

in *The Times* 18 December 1984

8 We got a really good consensus during the last election. Consensus behind my convictions.

attributed, 1984

9 We must try to find ways to starve the terrorist and the hijacker of the oxygen of publicity on which they depend.

speech to American Bar Association in London, 15 July 1985

10 I don't spend a lifetime watching which way the cat jumps. I know really which way I want the cats to go.

interview with Michael Charlton on BBC radio, 17 December 1985

11 No one would remember the Good Samaritan if he'd only had good intentions. He had money as well.

television interview, 6 January 1986

12 There is no such thing as Society. There are individual men and women, and there are families.

in *Woman's Own* 31 October 1987

13 No generation has a freehold on this earth. All we have is a life tenancy—with a full repairing lease.

speech to the Conservative Party Conference, 14 October 1988

14 We have become a grandmother.

in *The Times* 4 March 1989

15 Advisers advise and ministers decide.
*on the respective roles of her personal economic adviser, Alan Walters, and her Chancellor, Nigel **Lawson** (who resigned the following day)*

in the House of Commons, 26 October 1989

16 You don't reach Downing Street by pretending you've travelled the road to Damascus when you haven't even left home.
*of Neil **Kinnock***

in *Independent* 14 October 1989

1 I am naturally very sorry to see you go, but understand . . .
your wish to be able to spend more time with your family.
reply to Norman **Fowler**'s *resignation letter*

in *Guardian* 4 January 1990; see
Fowler 144:5

2 Others bring me problems, David brings me solutions.
of Lord Young

in *Observer* 1 July 1990

3 No! No! No!
*making clear her opposition to a single European currency, and
more centralized controls from Brussels*

in the House of Commons, 30
October 1990

4 I fight on, I fight to win.
having failed to win outright in the first ballot for party leader

comment, 21 November 1990

5 It's a funny old world.
*on withdrawing from the contest for leadership of the
Conservative party*

comment, 22 November 1990

6 I shan't be pulling the levers there but I shall be a very good
back-seat driver.
on the appointment of John **Major** *as the next Prime Minister*

in *Independent* 27 November 1990

7 Every Prime Minister needs a Willie.
at the farewell dinner for William **Whitelaw**

in *Guardian* 7 August 1991

8 *of being told by a majority of her Cabinet that she could not continue
as Prime Minister:*
Treachery with a smile on its face.

on 'The Thatcher Years' (BBC 1), 20
October 1993

9 *of the poll tax:*
Given time, it would have been seen as one of the most far-
reaching and beneficial reforms ever made in the working of
local government.

The Downing Street Years (1993)

10 I'm worried about that young man, he's getting awfully
bossy.
on Tony Blair

in *Irish Times* 6 February 1999 'This
Week They Said'

11 In my lifetime all our problems have come from mainland
Europe and all the solutions have come from the English-
speaking nations of the world.

in *Times* 6 October 1999

12 *asked if she thought Tony Blair's government was Thatcherite:*
There might have been a tincture of it but that is all. He has
a long way to come to be purely Thatcherite.

interview, 6 May 2005

William Roscoe Thayer 1859–1923

American biographer and historian

13 From log-cabin to White House.

title of biography (1910) of James
Garfield

Themistocles c.528–c.462 BC

Greek historian and Athenian statesman

14 The wooden wall is your ships.
*interpreting the words of the Delphic oracle to the Athenians,
before the battle of Salamis in 480 BC*

Plutarch *Parallel Lives*
'Themistocles' bk. 2, ch. 1; see
below

Yet Zeus the all-seeing grants to Athene's prayer
That the wooden wall only shall not fall, but help you and
your children.

words of the prophetess at Delphi;
Herodotus *Histories* bk. 7, sect.
141

Louis Adolphe Thiers 1797–1877
French statesman and historian

1 The king reigns, and the people govern themselves.

unsigned article in *Le National*, 20 January 1830; a signed article, 4 February 1830, reads: 'The king neither administers nor governs, he reigns'

Dylan Thomas 1914–53
Welsh poet

2 The hand that signed the paper felled a city;
Five sovereign fingers taxed the breath,
Doubled the globe of death and halved a country;
These five kings did a king to death.

'The Hand That Signed the Paper Felled a City'

3 The hand that signed the treaty bred a fever,
And famine grew, and locusts came;
Great is the hand that holds dominion over
Man by a scribbled name.

'The Hand That Signed the Paper Felled a City'

J. H. Thomas 1874–1949
British Socialist politician

4 And now 'ere we 'ave this obstinate little man with 'is Mrs Simpson. Hit won't do, 'arold, I tell you that straight.
*to Harold **Nicolson** on **Edward VIII** and the Abdication crisis*

Harold Nicolson letter 26 February 1936

5 They 'ate 'aving no family life at Court.
of the British people and the Abdication crisis

Harold Nicolson letter 26 February 1936

Norman Thomas 1884–1968
American Presbyterian minister and writer

6 I'd rather see America save her soul than her face.
protesting against the Vietnam War

speech in Washington, DC, 27 November 1965

Julian Thompson 1934–
British soldier, second-in-command of the land forces during the Falklands campaign.

7 You don't mind dying for Queen and country, but you certainly don't want to die for politicians.

'The Falklands War—the Untold Story' (Yorkshire Television) 1 April 1987

Robert Norman Thompson 1914–97
American-born Canadian mission worker, politician and academic

8 The Americans are our best friends whether we like it or not.

Peter C. Newman *Home Country: People, Places, and Power Politics* (1973)

Lord Thomson of Fleet 1894–1976
Canadian-born British newspaper and television proprietor

9 *on owning a commercial television station:*
It's just like having a licence to print your own money.

R. Braddon *Roy Thomson* (1965)

Henry David Thoreau 1817–62
American writer

1 I heartily accept the motto, 'That government is best which governs least' . . . Carried out, it finally amounts to this, which I also believe,—'That government is best which governs not at all.'

Civil Disobedience (1849); see **O'Sullivan** 298:7

2 Under a government which imprisons any unjustly, the true place for a just man is also a prison.

Civil Disobedience (1849)

3 The oldest, wisest politician grows not more human so, but is merely a grey wharf-rat at last.

Journal 1853

4 The government of the world I live in was not framed, like that of Britain, in after-dinner conversations over the wine.

Walden (1854) 'Conclusion'

5 It takes two to speak the truth,—one to speak, and another to hear.

A Week on the Concord and Merrimack Rivers (1849) 'Wednesday'

Jeremy Thorpe 1929–
British Liberal politician

6 *of Harold* **Macmillan***'s sacking seven of his Cabinet on 13 July 1962*
Greater love hath no man than this, that he lay down his friends for his life.

D. E. Butler and Anthony King *The General Election of 1964* (1965)

Thucydides c.455–c.400 BC
Greek historian

7 Happiness depends on being free, and freedom depends on being courageous.

Thucydides *History of the Peloponnesian War* bk. 2, ch. 4, sect. 43 (translated by Rex Warner)

James Thurber 1894–1961
American humorist

8 You can fool too many of the people too much of the time.

Fables for our Time (1940); see **Lincoln** 236:13

Lord Thurlow 1731–1806
English jurist; Lord Chancellor, 1778–83, 1783–92

9 Corporations have neither bodies to be punished, nor souls to be condemned, they therefore do as they like.
usually quoted as 'Did you ever expect a corporation to have a conscience, when it has no soul to be damned, and no body to be kicked?'

John Poynder *Literary Extracts* (1844) vol. 1

Tiberius 42 BC–AD 37
Roman emperor from AD 14

10 It is the part of the good shepherd to shear his flock, not skin it.
to governors who recommended burdensome taxes

Suetonius *Lives of the Caesars* 'Tiberius'

Kahn Tineta-Horn 1940–

American-born Canadian political activist, fashion model and civil servant

1 Why don't you all go back to where you came from? We own this land; we're your landlords. And the rent is due.
   on white Canadians occupying land belonging to Native Canadians

Myrna Kostash *Long Way From Home* (1980)

Tipu Sultan c.1750–99

Indian ruler

2 In this world I would rather live two days like a tiger, than two hundred years like a sheep.

Alexander Beatson *A View of the Origin and Conduct of the War with Tippoo Sultan* (1800) ch. 10

Buti Tlhagale 1947–

South African priest, Archbishop of Johannesburg

3 [The Catholic Church is] like a train that will not take a sharp turn.
   expressing the view that the election of an African Pope in 2005 was unlikely

in *Mail and Guardian* 4 April 2005

Alexis de Tocqueville 1805–59

French historian and politician

4 Where is the man of soul so base that he would prefer to depend on the caprices of one of his fellow men rather than obey the laws which he has himself contributed to establish?

The Ancien Régime (1856)

5 Despots themselves do not deny that freedom is excellent; only they desire it for themselves alone, and they maintain that everyone else is altogether unworthy of it.

The Ancien Régime (1856)

6 The French Revolution operated in reference to this world in exactly the same manner as religious revolutions acted in view of the other world. It considered the citizen as an abstract proposition apart from any particular society, in the same way as religions considered man as man, independent of country and time.

The Ancien Régime (1856)

7 History is a gallery of pictures in which there are few originals and many copies.

The Ancien Régime (1856)

8 When a nation abolishes aristocracy, centralization follows as a matter of course.

The Ancien Régime (1856)

9 The only substantial difference between the custom of those days and our own resides in the price paid for office. Then they were sold by government, now they are bestowed; it is no longer necessary to pay money; the object can be attained by selling one's soul.

The Ancien Régime (1856)

10 Centralization and socialism are native of the same soil: one is the wild herb, the other the garden plant.

The Ancien Régime (1856)

11 What do men need in order to remain free? A taste for freedom. Do not ask me to analyze that sublime taste; it can only be felt. It has a place in every great heart which God has prepared to receive it; it fills and inflames it. To try to explain it to those inferior minds who have never felt it is to waste time.

The Ancien Régime (1856)

1 No example is so dangerous as that of violence employed by well-meaning people for beneficial objects.

The Ancien Régime (1856)

2 He who desires in liberty anything other than itself is born to be a servant.

The Ancien Régime (1856)

3 It is not always by going from bad to worse that a society falls into revolution . . . The social order destroyed by a revolution is almost always better than that which immediately preceded it, and experience shows that the most dangerous moment for a bad government is generally that in which it sets about reform.

The Ancien Régime (1856)

4 The surface of American society is covered with a layer of democratic paint, but from time to time one can see the old aristocratic colours breaking through.

Democracy in America (1835–40) vol.1

5 Americans rightly think their patriotism is a sort of religion strengthened by practical service.

Democracy in America (1835–40) vol.1

6 The President may slip without the state suffering, for his duties are limited. Congress may slip without the Union perishing, for above Congress there is the electoral body which can change its spirit by changing its membership. But if ever the Supreme Court came to be composed of rash or corrupt men, the confederation would be threatened by anarchy or civil war.

Democracy in America (1835–40) vol.1

7 Providence has not created mankind entirely independent or entirely free. It is true that around every man a fatal circle is traced, beyond which he cannot pass; but within the wide verge of that circle he is powerful and free.

Democracy in America (1835–40) vol. 1

8 Of all nations, those submit to civilization with the most difficulty which habitually live by the chase.

Democracy in America (1835–40) vol. 1

9 What is understood by republican government in the United States is the slow and quiet action of society upon itself.

Democracy in America (1835–40) vol. 1

10 On my arrival in the United States I was struck by the degree of ability among the governed and the lack of it among the governing.

Democracy in America (1835–40) vol. 2

11 The French want no-one to be their *superior*. The English want *inferiors*. The Frenchman constantly raises his eyes above him with anxiety. The Englishman lowers his beneath him with satisfaction. On either side it is pride, but understood in a different way.

Voyage en Angleterre et en Irlande de 1835 (1958) 8 May 1835

Wolfe Tone 1763–98

Irish nationalist
see also **Last words** 226:10

12 I am sorry it was necessary.
on the execution of Louis XVI, 21 January 1793

Oliver Knox *Rebels and Informers* (1997)

13 To unite the whole people of Ireland, to abolish the memory of all past dissension and to substitute the common name of Irishman in place of the denominations of Protestant, Catholic and Dissenter.

in August 1796; Marianne Elliott *Wolfe Tone* (1989)

Robert Torrens 1780–1864
British economist

1 In the first stone which he [the savage] flings at the wild animals he pursues, in the first stick that he seizes to strike down the fruit which hangs above his reach, we see the appropriation of one article for the purpose of aiding in the acquisition of another, and thus discover the origin of capital.

An Essay on the Production of Wealth (1821) ch. 2

Arnold Toynbee 1889–1975
English historian

2 Civilization is a movement and not a condition, a voyage and not a harbour.

in *Readers Digest* October 1958

3 America is a large, friendly dog in a very small room. Every time it wags its tail it knocks over a chair.

attributed

4 The twentieth century will be remembered chiefly, not as an age of political conflicts and technical inventions, but as an age in which human society dared to think of the health of the whole human race as a practical objective.

attributed

Joseph Trapp 1679–1747
English poet and pamphleteer

5 The King, observing with judicious eyes
The state of both his universities,
To Oxford sent a troop of horse, and why?
That learned body wanted loyalty;
To Cambridge books, as very well discerning
How much that loyal body wanted learning.
  lines written on George I's donation of the Bishop of Ely's Library to Cambridge University

John Nichols *Literary Anecdotes* (1812–16) vol. 3; see **Browne** 58:6

Lord Trend 1914–87
British civil servant; Cabinet Secretary 1963–73

6 The acid test of any political decision is, 'What is the alternative?'

attributed, 1975

Charles Trevelyan 1807–86
British civil servant

7 *on the organization of a new system of admission into the civil service:*
It is proposed to invite the flower of our youth to the aid of public service.

to John Thadeus Delane, Editor of *The Times*, in 1853

G. M. Trevelyan 1876–1962
English historian

8 If the French noblesse had been capable of playing cricket with their peasants, their chateaux would never have been burnt.

English Social History (1942)

9 In a world of voluble hates, he plotted to make men like, or at least tolerate one another.
  *of Stanley **Baldwin***

in *Dictionary of National Biography 1941–50* (1959)

William Trevor 1928–

Irish novelist and short story writer

1 *of the troubles in Northern Ireland:*
A disease in the family that is never mentioned.

in *Observer* 18 November 1990

2 When you looked at the map Ireland and England seemed like lovers . . . 'Does the map remind you curiously of an embrace? A most extraordinary embrace to throw up all this.'

Fools of Fortune (1983)

Hugh Trevor-Roper 1914–2003

British historian

3 Those who exercise power and determine policy are generally men whose minds have been formed by events twenty or thirty years before.

From Counter-Reformation to Glorious Revolution (1992); introduction

4 How are we to disentangle religion from politics in a revolution? Religion may form the outlook of an individual. It may serve as an ideological intoxicant for a crowd. But in high politics it is a variable.

From Counter-Reformation to Glorious Revolution (1992)

5 Aristocracies . . . may preserve themselves longest, but only democracies, which refresh their ruling class, can expand.

Historical Essays (1952)

6 Historians in general are great toadies of power.

History and Imagination (1981)

7 Any reaction which is to be successful over a long period must have radical origins . . . A reaction which is to last, which is to be accepted as orthodoxy over several generations, must spring out of the same social circumstances as the progress which it resists.

The Rise of Christian Europe (1965)

David Trimble 1944–

Northern Irish politician, leader of the Ulster Unionist Party 1995–2005

8 We are not here to negotiate with them, but to confront them.
on entering the Mitchell talks on Northern Ireland with Sinn Féin

in *Guardian* 18 September 1997

9 The fundamental Act of Union is there, intact.
of the Northern Ireland settlement

in *Daily Telegraph* 11 April 1998

10 Once we are agreed our only weapons will be our words, then there is nothing that cannot be said, there is nothing that cannot be achieved.

in *Guardian* 4 September 1998

11 Mr Adams, it is over to you. We have jumped, you follow.
after the Ulster Unionist Council had voted to accept the setting up of the Northern Irish executive

in *Sunday Telegraph* 28 November 1999

Tommy Trinder 1909–89

British comedian

12 *of American troops in Britain during the Second World War:*
Overpaid, overfed, oversexed, and over here.

associated with Trinder, but probably not his invention

Anthony Trollope 1815–82

English novelist

1 I have hardly as yet met two Englishmen who were agreed as to the political power of the sovereign.

The American Senator (1877)

2 A man who entertains in his mind any political doctrine, except as a means of improving the condition of his fellows, I regard as a political intriguer, a charlatan, and a conjuror.

Autobiography (1883)

3 When taken in the refreshing waters of office any . . . pill can be swallowed.

The Bertrams (1859)

4 *of political life:*
The hatreds which sound so real when you read the mere words, which look so true when you see their scornful attitudes, on which for the time you are inclined to pin your faith so implicitly, amount to nothing.

The Landleaguers (1883)

5 But in truth the capacity of a man . . . [to be Prime Minister] does not depend on any power of intellect, or indomitable courage, or far-seeing cunning. The man is competent simply because he is believed to be so.

Lord Palmerston (1882)

6 To me it seems that no form of existing government—no form of government that ever did exist, gives or has given so large a measure of individual freedom to all who live under it as a constitutional monarchy.

North America (1862)

7 There is nothing more tyrannical than a strong popular feeling among a democratic people.

North America (1862)

8 I have sometimes thought that there is no being so venomous, so bloodthirsty as a professed philanthropist.

North America (1862)

9 [Equality] is a doctrine to be forgiven when he who preaches it is . . . striving to raise others to his own level.

North America (1862)

10 A fainéant government is not the worst government that England can have. It has been the great fault of our politicians that they have all wanted to do something.

Phineas Finn (1869)

11 *of the radical politician:*
It was his work to cut down forest-trees, and he had nothing to do with the subsequent cultivation of the land.

Phineas Finn (1869)

12 The first necessity for good speaking is a large audience.

Phineas Finn (1869)

13 It is the necessary nature of a political party in this country to avoid, as long as it can be avoided, the consideration of any question which involves a great change . . . The best carriage horses are those which can most steadily hold back against the coach as it trundles down the hill.

Phineas Redux (1874)

14 Newspaper editors sport daily with the names of men of whom they do not hesitate to publish almost the severest words that can be uttered; but let an editor be himself attacked, even without his name, and he thinks that the thunderbolt of heaven should fall upon the offender.

Phineas Redux (1874) ch. 27

15 A man destined to sit conspicuously on our Treasury Bench, or on the seat opposite to it, should ask the Gods for a thick skin as a first gift.

Phineas Redux (1874)

16 Equality would be a heaven, if we could attain it.

The Prime Minister (1876)

17 What Good Government ever was not stingy?

South Africa (1878)

1 How seldom is it that theories stand the wear and tear of practice!

Thackeray (1879)

2 Let the Toryism of the Tory be ever so strong, it is his destiny to carry out the purposes of his opponents.

Why Frau Frohmann Raised Her Prices (1882)

Leon Trotsky 1879–1940
Russian revolutionary

3 Old age is the most unexpected of all things that happen to a man.

Diary in Exile (1959) 8 May 1935

4 Civilization has made the peasantry its pack animal. The bourgeoisie in the long run only changed the form of the pack.

History of the Russian Revolution (1933) vol. 3

5 You [the Mensheviks] are pitiful isolated individuals; you are bankrupts; your role is played out. Go where you belong from now on—into the dustbin of history!

History of the Russian Revolution (1933) vol. 3

6 Where force is necessary, there it must be applied boldly, decisively and completely. But one must know the limitations of force; one must know when to blend force with a manoeuvre, a blow with an agreement.

What Next? (1932)

7 Not believing in force is the same thing as not believing in gravitation.

G. Maximov *The Guillotine at Work* (1940)

8 In a country where the sole employer is the State, opposition means death by slow starvation. The old principle: who does not work shall not eat, has been replaced by a new one: who does not obey shall not eat.

attributed

Pierre Trudeau 1919–2000
Canadian Liberal statesman, Prime Minister, 1968–79 and 1980–4

9 The state has no place in the nation's bedrooms.

interview, Ottawa, 22 December 1967

10 The twentieth century really belongs to those who will build it. The future can be promised to no one.

in 1968; see **Laurier** 228:11

11 Living next to you is in some ways like sleeping with an elephant. No matter how friendly and even-tempered the beast, one is affected by every twitch and grunt.
on relations between Canada and the US

speech at National Press Club, Washington D. C., 25 March 1969

Harry S Truman 1884–1972
American Democratic statesman, 33rd President of the US 1945–53
on Truman: see **Mencken** 267:13, **Newspaper headlines** 287:4; *see also* **Mottoes** 281:2, **Proverbs** 318:13

12 *to reporters the day after his accession to the Presidency on the death of Franklin* **Roosevelt**:
When they told me yesterday what had happened, I felt like the moon, the stars and all the planets had fallen on me.

on 13 April 1945

13 Sixteen hours ago an American airplane dropped one bomb on Hiroshima . . . The force from which the sun draws its power has been loosed against those who brought war to the Far East.
first announcement of the dropping of the atomic bomb

on 6 August 1945

1 Effective, reciprocal, and enforceable safeguards acceptable to all nations.

Declaration on Atomic Energy by President Truman, Clement **Attlee**, *and W. L. Mackenzie King, Prime Minister of Canada*

on 15 November 1945

2 All the President is, is a glorified public relations man who spends his time flattering, kissing and kicking people to get them to do what they are supposed to do anyway.

letter to his sister, 14 November 1947

3 What we are doing in Korea is this: we are trying to prevent a third world war.

after the recall of General **MacArthur**

address to the nation, 16 April 1951

4 Those who want the Government to regulate matters of the mind and spirit are like men who are so afraid of being murdered that they commit suicide to avoid assassination.

address at the National Archives, Washington, DC, 15 December 1952

5 He'll sit right here and he'll say do this, do that! And nothing will happen. Poor Ike—it won't be a bit like the Army.

of his successor **Eisenhower**

Harry S. Truman (1973) vol. 2; see **Schwarzkopf** 348:5

6 Once a decision was made, I did not worry about it afterward.

Memoirs (1955) vol. 2

7 I never give them [the public] hell. I just tell the truth, and they think it is hell.

in *Look* 3 April 1956

8 A politician is a man who understands government, and it takes a politician to run a government. A statesman is a politician who's been dead 10 or 15 years.

in *New York World Telegram and Sun* 12 April 1958

9 It's a recession when your neighbour loses his job; it's a depression when you lose yours.

in *Observer* 13 April 1958

10 Wherever you have an efficient government you have a dictatorship.

lecture at Columbia University, 28 April 1959

11 To me, party platforms are contracts with the people.

Memoirs (1955) vol. 2

12 If there is one basic element in our Constitution, it is civilian control of the military.

Memoirs (1955) vol. 2

13 Always be sincere, even if you don't mean it.

attributed

14 I didn't fire him [General MacArthur] because he was a dumb son of a bitch, although he was, but that's not against the law for generals. If it was, half to three-quarters of them would be in jail.

Merle Miller *Plain Speaking* (1974)

15 Secrecy and a free, democratic government don't mix.

Merle Miller *Plain Speaking* (1974)

Sojourner Truth c.1797–1883
American evangelist and reformer

16 That man . . . says that women need to be helped into carriages, and lifted over ditches, and to have the best place everywhere. Nobody ever helps me into carriages, or over mud puddles, or gives me any best place, and aren't I a woman? . . . I have ploughed, and planted, and gathered into barns, and no man could head me—and aren't I a woman? I could work as much and eat as much as a man (when I could get it), and bear the lash as well—and aren't I a woman? I have borne thirteen children and seen them most all sold off into slavery, and when I cried out with a mother's grief, none but Jesus heard—and aren't I a woman?

speech at Women's Rights Convention, Akron, Ohio, 1851

Morton Tsvangirai

Zimbabwean politician

1 This country is for blacks. But we need the knowledge of the whites to train people and create jobs.

in Times 15 April 2000 'Quotes of the Week'

Barbara W. Tuchman 1912–89

American writer

2 Dead battles, like dead generals, hold the military mind in their dead grip and Germans, no less than other peoples, prepare for the last war.

August 1914 (1962)

3 No more distressing moment can ever face a British government than that which requires it to come to a hard, fast and specific decision.

August 1914 (1962)

4 For one August in its history Paris was French—and silent.

August 1914 (1962)

A. R. J. Turgot 1727–81

French economist and statesman

5 *Eripuit coelo fulmen, sceptrumque tyrannis.*
He snatched the lightning shaft from heaven, and the sceptre from tyrants.
> *for a bust of Benjamin* **Franklin**, *inventor of the lightning conductor and one of those who drafted the Declaration of Independence*

inscription

Desmond Tutu 1931–

South African Anglican clergyman, Archbishop of Cape Town

6 I have struggled against tyranny. I didn't do that in order to substitute one tyranny with another.
> *on the ANC's attempt to prevent publication of the Truth Commission report*

in Irish Times 31 October 1998 'This Week They Said'

Mark Twain 1835–1910

American writer

7 It could probably be shown by facts and figures that there is no distinctly native American criminal class except Congress.

Following the Equator (1897)

8 It is by the goodness of God in our country that we have those three unspeakably precious things: freedom of speech, freedom of conscience, and the prudence never to practise either of them.

Following the Equator (1897)

9 Get your facts first, and then you can distort them as much as you please.

Rudyard Kipling *From Sea to Sea* (1899)

10 Suppose you were an idiot. And suppose you were a member of Congress. But I repeat myself.

A. B. Paine *Mark Twain* (1912)

William Magear ('Boss') Tweed 1823–78

American Democratic politician, Tammany 'boss' of New York City
on Tweed: see **Misquotations** 274:5

1 New York politics were always dishonest—long before my time . . . A politician coming forward takes things as they are.
  interviewed in prison a few months before his death

Richard Ackerman *Boss Tweed* (2005)

William Tyndale c.1494–1536

English translator of the Bible and Protestant martyr
see also **Last words** 227:6

2 If God spare my life, ere many years I will cause a boy that driveth the plough shall know more of the scripture than thou doest!
  to an opponent

in *Dictionary of National Biography* (1917–)

Harlan K. Ullman and James P. Wade

American strategic analysts

3 The basis for rapid dominance rests in the ability to affect the will, perception, and understanding of the adversary through imposing sufficient Shock and Awe to achieve the necessary political, strategic, and operational goals of the conflict or crisis that led to the use of force.

Shock and Awe: Achieving Rapid Dominance (1996) ch. 2

Kay Ullrich 1943–

Scottish Nationalist politician

4 As a lady of a certain age, I am willing to let the photographers and their zoom lenses stay, but only if they use their Joan Collins lens on me for close-ups.
  on the decision to ban photographers from the debating chamber of the Scottish Parliament

in *Scotsman* 18 March 2000

Universal Declaration of Human Rights

1948

5 All human beings are born free and equal in dignity and rights.

article 1

6 Everyone has the right to freedom of movement and residence within the borders of each State. Everyone has the right to leave any country, including his own, and to return to his country.

article 13

7 Everyone has the right to seek and to enjoy in other countries asylum from persecution.

article 14

John Updike 1932–

American novelist and short-story writer

8 Without the cold war, what's the point of being an American?

Rabbit at Rest (1990) pt. 3

Paul Valéry 1871–1945
French poet, critic, and man of letters

1 An attitude of permanent indignation signfies great mental poverty. Politics compels its votaries to take that line and you can see their minds growing more and more impoverished every day, from one burst of righteous anger to the next.

Tel Quel (1941–3)

2 Politics is the art of preventing people from taking part in affairs which properly concern them.

Tel Quel (1941–3)

William Henry Vanderbilt 1821–85
American railway magnate

3 The public be damned!
on whether the public should be consulted about luxury trains

A. W. Cole letter to *New York Times* 25 August 1918

Laurens van der Post 1906–96
South African explorer and writer

4 Human beings are perhaps never more frightening than when they are convinced beyond doubt that they are right.

The Lost World of the Kalahari (1958)

Raoul Vaneigem 1934–
Belgian philosopher

5 Never before has a civilization reached such a degree of a contempt for life; never before has a generation, drowned in mortification, felt such a rage to live.
of the 1960s

The Revolution of Everyday Life (1967) ch. 5

Robert Vansittart 1881–1957
British diplomat

6 The soul of our service is the loyalty with which we execute ordained error.

attributed; David Butler et al. *Failure in British Government* (1994)

Mordechai Vanunu 1954–
Moroccan-born Israeli nuclear technician, who made public Israel's nuclear progamme and was convicted of espionage

7 For all those calling me a traitor, I am proud of what I did and I'm glad I succeeded in what I did.

in *Independent* 22 April 2004

Bartolomeo Vanzetti 1888–1927
American anarchist, born in Italy

8 Sacco's name will live in the hearts of the people and in their gratitude when Katzmann's and yours bones will be dispersed by time, when your name, his name, your laws, institutions, and your false god are but a deem rememoring of a cursed past in which man was wolf to the man.
statement disallowed at his trial, with Nicola Sacco, for murder and robbery; both were sentenced to death on 9 April 1927, and executed on 23 August 1927

M. D. Frankfurter and G. Jackson *Letters of Sacco and Vanzetti* (1928)

Janet-Maria Vaughan 1899–1993
English scientist

1 I am here—trying to do science in hell.
working as a doctor in Belsen at the end of the war

letter to a friend, 12 May 1945; P. A. Adams (ed.) *Janet-Maria Vaughan* (1993)

Thorstein Veblen 1857–1929
American economist and social scientist

2 The first duty of an editor is to gauge the sentiment of his readers, and then tell them what they like to believe . . . His second duty is to see that nothing is said in the news items or editorials which may discountenance any claims made by his advertisers, discredit their standing, or expose any weakness or deception in any business venture that is or may become a valuable advertiser.

The Theory of Business Enterprise 1904

3 Conspicuous consumption of valuable goods is a means of reputability to the gentleman of leisure.

Theory of the Leisure Class (1899)

4 From the foregoing survey of conspicuous leisure and consumption, it appears that the utility of both alike for the purposes of reputability lies in the element of waste that is common to both. In the one case it is a waste of time and effort, in the other it is a waste of goods.

Theory of the Leisure Class (1899)

Vegetius fl. AD 379–95
Roman military writer

5 Let him who desires peace, prepare for war.
usually quoted as 'If you want peace, prepare for war'

Epitoma Rei Militaris

Pierre Vergniaud 1753–93
French revolutionary; executed with other Girondists

6 There was reason to fear that the Revolution, like Saturn, might devour in turn each one of her children.

Alphonse de Lamartine *Histoire des Girondins* (1847)

Hendrik Frensch Verwoerd 1901–66
South African statesman; Prime Minister from 1958

7 Up till now he [the Bantu] has been subjected to a school system which drew him away from his own community and practically misled him by showing him the green pastures of the European but still did not allow him to graze there . . . It is abundantly clear that unplanned education creates many problems, disrupts the communal life of the Bantu and endangers the communal life of the European.

speech in South African Senate, 7 June 1954

Vespasian AD 9–79
Roman emperor from AD 69
see also **Last words** 226:5

8 *Pecunia non olet.*

Money has no smell.
replying to Titus's objection to his tax on public lavatories; holding a coin to Titus's nose and being told it didn't smell, he replied, 'Atque e lotio est [Yes, that's made from urine]'

traditional summary of Suetonius *Lives of the Caesars* 'Vespasian'

1 Woe is me, I think I am becoming a god.
when fatally ill

Suetonius *Lives of the Caesars*
'Vespasian'

Queen Victoria 1819–1901
British monarch, Queen of the United Kingdom from 1837
on Victoria: see **Gladstone** 159:9

2 I will be good.
on being shown a chart of the line of succession, 11 March 1830

Theodore Martin *The Prince Consort*
(1875)

3 The Queen is most anxious to enlist every one who can
speak or write to join in checking this mad, wicked folly of
'Woman's Rights', with all its attendant horrors, on which
her poor feeble sex is bent, forgetting every sense of
womanly feeling and propriety.

letter to Theodore Martin, 29 May
1870

4 *on* **Gladstone**'s *last appointment as Prime Minister:*
The danger to the country, to Europe, to her vast Empire,
which is involved in having all these great interests
entrusted to the shaking hand of an old, wild, and
incomprehensible man of 82, is very great!

letter to Lord Lansdowne, 12
August 1892

5 The future Viceroy must . . . not be guided by the *snobbish*
and vulgar, over-bearing and offensive behaviour of our
Civil and Political Agents, if we are to go on peaceably and
happily in India . . . not trying to trample on the people and
continuously reminding them and making them feel they
are a conquered people.

letter to Lord **Salisbury**, 27 May
1898

6 We are not interested in the possibilities of defeat; they do
not exist.
on the Boer War during 'Black Week', December 1899

Lady Gwendolen Cecil *Life of
Robert, Marquis of Salisbury* (1931)

7 He speaks to Me as if I was a public meeting.
of **Gladstone**

G. W. E. Russell *Collections and
Recollections* (1898)

8 We are not amused.

attributed; Caroline Holland
Notebooks of a Spinster Lady
(1919), 2 January 1900

Gore Vidal 1925–
American novelist and critic

9 *of Ronald* **Reagan***:*
A triumph of the embalmer's art.

in *Observer* 26 April 1981

José Antonio Viera Gallo 1943–
Chilean politician

10 Socialism can only arrive by bicycle.

Ivan Illich *Energy and Equity* (1974)
epigraph

Virgil 70–19 BC
Roman poet

11 *Tantae molis erat Romanam condere gentem.*
So massive was the effort to found the Roman nation.

Aeneid

12   *Equo ne credite, Teucri.*
Quidquid id est, timeo Danaos et dona ferentes.
Do not trust the horse, Trojans. Whatever it is, I fear the
Greeks even when they bring gifts.

Aeneid

1   *Bella, horrida bella,*   *Aeneid*; see **Powell** 315:5
Et Thybrim multo spumantem sanguine cerno.

I see wars, horrible wars, and the Tiber foaming with much
blood.

Voltaire 1694–1778

French writer and philosopher
see also **Misquotations** 273:3

2 These two nations have been at war over a few acres of   *Candide* (1759)
snow near Canada, and . . . they are spending on this fine
struggle more than Canada itself is worth.
     of the struggle between the French and the British for the control
     of colonial north Canada

3 *Dans ce pays-ci il est bon de tuer de temps en temps un amiral*   *Candide* (1759)
pour encourager les autres.

In this country [England] it is thought well to kill an
admiral from time to time to encourage the others.

4 The art of government consists in taking as much money as   *Dictionnaire philosophique* (1764)
possible from one class of citizens to give to the other.   'Money'

5 Superstition sets the whole world in flames; philosophy   *Dictionnaire philosophique* (1764)
quenches them.   'Superstition'

6 This agglomeration which was called and which still calls   *Essai sur l'histoire générale et sur les*
itself the Holy Roman Empire was neither holy, nor Roman,   *moeurs et l'esprit des nations* (1756)
nor an empire.

7 Indeed, history is nothing more than a tableau of crimes   *L'Ingénu* (1767); see **Gibbon** 155:6
and misfortunes.

8 Governments need both shepherds and butchers.   'The Piccini Notebooks'
                                                     (*c.*1735–50)

9 God is on the side not of the heavy battalions, but of the best   'The Piccini Notebooks'
shots.   (*c.*1735–50); see **Tacitus** 385:8

10 Whatever you do, stamp out abuses, and love those who   letter to M. d'Alembert, 28
love you.   November 1762

11 If one must serve, I hold it better to serve a well-bred lion,   letter to a friend; Alexis de
who is naturally stronger than I am, than two hundred rats   Tocqueville *The Ancien Régime*
of my own breed.   (1856)

12 To succeed in chaining the crowd you must seem to wear   attributed
the same fetters.

13 *what Voltaire apparently said on the burning of* De l'esprit: James Parton *Life of Voltaire* (1881)
What a fuss about an omelette!   vol. 2; see **Misquotations** 273:3

William Waldegrave 1946–

British Conservative politician

14 In exceptional circumstances it is necessary to say   to a House of Commons select
something that is untrue in the House of Commons.   committee, in *Guardian* 9 March
                                                 1994

15 It was much more what cabinet government is supposed to   on *The Major Years* pt 2, BBC1, 18
be like . . . the problem was that when people began to be   October 1999
disloyal later on, they were not very frightened of him.
     of John **Major** *as Prime Minister*

Lech Wałęsa 1943–

Polish trade unionist and statesman, President since 1990

1 You have riches and freedom here but I feel no sense of faith or direction. You have so many computers, why don't you use them in the search for love?

in Paris, on his first journey outside the Soviet area, in *Daily Telegraph* 14 December 1988

Felix Walker fl. 1820

American politician

2 *excusing a long, dull, irrelevant speech in the House of Representatives, c.1820 (Buncombe being his constituency):* I'm talking to Buncombe ['bunkum'].

W. Safire *New Language of Politics* (2nd ed., 1972); see **Carlyle** 74:14

George Wallace 1919–98

American Democratic politician

3 Segregation now, segregation tomorrow and segregation forever!

inaugural speech as Governor of Alabama, January 1963

Henry Wallace 1888–1965

American Democratic politician

4 The century on which we are entering—the century which will come out of this war—can be and must be the century of the common man.

speech, 8 May 1942

Jim Wallace 1954–

Scottish Liberal Democrat politician, Party Leader 1992–2005, Deputy First Minister in the Scottish Parliament, 1999–2005

5 There is always a problem that party leaders have—of not quite knowing when you have overstayed your welcome. I don't want to encounter that problem.

announcing his resignation as Party Leader, 9 May 2005

William Wallace

American general

6 The enemy we're fighting is a bit different than the one we war-gamed against.
    of the campaign in Iraq

in *New York Times* 28 March 2003

Edmund Waller 1606–87

English poet

7 Others may use the ocean as their road,
Only the English make it their abode.

'Of a War with Spain' (1658)

8 Rome, though her eagle through the world had flown,
Could never make this island all her own.

'Panegyric to My Lord Protector' (1655)

9 Under the tropic is our language spoke,
And part of Flanders hath received our yoke.

'Upon the Late Storm, and of the Death of His Highness Ensuing the Same' (1659)

William Waller 1598–1668

English Parliamentary general

1 With what a perfect hatred I detest this war without an enemy.

letter to the Royalist Ralph Hopton, 16 June 1643; Samuel R. Gardiner *History of the Great Civil War* (1894)

Horace Walpole 1717–97

English writer and connoisseur, son of Robert **Walpole**

2 His speeches were fine, but as much laboured as his extempore sayings.
    *of Lord **Chesterfield**, 1751*

Memoirs of the Reign of King George II (1846) vol. 1

3 While he felt like a victim, he acted like a hero.
    of Admiral Byng, on the day of his execution, 1757

Memoirs of the Reign of King George II (1846) vol. 2

4 Perhaps those, who, trembling most, maintain a dignity in their fate, are the bravest: resolution on reflection is real courage.

in 1757; *Memoirs of the Reign of King George II* (1846) vol. 2

5 They seem to know no medium between a mitre and a crown of martyrdom. If the clergy are not called to the latter, they never deviate from the pursuit of the former. One would think their motto was, *Canterbury or Smithfield.*

in 1758; *Memoirs of the Reign of King George II* (1846) vol. 3

6 All his passions were expressed by one livid smile.
    *of George **Grenville**, 1763*

Memoirs of the Reign of King George III (1845) vol. 1

7 He lost his dominions in America, his authority over Ireland, and all influence in Europe, by aiming at despotism in England; and exposed himself to more mortifications and humiliations than can happen to a quiet Doge of Venice.
    *of **George III***

Memoirs of the Reign of King George III (1845) vol. 4

8 Our supreme governors, the mob.

letter to Horace Mann, 7 September 1743

9 Everybody talks of the constitution, but all sides forget that the constitution is extremely well, and would do very well, if they would but let it alone.

letter to Horace Mann, 18–19 January 1770

10 It was easier to conquer it [the East] than to know what to do with it.

letter to Horace Mann, 27 March 1772

11 By the waters of Babylon we sit down and weep, when we think of thee, O America!

letter to Revd William Mason, 12 June 1775

Robert Walpole 1676–1745

English Whig statesman; first British Prime Minister, 1721–42; father of Horace **Walpole**
on Walpole: see **Peel** 307:16, **Shippen** 364:2

12 Madam, there are fifty thousand men slain this year in Europe, and not one Englishman.
    to Queen Caroline, 1734, on the war of the Polish succession, in which the English had refused to participate

John Hervey *Memoirs* (written 1734–43, published 1848) vol. 1

1 We must muzzle this terrible young cornet of horse.
   *of the elder William **Pitt**, who had held a cornetcy before his
   election to Parliament, but whose speech in support of the
   congratulatory address on the Prince of Wales's marriage in
   1736 was regarded as so offensive through its covert satire that
   he was shortly afterwards dismissed from the army*

in *Dictionary of National Biography*
(1917-)

2 They now *ring* the bells, but they will soon *wring* their
   hands.
   on the declaration of war with Spain, 1739

W. Coxe *Memoirs of Sir Robert
Walpole* (1798) vol. 1

3 All those men have their price.
   of fellow parliamentarians

W. Coxe *Memoirs of Sir Robert
Walpole* (1798) vol. 1

4 [Gratitude of place-expectants] is a lively sense of future
   favours.

W. Hazlitt *Lectures on the English
Comic Writers* (1819) 'On Wit and
Humour'

5 *the normally imperturbable Walpole, having lost his temper at a
   Council, broke up the meeting:*
   No man is fit for business with a ruffled temper.

Edmund Fitzmaurice *Life of
Shelburne* (1875)

6 There is enough pasture for all the sheep.
   on his ability to spread round patronage satisfactorily

attributed

7 *on seeing Henry Fox (Lord **Holland**) reading in the library at
   Houghton:*
   You can read. It is a great happiness. I totally neglected it
   while I was in business, which has been the whole of my
   life, and to such a degree that I cannot now read a page—a
   warning to all Ministers.

Edmund Fitzmaurice *Life of
Shelburne* (1875) vol. 1

Claire Ward 1972-

British Labour politician

8 I don't always admit to being an MP. If I'm in a bar with
   people I don't know, to say you're a Labour MP isn't always
   a good move. I have said I'm a solicitor.

in *Independent on Sunday* 14 March
1999 'Quotes'

Charles Dudley Warner 1829–1900

American writer and editor

9 Politics makes strange bedfellows.

My Summer in a Garden (1871)

Earl Warren 1891–1974

American Chief Justice

10 In civilized life, law floats in a sea of ethics.

in *New York Times* 12 November
1962

Booker T. Washington 1856–1915

American educationist and emancipated slave

11 No race can prosper till it learns that there is as much
    dignity in tilling a field as in writing a poem.

Up from Slavery (1901)

12 You can't hold a man down without staying down with
    him.

attributed

George Washington 1732–99

American statesman, 1st President of the US
on Washington: see **Byron** 69:1, **Franklin** 146:3, **Lee** 230:2; *see also* **Last words** 227:3

1 I can't tell a lie, Pa; you know I can't tell a lie. I did cut it with my hatchet.

M. L. Weems *Life of George Washington* (10th ed., 1810)

2 The time is now near at hand which must probably determine whether Americans are to be freemen or slaves; whether they are to have any property they can call their own . . . The fate of unborn millions will now depend, under God, on the courage and conduct of this army. Our cruel and unrelenting enemy leaves us only the choice of brave resistance, or the most abject submission. We have, therefore, to resolve to conquer or die.

General orders, 2 July 1776, in J. C. Fitzpatrick (ed.) *Writings of George Washington* vol. 5 (1932)

3 Few men have virtue to withstand the highest bidder.

letter 17 August 1779

4 'Tis our true policy to steer clear of permanent alliances, with any portion of the foreign world.

President's Address . . . (17 September 1796)

5 Let me . . . warn you in the most solemn manner against the baneful effects of the spirit of party.

President's Address . . . (17 September 1796)

6 The nation which indulges toward another an habitual hatred or an habitual fondness is in some degree a slave. It is a slave to its animosity or to its affection, either of which is sufficient to lead it astray from its duty and its interest.

President's Address . . . (17 September 1796)

7 Liberty, when it begins to take root, is a plant of rapid growth.

attributed

Keith Waterhouse 1929–

English writer

8 Why should it take three times longer to elect a Mayor for London as it does to set up an entire Scottish Parliament?

in *Observer* 24 October 1999 'They Said What . . . ?'

William Watson c.1559–1603

English Roman Catholic conspirator

9 *Fiat justitia et ruant coeli.*
Let justice be done even though the heavens fall.

A Decacordon of Ten Quodlibeticall Questions Concerning Religion and State (1602), being the first citation in an English work of a famous maxim; see **Adams** 4:6, **Mottoes** 281:3

Evelyn Waugh 1903–66

English novelist

10 'In a democracy,' said Mr Pinfold, with more weight than originality, 'Men do not seek authority so that they may impose a policy. They seek a policy so that they may achieve authority.'

The Ordeal of Gilbert Pinfold (1957)

11 *The Beast* stands for strong mutually antagonistic governments everywhere . . . Self-sufficiency at home, self-assertion abroad.

Scoop (1938)

1 Remember that the Patriots are in the right and are going to win . . . But they must win quickly. The British public has no interest in a war that drags on indecisively. A few sharp victories, some conspicuous acts of personal bravery on the Patriot side and a colourful entry into the capital. That is *The Beast* Policy for the war.

Scoop (1938)

2 Other nations use 'force'; we Britons alone use 'Might'.

Scoop (1938)

3 I do not aspire to advise my sovereign in her choice of servants.
  on why he did not vote

in *Spectator* 2 October 1959

4 *it had been announced after an operation on Randolph Churchill that the trouble was 'not malignant':*
It was a typical triumph of modern science to find the only part of Randolph that was not malignant and remove it.

Michael Davie (ed.) *Diaries of Evelyn Waugh* (1976) 'Irregular Notes 1960–65', March 1964

5 The Conservative Party have never put the clock back a single second.

Frances Donaldson *Evelyn Waugh* (1967)

Beatrice Webb 1858–1943
English socialist

6 Restless, almost intolerably so, without capacity for sustained and unexcited labour, egotistical, bumptious, shallow-minded and reactionary, but with a certain personal magnetism, great pluck and some originality, not of intellect but of character.
  *in 1903, of Winston **Churchill***

Martin Gilbert *In Search of Churchill* (1994)

7 I never visualised labour as separate men and women of different sorts and kinds . . . labour was an abstraction, which seemed to denote an arithmetically calculable mass of human beings, each individual a repetition of the other.

My Apprenticeship (1926)

Sidney Webb 1859–1947
English socialist

8 Once we face the necessity of putting our principles first into Bills, to be fought through committee clause by clause; and then into the appropriate machinery for carrying them into execution from one end of the kingdom to the other . . . the inevitability of gradualness cannot fail to be appreciated.

presidential address to the annual conference of the Labour Party, 26 June 1923

9 Nobody told us we could do this.
  when the new National Government came off the Gold Standard in 1931, the outgoing Labour Government not having resorted to this tactic

Nigel Rees *Brewer's Quotations* (1994)

Max Weber 1864–1920
German sociologist

10 The Protestant ethic and the spirit of capitalism.

Archiv für Sozialwissenschaft Sozialpolitik vol. 20 (1904–5) (title of article)

11 In Baxter's view the care for external goods should only lie on the shoulders of the saint like 'a light cloak, which can be thrown aside at any moment.' But fate decreed that the cloak should become an iron cage.

Gesammelte Aufsätze zur Religionssoziologie (1920) vol. 1

1 The State is a relation of men dominating men, a relation supported by means of legitimate (i.e. considered to be legitimate) violence.

'Politik als Beruf' (1919)

2 The authority of the 'eternal yesterday'.

'Politik als Beruf' (1919)

3 The experience of the irrationality of the world has been the driving force of all religious revolution.

'Politik als Beruf' (1919)

4 The concept of the 'official secret' is its [bureaucracy's] specific invention.

'Politik als Beruf' (1919)

Daniel Webster 1782–1852

American politician
on Webster: see **Smith** 372:8

5 The people's government, made for the people, made by the people, and answerable to the people.

second speech in the Senate on Foote's Resolution, 26 January 1830; see **Lincoln** 235:8

6 Liberty *and* Union, now and forever, one and inseparable!

second speech in the Senate on Foote's Resolution, 26 January 1830

7 When my eyes shall be turned to behold for the last time the sun in heaven, may I not see him shining on the broken and dishonored fragments of a once glorious Union; on States dissevered, discordant, belligerent; on a land rent with civil feuds, or drenched, it may be, in fraternal blood.

second speech in the Senate on Foote's Resolution, 26 January 1830

8 Fearful concatenation of circumstances.
argument on the murder of Captain Joseph White

speech on 6 April 1830

9 He smote the rock of the national resources, and abundant streams of revenue gushed forth. He touched the dead corpse of the Public Credit, and it sprung upon its feet.
of Alexander **Hamilton**

speech 10 March 1831

10 Whatever government is not a government of laws, is a despotism, let it be called what it may.

at a reception in Bangor, Maine, 25 August 1835

11 One country, one constitution, one destiny.

speech 15 March 1837

12 Thank God, I—I also—am an American!
speech on the completion of Bunker Hill Monument, 17 June 1843

Writings and Speeches vol. 1 (1903)

13 The Law: It has honoured us, may we honour it.

speech at the Charleston Bar Dinner, 10 May 1847

14 I was born an American; I will live an American; I shall die an American.

speech in the Senate on 'The Compromise Bill', 17 July 1850

15 There is always room at the top.
on being advised against joining the overcrowded legal profession

attributed

Josiah Wedgwood 1730–95

English potter

16 Am I not a man and a brother.
legend on Wedgwood cameo, depicting a kneeling Negro slave in chains

reproduced in facsimile in E. Darwin *The Botanic Garden* pt. 1 (1791)

Simone Weil 1909–43
French essayist and philosopher

1 I would suggest that barbarism be considered as a permanent and universal human characteristic which becomes more or less pronounced according to the play of circumstances.

Écrits Historiques et politiques (1960) 'Réflexions sur la barbarie' (written c.1939)

2 A right is not effectual by itself, but only in relation to the obligation to which it corresponds . . . An obligation which goes unrecognized by anybody loses none of the full force of its existence. A right which goes unrecognized by anybody is not worth very much.

L'Enracinement (1949) 'Les Besoins de l'âme'

3 What a country calls its vital economic interests are not the things which enable its citizens to live, but the things which enable it to make war.

W. H. Auden *A Certain World* (1971)

Stanley Weiser and Oliver Stone 1946–

4 Greed—for lack of a better word—is good. Greed is right. Greed works.

Wall Street (1987 film); see **Boesky** 48:4

Chaim Weizmann 1874–1952
Russian-born Israeli statesman, President 1949–52

5 Something had been done for us which, after two thousand years of hope and yearning, would at last give us a resting-place in this terrible world.
   of the Balfour declaration

speech in Jerusalem, 25 November 1936; see **Balfour** 28:1

Joseph Welch 1890–1960
American lawyer

6 Until this moment, Senator, I think I never really gauged your cruelty or your recklessness . . . Have you no sense of decency, sir? At long last, have you left no sense of decency?
   *to Joseph **McCarthy**, 9 June 1954, defending the US Army against allegations of harbouring subversive activities; the televised confrontation was deeply damaging to McCarthy*

in *American National Biography* (online edition) 'Joseph McCarthy'

Orson Welles 1915–85
American actor and film director

7 In Italy for thirty years under the Borgias they had warfare, terror, murder, bloodshed—they produced Michelangelo, Leonardo da Vinci and the Renaissance. In Switzerland they had brotherly love, five hundred years of democracy and peace and what did that produce . . . ? The cuckoo clock.

The Third Man (1949 film); words added by Welles to Graham Greene's script

Duke of Wellington 1769–1852
British soldier and statesman
*on Wellington: see **Tennyson** 389:7, **Tennyson** 389:8, **Tennyson** 389:9*

8 As Lord Chesterfield said of the generals of his day, 'I only hope that when the enemy reads the list of their names, he trembles as I do.'
   usually quoted as 'I don't know what effect these men will have upon the enemy, but, by God, they frighten me'

letter, 29 August 1810

1 Trust nothing to the enthusiasm of the people. Give them a strong and a just, and, if possible, a good, government; but, above all, a strong one.

letter to Lord William Bentinck, 24 December 1811

2 Up Guards and at them!

letter from an officer in the Guards, 22 June 1815, in The Battle of Waterloo by a Near Observer [J. Booth] (1815); later denied by Wellington

3 Hard pounding this, gentlemen; let's see who will pound longest.
    at the Battle of Waterloo

Sir Walter Scott Paul's Letters (1816)

4 Publish and be damned.
    replying to Harriette Wilson's blackmail threat, c.1825

attributed; Elizabeth Longford Wellington: The Years of the Sword (1969)

5 *of his first Cabinet meeting as Prime Minister:*
An extraordinary affair. I gave them their orders and they wanted to stay and discuss them.

Peter Hennessy Whitehall (1990)

6 I used to say of him [Napoleon] that his presence on the field made the difference of forty thousand men.

Philip Henry Stanhope Notes of Conversations with the Duke of Wellington (1888) 2 November 1831

7 Ours [our army] is composed of the scum of the earth—the mere scum of the earth.

Philip Henry Stanhope Notes of Conversations with the Duke of Wellington (1888) 4 November 1831

8 I never saw so many shocking bad hats in my life.
    on seeing the first Reformed Parliament

William Fraser Words on Wellington (1889)

9 Nothing the people of this country like so much as to see their great men take part in their amusements. The aristocracy will commit a great error if they ever fail to mix freely with their neighbours.
    on foxhunting

in 1836; Philip Henry Stanhope Notes of Conversations with the Duke of Wellington (1888)

10 All the business of war, and indeed all the business of life, is to endeavour to find out what you don't know by what you do; that's what I called 'guessing what was at the other side of the hill'.

in The Croker Papers (1885) vol. 3

11 The battle of Waterloo was won on the playing fields of Eton.

*oral tradition, but not found in this form of words; C. F. R. Montalembert De l'avenir politique de l'Angleterre (1856); see **Orwell** 296:12*

12 *to a gentleman who had accosted him in the street saying, 'Mr Jones, I believe?'*
If you believe that, you'll believe anything.
    George Jones RA (1786–1869), painter of military subjects, bore a striking resemblance to Wellington

Elizabeth Longford Pillar of State (1972)

13 I have no small talk and Peel has no manners.

G. W. E. Russell Collections and Recollections (1898)

14 Next to a battle lost, the greatest misery is a battle gained.

in Diary of Frances, Lady Shelley 1787–1817 (ed. R. Edgcumbe); see S. Rogers Recollections (1859) for variations on the theme

1 There is no such thing as a little war for a great nation.
   to Fitzroy Somerset, urging military preparedness

attributed

2 You must build your House of Parliament upon the river . . .
   the populace cannot exact their demands by sitting down
   round you.

William Fraser *Words on Wellington* (1889)

H. G. Wells 1866–1946
English novelist

3 The Social Contract is nothing more or less than a vast
   conspiracy of human beings to lie to and humbug
   themselves and one another for the general Good. Lies are
   the mortar that bind the savage individual man into the
   social masonry.

Love and Mr Lewisham (1900)

4 The war that will end war.

title of book (1914); see **Lloyd George** 239:1

5 We fight not to destroy a nation, but a nest of evil ideas . . .
   Our business is to kill ideas. The ultimate purpose of this
   war is propaganda, the destruction of certain beliefs, and
   the creation of others.

The War That Will End War (1914) ch. 11

6 In England we have come to rely upon a comfortable time-
   lag of fifty years or a century intervening between the
   perception that something ought to be done and a serious
   attempt to do it.

The Work, Wealth and Happiness of Mankind (1931)

Rebecca West 1892–1983
English novelist and journalist

7 Having watched the form of our traitors for a number of
   years, I cannot think that espionage can be recommended
   as a technique for building an impressive civilization. It's a
   lout's game.

The Meaning of Treason (1982 ed.)

8 I myself have never been able to find out precisely what
   feminism is: I only know that people call me a feminist
   whenever I express sentiments that differentiate me from a
   doormat or a prostitute.

in *The Clarion* 14 November 1913

9 It was in dealing with the early feminist that the
   Government acquired the tact and skilfulness with which it
   is now handling Ireland.

in 1916; *The Young Rebecca* (1982)

10 Whatever happens, never forget that people would rather be
   lead to *perdition* by a man, than to *victory* by a woman.
   *in conversation in 1979, just before Margaret **Thatcher**'s first
   election victory*

in *Sunday Telegraph* 17 January 1988

William C. Westmoreland 1914–
American general

11 Vietnam was the first war ever fought without censorship.
   Without censorship, things can get terribly confused in the
   public mind.

attributed, 1982

John Fane, Lord Westmorland 1759–1841
English peer

12 *Merit*, indeed! . . . We are come to a pretty pass if they talk
   of *merit* for a bishopric.

noted in Lady Salisbury's diary, 9 December 1835

Charles Wetherell 1770–1846
English lawyer and politician

1 Then there is my noble and biographical friend who has added a new terror to death.
of Lord Campbell

Lord St Leonards *Misrepresentations in Campbell's Lives of Lyndhurst and Brougham* (1869); also attributed to Lord Lyndhurst

Grover A. Whalen 1886–1962

2 There's a lot of law at the end of a nightstick.

Quentin Reynolds *Courtroom* (1950)

Thomas, Lord Wharton 1648–1715
English Whig politician

3 I sang a king out of three kingdoms.
said to have been Wharton's boast after 'A New Song' became a propaganda weapon against James II

in *Dictionary of National Biography* (1917–); see **Songs** 375:3

E. B. White 1899–1985
American humorist

4 Democracy is the recurrent suspicion that more than half of the people are right more than half of the time.

in *New Yorker* 3 July 1944

5 The so-called science of poll-taking is not a science at all but a mere necromancy. People are unpredictable by nature, and although you can take a nation's pulse, you can't be sure that the nation hasn't just run up a flight of stairs.

in *New Yorker* 13 November 1948

Theodore H. White 1915–86
American writer and journalist

6 Johnson's instinct for power is as primordial as a salmon's going upstream to spawn.
*of Lyndon **Johnson***

The Making of the President (1964)

7 The flood of money that gushes into politics today is a pollution of democracy.

in *Time* 19 November 1984

William Allen White 1868–1944
American journalist and editor

8 Tinhorn politicians.

in *Emporia Gazette* 25 October 1901

9 Liberty is the only thing you cannot have unless you are willing to give it to others.

attributed

William Whitelaw 1918–99
British Conservative politician
*on Whitelaw: see **Thatcher** 392:7*

10 It is never wise to appear to be more clever than you are. It is sometimes wise to appear slightly less so.

attributed, 1975

11 The Labour Party is going around stirring up apathy.
recalled by Alan Watkins as a characteristic 'Willieism'

in *Observer* 1 May 1983

Gough Whitlam 1916–

Australian Labor statesman, Prime Minister 1972–5

1 *of the part played by the new Prime Minister, William McMahon,*
in the resignation of his predecessor John Grey Gorton:
He sat there on the Isle of Capri [at Surfers Paradise]
plotting his destruction—Tiberius with a telephone.

in the House of Representatives,
1971

2 *the Governor-General, Sir John Kerr, had dismissed the Labor*
government headed by Gough Whitlam in November 1975:
Well may he say 'God Save the Queen'. But after this
nothing will save the Governor-General . . . Maintain your
rage and your enthusiasm through the campaign for the
election now to be held and until polling day.

speech in Canberra, 11 November
1975

Walt Whitman 1819–92

American poet

3 O Captain! my Captain! our fearful trip is done,
The ship has weathered every rack, the prize we sought is
won,
The port is near, the bells I hear, the people all exulting.
allegorical poem on the death of Abraham **Lincoln**

'O Captain! My Captain!' (1871)

4 The ship is anchored safe and sound, its voyage closed and
done.
From fearful trip the victor ship comes in with object won;
Exult O shores, and ring O bells! But I with mournful tread
Walk the deck my Captain lies, Fallen cold and dead.

'O Captain! My Captain!' (1871)

5 Where the populace rise at once against the never-ending
audacity of elected persons.

'Song of the Broad Axe' (1881)

6 Where the city of the healthiest fathers stands,
Where the city of the best-bodied mothers stands,
There the great city stands.

'Song of the Broad Axe' (1881)

7 This dust was once the man,
Gentle, plain, just and resolute, under whose cautious hand,
Against the foulest crime in history known in any land or
age,
Was saved the Union of these States.

'This dust was once the man'
(1881)

8 The United States themselves are essentially the greatest
poem.

Leaves of Grass (1855) preface

9 Strange, (is it not?) that battles, martyrs, blood, even
assassination, should so condense—perhaps only really,
lastingly condense—a Nationality.
of the American Civil War

Geoffrey C. Ward *The Civil War*
(1991)

John Greenleaf Whittier 1807–92

American poet

10 'Shoot, if you must, this old grey head,
But spare your country's flag,' she said.
A shade of sadness, a blush of shame,
Over the face of the leader came.

'Barbara Frietchie' (1863)

Robert Whittington c.1480–1553?

English grammarian

1 As time requireth, a man of marvellous mirth and pastimes, and sometime of as sad gravity, as who say: a man for all seasons.
of Thomas **More**

in *Vulgaria* (1521) pt. 2; Erasmus famously applied the idea to More, writing in his prefatory letter to *In Praise of Folly* (1509) that he played 'omnium horarum hominem [a man of all hours]'

Ann Widdecombe 1947–

British Conservative politician

2 He has something of the night in him.
of **Michael Howard** *as a contender for the Conservative leadership*

in *Sunday Times* 11 May 1997 (electronic edition)

Elie Wiesel 1928–

Romanian-born American writer and Nobel Prize winner; Auschwitz survivor

3 Take sides. Neutrality helps the oppressor, never the victim. Silence encourages the tormentor, never the tormented.
accepting the Nobel Peace Prize

in *New York Times* 11 December 1986

4 God of forgiveness, do not forgive those murderers of Jewish children here.
at Auschwitz

in *The Times* 27 January 1995

William Wilberforce 1759–1833

British politician, philanthropist, and abolitionist

5 As soon as ever I had arrived thus far in my investigation of the slave trade, I confess to you, so enormous, so dreadful, so irremediable did its wickedness appear that my own mind was completely made up for the abolition.

speech, 12 May 1789; in W. Cobbett et al. (eds.) *The Parliamentary History of England* (1806–20) vol. 28

Oscar Wilde 1854–1900

Irish dramatist and poet

6 We have really everything in common with America nowadays except, of course, language.

The Canterville Ghost (1887); see **Misquotations** 272:6

7 If the country doesn't go to the dogs or the Radicals, we shall have you Prime Minister, some day.

An Ideal Husband (1895)

8 The English country gentleman galloping after a fox—the unspeakable in full pursuit of the uneatable.

A Woman of No Importance (1893) act 1; see **Zobel** 428:5

Wilhelm II 1859–1941

German monarch, emperor 1888–1918

9 We have . . . fought for our place in the sun and have won it. It will be my business to see that we retain this place in the sun unchallenged, so that the rays of that sun may exert a fructifying influence upon our foreign trade and traffic.

speech in Hamburg, 18 June 1901; see **Bülow** 60:5

John Wilkes 1727–97

English parliamentary reformer

1 EARL OF SANDWICH: 'Pon my soul, Wilkes, I don't know
   whether you'll die upon the gallows or of the pox.
   WILKES: That depends, my Lord, whether I first embrace
   your Lordship's principles, or your Lordship's mistresses.

Charles Petrie *The Four Georges* (1935); probably apocryphal

2 Give me a grain of truth and I will mix it up with a great
   mass of falsehood so that no chemist will ever be able to
   separate them.

Adrian Hamilton *The Infamous Essay on Women, or John Wilkes seated between Vice and Virtue* (1972)

William III 1650–1702

British monarch, King of Great Britain and Ireland from 1688
see also **Proverbs** 318:11

3 'Do you not see your country is lost?' asked the Duke of
   Buckingham. 'There is one way never to see it lost' replied
   William, 'and that is to die in the last ditch.'

Bishop Gilbert Burnet *History of M|
Own Time* (1838 ed.)

Roy Williamson 1936–90

Scottish folksinger and musician

4 O flower of Scotland, when will we see your like again,
   that fought and died for your wee bit hill and glen
   and stood against him, proud Edward's army,
   and sent him homeward tae think again.
   unofficial Scottish Nationalist anthem

'O Flower of Scotland' (1968)

Wendell Willkie 1892–1944

American lawyer and politician

5 Freedom is an indivisible word. If we want to enjoy it, and
   fight for it, we must be prepared to extend it to everyone,
   whether they are rich or poor, whether they agree with us
   or not, no matter what their race or the colour of their skin.

One World (1943)

6 The constitution does not provide for first and second class
   citizens.

An American Programme (1944)

A. N. Wilson 1950–

British novelist

7 I should prefer to have a politician who regularly went to a
   massage parlour than one who promised a laptop computer
   for every teacher.

in *Observer* 21 March 1999

Charles E. Wilson 1890–1961

American industrialist; President of General Motors, 1941–53
see also **Slogan** 366:8

8 For years I thought what was good for our country was
   good for General Motors and vice versa. The difference did
   not exist. Our company is too big. It goes with the welfare of
   the country.

testimony to the Senate Armed Services Committee on his proposed nomination to be Secretary of Defence, 15 January 1953

Harold Wilson 1916–95

British Labour statesman; Prime Minister, 1964–70, 1974–6
on Wilson: see **Anonymous** 9:5, **Benn** 34:5, **Birch** 43:2, **Bulmer-Thomas** 60:4, **Bush** 66:4, **Home** 187:8, **Junor** 208:13

1 All these financiers, all the little gnomes in Zurich and the other financial centres about whom we keep on hearing.

in the House of Commons, 12 November 1956

2 I think it's a trap, but I suppose you can always walk into a trap provided you are packing a Luger.
in 1961, when pressed by Hugh Gaitskell to exchange his successful shadow Treasury portfolio for Foreign Affairs

recalled by Anthony Howard; in *Times* 8 February 2005

3 I myself have always deprecated . . . in crisis after crisis, appeals to the Dunkirk spirit as an answer to our problems.

in the House of Commons, 26 July 1961; see **Wilson** 421:7

4 This party is a moral crusade or it is nothing.

speech at the Labour Party Conference, 1 October 1962

5 We are restating our socialism in terms of the scientific revolution . . . the Britain that is going to be forged in the white heat of this revolution will be no place for restrictive practices or outdated methods on either side of industry.

speech at the Labour Party Conference, 1 October 1963; see **Misquotations** 274:6

6 What I think we are going to need is something like what President Kennedy had when he came in after years of stagnation in the United States. He had a programme of a hundred days—a hundred days of dynamic action.

in a party political broadcast, 15 July 1964

7 I believe that the spirit of Dunkirk will carry us through . . . to success.

speech to the Labour Party Conference, 12 December 1964; see **Wilson** 421:3

8 The Smethwick Conservatives can have the satisfaction of having topped the poll, and of having sent here as their Member one who, until a further General Election restores him to oblivion, will serve his term here as a Parliamentary leper.
on the outcome of a by-election with racist overtones

in the House of Commons, 3 November 1964

9 A week is a long time in politics.
probably first said at a lobby briefing at the time of the 1964 sterling crisis

Nigel Rees *Sayings of the Century* (1984); see **Chamberlain** 79:4

10 [Labour is] the natural party of government.

in 1965; Anthony Sampson *The Changing Anatomy of Britain*

11 From now the pound abroad is worth 14 per cent or so less in terms of other currencies. It does not mean, of course, that the pound here in Britain, in your pocket or purse or in your bank, has been devalued.

ministerial broadcast, 19 November 1967

12 Get your tanks off my lawn, Hughie.
*to the trade union leader Hugh **Scanlon**, at Chequers in June 1969*

Peter Jenkins *The Battle of Downing Street* (1970)

13 I know what is going on. I am going on.
commenting on rumours of conspiracies against his leadership

at a May Day rally, 4 May 1969; Ben Pimlott *Harold Wilson* (1992)

14 One man's wage increase is another man's price increase.

speech at Blackburn, 8 January 1970

15 This party is a bit like an old stagecoach. If you drive along at a rapid rate, everyone aboard is either so exhilarated or so seasick that you don't have a lot of difficulty.
of the Labour Party, c.1974

Anthony Sampson *The Changing Anatomy of Britain* (1982)

1 Whichever party is in office, the Treasury is in power.
while in opposition, c.1974

Anthony Sampson *The Changing Anatomy of Britain* (1982)

2 I've buried all the hatchets. But I know where I've buried them and I can dig them up if necessary.
of the Cabinet in 1974

Lord Hunt in *Secret History. Harold Wilson: The Final Years* (Channel 4 TV) 15 August 1996

3 The trouble is when the old problems reappear I reach for the old solutions.
to his Press Secretary Joe Haines, July 1975

Peter Hennessy *The Prime Minister the Office and its Holders since 194* (2000)

4 The Monarchy is a labour-intensive industry.

in *Observer* 13 February 1977

5 The one thing we need to nationalize in this country is the Treasury, but no one has ever succeeded.

in 1984; Peter Hennessy *Whitehall* (1990)

Richard Wilson 1942–
British civil servant and Cabinet Secretary

6 There are occasions on which you have to say 'bollocks' to ministers.

in *Times* 10 February 2000

Woodrow Wilson 1856–1924
American Democratic statesman, 28th President of the US
on Wilson: see **Clemenceau** 96:4, **Keynes** 214:9

7 Prosperity is necessarily the first theme of a political campaign.

speech, 4 September, 1912; see **Slogans** 367:7

8 Liberty has never come from the government. Liberty has always come from the subjects of government. The history of liberty is the history of resistance. The history of liberty is a history of the limitation of governmental power, not the increase of it.

speech to the New York Press Club, 9 September 1912

9 The United States must be neutral in fact as well as in name.
at the outbreak of the First World War

message to the Senate, 19 August 1914

10 It is like writing history with lightning. And my only regret is that it is all so terribly true.
on seeing D. W. Griffith's film The Birth of a Nation

at the White House, 18 February 1915

11 No nation is fit to sit in judgement upon any other nation.

speech in New York, 20 April 1915

12 There is such a thing as a man being too proud to fight; there is such a thing as a nation being so right that it does not need to convince others by force that it is right.

speech in Philadelphia, 10 May 1915

13 We have stood apart, studiously neutral.

speech to Congress, 7 December 1915

14 America can not be an ostrich with its head in the sand.

speech at Des Moines, 1 February 1916

15 It must be a peace without victory . . . Only a peace between equals can last.

speech to US Senate, 22 January 1917

16 Armed neutrality is ineffectual enough at best.

speech to Congress, 2 April 1917

17 The day has come when America is privileged to spend her blood and her might for the principles that gave her birth and happiness and the peace which she has treasured.

speech to Congress, 2 April 1917

18 The world must be made safe for democracy.

speech to Congress, 2 April 1917; see **Wolfe** 424:1

19 The right is more precious than peace.

speech to Congress, 2 April 1917

1 Once lead this people into war and they will forget there ever was such a thing as tolerance.

John Dos Passos *Mr Wilson's War* (1917)

2 The programme of the world's peace . . . is this:
    I. Open covenants of peace, openly arrived at.

speech to Congress, 8 January 1918

3 America is the only idealistic nation in the world.

speech at Sioux Falls, South Dakota, 8 September 1919

4 A general association of nations must be formed . . . for the purpose of affording mutual guarantees of political independence and territorial integrity to great and small states alike.

speech to Congress, 8 January 1918

5 If I am to speak for ten minutes, I need a week for preparation; if fifteen minutes, three days; if half an hour, two days; if an hour, I am ready now.

Josephus Daniels *The Wilson Era* (1946)

William Windham 1750–1810
English politician

6 Those entrusted with arms . . . should be persons of some substance and stake in the country.

in the House of Commons, 22 July 1807

John Winthrop 1588–1649
American settler

7 We must consider that we shall be a city upon a hill, the eyes of all people are on us; so that if we shall deal falsely with our God in this work we have undertaken, and so cause Him to withdraw His present help from us, we shall be made a story and a byword through the world.

Christian Charity, A Model Hereof (sermon, 1630)

Robert Charles Winthrop 1809–94
American politician

8 A Star for every State, and a State for every Star.

speech on Boston Common, 27 August 1862

Humbert Wolfe 1886–1940
British poet

9 You cannot hope
to bribe or twist,
thank God! the
British journalist.

But, seeing what
the man will do
unbribed, there's
no occasion to.

'Over the Fire' (1930)

James Wolfe 1727–59
British general; captor of Quebec

10 The General . . . repeated nearly the whole of Gray's Elegy . . . adding, as he concluded, that he would prefer being the author of that poem to the glory of beating the French to-morrow.

J. Playfair *Biographical Account of J. Robinson* in *Transactions of the Royal Society of Edinburgh* vol. 7 (1815)

Thomas Wolfe 1900–38

American novelist

1 'Where they got you stationed now, Luke?' said Harry Tugman peering up snoutily from a mug of coffee. 'At the p-p-p-present time in Norfolk at the Navy base,' Luke answered, 'm-m-making the world safe for hypocrisy.'

Look Homeward, Angel (1929; see **Wilson** 422:18

Tom Wolfe 1931–

American writer

2 A liberal is a conservative who's been arrested.

The Bonfire of the Vanities (1987); see **Proverbs** 318:5

3 A cult is a religion with no political power.

In Our Time (1980)

Thomas Wolsey c.1475–1530

English cardinal; Lord Chancellor, 1515–29

4 Father Abbot, I am come to lay my bones amongst you.

George Cavendish *Negotiations of Thomas Wolsey* (1641)

5 Had I but served God as diligently as I have served the King, he would not have given me over in my grey hairs.

George Cavendish *Negotiations of Thomas Wolsey* (1641)

Lord Woolf 1933–

British judge, Lord Chief Justice

6 What is the difference between a Lord Chancellor and a Secretary of State, the man on Clapham Omnibus could, with reason, ask. After all, that engagingly friendly and cheerful chappie, Lord Falconer, seems to be quite happy playing both roles.

in *Guardian Unlimited* 4 March 2004. Quote from Lord Woolf's Squire Centenary Lecture 'The Rule of Law and a Change in the Constitution'

Alexander Woollcott 1887–1943

American writer

7 I think your slogan 'Liberty or Death' is splendid, and whichever one you decide on will be all right with me.

attributed

William Wordsworth 1770–1850

English poet

8 Bliss was it in that dawn to be alive,
But to be young was very heaven!

'The French Revolution, as it Appeared to Enthusiasts' (1809); also *The Prelude* (1850)

9   In our halls is hung
Armoury of the invincible Knights of old:
We must be free or die, who speak the tongue
That Shakespeare spake; the faith and morals hold
Which Milton held. In every thing we are sprung
Of Earth's first blood, have titles manifold.

'It is not to be thought of that the Flood' (1807)

10 Once did she hold the gorgeous East in fee,
And was the safeguard of the West.

'On the Extinction of the Venetian Republic' (1807)

Henry Wotton 1568–1639
English poet and diplomat

1 Dazzled thus with height of place,
Whilst our hopes our wits beguile,
No man marks the narrow space
'Twixt a prison and a smile.

'Upon the sudden restraint of the
Earl of Somerset' (1651)

2 An ambassador is an honest man sent to lie abroad for the
good of his country.

written in the album of
Christopher Fleckmore in 1604

Neville Wran 1926–
Australian politician

3 The average footslogger in the New South Wales Right . . .
generally speaking carries a dagger in one hand and a Bible
in the other and doesn't put either to really elegant use.

in 1973; Michael Gordon *A
Question of Leadership* (1993)

Nathaniel Wraxall 1751–1831
English traveller and memoirist

4 Eloquence, transcendent eloquence, formed the foundation
and the key-stone of Pitt's Ministerial greatness. Every other
quality in him was accessory.
*of William **Pitt** the Younger*

Historical and Posthumous Memoirs
(1884) vol. 4

Kenyon Wright 1932–
Scottish Methodist minister, Chairman of the Scottish
Constitutional Convention

5 What if that other single voice we know so well responds by
saying, 'We say No and we are the State.' Well, we say Yes
and we are the People!
*of Margaret **Thatcher** as Prime Minister*

speech at the inaugural meeting of
the Scottish Constitutional
Convention, 30 March 1989

Tony Wright 1948–
British Labour politician

6 *to the Prime Minister:*
Don't you think it's bizarre at all that the House of
Commons can have endless votes on whether it wants to kill
foxes, but not on whether it wants to kill people?

at a hearing of the House of
Commons Liaison Committee, in
Guardian 21 January 2003 (online
edition)

Harry Wu 1937–
Chinese-born American political activist

7 I want to see the word *laogai* in every dictionary in every
language in the world. I want to see the laogai ended. Before
1974, the word 'gulag' did not appear in any dictionary.
Today, this single word conveys the meaning of Soviet
political violence and its labour camp system. 'Laogai' also
deserves a place in our dictionaries.
the laogai *are Chinese labour camps*

in *Washington Post* 26 May 1996

Augustin, Marquis de Ximénèz 1726–1817
French poet

1 *Attaquons dans ses eaux*
   La perfide Albion!
   Let us attack in her own waters perfidious Albion!

'L'Ère des Français' (October 1793)

Isoroku Yamamoto 1884–1943
Japanese admiral, Commander-in-Chief responsible for planning the Japanese attack on Pearl Harbor

2 A military man can scarcely pride himself on having
   'smitten a sleeping enemy'; in fact, to have it pointed out is
   more a matter of shame.

letter, 9 January 1942; Hirosuki Asawa *The Reluctant Admiral* (1979, tr. John Bester)

William Yancey 1814–63
American Confederate politician

3 *of Jefferson **Davis**, President-elect of the Confederacy, in 1861:*
   The man and the hour have met.

Shelby Foote *The Civil War: Fort Sumter to Perryville* (1991)

W. B. Yeats 1865–1939
Irish poet

4 Too long a sacrifice
   Can make a stone of the heart.
   O when may it suffice?

'Easter, 1916' (1921)

5 I write it out in a verse—
   MacDonagh and MacBride
   And Connolly and Pearse
   Now and in time to be,
   Wherever green is worn,
   Are changed, changed utterly:
   A terrible beauty is born.

'Easter, 1916' (1921)

6 Those that I fight I do not hate,
   Those that I guard I do not love.

'An Irish Airman Foresees his Death' (1919)

7 I think it better that at times like these
   We poets keep our mouths shut, for in truth
   We have no gift to set a statesman right.

'A Reason for Keeping Silent' (1916)

8 Out of Ireland have we come.
   Great hatred, little room,
   Maimed us at the start.
   I carry from my mother's womb
   A fanatic heart.

'Remorse for Intemperate Speech' (1933)

9 Turning and turning in the widening gyre
   The falcon cannot hear the falconer;
   Things fall apart; the centre cannot hold;
   Mere anarchy is loosed upon the world,
   The blood-dimmed tide is loosed, and everywhere
   The ceremony of innocence is drowned;
   The best lack all conviction, while the worst
   Are full of passionate intensity.

'The Second Coming' (1920)

10 Romantic Ireland's dead and gone,
    It's with O'Leary in the grave.

'September, 1913' (1914)

11 Cast your mind on other days
    That we in coming days may be
    Still the indomitable Irishry.

'Under Ben Bulben' (1939)

1 *of the Anglo-Irish:*
We . . . are no petty people. We are one of the great stocks of
Europe. We are the people of Burke; we are the people of
Swift, the people of Emmet, the people of Parnell. We have
created most of the modern literature of this country. We
have created the best of its political intelligence.

speech in the Irish Senate, 11 June
1925, in the debate on divorce

David Yelland 1963–
British journalist, Editor of the *Sun*

2 I don't think the Blairs are *Sun* readers.

on *News from Number Ten* (BBC2
documentary), 15 July 2000

Boris Yeltsin 1931–
Russian statesman, President of the Russian Federation
1991–2000

3 Today is the last day of an era past.
at a Berlin ceremony to end the Soviet military presence in
Germany

in *Guardian* 1 September 1994

4 Europe is in danger of plunging into a cold peace.
at the summit meeting of the Conference on Security and
Co-operation in Europe, December 1994

in *Newsweek* 19 December 1994

Shoichi Yokoi 1915–97
Japanese soldier

5 It is a terrible shame for me—I came back, still alive,
without having won the war.
on returning to Japan after surviving for 28 years in the jungles of
Guam before surrendering to the Americans in 1972

in *Independent* 26 September 1997

Andrew Young 1932–
American clergyman and diplomat

6 Nothing is illegal if one hundred well-placed business men
decide to do it.

Morris K. Udall *Too Funny to be*
President (1988)

Michael Young 1915–
British writer

7 Today we frankly recognize that democracy can be no more
than aspiration, and have rule not so much by the people as
by the cleverest people; not an aristocracy of birth, not a
plutocracy of wealth, but a true meritocracy of talent.

The Rise of the Meritocracy (1958)

Israel Zangwill 1864–1926
Jewish spokesman and writer

8 America is God's Crucible, the great Melting-Pot where all
the races of Europe are melting and re-forming!

The Melting Pot (1908)

Emiliano Zapata 1879–1919
Mexican revolutionary

9 Many of them, so as to curry favour with tyrants, for a
fistful of coins, or through bribery or corruption, are
shedding the blood of their brothers.
on the maderistas *who, in Zapata's view, had betrayed the*
revolutionary cause

Plan de Ayala 28 November 1911

José Luis Rodriguez Zapatero 1960–

Spanish Socialist statesman, Prime Minister from 2004

1 You can't lead a war with lies.

in Independent 16 March 2004

Mikhail Zhvanetsky 1934–

Russian writer

2 We enjoyed . . . his slyness. He mastered the art of walking backward into the future. He would say 'After me'. And some people went ahead, and some went behind, and he would go backward.
*of Mikhail **Gorbachev***

in Time 12 September 1994; attributed

Ronald L. Ziegler 1939–

American government spokesman

3 *reminded of the President's previous statements that the White House was not involved in the Watergate affair:*
[Mr Nixon's latest statement] is the Operative White House Position . . . and all previous statements are inoperative.

in Boston Globe 18 April 1973

Grigori Zinoviev 1883–1936

Soviet politician

4 Armed warfare must be preceded by a struggle against the inclinations to compromise which are embedded among the majority of British workmen, against the ideas of evolution and peaceful extermination of capitalism. Only then will it be possible to count upon complete success of an armed insurrection.

letter to the British Communist Party, 15 September 1924, in The Times 25 October 1924 (the 'Zinoviev Letter', said by some to be a forgery)

Hiller B. Zobel 1932–

American judge

5 Asking the ignorant to use the incomprehensible to decide the unknowable.

*'The Jury on Trial' in American Heritage July–August 1995; see **Wilde** 419:8*

6 Judges must follow their oaths and do their duty, heedless of editorials, letters, telegrams, threats, petitions, panellists and talk shows.

judicial ruling reducing the conviction of Louise Woodward from murder to manslaughter, 10 November 1997

Émile Zola 1840–1902

French novelist

7 *La vérité est en marche, et rien ne l'arrêtera.*
Truth is on the march, and nothing will stop it.
on the Dreyfus affair

in Le Figaro 25 November 1897

8 *J'accuse.*
I accuse.
title of an open letter to the President of the French Republic, in connection with the Dreyfus affair

in L'Aurore 13 January 1898

Keyword Index

affairs conducted the public a. — NORT 292:3
taking part in a. — VALÉ 404:2
tide in the a. — SHAK 356:5
affection one a. left me — CARS 75:14
affirmative condemn a. action — POWE 315:1
affliction our unique a. — SALI 341:2
affluence influence into a. — JOHN 203:15
affluent a. society — GALB 149:5
afraid feel somewhat a. — DE V 116:5
not a. to go — LAST 227:3
afresh begins the world a. — MONN 276:6
Africa A. is a scar — BLAI 46:11
deported A. — GENE 152:8
new out of A. — PLIN 313:1
shape of A. — FANO 139:3
white man in A. — LESS 231:13
African A. is conditioned — KENY 214:3
[A.] national consciousness — MACM 253:3
A. people — MAND 258:2
I am an A. — MBEK 265:3
like an A. coup — ANON 10:7
against a. everything — KENN 213:13
He was a. it — COOL 103:10
never met anyone who wasn't a. war
— LOW 242:4
not with me is a. me — BIBL 41:21
people vote a. somebody — ADAM 2:6
those that work a. them — HALI 169:7
age a. fatal to Revolutionists — DESM 115:8
a. going to the workhouse — PAIN 302:1
a. is a dream that is dying — O'SH 298:6
a. of chivalry — BURK 63:1
a. we live in — BURK 63:14
Old a. — TROT 400:3
agenda any item of the a. — PARK 304:7
agents Civil and Political A. — VICT 406:5
ages belongs to the a. — STAN 378:11
aggression It is naked a. — POWE 316:1
aggressive being a. — HARN 173:8
agitation than to excite a. — PALM 303:3
agonizing a. reappraisal — DULL 128:7
agony a. is abated — MACA 247:9
agree appear to a. — PAIN 302:3
both a. is wrong — CECI 78:7
colours will a. in the dark — BACO 21:7
agreed they are not a. — SALI 341:10
you a. to evil — RODR 329:1
agreement a. between two men — CECI 78:7
a. with hell — GARR 152:3
blow with an a. — TROT 400:6
have reached a. — MITC 274:10
agrees a. with me in principle — SALI 344:14
agriculture taxes must fall upon a. — GIBB 155:9
ahead a. of your time — MCGO 250:1
aid Foreign a. — NIXO 291:3
Foreign a. is a system — BAUE 30:5
aids seventeen-year-olds dying of A. — GING 157:3
aim when you have forgotten your a. — SANT 346:2
aimez a. qui vous aime — VOLT 407:10
air a. power has prevailed — KEEG 210:8
to the Germans that of—the a. — RICH 326:8

airy world which is a.-fairy — BLUN 47:1
aitches nothing to lose but our a. — ORWE 297:1
Alamein Before A. — CHUR 91:1
Albert take a message to A. — LAST 227:
Albion perfidious A. — XIMÉ 426:
alcohol more out of a. — CHUR 92:1
aldermen divides the wives of a. — SMIT 369:1
alien damned if I'm an a. — GEOR 154:
fringe of a. populations — NEWS 287:1
quick to blame the a. — AESC 5.
alienation day of mental a. — RIEL 327:
alieni A. appetens — SALL 345:
alive a. I shall be delighted — HOLL 186.
came back, still a. — YOKO 427:
Not while I'm a. 'e ain't — BEVI 40:1
what keeps you a. — CAST 77
all a. men are evil — MACH 250
Fair shares for a. — SLOG 366:
man for a. seasons — WHIT 419
allegiance Alliance is not a. — BARN 29
flag to which you have pledged a. — BALD 26
alliance A. is not allegiance — BARN 29
morganatic a. — HARD 172
alliances entangling a. with none — JEFF 199:
permanent a. — WASH 411:
allies no a. to be polite to — GEOR 154:
no eternal a. — PALM 302:1
allons A., enfants de la patrie — SONG 375:
allow Government and public opinion a.
— SHAW 360:1
almighty A. had placed it there — LABO 223:
A. took seven — CHUR 89:
alone a. in the room — KEYN 215:1
cannot live a. — ROOS 331:
plough my furrow a. — ROSE 333:1
right to be let a. — BRAN 53:
would but let it a. — WALP 409:
altar lays upon the a. — SPRI 378:
altars a. to the ground — JORD 207:
alteration A. though it be — HOOK 187:1
alternative a. to war — KING 217:1
no real a. — THAT 390:
What is the a. — TREN 397:
alternatives decide between a. — BONH 50:
exhausted all other a. — EBAN 129:
always a. in the majority — KNOX 222:
Alzheimer he had A.'s disease — REAG 323:
amateurs nation of a. — ROSE 333:
we prefer rule by a. — ATTL 18:1
ambassador a. is an honest man — WOTT 425:
ambition A. can creep — BURK 63:
A., in a private man a vice — MASS 263:1
A.'s debt is paid — SHAK 354:1
A. should be made — SHAK 355:
fling away a. — SHAK 353:
not without a. — SHAK 357:
Vaulting a. — SHAK 357:
young a.'s ladder — SHAK 354:
ambitions ceiling put on our a. — PRES 316:
ambitious as he was a., I slew him — SHAK 355:1
says he was a. — SHAK 355:

amendment Fifth A.   DOUG 125:7
  First A. has erected a wall   BLAC 45:3
America A. is God's Crucible   ZANG 427:8
  A. is just ourselves   ARNO 15:8
  A. is the only idealistic   WILS 423:3
  A. our nation   DOS 125:6
  A.'s present need   HARD 173:1
  A., the land   GOLD 160:9
  A. thus top nation   SELL 349:11
  Australia looks to A.   CURT 107:9
  born in A.   MALC 257:2
  cannot conquer A.   PITT 311:12
  Don't sell A. short   PROV 318:7
  England and A. divided   MISQ 272:6
  glorious morning for A.   MISQ 274:4
  God bless A.   BERL 36:6
  I look upon North A.   SHIP 364:1
  in common with A.   WILD 419:6
  independence of A.   SHEL 362:1
  in the living rooms of A.   MCLU 252:3
  I, too, sing A.   HUGH 190:7
  loss of A.   FREE 147:7
  lost his dominions in A.   WALP 409:7
  makes A. what it is   STEI 379:5
  morning again in A.   SLOG 367:5
  primitive North A.   BROG 56:3
  see A. save her soul   THOM 393:6
  think of thee, O A.   WALP 409:11
  United States of A.   PAGE 299:7
  whole A.   BURK 62:1
American A. as cherry pie   BROW 58:2
  A. culture   COLO 100:1
  A. dream is   BYWA 69:4
  A. friends   BLAI 46:10
  A. government   JEFF 200:14
  A. people have spoken   CLIN 97:11
  A., this new man   CEÈV 104:8
  bad news to the A. people   KEIL 211:1
  changed in A. life   LAHR 223:8
  chief business of the A. people   COOL 103:7
  free man, an A.   JOHN 202:6
  Greeks in this A. empire   MACM 252:7
  I also—am an A.   WEBS 413:12
  I am A. bred   MILL 270:4
  in A. politics   MITC 274:8
  I shall die an A.   WEBS 413:14
  knocking the A. system   CAPO 74:2
  no A. infidels   SAHH 337:5
  not a Virginian, but an A.   HENR 181:4
  point of being an A.   UPDI 403:8
  Scratch any A.   RUSK 335:7
  send A. boys   JOHN 203:6
  welfare of the A. people   HEAR 178:7
Americanism A. with its sleeves rolled   MCCA 248:4
  hyphenated A.   ROOS 332:12
Americans A. are our best friends   THOM 393:8
  A. are to be freemen   WASH 411:2
  A. in and the Germans down   ISMA 195:8
  for A. it is just beyond   KISS 221:14
  let A. disdain   HAMI 171:11

  my fellow A.   KENN 212:8
  passed to new generation of A.   KENN 212:3
amiable in a. theories   SALI 338:2
amicably a. if they can   QUIN 320:5
ammunition pass the a.   FORG 143:3
amok patriotism run a.   RATH 322:5
amused We are not a.   VICT 406:8
amusements part in their a.   WELL 415:9
anarch Thy hand, great A.   POPE 314:1
anarchism A. is a game   SHAW 361:7
  A. stands for the liberation   GOLD 161:2
anarchy a. and competition   RUSK 336:6
  cure of a.   BURK 62:4
  democracy, call it a.   HOBB 185:11
  Mere a. is loosed   YEAT 426:9
anatomist am but a bad a.   LAST 226:10
ancestors If our a. had cared   SALI 340:4
  look backward to their a.   BURK 62:16
ancestry pride of a.   POWE 316:6
anchor firm a. in nonsense   GALB 149:7
anchored a. safe and sound   WHIT 418:4
angel a. of death   BRIG 55:2
  a. rides in the whirlwind   PAGE 299:6
  ape or an a.   DISR 120:13
angels better a. of our nature   LINC 234:13
  By that sin fell the a.   SHAK 353:6
  make the a. weep   SHAK 358:1
  plead like a.   SHAK 357:2
anger a. of the sovereign   MORE 278:7
  neither a. nor partiality   TACI 385:4
Anglicization demon of A.   HYDE 193:10
Anglo-Irishman He was an A.   BEHA 32:5
Anglo-Saxon natural idol of the A.   BAGE 23:6
anguish howls of a.   HEAL 177:3
animal by nature a political a.   ARIS 14:13
  insidious and crafty a.   SMIT 370:7
animals All a. are equal   ORWE 296:8
animated a. nature   SALI 343:9
ankle chain about the a.   DOUG 126:4
Anna Here thou, great A.   POPE 314:7
annihilating a. all civilization   SAKH 337:7
  a. nations   MONT 277:3
annus a. horribilis   ELIZ 134:3
anointed balm from an a. king   SHAK 358:8
answer a. is yes   DOLE 125:3
  a. to the Irish Question   SELL 349:10
answering about not a.   LYNN 244:3
antiblack a. laws   FRIE 148:1
Antichrist against the a. of Communism   BUCH 60:2
anticipate What we a.   DISR 122:22
antique traveller from an a. land   SHEL 362:4
anti-Semitic stupid as the a.   LLOY 239:15
antiwar ecology and a.   HUNT 192:6
Antony A. Would ruffle up   SHAK 356:1
anybody no one's a.   GILB 156:5
anywhere a. I damn well please   BEVI 40:10
apart have stood a.   WILS 422:13
apathy stirring up a.   WHIT 417:11
ape Is man an a.   DISR 120:13
aphrodisiac Power is the great a.   KISS 221:7

apologize Never a.   FISH 141:1
apology defence or a.   CHAR 81:2
apostles A. of freedom   CONN 101:4
  true a. of equality   ARNO 15:9
appeasement A. was a sensible   TAYL 387:16
appeaser a. is one who   CHUR 87:12
appeasers A. believe   BROU 57:4
appetite no a. for truth   PEEL 307:5
appetites chains upon their own a.   BURK 61:5
applause everyone is forced to a.   MILL 270:7
appointment a. by the corrupt few   SHAW 361:2
  create an a.   LOUI 241:8
appointments In making a.   SALI 342:11
apprenticeship a. for freedom   BARA 29:3
approbation a. of all their actions   HOBB 185:10
appropriate that was not a.   CLIN 97:9
après A. nous le déluge   POMP 313:8
Arab A. world together   ARAF 14:2
  like an A. horse   ROBE 327:6
Arabs seven hundred thousand A.   BALF 28:2
Arbeicht A. macht frei   SLOG 366:3
arbiter a. of others' fate   BYRO 69:2
arbitrary a. government   CHAR 82:3
  supreme power must be a.   HALI 170:3
arch a. of order   STRA 382:10
  triumphant a.   COMM 100:2
archbishop My Lord A.   BULL 60:3
archer attack Jeffrey A.   HUMP 192:4
archipelago Gulag a.   SOLZ 373:10
architecture What has happened to a.   LEVI 232:11
are A. you now   PROV 318:2
  A. you thinking   SLOG 366:4
  We a. what we are   DAVI 110:6
arena actually in the a.   ROOS 332:10
Argentina Don't cry for me, A.   RICE 326:4
Argentinian young A. soldiers   RUNC 335:4
argues Nobody a. now   SALI 341:7
argument a. for fisticuffs   CHUR 90:11
  a. of tyrants   PITT 312:2
  no a. but force   BROW 58:6
  no force but a.   BROW 58:6
  once in the use of an a.   BENN 35:3
  stir without great a.   SHAK 352:2
aristocracies A. . . . may   TREV 398:5
aristocracy abolishes a.   TOCQ 395:8
  a. glean honour   MACD 249:6
  a. is rather apt   DISR 123:1
  a. means government by   CHES 83:12
  a. of Great Britain   BRIG 55:3
  A. of the Moneybag   CARL 74:13
  a. the most democratic   MACA 246:12
  a. will commit   WELL 415:9
  called a.   PAIN 301:5
  displeased with a.   HOBB 185:11
  English a.   SALI 343:11
  love of a.   GLAD 158:12
  natural a. among men   JEFF 199:13
  not an a. of birth   YOUN 427:7
aristocrat A. who cleans   GILB 156:4

aristocratic distinguish clearly the a. class   ARNO 15:10
arithmetical a. ratio   MALT 257:8
armadillos dead a.   HIGH 183:7
Armageddon We stand at A.   ROOS 332:11
armaments bloated a.   DISR 120:8
  not a. that cause wars   MADA 254:4
armed a. conflict   EDEN 129:10
  A. neutrality is ineffectual   WILS 422:16
  A. warfare must be preceded   ZINO 428:4
armes Aux a., citoyens   SONG 375:1
armies interested in a. and fleets   AUDE 18:17
  standing a. of power   RADC 320:7
  stronger than all the a.   ANON 12:6
Arminian A. clergy   PITT 311:11
armistice It is an a. for twenty years   FOCH 142:4
armour a. of a righteous cause   BRYA 59:7
arms a. ye forge   SHEL 362:5
  it hath very long a.   HALI 170:9
  keep and bear a.   CONS 102:5
  This world in a.   EISE 131:5
  Those entrusted with a.   WIND 423:6
  world in a.   SHAK 356:8
army a. marches on its stomach   NAPO 284:14
  a. may be equal   SALI 340:11
  a. would be a base rabble   BURK 62:9
  command an a.   SHER 363:5
  Forgotten A.   MOUN 281:9
  formation of an Irish a.   GRIF 166:3
  French's contemptible little a.   ANON 8:11
  invasion by an a.   HUGO 191:2
  Irish Citizen a.   CONN 101:7
  with the A. you have   RUMS 335:3
  won't be a bit like the A.   TRUM 401:5
  Your poor a.   CROM 106:5
aroused a. every feeling   TAYL 387:3
arrange French a.   CATH 77:5
arrested who's been a.   WOLF 424:2
arrive barbarians are to a.   CAVA 78:2
arrogance a. of power   FULB 148:11
arrogant a., out-of-control   DELA 114:1
arse politician is an a. upon   CUMM 107:4
arsenal great a. of democracy   ROOS 331:2
art a. establishes   KENN 213:6
  a. of government   PEEL 308:4
  a. which one government sooner   SMIT 371:3
  great a. lies   MILT 271:4
  Minister that meddles with a.   MELB 266:6
  necessary a.   DULL 128:3
  Politics is not the a.   GALB 150:8
  Politics is the a.   GAND 150:14
  Politics is the a. of the possible   BISM 43:7
article first a. of my faith   GAND 151:4
artificial but an a. man   HOBB 185:1
artists A. are not engineers   KENN 213:7
arts France, mother of a.   DU B 128:3
  No a.; no letters   HOBB 185:6
ascendancy a. of the Whig party   MACA 246:8
ascent a. to greatness   GIBB 155:5
ascertainable a. facts   PEEL 308:9
Asian A. boys ought to be   JOHN 203:6

backward (*cont.*):
walking b. into future — ZHVA 428:2
bad almost always b. men — ACTO 1:12
B. laws — BURK 64:13
B. money drives out good — PROV 318:4
brave b. man — CLAR 93:15
from b. to worse — TOCQ 396:3
great men even under b. emperors — TACI 385:2
shocking b. hats — WELL 415:8
things were just as b. — KENN 212:10
When b. men combine — BURK 64:2
bag b. and baggage — GLAD 158:13
baggage bag and b. — GLAD 158:13
take some b. in — CALL 71:1
Baghdad B. is determined — HUSS 193:2
B. is safe — SAHH 337:5
baked b. cookies and had teas — CLIN 97:2
balance b. of our population — JOSE 207:5
b. of power — KISS 221:12
b. of power — NICO 286:8
b. of the Old — CANN 73:12
tongue in the b. — BISM 44:13
balanced b. spirit — GEOR 153:9
balancing B. the budget — GRAM 163:7
bald b. eagle had not been chosen — FRAN 145:10
fight between two b. men — BORG 51:7
young, b. Leader — KINN 219:2
Baldwin sandhills of the B. Cabinet — ASQU 16:8
Balfour of the B. declaration — WEIZ 414:5
Balkan in the B. peninsula — SALI 341:8
Balkans prevailed in the B. — KEEG 210:8
silly thing in the B. — BISM 44:8
trouble in the B. in the spring — KIPL 221:4
ballads permitted to make all the b. — FLET 141:8
ballot b. box in one hand — BRUT 59:6
b. is stronger than — MISQ 272:2
nuisances of the b. — SALI 340:3
rap at the b. box — CHIL 84:3
right of all to the b. — ANTH 14:1
Vote by b. — CARL 75:7
ballots peaceful b. — LINC 234:3
balm wash the b. — SHAK 358:8
ban B. the bomb — SLOG 366:5
banana disgrace a b. republic — MAWR 264:3
bang bigger b. for a buck — SLOG 366:8
If the big b. does come — OSBO 298:2
Not with a b. but a whimper — ELIO 132:2
banged heart's a little b. up — MACK 251:4
banish I b. you — SHAK 350:11
will b. myself — SHER 363:5
bank tyrannize over his b. balance — KEYN 215:8
banker as a Scotch b. — DAVI 110:4
bankrupts need more b. — JOSE 207:6
banner Freedom's b. — DRAK 126:9
star-spangled b. — KEY 214:6
Banquo as B.'s ghost — AITK 6:3
Bantu [B.] has been subjected — VERW 405:7
banyan like the great b. tree — PATI 306:1
bar judge is a member of the B. — BOK 48:6
barbarian He is a b. — SHAW 360:4
barbarians b. are to arrive — CAVA 78:2

B., Philistines, and Populace — ARNO 15:8
name the former *the B.* — ARNO 15:10
without the b. — CAVA 78:3
barbarism b. be considered — WEIL 414:1
lowest b. — SMIT 369:11
methods of b. — CAMP 72:9
barbarity b. of tyrants — SMIT 372:5
barbarous horrible and b. — SALI 339:3
bard goat-footed b. — KEYN 215:6
barefoot I was born b. — LONG 240:14
bark you don't b. yourself — ATTL 18:13
barrel grows out of the b. of a gun — MAO 259:7
barren I am but a b. stock — ELIZ 132:5
such b. terrain — NOON 291:9
base art thou b. — SHAK 352:9
man of soul so b. — TOCQ 395:4
people as b. as itself — PULI 317:5
basics time to get back to b. — MAJO 256:8
basket come from the same b. — CONR 101:9
bastard b. who gets the mail — KEAT 210:6
more b. children — SHAK 351:3
bastards Keep the b. honest — SLOG 367:8
Bastille Voltaire in the B. — DE G 113:17
bath sing in the b. — LAMO 224:4
bathing caught the Whigs b. — DISR 119:9
bathroom can't feel revolutionary in a b. — LINK 237:1
baton marshal's b. — LOUI 242:1
bats b. have been broken — HOWE 190:2
b. will squeak and wheel — NICO 286:8
like b. amongst birds — BACO 21:3
batsmen opening b. to the crease — HOWE 190:2
battalions not of the heavy b. — VOLT 407:9
battle b. for the mind — NOON 291:9
b. to the strong — BIBL 41:12
defeated in a great b. — LIVY 238:5
die in a b. — SHAK 352:11
France has lost a b. — DE G 113:3
in the B. of Britain — BEVI 40:7
Ireland's b. — CONN 101:6
Next to a b. lost — WELL 415:14
we b. for the Lord — ROOS 332:11
battles b., martyrs — WHIT 418:9
Dead b., like dead generals — TUCH 402:2
forced marches, b. and death — GARI 151:10
mother of all b. — HUSS 193:1
opening b. of subsequent wars — ORWE 296:12
baubles Take away these b. — MISQ 273:11
bayonet b. is a weapon — SLOG 366:6
bayonets throne of b. — INGE 195:3
beaches fight on the b. — CHUR 88:2
beacon b.-light is quenched — SCOT 348:8
bear any of us can b. — GIUL 157:8
b. those ills we have — SHAK 351:11
embrace the Russian b. — CHAN 81:1
Puritan hated b.-baiting — MACA 247:1
so b. ourselves that — CHUR 88:3
than it could b. — BUTL 67:11
beard King of Spain's B. — DRAK 126:7
bears b. the marks of the last person — HAIG 168:3
beast b. With many heads — SHAK 351:2

blond b.   NIET 289:9
either a b. or a god   ARIS 14:14
beat if the king b. us   MANC 257:11
money to even get b.   ROGE 329:3
beaten b. by strangers   DOS 125:6
being b. does not matter   STEP 379:7
hope that we should be b.   SALI 342:10
beating glory of b. the French   WOLF 423:10
beaut it's a b.   LA G 223:6
beautiful all that was b.   NEHR 286:1
b. country   LAST 228:3
Black is b.   SLOG 366:10
Small is b.   SCHU 348:2
beauty b. of the mountain rose   BEAV 31:9
bed never made my own b.   PU Y 317:7
bedfellows makes strange b.   WARN 410:9
strange b.   PROV 319:7
bedrock b. of Europe   POWE 315:2
bedrooms in the nation's b.   TRUD 400:9
bee b. on royal jelly   CHUR 92:7
b. produces honey   GOLD 161:1
Beeb game of chicken with the B.   KELL 211:3
beef roast b. of old England   BURK 64:1
Where's the b.   MOND 275:7
beer b. of a man in Klondike   CHES 83:11
warm b., invincible suburbs   MAJO 256:7
beg b. in the streets   FRAN 145:3
began believe that the world b.   CHUR 90:13
beggar b. would recognise guilt   PARS 305:10
begin b. the world over   PAIN 300:9
But let us b.   KENN 212:7
Wars b. when you will   MACH 250:7
beginning b. of the end   TALL 385:11
end of the b.   CHUR 89:1
I am only at the b.   NAPO 284:3
In my end is my b.   MARY 263:10
beginnings All b. are small   JOUB 207:9
time the b. and endings   BACO 20:9
begins b. the world afresh   MONN 276:6
begun b. to fight   JONE 206:1
behaviour b. was intolerable   MAJO 256:11
behind b. the throne   PITT 311:10
Belgium B. put the kibosh on the Kaiser
    SONG 375:4
until B. recovers in full   ASQU 16:5
Belgrano sinking of the B.   DALY 109:2
belief attacks my b.   JOHN 204:19
believe B. nothing until   COCK 98:9
b. what they wish   CAES 69:7
I could ever b.   BROW 57:9
professing to b.   PAIN 300:1
they b. intensely   SALI 338:2
you'll b. anything   WELL 415:12
believed b. to be so   TROL 399:5
if b. during three days   MEDI 265:4
Nothing can now be b.   JEFF 199:9
believes politician never b. what he says
    DE G 113:9
believing Not b. in force   TROT 400:7
bella B., *horrida bella*   VIRG 407:1
bells b. I hear   WHIT 418:3

now ring the b.   WALP 410:2
belong To betray, you must first b.   PHIL 310:3
belt no b. to tighten   PANK 303:11
see a b. without hitting   ASQU 17:3
bench only a simple b.   GARF 151:9
benches along Labour back b.   EWIN 138:4
asleep on the same b.   ONSL 295:11
beneficial b. reforms   THAT 392:9
benefit only true lasting b.   SALI 342:4
benevolence b. of the butcher   SMIT 370:2
Berliner *Ich bin ein B.*   KENN 213:5
best b. is like the worst   KIPL 220:4
b. lack all conviction   YEAT 426:9
b. man among them   CAST 77:1
b. Prime Minister we have   BUTL 68:2
b. rulers   LAO- 225:3
b. when we are boldest   BLAI 46:12
b. when we are boldest   BROW 57:8
It was the b. of times   DICK 118:1
Send forth the b.   KIPL 221:2
we will do our b.   CHUR 88:10
Whate'er is b. administered   POPE 314:4
bestow b. on every airth a limb   MONT 278:2
bestride b. the narrow world   SHAK 354:1
betray guts to b. my country   FORS 143:4
To b., you must first belong   PHIL 310:3
better b. angels of our nature   LINC 234:13
b. his own condition   SMIT 370:8
b. if he had never lived   CHUR 90:3
B. red than dead   SLOG 366:7
can only get b.   PETR 309:9
can only get b.   SLOG 368:9
from worse to b.   HOOK 187:12
illusion that times were b.   GREE 165:6
people can be b. off   DISR 123:4
see the b. things   OVID 298:11
We had b. wait and see   ASQU 16:4
would have done b.   SHOR 364:6
beware b. of the dog   BLIX 47:7
B. the ides of March   SHAK 353:10
bible B. in the other   WRAN 425:3
by B. readers *for* Bible readers   BAIN 25:7
bicycle arrive by b.   VIER 406:10
bicycling old maids b.   MAJO 256:7
bidder highest b.   WASH 411:3
big b. enough to take away everything
    FORD 142:10
b. tent   SLOG 366:9
fall victim to a b. lie   HITL 184:5
G.O.P.'s b. tent   NEWS 288:4
or a b. no   SARK 346:5
too b. for them   BULM 60:4
too b. to cry   LINC 235:5
bigger b. bang for a buck   SLOG 366:8
bigot mind of a b.   HOLM 187:5
bigotries b. that savage   LLOY 239:15
bike got on his b.   TEBB 388:13
biking Old maids b.   ORWE 297:1
bill B. of Rights was not   JORD 206:8
called upon to pay the b.   HARD 172:8
billet bullet has its b.   PROV 318:11

billion b. dollar country	FOST 143:7
bills pay my tax b.	HOLM 187:3
bind b. your sons to exile	KIPL 221:2
Obadiah B.-their-kings	MACA 247:3
bin Laden having one b.	MUBA 282:2
biographical noble and b. friend	WETH 417:1
biography B. should be written	BALF 28:6
nothing but b.	DISR 122:14
bird b.'s battling in its own home	AESC 5:6
catch the b. of paradise	KHRU 216:6
forgets the dying b.	PAIN 301:3
birds b. are flown	CHAR 81:3
for the high b.	HALI 171:5
like small b.	DISR 121:12
Birmingham B. Six released	DENN 115:3
birth accident of her b.	SHEL 362:9
disqualified by the accident of b.	CHES 83:4
one that is coming to b.	O'SH 298:6
bishop Another B. dead	MELB 266:5
B. of Rome	BOOK 50:4
hitting the niece of a b.	ORWE 297:11
No b., no King	JAME 197:1
bishopric *merit* for a b.	WEST 416:12
bite b. the hand that fed them	BURK 63:13
bites dead woman b. not	GRAY 165:3
bitterness fuelled by b.	BHUT 41:1
bizarre b. happening	HAUG 175:1
black b. domination	MAND 258:2
B. Hills belong to me	SITT 365:6
B. is beautiful	SLOG 366:10
b. kids get an education	POWE 315:1
b. majority rule	SMIT 372:1
b. men fought	MACA 245:6
B. Panther Party	NEWT 286:4
B. Power	CARM 75:8
B.'s not so black	CANN 73:7
not have the colour b.	MAND 259:1
one drop of b. blood	HUGH 190:8
with a b. skin	MALC 257:2
Blackpool this B. hot-house	HOME 187:6
blacks between whites and b.	LINC 234:6
country is for b.	TSVA 402:1
if b. get hurt	SEXW 350:5
bladders boys that swim on b.	SHAK 353:5
Blair one of B.'s babes	JACK 196:8
Sun backs B.	NEWS 288:6
Vote B.	SLOG 368:16
Blairs don't think the B.	YELL 427:2
blame does not mean I'm to b.	HOON 188:1
quick to b. the alien	AESC 5:7
blaming b. it on you	KIPL 219:10
blancmange multi-hued b.	MITC 274:7
blank political b. cheque	GOSC 163:3
blanket with the b. over his head	BABE 20:2
blasphemies truths begin as b.	SHAW 360:1
bleed b. in sport	SHAK 355:1
bleeper do not wear a b.	CLAR 94:12
Blenheim B. all over again	BEVA 38:7
blessed This b. plot	SHAK 358:6
blessing b. to the country	BISM 43:4
national b.	HAMI 171:8

blind country of the b.	ERAS 135:9
Like a b. man	O'NE 295:9
old, mad, b.	SHEL 362:8
too dangerous for b. partnership	STRO 383:2
blinked other fellow just b.	RUSK 335:5
bliss B. was it in that dawn	WORD 424:8
bloated b. armaments	DISR 120:8
block old b. itself	BURK 64:15
blocks he had b. to cut	PEEL 307:16
You b., you stones	SHAK 353:9
blond b. beast	NIET 289:9
blood b. be the price	KIPL 220:10
b.-dimmed tide is loosed	YEAT 426:9
b. drawn with the lash	LINC 236:6
b. is their argument	SHAK 352:11
b. of patriots	JEFF 198:6
b. of the socialist	CROS 106:14
b. on your hands	CARL 74:4
B. sport brought	INGH 195:4
B. sport brought	INGH 195:5
B., sweat, and tear-wrung	BYRO 68:10
b., toil, tears and sweat	CHUR 87:14
b. with guilt is bought	SHEL 362:5
defeated in b.	O'CO 293:6
enough of b. and tears	RABI 320:6
foaming with much b.	POWE 315:5
fraternal b.	WEBS 413:7
guiltless of his country's b.	GRAY 165:5
Here lies b.	EPIT 136:7
Man of B. was there	MACA 247:5
mingle my b.	BROW 58:4
my b. will invigorate India	GAND 151:1
one drop of black b.	HUGH 190:8
rivers of b.	JEFF 200:6
seas of b.	COBB 98:4
spend her b.	WILS 422:17
through b. and iron	BISM 44:5
Tiber foaming with much b.	VIRG 407:1
tincture in the b.	DEFO 112:8
watching a stream of b.	ANON 10:11
We, your b. family	SPEN 377:7
bloodhounds Seven b. followed	SHEL 362:3
bloodshed war without b.	MAO 259:6
bloodthirsty so venomous, so b.	TROL 399:8
bloody b. curtain	ELIS 132:3
no right in the b. circus	MAXT 264:4
blossom hundred flowers b.	MAO 259:9
blot b. on the escutcheon	GRAY 165:1
blow b. at the very principles	LINC 233:10
b. with an agreement	TROT 400:6
blubbering b. Cabinet	GLAD 159:8
blue b.-eyed devil white man	FARD 139:5
in the b. states	OBAM 292:10
True b. and Mrs Crewe	GEOR 153:4
blueprint Founding Fathers' b.	BIRC 43:3
blunder it is a b.	BOUL 52:5
wonder at so grotesque a b.	BENT 36:2
Youth is a b.	DISR 122:9
blunders Human b.	TAYL 387:8
blunt plain, b. man	SHAK 355:15
board carried on b.	HUME 191:6

bray Vicar of B.   SONG 376:3
Brazilian If I were a B.   STIN 381:7
bread b. and circuses   JUVE 209:4
  b. which it has earned   JEFF 199:1
  looked to government for b.   BURK 63:13
  should soon want b.   JEFF 200:8
  took the b. and brake it   ELIZ 133:13
break b. his spirit   HOLL 186:7
  b. your party   HEAD 177:2
breakfast found b. with difficulty   SALI 340:13
breast with dauntless b.   GRAY 165:5
breasts b. by which France is fed   SULL 383:7
breath b. can make them   GOLD 161:3
  b. of worldly men   SHAK 358:8
  taxed the b.   THOM 393:2
breathe yearning to b. free   LAZA 229:9
breathes B. there the man   SCOT 348:7
brewsters b. and baksters   LANG 225:2
bribe b. or gratuity   PENN 308:14
  cannot hope to b. or twist   WOLF 423:9
bribes asked Bacon how many b.   BENT 36:1
brick hardly throw a b.   ORWE 297:11
  inherited it b.   AUGU 19:7
bridge going a b. too far   BROW 58:7
  man on the b.   BALD 27:4
  promise to build a b.   KHRU 216:7
  to the b.-builders   MCAL 244:12
  Women, and Champagne, and B.   BELL 33:4
bridle b. and no spurs   TAYL 388:4
brief b. as I can be   O'CO 293:4
  little b. authority   SHAK 358:1
briefing b.is what *I* do   CALL 70:5
brigade of the Irish B.   DAVI 110:8
  Viva la the New B.   DAVI 110:9
brilliant B.—to the top of his boots   LLOY 239:17
brink walked to the b.   DULL 128:8
brinkmanship boasting of his b.   STEV 380:13
Britain boundary of B.   TACI 384:11
  B. a fit country   LLOY 239:2
  B. has lost an empire   ACHE 1:7
  B.'s stand alone   DE V 116:4
  B. will be honoured by historians   HARL 173:7
  B. will still be   MAJO 256:7
  dangerous man in B.   NEWS 287:11
  government of B.'s isle   SHAK 352:16
  Great B. has   CURZ 107:10
  I'm backing B.   SLOG 367:4
  speak for B.   BOOT 51:3
  Without B., Europe   ERHA 137:7
British as the B. public   MACA 246:2
  bones of one B. Grenadier   HARR 174:2
  B. government   HAMI 171:9
  B. is unique   CHUR 88:9
  B. king   MARK 260:8
  B. Minister sneezed   LEVI 232:10
  B. political system   TAYL 387:14
  B. pound   DYSO 129:5
  B. society of Bombay   SALI 342:9
  B. subject I was born   MACD 249:5
  destinies of the B. Empire   DISR 120:10
  from the B. government   MCAL 245:1

immobility of B. institutions   ASQU 16:6
  of the B. Empire   CHUR 88:14
  shield of B. fair play   AITK 6:2
  so also a B. subject   PALM 303:1
  thank God! the B. journalist   WOLF 423:9
Briton B., Saxon   HEWI 183:3
  glory in the name of B.   GEOR 153:1
Britons B. alone use 'Might'   WAUG 412:2
broccoli eat any more b.   BUSH 66:5
broke If it ain't b.   LANC 224:7
broken bats have been b.   HOWE 190:2
  b. window pane   PANK 303:10
  Can it be b.   JENK 201:2
  made to be b.   NORT 291:10
  taken up the b. blade   DE G 113:5
broker more that of an honest b.   BISM 44:2
bronze noontide was b.   CHUR 91:4
broomstick tether a b.   KEYN 215:7
brother BIG B. IS WATCHING YOU   ORWE 297:2
  Had it been his b.   EPIT 136:5
  man and a b.   WEDG 413:16
  want to be the white man's b.   KING 217:4
  what my b. will do   CHAR 82:2
brotherhood sit down at the table of b.   KING 217:7

brothers live together as b.   KING 217:9
brow b. of labour   BRYA 59:9
brown Get B.   SLOG 368:16
  John B.'s body   SONG 376:5
Browning safety-catch of my B.   JOHS 205:10
bruiser piratical old b.   HAIL 168:9
brute *Et tu, B.?*   SHAK 354:13
  finest b. votes in Europe   ANON 8:12
brutish nasty, b., and short   HOBB 185:6
Brutus B. is an honourable man   SHAK 355:8
  'B.' will start a spirit   SHAK 354:2
  You too, B.   CAES 69:12
buck bigger bang for a b.   SLOG 366:8
  b. stops here   MOTT 281:2
bud nip him in the b.   ROCH 328:12
budget Balancing the b.   GRAM 163:7
  b. should be balanced   MISQ 272:3
  look upon B. promises   SALI 344:3
bug thinks there'a b.   BUSH 66:4
bugger B. Bognor   LAST 226:8
build those who will b. it   TRUD 400:10
building finish b. it   RANK 322:4
builds b. on mud   MACH 250:10
  something that b. up a man   BENN 34:5
bullet b. has its billet   PROV 318:11
  stronger than the b.   MISQ 272:2
bullets bloody b.   LINC 234:3
bully by the bossy for the b.   SELD 349:4
  such a b. pulpit   ROOS 333:4
bulwark b. of continuing liberty   ROOS 330:12
  floating b. of the island   BLAC 45:6
bump b. in the road   BUSH 66:11
bums corporate welfare b.   LEWI 233:3
Buncombe talking to B.   WALK 408:2
  through reporters to B.   CARL 74:14
bungler good nature is a b.   HALI 171:2

Man is a b. — SHAW 360:17
burden bear any b. — KENN 212:4
  b. of the nation's care — PRIO 316:12
  impossible to carry the heavy b. — EDWA 130:5
  White Man's B. — KIPL 221:2
bureaucracy and the vast b. — DOUG 125:8
  [b.'s] specific invention — WEBE 413:4
  B., the rule of no one — MCCA 248:5
bureaucrats b. will care more for routine
                   — BAGE 23:12
  Guidelines for b. — BORE 51:6
burglar honest b. — MENC 267:9
burial any part, in its b. — MACM 253:6
buried b. all the hatchets — WILS 422:2
  b. at midnight — O'BR 293:3
  b. in the rain — MILL 270:3
burlesque b. and the newspapers — STON 382:1
burn B., baby, burn — SLOG 366:11
  b. its children to save — MEYE 268:9
burned b. women — BRAN 53:7
  men also, in the end, are b. — HEIN 179:7
burning b. the rain forest — STIN 381:7
  by b. him — CEAU 78:6
  Keep the Home-fires b. — SONG 376:6
burnt b., tortured, fined — JEFF 200:9
bury anything we want to b. — MOOR 278:3
  children b. their parents — HERO 182:2
  good day to b. bad news — MISQ 272:9
  I come to b. Caesar — SHAK 355:7
  We will b. you — KHRU 216:5
bus missed the b. — CHAM 80:5
  stepping in front of a b. — OSBO 298:2
buses more time on b. — STRU 383:4
bush B. wins it — NEWS 287:1
business big b. give people — SLOG 369:3
  b. as usual — THAT 391:5
  B. carried on as usual — CHUR 86:9
  create b. for itself — SALI 344:16
  do b. together — JEFF 200:5
  do b. together — THAT 391:7
  doing b. — HEAL 177:12
  fit for b. — WALP 410:5
  government of b. — LAWS 229:4
  Liberty is always unfinished b. — ANON 10:10
  neither b. nor rest — MORL 279:6
  of the American people is b. — COOL 103:7
  small b. party — BEAZ 32:2
  totter on in b. — POPE 314:2
  Treasury is the spring of b. — BAGE 22:4
  wheels of b. — TAWN 386:6
businessman b. has trampled — NICO 288:13
businessmen well-placed b. decide — YOUN 427:6
busy Government of the b. — SELD 349:4
butcher benevolence of the b. — SMIT 370:2
  Prime Minister has to be a b. — BUTL 68:4
  way to the b. — CHUR 87:6
butchers sacrificers, but not b. — SHAK 354:9
  shepherds and b. — VOLT 407:8
butter manage without b. — GOEB 160:3
  rather have b. or guns — GOER 160:5
butts b. me away — SHAK 351:2

buy b. a used car — SLOG 369:5
  b. it like an honest man — NORT 292:5
  Don't b. a single vote more — KENN 212:1
buyer b. can be found — SALL 345:6
bypass with a triple b. — HOWA 189:5
Byron movement needs a B. — POLL 313:6
bystander never be a b. — BAUE 30:7
byword story and a b. — WINT 423:7

cabinet blubbering C. — GLAD 159:8
  C. does not propose, it decides — ATTL 18:6
  c. government — WALD 407:15
  c. is a combining committee — BAGE 22:5
  C. meeting — LAWS 229:7
  C. ministers are educated — BENN 35:5
  C. minutes are studied — KAUF 209:10
  C.'s gone to its dinner — ANON 11:5
  consequence of c. government — BAGE 22:6
  group of C. Ministers — CURZ 108:1
  head of the C. — MORL 279:8
  mislead the C. — ASQU 16:10
  reluctance to consult c. — FRAS 146:10
  self-control in C. — SHEP 362:13
  To C. Ministers — SALI 344:9
  ways of getting into the C. — BEVA 39:10
Caesar always I am C. — SHAK 354:5
  Aut C., aut nihil — MOTT 281:1
  C. bleed in sport — SHAK 355:1
  C. hath wept — SHAK 355:9
  C.'s laurel crown — BLAK 47:1
  C.'s public policy — PLUT 313:5
  C.'s wife — CAES 69:8
  doth this our C. feed — SHAK 354:2
  I come to bury C. — SHAK 355:7
  in envy of great C. — SHAK 356:7
  loved C. less — SHAK 355:5
  O mighty C. — SHAK 355:3
  Render therefore unto C. — BIBL 41:22
  that C. might be great — CAMP 72:7
  Then fall, C. — SHAK 354:13
  unto C. shalt thou go — BIBL 41:27
  word of C. — SHAK 355:12
Caesars C. and Napoleons — HUXL 193:6
cage become an iron c. — WEBE 412:11
Caitlin C. Ni Uallachain — MACN 254:5
cake Let them eat c. — MARI 260:4
Calais 'C.' lying in my heart — MARY 263:5
Caledonia Mourn, hapless C. — SMOL 373:1
Caligula C.'s horse was made Consul — RAND 321:9
  eyes of C. — MITT 275:5
call Labour's c. — SLOG 366:15
  timeless c. — SCHL 347:10
  who do I c. — KISS 221:9
calling Germany c. — JOYC 208:3
calm c., rather than to excite — PALM 303:3
Calvinist Papist, yet a C. — EPIT 136:7
Calvinistic C. creed — PITT 311:11
Cambridge To C. books — TRAP 397:5
  to C. books he sent — BROW 58:6
came c. first for the Communists — NIEM 289:5

came (*cont.*):
  I c., I saw, I conquered   CAES 69:11
  I c. through   MACA 245:3
Camelot known As C.   LERN 231:11
  never be another C.   ONAS 294:8
campaign c. in poetry   CUOM 107:5
  capital in the c.   BUSH 67:7
  political c.   WILS 422:7
campaigns c. for public office   MORE 278:5
Canada C. could have enjoyed   COLO 100:1
  C. is not a real country   BOUC 52:4
  C. is ten   FOTH 144:2
  C. that shall fill   LAUR 228:11
  complex C.   STRO 383:3
  dedication to C.'s future   DIEF 118:9
  I see C.   DAVI 110:4
  more than C. itself is worth   VOLT 407:2
Canadian sense of doubt—a C.   LÉVE 232:2
cancer c. close to the Presidency   DEAN 111:8
  white race *is* the c.   SONT 374:4
candid c. friend   CANN 73:8
candidates c. for power   PAIN 302:5
  c. were not men   PAIN 301:11
candle better to light a c.   BENE 33:9
  c. in that great turnip   CHUR 90:10
  c. in the wind   JOHN 202:3
  c. to the sun   SIDN 364:9
  light such a c.   LAST 226:2
  rather light a c.   STEV 380:17
candles carry c. and set chairs   HERV 182:5
cannibals body of c.   MENC 267:13
cannon She is a loose c.   PIEN 311:1
Canossa not go to C.   BISM 43:10
cant c. of *Not men*   BURK 64:3
Canterbury C. or Smithfield   WALP 409:5
Cantuar how full of C.   BULL 60:3
capable c. of reigning   TACI 385:7
capers He c. nimbly   SHAK 359:3
capital c. in the campaign   BUSH 67:7
  C. must be propelled   BAGE 21:14
  destroy c.   MACA 247:2
  intellectual c.   CALL 71:1
  interests of c. and labour   ATKI 17:8
  origin of c.   TORR 397:1
capitalism C. has been singularly devoid   BERG 36:4
  C. is using its money   CAST 77:4
  c. of the working class   SPEN 377:8
  C., wisely managed   KEYN 215:2
  c. with the gloves off   STOP 382:6
  extermination of c.   ZINO 428:4
  monopoly stage of c.   LENI 230:8
  spirit of c.   WEBE 412:10
  unacceptable face of c.   HEAT 179:1
  Under c. man exploits man   ANON 13:1
capitalist c. system   MACM 253:6
  slave of the c. society   CONN 101:5
capitalists c. will sell us   MISQ 272:4
capitals series of c.   CURZ 107:10
Capri letter came from C.   JUVE 209:3
caprices depend on the c.   TOCQ 395:4

captain broken by the team c.   HOWE 190:2
  c. is in his bunk   SHAW 360:9
  my C. lies, Fallen   WHIT 418:4
  O C.! my Captain   WHIT 418:3
  plain russet-coated c.   CROM 105:9
  ship's c. complaining   POWE 315:11
captains c. and the kings   KIPL 220:6
car afford to keep a motor c.   SHAW 360:2
  buy a used c.   SLOG 369:5
  c. in every garage   HOOV 188:4
  whisky and c. keys   O'RO 296:3
caravan great c. of humanity   SMUT 373:2
carcases c. of unburied men   SHAK 350:11
carcasses c. of dead policies   SALI 339:14
card c. up his sleeve   LABO 223:4
  Orange c.   CHUR 86:1
  play the race c.   SHAP 359:16
  stood like a playing c.   MAIL 255:10
care c. of human life   JEFF 199:11
career c. in tatters   MAND 259:2
  C. open to the talents   CARL 74:8
  c. open to the talents   NAPO 284:16
  c. that lies before me   NAPO 284:3
  loyal to his own c.   DALT 108:8
  nothing in his long c.   NEWS 288:9
careless C. talk costs lives   OFFI 295:1
  c. trifle   SHAK 356:12
  have been a little c.   CRES 104:7
cares c. and pleasures   GIBB 155:7
carnivorous sheep born c.   FAGU 138:8
Caroline Queen C., not you   ANON 13:11
carpenter Between them, Walrus and C.   LEVI 232:8
carry c. a big stick   ROOS 332:5
Carthage C. must be destroyed   CATO 77:8
Carthaginian C. trustworthiness   SALL 345:7
cartoonist life as a c. wonderful   PETE 309:8
cash c. payment   CARL 74:7
  pay you c. to go away   KIPL 221:1
cast C. your mind on other days   YEAT 426:11
  die is c.   CAES 69:10
castle C. of lies   BOOK 50:8
  home is his c.   PROV 318:10
Castlereagh had a mask like C.   SHEL 362:3
casualties number of c.   GIUL 157:8
casualty is the first c.   PROV 320:1
cat big c. in a poodle parlour   PARR 305:5
  c.'s-paw must expect   COCK 98:8
  if a c. is black or white   DENG 114:8
  Like a powerful graceful c.   CHUR 91:3
  way the c. jumps   THAT 391:10
  which way the c. is jumping   SULZ 383:9
catalogue c. of human crime   CHUR 88:1
catch c. the weak and poor   ANAC 7:7
catched and not be c.   PEPY 309:1
categorical c. imperative   KANT 209:6
caterpillars c. of the commonwealth   SHAK 358:7
catholic Gentlemen, I am a C.   BELL 33:5
  Roman C. Church   MACM 253:11
Catholics When Hitler attacked the C.   NIEM 289:5
Cato losing one pleased C.   LUCA 243:1

Voice of C.	JONS 206:6
cats C. look down	CHUR 92:9
c. might play	CHUR 90:8
cattle thousands of great c.	BURK 63:5
cause armour of a righteous c.	BRYA 59:7
bad c. which cannot bear	LAST 227:2
good old C.	MILT 271:6
his c. being good	MORE 278:6
Our c. is just	DICK 118:5
winning c. pleased the gods	LUCA 243:1
causes aren't any good, brave c.	OSBO 298:2
tough on the c. of crime	BLAI 45:10
caution Speaking with that c.	PEEL 308:2
cavaliers C. (Wrong but Wromantic)	SELL 349:5
will not do with the c.	LAMB 224:1
cave political C. of Adullam	BRIG 55:6
Ceauşescus C.' execution	O'DO 293:9
Cecils C. always end up on top	BENN 35:1
cede c. to lawful authority	GIUL 157:6
celebrated Revolutions are c.	BOUL 52:6
Celt C., Briton, Saxon	HEWI 183:3
Celtic C. Tiger	MCAL 244:11
woods of C. antiquity	KEYN 215:6
cement like mixing c.	MOND 275:8
Palestine is the c.	ARAF 14:2
censorship extreme form of c.	SHAW 361:9
fought without c.	WEST 416:11
centralization C. and socialism	TOCQ 395:10
c. follows	TOCQ 395:8
centre c. cannot hold	YEAT 426:9
c. has always melted	HAIL 168:8
in the c. of politics	MOSL 280:6
My c. is giving way	FOCH 142:3
cents simplicity of the three per c.	DISR 122:20
centuries All c. but this	GILB 156:11
forty c. look down	NAPO 284:4
century c. of the common man	WALL 408:4
close the c.	MAND 258:8
cereal like breakfast c.	STEV 380:14
cerebellum If they've a brain and c.	GILB 156:9
ceremony c. of innocence is drowned	YEAT 426:9
c. that to great ones 'longs	SHAK 357:12
general c.	SHAK 352:14
certain four things c.	KIPL 219:8
you can be c.	KERR 214:5
chain c. about the ankle	DOUG 126:4
chaining c. the crowd	VOLT 407:12
chains better to be in c.	KAFK 209:5
c. upon their own appetites	BURK 61:5
deliverance from c.	DOUG 126:1
everywhere he is in c.	ROUS 334:6
lose but their c.	MARX 263:4
so debased by their c.	ROUS 334:7
chairman highly-paid c.	SALI 343:12
chairs carry candles and set c.	HERV 182:5
challenge times of c.	KING 218:1
Chamberlain Listening to a speech by C.	
	BEVA 39:9
chamberpot fortune empties her c.	MACD 249:4
chambers enchanted c. of Power	LAND 224:8
chameleon paint the c.	KEYN 215:7

champagne Women, and C.	BELL 33:4
chance c. to work hard	ROOS 332:7
in the last c. saloon	MELL 267:1
chancellor C. of the Exchequer	LOWE 242:6
Germany has a new C.	SLOG 366:13
two kinds of C.	BROW 57:10
change C. is constant	DISR 120:16
c. of persons	PAIN 301:12
c. their minds	HATT 174:8
involves a great c.	TROL 399:13
life can c. on a dime	LAHR 223:8
make c. our friend	CLIN 97:7
means of some c.	BURK 62:14
necessary not to c.	FALK 139:2
perils of c.	SALI 339:10
point is to c. it	MARX 262:9
things will have to c.	LAMP 224:6
time for a c.	DEWE 117:1
Times c., and we change	ANON 12:5
torrent of c.	CHES 83:5
wind of c. is blowing	MACM 253:3
changed changed, c. utterly	YEAT 426:5
If voting c. anything	LIVI 237:8
until I c. myself	MAND 258:9
changes c. we fear be thus irresistible	JOHN 204:1
to delay c.	SALI 342:3
channel [C.] is a mere ditch	NAPO 284:5
Fog in C.	BROC 55:10
Government . . . is simply not the c.	KENN 211:5
masters of the C.	NAPO 284:6
chaos dread empire, C.	POPE 314:1
grotesque c.	KINN 218:11
chappie cheerful c.	WOOL 424:6
chaps clever c. like you	BEVI 40:9
chapter write the next c.	JOHN 203:1
character about a fellow's c.	REAG 323:4
by the content of their c.	KING 217:7
did not have the c.	ROOS 330:2
excellence in our national c.	BAGE 24:10
characteristic c. vice	TAWN 386:4
characters great c. are formed	ADAM 2:2
charitably c. dispose of any thing	SHAK 352:11
charity c. for all	LINC 236:7
Keeping books on c.	PERÓ 309:5
charlatan c., and a conjuror	TROL 399:2
Charles C. II was always very merry	SELL 349:7
King C.'s golden days	SONG 376:3
charm northern c.	KENN 213:9
chase live by the c.	TOCQ 396:8
chasm c., a blank	FOX 144:10
chatter hare-brained c.	DISR 121:18
cheap done as c. as other men	PEPY 308:17
obtain too c.	PAIN 300:12
cheaper c. than we can	SMIT 370:5
cheating period of c.	BIER 42:5
check form a mutual c.	BLAC 45:9
checkers spaniel, named C.	NIXO 290:3
cheeks c. are drawn	PARR 305:8
cheer which side do they c. for	TEBB 388:14
cheerful as c. as any man could	PEPY 308:15
c. chappie	WOOL 424:6

What is the c. but the people — SHAK 350:10
civil c. to everyone — SISS 365:5
 dire effects from c. discord — ADDI 5:2
 Pray, good people, be c. — GWYN 167:10
civilian c. control — TRUM 401:12
civilization annihilating all c. — SAKH 337:7
 C. a movement — TOYN 397:2
 C. and profits — COOL 103:6
 c. of the Fabians — INGE 194:11
 C. was held together — TAYL 387:6
 elements of modern c. — CARL 74:9
 in a state of c. — JEFF 199:15
 pillars of c. — MONN 276:7
 submit to c. — TOCQ 396:8
 test of c. — JOHN 204:12
 thought of modern c. — GAND 151:6
civilizations eradicates autonomous c. — SONT 374:4
civilized c. community — MILL 269:9
 c. society — HOLM 187:3
 force another to be c. — MILL 269:13
 that are called c. — PAIN 302:1
civilizers two c. of man — DISR 121:6
civilizes Cricket c. people — MUGA 282:3
civil servant c. doesn't make jokes — IONE 195:7
 Give a c. a good case — CLAR 94:2
 Here lies a c. — SISS 365:5
 ideal c. — PEYR 309:10
civil servants conviction c. — BANC 29:1
 of c. — BRID 55:1
Civil Service business of the C. — ARMS 15:7
 C. doesn't do jokes — O'LE 294:6
 C. is a bit like — BUTL 68:3
 C. is deferential — CROS 107:2
 C. is like a rusty weathercock — BENN 34:11
 Reorganizing the C. — ANON 12:1
 Thank God for the C. — GEOR 154:8
civis C. Romanus sum — CICE 93:8
 C. Romanus sum — PALM 303:1
claim last territorial c. — HITL 184:8
claims c. are not false — RIEL 327:3
clamour c. for war — PEEL 307:14
 those who c. most — PEEL 307:17
clan c. and race — MILL 270:5
Clapham man on the C. omnibus — BOWE 52:7
clapped-out c., post-imperial — DRAB 126:6
class c. struggle — MARX 262:10
 first and second c. citizens — WILL 420:6
 hands of the ruling c. — STAL 378:4
 history of c. struggles — MARX 263:2
 use of *force* by one c. — LENI 231:1
 While there is a lower c. — DEBS 112:1
classes All c. of society — JEVO 201:8
 Clashing of C. — CONN 101:3
 c. and class antagonists — MARX 263:3
 lower c. had such white — CURZ 108:4
 masses against the c. — GLAD 159:5
classify Germans c. — CATH 77:5
cleaning c. the streets — LA G 223:7
clear c. in his great office — SHAK 357:2
clearing c.-house of the world — CHAM 79:6

Cleopatra C.'s nose been shorter — PASC 305:11
clergy Arminian c. — PITT 311:11
 c. are not called — WALP 409:5
 Established C. — GLAD 158:15
clergyman bookie or a c. — MUGG 282:6
clerks statesmen or of c. — DISR 122:5
clever become the c. country — HAWK 175:5
 Lord Birkenhead is very c. — ASQU 17:2
 lot of c. people — ATTL 18:15
 more c. than you are — WHIT 417:10
 to appear c. — HILL 183:8
 Too c. by half — SALI 339:9
 Too c. by half — SALI 345:2
cliché c. and an indiscretion — MACM 252:10
 used every c. — CHUR 88:6
clichés wreck it with c. — CLAR 94:2
cliffs white c. I never more must see — MACA 247:7
climax end a sentence with a c. — LASK 225:8
climb c. not at all — ELIZ 133:7
 Fain would I c. — RALE 321:5
climbs None c. so high — CROM 106:8
cloak c. become an iron cage — WEBE 412:11
 c. there is concealed — SALI 341:13
clock never put the c. back — WAUG 412:5
cloistered fugitive and c. virtue — MILT 271:3
cloned successfully c. a lamb — MARC 260:1
close c. my military career — MACA 245:5
 peacefully towards its c. — DAWS 111:6
 will not c. my politics — FOX 145:1
closed greatest c. shop — HOSK 189:1
closer Come c., boys — LAST 226:3
 could not have been c. — MART 261:7
cloth Republican c. coat — NIXO 290:2
cloud c. in the west — GLAD 158:2
 in C.-cuckoo-land — HEAL 177:7
cloudcuckooland How about 'C.' — ARIS 14:7
clutches c. of the law — SALI 341:9
CMG C. (Call Me God) — PROV 319:4
coach c. and six horses — RICE 326:3
 like being a football c. — MCCA 248:2
coal like miners' c. dust — BOOT 51:4
 shortage of c. and fish — BEVA 38:3
coalition rainbow c. — JACK 196:10
coalitions England does not love c. — DISR 120:6
coals c. to Newcastle — GEOR 154:2
coat doesn't have a mink c. — NIXO 290:2
 stick in his c. — BROW 59:1
cobwebs Laws are like c. — SWIF 384:5
cock Nationalism is a silly c. — ALDI 6:6
 Our c. won't fight — BEAV 31:2
cocksure c. of anything — MELB 266:7
 stupid are c. — RUSS 336:15
codified insincerity c. — SALI 344:6
coercion effect of c. — JEFF 200:9
coexistence peaceful c. — FULB 148:9
coffee c.-house — SWIF 384:4
 C. house babble — DISR 121:13
 put poison in your c. — ASTO 17:5
coffin silver plate on a c. — CURR 107:7
coins for a fistful of c. — ZAPA 427:9
cold c. relation — BURK 63:9

conservatism (*cont.*):

use of C.	SALI 342:3
What is c.	LINC 234:8

conservative become a c. on the day after

	AREN 14:4
bracing up the C. fibre	SALI 342:10
C. Associations	SALI 341:4
C. Government	DISR 120:1
c. is a liberal	PROV 318:5
c. is a man	ROGE 329:5
C. is a man	ROOS 330:14
C. Party	WAUG 412:5
C. Party always	MACL 251:9
C. Party at prayer	ROYD 334:8
c. who's been arrested	WOLF 424:2
is the C. Party leadable	HESE 182:12
it is really c.	FISH 140:8
make me c. when old	FROS 148:5
makes a man more c.	KEYN 215:4
most c. man in this world	BEVI 40:5
Or else a little C.	GILB 156:7
sound c. government	DISR 122:8

conservatives better with the C.

	SLOG 367:15
C. . . . being by the law	MILL 269:4
C. do not believe	HAIL 168:11
more formalistic than c.	CALV 71:8
night for the C.	PORT 314:13
trouble with c.	CARV 76:7

consistency I have no c. BYRO 69:3
conspicuous c. by its presence RUSS 337:3
  C. consumption VEBL 405:3
conspiracy c. against the public SMIT 370:3
  O c. SHAK 354:8
  party is but a kind of c. HALI 170:11
  perpetual c. SALI 340:6
  vast right-wing c. CLIN 97:3
conspirators All the c. save only he SHAK 356:7
constant c. as the northern star SHAK 354:12
constellation bright c. JEFF 199:5
constituencies go back to your c. STEE 379:1
  Parliament in their c. AMER 7:2
constituents c. in Parliament AMER 7:2
  views of my c. CADM 69:5
constitution boast of its c. PAIN 302:8

British C.	ELIZ 134:4
C. between friends	CAMP 72:8
c. does not provide	WILL 420:6
C., in all its provisions	CHAS 82:6
c. is extremely well	WALP 409:9
c. is to be amended	NEWS 287:2
construe the C.	LINC 234:11
essence of the c.	JUNI 208:6
establish this C.	CONS 102:1
genius of the C.	PITT 311:13
one c.	WEBS 413:11
people made the C.	MARS 261:4
principle of the English c.	BLAC 45:7
spirit of our c.	GEOR 153:9
support its C.	PAGE 299:7
When the C. was framed	BEAR 30:9
written c.	CALL 71:6

constitutional c. eyes LINC 236:9
  c. minuet SCAR 347:3
  c. monarchy TROL 399:6
  c. right LINC 234:12
constitutions such c. [as England's] BAGE 22:2
constrained by violence c. ELIZ 132:6
construction mind's c. SHAK 356:12
consul horse was made C. RAND 321:9
consulted right to be c. BAGE 23:4
consume c. more than HAYE 176:6
consumer c. society ILLI 194:9
consumes c. without producing ORWE 296:6
consumption Conspicuous c. VEBL 405:3
  C. is the sole end SMIT 371:1
  not increase its c. KEYN 215:9
contact come in personal c. TAYL 388:10
contemptible poor c. men CROM 106:5
contending let fierce c. nations know ADDI 5:2
content I am c. LAST 228:3
  Nothing less will c. me BURK 62:1
contented king shall be c. SHAK 358:12
continent Africa, drifting c. GENE 152:8
  brought forth upon this c. LINC 235:8
  C. isolated BROC 55:10
  overspread the c. O'SU 298:8
continental c. union PAIN 300:6
continentally think c. HAMI 172:3
continuation c. of politics CLAU 95:2
contract new social c. CALL 70:6
  social c. ROUS 334:5
  Social C. is nothing more WELL 416:3
  Society is indeed a c. BURK 63:6
contractors C. make profits MACD 249:6
contracts c. with the people TRUM 401:11
  preserve c. MELB 266:15
contradict I never c. DISR 123:20
  Never c. FISH 141:1
contrary trial is by what is c. MILT 271:3
contrive How Nature always does c. GILB 156:7
control cannot c. him BUTT 68:7
  c. of the military TRUM 401:12
  oblige it to c. itself MADI 255:4
  wrong members in c. ORWE 296:11
controls Who c. the past ORWE 297:4
controversies forged in c. FRAN 145:6
contumely proud man's c. SHAK 351:11
convenience 'Twixt treason and c. EPIT 136:7
conventional c. wisdom GALB 149:6
conversation c. perfectly delightful SMIT 372:9
conversations after-dinner c. THOR 394:4
  taping of c. NIXO 291:1
converted have not c. a man MORL 279:5
conveyance easy c. for men and goods

    BACO 21:11
convict c. stain HUGH 191:1
conviction best lack all c. YEAT 426:9
convictions behind my c. THAT 391:8
convince we c. ourselves JUNI 208:8
convinced c. me ROOS 331:11
cookies baked c. and had teas CLIN 97:2
cooperation Government and c. RUSK 336:6

courage (*cont.*):

One man with c.	JACK 196:6
on reflection is real c.	WALP 409:4
proud of their c.	DILL 119:2
salute your c.	GALL 150:11
test of c.	HAZL 176:9
two o'clock in the morning c.	NAPO 284:13
warm c.	BUSH 67:3
warm c.	ROOS 330:8

courageous describe it as *c.* — LYNN 244:5
freedom depends on being c. — THUC 394:7
course what c. thou wilt — SHAK 356:2
court arguments for having a mean C. — BAGE 23:1

art o' the c.	SHAK 351:6
bright lustre of a c.	CECI 79:1
no family life at C.	THOM 393:5
Say to the c., it glows	RALE 321:4

courtesy women with perfect c. — KITC 222:2
courtier Here lies a noble c. — EPIT 136:4
courts C. for cowards were erected — BURN 65:9
Coutts banks with C. — GILB 156:4
covenant c. with death — GARR 152:3
covenants Open c. of peace — WILS 423:2
Covent Garden committee on C. — KAUF 209:9
cover Duck and c. — OFFI 295:4
cow three acres and a c. — SLOG 368:13
cowardice C. asks the question — KING 218:4
cowards make c. of us all — SHAK 351:11
cowboy that damned c. — HANN 172:4
cozenage greatest c. — CROM 106:4
cradle from the c. to the grave — CHUR 89:3
rocking the c. — ROBI 328:7
crank c. is a small engine — SHEE 361:13
crash c. will come twenty years after — BISM 44:7
crazy Is that man c. — BUSH 66:4
should they go c. — PHOC 310:10
when I was c. — SHER 363:7
cream c. of the working-class — BEAZ 32:1
create c. business for itself — SALI 344:16
c. the current of events — BISM 44:9
genuinely *c.* Europe — MONN 276:2
created men are c. equal — JEFF 198:1
creation since the C. — NIXO 290:8
credit most c. — TAYL 388:9
credulity craving c. — DISR 120:12
season of c. — PITT 311:8
soften into a c. — BURK 63:17
creed article of my political c. — ADAM 3:12

Calvinistic c.	PITT 311:11
c. of slaves	PITT 312:2
fear their c.	HEWI 183:2
last article of my c.	GAND 151:4

creep Ambition can c. — BURK 63:12
Crewe True blue and Mrs C. — GEOR 153:4
cricket C.—a game which the English — MANC 258:1

C. civilizes people	MUGA 282:3
c. test	TEBB 388:14
c. with their peasants	TREV 397:8

cried little children c. — MOTL 280:7
poor have c. — SHAK 355:9

Crillon Hang yourself, brave C. — HENR 180:6
crime catalogue of human c. — CHUR 88:1

c. of being a young man	PITT 311:5
foulest c. in history	WHIT 418:7
parent of revolution and c.	ARIS 15:2
prevent c.	MELB 266:15
today's alarming c. rates	BOAZ 48:2
tough on the causes of c.	BLAI 45:10
worse than a c.	BOUL 52:5

crimes c. are committed in thy name — LAST 227:9
c., follies, and misfortunes — GIBB 155:6
Successful c. alone — DRYD 127:15
teems with c. — ANON 10:12
criminal American c. class — TWAI 402:7

c. it deserves	KENN 213:15
ends I think c.	KEYN 214:7
while there is a c. element	DEBS 112:1

criminals if there were no c. — SALI 344:4
Looney Tunes, and squalid c. — REAG 323:9
crimson c. thread of kinship — PARK 304:3
cringe to the cultural c. — KEAT 210:4
crises every age had consisted of c. — ATKI 17:7
crisis cannot be a c. — KISS 221:6

c. in American leadership	BALT 28:11
C.? What Crisis?	MISQ 272:5
C.? What crisis	NEWS 287:3
except in a c.	HOSK 189:2
fit for a great c.	BAGE 22:8
real c. on your hands	THAT 391:3

critic not the c. who counts — ROOS 332:10
critical at a c. moment — HARD 173:5
criticism c. of administration — BAGE 22:6
no c. of the president — ROOS 333:2
criticized to be c. is not always — EDEN 130:1
critics listen to their c. — GALB 150:5
crocodile feeds a c. — CHUR 87:12
Cromwell C., I charge thee — SHAK 353:6
C. said to the Long Parliament — AMER 7:5
Some C. guiltless — GRAY 165:5
cronies money-grabbing c. — HAGU 168:1
crony government by c. — ICKE 194:8
crook McAdoo his c. — SPRI 378:3
President is a c. — NIXO 290:12
crooked c. timber of humanity — KANT 209:7
crops experimental c. — HURD 192:9
cross c. of gold — BRYA 59:9
crosses tumbled down the c. — JORD 207:1
crossways understands everything c. — SALI 340:6
crowd chaining the c. — VOLT 407:12
electrically through a c. — SALI 343:10
riotousness of the c. — ALCU 6:5
crowds talk with c. — KIPL 220:1
crown Caesar's laurel c. — BLAK 47:1

conquer a c.	O'SH 298:5
c. in possession	PAIN 300:2
c. of thorns	BRYA 59:9
C., the symbol of permanence	JUAN 208:4
glory of my c.	ELIZ 133:4
head that wears a c.	SHAK 352:6
I give away my c.	SHAK 358:15
Indian C.	ROSS 334:1

influence of the C. — DUNN 129:1
king's c. — SHAK 357:12
neither abdicate the C. — JUAN 208:5
never wears the c. — HESE 182:8
No c. of thorns — SLOG 368:4
power of the c. — BURK 63:16
presented him a kingly c. — SHAK 355:10
wished to restore the c. — JOHN 204:16
Within the hollow c. — SHAK 358:11
crowned c. ruffians — PAIN 300:5
sitting c. upon the grave — HOBB 185:12
crowning c. mercy — CROM 105:13
crowns c. are empty things — DEFO 113:2
crucible America is God's C. — ZANG 427:8
crucified c. when alive — CONN 101:4
crucify c. mankind — BRYA 59:9
cruel c. and unusual punishment — CONS 102:7
c. men of Rome — SHAK 353:9
C. necessity — CROM 105:10
State business is a c. trade — HALI 171:2
cruelty never really gauged your c. — WELC 414:6
crusade faith in our united c. — ROOS 331:9
nor is c. — KENN 211:7
party is a moral c. — WILS 421:4
this 'c.', this war — BUSH 67:4
crush c. people to the earth — CHIL 84:2
cry Don't c. for me — RICE 326:4
rallied to that c. — BALD 27:1
Speechless still, and never c. — EPIT 136:7
too big to c. — LINC 235:5
crystal Why read the c. — BEVA 38:6
Cuban C. Missile Crisis — STOC 381:11
cuckoo c. clock — WELL 414:7
culling c. of First Secretaries — MORG 279:2
cult c. is a religion — WOLF 424:3
c. of the individual — KHRU 216:4
cultivation subsequent c. — TROL 399:11
cultural c. autonomy — GRAY 165:2
culture has an established c. — GREE 165:8
hears the word c. — GLEN 160:2
hear the word 'c.' — ESHE 137:9
hear the word c. — JOHS 205:10
men of c. — ARNO 15:9
cultures two great c. — LÉVE 232:2
cunctando c. restituit rem — ENNI 135:8
cunning c. men pass for wise — BACO 20:8
cure palliate what we cannot c. — JOHN 204:1
cured c. by more democracy — SMIT 371:5
curiosity You're a c. — KEEL 210:9
currency attitude to single c. — CLAR 94:11
debauch the c. — KEYN 215:1
single c. — NAPO 284:9
curs You common cry of c. — SHAK 350:11
curse is to me a c. — MASS 264:1
curst to all succeeding ages c. — DRYD 127:3
curtain bloody c. — ELIS 132:3
final c. comes down — MAJO 256:10
iron c. — CHUR 89:12
kept behind a c. — PAIN 301:14
lets the c. fall — POPE 314:1
cuss don't matter a tinker's c. — SHIN 363:10

custodes quis custodiet ipsos C. — JUVE 209:2
custodiet quis c. ipsos Custodes — JUVE 209:2
custom C., that unwritten law — D'AV 110:1
Lest one good c. — TENN 389:14
Office, and c. — SHAK 359:11
customers people of c. — SMIT 370:9
customs ancient c. and its manhood — ENNI 135:7
c. of his tribe — SHAW 360:4
cut c. his throat at last — BYRO 68:11
c. my conscience to fit — HELL 179:9
c. off my head — CHAR 81:4
most unkindest c. of all — SHAK 355:13
cute c. to have the British pound — DYSO 129:5
cutting c. each other's throat — ATKI 17:8
cuttlefish like a c. — ORWE 297:15
cycle c. of deprivation — JOSE 207:4
cyclops State policy, a c. — COLE 99:3
cynicism c. about Parliament — BOOT 51:5
healthy c. of MPs — CREW 105:1
cynics composed of c. — MENC 267:8
Czechoslovak C. government — NEWS 287:10

dabbling d. their fingers — MCGR 250:2
daddy D., what did you do — PROV 318:6
Look, D., no hands — HOGG 186:4
think his d. had trouble — IVIN 195:10
dagger d. in one hand — WRAN 425:3
hand that held the d. — ROOS 330:15
daggers they shall be d. — PITT 311:6
Dakotas D., I am for war — RED 324:1
damage MORAL OR INTELLECTUAL D. — KRUG 223:2
seriously d. your health — OFFI 295:7
Damascus road to D. — THAT 391:16
damn d. the consequences — MILN 270:9
d. you England — OSBO 298:4
with a spot I d. him — SHAK 356:3
damnation d. of his taking-off — SHAK 357:2
damned d. morality — MELB 266:11
d. to everlasting fame — POPE 314:5
lies, d. lies and statistics — DISR 124:8
not only dead, but d. — DISR 124:6
public be d. — VAND 404:3
Publish and be d. — WELL 415:4
Danaos timeo D. et dona ferentes — VIRG 406:12
dance d. with me in Ireland — ROBI 328:9
we can d. on pinheads — CAMP 72:5
dances it d. — LIGN 233:9
Dane paying the D.-geld — KIPL 221:1
danger big with d. and mischief — GIBB 155:2
d. from those that work — HALI 169:7
d. in this land — MITC 275:4
d. of her former tooth — SHAK 357:6
d. to the country — VICT 406:4
New Labour, new d. — SLOG 368:3
dangerous d. period of the year — SALI 341:8
left out would be d. — MELB 266:1
more d. than no parapet — SALI 344:8
most d. man — NEWS 287:11
most d. moment — TOCQ 396:3
such men are d. — SHAK 354:4

dangerous (*cont.*):
they are no longer d. — BOUL 52:6
dare none d. call it treason — HARI 173:6
Take me if you d. — PANK 303:9
daring d. pilot in extremity — DRYD 127:4
dark clean your teeth in the d. — JENK 201:1
colours will agree in the d. — BACO 21:7
people who live in the d. — SHOR 364:3
darker I am the d. brother — HUGH 190:7
darkness curse the d. — STEV 380:17
Go out into the d. — HASK 174:6
than curse the d. — BENE 33:9
there is d. everywhere — NEHR 285:7
universal d. buries all — POPE 314:1
Darwin evidence to upset D. — ADAM 3:1
date d. which will live in infamy — ROOS 331:5
dates matter of d. — TALL 386:1
daughter D. am I in my mother's house
— KIPL 220:5
d. of debate — ELIZ 132:10
daughters d. of the horse leech — SALI 342:5
dauntless with d. breast — GRAY 165:5
dawn in that d. to be alive — WORD 424:8
day Action this D. — PROV 318:1
d. I was meant not to see — THAT 391:6
d. of small nations — CHAM 79:8
not a second on the d. — COOK 102:8
not the purchase of a d. — PAIN 300:13
days brave d. of old — MACA 247:8
Cast your mind on other d. — YEAT 426:11
first 1,000 d. — KENN 212:7
hundred d. — WILS 421:6
our eleven d. — SLOG 367:1
two d. like a tiger — TIPU 395:2
dazzled D. thus with height — WOTT 425:1
dead Better red than d. — SLOG 366:7
carcasses of d. policies — SALI 339:14
D. battles, like d. generals — TUCH 402:2
d., but in the Elysian fields — DISR 123:19
d. he would like to see me — HOLL 186:8
d. minister weighs very light — TEMP 389:2
d. or really old — BUSH 66:3
D. Sea Fruit — LEVI 232:6
D. Sea fruit — MACM 253:9
d. shall not have died in vain — LINC 235:8
d. there is no rivalry — MACA 246:4
d. woman bites not — GRAY 165:3
democracy of the d. — CHES 83:3
dread a d.-level of income — TAWN 386:7
My d. king — JOYC 208:2
pay for my d. people — JOSE 207:3
thirteen men lay d. — HEAN 178:4
those who are d. — BURK 63:6
was alive and is d. — EPIT 136:5
we are all d. — KEYN 215:11
you're ten years d. — HAYE 176:7
deaf d. as an adder — ADAM 3:3
d., inexorable — SIDN 364:10
roomful of d. people — O'NE 295:9
deafness d., ignorance of French — SALI 340:6
deal new d. for the American people — ROOS 330:5

No d. — MORG 279:1
square d. — SLOG 369:3
square d. afterwards — ROOS 332:6
dealing d. with the modern media — MORR 279:9
dean no dogma, no D. — DISR 124:5
dear fault, d. Brutus — SHAK 354:1
dearest d. thing he owed — SHAK 356:9
death angel of d. — BRIG 55:2
consent to my own d. — RODR 329:2
covenant with d. — GARR 152:3
d. and taxes — FRAN 146:2
D. is a master from Germany — CELA 79:2
D. is the most convenient — LLOY 239:18
d. of Frederick the Great — BISM 44:7
d. of kings — SHAK 358:10
d., The undiscovered country — SHAK 351:11
d.-tick is audible — CURZ 108:1
D., without rhetoric — SIEY 365:3
disqualified by the accident of d. — CHES 83:4
evidence of life after d. — SOPE 374:5
forced marches, battles and d. — GARI 151:10
go on living even after d. — FRAN 145:5
I am become d. — OPPE 296:1
I signed my d. warrant — COLL 99:6
Keeps D. his court — SHAK 358:9
kiss of d. — SMIT 371:4
laws of d. — RUSK 336:5
Liberty or D. — WOOL 424:7
liberty, or give me d. — HENR 181:5
nearest thing to d. in life — ANON 11:2
new terror to d. — WETH 417:1
of the sovereign is d. — MORE 278:7
reaction to her d. — ELIZ 134:5
seeds of the d. of any state — HOBB 185:10
sentence of d. — CARS 76:1
sign her own d.-warrant — BAGE 23:2
studied in his d. — SHAK 356:12
suicide 25 years after his d. — BEAV 31:11
Those by d. are few — JEFF 199:7
timing of your d. — TACI 385:3
While there is d. — CROS 107:1
deaths million d. a statistic — STAL 378:9
debate daughter of d. — ELIZ 132:10
d. a question — JOUB 207:10
Rupert of D. — BULW 60:6
debout D.! les damnés — SONG 375:3
debt Ambition's d. is paid — SHAK 354:14
national d. — HAMI 171:8
National D. is a very Good Thing — SELL 349:4
public d. should be reduced — MISQ 272:3
war, an' a d. — LOWE 242:7
debts so we can pay our d. — NYER 292:7
decade fun to be in the same d. — ROOS 331:10
deceitful inconsequential, and d. — HELL 179:8
deceiving nearly d. your friends — CORN 103:13
decency d. to shoot me — MARK 260:6
Have you no sense of d. — WELC 414:6
decide Ministers d. — THAT 391:15
moment to d. — LOWE 242:8
decides Cabinet does not propose, it d. — ATTL 18:6
decision d. was made — TRUM 401:6

monologue is not a d. ATTL 17:10
specific d. TUCH 402:3
decisions make important d. ATTL 18:14
regard as important the d. PARK 304:8
decisive d. action CHEN 82:8
d. moment RETZ 324:7
deck from the bottom of the d. SHAP 359:16
Walk the d. my Captain lies WHIT 418:4
declaration no d. of war EDEN 129:10
decline orderly management of d. ARMS 15:7
decorated d., and got rid of CICE 93:10
decorum athwart Goes all d. SHAK 357:9
decree O king, establish the d. BIBL 41:16
deeds d. of the past DAVI 111:4
deep d. sleep of England ORWE 296:9
defeat D. doesn't finish a man NIXO 291:5
d. is an orphan CIAN 93:1
In d.; defiance CHUR 91:12
in D., Malice LYNN 244:4
In d. unbeatable CHUR 91:2
never had a d. CHUR 91:14
possibilities of d. VICT 406:6
defeated d. in a great battle LIVY 238:5
Down with the d. LIVY 238:4
defeats Dewey d. Truman NEWS 287:4
defence d. of the indefensible ORWE 297:16
greatest d. and ornament BLAC 45:6
Never make a d. CHAR 81:2
think of the d. of England BALD 26:10
defend d. as a man AYES 20:1
d. ourselves with guns GOEB 160:3
d. to the death your right MISQ 273:3
refuses to d. his rights JACK 196:1
defended God abandoned, these d. HOUS 189:3
defiance In defeat; d. CHUR 91:12
definition d. of the best government HALI 170:7
deflation or d. HOME 187:10
defraud d. his neighbour RUSK 335:10
defrauding d. of the State PENN 308:14
degree d. is shaked SHAK 359:12
dehumanizing d. the Negro LINC 234:7
deity top d. PIML 311:4
delay deny, or d. MAGN 255:8
to d. changes SALI 342:3
delayed Justice d. PROV 319:1
delaying One man by d. ENNI 135:8
delays most fatiguing d. BURK 65:5
worst is that which d. LLOY 239:5
delegate When in trouble, d. BORE 51:6
delenda D. est Carthago CATO 77:8
deleted Expletive d. ANON 8:10
delightful it can be d. SHAW 360:3
deliver d. a pizza ANON 13:5
if people don't d. HOWA 190:1
deliverance d. from chains DOUG 126:1
delivered God hath d. him BIBL 41:6
deluge Après nous le d. POMP 313:8
delusion under some d. BURK 64:17
demands cannot exact their d. WELL 416:2
demi-paradise other Eden, d. SHAK 358:6
democracies d. against despots DEMO 114:4

d., which refresh TREV 398:5
in d. it is the only sacred FRAN 145:2
democracy aspirant under d. MENC 267:11
basis of d. RUSS 336:8
before D. go CARL 74:10
cured by more d. SMIT 371:5
d. and proper drains BETJ 38:2
D. and socialism NEHR 285:9
D. a society TAWN 386:11
D. is the current suspicion WHIT 417:4
D. is the name we give FLER 141:7
D. is the theory MENC 267:5
D. is the worst form CHUR 90:5
D. means government by CHES 83:12
d. never lasts long ADAM 3:11
D. *not* identical with majority rule LENI 231:1
D. of the dead CHES 83:3
D. resumed her reign BELL 33:4
D. substitutes election SHAW 361:2
d. unbearable PERE 309:3
d. was renewed DEWA 116:10
D., which means despair CARL 75:6
extreme d. or absolute oligarchy ARIS 15:3
great arsenal of d. ROOS 331:2
grieved under a *d.* HOBB 185:11
justice makes d. possible NIEB 289:4
less d. to save ATKI 17:6
made safe for d. WILS 422:18
myth of d. CROS 107:3
not the voting that's d. STOP 382:2
pollution of d. WHIT 417:7
principle of d. MONT 277:7
property-owning d. SKEL 365:7
risk more d. BRAN 53:10
Russia an empire or d. BRZE 59:10
triumph for d. HOPE 188:7
Two cheers for D. FORS 143:5
Under d. MENC 267:7
understand d. STRU 383:4
Without d. TAYL 387:13
democrat D. is a fellow ROGE 329:5
I am a D. ROGE 329:6
Senator, and a D. JOHN 202:6
democratic among a d. people TROL 399:7
aristocracy the most d. MACA 246:12
D. or Republican way LA G 223:7
d. paint TOCQ 396:4
D. Party is like a mule DONN 125:5
democratically d. governed HAIL 168:12
democrats and a few D. BROG 56:4
D. object to men being disqualified CHES 83:4
saloon keepers were D. GREE 165:7
demolish can't really d. it RANK 322:4
demolition d. of a man LEVI 232:4
demon d. of Anglicization HYDE 193:10
d. you have roused LINC 234:7
demonstrations political d. SALI 341:6
denied Justice d. MILL 270:2
justice d. PROV 319:1
officially d. COCK 98:9
Denmark in the state of D. SHAK 351:9

deny d., or delay | MAGN 255:8
  I never d. | DISR 123:20
denying they were d. | FREE 147:5
departure point of d. | METT 268:8
deported would be d. | DE R 115:7
depose my state d. | SHAK 358:13
depositary d. of power | DISR 122:11
depression D. is when there is | PANK 303:11
  d. when you lose yours | TRUM 401:9
deprivation cycle of d. | JOSE 207:4
depth far beyond my d. | SHAK 353:5
depths unfathomable d. of insincerity | ANON 12:8
deputy d. elected by the Lord | SHAK 358:8
Derry oak would sprout in D. | HEAN 178:4
descent Irish d. | ROBI 328:8
desert Stand in the d. | SHEL 362:4
deserve and d. to get it | MENC 267:5
desiccated d. calculating machine | BEVA 39:2
desire d. for honour | CICE 93:5
  d. of power | HOBB 185:2
desires doing what one d. | MILL 269:14
desk modern man's subservience to the d. | FRAN 146:6
desolated province they have d. | GLAD 158:13
desolation years of d. | JEFF 200:6
desperate Diseases d. grown | SHAK 351:16
despise work for a Government I d. | KEYN 214:7
despot wise d. | HERB 182:1
despotism absolute oligarchy, or d. | ARIS 15:3
  D. accomplishes great things | BALZ 28:12
  d. in England | WALP 409:7
  D. is essential | CARL 75:3
  d., let it be called | WEBS 413:10
  d., or unlimited sovereignty | ADAM 3:12
  d. tempered by epigrams | CARL 74:12
  modern form of d. | MCCA 248:5
  present d. | HERZ 182:7
  root of d. | ROBE 328:4
despots against d.—suspicion | DEMO 114:4
  D. themselves do not deny | TOCQ 395:5
destiny manifest d. | O'SU 298:8
  one d. | WEBS 413:11
  rendezvous with d. | ROOS 330:9
destroy d. the town to save it | ANON 10:4
  in search of monsters to d. | ADAM 4:7
  my hand to d. | BURK 64:16
  power to d. | MARS 261:3
  then they d. us | BLUN 47:10
  Whom the mad would d. | LEVI 232:9
destroyed Carthage must be d. | CATO 77:8
  Prussia is wholly and finally d. | ASQU 16:5
  treated generously or d. | MACH 250:8
destroyer d. of worlds | OPPE 296:1
destruction means of total d. | SAKH 337:7
  whether the mad d. is wrought | GAND 151:2
destructive simply d. | MELB 266:1
deteriora D. sequor | OVID 298:11
determination d. of a quiet man | SMIT 371:12
  d. to overcome | SALI 343:6
  obstinate d. | FRAS 146:10
detest d. him more | MACA 247:13

detestation D. of the high | DICK 118:3
Deutschland D. über alles | HOFF 186:2
developed have a d. society | NYER 292:8
devil act like a d. | MALC 257:5
  blue-eyed d. white man | FARD 139:5
  d. shall not take it from us | RAND 321:8
  D. should have right | MORE 278:6
  first Whig was the D. | JOHN 205:3
  synonym for the D. | MACA 245:9
  white man was created a d. | MALC 257:1
devils d. would set on me | LUTH 243:8
devolution D. Day | SALM 345:8
  d. takes longer | BAIN 25:6
devour d. in turn each one | VERG 405:6
devourers become so great d. | MORE 278:4
diagram d. that accurately reflects | KEMP 211:4
diaper d. into the ring | ICKE 194:7
dictator Every d. uses religion | BHUT 40:14
dictators D. ride to and fro | CHUR 87:8
dictatorship d. impossible | PERE 309:3
  d. of the proletariat | MARX 262:10
  d. seriously violates | ROME 329:9
  elective d. | HAIL 168:7
  establish a d. | ORWE 297:9
  have a d. | TRUM 401:9
  inefficiencies of d. | GALB 150:6
  risk the d. | LINC 236:2
dictionary search for a d. | GLEN 160:2
die And shall Trelawny d. | HAWK 175:6
  better to d. on your feet | IBAR 194:3
  conquer or d. | WASH 411:2
  d. a Christian | CHAR 81:7
  d. for my country | KINN 218:12
  d. for politicians | THOM 393:7
  d. in my week | JOPL 206:7
  d. in the last ditch | WILL 420:8
  d. is cast | CAES 69:10
  d. like a true-blue rebel | LAST 227:4
  D., my dear Doctor | LAST 226:4
  d. to make men free | HOWE 190:5
  d. to vex me | MELB 266:5
  Don't d. of ignorance | OFFI 295:3
  Few d. and none resign | MISQ 272:8
  few d. well | SHAK 352:11
  he must d. | NICH 286:5
  I d. happy | LAST 226:9
  I d. hard | LAST 227:3
  I shall d. today | MORE 278:7
  I would rather d. | LEE 230:5
  last Jews to d. | MEIR 265:4
  Let us do—or d. | BURN 65:10
  love one another or d. | AUDE 19:3
  ought to d. standing | LAST 226:5
  prepare myself to d. | RIEL 327:5
  something he will d. for | KING 217:6
  we can d. but once | ADDI 5:1
  when you d. | HILL 184:1
  you asked this man to d. | AUDE 18:16
died Alan d. suddenly | CLAR 94:9
  D., has he | LOUI 242:3
  d. to save their country | CHES 83:7

'I never d.,' says he HAYE 176:7
Suppose Lenin had d. SCHL 347:9
What millions d. CAMP 72:7
dies king never d. BLAC 45:5
diet wholesome d. CHUR 92:13
difference d. of forty thousand WELL 415:6
tough-minded . . . respect d. BENE 33:8
What d. does it make GAND 151:2
differences end now our d. KENN 213:3
world made safe for d. BENE 33:8
different with a d. leader SHOR 364:6
differently freedom for the one who thinks d.
LUXE 243:9
difficult d. to speak BURK 65:2
difficulties d. about great thinkers SALI 344:7
d. in princes' business BACO 20:10
little local d. MACM 253:2
difficulty d. is often in their own mind
BACO 20:10
England's d. PROV 318:9
solving every d. PEEL 307:18
dig D. for victory OFFI 295:2
I could not d. KIPL 219:7
digging stop d. HEAL 177:9
dignity added to his d. CHUR 92:11
conciliate with d. GREN 166:5
d. and competence CLAR 94:8
d. in tilling a field WASH 410:11
d. of the office GEOR 153:8
d. which His Majesty BALD 27:3
maintain a d. in their fate WALP 409:4
no d. in persevering in error PEEL 307:15
dime life can change on a d. LAHR 223:8
diminished ought to be d. DUNN 129:1
diminishes d. my confidence JOHN 204:19
dimming d. of the lights NICO 286:10
dinner after-d. conversations THOR 394:4
asking it to d. HALS 171:6
bore people at d. parties KISS 222:1
not know where to find d. SALI 340:13
we expect our d. SMIT 370:2
dinosaurs day of the d. MCAL 244:12
diplomacist success of a d. SALI 338:8
diplomacy d. backed up by fairness ANNA 8:1
D. is about surviving LYNN 244:7
D. is saying CATL 77:7
D. is to do and say GOLD 160:8
diplomas d. they can't read GING 157:3
diplomat d. . . . is a person STIN 381:8
distinction of a d. PEAR 307:3
diplomatic d. boathook SALI 339:13
diplomatist d.'s vocabulary TAYL 387:16
diplomats D. tell lies KRAU 223:1
direct D. threats CHEN 82:8
direction move in a given d. HOUS 189:4
dirt D. is only matter GRAY 165:1
thicker will be the d. GALB 149:9
disappointments most mortifying d. BURK 65:5
disapprove d. of what you say MISQ 273:3
disarm d. a military capacity COOK 103:2
disaster Press lives on d. ATTL 18:10

triumph and d. KIPL 219:10
disastrous d. and the unpalatable GALB 150:8
discipline under such a d. HALI 170:13
discontent fund of d. PEEL 307:13
winter of d. CALL 70:9
Winter of d. NEWS 288:11
winter of our d. SHAK 359:2
discord d. doth sow ELIZ 132:10
hark! what d. follows SHAK 359:13
discover d. by his manner SMIT 372:7
discretion genius for d. BAGE 23:5
inform their d. JEFF 200:4
their happiness in thy d. ELIZ 133:3
discrimination acquiesce in the face of d.
BETH 38:1
detecting d. POWE 315:8
discuss stay and d. them WELL 415:5
discussion government by d. ATTL 18:11
reasonable d. CHUR 91:15
disease desperate d. FAWK 139:8
D., Ignorance, Squalor BEVE 40:3
d. in the family TREV 398:1
d. of opposition GALB 150:7
politics is a d. FOTH 144:1
diseases D. desperate grown SHAK 351:16
disgrace d. a banana republic MAWR 264:3
dishonesty allegation of d. LEVE 232:1
disjoins d. Remorse from power SHAK 354:6
dislike enough for me to d. MCCO 248:7
disloyal began to be d. WALD 407:15
disloyalty D. is the secret CRIT 105:6
dismal D. Science CARL 74:15
Disney Walt D. Corporation ANON 9:9
disobliging d. the few MACA 246:15
disorder to preserve d. DALE 108:7
dispossessed imprisoned or d. MAGN 255:7
disqualified d. for holding any office MORE 278:5
Disraeli D. school of Prime Ministers BLAI 46:5
dissatisfaction discontent and d. PEEL 307:13
dissent is called 'd.' HAVE 175:2
dissentious you d. rogues SHAK 350:7
dissimulation one word—d. DISR 122:15
dissolve d. the people BREC 54:7
distance proportion to his d. RAKO 321:3
distant relation of d. misery GIBB 155:13
distinction make no d. BUSH 67:2
distort then you can d. them TWAI 402:9
distress maiden in d. STEE 379:3
distressful most d. country SONG 376:2
distribute d. as fairly as he can LOWE 242:6
distribution d. of property SALI 338:4
most equitable d. ANON 12:13
distrust d. of government inspectors SALI 339:11
disturbed d. the sleep STEV 381:2
ditch [Channel] is a mere ditch NAPO 284:5
die in the last d. WILL 420:3
environed with a great d. CROM 106:6
diversity safe for d. KENN 213:3
divided d. by a common language MISQ 272:6
d. into three parts CAES 69:6
dividing by d. we fall DICK 118:6

divine government by d. right	HARR 174:4	d. of religion	GOLD 161:2
indefeasible, d. right	ADAM 4:1	d. of the English	DECL 112:4
say that D. providence	JOHN 202:4	d. of the master	HUME 191:6
divinity d. doth hedge a king	SHAK 352:3	d. of the world	MAHA 255:9
division d. in the House	CHUR 86:6	hand that holds d.	THOM 393:3
d. of Europe	GIBB 155:1	**dominions** His Majesty's d.	NORT 291:11
old wall of d.	GORE 162:7	**domino** 'falling d.' principle	EISE 131:7
divisions How many d. has *he* got	STAL 378:7	**dona** *timeo Danaos et d. ferentes*	VIRG 406:2
divorce d. between the leaders	DOWD 126:5	**done** great things are d.	BISM 44:6
grounds for d.	MEGU 265:6	If you want anything d.	THAT 390:4
do d. for the nation	HARD 172:10	surprised to find it d.	JOHN 204:9
d. something about it	CHOD 85:1	What is to be d.	LENI 231:3
d. what I please	FRED 147:3	what's d. is done	SHAK 357:6
going to d. about it?	MISQ 274:5	what should be d.	MELB 266:14
going to d. about it?	NAST 285:5	**donkeys** Lions led by d.	PROV 319:3
he'll say d. this	TRUM 401:5	**don't** D. you worry	BJEL 45:1
I can d. no other	LUTH 243:7	**doom** national d. is sealed	HEAR 178:7
Let us d.—or die	BURN 65:10	tongues d. men	SHAK 359:9
so much to d.	LAST 227:13	**door** open d.	HAY 175:9
supposed to d. anyway	TRUM 401:2	prejudices through the d.	FRED 147:2
we could d. this	WEBB 412:9	**doormat** d. or a prostitute	WEST 416:8
We must d. something	LYNN 244:8	**doors** Men shut their d.	SHAK 359:8
what can I d. for myself	NIXO 290:10	**doorstep** do this on the d.	JUNO 208:13
doctrine d. is something you kill for	BENN 34:9	**dossier** dodgy d.	NEWS 287:5
d. of ignoble ease	ROOS 332:1	d. on his past	HOWA 189:8
dodgy d. dossier	NEWS 287:5	draft d. produced	GILL 157:1
doer I am a d.	SMIT 372:2	**dots** damned d. meant	CHUR 86:5
doffed d. their lids	KEAT 210:5	**double** Labour's d. whammy	SLOG 367:11
dog beware of the d.	BLIX 47:7	**doublethink** D. means the power	ORWE 297:8
Black d. is back	CHUR 92:5	**doubt** in d. what should be done	MELB 266:14
called me an attack d.	REID 324:5	intelligent full of d.	RUSS 336:15
D. returns to his Vomit	KIPL 219:8	**down** born with D.'s syndrome	DE G 113:15
d.'s obeyed in office	SHAK 356:10	kicked d. stairs	HALI 171:6
d.'s walking on his hinder legs	JOHN 204:9	let the country d.	CALL 71:2
drover's d. could	HAYD 176:1	staying d. with him	WASH 410:4
get your d. back	LIEB 233:7	**downhearted** We are not d.	CHAM 79:9
good d. in Mr Ernest Bevin	ATTL 18:13	**Downing** reach D. Street	THAT 391:16
hard d. to keep	CLIN 97:4	room for me in D. Street	PITT 312:1
I must love the d.	GIBB 156:2	**dragons** political d.	MAJO 256:12
kids love that d.	NIXO 290:3	**drains** democracy and proper d.	BETJ 38:2
Labour's attack d.	PAXM 306:5	**drawers** hewers of wood and d. of water	
large, friendly d.	TOYN 397:3		BIBL 41:3
That d. won't hunt	RICH 326:6	**drawing-room** same men in the d.	HALI 170:1
Doge quiet D. of Venice	WALP 409:7	through my d.	EDEN 130:2
doggie saying 'Nice d.'	CATL 77:7	**drawn** died with their d. salaries	LLOY 240:6
dogma no d., no Dean	DISR 124:5	**dreadful** d. human beings sitting	NORR 291:10
dogs all their running d.	MAO 259:10	**dreadnoughts** as much to keep up as two D.	
D. look up	CHUR 92:9		LLOY 238:8
d. of Europe bark	AUDE 19:1	**dream** d. that is dying	O'SH 298:6
d. or the Radicals	WILD 419:7	I have a d.	KING 217:7
let slip the d. of war	SHAK 355:4	old men's d.	DRYD 127:6
Tom and the other d.	CLAR 94:9	One man with a d.	O'SH 298:5
doing d. business	HEAL 177:12	**dreamed** d. I saw Joe Hill	HAYE 176:7
necessity of d. something	JOHN 204:11	**dreams** d. of being Taoiseach	HAUG 174:9
dollar billion d. country	FOST 143:7	**dregs** d. are often filthy	CHUR 91:10
domestic d. business	MONT 276:10	d. of Romulus	CICE 93:2
Malice d.	SHAK 357:7	You would get the d.	LONG 241:3
pleasures of d. life	GIBB 155:7	**drest** D. in a little brief authority	SHAK 358:1
domination d. and equilibrium	KISS 221:11	**drift** adamant for d.	CHUR 87:7
domineered You d. too much	MELB 266:4	**drinking** d. is to continue	DEED 112:5
dominion d. of kings changed	PRIC 316:11	**drive** difficult to d.	BROU 57:2

driver back-seat d. — THAT 392:6
in the d.'s seat — BEAV 31:6
drizzle d. of Empires — CHUR 86:10
drollery fatal d. — DISR 123:7
drop *one* d. of black blood — HUGH 190:8
dropping D. the pilot — TENN 389:4
drought blame it for the d. — MORR 280:1
drover d.'s dog could — HAYD 176:1
drum d. out of the skin — LLOY 240:2
drunk d. with a theory — SALI 344:15
when he was d. — SHER 363:7
drunkard town d. — BROG 56:4
drunken d. man uses lampposts — LANG 225:1
Dublin those men in D. — DILL 119:2
to D. on a plate — PAIS 302:12
duchess every D. in London — MACD 249:9
duchesses what Grand D. are doing — NAPO 284:10
duck D. and cover — OFFI 295:4
just forgot to d. — DEMP 114:7
looks like a d. — REUT 325:3
ducking d. beneath it — CRIT 105:3
ducks d., produce bad parents — MORS 280:3
duke everybody praised the D. — SOUT 374:7
fully-equipped d. — LLOY 238:8
dullness D. in matters of government — BAGE 24:6
dumb d. son of a bitch — TRUM 401:14
So d. he can't fart — JOHN 203:14
duncery tyrannical d. — MILT 271:7
Dunkirk D. spirit — WILS 421:3
D. to Belgrade — DAVI 110:8
spirit of D. — WILS 421:7
dure *Pourvu que ça d.* — BONA 49:6
dust d. was once the man — WHIT 418:7
not without d. and heat — MILT 271:3
dustbin d. of history — TROT 400:5
Dutch fault of the D. — CANN 73:11
duty citizen's first d. — GRAS 164:8
do our d. as such — SALI 341:11
d. as a Member of Parliament — BIGG 42:8
d. of an Opposition — DERB 115:5
d. of a State — RUSK 336:1
d. of government — PAIN 300:10
every man's d. — COBB 98:6
Every subject's d. — SHAK 352:12
path of d. — TENN 389:12
dwarfs State which d. its men — MILL 269:15
dwellings d. shape us — CHUR 89:6
dying d. for Ireland — HUME 191:9
d. in the last dyke — BURK 65:3
Turkey is a d. man — NICH 286:5
unconscionable time d. — CHAR 82:5
words of a d. man — LAST 227:2
dyke last d. of prevarication — BURK 65:3
dyspepsia d. of society — CARL 75:7

eagle bald e. had not been chosen — FRAN 145:10
e. through the world had flown — WALL 408:8
ear hath the sow by the right e. — HENR 181:1
earl As far as the fourteenth e. — HOME 187:8
e. and a knight of the garter — ATTL 18:8

early Vote e. and vote often — MILE 269:2
earned e. on earth — THAT 390:7
earnest I am in e. — GARR 152:2
ears Enemy e. are listening — OFFI 295:8
lend me your e. — SHAK 355:7
earth earned on e. — THAT 390:7
e. of majesty — SHAK 358:6
end of e. — LAST 228:5
Everything on e. — GOGO 160:7
famous men have the whole e. — PERI 309:4
One does not sell the e. — CRAZ 104:5
shall inherit the e. — SMIT 371:9
surly bonds of e. — REAG 323:10
this e., this realm — SHAK 358:6
earthquake world-e., Waterloo — TENN 389:10
ease ignoble e. — ROOS 332:1
never at heart's e. — SHAK 354:5
easier will be e. for you — LAST 226:3
east Britain calls the Far E. — MENZ 267:14
E. is East — KIPL 219:4
E. of Suez — KIPL 220:4
face neither E. nor West — NKRU 291:8
gorgeous E. in fee — WORD 424:10
look the E. End in the face — ELIZ 134:8
people in the E. — SOLZ 373:12
politics in the E. — DISR 122:15
Easter like an E. Island statue — KEAT 210:2
easy ever said it would be e. — MITC 274:9
Life is not meant to be e. — FRAS 146:11
Life is not meant to be e. — SHAW 360:3
no e. walk-over — NEHR 285:12
woman of e. virtue — HAIL 168:5
eat E. and be eaten — SALI 343:9
e. him last — CHUR 87:12
e. my words — CHUR 92:13
e. up and swallow down — MORE 278:4
Let them e. cake — MARI 260:4
not obey shall not e. — TROT 400:8
eaten all was e. — MITC 271:11
ecclesiastic E. tyranny — DEFO 113:1
éclair chocolate é. — ROOS 332:3
ecological upset the e. balance — SONT 374:4
ecology e. and antiwar — HUNT 192:6
economic e. law — MARX 262:8
e. ones are incomprehensible — HOME 187:9
not purely e. — TAWN 386:10
vital e. interests — WEIL 414:3
economical e. with the *actualité* — CLAR 94:6
e. with the truth — ARMS 15:6
economics E. is the method — THAT 390:11
more about e. — KEYN 215:12
only the e. — MONN 276:4
speech on e. — JOHN 203:12
study of e. — SCHU 348:2
economist death of a political e. — BAGE 24:5
no e. should be denied it — GALB 149:14
economists e., and calculators — BURK 63:1
economy commanding heights of the e. — BEVA 39:3
e. of truth — BURK 64:6
fear of Political E. — SELL 349:8

economy (*cont.*):
general e. — EDEN 129:9
It's the e., stupid — SLOG 367:7
market e. — JOSP 207:8
Political E. — RUSK 335:10
There can be no e. — DISR 120:17
Eden other E. — SHAK 358:6
editor duty of an e. — VEBL 405:2
e. himself be attacked — TROL 399:14
News E. — ANON 9:5
educate e. our masters — LOWE 242:5
e. our masters — MISQ 274:3
e. our party — DISR 120:15
educated clothed, fed, and e. — RUSK 336:1
government by the badly e. — CHES 83:12
education black kids get an e. — POWE 315:1
discretion by e. — JEFF 200:4
e., education, and education — BLAI 46:1
E. makes a people — BROU 57:2
e. of a politician — CHUR 91:5
e. of the people — DISR 121:10
first part of politics? E. — MICH 269:1
parts of e. — SMIT 371:2
Standards of e. — DAY 111:7
unplanned e. creates — VERW 405:7
educationist e. is one of the daughters — SALI 342:5
EEC E. is a horse and carriage — DE G 113:16
eels like catching soaped e. — SALI 342:8
procreation of e. — SCHU 348:4
effective as e. as I should be — MORR 279:9
Being e. — BECK 32:3
efficiency e. of the post office — SULL 383:5
southern e. — KENN 213:9
where there is no e. — DISR 120:17
efficient have an e. government — TRUM 401:10
effort last e. of the patriots — ADAM 3:5
redoubling your e. — SANT 346:2
effusive don't be too e. — ELIZ 134:6
égalité É.! *Fraternité* — SLOG 367:14
egg e. on our face — BROK 56:5
lays an e. — NEWS 288:8
eggheads E. of the world — STEV 381:1
ego e. has landed — DOBS 125:1
eight We want e., and we won't wait — SLOG 369:4
elder to e. statesman — FOOT 142:8
elect dissolve the people and e. — BREC 54:7
e., and to reject — PAIN 302:4
e. the second chamber — JAY 197:11
mobs will not e. — SALI 339:6
elected audacity of e. persons — WHIT 418:5
e. by the manhood — ELLI 134:11
will not serve if e. — SHER 363:8
election Better lose the e. — STEV 380:4
e. by the incompetent many — SHAW 361:2
e. is coming — ELIO 132:1
good e. can't fix — NIXO 290:6
I've won the e. — GEOR 154:7
right of e. — JUNI 208:6
wanted an e. — ROOS 330:2
winning the e. — HOWA 190:1
elections e. are won — ADAM 2:6

fighting of e. — CHUR 91:5
I do not like e. — CHUR 92:1
You won the e. — SOMO 374:3
elective e. dictatorship — HAIL 168:7
electrically shoot e. through — SALI 343:10
electricity moral e. — O'CO 293:8
must use less e. — JENK 201:1
usefulness of e. — FARA 139:4
electrification e. of the whole country — LENI 231:5
elegant e. simplicity — STOW 382:8
elegy whole of Gray's E. — WOLF 423:10
elementary these e. schools — JEFF 200:1
elements e. So mixed in him — SHAK 356:7
elephant rogue e. — TAYL 387:14
sleeping with an e. — GRAV 164:11
sleeping with an e. — TRUD 400:11
elephants golden e. next — SHOR 364:4
eleven failing his e.-plus — PRES 316:7
our e. days — SLOG 367:9
elite power e. — MILL 270:8
elk hunted as an e. — RIEL 327:4
eloquence E., transcendent eloquence — WRAX 425:4
finest e. — LLOY 239:5
I admire his e. — GIBB 156:1
parliamentary e. — CARL 75:1
eloquent e. in a more sublime language — MACA 246:1
elsewhere There is a world e. — SHAK 351:1
Elysian in the E. fields — DISR 123:19
embalmer triumph of the e.'s art — VIDA 406:9
embarrassment financial e. — DISR 120:8
emblem e. of mortality — DISR 122:1
embrace e. your Lordship's principles — WILK 420:1
most extraordinary e. — TREV 398:2
emergency one e. following upon another — FISH 140:6
emigration e. system — JOHN 205:8
emotion dependable international e. — ALSO 7:1
e. will shoot electrically — SALI 343:10
emotional of being e. — HARN 173:8
emotions e. were riveted — FOOT 142:9
underlying e. — NAMI 284:1
emperor e. holds the key — CUST 108:5
E. is everything — METT 268:6
e. to die standing — LAST 226:5
emperors E. can do nothing — BREC 54:7
great men even under bad e. — TACI 385:2
empire All e. is no more — DRYD 127:7
Britain has lost an e. — ACHE 1:7
British E. would not have been — SALI 340:4
destinies of the British E. — DISR 120:10
E. is a commonwealth — ROSE 333:5
e., vast as it is — CUST 108:5
e. walking very slowly — FITZ 141:5
evil e. — REAG 323:6
found a great e. — SMIT 370:9
great e. and little minds — BURK 62:10
great Mother E. — FOST 143:8
Greeks in this American e. — MACM 252:7
How's the E. — LAST 226:8

meaning of E. Day CHES 83:11
metropolis of the e. COBB 98:7
nor Roman, nor an e. VOLT 407:6
of the British E. CHUR 88:14
Russia an e. or democracy BRZE 59:10
strength of the E. GLAD 159:1
this E. will perish DISR 124:10
trample an e. O'SH 298:5
unity of the e. BURK 62:8
way she disposed of an e. HARL 173:7
westward the course of e. BERK 36:5
wilderness into a glorious e. BURK 62:11
empires day of E. CHAM 79:8
drizzle of E. CHUR 86:10
e. of the future CHUR 89:5
employed innocently e. JOHN 204:15
employer sole e. is the State TROT 400:8
employers e. of past generations BALD 26:8
employment happily known as gainful e.
ACHE 1:6
empty e. taxi arrived CHUR 92:6
on an e. stomach BRAN 53:12
party in an e. room DEWA 116:8
enamoured So e. on peace CLAR 93:14
encompassed e. but one man SHAK 354:3
encourage right to e. BAGE 23:4
to e. the others VOLT 407:3
encourager e. les autres VOLT 407:3
encourages never vote. It only e. them
ANON 10:2
end ane e. of ane old song OGIL 294:3
beginning of the e. TALL 385:11
came to an e. all wars LLOY 239:1
do not e. when you please MACH 250:7
e. is not yet BIBL 41:23
e. of a thousand years of history GAIT 149:4
e. of earth LAST 228:5
e. of history FUKU 148:7
e. of the beginning CHUR 89:1
e. to bossing LENI 231:7
e. to the beginnings of all wars ROOS 331:12
e. to the old Britain BROW 57:6
In my e. is my beginning MARY 263:10
no e. of a lesson KIPL 220:3
reserved for some e. CLIV 98:3
sole e. for which mankind MILL 269:7
war that will e. war WELL 416:4
ended Georges e. LAND 224:9
ending way of e. a war ORWE 298:1
endings time the beginnings and e. BACO 20:9
endogenous neoclassical e. growth BROW 57:5
endure human hearts e. JOHN 204:5
enemies annihilate all his e. SALI 340:9
conquering one's e. GENG 152:9
e. are on your own side ANON 12:10
e. he has made BRAG 53:6
e. of Freedom do not argue INGE 194:10
e. of liberty HUME 191:7
e. to laws BURK 64:11
left me naked to mine e. SHAK 353:7
no perpetual e. PALM 302:14

not e. when we acquire them SENE 349:12
those e. they killed PEEL 307:9
you are now our e. MUGA 282:4
enemy belonged to the e. SALI 343:1
E. ears are listening OFFI 295:8
e. of my enemy PROV 318:8
e. we're fighting WALL 408:6
inveterate e. PITT 311:14
quieten your e. by talking CEAU 78:6
smitten a sleeping e. YAMA 426:2
than an acrimonious e. SALI 344:2
war without an e. WALL 409:1
will have upon the e. WELL 414:8
worst e. Ireland ever had MITC 271:13
written by an acute e. BALF 28:6
enfants e. de la patrie SONG 375:1
enforceable e. safeguards TRUM 401:1
engine crank is a small e. SHEE 361:13
Little E. that Could EDWA 130:7
not connected to the e. GOOD 162:3
Parliament is a potent e. SALI 342:2
engineering social e. POPP 314:12
engineers age of the e. HOGB 186:3
Artists are not e. KENN 213:7
e. of human souls STAL 378:6
e. of the soul GORK 163:2
engines e. to play a little BURK 62:13
England Church of E. CHAR 81:7
damn you E. OSBO 298:4
deep sleep of E. ORWE 296:9
end in the ruin of E. SHEL 362:1
E. and America divided MISQ 272:6
E. has saved herself PITT 312:5
E. is a disguised republic BAGE 24:2
E. is a nation of shopkeepers NAPO 285:1
E. is, I believe SALI 343:1
E. not the jewelled isle ORWE 296:11
E.'s difficulty PROV 318:9
E. shall perish ELIZ 133:8
E.'s native people BURN 65:12
E.'s not a bad country DRAB 126:6
E. to be the workshop DISR 119:6
E. was too pure an Air ANON 11:6
E. will have her neck wrung CHUR 88:12
God punish e. FUNK 149:1
Goodbye, E.'s rose JOHN 202:2
Gott strafe E. FUNK 149:1
history of E. MACA 246:7
Ireland and E. seemed like lovers TREV 398:2
keep your E. MUGA 282:5
last King of E. EDWA 130:3
Let not E. forget MILT 271:5
never have seen E. more CROM 105:7
O E.! model SHAK 352:7
old E.'s winding sheet BLAK 47:2
roast beef of old E. BURK 64:1
royal navy of E. BLAC 45:6
speak for E. AMER 7:4
strong arm of E. PALM 303:1
suspended in favour of E. SHAW 360:9
This E. never did SHAK 356:8

esse E. quam videri bonus SALL 345:5
essenced long e. hair MACA 247:5
essential Despotism is e. CARL 75:3
 give up e. liberty FRAN 146:4
established E. Clergy GLAD 158:15
estate fourth e. of the realm MACA 245:7
 ordered their e. ALEX 6:7
esteem e. too lightly PAIN 300:12
état L'É. c'est moi LOUI 241:5
eternal authority of the e. yesterday WEBE 413:2
eternity some conception of e. MANC 258:1
ethic protestant e. WEBE 412:10
ethical e. dimension COOK 103:1
 nuclear giants and e. infants BRAD 53:2
ethics law floats in a sea of e. WARR 410:10
Eton decry E. and Harrow BEVI 40:7
 playing-fields of E. ORWE 296:12
 playing fields of E. WELL 415:11
eunuch prerogative of the e. STOP 382:3
eunuchs seraglio of e. FOOT 142:5
Europe all the nations of E. SALM 345:9
 bedrock of E. POWE 315:2
 create a nation E. MONN 276:8
 division of E. GIBB 155:1
 dogs of E. bark AUDE 19:1
 E. a continent of energetic mongrels FISH 140:7
 E. by her example PITT 312:5
 E. has never existed MONN 276:2
 E. in danger of plunging YELT 427:4
 E. is a geographical concept BISM 43:11
 E. of nations DE G 113:10
 E. on the lips of politicians BISM 44:1
 E. will decide DE G 113:6
 from mainland E. THAT 392:11
 get out of E. BOOK 50:8
 glory of E. BURK 63:1
 great stocks of E. YEAT 427:1
 lamps are going out all over E. GREY 166:6
 liberation of E. EISE 131:4
 map of E. has been changed CHUR 86:12
 part of the community of E. SALI 341:11
 revival of E. CHUR 89:13
 salvation of E. PITT 312:3
 security of E. MITC 275:2
 smaller nationalities of E. ASQU 16:5
 spectre is haunting E. MARX 263:1
 sunk in E. BANK 29:2
 take over the whole of E. RIDL 327:1
 that's old E. RUMS 335:1
 United States of E. CHUR 90:1
 want to talk to E. KISS 221:9
 welfare of E. PEEL 308:1
 whole of E. NAPO 284:9
 Without Britain, E. ERHA 137:7
European e. integration KOHL 222:10
 E. system of nations SALI 339:1
 E. talks of progress DISR 123:9
 E. war might do it REDM 324:2
 E. wars PAIN 300:7
 green pastures of the E. VERW 405:7
 I'm E. HEWI 183:4

 involved in a E. war BEAV 31:3
 on E. Monetary Union CHIR 84:5
event greatest e. it is FOX 144:8
 not an e. TALL 385:12
 pseudo e. BOOR 51:1
eventide perfect e. home STOC 381:10
events create the current of e. BISM 44:9
 E., dear boy MISQ 272:7
 e. have controlled me LINC 236:3
 opposition of e. MACM 254:1
 train of e. has carried him AMER 7:3
 We cannot make e. ADAM 4:12
ever have you e. been PROV 318:2
Everest He is a Chimborazo or E. ASQU 16:8
evermore name liveth for e. EPIT 137:5
everyone like e. else DE G 113:15
everything against e. KENN 213:13
 knowledge of e. HERO 182:3
 Macaulay is of e. MELB 266:7
 robbed a man of e. SOLZ 373:9
evidence e. against their own understanding HALI 170:2
evil all government is e. O'SU 298:7
 all men are e. MACH 250:5
 axis of e. BUSH 67:5
 doing e. ROOS 333:3
 E. be to him who evil thinks MOTT 281:4
 e. effects are gradual DICE 117:6
 e. empire REAG 323:6
 e. reptilian kitten-eater ANON 8:8
 e. that men do lives SHAK 355:7
 for e. to triumph MISQ 273:5
 man produces e. GOLD 161:1
 meet e.-willers ELIZ 132:7
 necessary e. PAIN 300:3
 no e. in the atom STEV 380:8
 respond to e. HAVE 175:4
 root up any e. SALI 339:2
 where an e. exists SALI 341:6
 willed no e. STEP 379:8
 you agreed to e. RODR 329:1
evils enamoured of existing e. BIER 42:4
 no necessary e. JACK 196:4
evolution progress of e. ADAM 3:1
exact not to be e. BURK 61:13
 Politics is not an e. science BISM 43:6
exactitude L'e. est la politesse LOUI 242:2
examination e. of the acts HARR 174:5
examiners than my e. KEYN 215:12
example Europe by her e. PITT 312:5
 No e. is so dangerous TOCQ 396:1
excellence e. of the English government BLAC 45:9
excess poverty and e. PENN 308:13
excite e. those feelings ADAM 4:12
excited populace is e. LA B 223:5
excitement no e. like a big division CHUR 86:6
exclusion cannot be built on e. ADAM 2:8
excuse e. every man will plead SELD 349:1
 I will not e. GARR 152:2
excuses e. for our failures FULB 148:8

execution Ceauşescus' e.	O'DO 293:9
fascination of a public e.	FOOT 142:9
finally fail of e.	LINC 235:2
imminent e.	CLAR 94:4
stringent e.	GRAN 164:5
executioners shouting at her e.	O'DO 294:1
executive e. expression	BRIT 55:9
e. of this country	ACHE 1:10
hold the e. to account	BOOT 51:5
legislative and e.	ADAM 4:4
more corrupt than e.	MONT 277:12
new powers of the e.	DENN 115:4
nominated by the e.	GIBB 155:4
exercise desire to e. it	LEVI 232:12
exertions e. of private citizens	MACA 247:2
saved herself by her e.	PITT 312:5
exigency to the e. of the moment	PEEL 307:6
exile die in e.	LAST 226:12
exiled outlawed or e.	MAGN 255:7
exiles Politicians are e.	GRIG 167:3
existence e. as a nation	PITT 312:4
threatens the e. of life	SONT 374:4
existing enamoured of e. evils	BIER 42:4
e. state of things	SALI 339:10
paid for e.	KIPL 219:9
exit Such a graceful e.	JUNO 208:13
expectation E. of good news	MCAL 245:1
public e.	GALB 149:15
expectations revolution of rising e.	CLEV 96:11
expediency E. asks the question	KING 218:4
E. is everything	DEAN 111:9
ground of e.	ROOS 333:3
expedient not a principle, but an e.	DISR 119:10
not only necessary but e.	ARIS 15:1
expenditure annual e. nineteen	DICK 117:8
by e. of money	SALI 339:2
E. rises to meet income	PARK 304:4
particular e.	EDEN 129:9
tried to get e. under control	BIRC 42:12
expense regardless of e.	PEEL 308:6
expenses facts are on e.	STOP 382:4
expensive got so e.	ROGE 329:3
experience benefit of much e.	BENN 34:4
e. has taught me	EDEN 130:1
E. is the child of Thought	DISR 123:14
e. of nations	SALI 338:9
man of no e.	CURZ 108:2
experiment social and economic e.	HOOV 188:2
tide of successful e.	JEFF 199:3
experimental e. crops	HURD 192:9
expert e. in being a minority	EWIN 138:6
experts never trust e.	SALI 340:2
explain e. why it didn't happen	CHUR 92:3
Never complain and never e.	BALD 27:5
Never complain and never e.	DISR 124:1
Never e.	FISH 141:1
explained uneasiness when being e.	BALF 28:8
expletive E. deleted	ANON 8:10
explicit Frank and e.	DISR 123:5
exposure public e.	STON 382:1
extempore as his e. sayings	WALP 409:2

extend attempt to e. their system	MONR 276:9
exterminate e. a nation	SPOC 378:1
extermination e. of capitalism	ZINO 428:4
extraordinary e. man	JOHN 205:5
extravagant e. with his own	SALL 345:3
extreme e. equality is taken up	MONT 277:7
extremism e. in the defence of liberty	GOLD 161:8
E. in the pursuit	JOHN 203:7
extremists dangerous about e.	KENN 213:14
extremity daring pilot in e.	DRYD 127:4
exuberance irrational e.	GREE 166:1
exulting people all e.	WHIT 418:3
eye cast a longing e.	JEFF 198:12
e.-catching initiatives	BLAI 46:9
e. to the main chance	CECI 78:8
neither e. to see	LENT 231:10
spoils one's e.	HALI 171:5
eyeball e. to eyeball	RUSK 335:5
eyes constitutional e.	LINC 236:9
e. are full of tears	SHAK 359:1
e. of Caligula	MITT 275:5
King of England's e.	LAST 227:6
Mine e. have seen	HOWE 190:4
sun in his e.	CHUR 87:11
Fabians civilization of the F.	INGE 194:11
F. . . . found socialism	HEAL 177:7
good man fallen among F.	LENI 231:8
face construction in the f.	SHAK 356:12
f. neither East nor West	NKRU 291:8
socialism would not lose its human f.	
	DUBČ 128:2
stamping on a human f.	ORWE 297:10
than her f.	THOM 393:6
unacceptable f. of capitalism	HEAT 179:1
faction Liberty is to f.	MADI 255:1
made them a f.	MACA 246:13
party . . . is not a f.	POWE 315:9
shine in a f.	HALI 170:12
whisper of a f.	RUSS 337:1
factions good in canvasses and f.	BACO 20:7
factor Falklands F.	THAT 390:12
facts f. are on expenses	STOP 382:4
f. are sacred	SCOT 348:6
Get your f. first	TWAI 402:9
imagination for his f.	SHER 363:3
politics consists in ignoring f.	ADAM 3:2
report the f.	ROGE 329:7
very few f.	PEEL 308:9
faculties borne his f. so meek	SHAK 357:2
f. of men	MADI 255:2
From each according to his f.	BAKU 25:10
fade just f. away	MACA 245:5
fail shall not flag or f.	CHUR 88:2
Those who f.	BROW 57:10
failed they f. before	SLOG 369:7
failing from f. hands	MCCR 248:8
failure political lives end in f.	POWE 316:3
Success or f.	MACH 250:6
fain F. would I climb	RALE 321:5

fair F. shares for all — SLOG 366:15
  not being f. — FILK 140:4
fairness excellence as well as f. — ANON 13:4
faith f. and morals hold — WORD 424:9
  f. in a nation of sectaries — DISR 122:12
  f. in our united crusade — ROOS 331:9
  f. in The People — DICK 118:4
  f. is something you die for — BENN 34:9
  first article of my f. — GAND 151:4
  good sense and the good f. — GLAD 158:14
  if ye break f. — MCCR 248:8
  Marxism is now a world f. — BENN 34:6
faithful mentally f. to himself — PAIN 300:1
fake one you can f. that — PROV 319:11
Falklands F. Factor — THAT 390:12
  F. thing was a fight — BORG 51:7
fall Another thing to f. — SHAK 357:11
  by dividing we f. — DICK 118:6
  f. not out among yourselves — ASTL 17:4
  O! what a f. was there — SHAK 355:14
  Then f., Caesar — SHAK 354:13
  yet I fear to f. — RALE 321:5
fallacies f. of the present — SALI 338:6
fallacy f. in two lines — SALI 341:7
fallen F. cold and dead — WHIT 418:4
  good man f. among Fabians — LENI 231:8
  planets had f. on me — TRUM 400:12
fallible f. men in Whitehall — POWE 316:5
falling 'f. domino' principle — EISE 131:7
false f. report, if believed — MEDI 265:4
  getting it on f. pretences — SALI 339:7
  philosopher, as equally f. — GIBB 155:3
falsehood mass of f. — WILK 420:2
  strife of Truth with F. — LOWE 242:8
falsehoods f. which interest dictates — JOHN 204:3
falter not the time to f. — BLAI 46:13
falters love that never f. — SPRI 378:2
fame came here for f. — DISR 124:9
  damned to everlasting f. — POPE 314:5
  F. and tranquillity — MONT 276:11
  military f. — SHER 363:9
families Great f. of yesterday — DEFO 112:13
family disease in the f. — TREV 398:1
  f. with the wrong members — ORWE 296:11
  have a young f. — FOWL 144:5
  no f. life at Court — THOM 393:5
  running of a f. — MONT 276:10
  Selling off the f. silver — MISQ 273:8
  spend more time with f. — THAT 392:1
  We, your blood f. — SPEN 377:7
famine F. Queen — GONN 161:9
famous advantage of being f. — KISS 222:1
  f. men have the whole earth — PERI 309:4
  Let us now praise f. men — BIBL 41:18
  'twas a f. victory — SOUT 374:7
fanatic f. is a great leader — BROU 57:3
fanaticism f. consists in — SANT 346:2
fanatics Foolish f. — ROOS 333:1
far going a bridge too f. — BROW 58:7
  Mexico, so f. from God — DIAZ 117:3
  quarrel in a f. away country — CHAM 80:1

farce second as f. — MARX 262:7
fardels Who would f. bear — SHAK 351:11
farewell bid the company f. — LAST 226:11
  F.! a long farewell — SHAK 353:4
fart can't f. and chew gum — JOHN 203:14
  forgot the f. — ELIZ 133:12
fascination subject myself to his f. — GLAS 160:1
Fascism victims of American F. — ROSE 333:13
fascists 'Communists' to include F. — ANON 9:1
fashion f. in these things — FRAN 146:7
fashions fit this year's f. — HELL 179:9
fastidiousness f. a quality — LEVI 232:5
fat big f. wringer — MITC 275:3
  Butter merely makes us f. — GOER 160:5
  f. and long-haired — PLUT 313:4
  men about me that are f. — SHAK 354:4
  that f. gentleman — SHAW 361:12
fate arbiter of others' f. — BYRO 69:2
  decide the f. of the world — DE G 113:6
  f. of Abraham Lincoln — GRIG 167:2
  f. of this country — DISR 121:10
  F., thou art defied — MITC 271:12
  makers of our f. — POPP 314:8
  thy too rigid f. — MONT 278:1
father cut off thy f.'s head — CHAR 81:4
  f. was frightened of his mother — GEOR 154:5
  Had it been his f. — EPIT 136:5
  Lloyd George knew my f. — SONG 376:7
  politique f. — JAME 197:3
  sash my f. wore — SONG 377:2
fatherland unity of our f. — KOHL 222:9
fathers Founding F. — RICE 326:1
  Founding F.' blueprint — BIRC 43:3
  healthiest f. — WHIT 418:6
  Victory has a hundred f. — CIAN 93:1
  years ago our f. brought forth — LINC 235:8
fatness but not to f. — TAYL 388:11
fault f., dear Brutus — SHAK 354:1
Faust behind this shabby F. — HEAL 177:6
favour Fools out of f. — DEFO 112:9
  in f. of the people — BURK 63:15
favourite his f. flies — SHAK 351:15
  not the f. — RETZ 324:9
favours depends Upon your f. — SHAK 350:8
  f. from the great — TAYL 388:6
  sense of future f. — WALP 410:4
fear alive with f. — SCAR 347:7
  begins in f. — COLE 99:4
  concessions of f. — BURK 61:16
  eventide of f. — MORR 279:10
  F. God. Honour the King — KITC 222:2
  F. is, of all passions — RETZ 324:10
  f. is the foundation — ADAM 4:3
  f. to negotiate — KENN 212:6
  fourth is freedom from f. — ROOS 331:4
  not understand this f. — CHIR 84:8
  only thing we have to f. — ROOS 330:6
  Severity breedeth f. — BACO 20:13
  so long as they f. — ACCI 1:5
  try to have no f. — CHES 82:10
  what man living, freed from f. — AESC 5:5

feared neither f. nor flattered — EPIT 136:6
prince to be f. — MACH 250:9
fearful f. trip is done — WHIT 418:3
fears never of your f. — STEV 380:15
feast Nature's mighty f. — MALT 257:10
feature to be the striking f. — GEOR 153:3
fed clothed, f., and educated — RUSK 336:1
federal job of the F. Reserve — MART 261:8
Our F. Union — JACK 196:3
fee gorgeous East in f. — WORD 424:10
feeble f. can seldom persuade — GIBB 155:14
f. government — BURK 63:11
man of such a f. temper — SHAK 353:11
feed doth this our Caesar f. — SHAK 354:2
feeding F. the chooks — BJEL 45:2
feel How does it f. — CARL 74:4
making people f. good — CHRÉ 85:4
feeling appeals to diffused f. — BAGE 22:14
feelings governed more by their f. — ADAM 4:12
feet better to die on your f. — IBAR 194:3
hotbed of cold f. — EBAN 129:8
seven f. of English ground — HARO 173:9
Thabo has tiny f. — SEXW 350:4
where he put his f. — NICO 288:13
fell It f. by itself — JOHN 202:4
female f. worker slave of that slave — CONN 101:5
patriotic virtue in the f. — ADAM 2:3
feminist call me a f. — WEST 416:8
dealing with the early f. — WEST 416:9
fence sat on the f. so long — LLOY 240:1
fences barbed wire f. — JOHN 205:9
Good f. make good neighbours — FROS 148:6
Fenian grave of a dead F. — COLL 99:5
left us our F. dead — PEAR 306:7
fens reek o' the rotten f. — SHAK 350:11
Fermanagh dreary steeples of f. — CHUR 86:12
fermenting speech f. in me — GLAD 159:12
fertility by reason of their f. — MONT 277:15
fetish Militarism . . . is f. worship — TAWN 386:5
fetters f. rent in twain — DAVI 111:1
wear the same f. — VOLT 407:12
fever life's fitful f. — SHAK 357:7
treaty bred a f. — THOM 393:3
Février Janvier and F. — NICH 286:6
few as grossly as the f. — DRYD 127:9
disobliging the f. — MACA 246:15
so much owed by so many to so f. — CHUR 88:4
they shall be f. — PITT 311:6
fewer one man f. — METT 268:4
fiat f. justitia — MANS 259:4
F. justitia — MOTT 281:3
F. justitia — WATS 411:9
fiction f. lags after truth — BURK 61:17
one form of continuous f. — BEVA 39:5
fiddler f. after Paganini — NICO 288:12
fide Punica f. — SALL 345:7
fidelity f. to colleagues — LASK 225:7
pursues us with malignant f. — BALF 28:7
field only inhabitants of the f. — BURK 63:5
presence on the f. — WELL 415:6
fields In Flanders f. — MCCR 248:8

fiery f. trial through which we pass — LINC 235:6
fifth F. Amendment — DOUG 125:7
fifty F.-four forty — SLOG 366:16
fig f. for those by law protected — BURN 65:9
fight begun to f. — JONE 206:1
Citizen Army will f. — CONN 101:7
deadliness to f. Germany — CHUR 85:9
don't want to f. — SONG 377:3
Fifty-four forty, or f. — SLOG 366:16
f. against the future — GLAD 158:7
f. and fight again — GAIT 149:3
f. between a shark and a wolf — ANDR 7:8
f. for freedom — PANK 303:8
f. for freedom and truth — IBSE 194:5
f. for its King and Country — GRAH 163:6
f. for the living — JONE 206:2
f. for what I believe — CAST 77:2
f. I do not hate — YEAT 426:6
f. it out on this line — GRAN 164:2
f. no more — JOSE 207:2
f. on the beaches — CHUR 88:2
f. on to the end — HAIG 168:4
f. our country's battles — SONG 375:6
f. to maintain freedom — ROOS 331:3
I f. on — THAT 392:4
I will f. — SITT 365:6
I will not cease from mental f. — BLAK 47:5
put up as good a f. — DILL 119:2
refuse to f. — SLOG 369:2
those who bade me f. — EWER 138:3
too proud to f. — WILS 422:12
Ulster will f. — CHUR 86:2
We shall win this f. — PUTI 317:6
fighter f. not a quitter — MAND 259:2
fighting enemy we're f. — WALL 408:6
not f. does matter — STEP 379:7
two periods of f. — BIER 42:5
figures prove anything by f. — CARL 74:5
three sets of f. — ASQU 16:10
fils F. de Saint Louis — FIRM 140:5
final f. curtain comes down — MAJO 256:10
f. solution — HEYD 183:5
finality F. is not the language — DISR 120:7
finance F. is the stomach — GLAD 158:4
financial unsordid f. act — CHUR 89:8
with f. acumen — KAUF 209:9
fine walk a f. line — CLIN 97:12
finest f. hour — CHUR 88:3
finger burnt Fool's bandaged f. — KIPL 219:8
f. on the trigger — MACM 253:4
Whose f. — NEWS 288:10
fingers Five sovereign f. — THOM 393:2
pulled our f. out — PHIL 310:4
finish didn't let me f. — BABE 20:3
f. the job — CHUR 88:11
until they f. — RANK 322:4
finished f. in the first 100 days — KENN 212:7
f. when he quits — NIXO 291:1
world where England is f. — MILL 270:4
finita f. la commedia — MACM 253:13
fins swims with f. of lead — SHAK 350:8

fire f. brigade and the fire | CHUR 87:3
have kindled a f. | COBB 98:4
neighbour's house is on f. | BURK 62:13
shouting f. in a theatre | HOLM 187:1
take a walk into the f. | ENGE 135:6
wabbling back to the F. | KIPL 219:8
firebell f. in the night | JEFF 200:2
firmament fellow in the f. | SHAK 354:12
first culling of F. Secretaries | MORG 279:2
f. in a village | CAES 69:9
f. in the hearts | LEE 230:2
f. Kinnock in a thousand | KINN 218:13
F. rate men will not canvas | SALI 339:6
nothing done for the f. time | CORN 103:12
not to take the f. step | CLAU 95:1
to be called F. Lady | ONAS 294:7
firstborn f. the greatest ass | CARO 75:10
fish pretty kettle of f. | MARY 263:6
shortage of coal and f. | BEVA 38:3
fishes f. in a saucepan | KHRU 216:8
Men lived like f. | SIDN 364:8
fistful for a f. of coins | ZAPA 427:9
fisticuffs argument for f. | CHUR 90:11
fit I am f. for nothing | HERV 182:5
fitful life's f. fever | SHAK 357:7
Fitzdotterel F.'s eldest son | BROU 56:7
five f. per cent | MACA 246:3
fix don't f. it | LANC 224:7
good election can't f. | NIXO 290:6
fixed no such thing as a f. policy | SALI 342:6
flag brought back the f. | GRIF 166:8
carry the f. | CHOA 84:9
f. of the future | PEAR 307:1
f. of the United States | BELL 32:9
keep the red f. flying | SONG 377:1
national f. | SUMN 384:2
people's f. is deepest red | SONG 377:1
shall not f. or fail | CHUR 88:2
spare your country's f. | WHIT 418:10
flagpole run it up the f. | PROV 319:2
Flanders F. mare | HENR 181:2
part of F. | WALL 408:9
flashes f. of silence | SMIT 372:9
flashing f. out beams of light | JENK 201:5
flat debt, an' a f. | LOWE 242:7
flattered being then most f. | SHAK 354:10
neither feared nor f. | EPIT 136:6
flatterer hypocrite and f. | BLAK 47:3
flatterers sycophants and f. | HARD 172:8
tell him he hates f. | SHAK 354:10
within a week the same f. | HALI 170:1
flatteries against f. | MACH 251:1
flattering f., kissing and kicking | TRUM 401:2
flattery Everyone likes f. | DISR 123:17
f. corrupts | BURK 62:19
f. hurts no one | STEV 380:3
flaws Psychological f. | ANON 11:13
flesh flattered any f. | EPIT 136:6
flies catch small f. | SWIF 384:5
f. off the meat | CHUR 88:7
float f. lazily downstream | SALI 339:13

floating appeal to f. voters | COOK 103:4
f. vote lives up to | COLE 99:2
flog f. the rank and file | ARNO 15:12
flood just cause reaches its f.-tide | CATT 77:9
return it as a f. | GLAD 159:11
taken at the f. | SHAK 356:5
floor I could f. them all | DISR 119:3
flourish Princes and lords may f. | GOLD 161:3
flow blood must yet f. | JEFF 200:6
flower f. of our youth | TREV 397:7
f. of Scotland | WILL 420:4
flowers hundred f. blossom | MAO 259:9
flown birds are f. | CHAR 81:3
foaming f. with much blood | POWE 315:5
focus renewed f. of politics | HAVE 175:3
foe erect and manly f. | CANN 73:8
Where breathes the f. | DRAK 126:9
willing f. and sea room | ANON 13:9
fog F. in Channel | BROC 55:10
f. or moonlight | CLAU 94:14
sheep scattered in a f. | BRUT 59:5
fogies same old f. | KEAT 210:5
fogs insular country, subject to f. | DISR 122:17
folds f. rippling | SUMN 384:2
follies crimes, f., and misfortunes | GIBB 155:6
follow f. the worse | OVID 298:11
had to f. them | LEDR 229:10
followers find twenty f. | TAYL 388:1
folly as rapidly as f. | CHUR 90:4
ends in f. | COLE 99:4
f. of 'Woman's Rights' | VICT 406:3
He knew human f. | AUDE 18:17
fond f. of dear Ted | THAT 390:5
grow too f. of it | LEE 230:4
fondly F. do we hope | LINC 236:6
fondness habitual f. | WASH 411:6
food advertise f. to hungry people | GALB 149:10
give f. to the poor | CAMA 71:9
GM-free f. | MELC 266:16
room and f. | MALT 257:9
wholesome f. | SWIF 384:8
fool burnt F.'s bandaged finger | KIPL 219:8
f. all of the people | ADAM 2:5
f. all the people | LINC 236:13
f.'s bauble, the mace | CROM 106:2
f. too many | THUR 394:8
patriot yet, but was a f. | DRYD 127:10
wisest f. in Christendom | HENR 180:8
foolery little f. | OXEN 299:5
foolish did anything very f. | MELB 266:8
frantic boast and f. word | KIPL 220:9
never said a f. thing | EPIT 136:3
said something f. | ANON 9:6
fools F. out of favour | DEFO 112:9
f. said would happen | MELB 266:12
f., the fools, the fools | PEAR 306:7
let f. contest | POPE 314:9
millions mostly f. | CARL 74:9
not suffer f. gladly | PEAR 307:2
one half the world f. | JEFF 200:9
perish together as f. | KING 217:9

foot silver f. in his mouth — RICH 326:7
football like being a f. coach — MCCA 248:2
footslogger average f. — WRAN 425:3
forbearance f. ceases to be a virtue — BURK 61:12
force driving f. of all — WEBE 413:3
  employment of f. — SALI 344:12
  F., and fraud — HOBB 185:7
  F. is not a remedy — BRIG 55:8
  f. with a manoeuvre — TROT 400:6
  no argument but f. — BROW 58:6
  Not believing in f. — TROT 400:7
  Other nations use 'f.' — WAUG 412:2
  use of f. alone — BURK 61:18
  use of *f.* by one class — LENI 231:1
forced f. into some other line — HEAT 179:2
forces f. of conservatism — BLAI 46:8
forcibly f. if we must — CLAY 95:5
ford gave us Gerald F. — ABZU 1:4
  I am a F., not a Lincoln — FORD 142:11
forefathers Let us contemplate our f. — ADAM 4:9
  think of your f. — ADAM 4:5
foreign avoid f. collision — CLAY 95:4
  destroyed by a f. force — MONT 277:8
  disposed of f. enemies — PLAT 312:11
  events of f. places — BAGE 23:14
  far, f. fields — DAVI 110:8
  f. affairs — DISR 121:7
  F. aid — NIXO 291:3
  f. policy — COOK 103:1
  f. policy: I wage war — CLEM 96:3
  f. world — WASH 411:4
  from a f. yoke — MAZZ 265:1
  given us f. invasions — SALI 337:9
  idea behind f. policy — O'RO 296:4
  into any f. wars — ROOS 331:1
  journey to a f. land — HAGU 168:2
  My [f.] policy — BEVI 40:10
  on a f. strand — SCOT 348:7
  on f. policy — GALB 150:4
  shape its f. policy — HEAR 178:7
foreigners admit f. — HAMI 172:2
forest burning the rain f. — STIN 381:7
  country is like an American f. — BAGE 24:4
  cut down f.-trees — TROL 399:11
  f. laments — CHUR 85:11
forests found in the f. — MONT 277:11
foretell ability to f. — CHUR 92:3
forget do not quite f. — CHES 83:8
  f. there ever was such a thing — WILS 423:1
  I sometimes f. — DISR 123:20
  Lest we f. — KIPL 220:6
  make one set of people f. — HUXL 193:8
  never forgive but I always f. — BALF 28:9
forgetting consist in merely f. — MAND 258:6
forgive do not f. those murderers — WIES 419:4
  f. him anything — COLL 99:8
  f. those who were right — MACL 251:9
  Lord will f. me — CATH 77:6
  mercy to f. — DRYD 127:11
  never f. but I always forget — BALF 28:9
  Please f. us — PUTI 317:6

forgot Don't let it be f. — LERN 231:11
  f. the fart — ELIZ 133:12
  just f. to duck — DEMP 114:7
  Napoleon f. Blücher — CHUR 86:4
forgotten F. Army — MOUN 281:9
  f. man at the bottom — ROOS 330:4
  he himself had f. it — PALM 303:4
  learnt nothing and f. nothing — TALL 385:10
fork pick up mercury with a f. — LLOY 240:3
formal f. government is abolished — PAIN 301:13
formalistic more f. than conservatives — CALV 71:8
forms f. of government — POPE 314:4
fortnight beyond the next f. — CHAM 79:4
fortress f. built by Nature — SHAK 358:6
  f. rising above the horizon — LOUI 241:9
fortune f. empties her chamberpot — MACD 249:4
  leads on to f. — SHAK 356:5
fortunes f. in peace and war — CHUR 90:12
forty-five F. Minutes — NEWS 287:6
forward F., forward let us range — TENN 389:6
  F. not back — SLOG 366:17
  look f. to posterity — BURK 62:16
  to push things f. — MOWL 281:11
fought f. each other for — SOUT 374:6
  we f. at Arques — HENR 180:6
foully play'dst most f. for't — SHAK 357:5
found f. the Roman nation — VIRG 406:11
foundation fear is the f. — ADAM 4:3
  f. of all good things — BURK 63:10
founding F. Fathers — RICE 326:1
  F. Fathers' blueprint — BIRC 43:3
four F. lagging winters — SHAK 358:5
  F. legs good — ORWE 296:6
  say that two plus two make f. — ORWE 297:6
fourteenth f. Mr Wilson — HOME 187:8
fourth f. estate of the realm — MACA 245:7
  This is the F. — LAST 228:4
  your F. of July — DOUG 126:2
fox compared with f.-hunting — POWE 315:6
  f.-hunting—the wisest religion — HAIL 168:11
  galloping after a f. — WILD 419:8
  My God! They've shot our f. — BIRC 42:11
  Pitt as opposed to Fox — BUTL 68:1
  prince must be a f. — MACH 250:11
foxes f. have a sincere interest — ELIO 132:1
  wants to kill f. — WRIG 425:6
foxholes signs on the f. — KENN 213:4
fracture f. the Labour party — KINN 218:14
fragment not a geographical f. — PARN 304:11
fragrance Has she f. — CAUL 78:1
frailty concession to human f. — TAWN 386:9
France by which F. is fed — SULL 383:7
  F. and England — PEEL 308:1
  F. and Germany — CHUR 89:13
  F. has lost a battle — DE G 113:3
  F. has more need of me — NAPO 284:12
  F. is adequately secured — ASQU 16:5
  F. is the coachman — DE G 113:16
  F., mother of arts — DU B 128:3
  F. wants you to take part — CHIR 84:5
  F. was long a despotism — CARL 74:12

I now speak for F. — DE G 113:4
one illusion—F. — KEYN 214:8
safeguard against F. — ADEN 5:3
wield the sword of F. — DE G 113:5
frank F. and explicit — DISR 123:5
many f. words — COOK 102:9
fraternal f. blood — WEBS 413:7
fraternité *Égalité F.* — SLOG 367:14
fraud electoral f. — MAWR 264:3
Force, and f. — HOBB 185:7
f. and a liar — CONN 101:8
frauds all great men are f. — BONA 49:11
freak grotesque composite f. — HENN 180:2
Fred Here lies F. — EPIT 136:5
Frederick death of F. the Great — BISM 44:7
F. the Great lost — ANON 9:2
free as a f. lunch — PROV 319:10
be f. — SHEL 362:10
born f. — UNIV 403:5
both f. and equal — BAGE 24:12
By a f. country, I mean — SALI 341:1
Church shall be f. — MAGN 255:6
Comment is f. — SCOT 348:6
died that we might be f. — LARK 225:4
die to make men f. — HOWE 190:5
essence of f. government — CALH 70:2
forever f. — LINC 235:4
f. again — SOLZ 373:9
F. at last — EPIT 136:1
F. at last — KING 217:8
F. by '93 — SLOG 366:18
f. church — CAVO 78:5
f., democratic government — TRUM 401:15
f. development — MARX 263:3
freedom to the f. — LINC 235:7
f. lunch has still to be — GREE 166:3
f. man, an American — JOHN 202:6
f. press not a privilege — LIPP 237:5
f. society is a society where — STEV 380:10
half f. — LINC 234:4
I am not f. — DEBS 112:1
If a f. society cannot help — KENN 212:5
ignorant and f. — JEFF 199:15
in a f. country — BURK 62:6
in chains than to be f. — KAFK 209:5
land of the f. — KEY 214:6
leave their citizens f. — JEFF 200:14
man is either f. or he is not — BARA 29:3
Man was born f. — ROUS 334:6
men everywhere could be f. — LINC 235:3
Mother of the F. — BENS 35:6
naturally were born f. — MILT 271:9
No f. man shall be taken — MAGN 255:7
not a f. man — STEV 380:7
not a f. press but a managed — RADC 320:8
not f. either — SOLZ 373:11
not only to be f. — PANK 303:8
people are as f. as they want — BALD 25:11
prerogative of a f. people — PAIN 302:4
press is f. — JEFF 198:10
protection of f. speech — HOLM 187:1

should themselves be f. — BROO 56:6
so far kept us f. — JEFF 199:3
through f. trade — CHOD 85:2
to be f. to choose — BERL 37:2
truth which makes men f. — AGAR 5:8
unless he is f. — CUST 108:6
Was he f.? Was he happy — AUDE 19:5
We must be f. or die — WORD 424:9
wholly slaves or wholly f. — DRYD 127:12
will to be f. — LIPP 237:6
Work makes f. — SLOG 366:3
freed not be many f. men — HALI 170:16
freedom abridging the f. of speech — CONS 102:4
Apostles of f. — CONN 101:4
better organised than f. — PÉGU 308:11
cease to produce f. — SALI 338:3
conditioned to a f. — KENY 214:3
depends on f. of the press — JEFF 198:2
destroy the f. of thinking — ADAM 3:13
efficiencies of f. — GALB 150:6
enemies of f. do not argue — INGE 194:10
fight for f. and truth — IBSE 194:5
fight to maintain f. — ROOS 331:3
first is f. of speech — ROOS 331:4
for f. alone — DECL 112:4
f., and liberty — SHAK 355:2
F. and not servitude — BURK 62:4
F. and slavery are mental states — GAND 151:3
F. an English subject's — DRYD 127:17
F. cannot exist — METT 268:8
f. depends on being courageous — THUC 394:7
f. for the one who thinks differently — LUXE 243:9
f. for the pike — TAWN 386:8
F. hunted — PAIN 300:8
F. is about — GIUL 157:6
F. is an indivisible — WILL 420:5
f. is better than either — SALI 340:15
F. is excellent — TOCQ 395:5
F. is not a gift — NKRU 291:7
F. is slavery — ORWE 297:3
f. is something people take — BALD 25:11
F. is the freedom to say — ORWE 297:6
f. of movement — UNIV 403:6
f. of person — JEFF 199:5
f. of speech — TWAI 402:8
f. of the press — CHUR 92:4
F. of the press guaranteed — LIEB 233:8
F. of the press in Britain — SWAF 384:3
F.'s banner — DRAK 126:9
F. slowly broadens down — TENN 390:1
f. to the slave — LINC 235:7
f. worth the name — MILL 269:8
fundamental sense of f. — BERL 36:7
gave my life for f. — EWER 138:3
guarantee of f. — HAYE 176:3
I gave them f. — GORB 162:6
Let f. reign — BUSH 67:6
Let f. reign — MAND 258:5
let f. ring — KING 217:8
Let f. ring — SMIT 372:4
love not f., but licence — MILT 271:8

freedom (*cont.*):

love of f.	GLAD 158:12
neither equality nor f.	FRIE 147:10
not f. from, but freedom to	BERL 37:4
original source of f.	LIPP 237:2
participation of f.	BURK 62:8
peace from f.	MALC 257:4
plan for f.	POPP 314:9
riches and f.	WAŁĘ 408:1
rights of f.	JUNI 208:9
taste for f.	TOCQ 395:11
there can be no f.	LENI 231:2
walk-over to f.	NEHR 285:12

freedoms four essential human f. — ROOS 331:4
freehold f. on this earth — THAT 391:13
freeing f. some — LINC 235:3
freemen Americans are to be f. — WASH 411:2

great nursery of f.	SHIP 364:1
only f., are the only slaves	MASS 264:1
rule o'er f.	BROO 56:6

French F. are with equal advantage — CANN 73:11

F. arrange	CATH 77:5
F. government	COLO 100:1
F. Revolution operated	TOCQ 395:6
F. want no-one to be	TOCQ 396:11
glory of beating the F.	WOLF 423:10
If the F. noblesse	TREV 397:8
Paris was F.—and silent	TUCH 402:4
to the F. the empire of the land	RICH 326:8

fresh healthy f. air — GALB 150:2
fricassee f., or a ragout — SWIF 384:8
friend betraying my f. — FORS 143:4

candid f.	CANN 73:8
enemy is my f.	PROV 318:8
f. in power is a friend lost	ADAM 2:10
f. of every country	CANN 73:6
he's a f.	CHRÉ 85:7
He was my f.	SHAK 355:8
loss of a dear f.	SOUT 374:8
lost no f.	POPE 314:3
make one f.	TAYL 388:1
man, That love my f.	SHAK 355:15
most fatal f.	MITC 271:13
one f. left	LINC 236:5

friends Americans are our best f. — THOM 393:8

best f. are white	DURE 129:2
Constitution between f.	CAMP 72:8
f. of every country	DISR 121:14
F., Romans, countrymen	SHAK 355:7
lay down his f. for his life	THOR 394:6
makes f. of enemies	SHAK 351:15
nearly deceiving your f.	CORN 103:13
no true f. in politics	CLAR 94:5

friendship f. with all nations — JEFF 199:4

In f. false	DRYD 127:5
no f. at the top	LLOY 240:5

frigging no f. way — PARR 305:9
frighten by God, they f. me — WELL 414:8
frightened children are f. of me — GEOR 154:5

not very f. of him	WALD 407:15

frightening never more f. — VAN 404:4

fringe lunatic f. — ROOS 333:1
front for f. runners — BUSH 66:11

stabbed in the f.	INGH 195:6

frontier at its f. — CRIL 105:2

new f.	KENN 212:2

frontiers old f. are gone — BALD 26:10
frozen f. in an out-of-date mould — JENK 201:2
fructify f. in the pockets — GLAD 159:14
fruitcake we want a f. — PARR 305:7
frustrate F. their knavish tricks — SONG 376:1
frying-pan frizzled in my f. — ENGE 135:6
fudging f. and mudging — OWEN 299:3
fuelled f. by bitterness — BHUT 41:1
fugitive f. and cloistered virtue — MILT 271:3
Führer ein F. — SLOG 366:14
fulmen Eripuit coelo f. — TURG 402:5
fun f. to be in the same decade — ROOS 331:10

Gladstone read Homer for f.	CHUR 91:9
must not do things for f.	HERB 181:10
Politics has got to be f.	CLAR 94:7

function f. to perfection — MUSS 283:8
fund f. of discontent — PEEL 307:13
funny f. old world — THAT 392:5

f. thing happened	STEV 380:12

furnish f. the war — HEAR 178:6
furniture f. on the deck of the Titanic — MORT 280:4

too much of today's f.	LAWR 229:2

furrow plough my f. alone — ROSE 333:10
further but no f. — PIUS 312:7

f. you got from Britain	CALL 71:4

fuss f. about an omelette — VOLT 407:13
future controls the f. — ORWE 297:4

dedication to Canada's f.	DIEF 118:9
doubted your f.	MURR 283:2
empires of the f.	CHUR 89:5
fight against the f.	GLAD 158:7
flag of the f.	PEAR 307:1
f. can be promised to no one	TRUD 400:10
hopes of the f.	BURK 63:14
no faith in the f.	TAYL 387:15
no preparation for the f.	DISR 122:7
picture of the f.	ORWE 297:10
plan the f. by the past	BURK 61:4
promise of a bright f.	AHER 6:1
scaffold sways the f.	LOWE 242:9
seen the f. and it works	STEF 379:4
sense of f. favours	WALP 410:4
walking backward into f.	ZHVA 428:2

fuzzy-wuzzy f. colony — CAIR 70:1

Gael hearthstone of the G. — JOHN 205:9
gag tight g. of place — HEAN 178:5
gained misery is a battle g. — WELL 415:14
gains no g. without pains — STEV 380:5
Galileo feel like G. — LIVI 237:11

G. in two thousand years	PIUS 312:8

Gallia G. est omnis divisa — CAES 69:6
gallows die upon the g. — WILK 420:1

nothing but the g.	BURK 63:3

game Anarchism is a g. — SHAW 361:7

played the g.	SMIT 371:11
time to win this g.	DRAK 126:8
War is a very rough g.	MONT 277:16
gangrenous G. limbs cannot be	HEGE 179:5
gangsters great nations acted like g.	KUBR 223:3
garage to the full g.	HOOV 188:4
garlic clove of g. round my neck	O'BR 293:3
garment grasp the hem of his g.	BISM 44:11
garments Reasons are not like g.	ESSE 137:10
garter like about the Order of the G.	MELB 266:3
Order of the G.	CHUR 89:9
gas got as far as poison-g.	HARD 173:4
gate man at the g. of the year	HASK 174:6
gates g. are mind to open	KIPL 220:5
g. of opportunity	JOHN 203:9
suicide at its g.	HUSS 193:2
to the g. of Hell	PIUS 312:7
Gaul G. as a whole is divided	CAES 69:6
gear not got a reverse g.	BLAI 46:14
geese wild g.	BARR 29:7
Wild G. fly	DAVI 111:3
general feet of the great g.	OVID 299:1
generalities glittering and sounding g.	
	CHOA 84:10
General Motors good for G.	WILS 420:8
generals against the law for g.	TRUM 401:14
Dead battles, like dead g.	TUCH 402:2
g. who gain success	LINC 236:2
Russia has two g.	NICH 286:6
generation g. was stolen	FREE 147:5
g. which commences	JEFF 200:7
Had it been the whole g.	EPIT 136:5
never before has a g.	VANE 404:5
sleep of my g.	STEV 381:2
generosity g. of the politician	MAUG 264:2
generously treated g. or destroyed	MACH 250:8
genetic g. lottery comes up with	PIML 311:3
genetics human g.	JONE 206:4
Geneva G.'s strict limitations	GONZ 162:1
genius g. of its scientists	EISE 131:5
g. of the Constitution	PITT 311:13
g. would wish to live	ADAM 2:2
man of g. rules	STEP 379:6
talent and g.	KENN 213:2
touch of g.	MACM 253:10
Gentiles boasting as the G. use	KIPL 220:8
gentle g. rain from heaven	SHAK 358:2
His life was g.	SHAK 356:7
gentleman cannot make a g.	BURK 65:4
g. gets into the clutches	SALI 341:9
g. in Whitehall	JAY 197:7
Jack became a g.	SHAK 359:4
never a g.	DISR 124:4
real English g.	BAGE 24:5
gentlemen G. cease to be returned	DISR 124:10
G. do not take soup at luncheon	CURZ 108:3
g. of the press	SALI 340:1
nation of g.	MUGA 282:3
Not a religion for g.	CHAR 82:4
since g. came up	SHAK 352:17
geographical Europe is a g. concept	BISM 43:11

g. expression	METT 268:3
not a g. fragment	PARN 304:11
geography too much g.	KING 218:5
geometrical g. ratio	MALT 257:8
George accession of G. the Third	MACA 246:8
G. the Third	BENT 36:2
Georges G. ended	LAND 224:9
Georgia red hills of G.	KING 217:7
German all a G. racket	RIDL 327:1
every other G.	TAYL 387:9
G. dictator	CHUR 87:9
language of poems is G.	CELA 79:3
Germans G. . . . . are going to be squeezed	
	GEDD 152:5
G. classify	CATH 77:5
G. now have the historic chance	KOHL 222:9
government from the G.	MONT 277:11
They're G. Don't mention	CLEE 96:1
to the G. that of—the air	RICH 326:8
Germany at war with G.	CHAM 80:4
Christian life in G.	BONH 50:2
deadliness to fight G.	CHUR 85:9
Death is a master from G.	CELA 79:2
France and G.	CHUR 89:13
G. above all	HOFF 186:2
G. calling	JOYC 208:3
G. is the horse	DE G 113:16
offering G. too little	NEVI 286:3
put G. in the saddle	BISM 43:8
rebellious G.	OVID 299:1
remaining cities of G.	HARR 174:2
said that G. was rearming	BALD 27:1
get g. out in time	BROW 57:10
This is what you g.	LAW 228:13
want to g. along	RAYB 322:7
ghetto go into g. areas	AGNE 5:9
ghost as Banquo's g.	AITK 6:3
conjure a great g.	DANG 109:3
g. asked them to do	O'BR 293:1
g. of a great name	LUCA 243:2
g. of the deceased	HOBB 185:12
ghosts g. of a nation	PEAR 306:8
giant g.'s strength	SHAK 357:13
giants for war like precocious g.	PEAR 306:9
nuclear g. and ethical infants	BRAD 53:2
Want is one only of five g.	BEVE 40:3
gibes great master of g.	DISR 121:11
gift Freedom is not a g.	NKRU 291:7
thick skin is a g. from God	ADEN 5:4
gifts among God's greatest g.	BAGE 23:5
even when they bring g.	VIRG 406:12
gin torrent of g.	GLAD 158:10
Gipper Win just one for the G.	GIPP 157:5
girls Treaties like g. and roses	DE G 113:11
give us back	SLOG 367:1
given I would have g. gladly	JOHN 202:8
giving not in the g. vein	SHAK 359:7
glad Never g. confident morning	BROW 59:2
gladly I would have given g.	JOHN 202:8
Gladstone unprincipled maniac G.	DISR 124:4
Glasgow got a G. accent	REID 324:5

G. Government	TROL 399:17	right of g.	FOX 144:7
g. is oft interrèd	SHAK 355:7	**government** abandon a g.	JEFF 199:3
g. man to do nothing	MISQ 273:5	acts of g.	HARR 174:5
g. of subjects	DEFO 113:2	all g. is evil	O'SU 298:7
g. of the people	CICE 93:3	arbitrary g.	CHAR 82:3
g. old Cause	MILT 271:6	art of g.	PEEL 308:4
G. words do not last long	JOSE 207:3	art of g.	VOLT 407:4
Great and the G.	SAMP 345:11	art of g. is	SHAW 361:4
have a g. proof	CHRÉ 85:6	as well be in g.	HELL 179:8
have a g. thing	SHAK 352:5	attacks on g.	BREN 54:9
I will be g.	VICT 406:2	attack the G.	CHUR 90:6
making people feel g.	CHRÉ 85:4	become the most corrupt g.	JEFF 198:14
never had it so g.	MACM 253:1	bring the g. down	PARR 305:9
never had it so g.	SLOG 369:8	British g.	HAMI 171:9
never so g. or so bad	MACK 251:5	business of g.	LAWS 229:4
only g. Indians	SHER 362:14	consequence of good g.	SALI 339:8
policy of the g. neighbour	ROOS 330:7	constitution and its g.	PAIN 302:8
pursuing our own g.	MILL 269:8	corruption of each g.	MONT 277:6
than to seem g.	SALL 345:5	deal with the g.	HOLM 187:2
they were g. men	STEP 379:8	definition of the best g.	HALI 170:7
trying to do g.	SALI 344:5	distrust of g. inspectors	SALI 339:11
twelve g. men	BROU 57:1	duty of g.	PAIN 300:10
very g. day	MOOR 278:3	enable the g. to control	MADI 255:4
what g. came of it	SOUT 374:7	end of g.	ADAM 4:2
what was g. for our country	WILS 420:8	essence of free g.	CALH 70:2
would be a g. idea	GAND 151:6	Every g. will do	LEWI 233:5
would do g. to another	BLAK 47:3	Every Labour g.	CLAR 94:13
goods care for external g.	WEBE 412:11	excellence of the English g.	BLAC 45:9
when g. are private	TAWN 386:9	feeble g.	BURK 63:11
goodwill In peace; g.	CHUR 91:12	for a bad g.	TOCQ 396:3
goose on the ground at G. Green	KINN 218:9	forms of g.	POPE 314:4
steals a g.	ANON 12:12	for the federal g.	REAG 323:8
Gorbachev Mr G., tear down	REAG 323:12	four pillars of g.	BACO 21:1
Gore Vote for G.	SLOG 368:11	function of a g.	PALM 303:3
gorgeous g. East in fee	WORD 424:10	get all of the g.	FRIE 148:3
Goschen forgot G.	CHUR 86:4	Good G.	TROL 399:17
gossip I admit there is g.	DISR 121:18	g. above the law	SCAR 347:4
in the g. columns	INGH 195:4	G. acquired the tact	WEST 416:9
got we g. him	BREM 54:8	G. and co-operation	RUSK 336:6
gotcha G.	NEWS 287:7	G. and public opinion	SHAW 360:16
Götterdämmerung G. without the gods		g. as an adversary	BRUN 59:4
	MACD 249:3	G. at Washington lives	GARF 151:8
Gotto name is Ainsley G.	ERWI 137:8	g. been instituted	HAMI 172:1
gouverner G. c'est choisir	LÉVI 233:2	g. by crony	ICKE 194:8
govern easy to g.	BROU 57:2	g. by the people	CAMP 72:10
good enough to g. another	LINC 234:2	g. by the uneducated	CHES 83:12
g. according to the common	JAME 197:5	G., even in its best state	PAIN 300:3
g. in prose	CUOM 107:5	G. is a contrivance	BURK 62:18
No man is fit to g.	MACA 246:15	g. is best	THOR 394:1
not to g.	GLAD 158:5	G. is dangerously ill	BENN 35:4
people g. themselves	THIE 393:1	G. is influenced by	SMIT 370:9
right to g.	HARR 174:4	G. is like a big baby	REAG 322:9
to g. is to choose	LÉVI 233:2	G. . . . is simply not the channel	KENN 211:5
governed ability among the g.	TOCQ 396:10	g. it deserves	MAIS 256:3
g. by your inferiors	PLAT 312:10	G. of Britain's isle	SHAK 352:16
kings g. their rude age	BAGE 22:12	G. of laws, and not of men	ADAM 3:6
nation is not g.	BURK 61:18	G. of laws and not of men	FORD 143:1
not so well g.	HOOK 187:11	g. of statesmen	DISR 122:5
governess in the g. of a family	SALI 340:8	G. of the busy	SELD 349:4
governing incapable of g.	CHES 83:1	g. of the people	LINC 235:8
in the people g.	DICK 118:4	g. of the people	PAGE 299:7

government (*cont.*):

g. of the world	DISR 121:18
g. was a practical thing	BURK 61:9
g. which imprisons	THOR 394:2
g. which robs Peter	SHAW 360:7
g. will do for me	NIXO 290:10
great service to a g.	MEDI 265:4
have an efficient g.	TRUM 401:10
If the G. is big enough	FORD 142:10
I'm from the g.	REAG 323:11
important thing for G.	KEYN 215:5
in a disorderly g.	HALI 170:6
increase of his g. and peace	BIBL 41:15
inherit a g.	PAIN 301:9
institution of g.	BURK 64:16
intentions of a g.	GALB 149:12
I, we, the G.	BLAI 46:15
keep the g. in order	SCAR 347:5
King asks you to form a G.	ATTL 18:3
Labour G. does	MORR 279:12
land of settled g.	TENN 390:1
least g. was the best	FEIN 140:2
life of any g.	BOOK 50:5
maxim of a free g.	ADAM 3:4
meddling g.	MACA 247:11
members of the G.	SHAW 360:11
Monarchy is a strong g.	BAGE 22:11
natural party of g.	WILS 421:10
noblest g.	DISR 121:3
no British g. should be brought down	
	MACM 253:7
No G. can be long secure	DISR 122:13
no g. proper ever had	LINC 234:10
not a g. of laws	WEBS 413:10
not depend on g.	MISQ 272:3
not set by g.	DAY 111:7
not the worst g.	TROL 399:10
object of g. in peace and in war	BEVE 40:2
one form of g.	JOHN 204:13
one g. sooner learns	SMIT 371:3
on the side of the g.	RUSS 336:14
overdoes the quantity of g.	BAGE 23:13
Parliamentary g. is impossible	DISR 121:4
Peace, order, and good g.	ANON 11:8
people's g.	WEBS 413:5
powers of g.	JEFF 200:13
prefer that the g.	O'RO 296:4
prepare for g.	STEE 379:1
proceedings of g.	BURK 64:8
reins of g. are lodged	SHEL 361:14
representative g.	DISR 123:7
republican g.	HAMI 171:10
restraints of g.	GOLD 161:2
revealing the workings of g.	BLAC 45:4
reverence that form of g.	AESC 5:5
signifies the want of g.	HOBB 185:11
smack of firm g.	NEWS 288:2
support their g.	CLEV 96:10
system of G.	GLAD 158:3
they've elected a Labour G.	ANON 8:5
to run a g.	TRUM 401:8

under a g.	RAIN 321:2
understood by republican g.	TOCQ 396:9
Unfortunately, it's the g.	ALLE 6:8
uninteresting G.	HEAD 176:10
virtue of paper g.	BURK 61:15
vulgar arts of g.	PEEL 307:18
watch the g.	ROGE 329:7
wee pretendy g.	CONN 101:2
well-ordered g.	HALI 169:9
what the g. can do	HARD 172:10
work for a G. I despise	KEYN 214:7
worst form of G.	CHUR 90:5
worst g.	MENC 267:8
governments corrupted g.	HALI 170:5
foundation of most g.	ADAM 4:3
G. always want	RADC 320:8
G. are far more stupid	EISE 131:8
g. had better get out of the way	EISE 131:9
g. need both shepherds	VOLT 407:8
g. of Europe	JEFF 198:4
g. to gain ground	JEFF 198:7
In all tyrannical g.	BLAC 45:8
that the two g.	MITC 274:10
Visible g.	RUSK 335:11
governor save the G.-General	WHIT 418:2
governors supreme g., the mob	WALP 409:8
governs that which g. least	O'SU 298:7
which g. not at all	THOR 394:1
gowd man's the g.	BURN 65:8
grab all smash and no g.	NICO 289:1
Gracchos Quis tulerit G.	JUVE 209:1
grace but for the g. of God	CHUR 92:17
keep those of g.	MACH 251:3
retains the means of G.	BALF 28:5
graceful Such a g. exit	JUNO 208:13
gradualness inevitability of g.	WEBB 412:8
graft There's an honest g.	PLUN 313:2
grain choice g.	STOU 382:7
grammar destroy every g. school	CROS 106:12
erecting a g. school	SHAK 353:1
talking bad g.	DISR 122:2
grand what G. Duchesses are doing	NAPO 284:10
grandiose g. ideas and glory	MOSL 280:5
grandmother We have become a g.	THAT 391:14
grapes g. of the wine-press	MACA 247:4
g. of wrath	HOWE 190:4
grass everywhere nibble g.	FAGU 138:8
g. will grow in the streets	BRYA 59:8
g. will grow in the streets	HOOV 188:5
party comes from the g. roots	BEVE 39:11
two blades of g.	SWIF 384:7
grasses by short g.	PORT 314:14
checked by the g.	MONT 277:4
grasshopper Walton Heath with a g.	LLOY 238:11
grasshoppers half a dozen g.	BURK 63:5
gratitude G. is not a normal feature	KILM 217:1
G., like love	ALSO 7:1
gratuity bribe or g.	PENN 308:14
grave from the cradle to the g.	CHUR 89:3
g. of a dead Fenian	COLL 99:5
Is that ayont the g.	BURN 65:11

lead but to the g.	GRAY 165:4	My passport's g.	HEAN 178:2
life beyond the g.	KHRU 216:10	talking G. in the House	SALI 343:8
requires g. statesmen	DISR 122:17	wearin' o' the G.	SONG 376:2
sitting crowned upon the g.	HOBB 185:12	Wherever g. is worn	YEAT 426:5
walk on no g.	PAIS 302:10	**greenest** g. political party	JONE 206:3
gravedigger First G.	MACL 251:7	**Greenpeace** G. had a ring to it	HUNT 192:6
graveyard Poor Law, and a g.	JOHN 205:8	**grenadier** single Pomeranian g.	BISM 44:10
graveyards fills political g.	KINN 218:8	**grey** good g. head	TENN 389:8
gravitation not believing in g.	TROT 400:7	in my g. hairs	WOLS 424:5
grazing Tilling and g.	SULL 383:7	this old g. head	WHIT 418:10
greased wrestling with a g. pig	PATT 306:2	**grief** could I but rate My g.	MONT 278:1
greasy top of the g. pole	DISR 123:18	more worthy of g.	SHEL 362:9
great all g. men are frauds	BONA 49:11	**griefs** But not my g.	SHAK 358:13
favours from the g.	TAYL 388:6	soothed the g.	MACA 246:16
G. and the Good	SAMP 345:11	**grievance** deep-rooted g.	CRIL 105:2
g. break through	SHEN 362:12	desire to have a g.	PEEL 308:5
G. is the hand	THOM 393:3	**grievances** discovery of g.	SALI 340:14
g. man down	SHAK 351:15	**grind** Laws g. the poor	GOLD 161:6
g. man helped the poor	MACA 247:8	**grooves** ringing g. of time	TENN 389:6
g. men	ACTO 1:12	**grotesque** g. chaos	KINN 218:11
G. men are not always	BIBL 41:10	g. situation	HAUG 175:1
g. men even under bad emperors	TACI 385:2	**ground** gain a little patch of g.	SHAK 352:1
g. men make mistakes	CHUR 86:4	let us sit upon the g.	SHAK 358:10
g. ones devoured the small	SIDN 364:8	**grovelling** g. tyranny	DISR 123:12
g. qualities, the imperious will	BAGE 22:8	**groves** g. of *their* academy	BURK 63:3
G. Society	JOHN 203:4	**growth** children of a larger g.	CHES 82:11
g. things are done	BISM 44:6	neoclassical endogenous g.	BROW 57:5
grown so g.	SHAK 354:2	**guarantee** cannot g. it won't	HOWA 189:7
Ill can he rule the g.	SPEN 377:9	**guard** Be on your g.	OFFI 295:8
Madness in g. ones	SHAK 351:12	g. I do not love	YEAT 426:6
Men in g. place	BACO 20:11	**guards** Brigade of G.	MACM 253:11
no small steps in g. affairs	RETZ 324:8	Up G. and at them	WELL 415:2
Rightly to be g.	SHAK 352:2	who is to guard the g.	JUVE 209:2
weren't such a g. man	GLAD 158:1	**gubu** *acronym* G.	HAUG 175:1
with small men no g. thing	MILL 269:15	**Gucci** G. shoes	MURD 283:1
greater g. than a private citizen	TACI 385:7	**guerrilla** by means of g. bands	MAZZ 265:1
they behold a g.	SHAK 354:5	**guessing** g. what was at the other side	
greatest firstborn the g. ass	CARO 75:10		WELL 415:10
g. event it is	FOX 144:8	**guided** g. missiles	KING 218:2
g. week	NIXO 290:8	**guiding** g.-star of a whole brave nation	
life to live as the g. he	RAIN 321:2		MOTL 280:7
greatness abuse of g.	SHAK 354:6	**guilt** beggar would recognise g.	PARS 305:10
ascent to g.	GIBB 155:5	blood with g. is bought	SHEL 362:5
farewell, to all my g.	SHAK 353:4	g. of Stalin	GORB 162:4
G., with private men	MASS 264:1	**guilty** g. of some offence	FRIS 148:4
His g. weighed	SHAK 351:8	with Hitler g.	TAYL 387:9
nature of all g.	BURK 61:13	**guinea** but the g.'s stamp	BURN 65:8
Grecian G. horse	HAMI 172:2	g. you have in your pocket	RUSK 336:5
greed G. is healthy	BOES 48:4	**Guinness** pint of G.	MALL 257:6
g. of speculators	LAUR 228:10	**gulag** G. archipelago	SOLZ 373:10
G. works	WEIS 414:4	word 'g.' did not appear	WU 425:7
infectious g.	GREE 166:2	**gum** can't fart and chew g.	JOHN 203:14
greedy G. for the property	SALL 345:3	walk and chew g.	EDWA 130:6
Greek G. as a treat	CHUR 91:8	**gun** grows out of the barrel of a g.	MAO 259:7
Greeks G. in this American empire	MACM 252:7	g. in the other	BRUT 59:6
I fear the G.	VIRG 406:12	smoking g. to be a mushroom cloud	RICE 325:9
green England's g. and pleasant land	BLAK 47:5	we have got the Maxim G.	BELL 33:3
g. pastures of the European	VERW 405:7	**gunboat** send a g.	BEVA 38:7
g. shoots of economic spring	LAMO 224:3	**gunfire** towards the sound of g.	GRIM 167:4
g. shoots of recovery	MISQ 273:1	**gunpowder** G., Printing	CARL 74:9
Make it a *g.* peace	DARN 109:7	G. Treason and Plot	ANON 11:11

gunpowder (*cont.*):

invention of g.	MONT 277:3
printing, g., and the magnet	BACO 21:10

guns g. that are hidden FLEI 141:6
not found any smoking g. BLIX 47:6
rather have butter or g. GOER 160:5
sell him g. GALL 150:13
with g. not with butter GOEB 160:3

guts g. of the last priest DIDE 118:7
Mrs Thatcher 'showed g.' KINN 218:9
strangled with the g. MESL 268:2

gutter in the g. with that guy EISE 131:6

guy straight sort of guy BLAI 46:4

habeas corpus protection of *h.* JEFF 199:5

habits prejudices and h. GIBB 155:16

habitual h. hatred WASH 411:6

hack Do not h. me MONM 276:1

hair cutting h. BURN 65:6
h. blown about PRES 316:9
long essenced h. MACA 247:5

half h. slave LINC 234:4
Too clever by h. SALI 339:9
Too clever by h. SALI 345:2

halitosis h. of the intellect ICKE 194:6

Hallelujah H. . . . . Never again ALBR 6:4

hallow cannot h. this ground LINC 235:8

halls h. of Montezuma SONG 375:6

Hamlet putting on H. MACL 251:7

hamsters tigress surrounded by h. BIFF 42:6

hand bite the h. that fed them BURK 63:13
gladly shake your h. BRAN 54:1
h. impresses upon them SMIT 370:1
h. into the Hand of God HASK 174:6
h. that signed the paper THOM 393:2
h. that signed the treaty THOM 393:3
h. to execute CLAR 93:12
h. to execute GIBB 155:12
h.-up not a hand-out BLAI 46:7
h. which executes TAYL 388:5
invisible h. in politics FRIE 147:8
led by an invisible h. SMIT 370:6
lifted h. between HEWI 183:2
Thy h., great Anarch POPE 314:1

handbag hitting it with her h. CRIT 105:5

handkerchief lady's pocket h. LLOY 239:7

hands blood on your h. CARL 74:4
Look, Daddy, no h. HOGG 186:4
pair of h. BAUE 30:6
unproductive h. SMIT 370:4
With mine own h. SHAK 358:15

hang all h. together FRAN 145:8
didn't h. John C. Calhoun JACK 196:7
H. yourself, brave Crillon HENR 180:6
let him h. there EHRL 130:8
with which to h. them MISQ 272:4

hanged h., drawn, and quartered PEPY 308:15
h. for stealing horses HALI 170:17
if they'd been h. DENN 115:3

hanging h. men an' women SONG 376:2

hangman fit for the h. LASK 225:7

happen fools said would h. MELB 266:12
little should h. as possible SALI 340:7

happens Stuff h. RUMS 335:2

happiness H. depends on being free THUC 394:7
H. lies in conquering GENG 152:9
h. of an individual JOHN 204:13
h. of society ADAM 4:2
h. of the greatest number BENT 35:9
h. of the human race BURK 62:11
human life and h. JEFF 199:11
liberty and the pursuit of h. ANON 13:2
my people's h. ELIZ 133:3
no h. exists CUST 108:6
pursuit of h. JEFF 198:1
result h. DICK 117:8

happy Few people can be h. RUSS 336:13
I die h. LAST 226:9
none should be h. JOHN 205:1
someone, somewhere, may be h. MENC 267:3
splendid and a h. land GOLD 161:4
Was he free? Was he h. AUDE 19:5

harbour those who h. them BUSH 67:2
voyage not a h. TOYN 397:2

hard h. dog to keep CLIN 97:4

hare usually beat the h. MAJO 256:4

harlot prerogative of the h. KIPL 221:5

harm as much h. as it can LEWI 233:5
h. wercheth To the povere LANG 225:2
prevent h. to others MILL 269:6
What h. have I ever done TAWN 386:12

Harold H. knows best CROS 106:11

Harry little touch of H. SHAK 352:8

harvest h. in England BUTT 68:6

haste what h. I can to be gone LAST 227:7

hat man who doesn't wear a h. BEAV 31:13

hatchet cut it with my h. WASH 411:1

hatchets buried all the h. WILS 422:2

hate fight I do not h. YEAT 426:6
h. of those ye better KIPL 221:3
h. some other person RUSS 336:13
hearts that h. thee SHAK 353:6
I h. war ROOS 330:10
letter of h. OSBO 298:4
Let them h. ACCI 1:5
People must learn to h. MAND 258:7
roughness breedeth h. BACO 20:13
seen much to h. here MILL 270:4

hated rather h. the ruling few BENT 35:11

hates just heaven now h. EPIT 136:4
world of voluble h. TREV 397:9

hating By h. vices too much BURK 63:8

hatred Great h., little room YEAT 426:8
habitual h. WASH 411:6
mutual h. BURK 61:8
What we need is h. GENE 152:7
With what a perfect h. WALL 409:1

hatreds h. which sounded TROL 399:4
organization of h. ADAM 2:9

hats shocking bad h. WELL 415:8

Haughey H. buried at midnight O'BR 293:3

havoc Cry, 'H.!' and let slip — SHAK 355:4
hawk h. is in the air — DISR 121:12
hawking H. his conscience — MISQ 273:2
hay live on h. — HILL 184:1
he H. would, wouldn't he — RICE 326:5
head admirable h. of state — HAIL 168:12
  good grey h. — TENN 389:8
  h. beneath the feet — OVID 299:1
  h. in the sand — WILS 422:14
  h. of a party — RETZ 325:2
  h. of the Cabinet — MORL 279:8
  h. that wears a crown — SHAK 352:6
  h. to contrive — CLAR 93:12
  h. to contrive — GIBB 155:12
  h. which propounds — TAYL 388:5
  his brains go to his h. — ASQU 17:2
  ideas of its "h." — DISR 120:1
  If you can keep your h. — KIPL 219:10
  My h.'s clear — MACK 251:4
  On my h. — DISR 119:4
  proof of want of h. — PROV 319:5
  shorter by the h. — ELIZ 132:8
  show my h. to the people — DANT 109:6
  strike at the h. — BURK 65:1
  which way the h. lies — RALE 321:7
  your good h. — ELIZ 133:2
headache little men who have the h. — SALI 344:15
headline h. in the *Morning Star* — ANON 10:5
headmasters H. have powers — CHUR 91:7
healing not heroics, but h. — HARD 173:1
health h. of the whole human race — TOYN 397:4
  National H. Service — MACL 251:7
  National H. Service — THAT 391:1
  seriously damage your h. — OFFI 295:7
healthy Greed is h. — BOES 48:4
  h. state of political life — MILL 269:11
hear H. ye! Hear ye — ANON 9:8
  prefer not to h. — AGAR 5:8
  you will h. me — DISR 119:5
heard I will be h. — GARR 152:2
  right to be h. — HUMP 192:1
hearers attentive and favourable h. — HOOK 187:11
heart broken h. lies here — MACA 247:7
  committed adultery in my h. — CART 76:5
  examine my own h. — DE V 115:10
  Fourteen h. attacks — JOPL 206:7
  h. and stomach of a king — ELIZ 132:9
  h.'s a little banged up — MACK 251:4
  h. to resolve — GIBB 155:12
  If thy h. fails thee — ELIZ 133:7
  Irishman's h. — SHAW 360:13
  its h. should be — HUME 191:10
  just a h.-beat away — MISQ 273:6
  key of my h. — CLAY 95:8
  lying in my h. — MARY 263:5
  make a stone of the h. — YEAT 426:4
  occasional h. attack — CHEN 82:7
  proof of want of h. — PROV 319:5
  So the h. be right — RALE 321:7
  with a mighty h. — SHAK 352:7
heartbeat h. from the Presidency — STEV 380:11

hearth skeletons on their own h. — MITC 271:11
hearts all that human h. endure — GOLD 161:7
  h. of his countrymen — LEE 230:2
  Kind h. are more than coronets — TENN 389:5
  offspring of cold h. — BURK 63:2
  O you hard h. — SHAK 353:9
  queen in people's h. — DIAN 117:2
heat don't like the h. — PROV 318:13
  not without dust and h. — MILT 271:3
  white h. of revolution — WILS 421:5
  white h. of technology — MISQ 274:6
heather cries 'Nothing but h.' — MACD 249:2
heaven absolute h. — CALL 71:5
  ascend to h. — FIRM 140:5
  consent of h. — JONS 206:6
  Equality would be h. — TROL 399:16
  house as nigh h. — MORE 278:8
  just h. now hates — EPIT 136:4
  looketh this way to H. — CECI 79:1
  not go to H. — JEFF 198:8
  Pennies don't fall from h. — THAT 390:7
  sudden journey to h. — BEAV 31:8
  though h. perish — ADAM 4:6
  young was very h. — WORD 424:8
Hebrew H. conjuror — CARL 75:5
hedge divinity doth h. a king — SHAK 352:3
hedgehogs throwing h. under me — KHRU 216:9
heights commanding h. of the economy — BEVA 39:3
hell agreement with h. — GARR 152:3
  come hot from h. — SHAK 355:4
  do science in h. — VAUG 405:1
  H. has no terror for me — LARK 225:5
  H. of not making money — CARL 75:2
  H. or Connaught — CROM 106:7
  tell you to go to h. — STIN 381:8
  they think it is h. — TRUM 401:7
  to the gates of H. — PIUS 312:7
  War is h., and all that — HAY 175:7
helmsman change the h. — BAGE 22:9
help God h. me — LUTH 243:7
  h. and support of the woman — EDWA 130:5
  I'm here to h. — REAG 323:11
helped shall have h. it — DICK 118:2
helpless h. and ineffectual — HERB 182:1
helps Nobody ever h. me — TRUT 401:16
hemisphere portion of this h. — MONR 276:9
hen h.-roost to rob — LLOY 238:7
  take a wet h. — KHRU 216:6
heraldry boast of h. — GRAY 165:4
herd Morality is the h.-instinct — NIET 289:7
here H. I am — MACM 252:4
hereditary h. government — PAIN 301:9
  idea of h. legislators — PAIN 301:7
heresy mislike it, h. — HOBB 185:3
hero acted like a h. — WALP 409:3
  don't want to be a h. — STOP 382:6
  may be the H. of a novel — MACA 247:12
heroes fit country for h. — LLOY 239:2
  h. to govern you — CARL 75:6
  Unhappy the land that needs h. — BREC 54:2

heroics not h., but healing   HARD 173:1
Herr H. and there   COOK 102:9
hewers h. of wood and drawers of water
                                          BIBL 41:3
hidden guns that are h.   FLEI 141:6
hide something to h.   LAY 229:8
hiding bloody good h.   GRAN 164:1
high Be ye never so h.   DENN 115:1
  Detestation of the h.   DICK 118:3
  Men in h. places   TAYL 388:12
higher h. the monkey climbs   PROV 318:12
  not taking a h. road   NIXO 291:4
highest h. bidder   WASH 411:3
  to the h. office   MCCA 248:1
hill city upon a h.   WINT 423:7
  light on the h.   CHIF 84:1
hills Black H. belong to me   SITT 365:6
  red h. of Georgia   KING 217:7
hinterland She has no h.   HEAL 177:10
hip smote them h. and thigh   BIBL 41:4
hired They h. the money   COOL 103:9
hireling Pay given to a state h.   JOHN 204:2
Hiroshima bomb on H.   TRUM 400:13
historian h. looks behind   TAYL 387:4
historians H. in general   TREV 398:6
history admired your h.   MURR 283:2
  cancer of human h.   SONT 374:4
  cannot escape h.   LINC 235:6
  discerned in h. a plot   FISH 140:6
  dustbin of h.   TROT 400:5
  end of h.   FUKU 148:7
  fair summary of h.   FRAN 145:6
  hand of h.   BLAI 46:6
  H. came to a .   SELL 349:11
  H. gets thicker   TAYL 387:1
  H. is a gallery of pictures   TOCQ 395:7
  H. is almost always   NEHR 285:11
  H. . . . is, indeed, little more   GIBB 155:6
  h. is nothing more   VOLT 407:7
  h. is on our side   KHRU 216:5
  H. is past politics   FREE 147:6
  H. littered with the wars   POWE 315:3
  h. of class struggles   MARX 263:2
  h. of progress   MACA 246:7
  h. of the world   DISR 120:14
  H. teaches us   EBAN 129:7
  h. will record   MORS 280:2
  in the h. of the world   NIXO 290:8
  learned anything from h.   HEGE 179:6
  learning from our h.   BLAI 45:11
  more to shape h.   TAYL 387:8
  no h. of mankind   POPP 314:10
  pattern of h.   BOOK 50:6
  Phrases make h. here   MAFF 255:5
  Read no h.   DISR 122:14
  Thames is liquid h.   BURN 65:7
  thousand years of h.   GAIT 149:4
  too much h.   KING 218:5
  uses of h.   BORK 52:1
  War makes good h.   HARD 173:3
  What is h.   POWE 316:2

What will h. say   SHAW 360:5
  writing h. with lightning   WILS 422:10
Hitler didn't understand H.   ROBE 327:7
  H. swept out   NEWS 287:13
  H. thought he might   CHAM 80:5
  H. to make him PM   MACM 252:8
  H. was mad   LIVI 238:3
  When H. attacked the Jews   NIEM 289:5
hitting see a belt without h.   ASQU 17:3
hobgoblins series of h.   MENC 267:4
hocus accounting h.-pocus   TAUZ 386:3
hog root, h., or die   BROG 56:3
hoi polloi multitude, the h.   DRYD 128:1
hold can neither h. him   JEFF 200:3
  can't h. a man down   WASH 410:12
hole shell with a h.   HUME 191:10
  when you're in a h.   HEAL 177:9
holily wouldst thou h.   SHAK 357:1
hollow Within the h. crown   SHAK 358:1
holocaust Somme is like the H.   BARK 29:5
holy neither h., nor Roman   VOLT 407:6
homage h. of the low   DICK 118:3
home America, my h. sweet home   BERL 36:6
  as well as H. Rule   BALF 27:10
  battling in its own h.   AESC 5:6
  children who leave h.   SLOV 369:9
  Englishman's h.   PROV 318:10
  go back h.   BLUN 47:11
  h. of the brave   KEY 214:6
  Keep the H.-fires burning   SONG 376:6
  morning H. Rule passes   CARS 75:13
  princes are come h. again   SHAK 356:8
  Till the boys come h.   SONG 376:6
  White House or h.   DOLE 125:4
homeless h., tempest-tossed   LAZA 229:9
Homer Gladstone read H. for fun   CHUR 91:9
  prayers in H.   GLAD 158:11
homogeneous more h. State   NEWS 287:10
honest and remain h.   HOWE 190:6
  buy it like an h. man   NORT 292:5
  few h. men   CROM 105:8
  general h. thought   SHAK 356:7
  h. and intelligent   ORWE 297:18
  h. burglar   MENC 267:9
  h. man is laughed at   HALI 171:1
  h. politician   CAME 72:1
  Keep the bastards h.   SLOG 367:8
  more that of an h. broker   BISM 44:2
  one h. man   PAIN 300:5
  Robin and I are two h. men   SHIP 364:2
  There's an h. graft   PLUN 313:2
  two who are h.   MENC 267:6
honesty common sense and common h.
                                          SHEL 361:14
honey bee produces h.   GOLD 161:1
Hong Kong H.'s return to China   DENG 114:9
honi H. soit qui mal y pense   MOTT 281:4
honour All is lost save h.   MISQ 272:1
  As he was valiant, I h. him   SHAK 355:6
  cannot be maintained with h.   RUSS 337:2
  desire for h.   CICE 93:5

Fear God. H. the King — KITC 222:2
great peaks of h. — LLOY 238:9
He is the fountain of h. — BACO 20:5
h. and life — FRAN 145:4
h. would thee do — SHAK 352:7
in h. clear — POPE 314:3
king delighteth to h. — BIBL 41:9
louder he talked of his h. — EMER 135:2
may we h. it — WEBS 413:13
Office before h. — POWE 315:10
peace I hope with h. — DISR 121:15
peace with h. — CHAM 80:3
property or h. — MACH 250:12
reputation and h. — SOCR 373:6
roll of h. — CLEV 96:9
safety, h., and welfare — CHAR 81:8
throne *we* h. — SHER 363:2
When h.'s at the stake — SHAK 352:2
without an h. — PEEL 307:19
honourable Brutus is an h. man — SHAK 355:8
h. alike in what we give — LINC 235:7
h. by being necessary — HALE 169:5
honours Examine the H. List — BENN 35:4
excluded from h. — ADAM 2:3
neither h. nor wages — GARI 151:10
sale of h. — DISR 122:6
hope from rising h. — FOOT 142:8
h. — MACA 246:6
Land of H. and Glory — BENS 35:6
last best h. — LINC 235:8
Never to h. again — SHAK 353:5
ray of h. is blown out — LINC 234:7
there is h. — CROS 107:1
There is no h. — CHES 82:10
two thousand years of h. — WEIZ 414:5
hopes h. of its children — EISE 131:5
h. our wits beguile — WOTT 425:1
no h. but from power — BURK 64:11
hopping h. like so many fleas — O'HI 294:4
horizon fortress rising above the h. — LOUI 241:9
just beyond the h. — KISS 221:14
horizontal vertical to the eternal h. — GRAS 164:9
horny H.-handed sons of toil — SALI 339:12
horribilis annus h. — ELIZ 134:3
horrible h. and barbarous — SALI 339:3
horse Do not trust the h. — VIRG 406:12
feeds the h. enough oats — GALB 149:11
Grecian h. — HAMI 172:2
h. was made Consul — RAND 321:9
like an Arab h. — ROBE 327:6
Protestant with a h. — BEHA 32:5
sounds like a saddle h. — ONAS 294:7
young cornet of h. — WALP 410:1
horseleech daughters of the h. — SALI 342:5
horses if you cannot ride two h. — MAXT 264:4
swap h. when crossing — LINC 236:4
that h. may not be stolen — HALI 170:17
hostages h. to the fates — LUCA 243:3
hostile h. to the single currency — CLAR 94:11
hostility H. to Radicalism — SALI 343:13
hotbed h. of cold feet — EBAN 129:8

hothouse this Blackpool h. — HOME 187:6
hour finest h. — CHUR 88:3
man and the h. — YANC 426:3
preparation for this h. — CHUR 87:13
to serve the h. — TENN 389:11
hours better wages and shorter h. — ORWE 297:13
wearied me for two h. — GEOR 153:2
house admiring the H. of Lords — BAGE 23:7
cheer in the H. of Commons — BAGE 23:8
displeases this H. — O'CO 293:7
h. as nigh heaven — MORE 278:8
h. divided — LINC 234:4
H. of Peers — GILB 156:8
make a h. — CANN 74:1
put the H. in his pocket — GARV 152:4
This H. today is a theatre — BALD 27:3
When in that H. MPs divide — GILB 156:9
household centre of the h. — SHAW 360:8
housekeeping good h. to the winds — KEYN 215:13
houses Looking for h., Nye — ATTL 18:4
how H. do they know — PARK 304:1
howls h. of anguish — HEAL 177:3
huddled h. masses yearning — LAZA 229:9
huffiness h. which you see — SALI 340:8
huge shoes are h. — SEXW 350:4
human calculable mass of h. beings — WEBB 412:7
dreadful h. beings sitting — NORR 291:10
due to want of h. wisdom — BONA 49:7
health of the whole h. race — TOYN 397:4
H. blunders — TAYL 387:8
h. characteristic — WEIL 414:1
h. hearts endure — JOHN 204:5
h. life and happiness — JEFF 199:11
safeguard h. rights — SCAR 347:6
socialism would not lose its h. face — DUBČ 128:2
violates h. rights — ROME 329:9
humanitarian h. with an eye — CECI 78:8
humanity crooked timber of h. — KANT 209:7
H. does not consist — FOX 144:9
h., reason — BURK 62:3
not to their h. — SMIT 370:2
religion of h. — PAIN 300:14
teach governments h. — PAIN 301:4
truth, justice, and h. — GLAD 159:5
humbug H. or Humdrum — DISR 122:5
Yes we have. H. — PALM 303:6
humdrum Humbug or H. — DISR 122:5
humiliation five years' h. — HATT 174:7
humiliations mortifications and h. — WALP 409:7
hundred h. days — WILS 421:6
h. flowers blossom — MAO 259:9
one h. bin Ladens — MUBA 282:2
hunger against h., poverty — MARS 261:2
h. and poverty — LARK 225:5
offer you h., thirst — GARI 151:10
where mass h. reigns — BRAN 53:11
hungry advertise food to h. people — GALB 149:10
h. man is not — STEV 380:7
lean and h. look — SHAK 354:4
hunt h., and vote — BYRO 68:9
hunted h. as an elk — RIEL 327:4

hunted (*cont.*):
  h. round the globe PAIN 300:8
hunter from the h.-gatherer MCEW 249:12
hurry marks of h. SALI 340:9
  old man in a h. CHUR 86:3
hurt if blacks get h. SEXW 350:5
  Yes it h. SLOG 369:6
hurting If the policy isn't h. MAJO 256:5
husband My h. and I ELIZ 134:2
  pitied my h. MOWL 281:13
hustings reckless h. pledge SALI 338:5
hyphenated h. Americanism ROOS 332:12
hypocrisy organized h. DISR 120:1
  world safe for h. WOLF 424:1
hypocrite h. and flatterer BLAK 47:3
hypocrites other half h. JEFF 200:9
hypocritical h. cant of humanity FOX 144:9
hysteria thin whine of h. DIDI 118:8

I I am the State LOUI 241:5
  My husband and I ELIZ 134:2
iceberg ill-concealed i. LAWS 229:6
idea as near the central i. EVER 138:2
  good i., but it won't ROGE 329:8
  i. whose time has come ANON 12:6
  invasion by an i. HUGO 191:2
  would be a good i. GAND 151:6
idealism I. is the noble toga HUXL 193:7
idealist i. without illusions KENN 213:10
idealistic only i. nation WILS 423:3
ideals illusionist without i. MACL 251:10
  men without i. CAMU 73:1
ideas business is to kill i. WELL 416:5
  From it our i. are born GENE 152:7
  i. actually took root BORK 52:1
  political i. NAMI 284:1
  resistance of established i. BERL 37:5
  sound and original i. MACM 253:5
  still have the i. CHUR 91:1
ideology anchor of i. ANON 12:2
  country which loves i. RAFF 321:1
ides Beware the i. of March SHAK 353:10
  i. of March are come SHAK 354:11
idiot i. who praises GILB 156:11
  Suppose you were an i. TWAI 402:10
idiots fatuity of i. SMIT 372:5
idle add the vivacity of an i. man BAGE 24:16
  are not i. BUTT 68:6
idleness I. and pride FRAN 145:7
  Ignorance, Squalor and I. BEVE 40:3
idolatry organization of i. SHAW 361:4
if I. you can keep your head KIPL 219:10
ifs Talk'st thou to me of 'i.' SHAK 359:6
ignoble i. ease ROOS 332:1
ignorance Disease, I., Squalor BEVE 40:3
  Don't die of i. OFFI 295:3
  I. is an evil weed BEVE 40:1
  I. is strength ORWE 297:3
  I. of the law SELD 349:1
  sincere i. KING 217:12

ignorant Asking the i. ZOBE 428:5
  i. and free JEFF 199:15
  judgements of the i. BURK 65:5
  right of the i. man CARL 74:6
Ike I like I. SLOG 367:6
  Poor I. TRUM 401:5
ill ill-clad, i.-nourished ROOS 330:11
  I. fares the land GOLD 161:3
  i.-trained spaniel CRAN 104:3
  one-third of a nation i.-housed ROOS 330:11
  vain, i.-natured DEFO 112:10
  warn you not to fall i. KINN 218:10
illegal i. we do immediately KISS 221:8
  it is not i. NIXO 291:6
  Nothing is i. if YOUN 427:6
illegally accomplishes great things i. BALZ 28:12
illegitimate i. parents JOSE 207:7
illness i. should attend SHAK 357:1
ills i. of democracy SMIT 371:5
illusion one i.—France KEYN 214:8
illusionist i. without ideals MACL 251:10
illusions human i. LYND 244:2
  idealist without i. KENN 213:10
image Political i. MOND 275:8
  spelling the word i. PEYT 310:1
imagination i. cold and barren BURK 61:17
  i. for his facts SHER 363:3
  nothing but his i. SHAW 360:13
  Wanting i. DISR 123:2
immaturity expression of human i. BRIT 55:9
immobility i. of British institutions ASQU 16:6
immoral good and i. CHUR 86:11
impartial decline utterly to be i. CHUR 87:3
impeachment articles of i. ANON 9:8
  not grounds for i. DOWD 126:5
impediments i.—in common times BAGE 22:8
imperative categorical i. KANT 209:6
imperfect i. man JEFF 199:6
imperial our great I. family ELIZ 134:1
imperialism I. is the monopoly stage LENI 230:8
  wild-cat I. ROSE 333:7
imperialisms prey of rival i. KENY 214:9
imperialist i. system MAND 258:4
imperialists make the i. dance KHRU 216:8
imperially Learn to think I. CHAM 79:7
imperium I. et Libertas DISR 121:19
implacable i. in hate DRYD 127:5
importance taking decisions of i. PARK 304:8
important being less i. MONT 276:10
  no longer i. enough MCCO 248:7
importunate no less i. MONT 276:10
impossible i. to be silent BURK 65:2
  i. to carry the heavy burden EDWA 130:5
impostors treat those two i. KIPL 219:10
imprisoned taken or i. MAGN 255:7
improvement schemes of political i. JOHN 204:10
improvements no great i. MILL 269:3
impulses i. of populations SALI 341:5
  man's noblest i. KENN 211:5
impunity provokes me with i. MOTT 281:5
inactivity genius for i. LIPP 237:3

evacuation of I.	GRIF 166:8
God save I.	LAST 226:7
God save I.	SULL 383:6
have a united I.	DE V 116:2
how's poor ould I.	SONG 376:2
inhabiting island of I.	O'BR 293:1
I. and England seemed like lovers	TREV 398:2
I. bound to England	PARN 305:2
I., Ireland!	GLAD 158:2
I., Ireland, Ireland	GLAD 159:6
I. is mentioned	SMIT 372:5
I. is not a geographical	PARN 304:11
I., long a province	DAVI 111:1
I.'s battle	CONN 101:6
I.'s opportunity	PROV 318:9
I. unfree shall never be at peace	PEAR 306:7
I. we dreamed of	DE V 116:3
I. where people are not	MCAL 244:9
jurisdiction in I.	ADAM 2:7
knew I. too little	MACA 245:2
many parties in I.	PEEL 308:5
my love for I.	CARS 75:14
now handling I.	WEST 416:9
Out of I. have we come	YEAT 426:8
pacify I.	GLAD 158:8
parties in Northern I.	MITC 274:10
people of I.	TONE 396:13
Possession of I.	SALI 341:2
Romantic I.'s dead and gone	YEAT 426:10
split I.	BRUG 59:3
what I have got for I.	COLL 99:6
worst enemy I. ever had	MITC 271:13
would had been for I.	LAST 228:8
Irish answer to the I. Question	SELL 349:10
for an I. purpose	DAVI 111:5
I. are ashamed	MARV 262:2
I. Citizen Army	CONN 101:7
I. descent	ROBI 328:8
I. Question	DISR 119:7
of the I. Brigade	DAVI 110:8
serve the I. people	ROBI 328:11
what the I. people wanted	DE V 115:10
Irishman common name of I.	TONE 396:13
I'm an I.	HEWI 183:4
I. has no sense of	PEEL 308:8
I.'s heart	SHAW 360:13
Irishmen appeal to all I.	GEOR 153:6
I. in her Parliament	BALF 27:10
Irishry indomitable I.	YEAT 426:11
iron become an i. cage	WEBE 412:11
he's got i. teeth	GROM 167:6
i.-armed soldier	SONG 376:4
i. curtain	CHUR 89:12
i. curtain	CRIL 105:2
i. has entered into his soul	LLOY 240:1
i. lady	ANON 10:3
I. Lady	THAT 390:6
through blood and i.	BISM 44:5
wood painted to look like i.	BISM 44:3
irrational i. exuberance	GREE 166:1
irrationality i. of the world	WEBE 413:3

is what the meaning of 'i.' is	CLIN 97:10
Islam I. has established them	KHOM 216:2
island king of my own little i.	SMAL 369:10
never make this i. all her own	WALL 408:8
rough i.-story	TENN 389:12
isle sceptered i.	SHAK 358:6
isms All the i. are wasms	ANON 8:2
isolated Continent i.	BROC 55:10
splendidly i.	FOST 143:8
isolation Splendid i.	NEWS 288:5
isolationist find an i.	RUSK 335:7
Israel glory is departed from I.	BIBL 41:5
prophet in I.	BIBL 41:7
Italians I. have very much	SALI 340:8
Italy in I. for thirty years	WELL 414:7
I. is a geographical expression	METT 268:3
itch poor i. of your opinion	SHAK 350:7
itself contained nothing but i.	ADAM 2:11
jack J. became a gentleman	SHAK 359:4
jails not enough j.	HUMP 191:11
jam j. to-morrow	CARR 75:11
j. we thought was for tomorrow	BENN 34:3
James King J. stay behind	SONG 375:3
Jameson RAID BY DR J.	KRUG 223:2
Janvier J. and Février	NICH 286:6
Japan J.'s advantage	HIRO 184:3
jaw j.-jaw is always better	CHUR 90:16
jealousy neighbourly j.	SALI 338:10
jeers flouts and j.	DISR 121:11
jelly nail currant j.	ROOS 332:8
jellybeans way of eating j.	REAG 323:4
Jena lost the battle of J.	ANON 9:2
jeopardy twice put in j.	CONS 102:6
Jerusalem was J. builded here	BLAK 47:4
jests to his memory for his j.	SHER 363:3
Jesus bon Sansculotte J.	DESM 115:8
thinks he is J. Christ	CLEM 96:4
Jew especially a J.	MALA 256:13
J. and the language	CELA 79:3
J. of Tarsus	BIBL 41:26
old J.! That is the man	BISM 44:4
jewel j. in the crown	GRAY 165:1
Jewish murderers of J. children	WIES 419:4
national home for the J. people	BALF 28:1
total solution of J. question	GOER 160:6
Jews last J. to die	MEIR 265:7
When Hitler attacked the J.	NIEM 289:5
jingo Be a little J. if you can	CHAM 79:5
by j. if we do	SONG 377:3
job finish the j.	CHUR 88:11
hold down his j.	NICO 289:7
j. creation scheme	HENN 180:3
MP is the sort of j.	ABBO 1:1
neighbour loses his j.	TRUM 401:9
politician who has lost his j.	MENC 267:2
jobbing j., speculating	JEFF 198:13
jobs create j.	TSVA 402:1
jog as a man *might j. on with*	DURH 129:3
jogging alternative to j.	FITT 141:3

John more MPs called J. — JOWE 208:1
joint time is out of j. — SHAK 351:10
joints know the j. — BUTL 68:4
jokes civil servant doesn't make j. — IONE 195:7
   Civil Service doesn't do j. — O'LE 294:6
   don't know about j. — ROGE 329:7
Josephine Not tonight, J. — NAPO 285:3
Joshua like J. of old — FRAN 146:3
journalism but why j. — BALF 28:4
   cancer of bent and twisted j. — AITK 6:2
journalist thank God! the British j. — WOLF 423:9
journalists j. dabbling — MCGR 250:2
   tell lies to j. — KRAU 223:1
journey j. *really* necessary — OFFI 295:5
   j. to a foreign land — HAGU 168:2
   long j. to take — LAST 226:11
   now begin the j. — REAG 323:14
joy politics of j. — HUMP 192:2
   Strength through j. — SLOG 367:9
Judas J. was paid — POWE 315:7
   that of J. — STAL 378:8
judge j. is a member of the Bar — BOK 48:6
   J. not, that ye be not judged — BIBL 41:19
   j.'s robe — SHAK 357:12
   Justly to j. — BROO 56:6
   old priest, an old j. — CHAM 80:6
judged Judge not, that ye be not j. — BIBL 41:19
   nation is j. — LÉVE 232:3
judgement conclusive j. — GLAD 159:15
   everything except j. — ATTL 18:15
   fit to sit in j. — WILS 422:11
   functioning of a man's j. — SALI 344:10
   j. is a mere lottery — DRYD 128:1
   j. of his peers — MAGN 255:7
   j. was faultless — DISR 123:2
   j. will probably — MANS 259:5
   owes you his j. — BURK 64:10
   people's j. — DRYD 127:9
   weakens the j. most — RETZ 324:10
judges independence of j. — DENN 115:2
   j. can tap — MARS 261:6
   J. must follow their oaths — ZOBE 428:6
judicial j. power — ADAM 4:4
judiciary out-of-control j. — DELA 114:1
jumped We have j. — TRIM 398:11
jumps way the cat j. — THAT 391:10
jungle Law of the J. — KIPL 220:2
junto oligarchical j. — ADAM 3:12
jurisdiction j. in Ireland — ADAM 2:7
   j. in this Realm — BOOK 50:4
just God is j. — JEFF 200:10
   j. and old renown — TENN 390:1
   j. cause reaches its flood-tide — CATT 77:9
   'j.' or 'right' — PLAT 312:9
   may not be a j. peace — IZET 195:11
   Our cause is j. — DICK 118:5
   place for a j. man — THOR 394:2
justice call for j. — MORE 278:6
   J. delayed — PROV 319:1
   J. denied — MILL 270:2
   j. is ever lagging — GLAD 158:11

J. is in one scale — JEFF 200:3
J. is truth — DISR 120:3
j. makes democracy possible — NIEB 289:4
J. should not only be done — HEWA 183:1
let j. be done — ADAM 4:6
Let j. be done — MOTT 281:3
Let j. be done — WATS 411:9
liberty plucks j. — SHAK 357:9
loved j. — LAST 226:12
miracle of social j. — HAYE 176:2
moderation in the pursuit of j. — GOLD 161:8
moral good and of j. — JOHN 202:1
reason, and j. — BURK 62:3
right or j. — MAGN 255:8
think j. requires — MANS 259:5
threat to j. everywhere — KING 217:5
truth, j., and humanity — GLAD 159:5
victors' j. — SHAW 361:11
justifiable not a j. act of war — BELL 32:8
justitia *Fiat j.* — MOTT 281:3
   fiat j., pereat coelum — ADAM 4:6

Kaiser put the kibosh on the K. — SONG 375:4
keener with his k. eye — MARV 262:1
keep If you can k. your head — KIPL 219:10
   intention to k. my counsel — GLAD 159:3
   K. the bastards honest — SLOG 367:8
   k. your England — MUGA 282:5
Kennedy Senator, you're no Jack K. — BENT 36:3
kettle back to the tea-k. — DISR 120:2
   pretty k. of fish — MARY 263:6
key k. of the Union — CLAY 95:8
   possession of the k. — PAIN 300:2
keyholes screaming through the k. — LLOY 239:3
keystone foundation and the k. — WRAX 425:8
   k. which closeth — STRA 382:10
kibosh put the k. on the Kaiser — SONG 375:4
kick Nixon to k. around — NIXO 290:5
   will k. and fling — HALI 170:4
kicked k. up stairs — HALI 171:4
   no body to be k. — THUR 394:9
kicking flattering, kissing and k. — TRUM 401:2
kid comeback k. — CLIN 97:6
kids how many k. did you kill — SLOG 367:2
kill able to k. — RUMS 334:10
   Athenians will k. thee — PHOC 310:10
   how many kids did you k. — SLOG 367:2
   k. all the lawyers — SHAK 352:18
   k. animals and stick in stamps — NICO 288:14
   k. the world — MILL 270:5
   prepared to k. one another — SHAW 360:15
   wants to k. people — WRIG 425:4
   won't k. me — COLL 99:9
   you must k. him — EMER 135:3
killed don't mind your being k. — KITC 222:3
   Go to Spain and get k. — POLL 313:6
   I have k. my mother — ASQU 16:12
   k. in the war — POWE 315:13
   Suppose Hitler had been k. — SCHL 347:9
killers serial k. — LIVI 237:12

killing k. for Ireland HUME 191:9
  K. no murder SEXB 350:3
kills k. more people LIVI 238:3
kind K. hearts are more than coronets
    TENN 389:5

king As to the K. CHAR 81:6
  authority forgets a dying k. TENN 389:13
  authority of a K. STRA 382:10
  brightly as a k. SHAK 358:3
  British k. MARK 260:8
  Cotton is K. CHRI 85:8
  despised and dying k. SHEL 362:8
  divinity doth hedge a k. SHAK 352:3
  duty is the k.'s SHAK 352:12
  fight for its K. and Country GRAH 163:6
  five kings did a k. to death THOM 393:2
  God bless the K. BYRO 68:8
  God save our gracious k. SONG 375:7
  God save the k. SONG 375:7
  great and mighty k. EPIT 136:3
  greater than the K. PITT 311:10
  have served the K. WOLS 424:5
  If we beat the K. MANC 257:11
  K. and country need you PROV 320:2
  K. asks you to form a Government ATTL 18:3
  k. can do no wrong BLAC 45:7
  K. delighteth to honour BIBL 41:9
  K. enjoys his own again PARK 304:2
  k. is a thing men have made SELD 349:2
  k. is but a man SHAK 352:10
  k. is truly *parens patriae* JAME 197:3
  k. may make a nobleman BURK 65:4
  k. never dies BLAC 45:5
  K., observing with judicious TRAP 397:5
  K. of England cannot enter PITT 311:7
  K. of England's eyes LAST 227:6
  K. of Great Britain REED 324:3
  k. of my own little island SMAL 369:10
  K. over the Water ANON 10:9
  K. refused a lesser sacrifice MARY 263:8
  k. reigns THIE 393:1
  K.'s life moving peacefully DAWS 111:6
  K.'s Moll Reno'd NEWS 288:1
  k.'s name SHAK 358:9
  K. to have things done as cheap PEPY 308:17
  K. to Oxford sent BROW 58:6
  K. will get away with it CHAN 80:7
  last K. of England EDWA 130:3
  lay on the k. SHAK 352:13
  leave the K. EPIT 137:2
  leave without the k. ELIZ 134:9
  lessened my esteem of a k. PEPY 308:16
  loses the k. in the tyrant MAYH 264:8
  material for a constitutional k. BAGE 23:5
  Mrs Simpson's pinched our k. ANON 9:4
  My dead k. JOYC 208:2
  my life to make you K. CHAR 82:1
  mystery of the k.'s power JAME 197:4
  my true k. MACA 247:6
  neck of the last k. DIDE 118:7
  No bishop, no K. JAME 197:1

Northcliffe has sent for the K. ANON 9:7
not offended the k. LAST 228:2
not so much a k. SELL 349:7
O k., establish the decree BIBL 41:16
sang a k. out of three kingdoms WHAR 417:3
self-dedication of the King BLUN 48:1
still am I k. of those SHAK 358:13
stomach of a k. ELIZ 132:9
strike at a k. EMER 135:3
What is a K. PRIO 316:12
What must the k. do SHAK 358:12
whatsoever K. shall reign SONG 376:3
when thy k. is a child BIBL 41:13
you must not be a k. CHAR 81:4
your K. and your Country SONG 376:8
zeal I served my k. SHAK 353:7
kingdom but to mock the k. PYM 317:8
  k. against kingdom BIBL 41:24
  voice of the k. SWIF 384:4
kingdoms out of three k. WHAR 417:3
kingfish call me the K. LONG 240:13
kingly K. conclaves stern SHEL 362:5
kings captains and the k. KIPL 220:6
  change k. with us SARS 346:6
  death of k. SHAK 358:10
  dominion of k. changed PRIC 316:11
  end of k. DEFO 113:2
  five K. left FARO 139:7
  keep even k. in awe D'AV 110:1
  k. and parliaments FRAN 145:7
  k. are not only God's lieutenants JAME 197:2
  K. will be tyrants BURK 63:4
  last of the k. strangled MESL 268:2
  laws or k. JOHN 204:5
  laws or k. can cause GOLD 161:7
  politeness of k. LOUI 242:2
  puller down of k. SHAK 353:2
  ruin k. DRYD 127:2
  Through talk, we tamed k. BENN 34:7
  walk with K. KIPL 220:1
  War is the trade of k. DRYD 127:14
Kinnock If K. wins NEWS 287:9
kinship crimson thread of k. PARK 304:3
kiss k. my ass in Macy's window JOHN 203:13
  k. of death SMIT 371:4
  wanting to k. me MACD 249:9
kitchen get out of the k. PROV 318:13
  send me to eat in the k. HUGH 190:7
Kitchener K. is a great poster ASQU 16:11
kitten reptilian k.-eater ANON 8:8
Klondike beer of a man in K. CHES 83:11
knave epithet for a k. MACA 245:9
  foolish prating k. SHAK 351:13
  k. is not punished HALI 171:1
  man must be supposed a k. HUME 191:8
  To feed the titled k. BURN 65:11
knavery K. seems to be GEOR 153:3
knaves k. in place DEFO 112:9
knee down on one k. CALL 71:7
knees fell upon their own k. EVAR 138:1
  live on your k. IBAR 194:3

lass It came with a l.   JAME 197:6
last Free at l.   EPIT 136:1
  l. day of an era past   YELT 427:3
  l. great Englishman   TENN 389:7
  l. King of England   EDWA 130:3
  l. person who has sat on him   HAIG 168:3
  l. thing I shall do   LAST 226:4
  l. while they last   DE G 113:11
  without considering the l.   CLAU 95:1
  won the l. war   ROOS 330:1
lasts Lets hope it l.   BONA 49:6
late offering even that too l.   NEVI 286:3
later I'll let you know l.   ATTL 18:3
Latin L. as an honour   CHUR 91:8
laugh too badly hurt to l.   LINC 235:5
laughable very l. things   JOHN 204:10
laughed honest man is l. at   HALI 171:1
  l. at in the second   NAPO 284:7
laurels l. to paeans   CICE 93:4
  l. torn   SMOL 373:1
  Northern l.   LEE 230:1
lavender cured with l. water   HEGE 179:5
law against the l. for generals   TRUM 401:14
  Back the L. Lords   ANON 10:5
  books of l.   JOHN 203:1
  chief l.   CICE 93:3
  clutches of the l.   SALI 341:9
  Common L. of England   HERB 181:11
  Custom, that unwritten l.   D'AV 110:1
  dead-level of l. and order   TAWN 386:7
  economic l.   MARX 262:8
  enforce a l.   HUMP 191:11
  first is l.   DRYD 127:11
  government above the l.   SCAR 347:4
  had people not defied the l.   SCAR 347:1
  Ignorance of the l.   SELD 349:1
  judgement of the l.   JACK 196:12
  keystone of the rule of l.   DENN 115:2
  l. at the end   WHAL 417:2
  l. enforcement   KENN 213:15
  l. floats in a sea of ethics   WARR 410:10
  l. is above you   DENN 115:1
  l. is at a disadvantage   SCAR 347:7
  L. is boldly   BURR 66:1
  l. is contrary to liberty   BENT 35:10
  l. is established   SIDN 364:10
  L.: It has honoured us   WEBS 413:13
  L. of the Jungle   KIPL 220:2
  l.'s delay   SHAK 351:11
  lesser breeds without the L.   KIPL 220:8
  liberty under the l.   HAIL 168:6
  majestic equality of the l.   FRAN 145:3
  make a scarecrow of the l.   SHAK 357:10
  Necessity hath no l.   CROM 106:4
  not a l. at all   ROBE 328:1
  of a common l.   JEFF 198:14
  People crushed by l.   BURK 64:11
  respect for the l.   CHUR 92:12
  Right . . . is the child of l.   BENT 35:7
  this is the royal l.   CORO 104:1
  those by l. protected   BURN 65:9

  where no l. is   BIBL 42:1
lawful by 'l. authority'   MACD 249:7
lawfully acting l.   CLIN 97:12
lawn Get your tanks off my l.   WILS 421:12
  scooters off my l.   CLAR 94:10
laws are the l. of nature   SHAW 360:4
  arranges l.   MACH 250:5
  Bad l.   BURK 64:13
  bad or obnoxious l.   GRAN 164:5
  care who should make the l.   FLET 141:8
  country's planted thick with l.   BOLT 49:5
  dominion of l.   PRIC 316:11
  do with the l.   HORS 188:9
  everything the l. permit   MONT 277:9
  folly of human l.   SMIT 370:8
  government of l., and not of men   ADAM 3:6
  Government of l. and not of men   FORD 143:1
  If l. are needed   KHOM 216:2
  If the l. could speak   HALI 170:8
  l. and learning   MANN 259:3
  L. are generally found to be nets   SHEN 362:12
  L. are like cobwebs   SWIF 384:5
  l. are like spider's webs   ANAC 7:7
  L. are silent   CICE 93:9
  l. are their enemies   BURK 64:11
  L. grind the poor   GOLD 161:6
  L., like houses   BURK 64:4
  l. of God will be suspended   SHAW 360:9
  l. of the land   CHAR 81:6
  l. or kings   JOHN 204:5
  l. or kings can cause   GOLD 161:7
  L. were made to be broken   NORT 291:12
  l. which cannot be enforced   EINS 131:1
  l. which I was sworn   LINC 235:2
  more numerous the l.   TACI 385:5
  neither l. made   JOHN 201:9
  new code of l.   ADAM 2:1
  not a government of l.   WEBS 413:10
  part of the l. of England   HALE 169:4
  politics and our l.   DEWA 116:11
  rather than obey the l.   TOCQ 395:4
  taint pure l.   AESC 5:5
  their l. approve   DRYD 127:13
  trample bad l.   PHIL 310:7
  world abounds with l.   ANON 10:12
lawyer l. tells me I may   BURK 62:3
  middle-aged l.   SMIT 371:7
  to a corporate l.   COMM 100:2
lawyers complain of the l.   HALI 170:8
  kill all the l.   SHAK 352:18
  l. should do business   JEFF 200:5
Lazarus L. with a triple bypass   HOWA 189:5
lazy l., long, lascivious   DEFO 112:12
LBJ All the way with L.   SLOG 366:2
  Hey, L., how many kids   SLOG 367:2
lead cold l. and steel   O'DO 294:2
  easy to l.   BROU 57:2
  evening l.   CHUR 91:4
  l. a war with lies   ZAPA 428:1
leadable is the Conservative Party l.   HESE 182:12
leader fanatic is a great l.   BROU 57:3

leader (*cont.*):
  great and wonderful l.   LLOY 239:11
  I am their l.   LEDR 229:10
  l. of the Labour party   KINN 219:1
  no longer a political l.   BARU 30:2
  no Tory L. has spoken   SALI 340:12
  one people, one l.   SLOG 366:14
  right l. for the Labour Party   BEVA 39:2
  test of a l.   LIPP 237:4
  with a different l.   SHOR 364:6
leaders l. and their wives   HEAD 177:1
  l. and the people   MEGU 265:6
  l. Labour loves   HARR 174:3
  l. of a revolution   CONR 101:10
  party l. have   WALL 408:5
leadership L. is not about being nice   KEAT 210:7
  L. means making   CHRÉ 85:4
  successful l.   REAG 323:13
leaking L. is what you do   CALL 70:5
lean l. and hungry look   SHAK 354:4
  l. as much to the contrary   HALI 169:6
  l. on one another   BURK 64:4
  when you l. upon it   SALI 344:8
leap l. into the ocean   HUME 191:6
  l. to a hasty opinion   BAGE 25:1
learn l. men from books   DISR 123:14
  People must l. to hate   MAND 258:7
learned I've l.   BLAI 46:15
  l. anything from history   HEGE 179:6
learners slow l.   MALL 257:7
learning loyal body wanted l.   TRAP 397:5
  of liberty, and of l.   DISR 121:8
learnt They have l. nothing   TALL 385:10
least l. government was the best   FEIN 140:2
  what we l. expected   DISR 122:22
leave dying to l.   MITC 274:11
  l. the country   NEWS 287:9
  l. things alone you leave them   CHES 83:5
  l. without the King   ELIZ 134:9
  Once I l.   BALD 27:4
leaving like the l. it   SHAK 356:12
left l. out would be dangerous   MELB 266:1
  l.-wing, like humanity   DEBR 111:10
  No L.   MITC 274:7
  nothing l. for me   LEE 230:5
leg nor breaks my l.   JEFF 200:13
legacy l. from a rich relative   SMIT 371:10
legality any taint of l.   KNOX 222:6
legally accomplishing small things l.   BALZ 28:12
legend true l.   STAL 378:8
  Your l. ever will   JOHN 202:3
legions give me back my l.   AUGU 19:6
legislation foundation of morals and l.   BENT 35:9
legislative l. and executive   ADAM 4:4
  l. power   GIBB 155:4
  l. power   MONT 277:12
legislator people is the true l.   BURK 64:5
legislators idea of hereditary l.   PAIN 301:7
legislature no l. can manufacture   BAGE 22:1
  safe while the l. is in session   ANON 11:4
  work for a L.   ELLI 134:11

legitimate l. self-interest   BAST 30:3
legs dog's walking on his hinder l.   JOHN 204:9
  Four l. good   ORWE 296:7
  not for your bad l.   ELIZ 133:2
  old men who have good l.   SALI 344:13
  vast and trunkless l.   SHEL 362:4
  Walk under his huge l.   SHAK 354:2
Leicester Here lies the Earl of L.   EPIT 136:4
leisure conspicuous l.   VEBL 405:4
  increased l.   DISR 121:6
lend called L.-Lease   CHUR 89:8
  l. me your ears   SHAK 355:7
lenses zoom l.   ULLR 403:4
leper Parliamentary l.   WILS 421:8
lesser l. breeds   KIPL 220:8
lesson no end of a l.   KIPL 220:3
lessons l. to be drawn   ELIZ 134:5
lest L. we forget   KIPL 220:6
let L. freedom reign   BUSH 67:6
  L. freedom reign   MAND 258:5
  L. my people go   BIBL 41:2
  L. Reagan be Reagan   SLOG 367:13
  l. the country down   CALL 71:2
letter huge wordy l.   JUVE 209:3
letters No arts; no l.   HOBB 185:6
  writing inane l.   SALI 341:4
level Those who attempt to l.   BURK 62:17
levellers l. wish to level *down*   JOHN 204:8
levelling cannot bear l. *up*   JOHN 204:8
Leviathan L., called a commonwealth   HOBB 185:1
lex *Salus populi suprema l.*   SELD 349:3
  suprema est l.   CICE 93:3
liar l. should be outlawed   HALI 169:9
  proved l.   HAIL 168:5
liars L. ought to have good memories   SIDN 364:7
liberal between l. concessions   BOOK 50:6
  either a little L.   GILB 156:7
  first l. leader   STEE 379:1
  harm to the l. cause   HAYE 176:4
  ineffectual l.   FRAY 147:1
  l. is a conservative   WOLF 424:2
  L. is a man   ROOS 330:14
  l. who has been mugged   PROV 318:5
  particular L. Party   HERB 181:9
liberals Attacking the L.   PATT 306:2
liberation 'L.' in its title   LEVI 233:1
  l. of Europe   EISE 131:4
  l. of the human mind   GOLD 161:2
libertarian airy-fairy, l.   BLUN 47:10
libertas *Imperium et L.*   DISR 121:19
liberté *L.! Égalité*   SLOG 367:14
liberties give up their l.   BURK 64:17
  L. . . . . depend on the silence   HOBB 185:8
  not to have l.   PYM 317:8
liberty ardour for l.   PRIC 316:11
  be light! said L.   SHEL 362:2
  bulwark of continuing l.   ROOS 330:12
  by reason of the l.   MONT 277:15
  conceived in all l.   LINC 235:8
  contend for their l.   HALI 170:14
  cost of l.   DU B 128:4

life (*cont.*):
remaining years of l.   MAND 258:3
right to a dignified l.   JOHN 202:1
strenuous l.   ROOS 332:1
surrender of l.   CALH 70:3
voyage of their l.   SHAK 356:5
Who owns my life   RODR 329:2
Woolworth l. hereafter   NICO 286:9
your longer l.   ELIZ 133:3
light Give me a l.   HASK 174:6
Let there be l.   SHEL 362:2
l. has gone out of our lives   NEHR 285:7
l. on the hill   CHIF 84:1
more l. you pour   HOLM 187:5
place of l.   DISR 121:8
Put out the l.   LAST 227:11
switch peace on like a l.   MOWL 281:12
thousand points of l.   BUSH 66:8
lightest l. things swim at the top   HALI 170:6
lighthouse great l.   JENK 201:5
lightly esteem too l.   PAIN 300:12
lightning loosed the fateful l. HOWE 190:4
snatched the l.   TURG 402:5
writing history with l.   WILS 422:10
lights dimming of the l.   NICO 286:10
glare of l.   CHRÉ 85:5
turn out the l.   NEWS 287:9
like I L. Ike   SLOG 367:3
l. everyone else   DE G 113:15
l., or at least tolerate   TREV 397:9
l. this sort of thing   LINC 236:10
whether we l. it or not   THOM 393:8
liked wants to be l.   ANON 10:1
limb on every airth a l.   MONT 278:2
limpet l.-like Prime Ministers JENK 201:4
miserable l.   CRAN 104:4
Lincoln fate of Abraham L.   GRIG 167:2
I am a Ford, not a L.   FORD 142:11
L.'s conscience   BUSH 67:1
line l. will be drawn   AHER 6:1
met by the colour l.   DOUG 126:3
no Party l.   DJIL 124:13
problem of the colour l.   DU B 128:5
lines drawing l. upon maps   SALI 342:1
lining There's a silver l.   SONG 376:6
link destroyed the last l.   PARN 305:2
lion l. to frighten the wolves MACH 250:11
nation that had l.'s heart   CHUR 90:17
well-bred l.   VOLT 407:11
lions L. led by donkeys   PROV 319:3
lips Europe on the l. of politicians   BISM 44:1
my l. are not yet unsealed   BALD 26:12
My l. are sealed   MISQ 273:7
Read my l.   BUSH 66:9
Watch my l.   BLUN 47:8
liquid Thames is l. history   BURN 65:7
liquidation preside over the l. CHUR 88:14
list in my hand a l.   MCCA 248:3
There is no l.   STRA 382:12
listen don't l. to people   LAW 228:13
politicians have had to l.   FITT 141:4

listened have got to be l. to   KINN 219:3
I've l.   BLAI 46:15
literature L.'s always a good card to play
                                    BENN 35:5
Russian l. saved   RATU 322:6
little l. creep through   SHEN 362:12
L. Engine that Could   EDWA 130:7
Little man, l. man   ELIZ 133:6
l. people pay taxes   HELM 179:10
l. rich girl   ABBO 1:2
l. woman who wrote   LINC 236:1
obstinate l. man   THOM 393:4
offering Germany too l.   NEVI 286:3
So l. done   LAST 227:13
liturgy Popish l.   PITT 311:1
live enable its citizens to l. WEIL 414:3
he isn't fit to l.   KING 217:6
He shall not l.   SHAK 356:3
l. by positive goals   BERL 37:1
l. on your knees   IBAR 194:3
l. together as brothers   KING 217:9
nations how to l.   MILT 271:5
Sacco's name will l.   VANZ 404:8
sometimes l. apart   SAKI 337:3
would you l. for ever   FRED 147:4
lived better if he had never l. CHUR 90:3
lively l. Oracles of God   CORO 104:3
lives Careless talk costs l.   OFFI 295:1
evil that men do l.   SHAK 355:7
liveth name l. for evermore   EPIT 137:5
livid one l. smile   WALP 409:6
living against a l. one   TEMP 389:2
better l. conditions   BARU 30:1
fight for the l.   JONE 206:2
go on l. even after death   FRAN 145:5
l. to some purpose   PAIN 302:6
those who are l.   BURK 63:6
way of l. with the Negro   BALD 26:1
world does not owe us a l.   PHIL 310:4
Lloyd George L. knew my father SONG 376:7
L. would have a better   GRIG 167:2
loaf feel as a l. might   GLAD 159:2
lobby Orange in the L.   SALI 343:8
local enter l. politics   PARK 304:9
little l. difficulties   MACM 253:2
l. thing called Christianity   HARD 173:2
politics is l.   O'NE 295:10
locally act l.   SLOG 368:10
log Give me a l. hut   GARF 151:9
L.-cabin to White House   THAY 392:13
London City of L. remains   CHAM 79:6
L. is a modern Babylon   DISR 123:10
L. is to Paddington   CANN 73:9
lungs of L.   PITT 311:16
Mayor for L.   WATE 411:8
never the see L.   LIVI 237:9
Londoners rights of L.   LIVI 238:1
long continue for five years too l.   BIFF 42:7
has a l. way to come   THAT 392:12
How l. a time   SHAK 358:5
In the l. run   KEYN 215:11

it hath very l. arms HALI 170:9
night of the l. knives HITL 184:6
week is a l. time in politics WILS 421:9
longer devolution takes l. BAIN 25:6
your l. life ELIZ 133:3
longing cast a l. eye JEFF 198:12
look I l. at the senators HALE 169:3
l. at the record IVIN 195:9
l. forward to the trip STIN 381:8
l. the East End in the face ELIZ 134:8
L. to your Moat HALI 171:3
looked If you l. away, you knew SERE 350:1
looking no use l. beyond CHAM 79:4
looks l. like a duck REUT 325:3
looney L. Tunes, and squalid criminals
REAG 323:9
loose She is a l. cannon PIEN 311:1
loot To l. somebody SALI 344:11
lord Admit l. SHAF 350:6
coming of the L. HOWE 190:4
Praise the L. FORG 143:3
we battle for the L. ROOS 332:11
lords House of L. STOC 381:10
justification of the L. CAMP 72:6
l. who lay ye low SHEL 362:6
l. whose parents were DEFO 112:13
new unhappy l. CHES 83:10
reform the House of L. DANG 109:3
wit among L. JOHN 204:7
lordships good enough for their l. ANON 12:9
lose Better l. the election STEV 380:4
is to l. it ORWE 298:1
l. her as a friend GLAD 159:16
nothing to l. MARX 263:4
nothing to l. but our aitches ORWE 297:14
not to l. wars CHUR 90:2
on the right side and lose GALB 150:9
we don't want to l. you SONG 376:8
loser It is a l. politically NIXO 291:3
losing l. one pleased Cato LUCA 243:1
loss l. of innocence HOWA 189:6
l. of power RUSK 335:8
lost All is l. save honour MISQ 272:1
always l. it SMIT 371:11
and we are l. PYRR 320:3
Britain has l. an empire ACHE 1:7
France has not l. the war DE G 113:3
friend in power is a friend l. ADAM 2:10
Next to a battle l. WELL 415:14
OK. We l. MAJO 256:9
Vietnam was l. in MCLU 252:3
Lothian West L. DALY 108:9
West-L. DALY 109:1
lottery genetic l. comes up with PIML 311:3
judgement is a mere l. DRYD 128:1
l. of life RHOD 325:7
louder l. he talked of his honour EMER 135:2
lousy L. but loyal SLOG 368:1
lout l.'s game WEST 416:7
love all did l. him once SHAK 355:11
earth could never living l. EPIT 136:4

Gratitude, like l. ALSO 7:1
greater l. hath no man THOR 394:6
how I l. my country LAST 227:10
I must l. the dog GIBB 156:2
l. him most BRAG 53:6
l. men too little BURK 63:8
l. of freedom GLAD 158:12
l. of the people BURK 62:9
l. one another or die AUDE 19:3
l. that asks no question SPRI 378:2
L. the Beloved Republic FORS 143:5
l. those who love you VOLT 407:10
L. thyself last SHAK 353:6
Make l. not war SLOG 368:2
man, That l. my friend SHAK 355:15
my l. for Ireland CARS 75:14
pangs of disprized l. SHAK 351:11
party I l. LIVI 238:1
search for l. WAŁĘ 408:1
support of the woman I l. EDWA 130:5
You can only l. one war GELL 152:6
loved come to Washington to be l. GRAM 163:8
feared than l. MACH 250:9
l. Caesar less SHAK 355:5
l. the suffering many BENT 35:11
lovers same stuff as l.' oaths SALI 344:3
loves reigned with your l. ELIZ 133:4
low dost thou lie so l. SHAK 355:3
l. road to the highest MCCA 248:1
Malice is of a l. stature HALI 170:9
lower call the L. House DISR 122:4
l. classes had such white CURZ 108:4
While there is a l. class DEBS 112:1
lowliness l. is young ambition's SHAK 354:7
loyal Lousy but l. SLOG 368:1
l. to his own career DALT 108:8
loyalties l. which centre upon number one
CHUR 91:13
tragic conflict of l. HOWE 190:3
loyalty constitute l. BOSW 52:3
I want l. JOHN 203:13
learned body wanted l. TRAP 397:5
L. is a fine quality KINN 218:8
L. the Tory's secret weapon KILM 217:2
Lucifer falls like L. SHAK 353:5
lucky just the l. country HAWK 175:5
Luddite That's L. HURD 192:9
Luger packing a L. WILS 421:2
luggage flamboyant labels on empty l. BEVA 39:4
lunatic l. fringe ROOS 333:1
lunatics lunatic asylum run by l. LLOY 239:8
lunch as a free l. PROV 319:10
free l. has still to be GREE 166:3
luncheon take soup at l. CURZ 108:3
lungs l. of London PITT 311:16
Lupercal on the L. I thrice SHAK 355:10
lurk dangers to liberty l. BRAN 53:9
lurks l. a politician ARIS 14:9
lustre bright l. of a court CECI 79:1
lute pleasing of a l. SHAK 359:3
luxury Republics end in l. MONT 277:5

lying branch of the art of l.   CORN 103:13

Macaulay as Tom M.   MELB 266:7
mace fool's bauble, the m.   CROM 106:2
mackerel like rotten m.   RAND 322:1
mad half of the nation is m.   SMOL 372:11
  old, m., blind   SHEL 362:8
  We must be m.   POWE 315:4
  Whom the m. would destroy   LEVI 232:9
madam M. I may not call you   ELIZ 133:11
madame misunderstood M.   DE V 116:6
madmen M. in authority   KEYN 215:10
madness M. in great ones   SHAK 351:12
  m. of many   SWIF 384:9
  moment of m.   DAVI 110:5
  no cure for this sort of m.   SMIT 371:10
magic let in daylight upon m.   BAGE 23:3
  tightness of the m. circle   MACL 251:8
magistrate m. corruptible   ROBE 328:2
magna M. Charta is such a fellow   COKE 99:1
magnanimity M. in politics   BURK 62:10
magnet printing, gunpowder, and the m.   BACO 21:10
magnetism personal m.   WEBB 412:6
maiden m. in distress   STEE 379:3
maidens laughter of comely m.   DE V 116:3
maids Old m. biking   ORWE 297:1
mail gets the m. through   KEAT 210:6
maimed M. us at the start   YEAT 426:8
Maine As M. goes   FARL 139:6
  As M. goes   PROV 318:3
majestic m. equality of the law   FRAN 145:3
majesty earth of m.   SHAK 358:6
  no longer His M.'s Ministers   NORT 292:3
majorities parliamentary m.   BONA 49:8
majority always in the m.   KNOX 222:5
  black m. rule   SMIT 372:1
  however safe its m.   BOOK 50:5
  is a m.   PHIL 310:8
  large parliamentary m.   BUTL 67:10
  m. are wrong   DEBS 111:11
  m. in a small part   LYNC 244:1
  m. is always the best repartee   DISR 123:8
  m. never has right   IBSE 194:4
  m. . . . one is enough   DISR 122:18
  makes a m.   JACK 196:6
  makes a m.   PROV 319:6
  opinions of the m.   PEEL 307:11
  silent m.   NIXO 290:9
  slave of the m.   SALI 338:3
  tyrannical m.   BALF 27:9
  untutored m.   HEAD 176:10
  will of the m.   JEFF 199:2
make does not usually m. anything   PHEL 310:2
  M. do and mend   OFFI 295:6
  M. love not war   SLOG 368:2
  six men may m. five men   SALI 341:1
maker to meet my M.   CHUR 90:15
making always in the m.   SALI 342:6
malice M. domestic   SHAK 357:7

  M. is of a low stature   HALI 170:9
  m. toward none   LINC 236:7
malignant part of Randolph that was not m.   WAUG 412:4
malignity m. truly diabolical   BURK 63:17
man best m. among them   CAST 77:1
  century of the common m.   WALL 408:4
  defend as a m.   AYES 20:1
  demolition of a m.   LEVI 232:4
  encompassed but one m.   SHAK 354:3
  every m. against every man   HOBB 185:4
  every m. and nation   LOWE 242:8
  everyone has sat except a m.   CUMM 107:4
  extraordinary m.   JOHN 205:5
  for the sake of the m.   HALI 170:5
  God has more right than m.   JOHN 201:9
  good of m. must be the objective   ARIS 14:10
  happiness of the common m.   BEVE 40:2
  It's that m. again   NEWS 287:13
  led to *perdition* by a m.   WEST 416:10
  make a m. a woman   PEMB 308:12
  m. and a brother   WEDG 413:16
  m. and the hour   YANC 426:3
  m. at the gate of the year   HASK 174:6
  M. being . . . by nature all free   LOCK 240:8
  m. for all seasons   WHIT 419:1
  m. in the street   BALD 26:9
  M. is something to be surpassed   NIET 289:6
  m. is the only animal   JEFF 198:4
  M. is the only creature   ORWE 296:6
  M., proud man   SHAK 358:1
  M.'s laws, not God's   BOLT 49:5
  m.'s the gowd   BURN 65:8
  old Jew! That is the m.   BISM 44:4
  plain, blunt m.   SHAK 355:15
  right m. in the right place   JEFF 200:12
  said, ask a m.   THAT 390:4
  standing by my m.   CLIN 97:1
  This was a m.   SHAK 356:7
manage m. without butter   GOEB 160:3
managed not a free press but a m.   RADC 320:8
management m. of a balance   KISS 221:12
  orderly m. of decline   ARMS 15:7
Manchester committed at M.   PARN 304:12
  school of M.   DISR 124:7
  What M. says today   PROV 319:12
Mandy name is M.   PARR 305:8
manhood ancient customs and its m.   ENNI 135:7
  M. a struggle   DISR 122:9
manifesto m. written by Dr Mori   BENN 34:8
manifestoes in the party m.   ROTH 334:4
mankind has not created m.   TOCQ 396:7
  leave free the energies of m.   BAGE 23:13
  M. always sets itself   MARX 262:4
  M. is on the move   SMUT 373:2
  M. must put an end to war   KENN 212:11
  no history of m.   POPP 314:10
  one disillusion—m.   KEYN 214:8
manner discover by his m.   SMIT 372:7
manners Oh, the m.   CICE 93:7
  Peel has no m.   WELL 415:13

manoeuvre force with a m.   TROT 400:6
manufacture content to m. life   BERN 37:6
  m. the element   SALI 340:14
manufacturing m. the plausible   BALD 27:7
manure natural m.   JEFF 198:6
many fool too m.   THUR 394:8
  makes so m. of them   LINC 236:1
  so much owed by so m. to so few   CHUR 88:4
map Does the m. remind you   TREV 398:2
  Roll up that m.   PITT 312:6
maps drawing lines upon m.   SALI 342:1
marathon Politics is a m.   LIVI 237:10
marble left it m.   AUGU 19:7
march Beware the ides of M.   SHAK 353:10
  boundary of the m. of a nation   PARN 305:3
  do not m. on Moscow   MONT 277:17
  ides of M. are come   SHAK 354:11
  Let us m.   STEV 380:16
  m. as an alternative   FITT 141:3
  m. my troops towards   GRIM 167:4
  m. towards it   CALL 70:8
  Truth is on the m.   ZOLA 428:7
marche *congrès ne m. pas*   LIGN 233:9
marches forced m., battles and death   GARI 151:10
marching m. where it likes   ARNO 15:11
  people m. on   MORR 279:10
  soul is m. on   SONG 376:5
  truth is m. on   HOWE 190:4
marijuana experimented with m.   CLIN 97:5
market common m. is a process   MONN 276:3
  enterprise of the m.   ANON 8:6
  gathered in the m.-place   CAVA 78:2
  m. economy   JOSP 207:8
  m. has no morality   HESE 182:9
marquis there is the noble M.   HEAL 178:1
marriage Christian m.   MARG 260:3
  for a m. than a ministry   BAGE 22:13
married like other m. couples   SAKI 337:8
  time we got m.   CALL 71:7
  unhappily m.   PARK 304:9
Mars attack from M.   SALI 344:1
marshal m.'s baton   LOUI 242:1
martyr soul of a m.   BAGE 24:9
martyrdom crown of m.   WALP 409:5
  torches of m.   JEFF 199:12
martyred shrouded oft our m. dead   SONG 377:1
martyrs battles, m.   WHIT 418:9
Marx Karl M. and Catherine the Great   ATTL 18:9
  M is for M.   CONN 101:3
Marxian M. Socialism   KEYN 215:3
Marxism M. is now a world faith   BENN 34:6
  M. is only an episode   POPP 314:11
  monetarism, like M.   GILM 157:2
  more to Methodism than to M.   PHIL 310:5
Marxist I am not a M.   MARX 262:11
  tried to be a M.   TAYL 387:17
mask had a m. like Castlereagh   SHEL 362:3
masochism spirit of national m.   AGNE 5:10
mass Paris is well worth a m.   HENR 180:7
  two thousand years of m.   HARD 173:4
Massachusetts denied in M.   MILL 270:2

massage to a m. parlour   WILS 420:7
masses huddled m. yearning   LAZA 229:9
  m. against the classes   GLAD 159:5
  Movement of M.   CONN 101:3
master and no M.   ELIZ 133:1
  Death is a m. from Germany   CELA 79:2
  dominion of the m.   HUME 191:6
  I would not be a m.   LINC 234:5
  M. and Servant   CHUR 87:2
  M.-morality   NIET 289:8
  m. of the Party   HEAL 177:11
  slew his m.   BIBL 41:8
masterly m. inactivity   MACK 251:6
masters anything but new m.   HALI 170:14
  educate our m.   LOWE 242:5
  educate our m.   MISQ 274:3
  I have had two m.   BEAV 31:14
  m. of the Channel   NAPO 284:6
  people are the m.   BLAI 46:2
  people are the m.   BURK 64:14
  We are the m.   SHAW 361:10
  We are the m. now   MISQ 274:2
mastership All m. is not alike   RUSK 336:2
mastiff m.? the right hon. Gentleman's poodle   LLOY 238:6
matches have a box of m.   HOME 187:7
  with that stick of m.   MAND 258:11
material elementary m. wants   SALI 339:5
mateship as dearly as m.   ANON 13:4
matter m. out of place   GRAY 165:1
  not fighting does m.   STEP 379:7
maxim just political m.   HUME 191:8
  m. of a free government   ADAM 3:4
mayor if I was elected m.   LIVI 238:2
  M. for London   WATE 411:8
  running for m. of Toytown   SCAR 347:2
  tart who has married the M.   BAXT 30:8
maypole organ and the m.   JORD 207:1
MBEs M. and your knighthoods   KEAT 210:4
McCarthyism M. is Americanism with   MCCA 248:4
McNamara M.'s War   MCNA 254:3
me save thee and m.   OWEN 299:4
mean Happy the golden m.   MASS 264:1
  nothing common did or m.   MARV 262:1
meanest m. of mankind   POPE 314:5
means Increased m.   DISR 121:6
  m. just what I choose   CARR 75:12
  m. of rising   JOHN 204:18
  politics by other m.   CLAU 95:2
meant damned dots m.   CHUR 86:5
  what he m. by that   LOUI 242:3
measles m. of the human race   EINS 131:2
measure Shrunk to this little m.   SHAK 355:3
  ultimate m.   KING 218:1
measures Great public m.   PEEL 308:10
  M. not men   CANN 73:10
  Not men, but m.   BURK 64:3
  weights and m.   NAPO 285:2
meat appointed to buy the m.   SELD 349:2
  flies off the m.   CHUR 88:7

meat (*cont.*):
  teeth are in the real m.   GRIM 167:5
  Upon what m.   SHAK 354:2
meatballs spaghetti and m.   KEMP 211:4
Meath member from M.   BUTT 68:7
mechanical m. arts and merchandise   BACO 21:8
medal m. glitters   CHUR 88:13
meddle I m. not   CROM 105:11
  M. and muddle   DERB 115:6
meddles Minister that m. with art   MELB 266:6
meddling m. government   MACA 247:11
media dealing with the modern m.   MORR 279:9
  m. like an oil painting   INGH 195:5
  not m. driven   PEYT 310:1
medicine rotational m.   MORG 278:10
mediocre Titles distinguish the m.   SHAW 361:6
meek borne his faculties so m.   SHAK 357:2
  m. shall inherit   SMIT 371:9
meet to m. my Maker   CHUR 90:15
meeting loves m. people   LLOY 239:12
méfiez-vous *Taisez-vous!* M.   OFFI 295:8
Mein Kampf all in M.   ROBE 327:7
meliora *Video m.*   OVID 298:11
mellow ability to m.   MARG 260:2
melted centre has always m.   HAIL 168:8
melting M.-Pot where all the races   ZANG 427:8
member responsible for the m.   BUTT 68:7
memoirs write one's m. is to speak ill   PÉTA 309:7
memorable that m. scene   MARV 262:1
memorandum m. is written   ACHE 1:9
memorial whole earth as their m.   PERI 309:4
memories ought to have good m.   SIDN 364:7
memory m. for a politician   MORL 279:7
  my name and m.   LAST 226:6
  mystic chords of m.   LINC 234:13
  nation's collective m.   POWE 316:2
  no force can abolish m.   ROOS 331:6
  to his m. for his jests   SHER 363:3
men 200,000 m.   NAPO 284:15
  all m. would be tyrants   ADAM 2:1
  government of laws, and not of m.   ADAM 3:6
  Great m. are not always   BIBL 41:10
  innocent m., women, and children   JEFF 200:9
  learn m. from books   DISR 123:14
  Measures not m.   CANN 73:10
  m. and nations behave wisely   EBAN 129:7
  m. are created equal   JEFF 198:1
  M. lived like fishes   SIDN 364:8
  m. naturally were born free   MILT 271:9
  m. who will support me   MELB 266:13
  m. with the muck-rakes   ROOS 332:9
  Not m., but measures   BURK 64:3
  State is a relation of m.   WEBE 413:1
  twelve good m.   BROU 57:1
  wealth accumulates, and m. decay   GOLD 161:3
menace m. to be defeated   SCAR 347:4
mend Make do and m.   OFFI 295:6
mental day of m. alienation   RIEL 327:5
  Freedom and slavery are m. states   GAND 151:3
  m. decay   NICO 286:10
Mephistopheles who is the M.   HEAL 177:6

mercenary m. calling   HOUS 189:3
merchandise mechanical arts and m.   BACO 21:8
merchandize m. candidates   STEV 380:14
merchants M. have no country   JEFF 199:14
mercury pick up m. with a fork   LLOY 240:3
mercy crowning m.   CROM 105:2
  m. on my poor country   LAST 227:5
  m. to forgive   DRYD 127:11
  quality of m.   SHAK 358:2
  shut the gates of m.   GRAY 165:5
  so good a grace As m.   SHAK 357:12
  Thy m. on Thy People   KIPL 220:9
merit m. for a bishopric   WEST 416:1
  no damned m. about it   MELB 266:3
  What is m.   PALM 303:5
meritocracy m. of talent   YOUN 427:7
merry always very m.   SELL 349:7
  m. monarch   ROCH 328:13
  never m. world in England   SHAK 352:17
message ask me to take a m.   LAST 227:8
  if there is a m.   PAXM 306:4
messenger m.-boy Presidency   SCHL 347:8
met m. Saddam Hussein   GALL 150:13
Methodism more to M.   PHIL 310:5
metropolis m. of the empire   COBB 98:7
Mexico M., so far from God   DIAZ 117:5
MI5 head of M.   ANON 9:5
  M. is a job creation   HENN 180:3
Micawbers like inverted M.   GUED 167:7
mice as long as it catches m.   DENG 114:8
microphone paid for this m.   REAG 323:2
microscopic m. advantages   SALI 338:8
middle m. of the road   HIGH 183:7
  m.-sized are alone entangled   SHEN 362:12
  m. way is none at all   ADAM 3:7
middle class dregs of the m.   BEAZ 32:5
  m. is in control   ARIS 15:4
  M. was quite prepared   BELL 33:1
  Philistines proper, or m.   ARNO 15:10
  sinking m.   ORWE 297:14
Middlesex acre in M.   MACA 246:5
midnight stroke of the m. hour   NEHR 285:6
might Britons alone use 'M.'   WAUG 412:2
mighty thou art m. yet   SHAK 356:6
militarism M. . . . . is fetish worship   TAWN 386:5
military control of the m.   TRUM 401:12
  disarm a m. capacity   COOK 103:2
  entrust to m. men   CLEM 96:6
  m. fame   SHER 363:9
  m.-industrial complex   EISE 131:10
milk putting m. into babies   CHUR 89:4
mill lie so near the m.   CLEG 96:2
millennium m. is going to present us   DEED 112:5
  new m. approaches   ROBI 328:11
million m. deaths a statistic   STAL 378:9
millionaire m. has just as good a chance   HOPE 188:7
millionaires need more m.   JOSE 207:6
millions I will be m.   EPIT 137:1
  multiplying m.   O'SU 298:8
  What m. died   CAMP 72:7

millstone m. round our necks   DISR 120:5
Milton morals hold Which M. held   WORD 424:9
   mute inglorious M.   GRAY 165:5
mind absence of m.   SEEL 348:9
   battle for the m.   NOON 291:9
   Cast your m. on other days   YEAT 426:11
   [Charles] Sumner's m.   ADAM 2:11
   commonplace m.   HARD 173:5
   depth and compass of his m.   ADAM 4:8
   empires of the m.   CHUR 89:5
   liberation of the human m.   GOLD 161:2
   m. and truth   HEWI 183:2
   m. of the oppressed   BIKO 42:9
   m.'s construction   SHAK 356:12
   prepare the m. of the country   DISR 120:15
   retail mind   LLOY 239:10
mindful M. of the Church's teaching   MARG 260:3
minds great empire and little m.   BURK 62:10
   poison and warp men's m.   BUCH 60:1
miners like m.' coal dust   BOOT 51:4
mineworkers National Union of M.   MACM 253:11
minister As m. of the Crown   PEEL 307:6
   cheer the m.   CANN 74:1
   dead m. weighs very light   TEMP 389:2
   God help the M.   MELB 266:6
   last m. is strangled   NAIR 283:10
   m. going to run   HEND 179:12
   m. of a prince   RETZ 324:9
   M., whoever he at any time   PAIN 301:10
   m. who moves about   CHOI 85:3
   M. whose stubbornness   JENK 201:3
   wisdom of a great m.   JUNI 208:7
   Yes, M.! No, Minister   CROS 107:2
ministerial Pitt's M. greatness   WRAX 425:4
ministers 'bollocks' to m.   WILS 422:6
   group of Cabinet M.   CURZ 108:1
   how much my M. talk   THAT 390:8
   m. are behaving   BRUT 59:5
   M. decide   THAT 391:15
   M. go to baths   SALI 341:8
   M. say   HOGG 186:4
   my actions are my m.'   CHAR 81:9
   no longer His Majesty's M.   NORT 292:3
   To Cabinet M.   SALI 344:9
   warning to all M.   WALP 410:7
   worst possible M.   ATTL 18:12
ministries made many m.   BAGE 22:7
ministry m. of all the talents   ANON 10:15
   more for a marriage than a m.   BAGE 22:13
minnows death for the m.   TAWN 386:8
   Triton of the m.   SHAK 350:9
minorities M. . . . are almost always   SMIT 372:10
   treats its m.   LÉVE 232:3
   We are all m.   EWIN 138:6
minority efficient m.   STEP 379:6
   helpless m.   HEAD 176:10
   m. possess their equal rights   JEFF 199:2
   m. who happen to be a majority   LYNC 244:1
   smug m.   BERT 37:9
minuet constitutional m.   SCAR 347:3
minute in m. particulars   BLAK 47:3

minutes Cabinet m. are studied   KAUF 209:10
   Forty-Five M.   NEWS 287:6
   have the seven m.   COLL 99:7
   He who writes the m.   ANON 9:11
   Seventy m. had passed   BENN 35:3
   you did in two m.   EVER 138:2
miracle m. of social justice   HAYE 176:2
mire Sow returns to her M.   KIPL 219:8
mischief execute any m.   CLAR 93:12
   In every deed of m.   GIBB 155:12
   m., thou art afoot   SHAK 356:2
   no authority from God to do m.   MAYH 264:7
   sown the world with m.   BUCH 60:1
miserable m. limpet   CRAN 104:4
miseries in shallows and in m.   SHAK 356:5
misery m. is a battle gained   WELL 415:14
   m. which it is his duty   LOWE 242:6
   relation of distant m.   GIBB 155:13
   result m.   DICK 117:8
   splendid m.   JEFF 198:11
misfits m., Looney Tunes, and criminals
                           REAG 323:9
misfortunes crimes and m.   VOLT 407:7
   crimes, follies, and m.   GIBB 155:6
misgovernment stupidity and m.   GLAD 159:16
misguided m. men   KING 218:2
mislead than m. the people   STEV 380:4
misleading m. impression, not a lie   ARMS 15:6
misrule Thirteen years of Tory m.   SLOG 368:12
missed m. a good opportunity   CHIR 84:7
   m. the bus   CHAM 80:5
   No one would have m. her   EPIT 136:5
missile m. in the thatch   DE C 112:3
missing something m. in the world   FOX 144:10
mission My m. is to pacify   GLAD 158:8
missionaries free m.   MENC 267:13
Missouri admit M. to the Union   COBB 98:4
   God has given us M.   RAND 321:8
mistake every m. it makes   BOOK 50:5
   have made a great m.   MORS 280:2
   make a m.   LA G 223:6
   m. shall not be repeated   EPIT 137:3
mistaken possible you may be m.   CROM 105:12
mistakes great men make m.   CHUR 86:4
   If he makes m. they must be covered
                           CHUR 91:13
   man who makes no m.   PHEL 310:2
mistress but one M.   ELIZ 133:1
   m. I am ashamed to call you   ELIZ 133:11
   m. in my own   KIPL 220:5
   m. of the Party   HEAL 177:11
mistresses or your Lordship's m.   WILK 420:1
misunderstood m. Madame   DE V 116:3
mitre m. and a crown of martyrdom   WALP 409:5
mix fail to m. freely   WELL 415:9
   government don't m.   TRUM 401:15
mixture strange m. of blood   CEÈV 104:8
moat Look to your M.   HALI 171:3
mob do what the m. do   DICK 117:9
   each Tyrant, every M.   KIPL 219:5
   lied to please the m.   KIPL 219:7

mob (*cont.*):
  M., Parliament   COBB 98:5
  numerous assembly is a m.   RETZ 325:1
  supreme governors, the m.   WALP 409:8
mobs Talk of m.!   HAZL 176:8
  will not canvas m.   SALI 339:6
mock but to m. the kingdom   PYM 317:8
model forms the best m.   HAMI 171:9
moderate m. income   DURH 129:3
moderation astonished at my own m.   CLIV 98:2
  M. in the affairs   JOHN 203:7
  m. in the pursuit of justice   GOLD 161:8
  m. in war is imbecility   MACA 245:8
modern peace is a m. invention   MAIN 256:2
modest much to be m. about   CHUR 90:14
moll King's M. Reno'd   NEWS 288:1
Moloch great M., national sovereignty
                     MEYE 268:9
moment decisive m.   RETZ 324:7
  m. of madness   DAVI 110:5
monarch every hereditary m. was insane
                     BAGE 24:1
  merry m.   ROCH 328:13
  not so much a king as a M.   SELL 349:7
  relations with the M.   BLAI 46:5
monarchical utility of m. power   BOSW 52:3
monarchies elective m.   GIBB 155:2
  m., in poverty   MONT 277:5
monarchs m., whose power seems   MONT 277:4
  righteous m.   BROO 56:6
monarchy against absolute M.   PAIN 300:2
  characteristic of the English M.   BAGE 22:12
  constitutional m.   TROL 399:6
  discontented under *m.*   HOBB 185:11
  essential to a true m.   BAGE 22:1
  M. and succession   PAIN 300:4
  m. has become   ST J 381:9
  M. is a labour-intensive   WILS 422:4
  M. is a merchantman   AMES 7:6
  M. is a strong government   BAGE 22:11
  M. is only   SHEL 362:11
  state of m.   JAME 197:2
  US presidency a Tudor m.   BURG 61:1
monetarism m., like Marxism   GILM 157:2
money Bad m. drives out good   PROV 318:4
  by expenditure of m.   SALI 339:2
  Capitalism is using its m.   CAST 77:4
  draining m. from the pockets   SMIT 371:3
  getting m.   JOHN 204:15
  had m. as well   THAT 391:11
  Hell of not making m.   CARL 75:2
  If you have m. you spend it   KENN 214:1
  lost m. by underestimating   MENC 267:10
  make as much m.   FRIE 147:9
  m. and power   O'RO 296:3
  m.-grabbing cronies   HAGU 168:1
  m. gushes into politics   WHIT 417:7
  M. has no smell   VESP 405:8
  m. instead of political support   SALI 339:7
  M. is indeed the most important   SHAW 360:12
  M. . . . is none of the wheels   HUME 191:4

m. the sinews of war   BACO 21:4
m. to even get beat   ROGE 329:3
natural interest of m.   MACA 246:3
nobody ever lost m.   DEED 112:7
not spending m. alone   EISE 131:5
other people's m.   RAND 322:3
plenty of m.   ROGE 329:5
print your own m.   THOM 393:9
run out of m.   CLAR 94:13
spending the public m.   COOL 103:11
state is or can be master of m.   BEVE 40:4
They hired the m.   COOL 103:9
unlimited m.   CICE 93:6
use the m. for the poor   PERÓ 309:5
virtue does not come from m.   SOCR 373:7
moneybag Aristocracy of the M.   CARL 74:13
Mongols M. of our age   HUSS 193:2
mongrels continent of energetic m.   FISH 140:7
monk political old m.   MURD 283:1
monkey higher the m. climbs   PROV 318:12
  m. looking for fleas   LASK 225:8
  no reason to attack the m.   BEVA 38:11
monologue m. is not a decision   ATTL 17:10
monopolies only one M. Commission   ANON 13:8
monopoly best of all m. profits   HICK 183:6
  m. stage of capitalism   LENI 230:8
Monroe M. Doctrine   MONR 276:9
  mouth of Marilyn M.   MITT 275:5
monsters bastard brood of m.   BENT 35:7
  in search of m. to destroy   ADAM 4:7
monstrous m. regiment of women   KNOX 222:4
Montezuma halls of M.   SONG 375:6
  who imprisoned M.   MACA 246:10
moon defend the m.   SALI 344:1
  man on the M.   KENN 212:9
  m. the stars   TRUM 400:12
  Rising of the M.   LARK 225:4
moor in the middle of a m.   HUXL 193:9
moose strong as a bull m.   ROOS 332:2
moral attainment of m. good   JOHN 202:1
  It *is* a m. issue   NEWS 287:12
  m. electricity   O'CO 293:8
  m. imperative   DIDI 118:8
  most m.   MENC 267:8
  of some great m. effect   SALI 341:13
  party is a m. crusade   WILS 421:4
  single m. action   GLAD 159:15
morality damned m.   MELB 266:11
  fits of m.   MACA 246:2
  market has no m.   HESE 182:9
  M. is the herd-instinct   NIET 289:7
  national m. should have this   SHAW 360:12
  slave-m.   NIET 289:8
morals either m. or principles   GLAD 159:2
  faith and m. hold   WORD 424:9
  m. and legislation   BENT 35:9
more m. equal than others   ORWE 296:8
mores O tempora, O m.   CICE 93:7
morganatic m. alliance   HARD 172:8
Mori manifesto written by Dr M.   BENN 34:8
moribus *M. antiquis res*   ENNI 135:7

name (*cont.*):

n. things after you	BUSH 66:3
n. to all succeeding ages curst	DRYD 127:3
n. we give the people	FLER 141:7
no profit but the n.	SHAK 352:1
Not in my n.	SLOG 368:6
whistling of a n.	POPE 314:5
names man with three n.	CROM 106:9
n. of men	TROL 399:14
Napoleon thinks he is N.	CLEM 96:4
Napoleons Caesars and N.	HUXL 193:6
Narragansett Where are the N.	TECU 389:1
nastiest n. thing in the nicest way	GOLD 160:8
nasty n., brutish, and short	HOBB 185:6
n. party	MAY 264:5
nation AMERICA thus top n.	SELL 349:11
boundary of the march of a n.	PARN 305:3
broad mass of a n.	HITL 184:5
can deprive a n.	NAMI 284:2
conduct the affairs of the n.	AMER 7:5
create a n. Europe	MONN 276:8
every man and n.	LOWE 242:8
existence as a n.	PITT 312:4
exterminate a n.	SPOC 378:1
ghosts of a n.	PEAR 306:8
great n.	WELL 416:1
lift up sword against n.	BIBL 41:14
n. a le gouvernment	MAIS 256:3
n. at his service	POMP 313:9
n. expects to be ignorant	JEFF 199:15
n. grieve	DRYD 127:8
n. is judged	LÉVE 232:3
n. is not governed	BURK 61:18
N. is starving	O'CO 293:5
n. is the universality	MAZZ 265:2
n. of amateurs	ROSE 333:8
n. of shopkeepers	ADAM 4:11
n. of shopkeepers	NAPO 285:1
n. of shopkeepers	SMIT 370:9
N. once again	DAVI 111:1
n. shall rise against nation	BIBL 41:24
N. shall speak peace	REND 324:6
N. spoke to a Nation	KIPL 220:5
n. talking to itself	MILL 270:6
n. that had lion's heart	CHUR 90:17
n. which indulges toward another	WASH 411:6
new n.	LINC 235:8
No n. is fit	WILS 422:11
No n. was ever ruined	FRAN 146:5
no rainbow n.	MAND 259:1
not to destroy a n.	WELL 416:5
of the n.'s care	PRIO 316:12
of the whole n.	MACD 249:10
one n. under God	BELL 32:9
one-third of a n. ill-housed	ROOS 330:11
opt out of a n.	LYNC 244:1
pillars of the n. state	PROD 317:1
rich and lazy n.	KIPL 221:1
small n. that stood alone	DE V 116:4
so goes the n.	PROV 318:3
Still better for the n.	EPIT 136:5

terrorize a whole n.	MURR 283:4
things which make a n. great	BACO 21:11
unity of the n.	KOHL 222:8
voice of a n.	RUSS 337:1
what our N. stands for	BETJ 38:2
national n. debt	HAMI 171:8
N. Debt is a very Good Thing	SELL 349:8
n. flag	SUMN 384:2
n. language	DE V 116:2
n. morality should have this	SHAW 360:12
nationalism N. is an infantile sickness	EINS 131:2
N. is a silly cock	ALDI 6:6
Scottish and Welsh n.	BAKE 25:8
nationalist good N.	MARK 260:5
nationality condense—a N.	WHIT 418:9
Welsh n.	GLAD 159:7
nationalize need to n.	WILS 422:5
nations association of n.	WILS 423:4
commonwealth of n.	ROSE 333:5
danger of great n.	BAGE 25:4
day of small n.	CHAM 79:8
Europe of n.	DE G 113:10
friendship with all n.	JEFF 199:4
great n. acted like gangsters	KUBR 223:3
let fierce contending n. know	ADDI 5:2
N. have their infancy	BOLI 49:3
n. how to live	MILT 271:5
N. touch at their summits	BAGE 23:9
n. which have put mankind	INGE 195:2
other n. and states draw aside	GOGO 160:7
Other n. use 'force'	WAUG 412:2
place among the n.	EMME 135:4
three small n.	STRA 382:11
Two n.	DISR 123:3
two n. have been at war	VOLT 407:2
two n. warring	DURH 129:4
native England's n. people	BURN 65:12
my n. land	SCOT 348:7
n. stands on the edge	RIEL 327:3
our ideas about the n.	LESS 231:12
NATO N. exists for three reasons	ISMA 195:8
N. in	ROBE 327:8
Nato N. is the bedrock of Europe	POWE 315:2
natural n. party of government	WILS 421:10
n. propensities	BURK 64:7
N. rights is simple nonsense	BENT 35:8
nature better angels of our n.	LINC 234:13
How N. always does contrive	GILB 156:7
N. has not cure	SMIT 371:10
n. of war	HOBB 185:5
N.'s mighty feast	MALT 257:10
simply follow N.	LAO- 225:3
violates the order of n.	HERO 182:2
You know his n.	SHAK 353:3
naval N. tradition	CHUR 90:9
navies our n. melt away	KIPL 220:7
navy head of the N.	CARS 76:3
n. nothing but rotten timber	BURK 62:9
royal n. of England	BLAC 45:6
upon the n.	CHAR 81:8
Nazis N. were great believers	JONE 206:3

originated by the N.	BRUT 59:6
nearly n. kept waiting	LOUI 241:7
necessarily Not n. conscription	KING 218:6
necessary became n. to destroy the town	
	ANON 10:4
honourable by being n.	HALE 169:5
if it is deemed n.	BROW 58:4
journey *really* n.	OFFI 295:5
n. evil	PAIN 300:3
n. not to change	FALK 139:2
no n. evils	JACK 196:4
not only n. but expedient	ARIS 15:1
sorry it was n.	TONE 396:12
necessities great n. call out	ADAM 2:2
necessity Cruel n.	CROM 105:10
N. hath no law	CROM 106:4
N. is the plea	PITT 312:2
n. of being *ready*	LINC 235:1
n. of doing something	JOHN 204:11
pragmatic n.	DIDI 118:8
neck boil on the back of his n.	SALI 343:7
break thy n.	SHAK 356:9
had but one n.	CALI 70:4
Some chicken! Some n.	CHUR 88:12
necklace with our n.	MAND 258:11
necromancy mere n.	WHIT 417:5
need France has more n. of me	NAPO 284:12
needs according to his n.	MARX 262:6
to each according to his n.	BAKU 25:10
negation n. of God	GLAD 158:3
negativism nattering nabobs of n.	AGNE 5:11
neglect n. of governments	LAUR 228:10
negotiate n. out of fear	KENN 212:6
not here to n.	TRIM 398:8
negotiating N. with de Valera	LLOY 240:3
when I was n.	MAND 258:9
negotiation difficult n.	SALI 340:5
Negro one drop of N. blood	HUGH 190:8
root of the American N. problem	BALD 26:1
Negroes drivers of n.	JOHN 204:4
neighbour make war upon a n. nation	
	FAIR 139:1
n.'s house is on fire	BURK 62:13
policy of the good n.	ROOS 330:7
rob a n.	MACA 245:6
neighbours do not hurt their n.	SALI 341:1
Good fences make good n.	FROS 148:6
happening to our n.	CHAM 79:9
have good n.	ELIZ 132:7
look down on his n.	SALI 339:5
Nell Pretty witty N.	PEPY 309:2
Nemesis N. may spare the sagacious	SALI 338:1
nemesis just N.	SALI 338:12
Nemo N. *me impune lacessit*	MOTT 281:5
neoclassical n. endogenous growth	BROW 57:5
nephews Priests have n.	PEEL 308:7
Nero N. fiddled	MENC 267:12
nerve do not lose my n.	NEHR 285:8
nest I have no n.-eggs	LLOY 238:7
nets Laws are generally found to be n.	
	SHEN 362:12

neutral studiously n.	WILS 422:13
United States must be n.	WILS 422:9
neutrality Armed n. is ineffectual	WILS 422:16
Just for a word 'n.'	BETH 37:10
N. helps the oppressor	WIES 419:3
never N. explain	FISH 141:1
n. had it so good	MACM 253:1
n. had it so good	SLOG 369:8
N. in the field of human conflict	CHUR 88:4
n. surrender	PAIS 302:9
n. thought of thinking	GILB 156:6
new believes that n. Labour	DAVI 110:2
called the N. World	CANN 73:12
claims of something n.	SALI 343:3
n. and untried	LINC 234:8
n. deal for the American people	ROOS 330:5
n. frontier	KENN 212:2
N. Frontier was not	SCHL 347:10
N. Hampshire has long	BUSH 66:11
N. Labour brand	GOUL 163:4
New Labour, n. danger	SLOG 368:3
n. world order	BUSH 66:10
something n. out of Africa	PLIN 313:1
Newcastle coals to N.	GEOR 154:2
news good day to bury bad n.	MISQ 272:9
it is an item of n.	TALL 385:12
N. Editor	ANON 9:5
Six O'Clock N.	GEOR 154:7
told bad n. to American	KEIL 211:1
New South Wales revive in N.	BANK 29:2
newspaper never to look into a n.	SHER 363:1
N. editors	TROL 399:14
n. is a nation talking	MILL 270:6
seen in a n.	JEFF 199:9
newspapers burlesque and the n.	STON 382:1
n. I can't stand	STOP 382:5
n. nobly did precisely that	BLAC 45:4
Newspeak whole aim of N.	ORWE 297:5
New York N. politics were always	TWEE 403:1
New Zealanders When N. emigrate	MULD 282:8
next used to be the n. president	GORE 163:1
nexus n. of man to man	CARL 74:7
NHS corridors of the N.	GRIF 166:9
nice Leadership is not about being n.	KEAT 210:7
nicest nastiest thing in the n. way	GOLD 160:8
nickname Every n. is a title	PAIN 301:6
nigger 'damned n.' element	SALI 342:9
night coming for us that n.	BALD 26:3
n. of the long knives	HITL 184:6
something of the n.	WIDD 419:2
terrible n.	PORT 314:13
nightingale Florence N.	GRIF 166:9
nightmare long national n. is over	FORD 143:1
n. of the dark	AUDE 19:1
nightmares n. about two things	STOC 381:11
nightstick end of a n.	WHAL 417:2
nihil *Aut Caesar, aut n.*	MOTT 281:1
nineteenth n. century	LAUR 228:11
ninety glorious N.-two	REVE 325:5
n.-minute patriots	SILL 365:3
N. percent of the politicians	KISS 221:10

opponents purpose of his o.   TROL 400:2
opportunism principally o.   CHUR 85:10
opportunities grand o. all around   PLUN 313:3
    I seen my o.   PLUN 313:2
    one of those o.   GLAD 159:4
opportunity gates of o.   JOHN 203:9
    greatest o.   DISR 122:19
    Ireland's o.   PROV 318:9
    O. is more powerful   DISR 123:11
    o. to keep quiet   CHIR 84:7
oppose o. everything   DERB 115:5
opposed o. to any proposal   MACN 254:6
opposite on the o. side   ANON 12:10
opposition capacity in the Leader of the O.   BAGE 24:14
    decried in o.   SALI 338:12
    disease of o.   GALB 150:7
    duty of an O.   DERB 115:5
    effective means of o.   GOEB 160:4
    figure by o.   HALI 170:12
    Her Majesty's O.   BAGE 22:6
    His Majesty's O.   HOBH 185:13
    Leader of the O.   KINN 219:2
    O. is four or five   HATT 174:7
    o. of events   MACM 254:1
    O., on coming into power   BAGE 23:11
    O.'s about asking   LYNN 244:3
    period in o.   RIDL 326:9
    pleasure of the O.   MACL 252:1
    spell in O.   SALI 342:10
    without a formidable O.   DISR 122:13
oppressed barbarously o.   LAST 227:5
    mind of the o.   BIKO 42:9
oppression violate would be o.   JEFF 199:2
    war against o.   MCAL 244:13
oppressive o. and unjust   BURK 63:11
oppressor Neutrality helps the o.   WIES 419:3
    o.'s wrong   SHAK 351:11
opprobrium term of o.   MOYN 282:1
opt o. out of a nation   LYNC 244:1
option You had an o., sir   MULR 282:9
opulence degree of o.   SMIT 369:11
oracle when the o. has spoken   SALI 340:3
oracles lively O. of God   CORO 104:1
orange O. card   CHUR 86:1
    O. in the Lobby   SALI 343:8
Orangemen why the O. are not   O'HI 294:4
orator I am no o., as Brutus is   SHAK 355:15
    No o. ever made an impression   BAGE 22:3
orators greatest living o.   LLOY 239:5
oratory appetite for o.   GALB 150:3
    first in o.   DEMO 114:6
    object of o.   MACA 247:10
ordained not o. by nature   JORD 206:8
    o. error   VANS 404:6
ordeal fourteen years' o.   MITC 271:12
order defined by the word 'o.'   METT 268:8
    Good o. is the foundation   BURK 63:10
    keep the government in o.   SCAR 347:5
    new world o.   BUSH 66:10
    old o. changeth   TENN 389:14

o. of the boot   CHUR 89:9
O. reigns in Warsaw   ANON 11:7
party of o. or stability   MILL 269:11
Peace, o., and good government   ANON 11:8
renovation of the natural o.   PAIN 301:12
social o. destroyed   TOCQ 396:2
violates the o. of nature   HERO 182:2
war creates o.   BREC 54:3
orders gave them their o.   WELL 415:5
ordinary behaviour of o. people   TAYL 387:6
    o. men exercise initiative   TAWN 386:11
    warn you not to be o.   KINN 218:10
organ o. and the maypole   JORD 207:1
    o. of public opinion   DISR 120:4
organic committee is o.   PARK 304:6
organization o. of idolatry   SHAW 361:4
organize Don't waste time mourning—o.   LAST 227:4
organized o. hypocrisy   DISR 120:1
    o. political party   ROGE 329:6
    Party is o. opinion   DISR 120:11
organs other o. take their tone   GLAD 158:4
original sound and o. ideas   MACM 253:5
originality some o.   WEBB 412:6
originals few o. and many copies   TOCQ 395:7
ornament Nobility is a graceful o.   BURK 63:7
orphan defeat is an o.   CIAN 93:1
osprey o. to the fish   SHAK 351:4
ostracized old people are o.   MONB 275:6
ostrich can not be an o.   WILS 422:14
other o. Eden   SHAK 358:6
    Prudence is the o. woman   ANON 11:12
otherwise would wish o.   NEWS 288:9
ought didn't o. never to have done it   BEVI 40:11
out cannot o.-vote them   JOHN 205:2
    counted them all o.   HANR 172:5
    o. with the Stuarts   DISR 122:21
    will o.-argue them   JOHN 205:2
outdated o. methods   WILS 421:5
outdoor system of o. relief   BRIG 55:3
outlaw attacks from o. states   REAG 323:3
outlawed liar should be o.   HALI 169:7
    o. or exiled   MAGN 255:7
outlaws o. Russia   REAG 323:7
outrage Stupidity, o.   ROST 334:2
outside o. pissing in   JOHN 203:10
ovary let one o.   PARR 305:9
over it is all o.   NORT 292:2
    My war is o.   MCGU 250:3
    oversexed, and o. here   TRIN 398:12
    O. there   COHA 98:10
overbearing o. and offensive   VICT 406:5
overcome We shall o.   SONG 377:6
overpaid grossly o.   HERB 181:8
    O., overfed, oversexed   TRIN 398:12
overrule do not affect to o.   SALI 341:5
    threaten to o. him   PAXM 306:3
oversexed o., and over here   TRIN 398:12
overstayed o. your welcome   WALL 408:5
owed so much o. by so many to so few   CHUR 88:4

own my words are my o. CHAR 81:9
only to those who o. one LIEB 233:8
ownership o. of the means of production
ANON 12:13
Oxford academia in O. AUNG 19:8
King to O. sent BROW 58:6
secret in the O. sense FRAN 146:8
To O. sent a troop TRAP 397:5
oxygen o. of publicity THAT 391:9

pacify p. Ireland GLAD 158:8
pack running with the p. BUTL 68:5
packing p. a Luger WILS 421:2
Paddington London is to P. CANN 73:9
paeans laurels to p. CICE 93:4
Paganini fiddler after P. NICO 288:12
page foot of the first p. SAND 346:1
paid highly-p. chairman SALI 343:12
Judas was p. POWE 315:7
p. for this microphone REAG 323:2
we ha' p. in full KIPL 220:10
pain p. to the bear MACA 247:1
pains no gains without p. STEV 380:5
paint democratic p. TOCQ 396:4
p. the chameleon KEYN 215:7
painted wood p. to look like iron BISM 44:3
painting like a surrealistic p. MAND 258:10
palace p. is not safe DISR 124:2
pale turned p. SOUT 374:8
Palestine P. is the cement ARAF 14:2
Palladium P. of all the civil JUNI 208:12
palm bear the p. alone SHAK 353:11
Pandora If you open that P.'s Box BEVI 40:12
panem P. et circenses JUVE 209:4
pangs free of any p. CURT 107:9
panics Tory party never p. HOSK 189:2
pantheon Labour Party's p. PIML 311:4
panther Black P. Party NEWT 286:4
papacy p. is not other HOBB 185:12
paper All reactionaries are p. tigers MAO 259:8
built a p.-mill SHAK 353:1
here is the p. CHAM 80:2
virtue of p. government BURK 61:15
Papist P., yet a Calvinist EPIT 136:7
parade on the p. ground SMIT 371:7
parades produce victory p. HOBS 186:1
paradise catch the bird of p. KHRU 216:6
paralyses p. the social development CHUR 91:11
parapet could not see a p. CRIT 105:3
p. which gives way SALI 344:8
parchment should be made p. SHAK 352:19
pardon God may p. you ELIZ 133:5
parens king is truly p. patriae JAME 197:3
parents all working-class p. ABBO 1:1
children bury their p. HERO 182:2
illegitimate p. JOSE 207:7
In mine it was the p. SLOV 369:9
p. were the Lord knows who DEFO 112:13
produce bad p. MORS 280:3
Paris Hoares to P. GEOR 154:2

P. is well worth a mass HENR 180:7
P. was French—and silent TUCH 402:4
parish pension from his p. RUSK 336:4
parks p. are the lungs of London PITT 311:16
parliament build your House of P. WELL 416:2
function of P. BOOT 51:5
in a 21st-century p. ASHD 16:3
Irishmen in her P. BALF 27:10
let alone a P. ANON 13:5
look on the proceedings of P. BAGE 24:10
make P. work MART 261:7
minuet danced by P. SCAR 347:3
modern P. CONN 100:5
myths of the British P. MAYB 264:6
not even p. SCAR 347:6
object of P. CHUR 90:11
of [P.] BOOT 51:4
p. are a lot of hard-faced men BALD 26:4
p. can do any thing PEMB 308:12
P. is a potent engine SALI 342:2
P. itself would not exist SCAR 347:1
p. of whores O'RO 296:5
P., Rabble COBB 98:5
P. speaking through reporters CARL 74:14
representing P. AMER 7:2
returned to P. DISR 124:10
Rump P. SELL 349:6
Scots p. JOHN 205:8
Scottish P. EWIN 138:5
Scottish P. SALM 345:10
shall be a Scottish p. ANON 12:7
shall be a Scottish p. DEWA 116:9
three years in P. BROC 56:1
united P. FLET 142:1
voices in P. RUSK 336:3
parliamentarian safe pleasure for a p. CRIT 105:4
parliamentary large p. majority BUTL 67:10
old P. hand GLAD 159:3
p. eloquence CARL 75:1
P. Government DISR 121:3
P. leper WILS 421:8
p. majorities BONA 49:8
parliaments In p., men HALI 170:10
mother of P. BRIG 55:5
Parnell Poor P. JOYC 208:2
parrot has become a p. PAIS 302:13
parson Whig in a p.'s gown JOHN 204:6
world's p. HEAL 177:4
partiality neither anger nor p. TACI 385:4
participate refusing to p. PLAT 312:10
particular Did nothing in p. GILB 156:8
particulars in minute p. BLAK 47:3
parties P. come to power RIDL 326:9
P. must ever exist BURK 62:6
p. which divide the state EMER 135:1
that there are three p. MAYB 264:6
partnership too dangerous for blind p.
STRO 383:2
party break your p. HEAD 177:2
but with a p. JEFF 198:8
each p. is worse than ROGE 329:4

party (*cont.*):

educate our p.	DISR 120:15
extreme p. is most irritated	BAGE 25:2
greenest political p.	JONE 206:3
head of a p.	RETZ 325:2
I believe that without p.	DISR 121:4
in the p. manifestoes	ROTH 334:4
I wish p. government	SALI 344:6
judge a political p.	ROOS 331:7
master of the P.	HEAL 177:11
mood of the P.	CLAR 94:4
nasty p.	MAY 264:5
natural p. of government	WILS 421:10
nature of a political p.	TROL 399:13
none was for a p.	MACA 247:8
no P. line	DJIL 124:13
one p. always	MENC 267:7
organized political p.	ROGE 329:6
p. I love	LIVI 238:1
p. in an empty room	DEWA 116:8
p. is but a kind of conspiracy	HALI 170:11
p. is inherent in it	BAGE 23:10
P. is little less	HALI 170:13
p. . . . is not a faction	POWE 315:9
P. is organized opinion	DISR 120:11
P. is the madness	SWIF 384:9
p. like an old stagecoach	WILS 421:15
p. not to be brought down	HAIL 168:5
p. of order or stability	MILL 269:11
p. of two	BRIG 55:7
p. platforms	TRUM 401:11
P. shackled by tradition	SALI 343:2
p.'s over	CROS 106:13
p. which takes credit	MORR 280:1
political p. in power	SCAR 347:3
save the P. we love	GAIT 149:3
spirit of p.	WASH 411:5
Stick to your p.	DISR 123:16
stupidest p.	MILL 269:4
three-p. politics	KENN 211:8
voted at my p.'s call	GILB 156:6
Whichever p. is in office	WILS 422:1
without a p.	CHUR 92:2

pasarán *No p.* | IBAR 194:2

pass p. the ammunition | FORG 143:3
these things must come to p.	BIBL 41:23
They shall not p.	IBAR 194:2
They shall not p.	PROV 318:15

passengers p. trying to drive | ADCO 4:13

passer *de laisser p.* | QUES 320:4

passing as opposed to the p. | SALI 340:10

passion held with p. | RUSS 336:11
| in such a p. about | SHAW 361:12 |

Passionaria La P. | HEAL 177:8

passionate full of p. intensity | YEAT 426:9

passions Fear is, of all p. | RETZ 324:10
| p. of men | HAMI 172:1 |
| p. were expressed | WALP 409:6 |

passive p. obedience | BALF 27:9

passport My p.'s green | HEAN 178:2

past cannot remember the p. | SANT 346:3

comes out of the p.	PHIL 310:6
deeds of the p.	DAVI 111:4
dossier on his p.	HOWA 189:8
falsely imagined p.	BORK 52:1
ignorant of the p.	SPIE 377:10
knowledge of its p.	DIEF 118:9
lament the p.	BURK 63:13
last day of an era p.	YELT 427:3
never become the p.	BARK 29:5
nothing but the p.	KEYN 215:4
plan the future by the p.	BURK 61:4
remember what is p.	HALI 169:8
under the bloody p.	AHER 6:1
Utopia is a blessed p.	KISS 221:14
Who controls the p.	ORWE 297:4

pasture p. for all the sheep | WALP 410:6

paternal p., or in other words | MACA 247:11
| p. socialism | MACM 252:6 |

paternalism lessons of p. | CLEV 96:10

paths p. of glory | GRAY 165:4

patience my p. is now at an end | HITL 184:9

patrie *enfants de la p.* | SONG 375:1

patries *Europe des p.* | DE G 113:10

patriot honest p., in the full tide | JEFF 199:3
p. of the world	CANN 73:6
p. on an empty stomach	BRAN 53:4
p. yet, but was a fool	DRYD 127:10
Such is the p.'s boast	GOLD 161:5

patriotism history to his p. | ADAM 4:8
knock the p. out of the human race	SHAW 361:8
larger p.	ROSE 333:7
p. in the female sex	ADAM 2:3
P. is a lively sense	ALDI 6:6
p. is a sort	TOCQ 396:5
P. is not enough	CAVE 78:4
P. is the last refuge	JOHN 204:17
p. run amok	RATH 322:5

patriots 90-minute p. | SILL 365:3
blood of p.	JEFF 198:6
country p. born	BYRO 68:9
last effort of the p.	ADAM 3:5
P. are in the right	WAUG 412:1

paw accept its p. gingerly | CHAN 81:1

pawns p. are men | CARL 75:4

pay 4 Ulcer P. | EARL 129:6
Can't p., won't pay	SLOG 366:12
Equal P. for Equal Work	ANTH 13:13
Not a penny off the p.	COOK 102:8
p. any price	KENN 212:4
P. given to a state hireling	JOHN 204:2
p. later	HOLD 186:6
p. us, pass us	CHES 83:8
saved the sum of things for p.	HOUS 189:3
two-thirds of a nation p.	VOLT 407:4
we are made to p. for	FRIE 148:3
We won't p.	FO 142:2

paying P. the Dane-geld | KIPL 221:1
| price well worth p. | LAMO 224:2 |

peace arch of p. morticed | NICO 286:8
| banished p. | SMOL 373:1 |
| call it p. | TACI 385:1 |

people (*cont.*):
my p.'s happiness	ELIZ 133:3
new p. takes the land	CHES 83:9
no petty p.	YEAT 427:1
one p., one leader	SLOG 366:14
opinion of the p.	JEFF 198:3
opium of the p.	MARX 262:3
p. are the masters	BURK 64:14
p. as a source of power	SCAR 347:3
p. as base as itself	PULI 317:5
p. govern themselves	THIE 393:1
p. have spoken	FITT 141:4
p. is the true legislator	BURK 64:5
p. made the Constitution	MARS 261:4
p. marching on	MORR 279:10
P. die, but books never die	ROOS 331:6
p.'s prayer	DRYD 127:6
Power to the p.	SLOG 368:8
same as if they was p.	DURE 129:2
servants of the p.	BLAI 46:2
She was the P.'s Princess	BLAI 46:3
support of the p.	CLEV 96:10
suppose the p. good	ROBE 328:2
This was a p.'s war	TAYL 387:2
voice of the p.	ALCU 6:5
voice of the p.	BALD 27:2
wants to kill p.	WRIG 425:6
we are the p. of England	CHES 83:8
We the p.	CONS 102:1
What is the city but the p.	SHAK 350:10
What kind of a p.	CHUR 88:8
worship the p.	BACO 20:4

peopled conquered and p.	SEEL 348:9
Peoria play in P.	PROV 318:16
perdition led to *p.* by a man	WEST 416:10
perestroika restructuring [p.]	GORB 162:5
started the process of p.	GORB 162:6
perfect Entire and whole and p.	SPRI 378:2
most p. political community	ARIS 15:4
perfidious p. Albion	XIMÉ 426:1
performers no all the p.	MURR 283:6
perils p. of change	SALI 339:10
perish England shall p.	ELIZ 133:8
p. together as fools	KING 217:9
though the world p.	MOTT 281:3
venal city ripe to p.	SALL 345:6
permanent p. alliances	WASH 411:4
p. indignation	VALÉ 404:1
p. officials	HARC 172:7
represent the p.	SALI 340:10
will have p. results	SALI 343:14
permitted all is p.	MEGA 265:5
p. to make all the ballads	FLET 141:8
pernicious most p. race	SWIF 384:6
Perón have liked to be P.	PERÓ 309:6
perpetrator thou shalt not be a p.	BAUE 30:7
perpetual p. quarrel	BURK 62:5
persecution asylum from p.	UNIV 403:7
P. is not an original feature	PAIN 301:8
P. produced its natural effect	MACA 246:13
persevering no dignity in p. in error	PEEL 307:15

person most superior p.	ANON 11:1
personal p. is political	SLOG 368:7
personalities ten independent p.	FOTH 144:2
personality political p.	JENK 201:7
rocks of mere p.	ANON 12:2
personally should be p. associated	BLAI 46:9
perspire Gladstone may p.	CHUR 85:11
persuade p. a multitude	HOOK 187:11
persuading By p. others	JUNI 208:8
persuasion P. is the resource	GIBB 155:14
p. only	MILT 271:4
Peter government which robs P.	SHAW 360:7
petticoat out of the Realm in my p.	ELIZ 132:6
petty no p. people	YEAT 427:1
we p. men	SHAK 354:1
phantom embarrassed p.	DISR 122:16
pheasant make room for the p.	JOHN 205:9
philanthropist as a professed p.	TROL 399:8
philanthropy p. is a very good thing	SALI 340:15
Philistine run by a p.	KAUF 209:9
Philistines Barbarians, P., and Populace	ARNO 15:8
P. proper, or middle class	ARNO 15:10
philosopher p. may preach	GIBB 155:16
philosophers P. are very regardless	PEEL 308:6
philosophy p. quenches them	VOLT 407:5
study mathematics and p.	ADAM 3:9
photographers let the P. stay	SHER 363:4
p. and their zoom	ULLR 403:4
phrases *La mort, sans p.*	SIEY 365:1
P. make history here	MAFF 255:5
pickle weaned on a p.	ANON 12:11
pictures behind all the p.	BUSH 66:4
furnish the p.	HEAR 178:6
p. of their children	BUSH 67:8
pie p. in the sky	HILL 184:1
pies Bellamy's veal p.	LAST 227:10
piety bear witness to his p.	ADAM 4:8
pig wrestling with a greased p.	PATT 306:2
pigeon branded, p.-holed	PRES 316:7
pigs I am fond of p.	CHUR 92:9
pike freedom for the p.	TAWN 386:8
p. at the bottom	HEAL 178:1
p. in the thatch	DE C 112:3
Pilate What is truth? said jesting P.	BACO 21:6
pilgrims Land of the p.' pride	SMIT 372:4
pill any p. can be swallowed	TROL 399:3
pillar p. of the State	SOLZ 374:1
pillars four p. of government	BACO 21:1
p. of civilization	MONN 276:7
p. of the nation state	PROD 317:1
pillow like the feather p.	HAIG 168:3
pilot daring p. in extremity	DRYD 127:4
Dropping the p.	TENN 389:4
p. of the storm	BAGE 22:9
pinheads we can dance on p.	CAMP 72:5
pink p., quivering Ted	ANON 8:3
p. right down to	NIXO 290:1
pinstripe come in a p. suit	FEIN 140:1
pious varnish of p. phrases	SALI 344:11
pips until the p. squeak	GEDD 152:5

piratical p. old bruiser · HAIL 168:9
piss pitcher of warm p. · GARN 152:1
pissing inside the tent p. out · JOHN 203:10
  like p. down your leg · JOHN 203:12
pistol found the smoking p. · CONA 100:3
  I reach for my p. · JOHS 205:10
pitcher p. of warm piss · GARN 152:1
Pitt P. as opposed to Fox · BUTL 68:1
pity Scots deserve no p. · FLET 142:1
pixie some vanilla-flavoured p. · PARR 305:7
pizza deliver a p. · ANON 13:5
place All rising to great p. · BACO 20:14
  for the sake of the p. · HALI 170:5
  Get p. and wealth · POPE 314:6
  Gratitude of p.-expectants · WALP 410:4
  In p. of strife · CAST 77:3
  p. in the sun · BÜLO 60:5
  p. in the sun · WILH 419:9
  P., that great object · SMIT 369:12
  p. without power · ROSE 333:6
  right man in the right p. · JEFF 200:12
  rising unto p. is laborious · BACO 20:12
  thus with height of p. · WOTT 425:1
plagues of all p. · DEFO 113:1
plain p., blunt man · SHAK 355:15
plaintive p. treble · DISR 120:4
plan p. the future by the past · BURK 61:4
planets stars and all the p. · TRUM 400:12
planning resist all p. · OAKE 292:9
plant not a structure, but a p. · PARK 304:6
  p. of rapid growth · WASH 411:7
  p. of slow growth · PITT 311:8
planter of p. stock · HEWI 183:4
plates p. appear to be moving · PRES 316:10
platitude p. is simply a truth repeated · BALD 26:5
plausibility confer a dreadful p. · LAWS 229:3
plausible manufacturing the p. · BALD 27:7
plausibly p. maintained · BURR 66:1
play Better than a p. · CHAR 81:10
  cats might p. · CHUR 90:8
  may now sit and p. · ASTL 17:4
  only to p. fair · LABO 223:4
  p. in Peoria · PROV 318:16
played p. the game · SMIT 371:11
playedst p. most foully for't · SHAK 357:5
playing stood like a p. card · MAIL 255:10
  won on the p. fields · WELL 415:11
pleasant England's green and p. land · BLAK 47:5
please do what I p. · FRED 147:3
  not here to p. myself · HEND 179:11
  To tax and to p. · BURK 61:14
pleases do what he p. · RETZ 325:2
pleasure p. to their adversaries · SALI 341:12
  p. to the spectators · MACA 247:1
pleasures English take their p. · SULL 383:8
  two supreme p. · ROSE 333:11
plebeian of a p. leader · DISR 123:1
plebiscite justice by p. · ZOBE 428:6
pledge reckless hustings p. · SALI 338:5
plot discerned in history a p. · FISH 140:6
  Gunpowder Treason and P. · ANON 11:11

This blessèd p. · SHAK 358:6
plots P., true or false · DRYD 127:2
plotting p., and playing · CARL 75:4
plough boy that driveth the p. · TYND 403:2
  p. my furrow alone · ROSE 333:10
  wherefore p. · SHEL 362:6
ploughman wrong even the poorest p. · CHAR 81:5
plowshares beat their swords into p. · BIBL 41:14
pluck great p. · WEBB 412:6
plumage pities the p. · PAIN 301:3
plumber can't get a p. to come · SCHW 348:5
plumbers good p. · NIXO 290:13
plus Il n'y a p. de Pyrénées · LOUI 241:6
Plymouth pious ones of P. · EVAR 138:1
PM he ended P. CH and OM · ATTL 18:8
pocket guinea you have in your p. · RUSK 336:5
  in Britain, in your p. · WILS 421:11
  neither picks my p. · JEFF 200:13
  pecker in my p. · JOHN 203:13
  picking his p. · JOHN 202:7
pockets fructify in the p. · GLAD 159:14
poem being the author of that p. · WOLF 423:10
  essentially the greatest p. · WHIT 418:8
poet p.'s mouth be shut · YEAT 426:7
  p. will give up writing · CELA 79:3
poetical p. abstractions · MACN 254:5
poetry campaign in p. · CUOM 107:5
  writing p. · POWE 315:6
poets P. hope too much · LAWR 229:1
point different p. of view · NAPO 284:8
points p. upon which they are precise · SALI 341:10
  thousand p. of light · BUSH 66:8
poising p. every weight · MARV 261:9
poison food only a cover for p. · BURK 64:1
  got as far as p.-gas · HARD 173:4
  put p. in your coffee · ASTO 17:5
  strongest p. ever known · BLAK 47:1
poker tossed around like p. chips · ALBR 6:4
pole top of the greasy p. · DISR 123:18
polecat semi-house-trained p. · FOOT 142:7
police p. can beat you · SHAW 361:7
  p. were to blame · GRAN 164:1
policeman p. is there · DALE 108:7
  terrorist and the p. · CONR 101:9
  than a p. · SALI 344:4
  world's p. · HEAL 177:4
policemen p. of the world · BONA 49:10
policies but rarely p. · HURD 192:7
  carcasses of dead p. · SALI 339:14
  P. must 'grow' · BAGE 24:15
policy defend a bad p. · SALI 344:10
  determine p. · TREV 398:3
  English p. is to float · SALI 339:13
  foreign p. · COOK 103:1
  home p.: I wage war · CLEM 96:3
  If the p. isn't hurting · MAJO 256:5
  impose a p. · WAUG 411:10
  My [foreign] p. · BEVI 40:10
  national p. · BRIA 54:10
  no such thing as a fixed p. · SALI 342:6
  on foreign p. · GALB 150:4

p. is a disease   FOTH 144:1
P. is a marathon   LIVI 237:10
P. is a very long-run game   MAJO 256:4
P. is just like   REAG 322:10
p. is local   O'NE 295:10
P. is not the art   GALB 150:8
p. is present history   FREE 147:6
P. is the art   GAND 150:14
P. is the art of preventing   VALÉ 404:2
P. is the only profession   STEV 381:6
P. is war without bloodshed   MAO 259:6
P. is worse   MONT 277:16
P. makes strange   PROV 319:7
P. makes strange   WARN 410:9
p. of purpose   HUMP 192:2
p. of the left   JENK 201:2
P. supposed to be   REAG 322:11
P. too serious a matter   DE G 113:7
practical p.   ADAM 3:2
practice of p.   DISR 122:15
religion from p.   TREV 398:4
renewed focus of p.   HAVE 175:3
speak from above p.   MCAL 244:9
succeed in p.   LLOY 239:4
their p. usually stink   LAWR 229:1
this P. thing   ROGE 329:4
three-party p.   KENN 211:8
times in p.   GALB 150:9
week is a long time in p.   WILS 421:9
will not close my p.   FOX 145:1
zeal in p.   JUNI 208:8
politique p. father   JAME 197:3
poll of the p. tax   THAT 392:9
   science of p.-taking   WHIT 417:5
pollute p. now   HOLD 186:6
pollution p. of democracy   WHIT 417:7
Pomeranian single P. grenadier   BISM 44:10
pomp grinning at his p.   SHAK 358:11
   p. of pow'r   GRAY 165:4
   p. of yesterday   KIPL 220:7
Pompey Knew you not P.   SHAK 353:9
poodle in a p. parlour   PARR 305:5
   right hon. Gentleman's p.   LLOY 238:6
pool at the bottom of a p.   HEAL 178:1
poor better to be p. than rich   CECI 78:9
   cannot help the p.   LINC 236:12
   divided among the p.   SHAW 360:10
   faces of the p.   NICO 288:13
   give food to the p.   CAMA 71:9
   Laws grind the p.   GOLD 161:6
   make the p. poorer   NEHR 285:10
   many who are p.   KENN 212:5
   no peasant in my kingdom so p.   HENR 180:5
   p. did not   DE V 116:6
   p. have cried   SHAK 355:9
   p. have no right   RUSK 336:7
   p. man at his gate   ALEX 6:7
   p. man loved the great   MACA 247:8
   p. people in rich countries   BAUE 30:5
   p. who die   SART 346:7
   provision for the p.   JOHN 204:12

RICH AND THE P.   DISR 123:3
rich as well as the p.   FRAN 145:3
rich on the p.   JEFF 198:4
so p. to do him reverence   SHAK 355:12
statesman can give the p. man   SALI 342:4
To the p. people   LANG 225:2
your tired, your p.   LAZA 229:9
poorest p. he that is in England   RAIN 321:2
   p. man may in his cottage   PITT 311:7
pope against the P. or the NUM   BALD 27:6
   P.! How many divisions   STAL 378:7
   President, not a P.   STRE 383:1
popish P. liturgy   PITT 311:11
poppy not to wear a p.   MCAL 244:10
populace Barbarians, Philistines, and P.   ARNO 15:8
   clamours of the p.   ADAM 3:3
   give the name of P.   ARNO 15:11
   p. is excited   LA B 223:5
   p. rise at once   WHIT 418:5
popular p. in Scotland   DAVI 110:2
   p. institution   ST J 381:9
   p. politician   ARIS 14:8
   p. sentiments   PEEL 307:12
   strong p. feeling   TROL 399:7
population balance of our p.   JOSE 207:5
   p., when unchecked   MALT 257:8
populi Salus p.   CICE 93:3
   Salus p. suprema lex   SELD 349:3
porch keep on the p.   CLIN 97:4
porcupines throw p. under you   KHRU 216:9
port p. is near   WHIT 418:3
position p. must be held to the last man   HAIG 168:4
possessed world already p.   MALT 257:10
possessions All my p.   LAST 226:1
possibilities unlimited p.   GOLD 160:9
possible knowledge of the p.   BEVA 39:6
   Politics is the art of the p.   BISM 43:7
   p. you may be mistaken   CROM 105:12
poster Kitchener is a great p.   ASQU 16:11
posterity go down to p.   DISR 122:2
   hope of p.   POWE 316:6
   look forward to p.   BURK 62:16
   P. will do justice   DISR 124:4
   think of your p.   ADAM 4:5
   trustees of P.   DISR 123:6
postindustrial to the p.   MCEW 249:12
postmaster make him a p.   HIND 184:2
postponing simply by p. them   CHUR 92:14
pot chicken in every p.   HOOV 188:4
   chicken in his p.   HENR 180:5
potency evidence of his p.   DISR 124:3
potent Parliament is a p. engine   SALI 342:2
potential p. you actually have   BROW 57:6
Potomac quiet along the P.   MCCL 248:6
poultry lives of the p.   ELIO 132:1
pound British p.   DYSO 129:5
   p. here in Britain   WILS 421:11
pounding Hard p. this   WELL 415:3
poverty against hunger, p.   MARS 261:2

poverty (*cont.*):
amidst its p. and squalor — ARNO 15:11
conquer p. — JOHN 203:3
cost of setting him up in p. — NAID 283:9
hunger and p. — LARK 225:5
languishing in p. — MAND 258:8
mental p. — VALÉ 404:1
p. and excess — PENN 308:13
P. is the parent of revolution — ARIS 15:2
p. of individuals — HUME 191:5
war on p. — JOHN 203:2
power absolute p. corrupts — ACTO 1:11
acquisition of p. — RUSS 336:10
All p. to the Soviets — SLOG 366:1
any man who has p. — MONT 277:10
arrogance of p. — FULB 148:11
arts of p. — CLAY 95:7
balance of p. — KISS 221:12
balance of p. — NICO 286:8
Black P. — CARM 75:8
conception of the p. state — TEMP 389:3
considerable p. — BUTL 67:10
corridors of p. — SNOW 373:3
depositary of p. — DISR 122:11
desire of p. — HOBB 185:2
distribution of political p. — SALI 338:4
duty is to augment official p. — BAGE 23:13
enchanted chambers of P. — LAND 224:8
Everyone who desires p. — MILL 270:1
exaggerate their own p. — SALI 340:1
exercise p. — TREV 398:3
friend in p. is a friend lost — ADAM 2:10
greater the p. — BURK 64:9
greed for p. — LEVI 232:6
honour, command, p. — CICE 93:5
immense p. — DE V 116:5
in office but not in p. — LAMO 224:5
intoxicated with p. — BURK 61:2
jaws of p. are always opened — ADAM 3:13
Johnson's instinct for p. — WHIT 417:6
knowledge itself is p. — BACO 21:9
lay down the reins of p. — LINC 236:5
legislative p. — MONT 277:12
less the p. — LEVI 232:12
live without a common p. — HOBB 185:4
loss of p. — RUSK 335:8
mystery of the king's p. — JAME 197:4
no hopes but from p. — BURK 64:11
only have p. over people — SOLZ 373:9
outrun our spiritual p. — KING 218:2
Parties come to p. — RIDL 326:9
place without p. — ROSE 333:6
political p. of another — LOCK 240:8
politics of p. — HAIL 168:8
p. and glory, or happiness — ARIS 14:12
p. can be rightfully exercised — MILL 269:9
p. elite — MILL 270:8
p. grows out of the barrel of a gun — MAO 259:7
p. in trust — DRYD 127:7
p. is a trust — DISR 123:15
P. is not a means — ORWE 297:9

P. is so apt to be insolent — HALI 170:15
P. is the great aphrodisiac — KISS 221:7
P.? It's like Dead Sea fruit — MACM 253:9
p. of preventing — SALI 341:3
p. of suppress — NORT 292:4
p. of the crown — BURK 63:16
p. over nothing — HERO 182:3
p. should always be distrusted — JONE 206:5
p. to act — LOCK 240:11
p. to tax — MARS 261:3
P. to the people — SLOG 368:8
P., which has the ability — MARG 260:2
p. which stands on Privilege — BELL 33:4
P. without responsibility — KIPL 221:5
responsibility without p. — STOP 382:3
Sitting tight is p. — BELL 33:6
source of p. — MARS 261:6
Sovereign state p. — KEAN 210:1
standing armies of p. — RADC 320:7
supreme p. must be arbitrary — HALI 170:3
toadies of p. — TREV 398:6
Treasury is in p. — WILS 422:1
Unlimited p. — PITT 311:9
utility of monarchical p. — BOSW 52:3
What p. have you got — BENN 34:10
when it comes to p. — SNOW 373:5
wielding p. — GAND 150:14
with Eternal God for p. — TENN 389:11
powerful p. and free — TOCQ 396:7
powers accumulation of all p. — MADI 255:3
Headmasters have p. — CHUR 91:7
high contracting p. — BRIA 54:10
non-resistance to the higher p. — MAYH 264:8
real separation of p. — DENN 115:2
same p. as Scotland — JONE 205:11
ultimate p. of the society — JEFF 200:4
pox or of the p. — WILK 420:1
practical aim of p. politics — MENC 267:4
p. politics — ADAM 3:2
p. service — TOCQ 396:5
practice agree with me in p. — SALI 344:14
intention of putting it into p. — BISM 44:14
politics, as a p. — ADAM 2:9
wear and tear of p. — TROL 400:1
practise never to p. either — TWAI 402:8
pragmatism we need p. — RAFF 321:1
pragmatists p., who hoped — MCEW 249:11
praise Let us now p. famous men — BIBL 41:18
lived on p. — HEAT 179:2
P. the Lord — FORG 143:3
praised everybody p. the Duke — SOUT 374:7
happy when being p. — BALF 28:8
p., and got rid of — CICE 93:10
pray fervently do we p. — LINC 236:6
I p. for the country — HALE 169:3
P. for the dead — JONE 206:2
p. for them — LEE 230:6
p. you, master Lieutenant — MORE 278:9
Work and p. — HILL 184:1
prayer Conservative Party at p. — ROYD 334:8
One p. absorbs all others — GLAD 159:6

people's p.   DRYD 127:6
preaching woman's p.   JOHN 204:9
precedent is a dangerous p.   CORN 103:12
   p. embalms a principle   STOW 382:9
   p. to precedent   TENN 390:1
precious so p. it must be rationed   LENI 231:9
   This p. stone   SHAK 358:6
precise they are not p.   SALI 341:10
predicament not a position, it is a p.   BENN 35:2
pregnant being a little p.   HEND 180:1
prejudices Drive out p.   FRED 147:2
   p. and habits   GIBB 155:16
   proprietor's p.   SWAF 384:3
prelaty yoke of p.   MILT 271:7
preparation no p. is thought necessary   STEV 381:6
   p. for this hour   CHUR 87:13
   week for p.   WILS 423:5
prerogative English subject's sole p.   DRYD 127:17
   last p.   DRYD 127:11
   p. of the eunuch   STOP 382:3
   p. of the harlot   KIPL 221:5
   rotten as P.   BURK 63:16
   that which is called p.   LOCK 240:11
prescience lacked p.   DISR 123:2
presence conspicuous by its p.   RUSS 337:3
   p. on the field   WELL 415:6
present characteristic of the p. age   DISR 120:12
   fallacies of the p.   SALI 338:6
   live in the p.   SPIE 377:10
   no redress for the p.   DISR 122:7
   nothing but the p.   KEYN 215:4
   who controls the p.   ORWE 297:4
preservation p. of their property   LOCK 240:9
preserved Union: it must be p.   JACK 196:3
presidency away from the P.   MISQ 273:6
   cancer close to the P.   DEAN 111:8
   heart-beat from the P.   STEV 380:11
   I will seek the p.   DOLE 125:4
   messenger-boy P.   SCHL 347:8
   pursuit of the P.   JOHN 203:7
   Teflon-coated P.   SCHR 347:11
   US p. a Tudor monarchy   BURG 61:1
   wants the p. that much   BROD 56:2
   want the p.   MCCA 248:1
president All the P. is   TRUM 401:2
   All the P.'s men   BERN 37:7
   anybody could become P.   DARR 109:8
   any boy may become P.   STEV 380:9
   around the American P.   MAIL 256:1
   As P., I have no eyes   LINC 236:9
   come to the p.   EISE 131:11
   cowboy is P.   HANN 172:4
   first p. to be ousted   LIEB 233:6
   more than any other P.   MENC 267:12
   no criticism of the p.   ROOS 333:2
   nothing to hide from the P.   CHUR 89:11
   Office of P.   ROBI 328:11
   powers of P.   GALB 150:5
   P. can sing to you   ROBI 328:9
   P. is a crook   NIXO 290:12

   P. may slip   TOCQ 396:6
   P., not a Pope   STRE 383:1
   p. of Iraq   HUSS 193:3
   P. of the United States   ANON 12:4
   P.'s hardest task   JOHN 203:8
   P. should not wear   MCAL 244:10
   P.'s spouse   BUSH 66:2
   p. who can speak   MCAL 244:9
   rather be right than be P.   CLAY 95:9
   respect the p.   BUSH 67:8
   used to be the next p.   GORE 163:1
   vote for the best P.   PETE 309:8
   We are the P.'s men   KISS 221:13
   What did the P. know   ANON 13:6
   When the P. does it   NIXO 291:6
press as I believe, with the P.   MELB 266:4
   complain about the p.   POWE 315:11
   demagogic, corrupt p.   PULI 317:5
   depends on freedom of the p.   JEFF 198:2
   freedom of the p.   CHUR 92:4
   freedom of the p.   JEFF 199:5
   Freedom of the p. guaranteed   LIEB 233:8
   Freedom of the p. in Britain   SWAF 384:3
   free p. not a privilege   LIPP 237:5
   gentlemen of the p.   SALI 340:1
   liberty of the p.   JUNI 208:12
   lose your temper with the P.   PANK 303:7
   not a free p. but a managed   RADC 320:8
   Our Republic and its p.   PULI 317:4
   popular p. is drinking   MELL 267:1
   power of the p.   NORT 292:4
   p. is ferocious   DIAN 117:4
   p. is free   JEFF 198:10
   P. lives on disaster   ATTL 18:10
   to the p. alone   JEFF 200:11
   Viewed by the p.   CHIL 84:4
   with you on the free p.   STOP 382:5
pressure put p. on me   ROOS 331:11
prestige p. of government   EINS 131:1
   p. without distance   DE G 113:13
presumes p. more boldly   GLAD 158:14
pretended never p. to be   BEAZ 32:2
pretender blessing—the P.   BYRO 68:8
pretendy wee p. government   CONN 101:2
pretexts Tyrants seldom want p.   BURK 61:3
pretty p. straight sort   BLAI 46:4
   P. witty Nell   PEPY 309:2
prevarication last dyke of p.   BURK 65:3
prevent to p. war   MCGU 250:3
   try to p. it   MILN 270:9
preventing power of p.   SALI 341:3
   p. people from taking part   VALÉ 404:2
prey p. of the rich   JEFF 198:4
   to hast'ning ills a p.   GOLD 161:3
price another man's p. increase   WILS 421:14
   bought it at any p.   CLAR 93:14
   love that pays the p.   SPRI 378:2
   pay any p.   KENN 212:4
   p. of admiralty   KIPL 220:10
   p. of championing human   OWEN 299:2
   p. paid for office   TOCQ 395:9

price (*cont.*):

p. well worth paying	LAMO 224:2
those men have their p.	WALP 410:3
prices contrivance to raise p.	SMIT 370:3
rise in p.	HEAT 178:9
prick spur To p. the sides	SHAK 357:3
pride save its p.	MEYE 268:9
priest guts of the last p.	DIDE 118:7
rid me of this turbulent p.	HENR 180:9
priests dominion of p.	PRIC 316:11
p. by the imposition	MACA 246:1
p. have been enemies	HUME 191:7
P. have nephews	PEEL 308:7
with the guts of p.	MESL 268:2
priggish p. schoolgirl	GRIG 167:1
prigs p. and pedants	DISR 120:10
p. who attack	HUMP 192:4
Prime Minister best P. we have	BUTL 68:2
buried the Unknown P.	ASQU 16:9
fresh to be our war P.	BALD 26:11
have you P.	WILD 419:7
HOW DARE YOU BECOME P.	BONH 50:1
known every P.	HAIL 168:13
last British P.	ADAM 2:7
model of a modern P.	HENN 180:2
next P. but three	BELL 33:1
No woman will be P.	THAT 390:3
office of the P.	ASQU 16:7
P. has had a very difficult	GEOR 154:8
P. has nothing to hide	CHUR 89:11
P. has to be a butcher	BUTL 68:4
P. is like the banyan	PATI 306:1
P. needs a Willie	THAT 392:7
P. one day will	KEYS 216:1
to become P.	CALL 71:5
to be P.	TROL 399:5
turned-out P.	MELB 265:8
want to be p.	BROW 57:7
When P. he became	MARG 260:2
woman becoming a P.	ASQU 17:1
Prime Ministers birds, wild flowers, and P.	
	BALD 26:6
Disraeli school of P.	BLAI 46:5
Former P.	GLAD 159:10
like my P. to be	ANON 10:1
limpet-like P.	JENK 201:4
P. are wedded	SAKI 337:8
P. dissatisfied	JENK 201:6
P. have never yet been	CHUR 91:7
primitive call it a 'p. society'	GREG 166:4
prince bless the P. of Wales	SONG 375:2
dominion of a p.	HUME 191:6
in a p. the virtue	MASS 263:11
minister of a p.	RETZ 324:9
p. among my own people	BRAN 54:1
p. must be a fox	MACH 250:11
p. sets himself up above the law	MAYH 264:8
p. who gets a reputation	NAPO 284:7
safer for a p.	MACH 250:9
To be P. of Wales	BENN 35:2
princes P. and lords may flourish	GOLD 161:3

p. are come home again	SHAK 356:8
princess P. leave the Englishwoman	BISM 43:4
She was the People's P.	BLAI 46:3
principate p. and liberty	TACI 384:10
principis Indignatio p. mors est	MORE 278:7
principle agrees with me in p.	SALI 344:14
approves of something in p.	BISM 44:14
compass of p.	ANON 12:2
except from some strong p.	MELB 266:8
influenced by p.	RAKO 321:3
matter of p.	HEAD 177:2
precedent embalms a p.	STOW 382:9
p. of all social progress	FOUR 144:4
p. of the English constitution	BLAC 45:7
Protection is not a p.	DISR 119:10
rebels from p.	BURK 63:4
rise above p.	LONG 241:2
principles adjust their p.	HATT 174:8
begins with that of its p.	MONT 277:6
Damn your p.	DISR 123:16
either morals or p.	GLAD 159:2
embrace your Lordship's p.	WILK 420:1
need good p.	HAYE 176:5
no retreat from the p.	MURR 283:3
not men but p.	PAIN 301:11
p. are the same	JOHN 205:4
p., rather than persons	PAIN 302:5
p. that gave her	WILS 422:17
print p. your own money	THOM 393:9
printing caused p. to be used	SHAK 353:1
Gunpowder, P.	CARL 74:9
p., gunpowder, and the magnet	BACO 21:10
prison born in p.	MALC 257:2
is also a p.	THOR 394:2
only a p.	CUST 108:5
p. and a smile	WOTT 425:1
three years in p.	BROC 56:1
while there is a soul in p.	DEBS 112:1
prisoner object to your being taken p.	KITC 222:3
thoughts of a p.	SOLZ 373:11
prisoners enemy p.	GONZ 162:1
p. of addiction	ILLI 194:9
p. of Communism	SOLZ 374:2
private my p. will	ELIZ 132:4
P. faces in public places	AUDE 19:2
p. family	SMIT 370:5
p. opulence	GALB 149:8
P. property	LIPP 237:2
P. property is a necessary	TAWN 386:9
p. will governs	ROBE 327:11
sphere of p. life	MELB 266:10
system of p. property	HAYE 176:3
privilege Englishman's heaven-born p.	
	ARNO 15:11
free press not a p.	LIPP 237:5
power which stands on P.	BELL 33:4
privileges p. you were born with	BROW 57:6
prize p. in the lottery	RHOD 325:7
prizes glittering p.	SMIT 371:8
probabilities Human p. are not sufficient	
	FAIR 139:1

problem p. of the colour line   DU B 128:5
    you're part of the p.   CLEA 95:12
problems all our p.   THAT 392:11
    No *easy* p.   EISE 131:11
    old p.   WILS 422:3
    Others bring me p.   THAT 392:2
    p. as it can solve   MARX 262:4
    two p. in my life   HOME 187:9
process common market is a p.   MONN 276:3
    due p. of law   CONS 102:6
procreation p. of eels   SCHU 348:4
produce more than they p.   HAYE 176:6
producing consumes without p.   ORWE 296:6
production purpose of p.   SMIT 371:1
profaned desolated and p.   GLAD 158:13
profession politics as a p.   HOWE 190:6
    second oldest p.   REAG 322:11
professor p. of rotational medicine   MORG 278:10
profit no p. but the name   SHAK 352:1
profits best of all monopoly p.   HICK 183:6
    Civilization and p.   COOL 103:6
profusus *sui p.*   SALL 345:3
progress Congress makes no p.   LIGN 233:9
    history of p.   MACA 246:7
    illusion of p.   ANON 13:3
    march of social p.   BERT 37:9
    party of p. or reform   MILL 269:11
    principle of all social p.   FOUR 144:4
    p. depends on unreasonable man   SHAW 361:5
    P. to what   DISR 123:9
    Social P. began   KIPL 219:8
    social p., order, security   JOHN 201:10
progressive in a p. country   DISR 120:16
prohibited not expressly p.   MEGA 265:5
prohibition by the P. laws   EINS 131:1
    Communism is like p.   ROGE 329:8
    drug p.   BOAZ 48:2
    enacting P.   HOOV 188:2
    more successful than P. was   BOAZ 48:3
    P. law strikes a blow   LINC 233:10
proletarian p. socialist state   LENI 231:4
proletariat dictatorship of the p.   MARX 262:10
promise broke no p.   POPE 314:3
    Whose p. none relies on   EPIT 136:3
promised reach the p. land   CALL 70:8
    seen the p. land   KING 217:10
    weird women p.   SHAK 357:5
promises he is a young man of p.   BALF 28:10
    look upon Budget p.   SALI 344:3
    make good their p.   BAGE 23:11
    p. and panaceas   ROTH 334:4
    p. and understandings   TAYL 388:2
    p. nothing   ANON 9:14
    Vote for the man who p. least   BARU 29:9
proof p. is a proof   CHRÉ 85:6
propaganda on p.   CORN 103:13
    purpose of this war is p.   WELL 416:5
    ran the paper purely for p.   BEAV 31:5
propagandist p.'s purpose   HUXL 193:8
propensities natural p.   BURK 64:7
proper know our p. stations   DICK 117:7

property degrees and kinds of p.   MADI 255:2
    distribution of p.   SALI 338:4
    dominion of p.   GOLD 161:2
    not p. but a trust   FOX 144:7
    preservation of their p.   LOCK 240:9
    preserve his p.   LOCK 240:7
    Private p.   LIPP 237:2
    Private p. is a necessary   TAWN 386:9
    P. is theft   PROU 317:3
    p. of others   SALL 345:3
    p. of the rich   RUSK 336:7
    p. or honour   MACH 250:12
    p.-owning democracy   SKEL 365:7
    public p.   JEFF 199:10
    rank or p.   JUNI 208:9
    right of p.   TAFT 385:9
    system of private p.   HAYE 176:3
    through p. that we shall strike   PANK 303:9
    Where p. is in question   SALI 342:7
prophet not as a p.   MAND 258:3
    p. in Israel   BIBL 41:7
prophets ceased to pose as its p.   POPP 314:8
proportions by p. true   MARV 261:9
proprietor p.'s prejudices   SWAF 384:3
prose govern in p.   CUOM 107:5
prosper Treason doth never p.   HARI 173:6
prosperity p. and salvation   CARD 74:3
    P. is necessarily   WILS 422:7
prosperous p. or caring   HESE 182:10
prostitute doormat or a p.   WEST 416:8
prostitutes small nations like p.   KUBR 223:3
protect p. the writer   ACHE 1:9
protection great p. against war   BEVI 40:8
    P. is not a principle   DISR 119:10
    P. is not only dead   DISR 124:6
Protestant Hitler attacked the P. church   NIEM 289:5
    I am the P. whore   GWYN 167:10
    p. ethic   WEBE 412:10
    P. Province of Ulster   CARS 75:13
    P. Religion   CARL 74:9
    P. with a horse   BEHA 32:5
    'tis a P. wind   SONG 375:3
proud p. of their courage   DILL 119:2
    p. of what I did   VANU 404:7
    too p. to fight   WILS 422:12
prove p. anything by figures   CARL 74:5
proven because it's p.   CHRÉ 85:6
providence P. had sent a few men   RUMB 334:9
    P. has not created   TOCQ 396:7
    p. that protects idiots, drunkards   BISM 44:12
    way that P. dictates   HITL 184:7
province p. they have desolated   GLAD 158:13
provision p. for the poor   JOHN 204:4
provokes No one p. me   MOTT 281:5
prudence P. is the other woman   ANON 11:12
    What is p.   SMIT 370:5
Prussia military domination of P.   ASQU 16:5
    national industry of P.   MIRA 271:10
    put P. on the Rhine   ADEN 5:3
pseudo p. event   BOOR 51:1

psychological P. flaws ANON 11:13
p. rule KEYN 215:9
public admired in p. life ROOS 330:2
aggrandizes the p. HUME 191:5
aid of p. service TREV 397:7
as if I was a p. meeting VICT 406:7
assumes a p. trust JEFF 199:10
burn your fingers in p. life BEAV 31:1
carry on great p. schemes BURK 65:5
complainers for the p. BURK 61:11
Debate on p. issues BREN 54:9
exercises a p. trust CLEV 96:8
expense of p. interests TAYL 388:10
for the p. good LOCK 240:11
glorified p. relations man TRUM 401:2
Great p. measures PEEL 308:10
hand into the p. purse PEEL 307:18
holding p. office ACHE 1:6
in p. administration GALB 149:15
lifetime in p. office GALB 150:1
portion of the p. business MILL 269:5
Private faces in p. places AUDE 19:2
p. be damned VAND 404:3
p. liberty HENR 181:7
p. opinion concentrated O'CO 293:8
p. squalor GALB 149:8
p. will not stand HARC 172:7
researchers into P. Opinion AUDE 19:4
respect p. opinion RUSS 336:9
servants of the p. GOWE 163:5
tell the p. which way SULZ 383:9
'yields' to p. opinion SALI 339:4
publicity channels of modern p. BUCH 60:1
oxygen of p. THAT 391:9
qualities which create p. ATTL 18:5
publish P. and be damned WELL 415:4
pudding Take away the p. CHUR 92:16
pugna P. *magna victi sumus* LIVY 238:5
Pulitzer as a P. Prize CHIL 84:4
puller p. down of kings SHAK 353:2
pulling Here p. down MARV 261:9
pulpit such a bully p. ROOS 333:4
white glove p. REAG 322:8
punch p. above its weight HURD 192:8
take away the p. bowl MART 261:8
punctuality P. is the politeness LOUI 242:2
Punica P. *fide* SALL 345:7
punish God p. England FUNK 149:1
punishment cruel and unusual p. CONS 102:7
less horror than the p. GIBB 155:10
our peculiar p. SALI 341:2
punishments sanguinary p. PAIN 301:4
pupil p. of the eye HOLM 187:5
puppets not party p. CANA 73:5
purchasing not worth p. REED 324:3
puritan P. and Presbyterian GALB 150:2
P. hated bear-baiting MACA 247:1
puritanism P. The haunting fear MENC 267:3
Puritans P. from England KEIL 211:2
purpose for an Irish p. DAVI 111:5
politics of p. HUMP 192:2

purse hand into the public p. PEEL 307:18
pursue consistently p. SALI 338:9
pursuing p. our own good MILL 269:8
pursuit p. of happiness JEFF 198:1
p. of the uneatable WILD 419:8
push p. something HARN 173:8
put up with which I will not p. CHUR 90:7
puzzling has always been p. ELIZ 134:4
pyramid bottom of the economic p. ROOS 330:4
pyramids summit of these p. NAPO 284:4
pyre own funeral p. POWE 315:4
Pyrenees P. are no more LOUI 241:6

Quackocracy stages of Q. CARL 74:10
quaint renders q. some GONZ 162:1
qualification only great q. for CARS 76:3
quality q. of mercy SHAK 358:2
quarrel find q. in a straw SHAK 352:2
perpetual q. BURK 62:5
q. in a far away country CHAM 80:1
q. is now between light and darkness
LAMB 224:1
takes one to make a q. INGE 195:1
Quebec Long Live Free Q. DE G 113:12
Q. does not have opinions LAUR 228:12
Québécois I am a Q. LÉVE 232:2
queen choice of a Q. BALD 27:2
Famine Q. GONN 161:9
I have been to the Q. GLAD 159:9
Q. and country THOM 393:7
Q. Caroline, not you ANON 13:11
Q. drops in for tea BYWA 69:4
q. in people's hearts DIAN 117:2
Q. is most anxious VICT 406:3
q. of Scots ELIZ 132:5
take the Q. EPIT 137:2
To toast *The Q.* HEAN 178:2
unfitness for the Q.'s Throne NEWS 287:2
your anointed Q. ELIZ 132:6
queer All the world is q. OWEN 299:4
question debate a q. JOUB 207:10
greatest q. was decided ADAM 3:8
secretly changed the Q. SELL 349:10
questions awkward q. LYNN 244:3
quiet determination of a q. man SMIT 371:12
never have a q. world SHAW 361:8
opportunity to keep q. CHIR 84:7
q. along the Potomac MCCL 248:6
q. life HICK 183:6
quieta Q. *movere* SALL 345:4
quieten q. your enemy by talking CEAU 78:6
quietus q. make With a bare bodkin SHAK 351:11
quis q. *custodiet ipsos Custodes* JUVE 209:2
quits finished when he q. NIXO 291:5
quitter fighter not a q. MAND 259:2
quivering pink, q. Ted ANON 8:3

rabble army would be a base r. BURK 62:9
race clan and r. MILL 270:5

melted into a new r. — CEÈV 104:8
most pernicious r. — SWIF 384:6
No r. can prosper — WASH 410:11
nuclear arms r. — MOUN 281:10
play the r. card — SHAP 359:16
r. is not to the swift — BIBL 41:12
white r. *is* the cancer — SONT 374:4
races darker to the lighter r. — DU B 128:5
Of all the r. — GALB 150:3
racing r. tipster — TAYL 387:7
racism institutional r. — MACP 254:7
racket all a German r. — RIDL 327:1
radical Be as R. as you like — CHAM 79:5
commends a r. change — FISH 140:8
must have r. origins — TREV 398:7
never dared be r. when young — FROS 148:5
R. is a man — ROOS 330:14
radicalism Hostility to R. — SALI 343:13
r. and nothing else — DISR 123:4
radicals dogs or the R. — WILD 419:7
goddam r. — CAPO 74:2
trouble with r. — CARV 76:7
rafts r. floating untethered — GLAD 159:10
rage r. to live — VANE 404:5
ragout fricassee, or a r. — SWIF 384:8
raid R. BY DR JAMESON — KRUG 223:2
railway by r. timetables — TAYL 387:5
rain buried in the r. — MILL 270:3
command the r. — PEPY 308:16
credit for the r. — MORR 280:1
gentle r. from heaven — SHAK 358:2
rainbow no r. nation — MAND 259:1
r. coalition — JACK 196:10
raison r. *tonne en son cratère* — SONG 375:5
Raj sort of Scottish R. — PAXM 306:6
random chosen at r. — LLOY 238:10
rank distinguished by r. — JUNI 208:9
flog the r. and file — ARNO 15:12
r. is but the guinea's stamp — BURN 65:8
ranks must first close r. — CARM 75:9
rap r. at the ballot box — CHIL 84:3
rarest r. of all qualities — DISR 124:12
rascals R., would you live — FRED 147:4
rash r. and precipitate assent — PEEL 307:8
rat Anyone can r. — CHUR 87:1
grey wharf-r. — THOR 394:3
not worth a r.'s squeak — RUSK 336:3
r. out of the sewer — MOSL 280:5
smell a r. — ROCH 328:12
ratio geometrical r. — MALT 257:8
rational try to make it r. — CAMP 72:6
rationed so precious it must be r. — LENI 231:9
rats two hundred r. — VOLT 407:11
razor arse full of r. blades — KEAT 210:2
fitter instrument than a r. — PEEL 307:16
reach I r. for my pistol — JOHS 205:10
r. the promised land — CALL 70:8
reaction r. which is to be — TREV 398:7
reactionaries All r. are paper tigers — MAO 259:8
reactionary R. is a man — ROOS 330:14
recklessly r. steps — BOOK 50:6

read cannot now r. a page — WALP 410:7
not that I ever r. them — SHER 363:1
R. my lips — BUSH 66:9
want to r. a novel — DISR 124:11
readers sentiment of his r. — VEBL 405:2
Sun r. — YELL 427:2
reading Peace is poor r. — HARD 173:3
ready necessity of being r. — LINC 235:1
Reagan Let R. be Reagan — SLOG 367:13
R.'s optimism — BUSH 67:1
real Canada is not a r. country — BOUC 52:4
sounded so r. — TROL 399:4
their world is the r. one — ROTH 334:3
reality they are a r. — DEWA 116:9
too far from r. — SAHH 337:6
realm One r., one people — SLOG 366:14
this earth, this r. — SHAK 358:6
realms whom three r. obey — POPE 314:7
reap r. your old reward — KIPL 221:3
they shall r. the whirlwind — BIBL 41:17
when to r. — JEFF 200:8
reappraisal agonizing r. — DULL 128:7
reaps another r. — SHEL 362:7
reason influence of mere r. — PEEL 308:10
let us r. together — JOHN 203:11
r. and conscience — PRIC 316:11
r. and humanity — JEFF 200:11
r., and justice — BURK 62:3
r. and justice — HAMI 172:1
R. herself will respect — GIBB 155:16
R. to rule — DRYD 127:11
worst possible r. — CLIN 98:1
reasonable R. Man — HERB 181:11
r. man adapts — SHAW 361:5
will must be r. — JEFF 199:2
reasons R. are not like garments — ESSE 137:10
r. will certainly — MANS 259:5
twenty good r. why I can — BEVI 40:9
rebel die like a true-blue r. — LAST 227:4
I am *still* a r. — BROW 58:5
starve or r. — DUND 128:9
What is a r. — CAMU 73:2
rebelled have already r. — GIBB 155:8
rebellion little r. now and then — JEFF 198:5
R. lay in his way — SHAK 352:4
R. to tyrants — BRAD 53:5
R. to tyrants — MOTT 281:6
r. was the certain consequence — MANS 259:4
rum, Romanism, and r. — BURC 60:7
rebellions domestic r. — SALI 337:9
rebels r. are our countrymen — GRAN 164:3
subjects are r. — BURK 63:4
tip to r. — NICO 289:3
rebuilt requires to be r. — MILL 269:6
receiver r. and the giver — BURK 62:19
recession R. is when you have to — PANK 303:11
r. that Australia had to have — KEAT 210:3
r. when your neighbour — TRUM 401:9
spend way out of a r. — CALL 70:7
reckless r. hustings pledge — SALI 338:5
r. with our government — SHOR 364:5

recognized being r.   BECK 32:3
reconciliation bridge of r.   RUNC 335:4
  stability and r.   MITC 275:1
  True r. does not   MAND 258:6
reconstruction r. of Christian life   BONH 50:2
reconvened hereby r.   EWIN 138:5
record look at the r.   IVIN 195:9
  reversal of his r.   MARS 261:1
recreate r. their countries   BLUN 47:11
red Better r. than dead   SLOG 366:7
  get very r. in the face   BENT 36:1
  in the r. states   OBAM 292:10
  keep the r. flag flying   SONG 377:1
  people's flag is deepest r.   SONG 377:1
  raiment all r.   MACA 247:4
  r. men scalped each other   MACA 245:6
redtape r. talking-machine   CARL 75:1
reference within my terms of r.   HUTT 193:4
referendum r.? It'll be   SARK 346:5
referendums R. produce results   KINN 219:3
refined ruled in more r. ages   BAGE 22:12
reform innovate is not to r.   BURK 61:7
  party of progress or r.   MILL 269:11
  Peace, retrenchment, and r.   BRIG 55:4
  sets about r.   TOCQ 396:3
  thunder for r.   NEWS 288:7
  Universities never r. themselves   MELB 266:2
reformation plotting some new r.   DRYD 127:16
  total r.   PAIN 301:1
reforms beneficial r.   THAT 392:9
refuge Patriotism is the last r.   JOHN 204:17
refugees r. back   ROBE 327:8
refuse r. of your teeming tents   LAZA 229:9
  r. to fight   SLOG 369:2
  Which he did thrice r.   SHAK 355:10
regiment r. of women   KNOX 222:4
register r. of the crimes, follies   GIBB 155:6
regret Old Age a r.   DISR 122:9
  spoken with greater r.   BALD 26:12
regrets congratulatory r.   DISR 121:16
  I have no r.   CRES 104:6
regrette *Je ne r. rien*   CRES 104:6
regulations avalance of r.   BOOK 50:7
  ten thousand r.   CHUR 92:12
Reich *Ein R.*   SLOG 366:14
reign Let freedom r.   BUSH 67:6
  Let freedom r.   MAND 258:5
  Long to r. over us   SONG 375:7
  not you, that r.   ANON 13:11
reigned if he had not r.   TACI 385:7
  r. with your loves   ELIZ 133:4
reigns king r.   THIE 393:1
reinvent r. ourselves   HUMP 192:4
reject elect, and to r.   PAIN 302:4
  Minister will r. it   LYNN 244:5
  unelected r. politicians   RIDL 327:2
rejoice r. at that news   THAT 391:2
  r., rejoice   HEAT 179:3
relation cold r.   BURK 63:9
  State is a r. of men   WEBE 413:1
relations not have sexual r.   CLIN 97:8

  r. of life and death   DOUG 126:3
relationship r. that was not   CLIN 97:9
relief system of outdoor r.   BRIG 55:3
relieve chance to r. yourself   ANON 11:3
relieved By desperate appliances are r.
    SHAK 351:16
religio *Tantum r. potuit*   LUCR 243:5
religion As to r.   PAIN 300:10
  dominion of r.   GOLD 161:2
  establishment of r.   CONS 102:4
  Every dictator uses r.   BHUT 40:14
  feature of *any* r.   PAIN 301:8
  fox-hunting—the wisest r.   HAIL 168:11
  Freedom of r.   JEFF 199:5
  in Quebec a r.   FOTH 144:1
  Leave the matter of r.   GRAN 164:6
  much wrong could r. induce   LUCR 243:5
  Not a r. for gentlemen   CHAR 82:4
  on account of my r.   BELL 33:5
  politics as well as in r.   JUNI 208:8
  Politics, like r.   JEFF 199:12
  r. from politics   TREV 398:4
  r. is allowed to invade   MELB 266:10
  R. is the sigh   MARX 262:3
  r. is to do good   PAIN 302:2
  R. may in most   RUSS 336:14
  r. of humanity   PAIN 300:14
  r. of slaves   SALI 343:5
  r. of Socialism   BEVA 38:5
  reproach to r.   PENN 308:13
  sort of r.   TOCQ 396:5
religions r. considered man as man   TOCQ 395:6
religious all r. revolution   WEBE 413:3
  of some r. movement   SALI 341:13
  r. observance   DEED 112:5
reluctant r. obedience   MACA 246:9
remedies by violent r.   MONT 277:2
remedy applying the wrong r.   BENN 34:1
  dangerous r.   FAWK 139:8
  Force is not a r.   BRIG 55:5
  grievance to the r.   PEEL 308:5
  r. our *enemies* have chosen   SHER 363:6
  Things without all r.   SHAK 357:6
  'Tis a sharp r.   RALE 321:6
remember cannot r. the past   SANT 346:3
  knows what to r.   MORL 279:7
  R.   LAST 227:12
  r. the Fifth of November   ANON 11:11
  r. what is past   HALI 169:8
remembered like to be r.   POWE 315:13
remorse disjoins R. from power   SHAK 354:2
remunerated more highly r.   SMIT 371:7
render R. therefore unto Caesar   BIBL 41:22
rendezvous r. with destiny   ROOS 330:9
Reno King's Moll R.'d   NEWS 288:1
renounce I r. war   FOSD 143:6
rent r. is due   TINE 395:1
  R. is that portion   RICA 325:8
  r. we pay for our room   CLAY 95:11
reorganized we would be r.   ANON 13:3
repairing full r. lease   THAT 391:13

repartee always the best r.   DISR 123:8
repeal r. of bad or obnoxious laws   GRAN 164:5
repeat condemned to r. it   SANT 346:3
   I r. myself   TWAI 402:10
repeated mistake shall not be r.   EPIT 137:3
reporters speaking through r.   CARL 74:14
representation Taxation and r.   CAMD 71:10
   Taxation without r.   OTIS 298:9
representative r. assemblies   BEVA 39:7
   r. government   DISR 123:7
   Your r. owes you   BURK 64:10
repression price of r.   DU B 128:4
reproach leave affairs of r.   MACH 251:3
reproofs r. from authority   BACO 20:13
reptilian r. kitten-eater   ANON 8:8
republic destroyed the R.   DE V 115:11
   England is a disguised r.   BAGE 24:2
   essence of the R.   ROBE 328:4
   If a r. is small   MONT 277:8
   Love the Beloved R.   FORS 143:5
   Our R. and its press   PULI 317:4
   r., if you can keep it   FRAN 146:1
   R. is a government   BAGE 22:14
   r. is a raft   AMES 7:6
   r. with a wholly   HAIL 168:12
republican be a r. at twenty   PROV 319:5
   Democratic or R. way   LA G 223:7
   R. cloth coat   NIXO 290:2
   r. government   HAMI 171:10
   r. is the only form   JEFF 198:9
   understood by r. government   TOCQ 396:9
republics R. end in luxury   MONT 277:5
repulsive Right but R.   SELL 349:5
reputation r. and the favour   JEFF 199:6
requirement r. of a statesman   ACHE 1:8
rerat ingenuity to r.   CHUR 87:1
rescind NOT TO R.   REVE 325:5
rescued waiting to be r.   STEE 379:3
researchers Our r. into Public Opinion   AUDE 19:4
reservations no mental r.   LINC 234:11
reserve second profession in r.   NICO 289:3
reserved r. for some end   CLIV 98:3
resign Few die and none r.   MISQ 272:8
   more ready to r.   SALI 341:12
   says he won't r.   GALB 150:10
resignation Always threatening r.   BEAV 31:7
   by r. none   JEFF 199:7
   r. in him   BUTL 67:9
resigned r. commission   ANON 8:13
resistance break the r.   STAL 378:4
   history of r.   WILS 422:8
   intellectual r.   O'BR 293:2
   line of least r.   AMER 7:3
   r. by the *sword*   CLAY 95:3
   r. of established ideas   BERL 37:5
resolution r. on reflection   WALP 409:4
respect destroy all r.   CHUR 92:12
   fail to get r.   MACH 251:1
   r. each other   TAYL 387:10
   r. of the people   MARS 261:6
respected r. persons occasionally   HURD 192:7

respecter r. of persons   BROW 58:3
responsibility I accept r.   HOON 188:1
   Liberty means r.   SHAW 361:3
   Power without r.   KIPL 221:5
   r. without power   STOP 382:3
   slightest sense of r.   ANON 10:6
responsible personally r.   HIRO 184:4
rest neither business nor r.   MORL 279:6
   period of real r.   LAWS 229:7
   r. were little ones   ELIZ 133:10
resting give us a r.-place   WEIZ 414:5
restituit *cunctando r. rem*   ENNI 135:8
restored r. all that was beautiful   NEHR 286:1
restrain r. the popular sentiments   PEEL 307:12
restraint r. and punishment   MILT 271:4
restrictions finding greater r.   KEIL 211:2
restructuring r. [perestroika]   GORB 162:5
result r. happiness   DICK 117:8
results Referendums produce r.   KINN 219:3
   will have permanent r.   SALI 343:14
retail r. mind   LLOY 239:10
retaliation policy of r.   PARN 305:1
retard r. what we cannot repel   JOHN 204:1
reticence It is a R.   GLAD 159:13
   Northern r.   HEAN 178:5
retire r. from this station   JEFF 199:6
   r. gracefully   SALI 345:1
retirement r. from the stage   MACM 253:13
   there must be no r.   HAIG 168:4
retiring r. at high speed toward   HALS 171:7
retreat no r. from the principles   MURR 283:3
   not r. a single inch   GARR 152:2
retreating my right is r.   FOCH 142:3
retrenchment Peace, r., and reform   BRIG 55:4
retrograde no stronger r. force   CHUR 91:11
   r. if it does not advance   GIBB 155:15
retrospective r. or utopian   ARON 16:1
return I shall r.   MACA 245:3
   I will r.   EPIT 137:1
   r. of democratic control   STEE 379:2
revenge Gerald Ford as his r.   ABZU 1:4
   in Victory, R.   LYNN 244:4
   ranging for r.   SHAK 355:4
   r. for slight injuries   MACH 250:8
   r. what has happened   BISM 43:9
   tribal, intimate r.   HEAN 178:3
revengeful he's r.   SHAK 353:3
revenue Internal R. Service   SULL 383:5
   standing r.   BURK 62:5
reverence mystic r.   BAGE 22:1
   so poor to do him r.   SHAK 355:12
reverse not got a r. gear   BLAI 46:14
revive r. in New South Wales   BANK 29:2
revolt It is a big r.   LA R 225:6
revolution After a r.   HALI 170:1
   age of r.   JEFF 199:5
   commences a r. can rarely   JEFF 200:7
   destroyed by a r.   TOCQ 396:3
   entered into this R.   BROW 58:5
   French R. operated   TOCQ 395:6
   it is a big r.   LA R 225:6

revolution (*cont.*):

leaders of a r.   CONR 101:10
parent of r. and crime   ARIS 15:2
peaceful r.   KENN 213:1
restrained tyrants, averted r.   BENN 34:7
R. a parent of settlement   BURK 62:15
R., like Saturn   VERG 405:6
r. of rising expectations   CLEV 96:11
r. without revolution   ROBE 327:10
safeguard a r.   ORWE 297:9
served the cause of the r.   BOLÍ 49:4
You've had a r.   GEOR 154:9

revolutionaries R. are more formalistic
                                               CALV 71:8
r. potential Tories   ORWE 296:10
unmanageable r.   DE V 116:7

revolutionary can't feel r. in a bathroom
                                               LINK 237:1
Every r. ends as   CAMU 73:4
fine r. phrases   KHRU 216:10
forge his r. spirit   GUEV 167:9
most radical r.   AREN 14:4
r. government   ROBE 328:3
r. right   LINC 234:12

revolutionists age fatal to R.   DESM 115:8

revolutions All modern r.   CAMU 73:3
causes r.   SHEE 361:13
formerly called r.   PAIN 301:12
main cause of r.   INGE 194:11
R. are celebrated   BOUL 52:6
R. are not made   PHIL 310:6
R. are not made   PROV 319:8
R. have never lightened   SHAW 361:1
r. never go backward   SEWA 350:2
r. with rosewater   HEAL 177:13
share in two r.   PAIN 302:6

revolver reaches for a r.   GLEN 160:2
resembles a r.   FANO 139:3

reward fed with r.   TAYL 388:11
reap your old r.   KIPL 221:3

rhetoric Death, without r.   SIEY 365:1

rhetorician sophistical r.   DISR 121:17

Rhine R. is where our frontier lies   BALD 26:10

Rhodesia black majority rule in R.   SMIT 372:1

riband Just for a r.   BROW 59:1

rich better to be r. than poor   CECI 78:9
by destroying the r.   LINC 236:12
few who are r.   KENN 212:5
incomes of the r.   SHAW 360:10
little r. girl   ABBO 1:2
make the r. richer   NEHR 285:10
not r. enough   REED 324:3
of the powerful and r.   SALI 343:5
people can still get r.   REAG 323:5
poor people in r. countries   BAUE 30:5
R. AND THE POOR   DISR 123:3
r. as well as the poor   FRAN 145:3
r. enough to pay   HEAL 177:3
r. have no right   RUSK 336:7
r. in a more precious treasure   MACA 246:1
r. man in his castle   ALEX 6:7

r. men rule the law   GOLD 161:6
r. on the poor   JEFF 198:4
r., quiet, and infamous   MACA 246:11
r. wage war   SART 346:7
tax r. people   LLOY 239:18

rid decorated, and got r. of   CICE 93:10
How do we get r. of you   BENN 34:10
wishes to be r. of it   ROSE 333:9

riddle r. wrapped in a mystery   CHUR 87:10

riddles R. lie here   EPIT 136:7

ride if you cannot r. two horses   MAXT 264:4

ridiculous no sense of the r.   PEEL 308:8
no spectacle so r.   MACA 246:2
sublime to the r.   NAPO 284:11

Ridley good comfort, Master R.   LAST 226:2

rien R.   LOUI 241:10

right almost always in the r.   SMIT 372:9
be on the r. side   GALB 150:9
convinced that they are r.   VAN 404:4
defend to the death your r.   MISQ 273:3
doing what is r.   SALI 344:5
firmness in the r.   LINC 236:7
forgive those who were r.   MACL 251:9
if r., to be kept right   SCHU 348:3
I had rather be r.   CLAY 95:9
individual r.   TAFT 385:9
is it r.   KING 218:4
just not r.   PARK 304:10
'just' or 'r.'   PLAT 312:9
know what is r.   JOHN 203:8
Liberty is the r.   MONT 277:9
majority never has r.   IBSE 194:4
man of the r.   MOSL 280:5
more than half the people are r.   WHIT 417:4
my r. is retreating   FOCH 142:3
No R.   MITC 274:7
no r. in the circus   MAXT 264:4
not r. now   JAY 197:9
our country, r. or wrong   DECA 112:2
R. but Repulsive   SELL 349:5
r. is more precious   WILS 422:9
r. man in the right place   JEFF 200:12
r. of the ignorant man   CARL 74:6
r. of trampling on them   CHIL 84:2
r. to be heard   HUMP 192:1
r. to be let alone   BRAN 53:8
r. to be obeyed   JOHN 201:9
r. to govern   HARR 174:4
r. to rise up   LINC 234:1
r. to vote   ANTH 14:1
r. way to say things   ABBO 1:3
r. which goes unrecognized   WEIL 414:2
r.-wing, like nature   DEBR 111:10
Self-government is our r.   CASE 76:8
vast r.-wing conspiracy   CLIN 97:3
What is r.   PEEL 307:4

righteous armour of a r. cause   BRYA 59:7

rightful will to be r.   JEFF 199:2

rights all your r. become   CASE 76:9
asserting these r.   LAY 229:8
Bill of R. seems   COMM 100:2

certain unalienable r. ANON 13:2
championing human r. OWEN 299:2
equal in dignity and r. UNIV 403:5
extension of women's r. FOUR 144:4
from the South its dearest r. LEE 230:6
imaginary r., a bastard brood BENT 35:7
inalienable r. ROBE 328:1
respect for the r. of all BAGE 25:3
r. are disregarded BROW 58:4
r. bequeathed to us ADAM 4:9
r. inherent and inalienable JEFF 198:1
r. of an Englishman JUNI 208:12
r. of mankind JEFF 198:9
r. of other people SALI 340:4
Sovereign has three r. BAGE 23:4
talked about equal r. JOHN 203:1
rigid decisions that are r. PROD 317:2
thy too r. fate MONT 278:1
rigorously investigate anything too r. FILK 140:4
ring diaper into the r. ICKE 194:7
now r. the bells WALP 410:2
ringleaders r. from the Tarpeian rock
ARNO 15:12
riot r. is at bottom KING 218:3
rise people should never r. ADAM 3:5
right to r. up LINC 234:1
rising from r. hope FOOT 142:8
means of r. JOHN 204:18
revolution of r. expectations CLEV 96:11
r. hope MACA 246:6
R. of the Moon LARK 225:4
r. tide lifts all boats PROV 319:9
risk r. more democracy BRAN 53:10
risks just one of the r. he takes STEV 380:9
risky too r. and dangerous STRO 383:2
rivalry dead there is no r. MACA 246:4
river as in a r. HALI 170:6
Fame is like a r. BACO 20:16
House of Parliament upon the r. WELL 416:2
where there is no r. KHRU 216:7
rivers r. of blood JEFF 200:6
road in the middle of the r. BEVA 38:9
r. to Damascus THAT 391:16
roar called upon to give the r. CHUR 90:17
roast in boiled and r. SMIT 372:6
robber r.'s bundle SHEL 362:11
robe judge's r. SHAK 357:12
robes r. ye weave SHEL 362:7
robin R. and I are two honest men SHIP 364:2
robs government which r. Peter SHAW 360:7
rock smote the r. WEBS 413:9
until you find a r. CATL 77:7
rocked r. the system ROBI 328:7
rocket rose like a r. PAIN 301:2
rogue r. elephant TAYL 387:14
roi *que le roi* PROV 318:14
Roisin R. Dubh MACN 254:5
roll R. up that map PITT 312:6
Rolls like a R. Royce BUTL 68:3
Roman deceased R. Empire HOBB 185:12
found the R. nation VIRG 406:11

I am a R. citizen CICE 93:8
neither holy, nor R. VOLT 407:6
noblest R. of them all SHAK 356:7
R. people CALI 70:4
R.-Saxon-Danish-Norman DEFO 112:11
Romana *stat R. virisque* ENNI 135:7
Romanism rum, R., and rebellion BURC 60:7
Romans Friends, R., countrymen SHAK 355:7
R. were like brothers MACA 247:8
romantic R. Ireland's dead and gone YEAT 426:10
Wrong but R. SELL 349:5
Romanus *Civis R. sum* CICE 93:8
Civis R. sum PALM 303:1
Rome Bishop of R. BOOK 50:4
cruel men of R. SHAK 353:9
loved R. more SHAK 355:5
Men, I'm getting out of R. GARI 151:10
Now is it R. indeed SHAK 354:3
R., though her eagle WALL 408:8
R. under Sulla was like a bus ADCO 4:13
second at R. CAES 69:4
Treaty [of R.] DENN 114:10
voice of R. JONS 206:6
romping r. of sturdy children DE V 116:3
Romulus dregs of R. CICE 93:2
roof beneath whose r. I sleep BORR 52:2
roofs tiles on the r. LUTH 243:8
room always r. at the top WEBS 413:15
Great hatred, little r. YEAT 426:8
just entering the r. BROU 57:3
smoke-filled r. SIMP 365:4
struggle for r. MALT 257:9
rooms boys in the back r. BEAV 31:4
root axe to the r. PAIN 301:4
begins to take r. WASH 411:7
r., hog, or die BROG 56:3
roots lay bare its r. JOUB 207:9
party comes from the grass r. BEVE 39:11
rope sell us the r. MISQ 272:4
rose Goodbye, England's r. JOHN 202:2
R. shall fade DAVI 110:9
white r. of Scotland MACD 249:1
roses smells like r. JOHN 203:13
Treaties like girls and r. DE G 113:11
rosewater made with r. PROV 319:8
revolutions with r. HEAL 177:13
rotational r. medicine MORG 278:10
rotten like r. mackerel RAND 322:1
shines like r. wood RALE 321:4
Something is r. SHAK 351:9
rottenness r. begins in his conduct JEFF 198:12
Roundheads R. (Right but Repulsive) SELL 349:5
rout r. send forth a joyous shout MACA 247:4
routine care more for r. BAGE 23:12
royal bee on r. jelly CHUR 92:7
If you have a R. Family PIML 311:3
needed no r. title SPEN 374:9
R. authority MONT 277:13
r. throne of kings SHAK 358:6
this is the r. Law CORO 104:1
royalist more of a r. PROV 318:14

salutes see if anyone s.   PROV 319:2
salvation Mankind's s.   SOLZ 373:12
   prosperity and s.   CARD 74:3
   s. of Europe   PITT 312:3
Samaritan Good S.   THAT 391:11
same all say *the* s.   MELB 266:9
   Ever the s.   MOTT 281:7
sanctuary three classes which need s.   BALD 26:6
sandhills s. of the Baldwin Cabinet   ASQU 16:8
sang s. a king out of three kingdoms   WHAR 417:3
sansculotte *bon S. Jésus*   DESM 115:8
Santa Claus shoot S.   SMIT 371:6
sash s. my father wore   SONG 377:2
Saskatchewan on the banks of the S.   LAUR 228:10
sat everyone has s. except a man   CUMM 107:4
   s. too long here   CROM 106:1
Satanic dark S. mills   BLAK 47:4
satellite With s. TV   O'DO 293:9
satirist s. may laugh   GIBB 155:16
Saturn Revolution, like S.   VERG 405:6
saucepan fishes in a s.   KHRU 216:8
savaged s. by a dead sheep   HEAL 177:5
save God s. the king   SONG 375:7
   helped s. the world   KEYN 215:13
   less democracy to s.   ATKI 17:6
   Save me, oh, s. me   CANN 73:8
   s. the Governor-General   WHIT 418:2
   s. the Union   LINC 235:3
saved be s. in this World   HALI 171:3
   only s. the world   CHES 83:7
saw I came, I s., I conquered   CAES 69:11
Saxon S. will ever relax   O'DO 294:2
say all s. *the same*   MELB 266:9
   do as I s.   THAT 390:8
   s. nothing   HEAN 178:5
   s. what they please   FRED 147:3
   s. what you think   TACI 385:6
   that you could ever s.   BROW 57:9
   wrong way to s. things   ABBO 1:3
says What Manchester s. today   PROV 319:12
scabbard threw away the s.   CLAR 93:11
scabs Make yourselves s.   SHAK 350:7
scaffold forever on the s.   LOWE 242:9
scandal s. by a woman of easy virtue   HAIL 168:5
scandalous s. and poor   ROCH 328:13
scar s. on the conscience   BLAI 46:11
scarecrow make a s. of the law   SHAK 357:10
scarlet raise the s. standard   SONG 377:1
scent whiff of s.   LLOY 239:7
sceptered s. isle   SHAK 358:6
sceptre s. of George III   JOHN 205:6
schedule my s. is already full   KISS 221:6
schemes s. of political improvement   JOHN 204:10
Schleswig-Holstein S. question   PALM 303:4
scholarship indications of s.   CHUR 91:6
school destroy every grammar s.   CROS 106:12
   erecting a grammar s.   SHAK 353:1
   s. of Manchester   DISR 124:7
   went to s. without any boots   BULM 60:4
schoolboy Every s. knows   MACA 246:10

schoolgirl priggish s.   GRIG 167:1
schools hundred s. of thought contend   MAO 259:9
   s. will be better   JEFF 200:1
   some children, in some s.   BLUN 47:9
science Dismal S.   CARL 74:15
   do s. in hell   VAUG 405:1
   follow the progress of s.   SALI 343:3
   Politics is not an exact s.   BISM 43:6
   separation of state and s.   FEYE 140:3
   triumph of modern s.   WAUG 412:4
scientific s. power has outrun   KING 218:2
scoffing S. his state   SHAK 358:11
scold what a s. you are   BULL 60:3
scooters s. off my lawn   CLAR 94:10
scorn think foul s.   ELIZ 132:9
Scotch as a S. banker   DAVI 110:4
   like the S. terrier   BRIG 55:7
scotched s. the snake   SHAK 357:6
Scotchman count on a S.   SALI 342:11
Scotland flower of S.   WILL 420:4
   new voice of S.   CONN 101:1
   our infinite S.   MACD 249:2
   popular in S.   DAVI 110:2
   renewed in S.   DEWA 116:10
   same powers as S.   JONE 205:11
   S., land of omnipotent No   BOLD 48:7
   S.'s oil   SLOG 367:6
   S.'s rightful heritage   CONN 100:5
   S. will be reborn   NAIR 283:10
   sing Flower of S.   SILL 365:3
   Stands S.   SHAK 357:8
   white rose of S.   MACD 249:1
Scots S. deserve no pity   FLET 142:1
Scottish S. and Welsh nationalism   BAKE 25:8
   S. Parliament   EWIN 138:5
   S. parliament   SALM 345:10
   S. Parliament   WATE 411:8
   shall be a S. parliament   ANON 12:7
   shall be a S. parliament   DEWA 116:9
   sort of S. Raj   PAXM 306:6
   will of the S. people   SMIT 372:3
scoundrel plea of the s.   BLAK 47:3
   refuge of a s.   JOHN 204:17
scoundrels ten obvious s.   MENC 267:6
scout newly enrolled Boy S.   LEVI 232:7
scratch S. any American   RUSK 335:7
screaming s. through the keyholes   LLOY 239:3
scribbled by a s. name   THOM 393:3
scribbler academic s.   KEYN 215:10
scribblers Teenage s.   LAWS 229:5
scripture know more of the s.   TYND 403:2
scum glittering s.   CHUR 87:4
   s. of the earth   WELL 415:7
scurvy s. politician   SHAK 356:11
sea complaining about the s.   POWE 315:11
   dominion of the s.   COVE 104:2
   in a s. of glory   SHAK 353:5
   s.-change in politics   CALL 71:3
   s., which seems to want   MONT 277:4
   set in the silver s.   SHAK 358:6

sea (*cont.*):
slowly towards the s.   CHES 83:9
smiling surface of the s.   PLUT 313:5
to the English that of the s.   RICH 326:8
very much at s.   CARS 76:3
water in the rough rude s.   SHAK 358:8
willing foe and s. room   ANON 13:9
seagreen s. Incorruptible   CARL 74:11
sealed My lips are s.   MISQ 273:7
seals receives the s. of office   ROSE 333:11
sacrifice the s.   LLOY 239:13
seasons man for all s.   WHIT 419:1
seat in the driver's s.   BEAV 31:6
s. in the House   DISR 122:19
s. of Mars   SHAK 358:6
without a s.   CHUR 92:2
seated looked wiser when he was s.   KEYN 214:9
seats where we win s.   SALI 340:12
secession not towards union, but s.   SALI 338:10
second elect the s. chamber   JAY 197:11
In war there is no s. prize   BRAD 53:3
not a s. on the day   COOK 102:8
Politics comes at least s.   GIUL 157:7
s. at Rome   CAES 69:9
s.-class intellect   HOLM 187:4
s. oldest profession   REAG 322:11
s. profession in reserve   NICO 289:3
You would get s. raters   LONG 241:3
secrecy S., and a free   TRUM 401:15
secret concept of the official s.   WEBE 413:4
fit to be trusted with a s.   SALI 338:11
if you wish to keep a s.   SALI 344:9
is the s. weapon   CRIT 105:6
keeping the s.   TAYL 388:8
s. in the Oxford sense   FRAN 146:8
uncover some s.   MONT 277:3
secretary S. stays and gets thinner   ANON 11:5
secretive s. and authoritarian   GREE 165:8
secrets Official S. Act   LYNN 244:6
sect found them a s.   MACA 246:13
Persecute a s. and it holds   BAGE 24:13
sectaries in a nation of s.   DISR 122:12
security fear, otherwise styled s.   MADA 254:8
make s. secure   POPP 314:9
not much collective s.   CHUR 87:6
s. around the American President   MAIL 256:1
s. of Europe   MITC 275:2
s. of free states   DEMO 114:5
watchword is s.   PITT 311:15
seditione *de s. querentes*   JUVE 209:1
seditions surest way to prevent s.   BACO 21:2
see cannot s. the Speaker   ANON 9:12
could he s. you now   AUDE 18:16
day I was meant not to s.   THAT 391:6
We had better wait and s.   ASQU 16:4
seed s.-time of continental   PAIN 300:6
s. ye sow   SHEL 362:7
seeds s. of its own destruction   HARP 174:1
s. of the death of any state   HOBB 185:10
s. were waiting in the ground   BAGE 24:4
seeing *way* of s.   KEEN 210:10

seem to s. active   BONA 49:9
seen I have s. war   ROOS 330:10
should be s. to be done   HEWA 183:1
segregation S. now   WALL 408:3
selection no s. by examination   BLUN 47:8
self but their s.-love   SMIT 370:2
insult their s.-respect   TAWN 386:10
legitimate s.-interest   BAST 30:3
propelled by s.-interest   BAGE 21:14
s.-assertion abroad   WAUG 411:11
s.-censorship becomes   GALB 150:1
s.-control in Cabinet   SHEP 362:13
S.-government is our right   CASE 76:8
s.-preservation in the other   JEFF 200:3
s.-protection   MILL 269:7
S.-sufficiency at home   WAUG 411:11
starves your s.-respect   PARR 305:6
tyranny of s.-government   DISR 123:12
sell Don't s. America short   PROV 318:7
One does not s. the earth   CRAZ 104:5
s. Jack like soapflakes   KENN 213:12
s., or deny, or delay   MAGN 255:8
selling S. off the family silver   MISQ 273:8
semi s.-house-trained polecat   FOOT 142:7
semper *S. aliquid novi*   PLIN 313:1
S. eadem   MOTT 281:7
Sic s. tyrannis   MOTT 281:8
senator S., and a Democrat   JOHN 202:6
S., you're no Jack Kennedy   BENT 36:3
senators I look at the s.   HALE 169:3
send s. a gun-boat   BEVA 38:7
senior of a s. colleague   CLAR 94:4
sense good s. and the good faith   GLAD 158:14
Have you no s. of decency   WELC 414:6
question of competence and good s.   BIRC 43:1
talk s. to the American people   STEV 380:5
senseless worse than s. things   SHAK 353:9
senses come to their s.   PHOC 310:10
sensibilité equivalent to *s.*   PALM 303:6
sentence end a s. with a climax   LASK 225:8
life s. goes on   CONL 100:4
s. of death   CARS 76:1
what a s.   NEWS 288:3
sentiment Interest, not s.   CHES 82:12
sentiments not have opinions, only s.

                                               LAUR 228:12
popular s.   PEEL 307:12
separate can't s. peace   MALC 257:4
do not want to be s.   SALM 345:9
separately all hang s.   FRAN 145:8
separation fighting for s.   MALC 257:3
prepare for a s.   QUIN 320:5
real s. of powers   DENN 115:2
s. of state and science   FEYE 140:3
seraglio s. of eunuchs   FOOT 142:5
Serbs S. out   ROBE 327:8
serial s. killers   LIVI 237:12
serious War is too s.   CLEM 96:6
sermon rejected the S. on the Mount   BRAD 53:1
servant as a humble s.   MAND 258:3
born to be a s.   TOCQ 396:2

I was the S.	CHUR 87:2	**sharks** s. are circling	ANON 10:8
s. to the devil	SISS 365:5	s. circling, and waiting	CLAR 94:5
servants choice of s.	WAUG 412:3	**sharp** 'Tis a s. remedy	RALE 321:6
s. of business	BACO 20:11	will not take a s. turn	TLHA 395:3
s. of the people	BLAI 46:2	**shear** good shepherd to s. his flock	TIBE 394:10
s. of the public	GOWE 163:5	**shed** Burke under a s.	JOHN 205:5
talent of choosing his s.	MACA 246:14	**sheep** in s.'s clothing	CHUR 92:15
serve die but once to s. our country	ADDI 5:1	pasture for all the s.	WALP 410:6
If one must s.	VOLT 407:11	savaged by a dead s.	HEAL 177:5
love to s. my country	GIBR 156:3	s. born carnivorous	FAGU 138:8
s. until my last breath	GAND 151:1	s. on the way	CHUR 87:6
s. your captives' need	KIPL 221:2	s. scattered in a fog	BRUT 59:5
They also s.	MILT 271:2	s., that were wont to be	MORE 278:4
will not s. if elected	SHER 363:8	s. to pass resolutions	INGE 195:1
served Had I but s. my God	SHAK 353:7	two hundred years like a s.	TIPU 395:2
have them s. to him	CHUR 87:9	**sheet** old England's winding s.	BLAK 47:2
service at the s. of the nation	POMP 313:9	turn over the s.	SAND 346:1
devoted to your s.	ELIZ 134:1	**shell** s. with a hole	HUME 191:10
Every kind of s.	HALE 169:5	**shepherd** good s. to shear his flock	TIBE 394:10
s. of my love	SPRI 378:2	nation's s.	SPRI 378:3
s.? The rent we pay	CLAY 95:11	**shepherds** s. and butchers	VOLT 407:8
servitude Freedom and not s.	BURK 62:4	**shift** let me s. for myself	MORE 278:9
sets sun never s.	NORT 291:11	s. in what the public wants	CALL 71:3
setter Proud s. up	SHAK 353:2	**shines** s. and stinks	RAND 322:1
setting against a s. sun	SHAK 359:8	**shining** one brief s. moment	LERN 231:11
settled s. will	SMIT 372:3	**ship** desert a sinking s.	BEAV 31:10
s. will	STEE 379:2	s. has weathered every rack	WHIT 418:3
settlement through the Act of S.	RICE 326:3	S. me somewhere	KIPL 220:4
settling without s. it	JOUB 207:10	s. of the Union	LINC 234:9
seven Almighty took s.	CHUR 89:7	**ships** s. empty of men	NICI 286:7
have the s. minutes	COLL 99:7	s. have been salvaged	HALS 171:7
s. feet of English ground	HARO 173:9	storm-beaten ships	MAHA 255:9
seventy Palmerston is now s.	DISR 124:3	we've got the s.	SONG 377:3
spoilt child of s.	DAVI 110:3	wooden wall is your s.	THEM 392:14
to be s. again	CLEM 96:7	**shirt** in his s.	HUXL 193:9
sewer rat out of the s.	MOSL 280:5	**shit** chicken s.	JOHN 202:5
sex not even have to s. it up	HOWA 189:8	s. in a silk stocking	NAPO 285:4
subordination of one s.	MILL 269:16	**shits** knew who the s. were	CLAR 94:3
sexed The term 's.-up'	HUTT 193:5	**shock** characterized by s.	FRAN 146:9
sexes stronger, of the two s.	GIBB 155:7	S. and Awe	ANON 11:10
sexier make it s.	GILL 157:1	S. and Awe	ULLM 403:3
sexual not have s. relations	CLIN 97:8	we shall s. them	SHAK 356:8
shackled s. by tradition	SALI 343:2	**shoes** never tied my s.	PU Y 317:7
shackles s. of government	GOLD 161:2	president's s.	SEXW 350:4
shadow casts a s.	CHUR 88:13	**shoot** decency to s. me	MARK 260:6
shadows long s. on county grounds	MAJO 256:7	didn't s. Henry Clay	JACK 196:7
shake How s. them	TAWN 386:11	Don't s.	GUED 167:8
shaking entrusted to the s. hand	VICT 406:4	S., if you must	WHIT 418:10
shall mark you His absolute 's.'	SHAK 350:9	s. me in my absence	BEHA 32:6
shallows in s. and in miseries	SHAK 356:5	s. Santa Claus	SMIT 371:6
sham celebration is a s.	DOUG 126:2	they shout and they s.	INGE 194:10
shambles accountable s.	HUNT 192:5	**shoots** green s. of economic spring	LAMO 224:3
shame terrible s. for me	YOKO 427:5	green s. of recovery	MISQ 273:1
shamrock Apart from the s.	MCAL 244:10	if he s. you	BOGD 48:5
s. shine for ever	DAVI 110:9	man who s. him gets caught	MAIL 256:1
shape dwellings s. us	CHUR 89:6	**shop** talked s. like a tenth muse	ANON 9:10
shapely It wiggles, it's s.	ERWI 137:8	**shopkeepers** nation of s.	ADAM 4:11
share its ruin didst not s.	DODI 125:2	nation of s.	NAPO 285:1
shareholders good s.' dividend	SALI 343:12	nation of s.	SMIT 370:9
shares Fair s. for all	SLOG 366:15	**shopocracy** abuse the s.	NORT 291:13
shark between a s. and a wolf	ANDR 7:8	**short** by s. grasses	PORT 314:14

Englishmen never will be s.	SHAW 360:16	**smoke** can't see their s.	FLEI 141:6
freemen or s.	WASH 411:2	s.-filled room	DAUG 109:9
millions of royal s.	GENE 152:8	s.-filled room	SIMP 365:4
only freemen, are the only s.	MASS 264:1	**smoking** found the s. pistol	CONA 100:3
religion of s.	SALI 343:5	not found any s. guns	BLIX 47:6
S. become so debased	ROUS 334:7	S. can seriously damage	OFFI 295:7
sons of former s.	KING 217:7	s. gun to be a mushroom cloud	RICE 325:9
too pure an Air for S.	ANON 11:6	**smote** s. them hip and thigh	BIBL 41:4
wholly s. or wholly free	DRYD 127:12	s. the rock	WEBS 413:9
sledgehammer s. to miss a nut	BOOK 50:7	**smug** s. minority	BERT 37:9
sleek S.-headed men	SHAK 354:4	**snake** scotched the s.	SHAK 357:6
sleep deep s. of England	ORWE 296:9	**snatched** s. the lightning	TURG 402:5
disturbed the s.	STEV 381:2	**snatching** s. his victuals	CHUR 87:9
s. is so deep	CHAN 80:8	**sneezed** British Minister s.	LEVI 232:10
s. under bridges	FRAN 145:3	**snobbish** s. and vulgar	VICT 406:5
such as s. o' nights	SHAK 354:4	**snobs** effete corps of impudent s.	AGNE 5:10
We shall not s.	MCCR 248:8	**snow** few acres of s.	VOLT 407:2
sleeping s. with an elephant	GRAV 164:11	like the s. geese	OKPI 294:5
s. with an elephant	TRUD 400:11	s. before the summer sun	TECU 389:1
smitten a s. enemy	YAMA 426:2	**snows** our Lady of the S.	KIPL 220:5
sleeps it s. obedience	PAIN 301:10	**soaped** like catching s. eels	SALI 342:8
while the world s.	NEHR 285:6	**soapflakes** sell Jack like s.	KENN 213:12
sleepwalker assurance of a s.	HITL 184:7	**soar** creep as well as s.	BURK 63:12
sleeves Americanism with its s. rolled		**sobriety** S. is a very good thing	SALI 340:15
	MCCA 248:4	**social** new s. contract	CALL 70:6
slender s. indications	CHUR 91:6	paralyses the s. development	CHUR 91:11
slept s. more than any other	MENC 267:12	s. and economic experiment	HOOV 188:2
slew as he was ambitious, I s. him	SHAK 355:6	s. being that determines	MARX 262:5
s. his master	BIBL 41:8	s. contract	ROUS 334:5
slip President may s.	TOCQ 396:6	S. Contract is nothing more	WELL 416:3
slippery standing is s.	BACO 20:12	s. engineering	POPP 314:12
slob He was just a s.	LONG 241:4	s. progress, order, security	JOHN 201:10
slogans refuse to repeat s.	CLAR 94:12	with a s. position	ORWE 297:12
slovenliness Peace nothing but s.	BREC 54:3	**socialism** Centralization and s.	TOCQ 395:10
slow s. learners	MALL 257:7	Democracy and s.	NEHR 285:9
slowly twist s. in the wind	EHRL 130:8	Marxian S.	KEYN 215:3
slugs s. in the garden	MARK 260:5	paternal s.	MACM 252:6
slum if you've seen one city s.	AGNE 5:9	religion of S.	BEVA 38:5
slush mush and s.	OWEN 299:3	S. can only arrive	VIER 406:10
smack s. of firm government	NEWS 288:2	S. does not mean	ORWE 297:13
small day of s. nations	CHAM 79:8	s. has been singularly blessed	BERG 36:4
no s. steps	RETZ 324:8	S. is what	MORR 279:12
s. business party	BEAZ 32:2	S. *possibly* be	STAL 378:5
S. is beautiful	SCHU 348:2	s. wandering	HEAL 177:7
s. states—Israel, Athens	INGE 195:2	s. would be worth	TAYL 387:13
that cannot reach the s.	SPEN 377:9	s. would not lose its human face	DUBČ 128:2
with s. men no great thing	MILL 269:15	This is not S.	SNOW 373:4
smash all s. and no grab	NICO 289:1	trying to get s.	KINN 218:14
English never s. in a face	HALS 171:6	**socialist** be a s. at twenty	PROV 319:5
smell Money has no s.	VESP 405:8	blood of the s.	CROS 106:14
s. a rat	ROCH 328:12	build a s. society	NYER 292:8
smells s. like roses	JOHN 203:13	proletarian s. state	LENI 231:4
smile has a nice s.	GROM 167:6	signposts to s. Utopia	CROS 106:10
one livid s.	WALP 409:6	typical S.	ORWE 297:12
prison and a s.	WOTT 425:1	**socialists** s. throw it away	CAST 77:4
S. at us, pay us	CHES 83:8	We are all s. now	HARC 172:6
Treachery with a s.	THAT 392:8	**society** action of s. upon itself	TOCQ 396:9
smiling s. surface of the sea	PLUT 313:5	affluent s.	GALB 149:5
smith Chuck it, S.	CHES 83:6	bonds of civil s.	LOCK 240:10
Smithfield Canterbury or S.	WALP 409:5	call it a 'primitive s.'	GREG 166:4
smitten s. a sleeping enemy	YAMA 426:2	capital of polished s.	BURK 63:7

society (*cont.*):
dyspepsia of s.	CARL 75:7
Every s. gets	KENN 213:15
Great S.	JOHN 203:4
happiness of s.	ADAM 4:2
market s.	JOSP 207:8
modern s.	MARX 262:8
moves about in s.	CHOI 85:3
No human s.	MCEW 249:12
no letters; no s.	HOBB 185:6
No s. can survive	GING 157:3
no such thing as S.	THAT 391:12
of a great s.	SMIT 370:1
shape of s.	ORWE 296:10
s. begins to act	PAIN 301:13
S. is indeed a contract	BURK 63:6
S. needs to condemn	MAJO 256:6
s. requires to be rebuilt	MILL 269:6
s. where it is safe to be	STEV 380:10
unable to live in s.	ARIS 14:14

sodomy rum, s., prayers, and the lash   CHUR 90:9
soft s. under-belly of Europe   MISQ 273:9
soil Freedom's s. beneath our feet	DRAK 126:9
grows in every s.	BURK 62:7
powers of the s.	RICA 325:8
sold Never s. the truth	TENN 389:11
what cannot be s.—liberty	GRAT 164:10
would have s. all I had	CROM 105:7
soldier British s. can stand up to	SHAW 360:6
iron-armed s.	SONG 376:4
side of the Unknown S.	ASQU 16:9
s. of the Great War	EPIT 137:4
soldiers old s. never die	MACA 245:5
young Argentinian s.	RUNC 335:4
solicitor said I'm a s.	WARD 410:8
solidity appearance of s. to pure wind	
	ORWE 297:17
solution conditions for its s.	MARX 262:4
either part of the s.	CLEA 95:12
final s.	HEYD 183:5
kind of s.	CAVA 78:3
s. for world peace	MARS 261:1
total s.	GOER 160:6
solutions all the s.	THAT 392:11
David brings me s.	THAT 392:2
old s.	WILS 422:3
solve easy to s.	EISE 131:11
some fool s. of the people	LINC 236:13
somebody s. in his own right	BENN 34:5
When every one is s.	GILB 156:5
someone s., somewhere, may be happy	
	MENC 267:3
something S. must be done	MISQ 273:10
s. of the night	WIDD 419:2
S. should be done	EDWA 130:4
Somme S. is like the Holocaust	BARK 29:5
son do it for my s.	KEYS 216:1
leichter of a fair s.	ELIZ 132:5
S. of Saint Louis	FIRM 140:5
song ane end of ane old s.	OGIL 294:3
songs Gaelic s., and argument	DEWA 116:8

they know no s.	CHES 83:10
soon leave five minutes too s.	BIFF 42:7
sophisms string of s.	SHEL 361:15
sordid this s. saga	LIEB 233:6
sorry one day will say s.	KEYS 216:1
soul change the s.	THAT 390:11
engineers of the s.	GORK 163:3
engineers of the s.	KENN 213:7
every subject's s.	SHAK 352:12
iron has entered into his s.	LLOY 240:1
literature saved my s.	RATU 322:6
no s. to be damned	THUR 394:9
perfection of your s.	SOCR 373:6
save her s.	THOM 393:6
s. is marching on	SONG 376:5
with s. so dead	SCOT 348:7
souls common men have s.	TAWN 386:10
engineers of human s.	STAL 378:4
only in men's s.	STEV 380:8
open windows into men's s.	ELIZ 133:9
stuff of other people's s.	MCGR 250:2
times that try men's s.	PAIN 300:11
sound other half is not very s.	SMOL 372:1
s. and original ideas	MACM 253:5
s. and rumour	MORR 279:10
soundbite trade the s.	DOBS 124:15
soundbites can't speak in s.	CLAR 94:12
not a time for s.	BLAI 46:6
soup take s. at luncheon	CURZ 108:3
south S. is avenged	BOOT 51:2
wrest from the S.	LEE 230:6
sovereign advise my s.	WAUG 412:3
Here lies our s. lord	EPIT 136:3
he will have no s.	COKE 99:1
power of the s.	TROL 399:1
s. Nation	PAGE 299:7
S. state power	KEAN 210:1
subject and a s.	CHAR 81:6
subjects to the s.	HOBB 185:9
to be a S.	ELIZ 132:7
sovereigns what s. are doing	NAPO 284:10
sovereignties addition of s.	MONN 276:2
sovereignty s. is an artificial soul	HOBB 185:1
S. is unlimited	BARK 29:4
s. of nature	SHAK 351:4
soviet Communism is S. power	LENI 231:5
S. Union has indeed	FULB 148:3
soviets All power to the S.	SLOG 366:1
sow hath the s. by the right ear	HENR 181:1
S. returns to her Mire	KIPL 219:8
when to s.	JEFF 200:8
sown They have s. the wind	BIBL 41:17
space more s. where nobody is	STEI 379:5
spaghetti s. and meatballs	KEMP 211:4
Spain Go to S. and get killed	POLL 313:6
nor leave S.	JUAN 208:5
permanence and unity of S.	JUAN 208:4
Spaniards not the power of the S.	SCHU 348:1
thrash the S. too	DRAK 126:8
spaniel ill-trained s.	CRAN 104:3
little cocker-s.	NIXO 290:3

spare s. your country's flag — WHIT 418:10
spark s.-gap is mightier — HOGB 186:3
sparrows pass through for the s. — GALB 149:11
Spartans Go, tell the S. — EPIT 136:2
spasm I call it an emotional s. — BEVA 39:1
speak didn't s. up — NIEM 289:5
  difficult to s. — BURK 65:2
  I now s. for France — DE G 113:4
  I only s. right on — SHAK 355:16
  one to s. — THOR 394:5
  s. for Britain — BOOT 51:3
  s. for England — AMER 7:4
  s. for ten minutes — WILS 423:5
  s. ill of everybody except oneself — PÉTA 309:7
  S. Out — GRAS 164:8
  S. softly — ROOS 332:5
speaker cannot see the S. — ANON 9:12
speaking necessity for good s. — TROL 399:12
speaks He s. to Me — VICT 406:7
specific s. decision — TUCH 402:3
spectacle no s. so ridiculous — MACA 246:2
spectator disposition of the s. — PHIL 310:9
  s. sport — GALB 149:13
spectre s. is haunting — HAVE 175:2
  s. of Communism — MARX 263:1
speech abridging the freedom of s. — CONS 102:4
  freedom of s. — TWAI 402:8
  function of s. to free — BRAN 53:7
  little other use of their s. — HALI 170:2
  make a s. on conservation — STEV 381:3
  nonpolitical s. — NIXO 290:4
  s. fermenting in me — GLAD 159:12
  s. from Ernest Bevin — FOOT 142:9
  s. on economics — JOHN 203:12
  utterance, nor power of s. — SHAK 355:16
speeches old s. burnt — SNOW 373:5
  s. were fine — WALP 409:2
speechless let it lie S. still — EPIT 136:7
spend If you have money you s. it — KENN 214:1
  I intend to s. it — BUSH 67:7
  s. more time with my family — FOWL 144:5
  s. your way out — CALL 70:7
spending s. other people's money — RAND 322:3
  s. the public money — COOL 103:11
spies paid s. — SHER 363:5
spin great world s. for ever — TENN 389:6
  Labour s. doctors — CAMP 72:2
  s.-doctors in spin clinics — BENN 34:13
spine s. to run up — EWIN 138:4
spirit break his s. — HOLL 186:7
  'Brutus' will start a s. — SHAK 354:2
  forge his revolutionary s. — GUEV 167:9
  never approached my s. — METT 268:5
  s. of Dunkirk — WILS 421:7
  s. of party — WASH 411:5
  Thy s. walks abroad — SHAK 356:6
spirits insult to the s. — RED 324:1
  ruffle up your s. — SHAK 356:1
spiritual not being a s. people — MANC 258:1
  outrun our s. power — KING 218:2
spit s. on the deck — BALD 27:4

splendid s. and a happy land — GOLD 161:4
  S. isolation — NEWS 288:5
  s. little war — HAY 175:8
  s. misery — JEFF 198:11
splendidly s. isolated — FOST 143:8
splendour s. of hawthorn buds in spring — BEAV 31:9
split s. Ireland — BRUG 59:3
spoilt s. child of seventy — DAVI 110:3
spoke How well he s. — STEV 380:16
  s. for an hour — GARV 152:4
spoken American people have s. — CLIN 97:11
  never been s. to like this — CHIR 84:6
  never have s. yet — CHES 83:8
  when the oracle has s. — SALI 340:3
spoons counted our s. — EMER 135:2
sport bleed in s. — SHAK 355:1
  spectator s. — GALB 149:13
spot with a s. I damn him — SHAK 356:3
spouse President's s. — BUSH 66:2
spread be made to s. — CHUR 90:4
spring s. that should move easily — MONT 277:13
  trouble in the Balkans in the s. — KIPL 221:4
sprint marathon not a s. — LIVI 237:10
spur I have no s. — SHAK 357:3
spurs bridle and no s. — TAYL 388:4
squalid s. nuisance — CHUR 89:10
squalor Ignorance, S. and Idleness — BEVE 40:3
square s. deal — SLOG 369:3
  S. deal afterwards — ROOS 332:6
  turn s. corners — HOLM 187:2
squeak until the pips s. — GEDD 152:5
squeamish consist in a s. ear — FOX 144:9
squire s. and his relations — DICK 117:7
squires last sad s. ride — CHES 83:9
stabbed s. in the front — INGH 195:6
stability natural s. of gold — SHAW 360:11
  party of order or s. — MILL 269:11
  political s. — MITC 275:1
  s. pact is stupid — PROD 317:2
stables S. are the centre — SHAW 360:8
stage get off the s. — MAJO 256:10
  performs upon the s. — TAYL 387:4
stagecoach party like an old s. — WILS 421:15
stain convict s. — HUGH 191:1
stake deep s. they have — BURK 62:9
  s. driven through his heart — O'BR 293:3
  s. in the country — WIND 423:6
  what it is we have at s. — PITT 312:4
Stalin guilt of S. — GORB 162:4
stamp but the guinea's s. — BURN 65:8
stamps can lick the s. — HIND 184:2
  kill animals and stick in s. — NICO 288:14
stand By uniting we s. — DICK 118:6
  Here s. I — LUTH 243:7
  intended to s. — DISR 119:4
  I will s. by — GRIF 166:7
  Never s. when you could sit — ANON 11:3
  s. by each other — SHER 363:7
  s. up to anything except — SHAW 360:6
  who only s. and wait — MILT 271:2

standard float that s. sheet — DRAK 126:9
raise the scarlet s. — SONG 377:1
standing by s. on it — CHUR 92:11
ought to die s. — LAST 226:5
s. armies of power — RADC 320:7
s. by my man — CLIN 97:1
stands S. Scotland — SHAK 357:8
sun now s. — JOSE 207:2
where he s. — KING 218:1
star constant as the northern s. — SHAK 354:12
guiding s. — CARS 76:2
S. for every State — WINT 423:8
s.-spangled banner — KEY 214:6
stare rule never to s. at people — BALF 28:3
stars not in our s. — SHAK 354:1
seen the s. — MARK 260:7
start 'Brutus' will s. a spirit — SHAK 354:2
s. in the streets — KENN 211:9
starvation S. Dundas — DUND 128:9
starve let our people s. — NYER 292:7
s. or rebel — DUND 128:9
starving choice of working or s. — JOHN 203:16
NATION is s. — O'CO 293:5
you have a s. population — DISR 119:7
state all were for the s. — MACA 247:8
bosom of a single s. — DURH 129:4
church and s. forever separate — GRAN 164:6
defrauding of the S. — PENN 308:14
duty of a S. — RUSK 336:1
each S. has a vested right — SALI 339:1
faithful to the s. — ELIZ 132:4
Founding a firm s. — MARV 261:9
I am the S. — LOUI 241:5
in a free s. — CAVO 78:5
my glories and my s. — SHAK 358:13
no such thing as the S. — AUDE 19:3
pillar of the S. — SOLZ 374:1
put the s. to rights — ENNI 135:8
reinforcement of the S. — CAMU 73:3
rule the s. — DRYD 127:5
Scoffing his s. — SHAK 358:11
separation of s. and science — FEYE 140:3
Sovereign s. power — KEAN 210:1
S. business is a cruel trade — HALI 171:2
S. for every Star — WINT 423:8
s. has no place — TRUD 400:9
s. intervention — DICE 117:6
S. is an instrument — STAL 378:4
S. is a relation of men — WEBE 413:1
S. is not 'abolished' — ENGE 135:5
s. is or can be master of money — BEVE 40:4
s. of the Union — CONS 102:3
S. policy, a cyclops — COLE 99:3
S. which dwarfs its men — MILL 269:15
s. without the means — BURK 62:14
usurped the powers of the s. — GIBB 155:7
wall between church and s. — BLAC 45:3
While the S. exists — LENI 231:2
statements all previous s. inoperative — ZIEG 428:3
states free and independent S. — ADAM 3:8
indestructible S. — CHAS 82:6

many sovereign S. — PAGE 299:7
more s. there are to suffer — BAGE 25:5
rights of s. — BROW 58:5
thirteen S. — HAMI 171:11
Union of these S. — WHIT 418:7
United S. of Europe — CHUR 90:1
statesman de-intellectualize a s. — BAGE 24:11
gift of any s. — METT 268:7
great s. is one — MONN 276:5
he was a s. — LLOY 239:9
importance to a s. — TAYL 388:1
requirement of a s. — ACHE 1:8
set a s. right — YEAT 426:7
s. can give the poor man — SALI 342:4
s. is a politician — TRUM 401:8
s. is a politician who — POMP 313:9
S., yet friend to Truth — POPE 314:3
statesmanship You call that s. — BEVA 39:1
statesmen government of s. — DISR 122:5
stations know our proper s. — DICK 117:7
statistic million deaths a s. — STAL 378:9
statistics lies, damned lies and s. — DISR 124:8
uses s. as a drunken man — LANG 225:1
stature Malice is of a low s. — HALI 170:9
status quo ladder called 'the s.' — BENN 34:12
stay here I s. — MACM 252:4
s. of execution — CARS 76:1
things to s. as they are — LAMP 224:6
stays never s. too long — MACA 246:4
steaks s. to a tiger — BROU 57:4
steal s. bread — FRAN 145:3
stealing hanged for s. horses — HALI 170:17
steals politician who s. — PLUN 313:3
steam s.-engine in trousers — SMIT 372:8
traces the s.-engine — DISR 120:2
steeds mounting barbèd s. — SHAK 359:3
steel cold lead and s. — O'DO 294:2
steeple North Church s. — REVE 325:6
steeples dreary S. of Fermanagh — CHUR 86:12
steer s. by the compass — TAYL 388:7
steering s. wheel that's not — GOOD 162:3
step not to take the first s. — CLAU 95:1
One s. forward — LENI 230:9
steps hears the s. of God — BISM 44:11
no small s. — RETZ 324:8
stern s. without being obstinate — SALI 338:7
sterner made of s. stuff — SHAK 355:9
stick carry a big s. — ROOS 332:5
fell like the s. — PAIN 301:2
s. that he seizes — TORR 397:1
still s. it is not we — CHES 83:9
stingy was not s. — TROL 399:17
stink their politics usually s. — LAWR 229:1
stir s. men's blood — SHAK 355:16
s. up undisputed matters — SALL 345:4
s. without great argument — SHAK 352:2
stirring s. up apathy — WHIT 417:11
stock Woman s. is rising — CHIL 84:3
stockholders money for their s. — FRIE 147:9
stolen generation was s. — FREE 147:5
stomach army marches on its s. — NAPO 284:14

on an empty s.   BRAN 53:12
s. of a king   ELIZ 132:9
s. of the country   GLAD 158:4
stone bomb them back into the S. Age
    LEMA 230:7
make a s. of the heart   YEAT 426:4
s. which he flings   TORR 397:1
This precious s.   SHAK 358:6
Under every s.   ARIS 14:9
stones move The s. of Rome   SHAK 356:1
stood s. against the world   SHAK 355:12
s. four-square to all the winds   TENN 389:9
stop nothing will s. it   ZOLA 428:7
stories tell sad s.   SHAK 358:10
storm coming s.   GLAD 158:2
directs this s.   PAGE 299:6
Stormont Ulster Parliament at S.   GEOR 153:6
storms He sought the s.   DRYD 127:4
story s. and a byword   WINT 423:7
Strafford S., who was hurried hence   EPIT 136:7
straight no s. thing   KANT 209:7
pretty s. sort   BLAI 46:4
strain s. is awful   MACM 254:2
strangers beaten by s.   DOS 125:6
strangled last minister is s.   NAIR 283:10
s. with the guts   MESL 268:2
strategy developing our industrial s.   BENN 34:4
strawberry Like s. wives   ELIZ 133:10
stream watching a s. of blood   ANON 10:11
street both sides of the s.   ROOS 331:7
streetcars common as s.   REUT 325:4
streets grass will grow in the s.   BRYA 59:8
grass will grow in the s.   HOOV 188:5
start in the s.   KENN 211:9
s. being paved with gold   LOUI 241:9
strength exhausting its s.   MONT 277:2
giant's s.   SHAK 357:13
S. through joy   SLOG 367:9
that tower of s.   TENN 389:9
strenuous s. life   ROOS 332:1
strife In place of s.   CAST 77:3
step towards an end of s.   GEOR 153:6
strike s. against public safety   COOL 103:5
s. at a king   EMER 135:3
s. at the head   BURK 65:1
S. the tent   LAST 228:1
string s. of sophisms   SHEL 361:15
s. that ties   SHEL 362:11
untune that s.   SHAK 359:13
stringent s. execution   GRAN 164:5
stripes s. on their ties   GUED 167:8
stroke at a s.   HEAT 178:9
stroked if not s.   HALI 170:4
stroll s. round Walton Heath   LLOY 238:11
strong Belinda's s. point   HARP 173:10
nature of s. people   BONH 50:3
not to the s. alone   HENR 181:6
people s. enough   ROOS 330:12
s. as a bull moose   ROOS 332:2
s., silent man   MORL 279:3
stronger interest of the s.   PLAT 312:9

on the side of the s.   TACI 385:8
struggle class s.   MARX 262:10
Manhood a s.   DISR 122:9
s. for room   MALT 257:9
s. of the African   MAND 258:2
s. was of blood   O'CO 293:6
struggled s. against tyranny   TUTU 402:6
struggles history of class s.   MARX 263:2
Stuarts out with the S.   DISR 122:21
stubbornness self-righteous s.   JENK 201:3
stud retired s.-horse   MENC 267:2
students S. accept   JONE 206:4
studiously s. neutral   WILS 422:13
stuff made of sterner s.   SHAK 355:9
S. happens   RUMS 335:2
stumbled s. over the truth   CHUR 92:8
stumbles how the strong man s.   ROOS 332:10
stump mount the s.   STEV 381:3
stupid It's the economy, s.   SLOG 367:7
more s. than their people   EISE 131:8
safe not to be s.   SALI 342:11
stability pact is s.   PROD 317:2
s. are cocksure   RUSS 336:15
Would it be s.   RUMS 334:10
stupidest s. party   MILL 269:4
stupidity alcoholic s.   HILL 183:8
conscientious s.   KING 217:12
explanation of s.   LEVE 232:1
S., outrage   ROST 334:2
subject British s. I was born   MACD 249:5
Every s.'s duty   SHAK 352:12
s. and a sovereign   CHAR 81:6
what it is to be a s.   ELIZ 132:7
subjection some are marked for s.   ARIS 15:1
subjects among his s.   HERB 182:1
good of s.   DEFO 113:2
obligation of s.   HOBB 185:9
s. are rebels   BURK 63:4
sublime s. to the ridiculous   NAPO 284:11
submission s. of men's actions   HOBB 185:10
submit Must he s.   SHAK 358:12
subordination inequality and s.   JOHN 205:7
s. of one sex   MILL 269:16
subsistence S. only increases   MALT 257:8
substance persons of some s.   WIND 423:6
substitute no s. for victory   MACA 245:4
s. shines brightly   SHAK 358:3
subtlety s. of intellect   MORL 279:4
subversion Gracchi complaining about s.
    JUVE 209:1
succeed s. in politics   LLOY 239:4
succeeded glad I succeeded   VANU 404:7
success ask of you is military s.   LINC 236:2
Confidence of s.   SALI 343:6
S. or failure   MACH 250:6
successful S. crimes alone   DRYD 127:15
successors dissatisfield with s.   JENK 201:6
none of my s.   MAJO 256:11
Sudeten problem of the S. Germans   HITL 184:9
Suez East of S.   KIPL 220:4
S.—a smash and grab raid   NICO 289:1

Suez (*cont.*):
S. Canal — EDEN 130:2
suffer Better one s. — DRYD 127:8
not s. fools gladly — PEAR 307:2
s. most — PEEL 307:17
suffering sorrow and s. — CONN 101:8
untold s. — MAND 258:4
sufficient S. conscience to bother him — LLOY 240:4
suffrage Women's s. — DILL 119:1
suicide commit s. — TRUM 401:4
democracy that did not commit s. — ADAM 3:11
it is s. — MACD 249:8
longest s. note — KAUF 209:8
s. 25 years after his death — BEAV 31:11
sui generis say that I am *s.* — LONG 241:1
suis *J'y s.* — MACM 252:4
suit wear a dark s. — ROSS 333:14
suites get to the s. — KENN 211:9
suits omelette all over our s. — BROK 56:5
summer best s. Town House — PITT 312:1
if it takes all s. — GRAN 164:2
summits Nations touch at their s. — BAGE 23:9
sun against a setting s. — SHAK 359:8
candle to the s. — SIDN 364:9
commanded the s. — FRAN 146:3
place in the s. — BÜLO 60:5
place in the s. — WILH 419:9
S. backs Blair — NEWS 288:6
s. doesn't revolve — LIVI 237:11
s. in his eyes — CHUR 87:11
s. never sets — NORT 291:11
s. now stands — JOSE 207:2
s. of York — SHAK 359:2
S. readers — YELL 427:2
S. wot won it — NEWS 287:14
Sunningdale S. for slow — MALL 257:7
sunset s. of my life — REAG 323:14
superior embarrass the s. — SHAW 361:6
most s. person — ANON 11:1
no-one to be their s. — TOCQ 396:11
superiors want it with our s. — BECQ 32:4
superman I teach you the s. — NIET 289:6
superstition s. sets the whole world — VOLT 407:5
suppliant s. for his own — BYRO 69:2
supplies just bought fresh s. — BREC 54:6
support depend on the s. of Paul — SHAW 360:7
expect political s. — SALI 339:8
help and s. of the woman — EDWA 130:5
money instead of political s. — SALI 339:7
s. me when I am in the wrong — MELB 266:13
s. of the people — CLEV 96:10
without the s. of all — LULA 243:6
supported not s. by the people — HUMP 191:11
suppress power of s. — NORT 292:4
supreme if ever the S. Court — TOCQ 396:6
s. power must be arbitrary — HALI 170:3
surrealistic like a s. painting — MAND 258:10
surrender entire s. — BELH 32:7
I s. to you — GERO 154:11
never s. — PAIS 302:9
No s. — SLOG 368:5

we shall never s. — CHUR 88:2
surrendered never s. her soul — DE V 116:4
survival s. game — CHRÉ 85:5
survived I s. — SIEY 365:2
survives still s. — LAST 228:6
surviving s. till the next century — LYNN 244:7
suspicion above s. — CAES 69:8
against despots—s. — DEMO 114:4
common s. of Ottawa — FOTH 144:2
s. that more than half — WHIT 417:4
suspicions S. amongst thoughts — BACO 21:3
swap s. horses when crossing — LINC 236:4
swayed s. by the basest men — CLAY 95:6
sweat Blood, s., and tear-wrung — BYRO 68:10
blood, toil, tears and s. — CHUR 87:1
s. of its labourers — EISE 131:5
sweep he'd s. the country — DISR 124:3
sweet technically s. — OPPE 296:2
sweets bag of boiled s. — CRIT 105:4
s. of place with power — ROSE 333:6
swift race is not to the s. — BIBL 41:12
swimming S. for his life — GLAD 158:9
Switzerland in S. they had — WELL 414:7
sword first drew the s. — CLAR 93:11
his s. Hath a sharp edge — SHAK 353:3
I gave them a s. — NIXO 291:2
lift up s. against nation — BIBL 41:14
not to send peace, but a s. — BIBL 41:14
resistance by the s. — CLAY 95:3
s. and the currency — PROD 317:1
s. the axis of the world — DE G 113:14
terrible swift s. — HOWE 190:4
We shall never sheath the s. — ASQU 16:5
wield the s. of France — DE G 113:5
swords s. In our own proper entrails — SHAK 356:6
s. into plowshares — BIBL 41:14
ten thousand s. leapt — BURK 62:20
sworn s. to execute — LINC 235:2
sycophants s. and flatterers — HARD 172:8
syllable never used one s. — JAY 197:8
sympathy just enough s. — GALB 150:5
no s. in politics — THAT 390:5
s. is cold — GIBB 155:13
Syria S. isn't on it — STRA 382:12
system rocked the s. — ROBI 328:7
s. of Government — GLAD 158:3
s. of outdoor relief — BRIG 55:3

table at whose t. I sit — BORR 52:2
tableau t. of crimes — VOLT 407:7
tail more he shows his t. — PROV 318:12
sensations of its "t." — DISR 120:1
wags its t. — TOYN 397:3
taint any t. of legality — KNOX 222:6
taisez-vous *T.! Méfiez-vous* — OFFI 295:8
take big enough to t. away — FORD 142:10
t. away the punch bowl — MART 261:8
t. the Queen — EPIT 137:2
T. up the White Man's Burden — KIPL 221:2
t. you in the morning — BALD 26:3

takes if it t. all summer   GRAN 164:2
talent concentration of t.   KENN 213:2
   t. of choosing his servants   MACA 246:14
talents career open to the t.   NAPO 284:16
   ministry of all the t.   ANON 10:15
   virtue and t.   JEFF 199:13
talk Careless t. costs lives   OFFI 295:1
   how much my Ministers t.   THAT 390:8
   I have no small t.   WELL 415:13
   want to t. to Europe   KISS 221:9
talking if you can stop people t.   ATTL 18:11
   nation t. to itself   MILL 270:6
   quieten your enemy by t.   CEAU 78:6
   redtape t.-machine   CARL 75:1
talks t. frankly only with his wife   BABE 20:2
tall don't look t.   PORT 314:14
tamed in one year t.   MARV 262:2
Tandy met wid Napper T.   SONG 376:2
tanks Get your t. off my lawn   WILS 421:12
tantae T. molis erat   VIRG 406:11
tantum T. religio potuit   LUCR 243:5
taoiseach dreams of being T.   HAUG 174:9
taping t. of conversations   NIXO 291:1
Tarsus Jew of T.   BIBL 41:26
tart t. who has married the Mayor   BAXT 30:8
tarts action of two t.   MACM 253:7
taste t. for freedom   TOCQ 395:11
   underrating public t.   DEED 112:7
tasteless odourless and t.   PEYR 309:10
tax pay my t. bills   HOLM 187:3
   power to t.   MARS 261:3
   soon be able to t. it   FARA 139:4
   t.-paying Americans   GING 157:4
   t. rich people   LLOY 239:18
   t. with a heavier hand   FRAN 145:7
   To t. and to please   BURK 61:14
taxation heavy t.   MACA 247:2
   modes of t.   PEEL 308:3
   T. and representation   CAMD 71:10
   T. without representation   OTIS 298:9
taxes compensation for heavy t.   MONT 277:14
   death and t.   FRAN 146:2
   little people pay t.   HELM 179:10
   no new t.   BUSH 66:9
   peace, easy t.   SMIT 369:11
   people overlaid with t.   BACO 21:5
   t. must fall upon agriculture   GIBB 155:9
   t. shall be apportioned   CONS 102:2
taxi driving t. cabs   BURN 65:6
   empty t. arrived   CHUR 92:6
taxidermist veterinarian and the t.   LIEB 233:7
taxing t. machine   LOWE 242:6
taxpayer at the t.'s expense   MENC 267:13
   t.—that's someone   REAG 323:8
tea and sometimes t.   POPE 314:7
   damned t. parties   LODG 240:12
   Queen drops in for t.   BYWA 69:4
teaching for the t. of which   SMIT 371:2
   t. nations how to live   MILT 271:5
tear t. down this wall   REAG 323:12
tearing t. down an old wall   GORE 162:7

tears blood, toil, t. and sweat   CHUR 87:14
   enough of blood and t.   RABI 320:6
   With mine own t.   SHAK 358:15
technically t. sweet   OPPE 296:2
technology Sixties t.   LEVI 232:7
   white heat of t.   MISQ 274:6
Ted pink, quivering T.   ANON 8:3
teddy Now T. must run   KENN 214:2
teenage T. scribblers   LAWS 229:5
teenagers unemployment among t.   FRIE 148:1
teeth clean their t. in the dark   JENK 201:1
   he's got iron t.   GROM 167:6
   kick them in the t.   BEVA 39:10
   t. are in the real meat   GRIM 167:5
   t. taken out   HITL 184:10
teetotaller secret t.   ORWE 297:12
Teflon T.-coated Presidency   SCHR 347:11
telephone Tiberius with a t.   WHIT 418:1
telephones Tudor monarchy with t.   BURG 61:1
television accomplishments of t.   GALB 149:13
   t. and radio   DE V 116:5
   T. brought brutality   MCLU 252:3
   T. has made dictatorship   PERE 309:3
tell Don't ask, don't t.   NUNN 292:6
   Go, t. the Spartans   EPIT 136:2
   t. sad stories   SHAK 358:10
   t. them of us and say   EPIT 137:6
temper enforce with t.   GREN 166:5
   including my t.   NEHR 285:8
   lose your t. with the Press   PANK 303:7
   with a ruffled t.   WALP 410:5
temperament first-class t.   HOLM 187:4
tempest occurrence of a grave t.   BAGE 22:9
tempora O t., O mores   CICE 93:1
temporary force alone is but t.   BURK 61:18
temptation t. to a rich and lazy nation
      KIPL 221:1
temptations t. both in wine and women
      KITC 222:2
tempted one thing to be t.   SHAK 357:11
ten amend the T. Commandments   BIGG 42:8
   aren't no T. Commandments   KIPL 220:4
   t. minutes notice   SMIT 372:7
tenancy is a life t.   THAT 391:13
tenants feudal landlord abusing t.   ATTL 17:9
tent big t.   SLOG 366:9
   G.O.P.'s big t.   NEWS 288:4
   inside the t. pissing out   JOHN 203:10
   Strike the t.   LAST 228:1
tents t. have been struck   SMUT 373:2
termination law for its own t.   LINC 234:10
terminological t. inexactitude   CHUR 86:7
terrible t. night   PORT 314:13
terrier like the Scotch t.   BRIG 55:7
territorial last t. claim   HITL 184:8
terror new t. to death   WETH 417:1
   t. attack   HOWA 189:7
   t. instituted   MACD 249:7
   t. of the world   PITT 311:14
   unity against t.   BUSH 67:3
terrorism democratic world and t.   BLAI 46:10

terrorism (*cont.*):
  international t.   PUTI 317:6
  subtle t. of words   GAIT 149:2
  this war on t.   BUSH 67:4
terrorist t. and the hijacker   THAT 391:9
  t. and the policeman   CONR 101:9
terrorists t. who committed   BUSH 67:2
terrorize t. a whole nation   MURR 283:4
test cricket t.   TEBB 388:14
testators T. would do well   HERB 181:9
testifying t. falsely   CLIN 97:12
testimony t. against slavery   DOUG 126:1
Thames T. is liquid history   BURN 65:7
thatch pike in the t.   DE C 112:3
Thatcher it is for Mrs T.   CALL 71:3
Thatcherite to be purely T.   THAT 392:12
theatre shouting fire in a t.   HOLM 187:1
  t. of the world   MARY 263:9
  t. where no-one allowed   MILL 270:7
  This House today is a t.   BALD 27:3
thee save t. and me   OWEN 299:4
theft Property is t.   PROU 317:3
theme first t.   WILS 422:7
  it has no t.   CHUR 92:16
themselves thinking about t.   MACM 253:8
theories in amiable t.   SALI 338:2
  t. stand the wear   TROL 400:1
theorists divided between the t.   MCEW 249:11
theory *Died of a T.*   DAVI 110:7
  drunk with a t.   SALI 344:15
there Over t.   COHA 98:10
  T. you go again   REAG 323:3
  you were not t.   HENR 180:6
thick ask the Gods for a t. skin   TROL 399:15
  t. skin is a gift from God   ADEN 5:4
thicker History gets t.   TAYL 387:1
thigh smote them hip and t.   BIBL 41:4
thin pale and t. ones   PLUT 313:4
thing sort of t. they like   LINC 236:10
things T. can only get better   PETR 309:9
  T. can only get better   SLOG 368:9
  T. fall apart   YEAT 426:9
think easier to act than to t.   AREN 14:5
  might very well t. that   DOBB 124:14
  t. alike who think at all   PAIN 302:3
  t. globally   SLOG 368:10
  t. of your forefathers   ADAM 4:5
  t. other men's thoughts   BAGE 24:8
  T. some more   SLOG 368:11
  t. what you like   TACI 385:6
thinkers difficulties about great t.   SALI 344:7
thinking All t. for themselves   GILB 156:10
  every t. man   ADAM 2:4
  modes of t. are different   JOHN 205:4
  own way of t.   NAPO 284:8
  t., speaking, and writing   ADAM 3:13
  t. what we're thinking   SLOG 366:4
thinks He t. too much   SHAK 354:4
  t. he knows everything   SHAW 360:14
thirst man can raise a t.   KIPL 220:4
  offer you hunger, t.   GARI 151:10

thirteen t. States   HAMI 171:11
  T. years of Tory misrule   SLOG 368:12
this T. was a man   SHAK 356:7
thorn t. in Charles's side   FOX 144:6
thorns can't have the crown of t.   BEVA 38:10
  crown of t.   BRYA 59:9
  No crown of t.   SLOG 368:4
thought investigation and t.   HALD 169:1
  modes of t.   MILL 269:3
  never t. of thinking   GILB 156:6
  Political t., in France   ARON 16:1
  put t. in a concentration camp   ROOS 331:6
  they think they ought to have t.   ANON 11:5
  T. is the child of Action   DISR 123:14
  troubled seas of t.   GALB 149:7
thoughtcrime t. literally impossible   ORWE 297:5
thoughts t. of a prisoner   SOLZ 373:11
thousand Empire lasts for a t. years   CHUR 88:3
  first t. days   KENN 212:7
  not in a t. years   SMIT 372:1
  t. points of light   BUSH 66:8
  t. years of history   GAIT 149:4
thread crimson t. of kinship   PARK 304:3
threaten t. to overrule him   PAXM 306:3
threatened covertly t.   SALI 344:12
threats Direct t.   CHEN 82:8
three divided into t. parts   CAES 69:6
  T. acres and a cow   SLOG 368:13
  t. corners of the world   SHAK 356:8
  t. fifths of all other persons   CONS 102:2
  t.-fifths of a man   RICE 326:1
  t.-party politics   KENN 211:8
  T. Wise Men   DE R 115:7
thriftless t. and hopeless   DAVI 111:4
throat cut his t. at last   BYRO 68:11
  murder by the t.   LLOY 239:6
throne behind the t.   PITT 311:10
  On the highest t.   MONT 277:1
  royal t. of kings   SHAK 358:6
  t. of bayonets   INGE 195:3
  t. sent word to a Throne   KIPL 220:5
  t. *we* honour   SHER 363:2
  T. will sway a little   CHAN 80:7
  through slaughter to a t.   GRAY 165:5
  vacancy of the t.   GIBB 155:2
  worthy of the t.   GIBB 155:8
throw t. away   SHAK 356:12
thrown All *this* t. away   MARY 263:7
thumbed t. their nose at Congress   DELA 114:1
thunder t. for reform   NEWS 288:7
  voice like t.   DAVI 111:2
Tiber River T. foaming   POWE 315:5
  T. foaming with much blood   VIRG 407:1
Tiberius T. with a telephone   WHIT 418:1
tide influence the t.   COLE 99:2
  rising t. lifts all boats   PROV 319:9
  t. in the affairs   SHAK 356:5
  Treaty like an incoming t.   DENN 114:10
ties stripes on their t.   GUED 167:8
tiger atom bomb is a paper t.   MAO 259:8
  Celtic T.   MCAL 244:11

steaks to a t.	BROU 57:4
two days like a t.	TIPU 395:2
tigers t. are getting hungry	CHUR 87:8
wilderness of t.	SHAK 359:10
tight Sitting t. is power	BELL 33:6
t. gag of place	HEAN 178:5
tigress t. surrounded by hamsters	BIFF 42:6
tiles t. on the roofs	LUTH 243:8
tilt We do not t. on either side	GAND 150:15
timber crooked t. of humanity	KANT 209:7
navy nothing but rotten t.	BURK 62:9
time devote more t.	FOWL 144:5
for a moment of t.	LAST 226:1
idea whose t. has come	ANON 12:6
in a limited t.	ATTL 18:14
leave exactly on t.	MUSS 283:8
not the t. to falter	BLAI 46:13
peace for our t.	CHAM 80:3
ringing grooves of t.	TENN 389:6
spend more t. with family	THAT 392:1
that it will be on t.	CONN 101:7
t. for a change	DEWE 117:1
t. has come	LONG 241:2
t. is money	HUGO 191:3
T. is on our side	GLAD 158:7
t. is out of joint	SHAK 351:10
t.-lag of fifty years	WELL 416:6
T. spent on any item	PARK 304:7
t. to win this game	DRAK 126:8
t. will come	DISR 119:3
to fill the t. available	PARK 304:5
unconscionable t. dying	CHAR 82:5
waste of t. and effort	VEBL 405:4
well to t. the beginnings	BACO 20:9
whips and scorns of t.	SHAK 351:11
timeless t. call	SCHL 347:10
timeo t. Danaos et dona ferentes	VIRG 406:12
times illusion that t. were better	GREE 165:6
It was the best of t.	DICK 118:1
Oh, the t.	CICE 93:7
T. change, and we change	ANON 12:5
t. that try men's souls	PAIN 300:11
t. will not mend	PARK 304:2
timetables by railway t.	TAYL 387:5
timing real bad sense of t.	MCGO 250:1
t. of your death	TACI 385:3
tincture might have been a t. of it	THAT 392:12
t. in the blood	DEFO 112:8
tinhorn T. politicians	WHIT 417:8
tinker don't matter a t.'s cuss	SHIN 363:10
Tippecanoe soldier of T.	SONG 376:4
T. and Tyler, too	SLOG 368:14
tipster racing t.	TAYL 387:7
tired Give me your t., your poor	LAZA 229:9
I was t. of it	PARK 304:10
tireless sound of t. voices	STEV 381:5
tit get her t. caught	MITC 275:3
titanic furniture on the deck of the T.	MORT 280:4
title gained no t.	POPE 314:3
needed no royal t.	SPEN 374:9
titles T. are but nick-namess	PAIN 301:6

T. are shadows	DEFO 113:2
T. distinguish the mediocre	SHAW 361:6
with 15th-century t.	ASHD 16:3
toadies t. of power	TREV 398:6
today doubts of t.	ROOS 331:13
never jam t.	CARR 75:11
standing here t.	JOHN 202:8
T. is the last day	YELT 427:3
we gave our t.	EPIT 137:6
What Manchester says t.	PROV 319:12
toga Idealism is the noble t.	HUXL 193:7
toil blood, t., tears and sweat	CHUR 87:14
Horny-handed sons of t.	SALI 339:12
unrequited t.	LINC 236:6
told Nobody t. us	WEBB 412:9
tolerance such a thing as t.	WILS 423:1
tolerate like, or at least t.	TREV 397:9
tolerated women not merely t.	AUNG 19:9
toleration t. produced mutual indulgence	
	GIBB 155:3
tombstone written on its t.	DAVI 110:7
Tomnoddy My Lord T.	BROU 56:7
tomorrow For your t. we gave	EPIT 137:6
jam t.	CARR 75:11
jam we thought was for t.	BENN 34:3
realization of t.	ROOS 331:13
tongue nor t. to speak	LENT 231:10
speaking the same t.	MAZZ 265:2
t. In every wound	SHAK 356:1
t. in the balance	BISM 44:13
t. of Fox	JOHN 205:6
t. That Shakespeare spake	WORD 424:9
t. to persuade	CLAR 93:12
yield to the t.	BIER 42:3
tongues t. doom men	SHAK 359:9
tonight Not t., Josepehine	NAPO 285:3
Tony straight from T.	PARR 305:8
tools Give us the t.	CHUR 88:11
t. to him that can handle them	CARL 74:8
tooth danger of her former t.	SHAK 357:6
toothpaste t. is out of the tube	HALD 169:2
top always room at the t.	WEBS 413:15
end up on t.	BENN 35:1
no friendship at the t.	LLOY 240:5
torch t. passed to a new generation	KENN 212:3
we throw The t.	MCCR 248:8
torches t. of martyrdom	JEFF 199:12
Tories both T.	BOSW 52:3
Mamma, are T. born wicked	ANON 10:13
revolutionaries potential T.	ORWE 296:10
T. must have a bogy man	BEVA 38:8
T. own no argument	BROW 58:6
unbending T.	MACA 246:6
torment most hateful t. for men	HERO 182:3
torrent t. of gin	GLAD 158:10
torso remain only a t.	ERHA 137:7
tortoise t. will usually beat	MAJO 256:4
Tory burning hatred for the T. Party	BEVA 38:4
Loyalty the T.'s secret weapon	KILM 217:2
my favourite T.	FOOT 142:6
no T. Leader has spoken	SALI 340:12

Tory (*cont.*):

Thirteen years of T. misrule	SLOG 368:12
to like T. MPs	CAMP 72:2
T. and Whig in turns	SMIT 372:6
T. Corps d'Armée	GLAD 158:15
Toryism of the T.	TROL 400:2
T. is someone who	POWE 315:12
T. men and Whig measures	DISR 122:8
T. party never panics	HOSK 189:2
t. recognizes	HESE 182:11
violent T.	RUSK 335:12
weapon of the T. Party	CRIT 105:6
what a T. he is	SHER 363:4
what T. Democracy is	CHUR 85:10
wise T.	JOHN 205:4

Toryism T. has always been   MACM 252:6

T. of the Tory	TROL 400:2

total t. reformation   PAIN 301:1

t. solution	GOER 160:6

totalitarian lead to the t. state   DENN 115:4

t. innovation	O'BR 293:2

totalitarianism under the name of t.   GAND 151:2

touch nothing, Can t. him further   SHAK 357:7

touchstone t. of our judgement   KENN 213:6

tough t. on the causes of crime   BLAI 45:10

When the going gets t.	PROV 319:13

toughness T. doesn't have to come   FEIN 140:1

tower fall'n at length that t.   TENN 389:9

town best summer T. House   PITT 312:1

destroy the t. to save it	ANON 10:4

Toytown running for mayor of T.   SCAR 347:2

trade autocrat: that's my t.   CATH 77:6

ever ruined by t.	FRAN 146:5
great t.	BURK 61:13
People of the same t.	SMIT 370:3
There isn't any T.	HERB 181:8
War is the t. of kings	DRYD 127:14
wheels of t.	HUME 191:4

tradition shackled by t.   SALI 343:2

T. means giving votes to	CHES 83:3
t. objects to their being disqualified	CHES 83:4

tragedy first time as t.   MARX 262:7

trahison *La t. des clercs*   BEND 33:7

train like a runaway t.   CONL 100:4

like a t. that will not	TLHA 395:3

trained We t. hard   ANON 13:3

traitor calling me a t.   VANU 404:7

hate the t.	DANI 109:4
t. to myself	SHAK 359:1

traitors form of our t.   WEST 416:7

hate t. and the treason love	DRYD 127:13

trample t. bad laws   PHIL 310:7

t. the very values	RATH 322:5

trampling right of t. on them   CHIL 84:2

tranquillity Fame and t.   MONT 276:11

transgression where no law is, there is no t.

   BIBL 42:1

transient t. and embarrassed   DISR 122:16

trap walk into a t.   WILS 421:2

traps recognize the t.   MACH 250:11

travel obliged to t. again   CHAR 82:2

traveller No t. returns   SHAK 351:11

t. from an antique land	SHEL 362:4

treacherous Exterminate . . . the t. English

   ANON 8:11

treachery mother of all t.   PAIS 302:11

not an absolution for t.	ASHC 16:2
t. cannot trust	JUNI 208:11
t. of the intellectuals	BEND 33:7
t. or meanness	DISR 123:13
T. with a smile	THAT 392:8

treason bloody t. flourished   SHAK 355:14

condoned high t.	DISR 121:2
Gunpowder T. and Plot	ANON 11:11
hate traitors and the t. love	DRYD 127:13
In trust I have found t.	MISQ 273:4
love the t.	DANI 109:4
none dare call it t.	HARI 173:6
t. a matter	TALL 386:1
t. can but peep	SHAK 352:3
T. has done his worst	SHAK 357:7
t. is not owned	DRYD 127:15
t., make the most of it	HENR 181:3
t. to his country	JOHN 204:2
'Twixt t. and convenience	EPIT 136:7

treasure day we should t.   AHER 6:1

treasury nationalize is the T.   WILS 422:5

our T. Bench	TROL 399:15
T. is in power	WILS 422:1
T. is the spring of business	BAGE 22:4
treble of the T. Bench	DISR 120:4

treaties T. do not affect   SALI 341:5

T. like girls and roses	DE G 113:11

treaty against this T.   DE V 115:9

good t. with Russia	BISM 43:5
hand that signed the t.	THOM 393:3
not a peace t.	FOCH 142:4
t. is in most cases	SALI 344:12
T. like an incoming tide	DENN 114:10

tree cut down a redwood t.   STEV 381:3

killing a t.	JOUB 207:9
t. of liberty	JEFF 198:6

trees apple t. will never get across   FROS 148:6

cut down forest-t.	TROL 399:11

Trelawny And shall T. die   HAWK 175:6

tremble t. for my country   JEFF 200:10

trembles t. as I do   WELL 414:8

trembling t. most, maintain a dignity

   WALP 409:4

trenches t. in the Great War   STOC 381:11

trial t. by juries   JEFF 199:5

t. is by what is contrary	MILT 271:3

tribal t., intimate revenge   HEAN 178:3

tribalism pure t.   FITT 141:3

tribunes t. with their tongues   SHAK 359:9

tribute Why should we pay t.   SHAK 351:5

trick to win the t.   LABO 223:4

trickle T.-down theory   GALB 149:11

tricks Frustrate their knavish t.   SONG 376:1

trifle careless t.   SHAK 356:12

trigger finger on the t.   MACM 253:4

want on the t.	NEWS 288:10

trimmer innocent word T. HALI 169:6
trip forward to the t. STIN 381:8
  from fearful t. WHIT 418:4
triple t. cord BURK 61:6
  with a t. bypass HOWA 189:5
Triton T. of the minnows SHAK 350:9
triumph for evil to t. MISQ 273:5
  shall not see the t. DICK 118:2
  t. and disaster KIPL 219:10
  t. from the north MACA 247:4
  t. of modern science WAUG 412:4
  t. of the embalmer's art VIDA 406:9
trivial t., inconsequential HELL 179:8
troika like a spirited t. GOGO 160:7
Trojan what T. 'orses will jump out BEVI 40:12
troops t. towards the sound GRIM 167:4
tropic Under the t. is our language WALL 408:9
trouble art of looking for t. BENN 34:1
  T. in the Balkans in the spring KIPL 221:4
  t. with 'the vision thing' IVIN 195:10
  When in t., delegate BORE 51:6
  with the least t. TAYL 388:9
  you are the one in t. ROOS 329:10
trousers have your best t. on IBSE 194:5
  steam-engine in t. SMIT 372:8
trowel lay it on with a t. DISR 123:17
true by the people as equally t. GIBB 155:3
  my t. king MACA 247:6
  to itself do rest but t. SHAK 356:8
  T. blue and Mrs Crewe GEOR 153:4
  t. legend STAL 378:8
Truman T.'s integrity BUSH 67:1
trumpet t.'s silver sound SCOT 348:8
trunkless vast and t. legs SHEL 362:4
trust assumes a public t. JEFF 199:10
  built An absolute t. SHAK 356:12
  does not t. himself RETZ 324:11
  except t. TAYL 387:3
  In t. I have found treason MISQ 273:4
  never t. experts SALI 340:2
  not property but a t. FOX 144:7
  power in t. DRYD 127:7
  power is a t. DISR 123:15
  treachery cannot t. JUNI 208:11
trusted fit to be t. with a secret SALI 338:11
  not to be t. with the office BROD 56:2
  unfit to be t. CHES 83:1
trustworthiness Carthaginian t. SALL 345:7
truth can tell you the t. MACH 251:1
  diminution of the love of t. JOHN 204:3
  economical with the t. ARMS 15:6
  economy of t. BURK 64:6
  fiction lags after t. BURK 61:17
  fight for freedom and t. IBSE 194:5
  forsake this t. ROSE 333:12
  grain of t. WILK 420:2
  just tell the t. TRUM 401:7
  Never sold the t. TENN 389:11
  no appetite for t. PEEL 307:5
  One man plus the t. PROV 319:6
  opinion is t. filtered PHIL 310:9

simple sword of t. AITK 6:2
speak the t. HAZL 176:9
Statesman, yet friend to T. POPE 314:3
stop telling the t. STEV 380:6
strife of T. with Falsehood LOWE 242:8
stumbled over the t. CHUR 92:8
there *is* such a thing as t. BAGE 24:9
to speak the t. NIXO 290:7
T. against the world LLOY 239:14
T. forever on the scaffold LOWE 242:9
t. in action DISR 120:3
t. is marching on HOWE 190:4
T. is on the march ZOLA 428:7
t. is the first PROV 320:1
t. is the glue FORD 143:2
T. itself becomes suspicious JEFF 199:9
t., justice, and humanity GLAD 159:5
t. which makes men free AGAR 5:8
two to speak the t. THOR 394:5
wedded to the t. SAKI 337:8
truths basic human t. KENN 213:6
  these t. to be self-evident ANON 13:2
  t. begin as blasphemies SHAW 360:1
  We hold these t. JEFF 198:1
try here to t. BLAI 46:6
  Nice t. MORG 279:1
tu Et t., Brute? SHAK 354:13
tube toothpaste is out of the t. HALD 169:2
Tudor US presidency a T. monarchy BURG 61:1
tumult t. and the shouting KIPL 220:6
tunnel back down the time t. KEAT 210:4
turbulent rid me of this t. priest HENR 180:9
turkey T. is a dying man NICH 286:5
turkeys t. vote for Christmas CALL 70:10
Turks Let the T. now carry GLAD 158:13
turn t. over the sheet SAND 346:1
  will not take a sharp t. TLHA 395:3
turned t. from one's course FABI 138:7
  t. out of the Realm ELIZ 132:6
turning lady's not for t. THAT 390:10
turnip in that great t. CHUR 90:10
TV T. has merely demonstrated MURR 283:6
twelve ruin himself in t. months GEOR 154:3
  t. good men BROU 57:1
twentieth fill the t. century LAUR 228:11
  t. century belongs to those TRUD 400:10
  t. century have looked SCHL 347:9
  t. century will be TOYN 397:4
twist t. slowly in the wind EHRL 130:8
two Canada is t. nations BOUC 52:4
  I see t. ANON 9:12
  say that t. plus two make four ORWE 297:6
  t. ears of corn SWIF 384:7
  t. hundred thousand men NAPO 284:15
  T. nations DISR 123:3
  t. o'clock in the morning NAPO 284:13
  t. to speak the truth THOR 394:5
  you did in t. minutes EVER 138:2
Tyler Tippecanoe and T., too SLOG 368:14
tyrannical In all t. governments BLAC 45:8
  nothing more t. TROL 399:7

tyrannical (cont.):
  t. majority   BALF 27:9
tyrannis Sic semper t.   BOOT 51:2
  Sic semper t.   MOTT 281:8
tyrannize t. over his bank balance   KEYN 215:8
tyrannous t. To use it like a giant   SHAK 357:13
tyranny burden of t.   SHAW 361:1
  call it t.   HOBB 185:11
  caused by some one's t.   BAGE 22:3
  definition of t.   MADI 255:3
  Ecclesiastic t.   DEFO 113:1
  freed from t.   BLUN 47:11
  grovelling t.   DISR 123:12
  liberty against t.   ROBE 328:3
  specious disguise for brutal t.   BERL 37:4
  struggled against t.   TUTU 402:6
  T. entrenches   SHEL 362:10
  T. is always better organized   PÉGU 308:11
  Under conditions of t.   AREN 14:5
  unnecessary t.   RUSS 336:9
  wage war against a monstrous t.   CHUR 88:1
  without representation is t.   OTIS 298:9
  worst sort of t.   BURK 64:13
tyrant each T., every Mob   KIPL 219:5
  loses the king in the t.   MAYH 264:8
  No t. need fear   ARIS 15:5
  t. has disposed   PLAT 312:11
  t. of his fields withstood   GRAY 165:5
tyrants all men would be t.   ADAM 2:1
  all men would be t.   DEFO 112:8
  argument of t.   PITT 312:2
  barbarity of t.   SMIT 372:5
  Excessive dealings with t.   DEMO 114:5
  Kings will be t.   BURK 63:4
  patriots and t.   JEFF 198:6
  reasoning of t.   GIBB 155:8
  Rebellion to t.   BRAD 53:5
  Rebellion to t.   MOTT 281:6
  restrained t., averted revolution   BENN 34:7
  sceptre from t.   TURG 402:5
  stuff of which t. are made   BEAV 31:12
  T. seldom want pretexts   BURK 61:3
Tyre Nineveh and T.   KIPL 220:7

UK within the U.   STRA 382:11
ulcer 8 U. Man   EARL 129:6
Ulster betrayal of U.   CAIR 70:1
  Province of U.   CARS 75:13
  title deeds of U.   PAIS 302:12
  to which U. will not go   BONA 49:8
  U. says no   SLOG 368:15
  U.'s honoured dead   PAIS 302:10
  U. will fight   CHUR 86:2
Ulsterman I'm an U.   HEWI 183:4
umbra magni nominis u.   LUCA 243:2
unacceptable u. face of capitalism   HEAT 179:1
unaided country's u. strength   STAL 378:5
unbearable in victory u.   CHUR 91:2
unbeatable In defeat u.   CHUR 91:2
unconscionable u. time dying   CHAR 82:5

unconstitutional u. takes a little longer
     KISS 221:8
uncreating U. word   POPE 314:1
undaunted we must be u.   CHUR 88:5
under those that work u. them   HALI 169:7
underbelly soft u. of Europe   MISQ 273:3
  u. of the Axis   CHUR 89:2
underestimated u. for decades   KOHL 222:7
underestimating lost money by u.   MENC 267:10
underlings ourselves, that we are u.   SHAK 354:1
underrating u. public taste   DEED 112:7
understand doesn't u. the situation   MURR 283:7
  do not u.   CHIR 84:8
  u. a little less   MAJO 256:6
  u. the country   LESS 231:1
  u. what is happening   CHAM 79:9
  u. what it is   HALI 170:16
understanding evidence against their own u.
     HALI 170:2
understandings muddy u.   BURK 63:2
understatement that was an u.   MITC 274:9
undertaking no such u. has been received
     CHAM 80:4
  u. of Great Advantage   ANON 8:7
underwear right down to her u.   NIXO 290:1
undiscovered death, The u. country   SHAK 351:11
undo will u. myself   SHAK 358:14
uneasy makes me u.   JOHN 204:19
  U. lies the head   SHAK 352:6
  You are u.   JACK 196:5
uneatable pursuit of the u.   WILD 419:8
uneducated government by the u.   CHES 83:12
unelected u. reject politicians   RIDL 327:2
unemployed from among the u.   LLOY 238:10
unemployment u. among teenagers   FRIE 148:1
unequal equal division of u. earnings   ELLI 134:10
unexpected age is the most u.   TROT 400:3
unfinished Liberty is always u. business
     ANON 10:10
unfit u. to be trusted   CHES 83:1
  u. to rule   MENC 267:7
unfitness u. for the Queen's Throne   NEWS 287:2
unforeseen situations as yet u.   MONN 276:5
ungraceful no more u. figure   CECI 78:8
unhappily u. married   PARK 304:9
unhappy have died u.   HAIL 168:13
  some should be u.   JOHN 205:1
  U. the land that needs heroes   BREC 54:2
unheard language of the u.   KING 218:3
uniformity u. [of opinion]   JEFF 200:9
uninspiring may be u.   GEOR 154:4
union Act of U. is there   TRIM 398:9
  destroyed the Act of U.   PAIS 302:12
  determined to preserve this U.   HOUS 189:4
  devotion to the u.   CARS 76:2
  England to carry the U.   O'CO 293:6
  indestructible U.   CHAS 82:6
  Join the u., girls   ANTH 13:13
  key of the U.   CLAY 95:8
  knell of the u.   JEFF 200:2
  Liberty and U.   WEBS 413:6

vermin little odious v.	SWIF 384:6	**vigilance** eternal v.	CURR 107:6
Tory Party are lower than v.	BEVA 38:4	**vigilant** v., the active	HENR 181:6
Vermont so goes V.	FARL 139:6	**vile** V., but viler George the Second	LAND 224:9
Versailles politics of V.	MONN 276:4	you are a v. Whig	JOHN 204:14
verse write it out in a v.	YEAT 426:5	**village** first in a v.	CAES 69:9
vertical v. to the eternal horizontal	GRAS 164:9	Like a v. fiddler	NICO 288:12
vessel remaining in a v.	HUME 191:6	Some v.-Hampden	GRAY 165:5
veterinarian v. and the taxidermist	LIEB 233:7	**vine** Under his own v.	SHAK 353:8
vex die to v. me	MELB 266:5	**vintage** trampling out the v.	HOWE 190:4
vibration v. of a pendulum	JUNI 208:7	**violate** v. would be oppression	JEFF 199:2
vicar V. of Bray	SONG 376:3	**violence** legitimate v.	WEBE 413:1
vice defence of liberty is no v.	GOLD 161:8	v. employed	TOCQ 396:1
in a private man a v.	MASS 263:11	v. is necessary	BROW 58:2
render v. serviceable	BOLI 49:2	**violent** anything that is v.	SALI 343:14
vice-presidency v. isn't worth	GARN 152:1	policy is v.	HUME 191:5
viceroy every other V.	NEHR 286:1	v. revolution	KENN 213:1
future V. must . . . not be	VICT 406:5	v. Tory	RUSK 335:12
vices By hating v. too much	BURK 63:8	**violently** v. if they must	QUIN 320:5
vicious didn't know what v. was	AUNG 19:8	**violet** v. smells to him	SHAK 352:10
victa sed v. Catoni	LUCA 243:1	**Virginian** I am not a V.	HENR 181:4
victi Pugna magna v. sumus	LIVY 238:5	**virisque** stat Romana v.	ENNI 135:7
victim felt like a v.	WALP 409:3	**virtue** in a prince the v.	MASS 263:11
oppressor, never the v.	WIES 419:3	practise v. afterwards	HORA 188:8
thou shalt not be a v.	BAUE 30:7	serviceable to the cause of v.	BOLI 49:2
victims They are its v.	CONR 101:10	v. and talents	JEFF 199:13
v. of American Fascism	ROSE 333:13	v. does not come from money	SOCR 373:7
victis Vae v.	LIVY 238:4	v. is the essence	ROBE 328:4
Victorian stuffy V. family	ORWE 296:11	v. of Englishmen	TAWN 386:4
V. values	THAT 391:4	without v.	ROBE 328:6
victories few sharp v.	WAUG 412:1	woman of easy v.	HAIL 168:5
Peace hath her v.	MILT 271:1	**virtues** v. Will plead	SHAK 357:2
proper use of v.	POLY 313:7	**virtuous** looking upon men as v.	BOLI 49:1
victorious Send him v.	SONG 375:7	**visible** V. governments	RUSK 335:11
victors v.' justice	SHAW 361:11	**vision** hold a v.	REAG 323:13
written by the v.	NEHR 285:11	trouble with 'the v. thing'	IVIN 195:10
victory Dig for v.	OFFI 295:2	v. thing	BUSH 66:6
In v.; magnanimity	CHUR 91:12	Where there is no v.	BIBL 41:11
in V., Revenge	LYNN 244:4	young men's v.	DRYD 127:6
in v. unbearable	CHUR 91:2	**visionary** v. politicians	BURK 61:9
Labor Party to v.	HAYD 176:1	**vive** V. différence	ELIZ 134:7
Liberals bought a v.	HARP 174:1	**vocabulary** diplomatist's v.	TAYL 387:16
never had a v.	CHUR 91:14	**voice** horrible v.	ARIS 14:8
no substitute for v.	MACA 245:4	It is my inner v.	GAND 151:7
One more such v.	PYRR 320:3	new v. of Scotland	CONN 101:1
peace without v.	WILS 422:15	No 'v. of the people'	SALI 339:4
produce v. parades	HOBS 186:1	v. of a nation	RUSS 337:1
'twas a famous v.	SOUT 374:7	v. of Rome	JONS 206:6
v. by a woman	WEST 416:10	v. of the kingdom	SWIF 384:4
V. has a hundred fathers	CIAN 93:1	v. of the people	BALD 27:2
v. in war	KEEG 210:8	v. was that of Mr Churchill	ATTL 18:1
wallow in our v.	PRES 316:8	v. we know so well	WRIG 425:5
victrix V. causa deis placuit	LUCA 243:1	**voices** sound of tireless v.	STEV 381:5
vidi Veni, v., vici	CAES 69:11	v. in Parliament	RUSK 336:3
Vienna at the Congress of V.	ADEN 5:3	**volcanoes** range of exhausted v.	DISR 121:5
V. is nothing	METT 268:6	**Volk** ein V.	SLOG 366:14
Vietnam led to the V. War	BLAC 45:4	**volley** v. we have just heard	COLL 99:5
To win in V.	SPOC 378:1	**Voltaire** V. in the Bastille	DE G 113:17
V. as a war	PILG 311:2	**volumes** thirty fine v.	MORL 279:3
V. was lost in	MCLU 252:3	**vomit** Dog returns to his V.	KIPL 219:8
V. was the first	WEST 416:11	**vote** Don't buy a single v. more	KENN 212:1
views v. of my constituents	CADM 69:5	floating v. lives up to	COLE 99:2

I never v. — ANON 10:2
inspire them to v. — JACK 196:11
One man shall have one v. — CART 76:6
people v. against somebody — ADAM 2:6
right to v. — ANTH 14:1
turkeys v. for Christmas — CALL 70:10
V. Blair — SLOG 368:16
v. could not have been closer — MART 261:7
V. early and vote often — MILE 269:2
V. for Gore — SLOG 368:11
v. for the best President — PETE 309:8
V. for the man who promises least — BARU 29:9
v. is to perform — PAIN 302:5
v. just as their leaders tell 'em — GILB 156:9
voted v. at my party's call — GILB 156:6
v. cent per cent — BYRO 68:10
voter every intelligent v. — ADAM 2:4
every v. — CLEV 96:8
voters appeal to floating v. — COOK 103:4
v. don't know — FOTH 144:3
votes finest brute v. in Europe — ANON 8:12
gather v. like box tops — STEV 380:14
V. for women — SLOG 369:1
voting If v. changed anything — LIVI 237:8
not the v. that's democracy — STOP 382:2
vow v. to thee, my country — SPRI 378:2
vox V. populi, vox Dei — ALCU 6:5
voyage v. not a harbour — TOYN 397:2
v. of their life — SHAK 356:5

wage home policy: I w. war — CLEM 96:3
One man's w. increase — WILS 421:14
wages better w. and shorter hours — ORWE 297:13
neither honours nor w. — GARI 151:10
took their w. — HOUS 189:3
wags w. its tail — TOYN 397:3
wait may indeed w. for ever — MACA 245:10
We had better w. and see — ASQU 16:4
We want eight, and we won't w. — SLOG 369:4
who only stand and w. — MILT 271:2
waited w. nearly 300 years — CONN 101:1
waiting keeping you w. — LAST 226:8
nearly kept w. — LOUI 241:7
w. seven hundred years — COLL 99:7
What are we w. for — CAVA 78:2
wake W. up, England — GEOR 153:5
Wales bless the Prince of W. — SONG 375:2
To be Prince of W. — BENN 35:2
W.'s own annual blood sport — MORG 279:2
W. to gain the same powers — JONE 205:11
womanhood of W. — ELLI 134:11
walk no easy w.-over — NEHR 285:12
upon which the people w. — CRAZ 104:5
w. and chew gum — EDWA 130:6
W. under his huge legs — SHAK 354:1
walking empire w. very slowly — FITZ 141:5
wall tear down this w. — REAG 323:12
w. of division — GORE 162:7
W. Street lays an egg — NEWS 288:8
w. to a layman — COMM 100:2

when the w. opened — MERK 268:1
With our backs to the w. — HAIG 168:4
wooden w. is your ships — THEM 392:14
wallow w. in our victory — PRES 316:8
walls not in w. — NICI 286:7
wooden w. are the best — COVE 104:2
walrus Between them, W. and Carpenter — LEVI 232:8
want that people know what they w. — MENC 267:5
third is freedom from w. — ROOS 331:4
wants elementary material w. — SALI 339:5
provide for human w. — BURK 62:18
war ain't gonna be no w. — MACM 252:9
alternative to w. — KING 217:11
at w. with Germany — CHAM 80:4
better than to w.-war — CHUR 90:16
business of w. — WELL 415:10
calamities of w. — JOHN 204:3
clamour for w. — PEEL 307:14
cold w. warrior — THAT 390:6
condition which is called w. — HOBB 185:4
cruellest and most terrible w. — LLOY 239:1
desolation of w. — GEOR 153:7
done very well out of the w. — BALD 26:4
Don't mention the w. — CLEE 96:1
during a great w. — SALI 343:1
easier to make w. — CLEM 96:5
enable it to make w. — WEIL 414:3
essence of w. is violence — MACA 245:8
European w. might do it — REDM 324:2
ever another w. in Europe — BISM 44:8
except the British W. Office — SHAW 360:6
first w. fought without — WEST 416:11
First World W. had begun — TAYL 387:5
France has not lost the w. — DE G 113:3
furnish the w. — HEAR 178:6
go to w. with the Army — RUMS 335:3
great protection against w. — BEVI 40:8
Grim-visaged w. — SHAK 359:3
hand of w. — SHAK 358:6
harder than making w. — STEV 380:2
home policy: I wage w. — CLEM 96:3
I am for w. — RED 324:1
If w. should ever come — BONA 49:7
I hate w. — ROOS 330:10
I have seen w. — ROOS 330:10
in peace and w. — CHUR 90:12
in time of peace thinks of w. — ANON 9:3
involved in a European w. — BEAV 31:3
involve us in the wrong w. — BRAD 53:4
In w. it is necessary — BONA 49:9
In w.; resolution — CHUR 91:12
In w. there is no second prize — BRAD 53:3
in w. the two cardinal virtues — HOBB 185:7
I renounce w. — FOSD 143:6
It's the wrong w. — KERR 214:4
killed in the w. — POWE 315:13
lead a w. with lies — ZAPA 428:1
lead this people into w. — WILS 423:1
Let me have w. — SHAK 351:3
let slip the dogs of w. — SHAK 355:4

war (*cont.*):

Let w. stay abroad	AESC 5:6
Let w. yield to peace	CICE 93:4
little w.	WELL 416:1
made this great w.	LINC 236:11
Make love not w.	SLOG 368:2
make w. on a kindred nation	BETH 37:10
Mankind must put an end to w.	KENN 212:11
man of w.	DE V 115:9
McNamara's W.	MCNA 254:3
midst of a cold w.	BARU 29:8
money the sinews of w.	BACO 21:4
My w. is over	MCGU 250:3
nature of w.	HOBB 185:5
never met anyone who wasn't against w.	
	LOW 242:4
never to go to w.	CHAM 80:2
never was a good w.	FRAN 145:9
no declaration of w.	EDEN 129:10
not a justifiable act of w.	BELL 32:8
Older men declare w.	HOOV 188:6
open or secret w.	JEFF 198:9
page 1 of the book of w.	MONT 277:17
prepare for w.	VEGE 405:5
recourse to w.	BRIA 54:10
rich wage w.	SART 346:7
seek no wider w.	JOHN 203:5
short decisive w.	LYND 244:2
silent in time of w.	CICE 93:9
sinews of w.	CICE 93:6
special problem in w.	CLAU 94:14
splendid little w.	HAY 175:8
stirring up some w.	PLAT 312:11
study politics and w.	ADAM 3:9
tell us all about the w.	SOUT 374:6
tempered by w.	KENN 212:3
third world w.	TRUM 401:3
this w. on terrorism	BUSH 67:4
This was a people's w.	TAYL 387:2
two nations have been at w.	VOLT 407:2
Vietnam as a w.	PILG 311:2
wage w. against a monstrous tyranny	
	CHUR 88:1
W. always finds a way	BREC 54:5
w., an' a debt	LOWE 242:7
w. and peace in the 21st century	KOHL 222:10
W. appears to be	MAIN 256:2
w. creates order	BREC 54:3
w. for independence	MCAL 244:13
w.-gamed against	WALL 408:6
W., in whatever form	SALI 339:3
W. is a very rough game	MONT 277:16
W. is capitalism with	STOP 382:6
W. is continuation of politics	CLAU 95:2
W. is hell, and all that	HAY 175:7
W. is not the word	KENN 211:7
w. is over	GRAN 164:3
W. is peace	ORWE 297:3
w. is politics with bloodshed	MAO 259:6
w. is so terrible	LEE 230:4
W. is the national industry	MIRA 271:10

W. is the remedy	SHER 363:6
W. is the trade of kings	DRYD 127:14
W. is too serious	CLEM 96:6
W. makes good history	HARD 173:3
W. Office kept three sets	ASQU 16:10
w. on 23 million Americans	BOAZ 48:3
w. on poverty	JOHN 203:2
w. regarded as inevitable	KENN 211:6
w. run to show the world	BERR 37:8
w. situation	HIRO 184:3
w. that drags on	WAUG 412:1
w. that we may live in peace	ARIS 14:11
w. that will end war	WELL 416:4
w. that would not boil	TAYL 387:11
w. which existed to produce	HOBS 186:1
W. will cease	SLOG 369:2
w. without an enemy	WALL 409:1
way of ending a w.	ORWE 298:1
We hear w. called murder	MACD 249:8
we prepare for w.	PEAR 306:9
what did you do in the W.	PROV 318:6
When is a w. not a war	CAMP 72:9
when it's at w.	KING 218:7
when there was w., he went	AUDE 19:4
When w. enters a country	ANON 13:7
When w. is declared	PROV 320:1
will not have another w.	GEOR 154:1
win an atomic w.	BRAD 52:8
without having won the w.	YOKO 427:5
won the last w.	ROOS 330:1
You can only love one w.	GELL 152:6
warder w. silent on the hill	SCOT 348:8
warfare Armed w. must be preceded	ZINO 428:4
true method of w.	MAZZ 265:1
warm w. courage	BUSH 67:3
w. courage	ROOS 330:8
warn right to w.	BAGE 23:4
w. you not to be ordinary	KINN 218:10
warning w. to all persons	BALD 26:7
warring two nations w.	DURH 129:4
warrior cold war w.	THAT 390:6
Here lies a valiant w.	EPIT 136:4
wars came to an end all w.	LLOY 239:1
end to the beginnings of all w.	ROOS 331:12
European w.	PAIN 300:7
History littered with the w.	POWE 315:3
how do w. start	KRAU 223:1
into any foreign w.	ROOS 331:1
most w. in history	CHUR 92:14
not armaments that cause w.	MADA 254:8
not to lose w.	CHUR 90:2
W. are popular	MACD 249:6
W. begin when you will	MACH 250:7
w., horrible wars	VIRG 407:1
w. planned by old men	RICE 326:2
Warsaw Order reigns in W.	ANON 11:7
warts w. and all	MISQ 274:1
Warwick impudent and shameless W.	
	SHAK 353:2
wash w. the balm	SHAK 358:8
washed never w. my own feet	PU Y 317:7

wheels w. of trade — HUME 191:4
where fixed the w. and when — HAWK 175:6
Whig ascendancy of the W. party — MACA 246:8
  first W. was the Devil — JOHN 205:3
  Tory and W. in turns — SMIT 372:6
  Tory men and W. measures — DISR 122:8
  W. in any dress — JOHN 204:6
  wise W. — JOHN 205:4
  you are a vile W. — JOHN 204:14
Whigs caught the W. bathing — DISR 119:9
  W. admit no force — BROW 58:6
whimper Not with a bang but a w. — ELIO 132:2
whine thin w. of hysteria — DIDI 118:8
whip W.'s duty is — CANN 74:1
whips Like most Chief W. — CLAR 94:3
  w. and scorns of time — SHAK 351:11
  W. want the safe men — MACM 252:8
whirlwind angel rides in the w. — PAGE 299:6
  they shall reap the w. — BIBL 41:17
whisky large w. — MALL 257:6
  w. and car keys — O'RO 296:3
whisper w. of a faction — RUSS 337:1
whist ignorance of w. — TALL 386:2
whistle shrimp learns to w. — KHRU 216:3
white best friends are w. — DURE 129:2
  blue-eyed devil w. man — FARD 139:5
  lowest w. man — JOHN 202:7
  nor w. so very white — CANN 73:7
  no w. man's foot — SALI 342:1
  no 'w.' or 'coloured' signs — KENN 213:4
  say this for the w. race — GREG 166:4
  want to be the w. man's brother — KING 217:4
  w. cliffs I never more must see — MACA 247:7
  w. domination — MAND 258:2
  w. heat of technology — MISQ 274:6
  w. man in Africa — LESS 231:13
  W. Man's Burden — KIPL 221:2
  w. man's cruelties — MALC 257:5
  w. man was *created* a devil — MALC 257:1
  w. race *is* the cancer — SONT 374:4
Whitehall condottiere through W. — HURD 192:7
  fallible men in W. — POWE 316:5
  gentleman in W. — JAY 197:7
  [W.] will create — SALI 344:16
White House imported the W. — ANON 9:13
  Log-cabin to W. — THAY 392:13
  no whitewash at the W. — NIXO 290:11
  way to the W. — STEV 380:12
  W. is another world — DEAN 111:9
  W. or home — DOLE 125:4
whiter w. than white — SANT 346:4
whites between w. and blacks — LINC 234:6
  if w. get hurt — SEXW 350:5
  need the knowledge of w. — TSVA 402:1
whitewash no w. at the White House — NIXO 290:11
who W.? Whom — LENI 231:6
whom Who? W. — LENI 231:6
whore I am the Protestant w. — GWYN 167:10
whores parliament of w. — O'RO 296:5
whoring w. herself out — ABBO 1:2

whose W. finger — NEWS 288:10
wicked all the world w. — BURK 63:17
  Mamma, are Tories born w. — ANON 10:13
  w. and moral — CHUR 86:11
wickedness than human w. — TAYL 387:8
  W. is the root — ROBE 328:4
wider seek no w. war — JOHN 203:5
widow actions of a retired w. — BAGE 22:10
wields he who w. the knife — HESE 182:8
wife Caesar's w. — CAES 69:8
  I have a w. — LUCA 243:3
  joined me as my w. — HEAT 179:4
  talks frankly only with his w. — BABE 20:2
  w. does not like — PRES 316:9
Wigan mothers-in-law and W. Pier — BRID 55:1
wiggles It w., it's shapely — ERWI 137:8
wild one is the w. herb — TOCQ 395:10
  w. geese — BARR 29:7
  W. Geese fly — DAVI 111:3
  W. men screaming — LLOY 239:3
wilderness grain into the w. — STOU 382:7
  They make a w. — TACI 385:1
  w. into a glorious empire — BURK 62:11
  w. of tigers — SHAK 359:10
will according to the common w. — JAME 197:5
  cannot resist the w. — SCAR 347:7
  general w. rules — ROBE 327:11
  not obey the w. — PEEL 307:10
  One single w. — ROBE 328:5
  settled w. — SMIT 372:3
  settled w. — STEE 379:2
  w. is not his own — SHAK 351:8
  w. of the majority — JEFF 199:2
  w. o' the wisp — MARK 260:7
  w. to be free — LIPP 237:6
  w. to carry on — LIPP 237:4
Willie needs a W. — THAT 392:7
willows Southern w. — LEE 230:1
win know how to w. — POLY 313:7
  might never w. — SMIT 372:2
  spend it, and w. — KENN 214:1
  To w. in Vietnam — SPOC 378:1
  w. an atomic war — BRAD 52:8
  W. just one for the Gipper — GIPP 157:5
wind appearance of solidity to pure w. — ORWE 297:17
  lie with the w. — TAYL 388:7
  moved about like the w. — GERO 154:11
  They have sown the w. — BIBL 41:17
  'tis a Protestant w. — SONG 375:3
  twist slowly in the w. — EHRL 130:8
  w. of change is blowing — MACM 253:3
winding by a w. stair — BACO 20:14
  old England's w. sheet — BLAK 47:2
window kiss my ass in Macy's w. — JOHN 203:13
  return through the w. — FRED 147:2
windows open w. into men's souls — ELIZ 133:9
winds W. of the World — KIPL 219:6
wings beating of his w. — BRIG 55:2
winning w. cause pleased the gods — LUCA 243:1
  w. the election — HOWA 190:1

working (*cont.*):

it isn't w.	MAJO 256:5
Labour isn't w.	SLOG 367:10

working class capitalism of the w.   SPEN 377:8

cream of the w.	BEAZ 32:1
into the w.	ORWE 297:14
vast portion . . . of the w.	ARNO 15:11

works it w., doesn't it   CALL 71:6

seen the future and it w.   STEF 379:4

workshop nation may be its w.   CHAM 79:6

w. of the world   DISR 119:6

world begins the w. afresh   MONN 276:6

begin the w. over	PAIN 300:9
believe that the w. began	CHUR 90:13
bestride the narrow w.	SHAK 354:1
citizen of the w.	SOCR 373:8
country is the w.	PAIN 302:2
decide the fate of the w.	DE G 113:6
enthusiasm moves the w.	BALF 27:8
funny old w.	THAT 392:5
governs the whole w.	OXEN 299:5
great w. spin for ever	TENN 389:6
interpreted the w.	MARX 262:9
loosed upon the w.	YEAT 426:9
new w. order	BUSH 66:10
one half the w. fools	JEFF 200:9
only saved the w.	CHES 83:7
start of the majestic w.	SHAK 353:11
There is a w. elsewhere	SHAK 351:1
third w. war	TRUM 401:3
though the w. perish	MOTT 281:3
three corners of the w.	SHAK 356:8
Thus passes the glory of the w.	ANON 12:3
Truth against the w.	LLOY 239:14
turned the w. upside down	BIBL 41:25
way the w. ends	ELIO 132:2
way to a w. society	CHOD 85:2
Winds of the W.	KIPL 219:6
workshop of the w.	DISR 119:6
w. becoming like a lunatic asylum	LLOY 239:8
w. must be made safe	WILS 422:18
w. safe for hypocrisy	WOLF 424:1
w.'s policeman	HEAL 177:4
w. stood like a playing card	MAIL 255:10
written for the w. of 1918	BLAI 45:11

worldly breath of w. men   SHAK 358:8

worlds destroyer of w.   OPPE 296:1

worms set on me in W.   LUTH 243:8

worry did not w. about it   TRUM 401:6

Don't W. Me	EARL 129:6
Don't you w.	BJEL 45:1

worse follow the w.   OVID 298:11

from w. to better	HOOK 187:12
will be for the w.	SALI 340:7
w. off for having known	STEP 379:8
w. than a crime	BOUL 52:5

worship second is freedom to w.   ROOS 331:4

various modes of w.	GIBB 155:3
w. the people	BACO 20:4

worst be told the w.   CHUR 88:9

it was the w. of times   DICK 118:1

While the w. are full	YEAT 426:9
w. form of Government	CHUR 90:5
w. possible reason	CLIN 98:1
You do your w.	CHUR 88:10

worth confident of their own w.   AUNG 19:9

nor words, nor w.   SHAK 355:16

would He w., wouldn't he   RICE 326:5

wound help to w. itself   SHAK 356:8

tongue In every w.	SHAK 356:1
w. had been for Ireland	LAST 228:8

wounds bind up the nation's w.   LINC 236:7

wrangle men w.   HALI 170:10

wrath grapes of w.   HOWE 190:4

wreckers not the w.   MCAL 244:12

wrestled w. for perhaps too long   HOWE 190:3

wring soon w. their hands   WALP 410:2

wringer big fat w.   MITC 275:3

write I w. one   DISR 124:11

written w. by the victors   NEHR 285:11

wrong both agree is w.   CECI 78:7

chose the w. way	ABBO 1:3
disastrously w.	GALB 149:14
if w., to be set right	SCHU 348:3
involve us in the w. war	BRAD 53:4
It's the w. war	KERR 214:4
majority are w.	DEBS 111:11
much w. could religion induce	LUCR 243:5
never in the w.	BURK 63:15
not always to be w.	EDEN 130:1
often think w.	SALI 344:7
only an accumulated w.	CASE 76:9
our country, right or w.	DECA 112:2
This is w. for Canada	MULR 282:9
We were w.	MCNA 254:4
when I am in the w.	MELB 266:13
W. but Wromantic	SELL 349:5
w. even the poorest ploughman	CHAR 81:5
W. forever on the throne	LOWE 242:9
w. members in control	ORWE 296:11
you can be w.	KERR 214:5

Yanks Y. are coming   COHA 98:10

year man at the gate of the y.   HASK 174:6

years two hundred y. like a sheep   TIPU 395:2

two thousand y. of hope	WEIZ 414:5
y. of desolation	JEFF 200:6

yellow y. stripes   HIGH 183:7

yelps loudest y. for liberty   JOHN 204:4

yes answer is y.   DOLE 125:3

We say Y.	WRIG 425:5
Y. it hurt	SLOG 369:6
Y., Minister! No, Minister	CROS 107:2

yesterday authority of the eternal y.   WEBE 413:2

Y.'s men   SLOG 369:7

yielding y. without ever being weak   SALI 338:7

yields 'y.' to public opinion   SALI 339:4

yoke hath received our y.   WALL 408:9

y. of prelaty   MILT 271:7

yolks lose but your y.   STEV 381:1

you Y. too, Brutus   CAES 69:12

young crime of being a y. man   PITT 311:5
    defrauded y.   KIPL 219:7
    too y. to understand   BROW 58:3
    what the world would call y. men   PEEL 307:7
    y., bald Leader   KINN 219:2
    y. men's vision   DRYD 127:6
    y. was very heaven   WORD 424:8
younger curse of the y. generation   MACM 253:8
youth flower of our y.   TREV 397:7
    In the y. of a state   BACO 21:8
    it is y. who must fight   HOOV 188:6
    today's y.   SPIE 377:10
    widow and an unemployed y.   BAGE 22:10
    Y. is a blunder   DISR 122:9
    Y. is not an absolution   ASHC 16:2

    y. is the season of credulity   PITT 311:8
    Y. of a Nation   DISR 123:6
    y. of the realm   SHAK 353:1
    y. to the gallows   PAIN 302:1

Zane works by Mr Z. Grey   ACHE 1:10
zeal by men of z.   BRAN 53:9
    holy mistaken z.   JUNI 208:8
    not the slightest z.   TALL 385:13
zealous z. citizen   BURK 63:9
Zimbabwe keep my z.   MUGA 282:5
Zionism Z. is rooted in traditions   BALF 28:2
zoom z. lenses   ULLR 403:4
Zurich gnomes in Z.   WILS 421:1